G. R. Kirk.

4:5 Moberly Tower

Manchester M15

061-273-2875

£23.75

Ig chn - retrieval - p 162

Cognitive Psychology

Darlene V. Howard

GEORGETOWN UNIVERSITY

Cognitive

Memory, Language,

MACMILLAN PUBLISHING CO., INC.
New York

COLLIER MACMILLAN PUBLISHERS
London

Psychology

and Thought

Macmillan Publishing Co., Inc.
866 Third Avenue, New York, New York 10022

Collier Macmillan Canada, Inc.

Library of Congress Cataloging in Publication Data

Howard, Darlene V.
  Cognitive psychology.

  Includes index.
  1. Cognition.   I. Title.
BF311.H66   153   82-15158
ISBN 0-02-357320-1   AACR2

Printing: 1 2 3 4 5 6 7 8   Year: 3 4 5 6 7 8 9 0

ISBN   0-02-357320-1

To my parents
Jane and Lawrence Vaglia
with love and gratitude

I suppose that all textbook authors try to make converts of their readers, and I am no exception. Not only do I think cognition is the most fascinating topic within psychology, but I believe that no undergraduate education is complete without a course in cognitive psychology. Cognitive psychology's inherent interest and its importance in a liberal arts education stem from the same sources. First, since it is concerned with the nature of human knowledge, cognitive psychology addresses the same philosophical questions that have intrigued Mankind for centuries and continue to form the heart of a college education. Second, relying as it does on experimental methods and on precise, often computer-based models, the content matter of cognitive psychology courses is appropriate for introducing students to the kinds of scientific reasoning that are of increasing importance for the educated layman. Third, the topic offers student and professor alike an excuse for engaging in some thoughtful introspection about the workings of their own minds. Finally, consideration of mnemonic techniques and problem-solving strategies enables students to develop skills that are of use in their other courses and outside the classroom as well.

I have tried to take advantage of these characteristics of cognitive psychology in teaching my courses on the subject and in writing this text. The reader I have in mind is not only the rare (though welcome!) psychology major who seeks to become a cognitive psychologist, but just as importantly, the intelligent non-psychology major who wants to gain a critical understanding of how the workings of our minds can be investigated using scientific methods, and who hopes to consider how the knowledge so gained can be applied outside the laboratory.

Keeping this reader in mind has led to several features of this book. Since it is designed to serve as an integrated introduction to cognition, not as a review of theories and data, the first chapter presents a general information-processing theory which encompasses memory, language, and thought. This theory is elaborated throughout the book providing an organization to which new material is related. Each chapter includes the major issues, theory, and experimental procedures that are central to the topic being discussed, but emphasis is placed, not on providing an exhaustive survey, but rather on devel-

Preface

oping a critical understanding of the reasoning upon which the research is based. Therefore, usually only one or two key experiments
are presented for a given topic. At the end of each chapter, a "Suggested Reading" section sends the interested reader to additional
sources. These sections also suggest topics and controversial issues
that would make interesting and challenging term papers.

In order to encourage students to think, and to heighten interest
in the topic at hand, each chapter begins with a "Food for Thought"
demonstration phenomenon or experiment which the reader is asked
to attempt. Descriptions of how certain key phenomena and experiments can be replicated by the reader are also contained throughout
most chapters. These suggestions are based on demonstrations I have
used during the nine years I have been teaching cognitive psychology.
Not only do these exercises help students to remember and understand the material, but they stimulate in-class (and out of class) discussion.

Throughout the book whenever appropriate, actual and potential
applications of theory and research are presented. These include both
applications to general problems (such as what contemporary research
on memory and language processing suggests about the potential uses
and abuses of advertising), as well as applications for developing the
reader's own skills at remembering and thinking.

For the most part, the order in which topics are introduced and
the extent to which individual topics are stressed conforms to the organization used in most cognitive psychology courses. However, my
experience at teaching has led me to depart from this standard in a
few cases. Pattern recognition is discussed, not in an early chapter,
as is the usual practice, but rather midway through the book in the
chapter on speech perception, where the perception of speech sounds
is used as a particularly important example of the general problem of
pattern recognition. Rather than adopting the usual practice of discussing perception of the sounds of speech prior to the perception of
meaningful units such as sentences and paragraphs, I have reversed
the order. After discussing language comprehension in general in
Chapter 9, I consider the modality specific aspects of language in the
immediately following "Language by Ear" and "Language by Eye"
chapters. In the latter, I spend considerably more space on sign language than is typical. This is, in part, because of the fascination this
topic holds for me (a fascination I've found to be shared by my students), but also because it provides an excellent vehicle for differentiating those characteristics of language that are specific to a particular modality from those that are universal. One final departure from
the usual order of presentation is that the Thinking section introduces
problem solving before deduction and conceptual thinking rather than
the reverse, an ordering which allows me to discuss general phenom-

ena of problem solving and then to treat deduction and conceptual thinking as special cases.

Many people helped this book come into being. I am grateful to my students at Georgetown whose comments and interests have helped to shape the contents of this book, and to my colleagues in the psychology department who not only provided encouragement, but also took over my duties for a sabbatical year during which I finally found time to complete the manuscript. I wish especially to acknowledge my colleague Dan Robinson who first talked me into undertaking this book, and who has encouraged me to keep at it ever since. I am indebted to William Banks and Earl Hunt who read the whole manuscript and to Ralph Haber who read a large part of it. Their suggestions have improved the book tremendously, though, of course, they are not responsible for any errors of omission or commission that remain. I am grateful to Clark Baxter, Senior Editor at Macmillan, with whom it has been a pleasure to work, and to Dave Novack at Macmillan who has supervised production of the final product. The Georgetown University Academic Computation Center has provided computer funds for word processing. I am particularly grateful to Allen Tucker for making these funds available, and to Charlotte Kaufer for her most capable handling of the details. My husband Jim deserves far more than the usual credit given spouses. Not only did he provide encouragement, but he also read and criticized the manuscript, offering advice based on his own experience at teaching courses on cognition. It was also Jim who suggested that I use a word processing system to prepare the manuscript and who taught me how to do so. Finally, both Jim and I are grateful to our newborn son Jeffrey Matthew, who was wise enough to delay his eagerly anticipated arrival until after the manuscript had been completed.

Darlene V. Howard

Contents

ONE

Introduction

An Overview

FOOD FOR THOUGHT

Begin by answering each of these questions:

> **Is *rimmelnode* a word you know?**
>
> **How many animals of each kind did Moses take on the Ark?**

You probably answered the first question effortlessly within a fraction of a second, and were little impressed with your ability to do so. But how did you determine that you don't know *rimmelnode*? It is unlikely that you looked through all the thousands of words stored in your memory in so short a time. This ability suggests that your knowledge of words is organized in such a way that the physical appearance of a string of letters tells you where the string would be stored in memory if you knew it. Apparently, you looked where *rimmelnode* should be and you didn't find it there. We will have more to say about how memory is organized later in the book, but the point now is that we can often gain insights into the workings of our own minds by taking notice of the kinds of judgments all of us make without apparent effort.

Did you answer "two" to the second question? If so, look at the question again, perhaps reading it aloud. Are you still sure of your answer? Most of you probably succumbed to the so-called *Moses illusion* which was discovered by Erickson and Mattson (1981). Of course, Moses didn't sail the Ark, Noah did; yet even those of us who know this very well usually get caught. People often fail to see the problem with this sentence (and others such as "In the biblical story, what was Joshua swallowed by?") even after reading it carefully several times. The illusion works only if the name that is substituted is similar in meaning to the correct name. No one is fooled by "How many animals of each kind did Nixon take on the Ark?", though many are fooled by "How many animals of each kind did Adam take on the Ark?" Why are we so vulnerable? Try out this Moses illusion and variations of it on a few friends. You might also ask a few children too, to find out whether they are as susceptible. What does this illusion tell us about how we comprehend language? We'll return to this question in later chapters, but my purpose now is simply to encourage you to begin noticing some of the errors we all make, and to consider what these reveal about the workings of our minds.

Everyone is fascinated by unusual feats of cognition (such as the rare ability to report the day of the week instantaneously given any date in history), yet we usually take little note of the equally remarkable and much more important cognitive feats (and errors) that we all exhibit every day. One of the purposes of this book is to change that. Though we will sometimes consider individuals with rare abilities, we will more frequently focus on people like ourselves who, as you will learn, are puzzling enough. We will examine how our minds work; how they enable us to remember and forget, to comprehend language, and to think and reason.

A SCIENTIFIC REVOLUTION

The questions that will concern us throughout the book have intrigued philosophers for centuries, but for several decades these issues were largely ignored by American experimental psychologists.

The radical *behaviorists* led first by John B. Watson (1913) and later by B. F. Skinner (1938) argued that science must investigate public, observable events. The behaviorists concluded that since mental events such as thoughts and images and consciousness cannot be observed directly, they have no place in the science of psychology.

The behaviorists' arguments had tremendous impact on American psychology and, indeed, on American society. From the early 1920's through the late 1950's almost all experimental psychologists abandoned the investigation of mental events and substituted the study of behavior, the latter being more readily observable and, thus, more amenable to study by scientific methods. As a consequence of this choice of subject matter, these decades led to many statements about the effects of reinforcement on the behavior of people and laboratory animals, but they provided little insight into the mysteries of memory, language, and thought. Since the late 1950's, however, a revolution has occurred. Experimental psychologists have turned their talents increasingly to the investigation of the mind, and there has been a rebirth of interest in what is now called the cognitive approach to psychology.

THE COGNITIVE APPROACH

The essence of the cognitive approach can be summarized by considering three of the major characteristics that distinguish it from behaviorism. First, it emphasizes knowing, rather than responding. Cognitive psychologists are concerned with finding scientific means for studying the mental processes involved in the acquisition and application of knowledge. This means that their major emphasis is not upon stimulus-response bonds, but on mental events. This stress on mind as opposed to behavior is consistent with intuition; we define ourselves at least as much by our thoughts as by our actions. Descartes said "*Cogito ergo sum*" ("I think; therefore I am"). His words would not have rung so true had he proclaimed, "I behave; therefore I am."

Of course, the cognitive approach does not ignore behavior, but rather than being the object of study, responses are used as indicators that enable inferences regarding mental events. Perhaps the best way to state the distinction is to paraphrase Noam Chomsky, the great linguist, who wrote that calling psychology "behavioral science" is like designating natural science "the science of meter readings" (Chomsky, 1968, p. 58). Chomsky eloquently expresses the cognitive viewpoint: to call psychology the *science of behavior* is to confuse the evidence studied (behavior) with the goal of the study (an understanding of the mind). Indeed, in attempting to banish unobservables from the realm of psychology, the behaviorists were striving to impose a restriction on psychological theorizing that is not imposed in any of the other sciences. No one has ever observed directly either gravity or a quark, yet physicists are not deemed unscientific for including these concepts in their theories.

A second characteristic of the cognitive approach is that it emphasizes *mental structure* or *organization*. It is argued that an individual's knowledge is organized and that new stimuli are interpreted in light of this knowledge. This stress on organization is particularly apparent in the theory of Jean Piaget, the Swiss scholar who has contributed so much to our understanding of human development. Piaget has argued that all living creatures are born with an invariant tendency—to organize experience—and that this tendency provides an important impetus for cognitive development.

The third characteristic of the cognitive approach is that the individual is viewed as being active, constructive, and planful, rather than as being the passive recipient of environmental stimulation. The analogies frequently used by the behaviorist reveal a passive view of the organism. Humans are described as blank slates upon which the environment writes, wax upon which the environment impresses itself, and mirrors that reflect the environment. On the other hand, the cognitive theorist views the individual as an active participant in the process of acquiring and using knowledge. The individual is thought of as actively constructing a view of reality, selectively choosing some aspects of experience for further attention, and attempting to commit some information to memory. The cognitive theorist assumes that any complete theory of human cognition must include an analysis of the plans or strategies people use for thinking, remembering, and understanding and producing language.

A good way to highlight the distinctions between the behaviorist and the cognitive views of human nature is to examine how proponents of each approach have attempted to study morality, a topic outside the realm of this book. Behaviorists have focused on certain moral (or immoral) behaviors, such as cheating, helping others, and disobeying authority (reflecting characteristic 1). They have assumed that moral development involves nothing more than the learning of additional moral behaviors (characteristic 2), and have viewed such moral development as the result of reinforcement and punishment to which the individual has been subjected (characteristic 3). Cognitive theorists, on the other hand, have focused on the thought processes by which people decide between right and wrong (characteristic 1). They have argued that moral development brings with it increasingly complex and organized rules for making moral decisions (characteristic 2), and that such development is dependent upon the active construction of the individual (characteristic 3). It is hard to imagine two more radically different approaches to the same topic!

INSTIGATORS OF THE REVOLUTION: LINGUISTICS AND COMPUTER SCIENCE

Why, after decades of indifference, have experimental psychologists begun to devote more and more intellectual energy to the analysis of the mind? Two concurrent events were particularly important in leading to the current revolution. It is characteristic of the interdisciplinary nature of contemporary research that neither of these originated within the discipline of psychology itself.

The contribution of linguistics. The first event took place in linguistics, a discipline concerned with specifying the structure of language. In the late 1950's Noam Chomsky published several works which were to have great impact not only on linguistic theory, but also on psychological investigations of cognition. As we shall discuss in more detail in later chapters, Chomsky argued that traditional stimulus-response and behavioristic theories are *in principle* inadequate to account for the acquisition and use of human language. Since language plays such a central role in human thought and human affairs, a theoretical approach that cannot encompass language must, of necessity, be inadequate for understanding human cognition.

Chomsky's work had major impact on psychology in that it highlighted the inadequacies of behaviorism. Scientific theories are rarely discarded simply because they are shown to be inadequate, however. Indeed, even the scientist who proposes a theory is usually quite aware that the theory is inadequate in that there are phenomena for which it cannot account. In order for a theoretical approach to be abandoned, a better alternative must be available, and, unfortunately, Chomsky did not offer the experimental psychologist a satisfactory alternative.

The theory Chomsky espoused was a linguistic, not a psychological, theory; i.e., it was more concerned with specifying the structure of language than with explaining how people produce and comprehend language. It was the second event—rapid developments in computer science—that led psychologists to propose a particular kind of cognitive theory which seemed to offer new and exciting possibilities for the investigation of human cognition. Before focusing on this new theoretical perspective, which has been termed the information-processing approach, let's examine the contributions of computer science in more detail.

The contributions of computer science. The mid-1940's witnessed the birth of the first experimental computers, and by 1950 the first commercial computer was available. The subsequent rapid development of these high speed computers has affected psychology in many ways. For one thing, laboratory computers have made it easier for psychologists to do experiments and analyze their results. Whereas graduate students used to spend long hours pushing buttons and recording responses every time a subject was tested, now computers can be programmed to present stimuli in specified orders for specified lengths of time, and to record responses accurately and tirelessly. (Computers, unlike graduate students, never get bored.) Indeed, many of the studies you will be reading about later in the book were controlled by computers. Furthermore, researchers used to spend hours and hours doing various computations on their results, but now computer programs are available which enable these same analyses to be completed in fractions of a second. Virtually every study you read about in this book will have involved such computer analyses.

The ease with which computers can be coerced into doing tedious laboratory tasks, however, is the least important of their contributions to psychology. Much more noteworthy is the fact that computer science has provided both (1) a thought-provoking analogy for human cognition, and (2) a new means of stating and testing theories of cognition. Although everyone is aware of the tremendous impact computers have had on our everyday lives, most laymen are unaware of the extent to which computer science has influenced psychological theories. In order to understand this impact, it's best to begin by considering computers themselves.

Computers: Hardware and software. A *computer* is a high speed, general purpose symbol-manipulating machine, or, in other words, a high speed, general purpose machine for processing information. A distinction is often drawn between the *hardware* and the *software* of the computer. The hardware is the physical equipment (the nuts and bolts, as it were) of the computer. Although the actual components vary among computers, each computer's hardware is composed of three functional units. That is, each part of the hardware could be classified as contributing to one or more of the following three functional components: the *memory,* the *central processing unit,* and the *input-output equipment.*

The memory consists of a physical device that can store many numbers (or symbols). Each location in the memory has an "address" so that it is possible to refer to any given location. The central processing unit does the manipulating of the symbols, so it forms the heart of the system. Finally, the input-output devices enable the computer and the outside world to communicate. For example, there are often teletypes or card readers that enable the computer to receive (input) symbols from the external world, and there are also line-printers and card punches that enable the computer to report (output) the results of its symbol manipulations.

Although the hardware components we've described are necessary, they would be nothing but an empty, useless skeleton without the software. The software of the computer consists of programs. A *program* is a numbered list of instructions (or, to borrow Neisser's [1967] analogy, a recipe) for manipulating symbols. The computer can be instructed (through its input devices) to run any of its stored programs. This instruction will cause the central processing unit to find the requested program in memory and to carry out, or *execute,* each of the instructions in the program in turn.

Computer programs are much more important than computer hardware for contemporary theories of human thought, so it is worth considering the way a program works in a little more detail. Consider, for example, a program that is designed to search through a list of letters and report whether or not the list contains a specified letter. For example, the program is designed to report "yes" if the list contains an *A,* and "no" otherwise. Of course, in order for a computer to be able to store away and execute the program it would have to be written in a special language that the computer is able to interpret. For our purposes, though, it is sufficient to consider how the program would look if written in English. A program that would perform the task described is shown in Table 1–1.

The best way to understand the program is to set up a sample list to be searched, e.g., *BDA,* and then step through the program obeying each of the instructions in turn. Step 1 would lead us to get the letter *B.* Step 2 would lead us to determine whether or not the current letter is an *A* and, since it is not, would send us to Step 3. Step 3 would have us look to see if there is another item in the list and, since there is, would send us to Step 4. Step 4 instructs us to get the next item, which is a *D* in our example. Step 5 then sends us back to Step 2, and so on. Eventually, for the current list *BDA* the program

TABLE 1–1.   A Sample Program.

Step Number	Instruction
1	Get the first item in the list.
2	If the item is an *A*, then go to Step 6. Otherwise go to Step 3.
3	If this is the last item go to Step 8. Otherwise go to Step 4.
4	Get the next item.
5	Go to Step 2.
6	Report "Yes."
7	Stop.
8	Report "No."
9	Stop.

will lead us to Step 6 which would result in the report of the answer "yes" and then to Step 7 which would stop execution of the program. On the other hand, the list "KVL" would lead us to search through the whole list and, failing to find a match, to Step 8 and, finally, Step 9.

Notice that instructions are usually executed in numerical order, but there are important exceptions. Particularly important are instructions like numbers 2 and 3, which indicate that a comparison or other test should be made, with the outcome determining which step should be executed next. Thus, the program has the capability of making subsequent actions dependent upon the outcome of certain decisions.

Another way of depicting the sequence of symbol manipulations specified in a particular computer program is to draw a *flowchart*. The flowchart depicted in Figure 1–1 is equivalent to the program in Table 1–1. In the flowchart the sequence in which the steps should be executed is depicted by directional arrows. By convention, decision points (in steps 2 and 3) are indicated by diamonds, with arrows indicating the next step that should be taken in the event of each of the possible outcomes of the decision.

The program analogy.   It may already have occurred to you that the human mind, like the computer, might be thought of as a general purpose device for manipulating symbols. That is, both people and computers take in large amounts of information from the environment, manipulate that information, and then (at least sometimes) report and act on the outcomes of these manipulations. This insight led psychologists to draw an analogy between computer information processing and human thought. Although this analogy is often termed the *computer analogy*, Neisser (1967) has said that it is more accurately termed the *program analogy*. The analogy focuses the attention of the theoretician not upon the hardware, or physiology, of human cognition, but rather on the sequence of symbol manipulations that

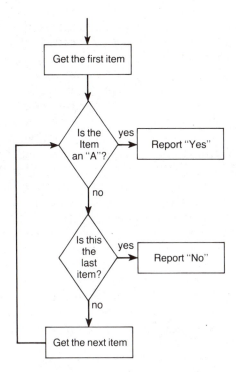

Figure 1–1. A flowchart which is equivalent to the program in Table 1–1.

underlies thought. The task of the psychologist who is trying to understand human cognition is viewed as the problem of determining the library of programs the human has stored away in memory—programs that enable the person to understand and produce sentences, to commit certain experiences and rules to memory, and to solve novel problems.

The program analogy is useful because drawing analogies between the phenomenon of interest and some other better understood phenomenon often provides a fruitful source of hypotheses about the former. Psychology is not unique in this regard; Neils Bohrs' atomic theory rested on drawing an analogy between the little known structure of the atom and the more precisely specified structure of the solar system. Similarly, since computer information processing is better understood than the human mind, it is hoped that drawing an analogy between the two will suggest new ways in which to theorize about human thought. For example, flowcharts are useful for analyzing the sequence of steps in a computer program and they are also proving useful for describing sequences of mental events.

The program analogy is often thought to imply that the mind is nothing more than a computer. Such misinterpretations have, quite understandably, led to emotional denials of any similarity and to the accusation that the analogy robs people of their humanity. You will notice, however, that the program analogy does *not* imply an attempt to equate Man and computer any more than Neils Bohr meant to equate the atom with the solar system. Nor does the analogy even require the assumption that *all* aspects of human thought are analogous to computer information processing. The argument is simply that both humans and computers remember, and both engage in symbol manipulation. Since we understand computer information processing better than we understand human thought, we may gain insightful hypotheses about the latter by using our knowledge of the former.

Thus, the argument that the program analogy necessarily dehumanizes people is unfounded. There is another danger in using the program analogy that cannot be so readily dismissed, however, and that is the possibility that the analogy is inappropriate. It is possible that the principles that underlie human thought are dramatically different from those involved in computer information processing, and if this is the case, then the program analogy will lead us down a blind alley. This, of course, is the danger inherent in proposing any theory, i.e., it may be wrong.

Throughout the rest of the book we will examine information-processing theory—an approach to the study of human cognition that has grown out of the program analogy. We will argue that this approach has already provided insights into the nature of human memory, language, and thought. On the other hand, we will also see that many questions remain. Whether these questions can be answered within the information-processing framework, or whether a new and as yet unforeseen approach will be needed is unknown. Thus, the program analogy and the particular theories that build upon it may ultimately prove inadequate. Such is the way of science. Fortunately, in scientific endeavors as well as in the rest of life, we often learn as much from mistakes as from successes. If the information-processing approach fails ultimately, we will at least have specified more precisely the senses in which the program analogy is inadequate and will, thereby, have increased our understanding of human cognition.

Computer simulation. Not only has the development of computer science provided cognitive psychology with an analogy, but it has also provided a new means of stating and testing theories of human cognition. This application of computers is often called computer simulation.

In the past, theories about human thought were usually phrased in words. For example, the theorist who wished to propose a theory of how people solve problems would state a series of assumptions.

The theory might specify that solving a problem is assumed to require the following four stages: (1) setting up a representation of the problem, (2) devising some plan for solving the problem, (3) carrying out the plan, and (4) checking the solution obtained to make sure that it is adequate.

Although the sequence of assumed stages seems reasonable, this theory is vague. Exactly what is meant by the term *representation* and exactly what determines which representation will be chosen? What criteria are used to determine whether the solution is adequate? Such vagueness is troublesome, because it makes the theory difficult to test. Another difficulty with theories that are stated only in words is that it is very difficult to determine whether or not the assumptions of the theory are *sufficient* to explain the phenomenon in question. That is, our foregoing theorist is arguing that by making only a few simple assumptions he can explain human problem solving. The skeptic, however, might argue that if the human mind embodied only those principles it would never be able to solve problems in the way people are observed to do everyday. In other words, the skeptic might argue that the assumptions of the theory are not sufficient. Notice that as long as the theory is only stated in words, this debate would be difficult to resolve.

Since the late 1950's an increasing number of theorists have argued that such problems can be alleviated by stating theories in the form of computer programs. In this case, then, a theory of problem solving would be stated as a list of instructions that represents the sequence of steps people are assumed to use when solving a problem. The resulting program would then be stored in a computer's memory and tested by giving the program problems to solve. If the program is able to solve the problems, then both of the difficulties we discussed have been overcome. First, the theory has been stated precisely and unambiguously. If it were not, the computer would not have been able to carry out the sequence of instructions. Computers, unlike people, do not fill in the vague parts automatically. Second, we have shown that the theory is sufficient in the sense that it does solve problems.

The technique just described involves testing a theory by attempting to program a computer to simulate or imitate the human activity about which we are theorizing. This method of theory testing is called computer simulation, and, as we have seen, it avoids some of the inadequacies of theories stated in words. As the pessimist will already have suspected, however, computer simulation raises other problems. One of these is that it is difficult to communicate the theory to other people, particularly those who do not know the computer language in which the program is written.

A more interesting difficulty presented by computer simulation becomes apparent whenever we try to decide whether or not the computer program is doing the task in the same way as the human. The difficulty is that it is quite possible to write a program that solves problems, but uses a method completely different from that used by humans. To see that this is possible, consider *cryptarithmetic problems,* that is, arithmetic problems that contain letters instead of digits. Here is an example.

```
  DONALD
 +GERALD
  ROBERT
```

The subject is told that each of the 10 different letters stands for one of the digits between 0 and 9, with each of the letters standing for a different digit. The problem is to determine which digit corresponds to each of the letters. (To make the problem a little less challenging, subjects are usually given a hint. For example, in this problem they are told that D = 5. At this point you should stop reading for a few minutes and try to solve the problem yourself—only 9 more pairs to go.)

It would be possible to write a program that solved this problem by blindly trying out, in random order, all 362,880 (i.e., 9!) possible combinations of digits and letters until it found one that worked. Such a program would always come up with the correct solution, and, given the speed of contemporary computers, it would solve the problem more quickly than you would—probably in less than one second. Despite the program's success, however, no one would claim that this program offers a reasonable theory of how people solve the problem.

The general question this example highlights is: once we have written a program that solves problems, how can we determine whether it is solving them the way humans do? That is, how can we determine whether the program offers an accurate theory of human problem solving? In 1950 the British mathematician A. M. Turing suggested the general form such a test might take. Turing, in fact, was concerned with how we might answer the question, "Can machines think?", but the solution he offered to this dilemma is applicable to the question at hand and has come to be called *Turing's test.* Turing proposed that to test a theory of human thought, we should place both a human and a computer programmed with our theory in Room *A.* A human interrogator would be placed in Room *B* with two teletypes— one hooked up to the human in Room *A* and the other to the computer in Room *A.* The interrogator would be able to send questions to each of the occupants of the other room and receive answers from them through these two teletypes, and his task would be to determine which of the teletypes was hooked up to the computer and which was hooked up to the other person. If the interrogator finds it easy to tell the difference, then the computer program does not embody an adequate theory of human thought.

Turing's test suggests, then, that we test our theory by determining whether or not it is possible to distinguish between the behavior (output) of the computer program and the behavior of a human subject. If you give this issue more thought, however, you will realize that ambiguity still remains, for it is necessary to decide exactly which aspects of behavior the program should be required to imitate, and which are irrelevant.

To appreciate this distinction, consider how we might apply Turing's suggestion to test our (hypothetical) theory of how people solve cryptarithmetic problems. We might compare the output of the program (which solves the problem by trying randomly all possible combinations of letters and digits) with the performance of humans on a large number of cryptarithmetic problems. Our earlier discussion of this program suggests that there would, in fact, be at least some differences between the behavior of our program and human behavior. In particular, the computer would produce its solution much more quickly than people would. This difference in the overall time required for solution, however, would not necessarily disprove our theory, for the difference in time might simply be due to hardware differences between the human and the computer. We want to know if the *programs* (i.e., the sequence of symbol manipulations) of the computer program and the human are the same. The point, in general, is that some differences between the computer output and human behavior are irrelevant.

One kind of behavior that would seem much more relevant for our purposes would be the order in which components of the solution are produced. Look back again at the cryptarithmetic problem. The first part of the solution you would expect a human to produce (having been told that D = 5) is that T = 0. This, of course, is because the strategy that humans use leads them to add the two D's and conclude that the T must be equal to 0. If the computer program is using the same strategy as the human, it should do likewise. If the program does not produce T = 0 before the other parts of the solution, then we have strong evidence that the strategy embodied in the program is different from the human's strategy. Given that the hypothetical program we have discussed generates the solution by trying all possible random pairings in turn, if we actually ran the program we would find that it would usually not generate the T = 0 part of the solution first. This difference between human and computer output would tell us that we must either modify the program or throw it out and begin again.

To carry the example further, imagine that we constructed a different theory (and a different program) that produced the parts of the solution in the same order as humans. Would this prove the new theory? No, but it would give us enough confidence in the feasibility of the theory to test it further. In general, we would analyze more and more detailed components of the performance of both human and computer program. For example, we might compare the pattern of incorrect attempts each generated in the course of solution.

The major point of this extended example, then, is that the logic behind computer simulation requires not only that the program be able to exhibit the phenomenon of interest (whether that phenomenon be solving problems, memorizing lists, or comprehending sentences), but also that it simulate the *relevant* characteristics of human performance.

This section began by asking why the cognitive approach received so much impetus during the late 1950's, and we stated that some of the most important contributions came from the field of computer science. The behaviorists had abandoned the study of mental events because they believed that theories of the mind must of necessity be vague and untestable since they postulate unobservable processes and structures. The outcome of both the program analogy and computer simulation has been to render theories of cognition more specific and, hence, more subject to empirical test. To what extent has this analogy and simulation advanced our understanding of the nature of the mind? This question will form the heart of our inquiry.

ASSUMPTIONS OF INFORMATION-PROCESSING THEORIES

It is now time to consider the information-processing approach in more detail. Since information-processing theories are cognitive theories, they share the three characteristics discussed earlier in this chapter. That is, they stress knowing rather than responding, they emphasize mental structure and organization, and they view the individual as active, constructive, and planful. In addition, however, information-processing theories make the following three assumptions, all of which reveal the influence of the program analogy on this theoretical approach.

First, it is assumed that between stimulus and response there is a series of stages of processing, each of which requires a finite amount of time. The assumption that each stage requires time is extremely important, because it implies that measuring the amount of time people take to perform various kinds of tasks will enable us to make inferences about the stages involved. Second, when a stimulus is processed through these stages, the form and content of the stimulus are assumed to undergo a series of changes or transformations. Third, it is assumed that at one or more of these stages the processing system has a limited capacity in the sense that there is a limit on the amount of processing that can occur simultaneously. According to the information-processing approach, then, in order to understand human cognition, it is necessary to determine the series of stages that make up a given act of cognition, and to determine the nature of the changes or transformations that occur at each stage. For example, the information-processing theorist would study problem solving by attempting to determine the stages that occur during problem solving and how information is represented at each of these stages.

As the generality of the three assumptions suggests, the information-processing approach encompasses a wide range of theories. Some of these are global, attempting to describe broad aspects of human cognition; others are concerned with providing detailed models of narrower topics, e.g., how letters are recognized or memory is searched. Throughout the later chapters we will have occasion to examine both global and restricted theories. I begin in the next section by outlining a very general information-processing theory of human cognition, which encompasses memory, language, and thought. This theory contains components of the seminal memory model Atkinson and Shiffrin proposed in 1968 and modified in 1971, but it also draws heavily on more recent formulations (including those of Bjork, 1975; Bower, 1975; Craik & Jacoby, 1975; Craik & Levy, 1976; Hunt, 1971; Hunt & Poltrock, 1974; Shiffrin, 1975; Shiffrin, 1976).

I present such a general theory now to provide an overview of what lies ahead. Since it is meant to be a roadmap, most of the details and virtually all justifications for proposing the theory are left unstated. The point now is to provide you with a preview of what is to come and, more important, an organization that you should keep in mind throughout the more detailed chapters that follow. My goal throughout the book will be to help you understand how the parts of information-processing theories relate to the whole of cognition.

AN INFORMATION-PROCESSING THEORY

The theory that will form the skeleton of this book is depicted in Figure 1–2. The theory assumes that the human information-processing system consists of three functionally distinct kinds of memory systems: the *sensory registers, working memory,* and *long-term memory.* These systems are similar to the hardware of a computer in that they are assumed to be permanent, built in components.

In addition to these *structural components,* the system is also assumed to contain *control processes* which are analogous to the programs of a computer. The "control" part of this term refers to the fact

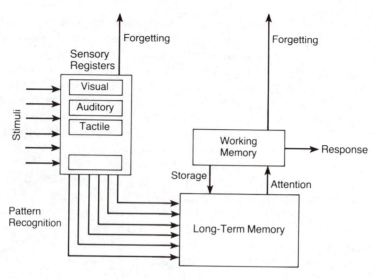

Figure 1–2. A diagram of the overview theory which will form
the framework of this book. We will view remembering,
thinking, and comprehending and producing language as
taking place in such an information-processing system.

that these processes are assumed to govern or control the flow of information within the information-processing system. The control processes may be thought of as strategies that are stored in memory and
may be called into action (i.e., "executed" to use the program analogy) when the occasion demands. We will discuss many kinds of control processes later, but one of the most common is *rehearsal,* which
means overt or covert repetition of an item. Adults often use this particular control process when trying to commit new information to
memory. Other control processes include strategies for solving problems, techniques for searching through memory, and strategies for understanding and producing speech.

Many of the control processes can be adopted or not at the dis-
cretion of the person, and, as such, the control processes embody the
active, planful aspect of human thought that is such an important
component of the cognitive view of human nature. This does not mean,
however, that the person *always* exerts conscious control over which
process to call into action, nor does it mean that the person is capable
of describing all control processes in detail. For example, when engaged in conversation you are using control processes for understanding and producing sentences, yet if I asked you to explain exactly how
you go about doing so, you probably would not be able to tell me.
Using the program analogy, then, we would say that you have stored
programs (i.e., control processes) in memory which enable you to un-

derstand and produce language. You are able to execute these programs when you wish to do so, but you are not able to examine and report the details of the programs.

Characteristics of the structural components. The distinctions among the three kinds of memory systems can be revealed most clearly by examining three characteristics of each. The first characteristic concerns each system's *capacity*. The capacity of a system refers to how much information it can hold at any one time.

The second characteristic concerns the form of representation each system is assumed to contain. When someone sees a tree and later remembers details of the tree, it is obvious that the tree itself is not lodged in the cerebral cortex. Rather, some *representation* that *stands for* the tree is set up in the person's memory and later called to mind when the person recalls that specific tree. There are a number of different ways in which a given event might be represented or *coded*. For example, if you are shown the letters *CAT* you might store in memory a representation of the sound of the word or, alternatively, a representation of the visual image of the word's referent (i.e., a mental picture of a cat). Of course, there are other possibilities as well, the main point here being simply that any given stimulus could be represented in the mind in several different forms. Information-processing theories assume that the representation of a stimulus undergoes changes as it is transferred from one memory system to another.

The third characteristic concerns the cause of *forgetting* from each of the memory systems. All of us are aware of the failures of memory that we call forgetting, and we often think of all instances of forgetting as being similar. As we shall discuss, however, there is good reason to assume that the three kinds of memory systems differ in the causes of forgetting.

Let's now consider each of the systems in turn. The following discussion is summarized in Table 1–2, which displays the assumed characteristics of each.

We begin with the sensory registers because all stimuli presented to the person are assumed to be recorded here first, before they are processed further. In fact, there are assumed to be several sensory registers—one for each of the sensory modalities. As their name suggests, these hold the stimulus information in a form that is closely related to the actual sensory stimulus. That is, the visual sensory register holds an image of the latest visual experience to which the person was exposed, whereas the auditory sensory register holds an echo of the last sounds. The capacity of the sensory registers is large. For example, the visual sensory register keeps a brief record of all visual stimulation that reaches the person's eyes.

One of the most important characteristics of sensory storage is

TABLE 1–2. **Assumed Characteristics of Each Kind of Memory System.**

	Sensory Registers	**Working Memory**	**Long-Term Memory**
Capacity	Large	Small	Functionally infinite
Cause of Forgetting	Primarily decay, but also interference	Primarily interference, but also decay	Retrieval failures
Kind of Representation	Closely tied to form of external stimulus	Flexible, probably including verbal, visual, and semantic	Semantic, verbal, and visual

its extremely brief duration. For example, information resides in the visual sensory register for less than one second. There are two causes of forgetting from sensory memory. The first and most important is automatic *decay*. This means that the memory for an item fades or decays with the passage of time, even if no new stimulus is presented. The second is *interference* or *displacement*. If a given sensory register contains some item, then placing some new item in the same sensory register can interfere with, or displace, the original item.

Thus, the sensory registers hold rapidly fading replicas of external stimulation. Unlike the remaining systems, control processes have little effect on either the duration or the contents of the sensory registers; the individual cannot use strategies to keep information in the sensory registers from decaying or being displaced. Because of the brief duration of sensory storage, we are seldom aware of this memory system. Nonetheless, it performs the important function of prolonging external stimulation long enough for the person to have time to process it further.

The next system to be described, working memory, differs dramatically from the sensory registers. Working memory is assumed to hold information to which the person is attending. The most important characteristic of this system is that it has a very limited capacity. For the moment, it will be helpful to think of this system as containing approximately 7 slots (or drawers) each of which can contain one item. You have probably noticed this limitation when you have looked up a new telephone number. If you need remember only the last 7 digits of the number, there is usually no problem because they do not exceed the capacity limits of working memory. But if you are forced to remember a new area code as well, you often make errors, presumably because you haven't enough slots to hold all these items without error.

Once the capacity of working memory has been reached, if new items are placed in this system they must compete with items already there for the limited space. Usually this will result in some of the items—either the old or the new—being displaced. Such displacement or interference is the major cause of forgetting from working memory. Even if the capacity is not exceeded, however, there is some evidence that items decay from working memory within 15 seconds or so if they are not rehearsed. As long as the items are rehearsed, and the capacity limits of working memory are not exceeded, items can be maintained in this system indefinitely.

In contrast with the sensory registers, which hold replicas of the sensory stimulation, the form of representation of an item in working memory may be different from the form of the external stimulus. For example, a visual stimulus, such as a picture, may lead to a label for that picture (i.e., a *verbal representation*) being placed in working memory. Such verbal coding is a particularly important form of representation in working memory. However, coding in working memory can be not only verbal, but also *visual* (particularly for stimuli that are not easily labeled, such as the face of a stranger), and *semantic*, i.e., a representation of the meaning of the item. The important point for now is that coding in working memory is flexible and can be independent of the type of external stimulus to which the person was exposed.

You will notice that I hedged in the preceding paragraph, using such phrases as "may be different" and "can be independent." I have done so because the form in which a stimulus is represented in working memory varies a great deal depending on the control processes the person adopts in a particular situation; indeed, people are able to exert conscious control over the form of representation in working memory. This contrasts with the sensory registers, since the person has no control over the form of representation in these.

We turn now to the most intriguing structural component of the proposed information-processing system, long-term memory. This is the system that corresponds to what most people have in mind when they speak of memory. Long-term memory is assumed to contain all of an individual's permanent knowledge. The capacity of this system is, for practical purposes at least, unlimited. That is, as far as we know, no one has ever reached the point at which his long-term memory was full to capacity.

It is further assumed that once an item has been stored in long-term memory, it is never erased. Rather, the frequent forgetting we experience is attributed to difficulties in finding—or *retrieving*—material that has been stored. All of us have experienced such *retrieval difficulties*, particularly when taking examinations. After having searched high and low through the backroads of memory for some name or date and finally given up, the sought-after item, seemingly of its own accord, may pop into mind as you walk out of the examination room.

The form of representation in long-term memory is a subject of considerable controversy, but it is clear that this system contains many kinds of information. Perhaps the most important is semantic, for long-term memory contains our knowledge about the meaning of words and experiences. In addition, long-term memory is also assumed to contain verbal codes, in part because most of us feel as though we think in words. It is clear, however, that we have stored away much information that could not be coded verbally. For example, we recognize faces even though we may not have attached any label to them. Similarly we recognize the voices of many people on the telephone, even after years of separation. We remember melodies and odors and tastes. We know not only word meanings, but also how words sound and how they look.

We have still not touched on all the kinds of information contained in long-term memory, for not only do we remember the kinds of facts and experiences described, but we also remember how to do a variety of things. Many of us know how to type and how to ride a bike. We know how to solve arithmetic problems, how to compose a comprehensible paragraph, how to commit new facts to memory, and so on. These observations suggest that long-term memory contains not only *facts*, but also *procedures*. In fact, the control processes we discussed earlier are assumed to be stored in long-term memory as procedures. Considering a computing system will help to make the distinction between facts and procedures clear, because a computer also stores both data (i.e., facts) and programs for manipulating the data (i.e., procedures). For example, the registrar at your college or university probably uses a computer to perform the mysterious machinations that result in the computation of your grade point average. The computer's memory stores both your course grades (facts) and a program (procedure) that tells the central processor how to operate on these data to compute your overall average.

Given the amount of information contained in long-term memory and the rapidity with which most of it can be located (recall our discussion of "rimmelnode"), it is clear that long-term memory must be highly and flexibly organized. In fact, any large capacity storage system must be organized if it is to be useful. Imagine a library that lacked a card catalogue, and shelved books randomly. (Such libraries do exist, my personal collection being a case in point.) If the library contains only a small number of volumes, it is still worth having. If the number of volumes is large, however, the library is almost useless until some organizing scheme is adopted. Not only must the volumes be arranged systematically, but it is also necessary to provide some flexible system for finding (or retrieving) them. A library that contained only an author index in the card catalogue would not help the student who knew only the title of a book. By providing author, title, and subject cards, libraries attempt to provide more flexibility for their users. Similarly, our long-term memory appears to be organized flexibly, because we are able to find a particular item of information given many different kinds of cues. For example, either seeing a bird, seeing the letters *BIRD*, hearing the sound *burd*, or being asked "What has feathers and flies?" all lead us to the location in long-term memory that contains our knowledge about birds. Determining exactly how long-term memory is organized to enable such flexible retrieval has proven a fascinating challenge for cognitive psychologists, and we'll examine these attempts in later chapters.

Relations among the systems.   Now that we have discussed the major characteristics of each memory system, let's consider how they operate together, by tracing the sequence of events assumed to take place between presentation of a stimulus and generation of a response. Frequent reference to Figure 1–2 is particularly important for this discussion.

At any one moment many stimuli (and hence the several incoming arrows in Figure 1–2) impinge on the person's sensory organs. Sensory representations of all these stimuli reside briefly in the appropriate sensory registers. We also assume that each of these representations automatically contacts a place in long-term memory where information about it is kept, that is, where some of the permanent knowledge about the stimulus is located. This process of identifying a stimulus is termed *pattern recognition*. For example, when the letter *Q* is presented, we assume that a visual replica of the letter is automatically stored in the visual sensory register and that this visual representation automatically activates, or excites, the place in long-term memory at which information about the letter (e.g., its name) is stored. Notice, then, that we assume pattern recognition to take place automatically regardless of whether the person actively attends to the item or not. For this reason Figure 1–2 depicts many arrows going from the sensory registers to long-term memory, to indicate that at this point in information processing there are not severe capacity limitations; we can pattern recognize many items simultaneously.

Be sure that you do not misinterpret the arrows going from the sensory registers to long-term memory. We assume that part of the long-term memory representation of an item is automatically contacted whenever that item is placed in the sensory register, but we do *not* assume that a permanent record of that occurrence is stored in long-term memory. You might think of this pattern recognition process as similar to looking up an item in the dictionary, in that looking up the item does not change what is stored in the dictionary (or long-term memory) itself.

We assume that new information is stored permanently in long-term memory *only if* further *attention* is given to the item, i.e., only if it is placed in working memory. Notice, then, that capacity limitations come into play at this point. Since working memory represents the limited capacity component of the information processing system, there will be a limit to how many items this system can maintain at once. Therefore, if the person is exposed to many stimuli simultaneously, only some of these will receive the attention that is necessary for them to be remembered later. To depict this severe limitation, we have drawn only one arrow from long-term memory to working memory, and one from working memory to long-term memory. In sum, all stimuli that impinge on a person's sensory organs are assumed to have some temporary effect on the information processing system, but most of these make no permanent impression, fading away before the person has a chance to attend to them (i.e., place them in working memory). Only items that receive such attention are assumed to be placed in long-term memory.

Consider what is assumed to happen in the information processing system when the person makes a response. For example, the person may say "That's a Q" when presented with the letter Q. Figure 1–2 depicts the response being generated from working memory, because the production of a response is also assumed to require some of the person's limited capacity.

Having completed a brief survey of the major characteristics of the human information processing system and the ways in which the various components are assumed to interact, it is important to make three general points about the theory outlined here. First, you should always keep in mind that information about a given experience or fact may be in more than one system simultaneously. For example, you have a record of your telephone number stored in your long-term memory. When you have occasion to tell that number to someone else, you copy a representation of the number into working memory, but you do *not* remove the representation of the number from long-term memory.

A second general point is that information processing frequently occurs in the absence of any external stimulus and without leading to any external response. For example, you may be sitting in a quiet, darkened room (or, for that matter, in a noisy bar) and decide to think about the history of China, or to daydream about the weekend ahead. In the former case you might dredge up what you know about China's history, perhaps noticing a relation between stored events that you had never noticed before, and then modify the contents of your long-term memory to reflect this new insight. In the latter case, you might create elaborate and detailed mental scenarios of what you imagine yourself doing and, more practically, you might devise plans for how you will go about making these daydreams come true. In both cases, you would have called into action various control processes, placed some information into working memory and changed the contents of long-term memory without having processed any external stimulus or made any overt response. In fact, the only system that is closely tied to the external world is sensory storage. The sensory register for any sensory modality will contain information *only* if that modality has just received stimulation. Thinking about the picture of a sunset will not result in the representation of a sunset being placed in the sensory register. It will, however, result in some representation of a sunset being placed in working memory.

A third general point is that although the theory I've outlined emphasizes memory, it encompasses language and thinking as well. In fact, when multi-store (or multi-system) models of the sort described here were first proposed (e.g., Atkinson and Shiffrin, 1968), they were designed to be theories of memory, and to the present day, information-processing theorists view memory as the central component of cognition. More recently, however, multi-store models have been elaborated to make them not only theories of memory, but theories of cognition. Throughout the book I will elaborate the overview theory to describe the series of processes and the organization of knowledge that are involved in understanding and producing language as well as in thinking.

In fact, you should already have some understanding of how language and thinking may be viewed in the theory outlined. For example, long-term memory is assumed to store procedures or programs that can be called into action for understanding and producing language and for solving problems. Long-term memory also contains knowledge about the spelling, sound, and meaning of words, knowledge which is critical for reading, listening, and communicating. When we examine language and thinking in later chapters we will be attempting to specify the nature of these procedures and knowledge more precisely. Furthermore, the limited capacity working memory places severe limitations on the number of things we can think about at once, limitations which influence problem solving and the ability to comprehend and produce language.

Three kinds of store or three kinds of activation?   We have postulated three distinct kinds of memory system, but it is important to realize that these systems need not be physically separate structures. That is, we need not assume that working memory is located in one part of the brain and long-term memory in another. In fact, these three systems may be thought of as different kinds of activation of the same location. For example, we might postulate that there is only one memory store, but that it contains three different kinds of storage. One of these (i.e., long-term storage) is permanent and represents a permanent change in the nervous system. We could further assume that there are two kinds of temporary excitation (or activation) of this same memory store. One of these temporary kinds of activation usually lasts for a second or less and emphasizes the physical characteristics of any presented stimulus. There is no limit to how many locations can be activated at once for this sensory storage activation, but the person has no control over what items will be activated in this way, nor can he control how long the activation lasts. This kind of activation, of course, corresponds to the sensory registers depicted in Figure 1–2. Finally, we might postulate a second kind of temporary activation that can emphasize any of a number of characteristics of the stimulus (i.e., many possible forms of representation) and that can be continued indefinitely via rehearsal. This second kind of temporary activation, which corresponds to the working memory of Figure 1–2, would be assumed to have a limited capacity in that only a small number of items can be activated at once.

At the present stage of development of information-processing theories, we cannot distinguish between the three-kinds-of-store model and the three-kinds-of-activation model. That is, no one has been able to think of an experimental test that would enable us to decide between these two possibilities. Therefore, for our purposes at least, they may be thought of interchangeably. Throughout the book I will usually use the three stores terminology, because it simplifies the discussion

INFORMATION-PROCESSING THEORY AND THE ANALYSIS OF INDIVIDUAL DIFFERENCES

So far the information-processing approach has contributed primarily to basic research and theory. Within the last few years, however, it has become clear that information-processing theory offers a promising perspective for addressing practical questions as well. One such application to which we will return frequently is the analysis of individual differences in cognition.

For many years psychologists and educators alike have been concerned with determining how people differ from each other. For example, educators have wished to determine how the thinking of the child who does well in school differs from that of the child who does not. Clinical psychologists have wanted to know how the thought patterns of the schizophrenic person differ from those of the non-schizophrenic. Unfortunately, during the last century experimental psychologists have contributed little to our understanding of such individual differences. Instead, a separate subdivision of psychology—often called *psychometrics* or psychological tests and measurements—has emerged. Psychometricians have developed standardized tests (such as IQ tests and SAT tests) which are especially designed to measure individual differences. Usually such tests have been developed for the purpose of predicting how well the person tested is likely to do in some later academic situation. For example, IQ tests have been constructed by choosing a set of questions which differentiate children who will later do well in school from those who will not. Such tests, then, are pragmatically, not theoretically, based. A given question is included in the test, not because it is assumed to reflect some particular thought process, but rather because the extent to which it is answered correctly predicts later school performance.

Within the past few years the situation has changed. The recent development of information-processing theories has encouraged an increasing number of experimentalists to attempt a theoretically based analysis of individual differences in cognition. Notice that the information-processing theory outlined suggests the kinds of questions one might ask about individual differences. For example, at what stages of information processing are there individual differences: in sensory storage, working memory, or in long-term memory? Are any differences that emerge attributable primarily to changes in the structural components of the system or in the control processes? Are there individual differences in the capacity of the various systems, in their duration, in the form of representation that is likely to be used, and so on?

Foremost among the cognitive psychologists investigating individual differences in information processing is Professor Earl Hunt. He and his students and colleagues have taken advantage of the fact that all entering freshmen at the University of Washington take a battery of tests (similar to the SATs) which yields a Quantitative Ability and a Verbal Ability score for each student. These tests were designed atheoretically in the psychometric tradition. Hunt has administered many of the information-processing tasks we will be discussing throughout this book to University of Washington students to determine which such tasks distinguish between students who score high and low on these standardized tests. As we shall see later, his work is already suggesting some interesting hypotheses about the nature of individual differences in cognition. In addition, Hunt has extended his work to study individuals with extraordinarily accurate memory in an attempt to determine exactly what components of information processing distinguish them from the rest of us ordinary and forgetful mortals.

All of this is to anticipate our story a bit, for we will return to

Hunt's and others' analyses of individual differences throughout the book. Before concluding the present discussion, however, it is important to address one further question: why attempt to develop theoretically based analyses of individual differences?—that is, since we already have IQ tests that predict later school performance reasonably well, why try to analyze such individual differences from the information-processing perspective? There are two major reasons, one practical and the other theoretical. First, it is true that the psychometrically designed tests are predictive and diagnostic, but since they do not reveal what is different about the thought processes of "high IQ" as opposed to "low IQ" individuals, they offer no guidance if we wish to design educational techniques to help the low-scoring person. The point is particularly obvious in the case of the mentally retarded individual; the standardized IQ test enables us to classify this person as subnormal in intelligence, but it does not tell us how to help the person function more adequately. On the other hand, if we were able to isolate exactly what aspects of information processing differentiate the retarded individual from the person of normal intelligence, then it might be possible to design educational experiences that would improve that aspect of information processing and lead to a corresponding improvement in cognitive functioning. Indeed, Ann Brown and her colleagues (e.g., Brown, Campione, Bray, & Wilcox, 1973; Brown, Campione, & Murphy, 1974) have already reported some success in working with retarded children.

The second advantage of looking at individual differences is theoretical. Eventually an adequate understanding of human cognition must specify both those aspects of thought that are similar across individuals and those which differ from one person to another. As long as we attempt to examine only the similarities, our theories will be incomplete. Indeed, by averaging the results from many different people and looking only at the final averages, we may be obtaining results that are not representative of any one individual. This is somewhat akin to using census figures to conclude that the average American family contains 2.3 children. Although this may, indeed, be the average, it is clear that no one family has ever had 2.3 children.

UNIVERSAL PATTERNS OF HUMAN THOUGHT?

Ever since missionaries and explorers returned from exotic lands reporting the "strange" thought processes of the natives, people have been intrigued by the notion that there might be important cultural differences in human cognition. To what extent are the theories and research findings we will be discussing applicable to all human beings? Are there certain universals of human information processing that remain relatively unchanged across enormous differences in physical environment, social setting, and educational system?

Unfortunately, most research has been conducted with college students in the United States as subjects, so the extent to which there are cultural universals of information processing is unclear, and a topic very much in need of more investigation. Throughout the book whenever possible we will examine cross-cultural research that might give some indication of the universality of the processes we are studying.

CHAPTER SUMMARY

Psychology is undergoing a scientific revolution. Behaviorism had dominated the discipline during the first half of the twentieth century, but the last two decades have brought a rebirth of interest in the cognitive approach to psychology. This approach has three characteristics which distinguish it from behaviorism. It emphasizes the study of knowledge, rather than behavior. It stresses mental structure and organization, rather than simple associations, and it views the individual as being active, constructive, and planful, rather than the passive recipient of environmental stimulation.

Contributions from two other disciplines were instrumental in precipitating the revolution. On the one hand linguists, such as Noam Chomsky, argued that behaviorism was, in principle, inadequate to explain how people acquire and use language. The linguists' criticisms came to the attention of psychologists in the late 1950's. At about the same time, rapid developments in computer science provided psychology with both a new way of testing theories (computer simulation), and with a new analogy for human thought (the program analogy).

The new kind of theory that grew out of the program analogy is called information-processing theory. In addition to the three characteristics of all cognitive theories, information-processing theories make three assumptions: (1) Between stimulus and response there is a series of stages of processing, each of which requires a finite amount of time. (2) When a stimulus is processed through these stages it undergoes a series of transformations. (3) At one or more of these stages there is limited capacity, i.e., a limit on how much can be done at once.

Throughout the rest of the book we will examine information-processing theory in more detail, and this chapter presented an overview theory which will provide an organizing framework for the more detailed discussions ahead. This overview theory assumes that there are three functionally distinct memory systems. These systems differ from each other in their capacity, the form of representation they contain, and the nature of the forgetting that occurs. Remembering, comprehending and using language, and thinking are all assumed to reflect the interactions among these three systems.

Not only does the information-processing approach offer insights into the universal characteristics of human cognition, but it also suggests a promising new way of analyzing individual and cultural differences.

SUGGESTED READING

(Full references for all the suggested readings are included under the author's name in the References section at the end of the book.) Two books published in the 1960's captured the interest and imagination of many experimental psychologists and converted many behaviorists to the cognitive approach. The first is *Plans and the Structure of Behavior* by Miller, Galanter, and Pribram, and the second is Ulric Neisser's *Cognitive Psychology*. Both provide thought-provoking and enjoyable reading. Chapter 3 of Miller, Galanter, and Pribram offers a particularly good historical introduction to simulation. If you'd like to find out what Neisser thinks of his own book a decade after he wrote it, read his *Cognition and Reality* published in 1976.

A detailed account of the historical antecedents of the information-processing approach may be found in the Appendix of Newell and Simon's *Human Problem Solving* and in a 1974 chapter by Haber in the *Handbook of Perception*. In addition, you will find an interesting account of the cognitive revolution in the first chapter of Palermo's recent text *The Psychology of Language*.

The best sources for additional reading on the contribution of computers to psychology are *The Thinking Computer* by Bertram Raphael, the book edited by Feigenbaum and Feldman entitled *Computers and Thought*, and the text by Patrick Winston entitled *Artificial Intelligence*. For a more skeptical account see Dreyfus' *What Computers Can't Do*. You may also wish to read Walter Reitman's *Cognition and Thought* which provides a useful discussion of the promise and problems inherent in computer simulation.

If you wish to read some of the original papers in which general information-processing theories are presented, I suggest that you begin with the two papers by Atkinson and Shiffrin mentioned in the current chapter. Of the more recent papers, I particularly recommend Bower, 1975, because it is broader in scope than most, and Hunt's 1971 paper entitled "What kind of computer is Man?"

Additional discussion of both individual differences and cross-cultural research will be included in later chapters, but if you want to get a preview of the work on individual differences, you might read Hunt's 1978 article in the *Psychological Review*, the 1975 paper by

Hunt and Lansman published in one volume of a series edited by William Estes, and an article on testing and cognitive psychology by Robert Sternberg in the *American Psychologist*. In the Estes volume Medin and Cole emphasize the importance of cross-cultural research on human cognition. If you are particularly interested in the latter topic, you must read *Culture and Thought* by Cole and Scribner. Not only does it provide a fascinating review of many cross-cultural studies, but it offers an excellent critical discussion of cross-cultural research and theory.

Memory TWO

The Sensory Registers

FOOD FOR THOUGHT

Consider what the following three phenomena have in common. First, if you are in a darkened room with someone who is waving a brightly lit cigarette, you will notice that the cigarette seems to leave a trail of light behind it. In fact, if the conditions are right, it is often possible to write letters or forms in the air. A second more common experience is the "What did you say" phenomenon. You experience this when, thinking you have missed part of a conversation, you ask the speaker to repeat a sentence. Before the speaker finishes doing so, however, you realize that the repetition wasn't necessary after all, because in the interim you finished understanding the rest of the sentence. The third phenomenon occurs when you suddenly become aware of an abrupt silence, even though you had not previously noticed the presence of a background noise. This detection of a change in the ambient noise level leads you to think back to identify the nature of the background noise that just stopped (e.g., to realize an air conditioner had been running). The important point here is that the listener identifies the sound only *after* it has ceased.

According to the information-processing model described in the previous chapter, all of these phenomena have at least one feature in common; they reflect the operation of the sensory registers which are the focus of this chapter.

The sensory registers are of extremely brief duration and this brevity renders them particularly mysterious, for we have difficulty introspecting about such short-lived memories. Until you read the previous chapter you were probably completely unaware of their existence.

THE VISUAL SENSORY REGISTER

We begin by considering the visual sensory register because it has been the most widely studied and, consequently, is the best understood of the sensory memories. The visual sensory register has been given many different names including the *visual information store,* the *visual sensory store,* and the *visual preperceptual store,* but the most graphic of all is *iconic memory.* Neisser (1967) suggested this designation when he concluded that this short-lived sensory memory contains an icon, or picture, of the external stimulus. We will use the terms visual sensory register, visual sensory store, and iconic memory interchangeably, and the term *icon* to refer to the contents of the store.

Sperling's partial report studies. The notion that there is a visual trace that outlasts the external stimulus is not new, but recent interest in the properties of the icon began in earnest in 1960 when George Sperling published a monograph which was based on his doctoral dissertation at Harvard University. Sperling's original goal was not so much to study memory as it was to study perception, and indeed one of the most important contributions of Sperling's work was to demonstrate the intimate relation between memory and perception.

Sperling's monograph begins with a statement of the question that concerned him, "How much can be seen in a single brief exposure?" (Sperling, 1960, p. 1) He noted that this question has long fascinated psychologists, because it has been known since before the turn of the century that visual perception consists of a series of brief exposures. When you scan a room or read a paragraph, your eyes do not move continuously across the scene. Rather, they are stationary for a brief period, which is called a *fixation*, then they move rapidly in what is called a *saccadic eye movement* to a new fixation. Thus, during scanning your eyes literally jump across the scene. During the saccadic movements very little information is taken in, so our knowledge of the visual world must be built up from a series of brief fixations, each of which can last as little as one-quarter of a second. It is for this reason that it is important to determine how much can be taken in during a single brief exposure.

In all of Sperling's studies subjects peered into a *tachistoscope*, which is a device that enables the experimenter to present visual stimuli for precisely specified durations. Each subject in Sperling's first experiment participated in a series of trials. On each trial he was shown an array of letters for 50 milliseconds (msec). A *millisecond* is 1/1000 of a second, so Sperling's subjects saw the array for only 1/20 of a second, a brief duration to be sure. Sperling also varied the number of letters presented to the subject, with the array containing as few as 3 letters on some trials and as many as 12 letters on others. The subject's task was to report immediately as many of the letters as possible. Sperling's results are depicted by the lowest curve in Figure 2–1, which shows the number of letters correctly reported as a function of the number of letters in the array. Before examining the results, notice that if subjects were able to report the entire array, then the results would fall on the diagonal of this figure, i.e., subjects would report 3 letters when 3 had been presented and 12 letters when 12 had been presented. The data Sperling actually obtained are shown in the function labeled "whole report." Notice that performance was perfect for arrays of 4 items or less, but for larger arrays the subjects were able to report only about 4.5 items correctly, regardless of how many items were presented. This limitation doesn't hold only for 50 msec presentations; in a second study Sperling showed that reducing the duration of the array to 15 msec or extending it to 500 msec made no difference. As Sperling noted, this limit of 4 to 5 on the number of items

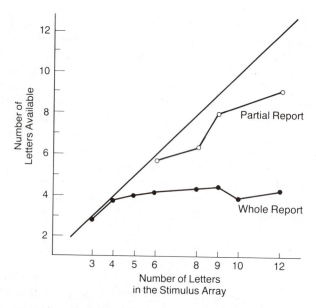

Figure 2–1. Performance in Sperling's experiment when subjects were asked to report part of the array (open circles) compared with when they were to report the whole array (closed circles). The graph shows the number of letters that were available as a function of the number of letters contained in the stimulus array. If the entire array were available, the data points would fall along the diagonal line. (After Sperling, 1960. Copyright 1960 by the American Psychological Association. Reprinted by permission of the publisher and author.)

that can be reported from a brief display had been known since the turn of the century and is usually termed the *span of apprehension.*

Does this span of apprehension indicate that we are able to take in no more than 4 or 5 items in each fixation? Sperling suspected not. He knew that ever since Cattell's study in 1883, subjects had been insisting that they were able to see more than they could report. Sperling's subjects were no exception. They reported that they perceived a complete visual array, but that it faded away before they were able to report all the letters they had seen. In other words, subjects over the decades had been insisting that the span of apprehension reflected a limit on how many items they could report, not a limit on how many items they could perceive.

Sperling developed a simple, but ingenious way of overcoming this report limitation. He asked the subject to report only a sample of the array on each trial. Sperling reasoned that if the experimenter chose the portion randomly, so that the subject could not predict which part of the array would be tested, then it would be possible to use the per cent correct on the tested portion to estimate how much of the whole array the subject must have perceived.

Sperling's reasoning here is exactly that employed in most testing situations. If you are taking a course, the professor wishes to determine how much of the material you have mastered. It is not practical to ask you to report everything you know, however, so instead you are asked about only a sample of the material. The professor then assumes that if you answered 100% of the test questions correctly, you probably know 100% of the material covered in the course. In order for this assumption to be valid, of course, it is important that the student not know exactly what questions will be asked ahead of time, for then it would be possible to get 100% of the questions correct knowing only a fraction of the material in the course—i.e., exactly that fraction tested.

Using this reasoning, then, Sperling developed what he called the *partial report procedure*. The following sequence of events occurred on each trial. The subject was shown a visual array with either 9 or 12 letters (3 rows of either 3 or 4 letters each) for 50 msec. Immediately *after* the array was turned off, the subject was presented with a cue that specified which one of the 3 rows should be reported. This cue consisted of a tone of high, medium, or low frequency (i.e., pitch), signaling the subject to report the top, middle, or bottom row, respectively. Sperling recorded the number of correct responses on each trial. He estimated how much of the entire array the subject perceived (i.e., how much of the entire array was available) by calculating the per cent correct on the partial test. For example, if on the 12 item array subjects got ¼ or 25% of an individual row correct, Sperling would estimate that they must have perceived 25% of the entire array, or .25 × 12 = 3 items. In general, then, it is possible to calculate the number of items available on partial report trials by determining the per cent correct on the sample tested, and multiplying this percentage times the number of items in the whole array.

When Sperling examined his partial report data, he found that more items were available than the 4 or 5 revealed in the full report procedure. On the 12 item array, for example, subjects usually got slightly more than 3 of the 4 tested items correct, suggesting that they had available about 76% of the whole array or 9.1 items. These results are shown by the upper curve in Figure 2–1 which plots the number of items available for partial report trials.

Sperling's partial report data reveal that the protests of subjects throughout the decades were quite correct; they did perceive many more items than the span of apprehension would indicate. Indeed, the function of number of items available derived from the partial report data indicates performance that is almost perfect. Apparently, then, subjects are able to take in a large part of the array in one glance, but in the time available for reporting they are able to produce only about 4 items.

Sperling's subjects reported another observation that we haven't investigated yet, and it is this observation that takes us to the evidence for a brief duration iconic memory. People reported that they perceived the visual array as fading away, rather than terminating abruptly. This led Sperling to hypothesize that the entire array might be available, not only immediately at the offset of the stimulus, but also for some time afterward. In other words, there might be a sensory memory that outlasts the external stimulus. Sperling sought evidence for such a sensory memory by administering the partial report cue, and determining how many items were available, at various delays after the array itself had been turned off. By doing so he hoped to be able to follow the time course of any such short-lived memory. Figure 2–2 depicts Sperling's results for the 12 item array, and it also includes the whole report performance for comparison. Notice that for cues which occur as late as 300 msec after the array is turned off the subject still has a considerable proportion of the array available, but by 1 second, performance is little better than it would be on whole report trials.

Combining the results of all the research we've discussed so far, Sperling concluded that there is a rapidly fading visual sensory memory that outlasts the stimulus for approximately ¼ of a second. This sensory memory is of large capacity since it contains virtually all of the items in a visually presented array. In fact, in a later partial report study, Averbach and Sperling (1961) presented 16 items and found that subjects had almost all of this larger array available as well.

Consider Sperling's findings in the context of the information-processing model outlined in the previous chapter. Upon presentation, a record of the visual stimulus array is set up in the visual sensory memory. As Figure 1–2 suggests, however, responses cannot be generated directly from this large capacity store. In order for a letter to be reported, it must first be recognized and processed through the limited capacity working memory. The latter process takes time, during which the sensory memory is decaying quite rapidly. Thus, if whole report of the entire array is requested, the subject has time to identify and report only about 4.5 items before the array fades away. On partial report trials, however, if the cue arrives before the array has completely faded away, then the subject is able to selectively identify and report the particular part of the array requested. If the partial report cue is delayed until after the icon has faded away, however, then the subject will be able to report only those items he had already identified and placed in working memory.

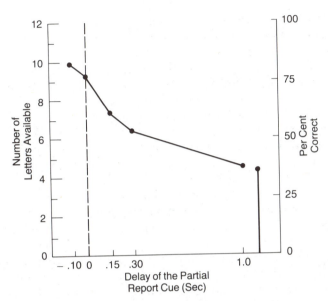

Figure 2–2. Performance in Sperling's experiment for 12-item stimulus arrays when the cue for partial report was presented at varying intervals before and after offset of the stimulus array. The graph shows the number of letters that were available (on the left axis) and the per cent correct (on the right axis) as a function of the delay of the partial report cue. The solid vertical bar at the right shows performance on whole report trials, for comparison. (After Sperling, 1960. Copyright 1960 by the American Psychological Association. Reprinted by permission of the publisher and author.)

Form of representation. The findings we have considered so far provide evidence for the existence of a large-capacity but short-lived memory for visually presented stimuli, but as yet we have not discussed evidence that bears directly on a very important question: what kind of representation does this memory contain?

Sperling argued that the visual sensory memory contains a veridical, mental "picture" or icon of the visual stimulus array. Thus, the representation stored in visual sensory memory is assumed to be *precategorical* in that it has not yet been categorized or classified. Categorization requires the use of knowledge stored in long-term memory, and as Figure 1–2 suggests, sensory storage is assumed to occur before long-term memory becomes involved.

The conclusion that sensory memory contains a fading precategorical visual image is consistent with the introspections subjects have reported, but the experimental evidence we have discussed so far does not necessarily imply this conclusion. For example, it is possible that rather than containing a precategorical visual icon of the array, this large capacity, brief duration store contains a verbal description, e.g., a representation of the sounds of all the letters in the array.

In fact, there are several forms of evidence which argue against the latter verbal encoding hypothesis. We will now consider five of these because this discussion will provide an opportunity to introduce some important experimental techniques for investigating how the mind represents external experience. In addition, along the way we will discover more about the duration of this memory and about the causes of forgetting from it.

The first kind of evidence comes from studies of *visual persistence*. If visual sensory memory contains an icon, then it should be possible to observe such persistence of vision in situations other than Sperling's task. In fact, for at least two centuries it has been known that the subjective impression of a visual stimulus often seems to outlast the stimulus itself. Such persistence of vision is experienced in the case of the cigarette in the darkened room discussed at the beginning of the chapter. As long ago as 1740, Segner (reported in Baddeley, 1976) used this phenomenon to measure the duration of visual persistence. He attached a glowing ember to the spoke of a wheel. After determining the rate at which the wheel had to be rotated in order for a complete circle to be seen, he calculated how long it took for one such rotation. Segner obtained an estimate of 100 msec for visual persistence in this situation—a duration amazingly similar to Sperling's estimate, given the substantial differences in the situation of testing.

More recently, Haber and his colleagues at the University of Rochester have reported the results of a number of studies reminiscent of Segner's early attempt. In one such study (Haber & Standing, 1969) subjects were presented with a black outlined form which was flashed on and off several times. Each time the form was on, it lasted for exactly 10 msec, but the experimenter could vary the duration of the intervening off periods. Subjects were asked to view this display and report when the form had completely faded away before it reappeared. If there is a veridical fading image of the stimulus that lasts for about ¼ of a second, then when the interstimulus interval is less than 250 msec, the stimulus should never disappear completely since the person would continue to see the icon. In fact, this is exactly what Haber and Standing found. The shortest interstimulus interval at which subjects reported that the circle disappeared completely was about 250 msec.

A very different technique for measuring visual persistence also yielded results consistent with this ¼ second estimate. In this study (Haber & Standing, 1970) subjects were again presented with a brief duration visual stimulus. In this case, however, they were simply asked to adjust auditory clicks so that they corresponded with the onset and offset of the visual stimulus. Haber and Standing calculated the subjective duration of the visual stimulus by recording the difference in time between the two auditory clicks set by the subject. Once again the results suggested that visual stimuli which are presented for a brief duration (e.g., 50 msec) are perceived as lasting approximately 250 msec.

One additional kind of visual persistence study is particularly interesting. An example of the stimuli used in this experiment is shown in Figure 2–3. Each of the top two panels of this figure seems to consist of a random set of dots, but when superimposed, as they are in the lowest panel, the dots spell out the syllable VOH.

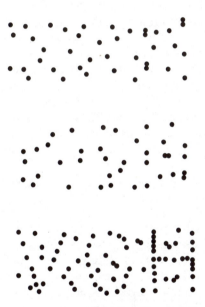

Figure 2–3. The stimuli used in Eriksen and Collin's (1967) study of visual persistence. The items in the top two panels were presented sequentially. When superimposed, they spell out the nonsense syllable VOH, as shown in the bottom panel. (After Eriksen & Collins, 1967. Copyright 1967 by the American Psychological Association. Reprinted by permission of the publisher and author.)

If there is a persisting icon, then the subject should be able to report the nonsense syllable, even if there is a delay of up to 250 msec between offset of the first panel and onset of the second superimposed panel. Eriksen and Collins (1967; 1968) tested this prediction by presenting subjects with the two halves of the stimulus (i.e., the two top panels of Figure 2–3) for 6 msec each, one after the other, and they varied the duration between offset of the first half and onset of the second half (the interstimulus interval). Their findings were consistent with the assumption that there is a decaying visual trace of approximately ¼ second duration. Subjects were most accurate at reporting the nonsense syllable when the two arrays were presented simultaneously, and the probability of correctly identifying the syllable declined as the interstimulus interval increased, with the rate of decline in performance leveling off at between 100 and 300 msec.

These studies of visual persistence are particularly important for two reasons. First, they provide a different way of assessing the duration of visual sensory storage. The fact that the durations obtained are consistent with those from Sperling's partial report method gives us added confidence in the generality of Sperling's findings. Second, and more important, they suggest that this sensory memory does contain an icon, or visual persistence of the stimulus. It would be difficult to account for any of these phenomena by postulating a verbally encoded memory. Indeed, in visual persistence studies, subjects do not seem to differentiate between the external stimulus and their sensory memory of it.

A second kind of evidence for the conclusion that visual sensory memory contains a fading sensory impression of the stimulus is that even though its duration is usually approximately 250 msec, the exact duration of the icon is affected by the physical conditions under which the stimulus is presented. It has been demonstrated (Averbach & Sperling, 1961) that if the blank displays immediately preceding and following the array in Sperling's task are very dark, then the icon may persist for more than a second, but if these pre- and post-exposure displays are very bright, then the duration of the icon may be less than ¼ of a second. Subjects report that in the latter condition, the letter display seems to be washed out by the bright light.

Another important characteristic of the presentation conditions in Sperling's procedure is the brightness of the display of letters itself. A bright display of letters results in a longer duration icon than does a dimmer display (e.g., Keele & Chase, 1967). Furthermore, in studies of visual persistence the duration of visual persistence is also found to depend on such characteristics of the stimulus, a finding that is in keeping with the conclusion that visual persistence studies and Sperling's partial report procedure are both tapping the same high capacity, brief duration sensory memory. This intimate relation between the conditions of presentation and the duration of the icon is consistent with the notion that the icon is closely tied to the external world, and as we will see in later chapters, is a feature of sensory memory that stands in sharp contrast to the other memory systems.

A third form of evidence which argues for the visual nature of the icon is that under certain conditions, subsequent presentations of new visual stimuli degrade or interfere with the icon (Averbach, 1963; Sperling, 1963), whereas subsequent auditory stimuli do not. Suppose that we conduct Sperling's partial report study, but instead of following the display of letters with a blank display, we follow it with some sort of patterned stimulus, e.g., a closely meshed grid. We would find that this subsequent stimulus severely degrades or even terminates the icon of the letters. It is clear that this is a visual phenomenon because subsequent auditory stimuli do not affect the icon. Notice that the *visual masking* just described also reveals a second cause of forgetting from the visual sensory memory. Not only does the image decay spontaneously within 250 msec or so, but if a second visual stimulus is presented before the icon has faded, this new stimulus interferes with the icon of the first.

A fourth kind of evidence for the precategorical nature of the icon comes from studies concerning the kind of partial report cue that is effective. If the icon contains a visual trace in unrecognized sensory form, then the only kind of information that has been extracted from the stimulus is the physical properties of the array. If this is the case, then the only kind of partial report cue that people should be able to use effectively is a cue based on visual aspects of the array. Cues that are based on some non-visual aspect of the items in the array, and hence require reference to long-term memory, should not be helpful, since you can't know which items to report until after you have identified them. By that time, most of the rest of the icon will have decayed.

Coltheart, Lea, and Thompson (1974) reported one study in which this prediction was tested. These researchers used Sperling's whole and partial report techniques, but on each trial the array consisted of two rows of four letters each. Half of the letters were red and half were black, and half had a long e sound (e.g., *BCDGPT*) whereas the other half had a short e sound (e.g., *FLMNSX*). On partial report trials subjects could be presented with one of three different kinds of cues, all of which were conveyed by tones. On trials with the Row partial report cue, subjects were instructed to report either the top or the bottom row. This is a replication of Sperling's original procedure. On trials with the Color partial report cue, subjects were instructed to report either all the red letters or all the black. Finally, with Sound partial report cues the subjects were instructed to report either all the letters with the long e sound or all the letters with the short e sound.

If the visual sensory memory contains relatively unprocessed visual information, then either the Row or the Color partial report cues should reveal performance superior to whole report. The visual image contains that information and so the subject should be able to read off the requested letters. The Sound cue is very different, however, for it is not contained directly in the visual image. In order to know whether or not to report a particular letter, it would be necessary to first identify the letter, because the visual form alone doesn't reveal whether a letter has a long or short e sound. Thus, for the Sound partial report cue, partial report should not be superior to whole report. This is exactly the pattern Coltheart et al. obtained. Partial report was better than whole report for both the Row (as in Sperling) and the Color cues, but not for the Sound cue. Other studies have revealed similar findings (e.g., Sperling, 1960; Turvey & Kravetz, 1970; von Wright, 1968; 1972); cues based on a visual characteristic of the array, such as shape, position, size, and color, are effective, but partial report cues which require that the items be identified, such as consonants vs. digits, are not.

A final kind of evidence for the visual nature of the information in the visual sensory register comes from the study of the kinds of confusion errors people make. This is a particularly important technique, for analyzing patterns of errors is useful for revealing many characteristics of mental events. Consider once more Sperling's partial and whole report studies, but rather than examining how many correct responses the subject makes, instead we will look only at the errors, to see how the letter the subject reports is related to the letter that was, in fact, correct. Sperling himself (and later Keele and Chase, 1967) reported that many of these errors reflected what seemed to be visual confusions. That is, subjects would recall the letter E when the correct letter was F, or the letter O when the correct letter was Q. If subjects are holding a rapidly decaying visual image of the stimulus and reporting the parts requested by the experimenter, this is exactly the kind of error we would expect. Parts of the image would become blurred, leading visually similar letters to be confused. As we will see later, the predominance of such visual confusions is another feature of the visual sensory register that distinguishes it from both working and long-term memory.

Summary. We have considered a number of kinds of evidence which suggest the existence of a short-lived, high capacity sensory memory that prolongs the duration of brief visual stimuli. This discussion also reveals the generality of a property of human information processing referred to in Chapter 1. We noted there that human information processing must be thought of as an active process, the outcome of which is not dependent solely upon the external stimulus.

Now it is true that the visual sensory register is quite closely linked to the external stimulus. That is, the icon contains a veridical depiction of the external stimulus, and the visual sensory register will contain an icon if and only if a visual stimulus reaches the retina. Furthermore, strategies and past experience exert little influence on the contents or duration of the icon. These characteristics make sensory storage very different from later stages of information processing.

Nonetheless, even at this level of information processing, we find a discontinuity between the external world and cognition. Indeed, we mistake the icon for the external world; Sperling's subjects thought that the stimulus itself was fading away gradually, but in reality it was their memory of the stimulus that was fading. The stimulus itself had been turned off much more abruptly ¼ of a second before. Similarly, in all of the visual persistence studies we discussed, people interpreted their sensory memory of a stimulus as an extension of the external stimulus itself. Even at this early stage of information processing, then, our perception of the external world is not dependent solely upon the stimulus presented, but is influenced by the characteristics of memory.

THE AUDITORY SENSORY REGISTER

The auditory sensory memory has been given many names including the *auditory sensory store*, the *auditory preperceptual store*, the *precategorical acoustic store*, and the *auditory information store*, but as in the case of vision, Neisser's (1967) terminology is most descriptive. He called it *echoic memory* in recognition of the fact that it is assumed to contain a brief echo of the auditory stimulus.

The role of the auditory sensory register in information processing.   The need for a sensory memory is even more obvious in the case of audition than it was for vision; whereas vision is inherently spread out in space, audition is spread out in time. Many of the important auditory signals in our lives consist of changes over time. For example, the intonation pattern of a sentence can be as important in conveying the speaker's intent as are the words. The statement, "Dr. Livingston," can take on many meanings depending upon whether the words are spoken with rising intonation (suggesting a question), with emphasis (suggesting shock at the good doctor's behavior, or, perhaps, surprise at seeing him), or with a more level intonation pattern (simply acknowledging the doctor's presence). In order to be aware of these important differences in intonation, you must be able to compare the loudness and pitch of the beginning of the sentence with that at the end. Furthermore, it is necessary to compare different speech sounds in order to learn how words should be pronounced, yet in almost all circumstances the sounds are not simultaneous. Therefore, comparison requires that you keep one sound in memory long enough to compare it with the other. Neisser (1967) has suggested the example of the immigrant who is trying to learn to speak English. When told, "No, not zeal, seal," he must be able to hold the sound of "zeal" in memory so that it can be compared with "seal."

The statement that audition is spread out in time not only reflects the fact that comparison of sounds across time is important, but also indicates that unlike vision, an auditory stimulus usually cannot be prolonged by the simple expedient of reorienting the receptor organs. This point is clearest when reading and listening are compared. In the case of reading, the words are on the printed page, and if you are an unskilled reader it is possible to prolong the stimulus simply by scanning the lines more slowly. If later in a sentence you discover that you missed a particular word, you can simply scan back to see what the word was. In the case of listening to someone speak, however, the stimulus is spread out over time, so you must deal with it as it is presented. If you later find that you missed a word, you can't turn your ears back in the hope of finding the sound still lurking in the external world. An auditory memory that prolonged the stimulus for even a brief period would be extremely useful in enabling us to deal with these characteristics of auditory stimuli.

Auditory analogues of Sperling's partial report procedure.
Moray, Bates, and Barnett (1965) first reported an analogue of Sperling's partial report procedure in audition, but we will consider a later replication and extension by Darwin, Turvey, and Crowder (1972), since the latter work overcame some difficulties which clouded interpretation of the Moray et al. results.

Darwin and his colleagues used a *three-eared man* procedure. Subjects were presented simultaneously with three sequences of three items each (digits and letters). One sequence was presented to the right ear, one to the left, and one to both. The last of these sounded as though it was in the center of the head, hence the designation "three-eared man." Each string of items was presented at the rate of 3 per second, so it took exactly one second for stimulus presentation. On whole report trials subjects were to report as many of the 9 items as they could. On partial report trials the subject was presented with a visual marker projected on a screen either to the left, in the center, or to the right, indicating respectively, that the subject should report the letters in the left, middle, or right ear. The partial report cue was presented either 0, 1, 2, or 4 seconds after offset of the last stimulus presentation.

Using the reasoning we discussed for Sperling's experiments, if there is a large capacity auditory sensory memory that decays rapidly, then with brief delays between stimulus offset and the cue, partial report should reveal more items available than whole report. Furthermore, the relative advantage of partial report should decline as the delay of the cue is increased. The results are depicted in Figure 2–4, which shows the number of items available at the various cue delays. The figure shows that there is an advantage of partial over whole report, and this advantage declines with cue delay, providing evidence for the existence of a decaying auditory memory. The time course of the decay is much more extended than it was for vision; even after 2 seconds, partial report is considerably better than whole report. So far, then, these results suggest the existence of a large capacity auditory memory lasting for 2 seconds or more.

What is the form of information in this auditory memory? Is the memory sensory in that it contains a relatively unprocessed echo of auditory stimulation? In the case of vision, we discussed evidence which suggested the sensory nature of the memory tapped by Sperling's task. One such kind of evidence was the finding that only cues

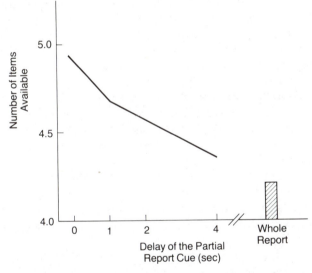

Figure 2–4. Performance in Darwin, Turvey, and Crowder's (1972) three-eared man study of auditory sensory memory. The graph shows the number of items available on partial report trials when the cue occurred at varying intervals after offset of the stimulus items. The vertical bar at the right shows performance on whole report trials for comparison. (After Darwin, Turvey, & Crowder, 1972. Copyright 1972 by Academic Press. Reprinted by permission.)

based on visual characteristics of the stimulus array are effective partial report cues. If the memory tapped in the three-eared man study is an analogous auditory sensory memory, then we would expect that the only partial report cues that would be effective would be those based on auditory characteristics of the stimulus array. The location cue used in the study we just discussed is certainly based on such an auditory characteristic, in that one need not categorize or identify the items in order to report from one of the three positions.

Darwin and his colleagues attempted to determine whether a cue that would require categorization would be effective. They cued their subjects to recall either all the digits or all the letters, again by using a visual marker cue which, by prearrangement with the subject, indicated either that the digits or the letters should be reported. Their results were equivocal. At brief cue delays there was a very slight advantage of partial over whole report trials for this categorical cue, but the partial report advantage was considerably smaller than with the partial report cue based on location. Thus, Darwin et al. found that cues based on the auditory characteristics of the array are much more effective than those based on categorical membership of the items—a finding in keeping with the postulation of a relatively unprocessed auditory echo. Nonetheless, the fact that there was a small partial report advantage with the categorical cue suggests the possibility that the memory tapped in the three-eared man experiment is not entirely precategorical. We shall return to this question later.

Recency, modality, and suffix effects. It would be unparsimonious in the extreme to postulate a new memory store or system for every experimental procedure that is invented, so again, as in the case of the visual sensory memory, we seek other observations which suggest the existence of echoic memory.

In 1969 Crowder and Morton published an influential paper in which they argued that the pattern of results typically obtained in certain immediate serial recall experiments suggests the existence of an auditory sensory memory, which they termed the *precategorical acoustic store* (or PAS).

In the *immediate serial recall* experiment the person is presented with a short series, usually of 10 or fewer items, and is asked to recall them immediately in the serial order in which they were presented. Usually the items are presented at the rate of about 2 per second. The experimenter could, of course, simply record the total number of items recalled correctly (which is exactly what is done in many standardized IQ tests, such as the WAIS), but a much more informative component of the results emerges when the researcher examines recall as a function of the serial position in which the item was presented. This is called a *serial position function*. For example, if the subject was presented with the series 986529763, the first 9 is in serial position 1, the 8 in serial position 2, and so on. If the subject reported 987529763, we would record that he was correct in all serial positions except serial position number 3.

When the list of digits is presented auditorilly, or if the subject is required to read aloud a visually presented list, a typical serial position function emerges, as is depicted by the filled circles in Figure 2–5. This Figure displays the percent of recall errors as a function of serial position. Notice that there are three parts to this function. The superior recall for items in the first few serial positions is called the *primacy effect*. There is also superior recall for the item presented in the last serial position, and this is termed the *recency effect*. Finally, items in the central few positions yield poorest recall. The serial position function will come up again and again because it is one of the most general characteristics of human memory, showing up reliably both in the laboratory and in many more common situations.

For the moment, one aspect of the serial position function is particularly interesting. It has been known since at least the turn of the century that the modality in which a list is presented for immediate serial recall is important. The open circles in Figure 2–5 show the

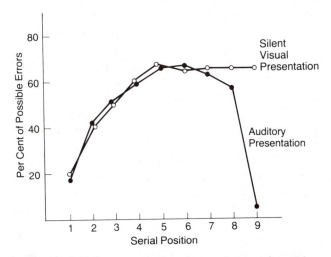

Figure 2–5. Idealized data depicting the serial position functions obtained in the immediate serial recall task when stimulus presentation is auditory (filled circles) or silent visual (open circles). The curves show per cent errors as a function of serial position. Note that the recency effect is obtained only for auditory presentation. This difference between auditory and visual presentation is termed the modality effect.

serial position function obtained when the list is presented visually and the subject is *not* permitted to read the list aloud. In contrast to the auditory curve, this visual curve exhibits little recency. This superiority of auditory over visual presentation in the recency portion of the serial position curve is termed the *modality effect*, because it reflects the modality in which the information was presented.

Before we go on, it is worth noting that the modality effect is easy to demonstrate without any equipment at all. Enlist one or more friends to be your subject(s) and replicate the effect. Begin by preparing about 6 lists of 9 digits each, with the digits arranged in a haphazard order. Make sure your subject has a pencil and a piece of paper for writing responses. The paper should contain 6 rows of 9 blanks each, one row for each trial. Explain that the subject will either hear or see a series of digits on each trial, and that at the end of the sequence you will tap a pencil on the table signaling that the person should begin to write down the sequence of letters in the blanks in the order in which they were presented. Explain that a letter will be counted as correct only if it is written in the correct blank. As experimenter, on three of the trials you should use auditory presentation. Read the list for that trial at approximately the rate of 2 digits per second, and after the ninth digit tap a pencil on the table signaling your subject to write down the remembered list. For the next three trials try visual presentation. A rather awkward, but adequate technique for doing this is to print each of the three lists you'll be using on a piece of paper. Cover them with an index card and then move the card so that the letters are exposed from left to right, at approximately the rate of 2 items per second. Immediately after the last letter has become visible, tap the pencil to signal recall.

After you've collected your data, divide the trials into two sets, one in which auditory presentation was used and the other in which visual presentation was used. Score each trial by circling the digits the subject missed. Then calculate the percentage of errors the subject made at each serial position, and draw your own graph like the one displayed in Figure 2–5. Your serial position functions will undoubtedly be quite variable, unlike the neat ones displayed in previous figures, because you have so few trials. Nonetheless, you will probably find evidence for primacy in both kinds of presentations, and for a strong recency effect with auditory presentation, but a much weaker recency effect with visual presentation—the modality effect. It would be interesting to ask your subjects which of the two kinds of lists they thought was easier and why. If possible, have someone else test you as a subject, using new lists of course, so you can examine your own introspections.

Ever since it was discovered, the modality difference you've just attempted to replicate has puzzled and intrigued students of human memory. Why does auditory presentation lead to better recall of the last few serial positions than silent visual presentation? Crowder and Morton proposed that the difference may be attributed to the existence of an auditory sensory memory that is of longer duration than visual sensory memory. They argued that the earlier portions of the serial position function reflect storage in working and/or long-term memory, and thus are relatively uninfluenced by the modality of presentation. The recency portion of the curve, they argued, reflects the operation of the sensory registers as well. In the case of vision we have already seen that the visual icon lasts for less than one second and is interfered with by subsequent visual presentations. The icon gives little if any advantage to the last few items in the immediate serial recall task, because it will either decay while the subject is reporting earlier items, or it will be masked by the subsequent visual stimuli the subject perceives while he is reporting the earlier items.

In the case of auditory presentation, however, Crowder and Morton argue that the auditory sensory register is of longer duration, perhaps on the order of several seconds in length. Thus, the last few items in the list are likely to have an advantage over middle items in that they can be read either from the more permanent stores or from the auditory sensory register. The auditory sensory register does not improve memory for the earlier items in the list because it is assumed that new auditory presentations interfere with or displace the old. You will notice that the argument that echoic memory is of longer duration than iconic is quite consistent with the results of the auditory partial report experiment we discussed earlier.

Notice that, according to Crowder and Morton's argument, auditory sensory memory assists recall in the usual immediate serial recall task whereas visual sensory memory does not for two reasons. First, auditory sensory memory has a longer duration than visual, and second, since the person is surrounded by other visual events, even if the visual memory didn't decay it would be masked by these intervening visual experiences. In contrast, the usual immediate serial recall experiment does not involve any additional auditory stimulation between the end of the list and the subject's recall, except for the brief recall cue of a tap. Thus, the longer duration auditory sensory memory is usually not masked.

Crowder and Morton reasoned that if their analysis is correct, then it should be possible to erase the advantage of auditory presentation by presenting some additional auditory stimulus at the end of the auditorilly presented list. Since this stimulus would also enter the auditory sensory memory, it would be expected to interfere with the echoic representation of the last few items in the list. Crowder and Morton accomplished this by adding what they called an *auditory suffix* to the end of the list. In their main experiment, this suffix consisted of the spoken word *zero* following the last item in the list. The subject was told that he did not need to remember this item, but that it should simply be interpreted as a cue to recall the rest of the list. The open circles in Figure 2–6 present the results of an auditory suffix condition. The results confirm Crowder and Morton's predictions. When an auditory suffix is presented, the recency portion—and only the recency portion—of the auditory serial position function is disrupted. Apparently this suffix degrades the sensory representation of the last stimulus item, thereby reducing the contribution of the auditory sensory register. As a result, recall is limited to the information that was placed in one or more of the more permanent memory stores. This decrease in the recency effect that occurs when a suffix follows presentation of the stimulus list is called the *suffix effect*. Like the modality effect, the suffix effect is quite easy to replicate, so try doing three trials with auditory presentation followed by the spoken suffix *zero*.

If the suffix effect and the modality effect reflect information stored in an echoic, precategorical memory, then the meaning of the suffix should not influence the magnitude of the suffix effect. In particular, the relationship between the meaning of the items in the list

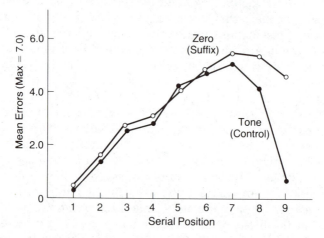

Figure 2–6. The effect of an auditory suffix on the immediate serial recall serial position function. For both conditions depicted, presentation was auditory. For the suffix condition (open circles) an auditory presentation of the word *zero* served as the recall cue, but for the control condition (filled circles) a tone served as the recall cue. Notice that the auditory suffix disrupts the recency portion of the curve, an effect which is called the suffix effect. (After Crowder, 1972. Copyright 1972 by MIT Press. Reprinted by permission.)

and the meaning of the suffix items should not influence the extent to which the suffix displaces the items in echoic memory. Notice that in the original studies the suffix (zero) was similar in meaning to the items to be remembered (the digits from 1 to 9), but if the store is indeed precategorical then, regardless of its meaning, any other word should interfere to the same degree. Crowder and Morton showed that this prediction is upheld; presenting the suffix word rosy (the two syllables of zero reversed) led to just as great a suffix effect, even though there is much less semantic similarity between the suffix and the memory list.

If the suffix and modality effects reflect a sensory precategorical store, then auditory similarity between the suffix and the to-be-remembered list should influence the degree to which the suffix effect is obtained. Once again, Crowder and Morton have reported evidence confirming this prediction. If the memory list is presented in a female voice, and the suffix in a male voice, the suffix effect is much reduced, relative to a condition in which both list and suffix are in the same voice. Further, if the stimulus list is spoken in a human voice, then an acoustically dissimilar suffix like a click or a burst of static (or the pencil tap you used) does not yield a suffix effect. In general, the greater the acoustic similarity between list and suffix, the greater the magnitude of the suffix effect (i.e., the greater the disruption of the recency portion of the serial position curve).

More recently, other researchers have examined the suffix effect when the list to be remembered consists of nonspeech sounds such as tones (Foreit, 1976) or meaningful environmental sounds such as car horns (Rowe & Rowe, 1976). These results reveal that when the subject is attempting to remember nonspeech sounds, nonspeech suffixes lead to a suffix effect, whereas speech sound suffixes do not. In general, then, whether speech or nonspeech sounds are investigated, the greater the acoustic similarity between list and suffix, the greater the magnitude of the suffix effect.

Selective impairment of auditory sensory storage. We have discussed several phenomena, all of which indicate that there is a form of auditory sensory storage that contains a veridical, though short-lived record of the most recent acoustic stimuli to which an individual is exposed. The evidence discussed has included the findings from partial report studies and from analyses of the recency, modality and suffix effects obtained in immediate serial recall studies.

There is yet another highly tentative, but particularly interesting form of evidence suggesting that this auditory sensory storage is functionally distinct from other aspects of memory. Saffran and Marin (1975) have reported a case study of a patient at the Johns Hopkins University School of Medicine who suffered a lesion in the left posterior parietal cortex. Despite this brain injury, many aspects of the patient's cognitive processing appear to be unimpaired. He reveals good comprehension of spoken and written language and little difficulty in expressing himself in speaking or writing. In immediate serial recall for visually presented lists of items, he was able to recall approximately 6 items perfectly, a score quite similar to that obtained by normal people. He also reveals the usual primacy effect obtained in such studies. In general, then, this patient performs as though working and long-term memory functioning are normal.

The pertinent observation for the issue at hand is that the patient's performance on certain other tasks is decidedly different from that of normals. If a list of items is presented auditorilly for immediate serial recall the patient makes errors on any lists that exceed a length of 3 items—performance far poorer than normal. Furthermore, his recall does not reveal even a hint of recency. If the patient is asked to vocalize a visually presented list, his recall is no better than it is for silent visual presentation. When asked to repeat verbatim sentences which are auditorilly presented, the patient is unable to do so when the sentence contains as few as 6 words—despite the fact that he is usually able to paraphrase the sentences correctly.

This patient's pattern of difficulties suggests that he is suffering from impairment of the auditory sensory memory, but that the other memory systems are undisturbed. This suggests that the auditory sensory register is indeed a system that is functionally distinct from the other memory stores; its functioning can be radically impaired in an individual while other aspects of that person's memory are apparently normal.

Puzzles. Despite the consistent pattern of research findings we have just discussed, many questions remain regarding the auditory sensory register. Research on the echo has generated considerably more controversy than has research on the icon.

It's not that anyone seriously questions the existence of a short-lived sensory memory from which old information is displaced by new auditory inputs. Both logic and research evidence argue too strongly for its existence. Rather, the main question that underlies most of the controversy is whether the effects we have just discussed all reflect the operation of a precategorical sensory store as opposed to a more highly processed memory. On the one hand there are researchers like Crowder (1976) who argue that there is an auditory sensory register of longer duration than the visual that retains relatively unprocessed sensory impressions and causes the partial report advantage, the suffix effect, and the modality effect. On the other hand there are those, like Massaro (1972) who agree that there is a relatively unprocessed sensory memory, but argue that it lasts for only 250 msec or so—approximately the same duration as the visual sensory register—and that the phenomena we have just discussed reflect the operation of a different memory—still acoustic, but more highly processed.

This second position is tenable because of several kinds of puzzling findings, of which I will mention only two. You are already familiar with the first of these—the finding that there is some small partial report advantage for categorically based cues in studies using the three-eared man procedure. There should be no such advantage if the memory we are tapping with this technique is truly nothing more than an acoustic echo, and you will recall that such categorical cues never lead to a partial report advantage when we study the visual sensory register.

Second, Watkins and Watkins (1973) have compared the modality effect in serial recall of lists that contain words of either one or four syllables. If the modality effect is due to a store that simply retains an echo or tape-recording of acoustic stimuli, then for words of four syllables we would expect the modality effect to occur only for the last word (since it contains four syllables and later syllables should interfere with earlier ones) or at most two, whereas for word lists of one syllable it should extend over the last several words. Contrary to prediction, however, Watkins and Watkins found that the effect extended over the last few words in a list regardless of whether the words were one or four syllables long. This finding suggests, of course, that the memory system that is responsible for the modality effect is influenced by more than simply the number of sounds—some linguistic segmentation or categorization seems to have taken place already.

Further research will be necessary to resolve these puzzling findings, but two conclusions are clear. First, there is considerable evidence for an auditory sensory memory that is analogous to the visual sensory register. Second, there is some form of auditory memory that outlasts the visual sensory memory. Whether this memory contains only a sensory code or whether some analysis of the meaning of the items stored has already occurred is still unclear.

THE TACTUAL SENSORY REGISTER

The theory of cognition outlined in Chapter 1 assumes that there is a sensory register for each of the sensory modalities. Nonetheless, virtually all research and theorizing has focused on vision and audition. Indeed, if research energies must be focused, these modalities are excellent choices because of their apparent predominance in human cognition. (Presumably if we were primarily interested in canine cognition more emphasis would have been placed on sensory memory for odors.)

Despite current concentration on audition and vision, two interesting preliminary investigations of tactual sensory memory have been reported. One series (Bliss, Crane, Mansfield, & Townsend, 1966) used the partial report technique. Using a rather elaborate array of equipment, subjects were presented simultaneously with a number of air blasts to randomly chosen finger joints. They were then required either to report all the joints that had been stimulated (whole report), or they saw a visual cue which instructed them that they need only report whether or not a specified subset of the joints had been stimulated (partial report). The findings were quite similar to those obtained in studies of visual and auditory sensory memory. Partial report was superior to whole report when the cue occurred immediately after offset of the array, suggesting that more touches were available than could be reported. Furthermore, partial report was significantly better than whole report whenever the cue occurred within 800 msec after offset of the air blasts, suggesting that the memory may be of slightly longer duration than visual sensory memory.

If we are correct in hypothesizing that tactual sensory memory is of longer duration than visual, then tactual sensory memory should prove to be helpful in immediate serial recall of tactual stimulation, and so we would expect to find a recency effect. Furthermore, if subsequent tactual stimuli enter this store and interfere with previous sensory memory, then following the tactual list with a tactual suffix should eliminate this recency. In other words, we should also obtain a suffix effect. A study by Watkins and Watkins (1974) tested these predictions. Unlike the previous study, these experiments required equipment no more elaborate than a pencil, so it would be informative to attempt to replicate it with a friend or two.

In one of these studies the experimenter used a pen to tap a predetermined sequence of fingers on the person's writing hand. Each such sequence contained a series of 7 taps. Immediately after the taps the experimenter tapped the pen on the table as a recall signal, and the subject was shown a pictured hand on which he was to point to the fingers in the same order he had just experienced. This, of course, was the recall test. When serial position functions were plotted, the researchers found a serial position curve much like that obtained with auditory presentations. For our purposes the most important component of this function was the strong recency effect obtained. Subjects were more accurate in identifying the last couple of touches than they were at identifying the middle few touches.

In addition, the researchers administered another series of trials which were identical to those described except that the recall cue was a brisk stroke of the pen across the critical parts of the fingers of the writing hand. If the recency effect is caused by a tactual sensory memory, then such a tactual suffix should decrease the magnitude of the recency effect, and that is exactly what happened.

Therefore, although research on tactual sensory memory is just beginning, the preliminary results are consistent in suggesting the existence of a sensory register of slightly longer duration than the visual sensory register.

DIFFERENCES AMONG INDIVIDUALS

There is evidence that the duration of the icon varies slightly among college students. For example, of Sperling's original five subjects, one appeared to have a slightly longer duration sensory memory than the others. It would be interesting to know (1) whether this longer duration icon is related to any other aspects of cognitive functioning (e.g., Does this person score higher or lower on IQ tests or on other information-processing tasks than the other subjects?), (2) how the difference arose (e.g., Did this individual always have a longer duration store, or was it acquired as a result of experience?), and (3) whether this longer duration sensory storage is restricted to the visual modality (e.g., Does this individual also have a longer duration echoic memory?). At the moment, all these questions remain unanswered.

A few developmental studies have been conducted in which individuals of various ages were compared. The duration of auditory sensory storage seems the same for elementary school children as it is for adults (e.g., Frank & Rabinovitch, 1974). However, there is some indication that in the case of visual sensory storage, young children may have a slightly *longer* duration icon than adults. This conclusion comes from studies of visual persistence (e.g., Pollack, Ptashne, & Carter, 1969) and partial report (e.g., Gummerman & Gray, 1972). The influence this age difference might have on other aspects of cognition is unknown. It is of particular interest, though, that children of normal intelligence who have reading difficulties apparently have a *longer* duration icon than normal children of the same age. In one study (Stanley, 1975), such dyslexic children were found to have icons of 30 or 50 msec longer duration than normal children.

Despite the individual and developmental differences cited, the similarities among individuals are far more impressive than the differences. For all Sperling's subjects, partial report was superior to whole report for brief cue delays, and the partial report advantage decreased dramatically when the cue delay increased from 0 msec to

500 msec. Furthermore, the few published studies of children (e.g., Morrison, Holmes, & Haith, 1974) indicate that the capacity of the icon is the same for six-year-olds as it is for adults.

Any conclusion based on such scattered findings can represent nothing more than an educated guess regarding individual differences in sensory storage. I shall venture one, nonetheless. At this point, the best guess is that the characteristics of sensory storage, particularly its duration, reveal some variation among individuals. These differences, however, are small and of currently unknown importance for the rest of cognition.

CHAPTER SUMMARY

Though the sensory registers are usually neither noticed nor appreciated, they are absolutely essential, because they prolong stimuli long enough to give us a second chance to perceive them, just in case the stimuli are important. All the sensory registers have several characteristics in common. First, all are of extremely brief duration, though the durations vary from ¼ of a second or less in the case of vision, to perhaps 1 second in touch, to 2 or even 4 seconds in the case of audition. Second, subsequent stimuli presented in the same sensory modality interfere with any remaining sensory information that has not already decayed. Third, all have a large capacity, holding a brief record of virtually all the stimuli that reach our senses. Fourth, the sensory registers are outside the voluntary, strategic control of the individual. The person can neither prolong the duration of the sensory memory, nor change its form. The form of representation is determined by the modality of the external stimulus, e.g., the icon contains a visual image of the external visual stimulus. Furthermore, a given sensory register will contain information *only if* a stimulus has been encountered recently in the appropriate sensory modality. Fifth, the properties of sensory storage, such as its duration and capacity, seem to vary little across individuals and developmental levels.

SUGGESTED READING

More detailed, but still wide-ranging discussions of visual sensory storage may be found in the texts by Baddeley (1976, Chapter 9) and Crowder (1976, Chapter 2) as well as in review articles by Dick (1974) and Turvey (1978). More specifically, there are three current areas of controversy with which you may wish to become familiar.

The first concerns the issue of whether or not the visual sensory register as we have described it actually exists. Holding (1975) has argued that the evidence we've discussed in this chapter is amenable to alternative interpretations, and so he questions the necessity for postulating the visual sensory register. Coltheart (1975) has offered a cogent criticism of Holding's argument, though Coltheart himself (1980) has offered his own reinterpretation in a wide-ranging review. Also relevant here is an article by Triesman, Russell, and Green (1975) showing that there is iconic storage of movement.

The second issue concerns the locus of visual sensory storage. Sakitt (1975, 1976; Sakitt & Long, 1979) has presented fascinating evidence which she interprets as indicating that iconic storage is retinal, and, for the most part, confined to the rods. On the other hand, Banks and Barber (1977; 1980) have presented equally interesting data and arguments for the conclusion that it is more centrally located (after integration of information from the two eyes has taken place), and that it is virtually unchanged when there is no rod component at all.

The third issue concerns the nature of masking. Since the precise mechanisms underlying masking are not important here, I have avoided detailed discussion of this topic, but excellent sources for more information are Chapter 2 of the text by Reynolds and Flagg (1977) and, at a more advanced level, an article by Turvey (1978).

For further general discussion of the auditory sensory register I recommend again the texts by Baddeley (1976, Chapter 10) and Crowder (1976, Chapter 3). Two other chapters by Crowder (1972, 1975) will also be helpful. The following readings are more advanced and limited in scope than those just suggested and will be useful if you wish to pursue certain issues in more depth. For further elaboration of the view that auditory sensory memory is *not* of longer duration than visual, see Massaro (1972; 1975). If you wish to examine the extent to which the auditory sensory memory is precategorical, consult the articles mentioned in the "Puzzles" section, as well as articles by Balota and Engle (1981), Crowder (1982), Morton, Marcus, and Ottley (1981), and Watkins and Watkins (1980). There is also an interesting debate concerning the kinds of sounds that are held in echoic memory. The experimental papers by Darwin and Baddeley (1974), Morton and Chambers (1976), and Hall and Blumstein (1977) are illustrative examples. Finally, in a paper relevant to several of these issues, Shand and Klima (1981) have reported evidence of a nonauditory suffix effect in the congenitally deaf.

Attention

FOOD FOR THOUGHT

Many conversations take place in less than optimal settings. In crowded bars, restaurants, and buses, the voices we are trying to ignore are often louder than the one to which we are listening. The next time you find yourself in such a situation try to block out completely all the surrounding conversations. Are you able to do so? Then try to listen to two conversations at once. Can you do so without missing parts of either?

The ability to focus on one voice in a mélange of others is only one example of the extent to which you attend selectively to certain aspects of the environment while ignoring others. Such selection occurs every minute of your life, for at any given instant you are exposed to a wide range of stimulation to which your sense organs are capable of responding, yet you are usually conscious of only a small part of it. As you read you have probably been concentrating your efforts on the page in front of you and if you are working efficiently, you've been oblivious to most of the world around you. Stop reading at the end of this sentence, though and without moving from your present position notice all the stimulation to which you've been exposed—the sounds of noise in the next room, or perhaps birdsong or air conditioners, and notice how you can feel your clothes touching your body. Until this moment, you'd been ignoring all of these extraneous stimuli, and if you had not, your comprehension would have been affected.

SELECTIVE ATTENTION

These instances are examples of *selective attention*, i.e., the ability to focus on a chosen part of a situation while ignoring other parts. The word *situation* here is intentionally vague for we can attend selectively not only to external stimuli, such as a certain voice, but also to internal stimuli, such as our own thoughts. Selective attention is of central importance for human existence, because it enables us to free ourselves from the domination of the surrounding world. You manage to read in the library or drive a car filled with six-year-olds because you are able to focus your attention on the important components of the situation at hand.

Selective attention actually alters our perception of many aspects of experience. One example is a phenomenon Titchener reported in 1908. Titchener noticed that if a person is exposed to two simultaneous or nearly simultaneous stimuli, he will think that the stimulus to which he is attending occurred first. For example, if a light and a touch are presented simultaneously, the observer will think the light occurred first if he is attending to the light, but he will judge that the touch occurred first if he is attending to the touch. Thus, the same configuration of external stimuli can be perceived in two different ways depending upon the focus of attention. Titchener termed this effect of the direction of attention on perceived order *The Law of Prior Entry*. Though Titchener's phenomenon may not seem particularly noteworthy when phrased in terms of a light and a touch, consider its potential impact when the witness to a crime is asked, "Who shot first?" or "Who threw the first punch?" The Law of Prior Entry suggests that two eyewitnesses, both of whom are telling the truth as they see it, might give reports at odds with each other simply because each was attending to a different actor during the crime.

What role does attention play in human cognition? For example, does unattended material to which we are exposed influence our thoughts and actions without our being aware of it? Is there permanent memory for unattended stimuli? Notice that the overview theory depicted in Figure 1–2 assumes that when a stimulus is presented to an individual some of the person's long-term knowledge about the stimulus is looked up in long-term memory, regardless of whether or not the person is attending to the object, but that no permanent change in long-term memory (i.e., no permanent learning) occurs unless the stimulus is attended to. Furthermore, it is assumed that when an item is attended to it is placed in working memory. There, special control processes such as rehearsal may be called into play, resulting in the item being permanently stored in long-term memory.

In fact, the theory of attention assumed in our overview model is only one of a number of possible theories we might have adopted. In this chapter we will examine several alternative theories and the research that inspired their development. By the end of the chapter not only will we have considered the evidence that makes the overview theory more plausible than the alternatives, but we will also have found reason to elaborate and extend our theory.

THE LEGACY OF THE FIFTIES

At the turn of the century many psychologists realized the importance of attention in everyday affairs as witnessed by Titchener's discovery of the Law of Prior Entry and by the fact that in 1890 William James devoted an entire chapter of his text *The Principles of Psychology* to a discussion of attention. Nonetheless, once behaviorism came to dominate American experimental psychology the study of attention was banished. Notice that if one admits that an animal is capable of attending selectively to a certain subset of the total stimulus environment, then the mapping of precise relations between stimuli and responses becomes difficult, for one can no longer know exactly what the stimulus is. Thus, for several decades attention went the way of mental images and strategies—a topic considered to be outside the realm of scientific investigation.

In the early 1950's, however, several studies of selective attention by British researchers captured the interest of experimental psychologists. They are still among the most influential studies in the literature on cognition, so we will consider some of them before discussing the theories and controversies they spawned.

Selective listening: Cherry's cocktail party experiments.

In 1953 and 1954 E. Colin Cherry published two studies of what he termed the "cocktail party problem." Out of a sea of voices the partygoer must focus on only one. Cherry set out to determine how effective people are at ignoring extraneous conversations.

Cherry devised a shadowing technique that would capture the important characteristics of the cocktail party problem in a controlled laboratory setting. The *shadowing technique* involves presenting the subject with two or more simultaneous messages and instructing him to shadow, or repeat aloud, one of these while ignoring the other. The message the subject is instructed to shadow is usually termed the *shadowed, relevant,* or *attended* message, whereas the one to be ignored is called the *irrelevant, rejected,* or *unattended* message. By requiring the subject to shadow, and then monitoring his accuracy at doing so, the experimenter attempts to ensure that the subject is, in fact, focusing on the relevant message.

In one condition, Cherry presented both messages *binaurally,* that is, both messages were presented through earphones to both ears. He found that subjects were able to shadow one of the messages accurately as long as the messages differed in some physical characteristic, (e.g., one was in a male voice and the other in a female voice), but when the messages differed only in meaning (e.g., a Hemingway novel versus a biology text) the task became more difficult and subjects frequently made mistakes, shadowing some words from the irrelevant passage.

In contrast, Cherry found that subjects shadowed almost perfectly regardless of message content in a different condition in which the two messages were presented *dichotically,* that is one message was presented to the left ear and another to the right. Despite his subjects' perfect shadowing, other aspects of their performance reveal that the task was not exactly easy. Cherry notes that his subjects always shadowed in a monotonous tone without the usual intonation patterns that accompany reading or speaking. This indicates that the task was so difficult that subjects were little aware of the content of the message they were reporting verbatim. Indeed, when at the end of shadowing Cherry asked his subjects to describe the meaning of the message they had just shadowed, they were usually very poor at doing so.

To become convinced of the challenging nature of Cherry's task, you should experience it yourself. You might try the technique mentioned at the beginning of the chapter, i.e., focusing on one conversation of two occurring near you in a line or waiting room. In this case, I recommend that you shadow silently lest you be arrested. Better yet, have two friends sit on either side of you, each reading a passage from a different book. (Both passages should be unfamiliar to you.) Try to shadow one of them aloud for 2 or 3 minutes. If you have already depleted your supply of friends as a result of earlier replications, then two radios placed in strategic positions and tuned to two different news broadcasts will do. After you've finished shadowing, try to summarize the message you just repeated.

So far we've been concerned with the accuracy of shadowing and with memory for the shadowed message. For our purposes, though, the most important aspect of Cherry's findings concerns what subjects are able to report about the unshadowed message. In order to find out, Cherry presented his subjects with a dichotic listening task in which they were to shadow a male voice presented to one ear, while ignoring a message presented to the other ear. The message on this rejected ear always began and ended with a passage read in a male voice. However, the middle of the irrelevant message was altered in a number of ways. For example, the voice was switched from male to female or the meaning of the passage was changed, or the language was changed from English to French. At the end of the shadowing task, Cherry asked his subjects what they could tell him about the message in the *rejected* ear. Cherry found they were able to report amazingly little. His subjects did notice physical characteristics of the rejected message; they were able to identify whether the voice was male or female, and whether the center portion consisted of speech sounds or pure tones. However, subjects were unable to report the meaning of the rejected message, nor could they report even a few words or a single phrase. In fact, they failed to notice a change in the language of the rejected message.

The subject's lack of memory for the content of an unattended message was later confirmed by Moray (1959) who showed that even if a small set of words was repeated as many as 35 times in the unattended message, the subject was still unable to report any of them. Indeed, warning the subject that he would be asked to report the words made little difference; still the shadowing task was so demanding that subjects were unable to do so.

Cherry's experiments thus led to two important conclusions about selective listening. First, when people are presented with simultaneous messages that differ in some physical characteristic, such as voice or location, it is possible to separate the two messages and attend to only one of them. Second, when the person focuses on one message, only gross physical characteristics of the other are noticed and reported later.

Selective looking.　Cherry studied only selective listening. Would his conclusions hold for selective looking as well? Recently, researchers at Cornell University (Neisser & Becklen, 1975) asked this question by conducting a visual analogue of Cherry's selective listening experiments. Neisser and Becklen superimposed two video displays on which two different episodes were taking place, as depicted in Figure 3–1c. You can experience the nature of the stimulus array by looking out a window from a lighted room at dusk. If the conditions are right, you will see two scenes superimposed—the one in the room (reflected by the glass) and the one outside. Try attending to one or the other.

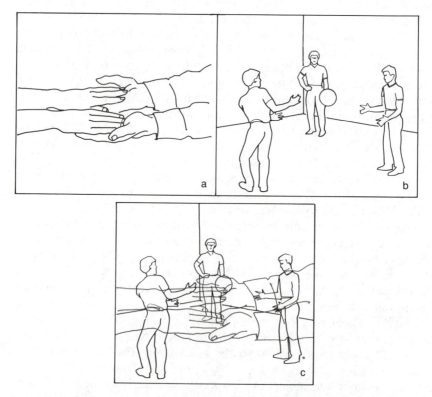

Figure 3–1. The stimulus arrays Neisser and Becklen used in their study of selective looking. Picture a displays the handgame alone, Picture b the ballgame alone, and Picture c the handgame and ballgame superimposed. (After Neisser & Becklen, 1975. Copyright 1975 by Academic Press. Reprinted by permission.)

In the Neisser and Becklen study, one of the scenes was an episode of a familiar handgame in which the person whose palms are up tries, through a rapid movement, to hit the tops of the other player's hands. The other player, of course, tries to move his hands so as to prevent a hit. The superimposed visual sequence was an episode from a ballgame in which a ball was tossed among three persons. In one condition Neisser and Becklen had their subjects monitor the events of one episode while ignoring the other visually superimposed episode. Subjects had no difficulty doing so. In fact, they failed to notice bizarre events which occurred in the simultaneous nonattended episode. For example, on some trials the handgame episode would contain the rather incongruous event of the two people shaking hands in the middle of the game. Subjects who were attending to the ballgame episode virtually never noticed this event.

These findings suggest, then, that there is some generality to the findings obtained in Cherry's studies of selective listening. People can attend selectively to one of two simultaneous signals, whether auditorily or visually presented, and when they do so they seem oblivious to much of the unattended material.

STIMULUS-SELECTION VERSUS RESPONSE-SELECTION THEORIES OF ATTENTION

Broadbent's sensory filter theory. In 1958 Donald Broadbent proposed a theory of selective attention, a theory inspired by Cherry's cocktail-party findings and by Broadbent's own research. Broadbent's theory was particularly influential because it was one of the first information-processing theories of human cognition, providing a preview of what was to come.

Some of the major components of Broadbent's filter theory are depicted in Figure 3–2. Broadbent assumed that all stimuli that reach the individual's sense organs reside briefly in sensory storage of the sort we discussed in the previous chapter. Next, information reaches a sensory filter, which blocks out certain input channels while allowing other (attended) inputs to pass through. The filter is termed a *sensory filter* because it may be tuned to select stimuli for further processing on the basis of certain physical characteristics (e.g., ear of arrival, pitch of the voice). The attended message is then processed through a *limited capacity channel*. Information in this limited capacity channel is assumed to have access to the individual's long-term memory, and to a response system that enables the person to produce responses.

Notice several central predictions of Broadbent's theory. First, there should be some very short-lived memory even for unattended

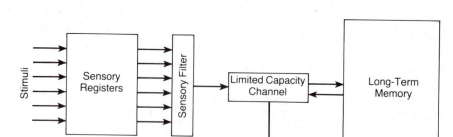

Figure 3–2. A block diagram showing some of the major components of Broadbent's sensory filter theory of attention.

inputs since information from all input channels is assumed to reside briefly in the sensory registers. This prediction was confirmed in a study (Norman, 1969) in which subjects were interrupted in the midst of shadowing during a dichotic listening task, and asked to report the last few words from the rejected message. They were always able to do so, a finding in keeping with our previous discussion of the sensory registers.

Second, the theory assumes that long-term knowledge is contacted only for attended stimuli (i.e., those accepted by the filter), so the meaning of unattended stimuli is never determined. Therefore, Broadbent's theory predicts that the subject should not be able to tune the filter to accept only one of two messages if the messages differ only in meaning, because meaning is not determined until *after* the filter. This prediction of the model is consistent with Cherry's finding that shadowing one of two simultaneous messages is quite poor when they differ only in meaning. Furthermore, since the rejected message is assumed to be filtered prior to analysis of its meaning, the theory predicts that the subject should not be able to report the meaning of the rejected message—a finding consistent with the ignorance Cherry's subjects displayed when asked about characteristics of the rejected message. Finally, Broadbent's filter theory predicts that there should be no long-term memory for material in unattended channels, because information is assumed to gain access to long-term memory only if it is passed through the limited capacity channel. Thus, the finding that subjects are not able to report any words or phrases from the rejected passage if they are questioned at the end of shadowing is consistent with Broadbent's theory.

Broadbent's original (1958) theory and more recent modifications of it (Broadbent, 1971; Treisman, 1960) are usually termed *stimulus-selection theories* because they assume that selective attention affects information processing near the stimulus end of the series of stages intervening between overt stimulus and overt response.

Problems with the filter theory. Broadbent's theory was elegant in its simplicity, but experimental results which appeared soon after the theory was published demonstrated that it was inadequate. We will mention only two such findings here. First, Moray (1959) demonstrated a phenomenon you have probably noticed at our now familiar cocktail party. Although people usually are unaware of the identity of words in nonattended messages there is one notable exception—one's own name. Moray found that subjects detected their own name in the rejected channel in a dichotic listening task, even though they had been unaware of previous items in the unattended ear. If the nonattended message is filtered out, as Broadbent's theory assumes, this effect should not occur. Broadbent's theory might be able to account for the latter phenomenon with minor modifications of assumptions, but another result gave it even more difficulty.

Treisman (1960) reported a dichotic listening shadowing study in which the messages were switched halfway through the shadowing task. For example, consider a task in which the subject was instructed to shadow the right ear. The experiment might begin with the right ear containing a passage from a novel and the left ear containing a passage from a biology text. Halfway through shadowing, however, Treisman would switch the two messages so that the novel was in the left ear whereas the biology passage was in the right, to-be-shadowed ear. Treisman found that when the break came in the shadowed message, most subjects switched over to shadow the other ear for a few words (thus making errors) before going back to the message now on the to-be-attended ear. Treisman was able to show that this switchover didn't occur simply because of a break in the meaning of the attended message, because she found that if the shadowed message was broken, but was not continued on the rejected ear, no such momentary switchover to shadowing the rejected ear occurred. Therefore, it is clear that the subject's performance was being influenced by the meaning of the message in the rejected ear, a finding inconsistent with Broadbent's filter theory.

Response-selection theories. Since the experiments just described indicated that the meaning of unattended material is processed, other theorists (e.g., Deutsch and Deutsch, 1963 and Norman, 1968) proposed theories in which there is no filter at all prior to recognition.

Figure 3–3 depicts several features of the model proposed by Norman. All sensory inputs are assumed to undergo some perceptual processing and to contact their representations in long-term memory,

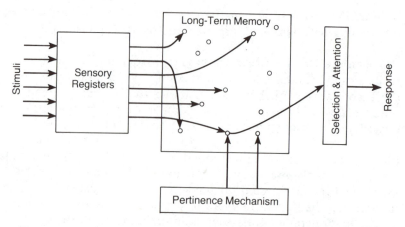

Figure 3–3. A block diagram showing some of the major components of Norman's response-selection theory of attention. The circles in long-term memory depict memory locations or dictionary units.

causing a temporary excitation or activation of their corresponding memory locations. Thus it is assumed that all stimuli presented to the person are recognized automatically and in parallel (i.e., simultaneously). Up to this point, then, attention has not influenced processing.

According to Norman's model in Figure 3–3 this activation resulting from a sensory input is only one of two sources of activation of long-term memory units. The other is a pertinence mechanism which activates items that are pertinent, or important, for the individual. Some units (e.g., one's own name) are assumed to always receive some input from the pertinence mechanism because they are always important. Others are excited momentarily by the pertinence unit (e.g., a word that is likely in context, or all stimuli coming in by the right ear if one is in a shadowing task). The unit that receives the highest total excitation from the sensory input and pertinence mechanisms combined then reaches consciousness and is selected for further processing, which may include an overt response (such as pronouncing the word) or a mental operation (such as storing the word permanently in long-term memory). Thus selective attention is assumed to limit how many items can be responded to (either covertly or overtly), but not to influence recognition.

In summary, stimulus-selection models (Broadbent, Treisman) differ from response-selection models (Deutsch and Deutsch, Norman) in the stage of processing at which selective attention is assumed to occur. According to stimulus-selection theories, selective attention occurs early in processing, prior to recognition of stimulus input. According to response-selection theories, attention does not influence recognition; it occurs late in processing, operating only to choose among competing responses. The stimulus- and response-selection theories have in common the assumption that there is no permanent memory for unattended items. Even in Norman's theory, the automatic activation that accompanies perceptual processing is only temporary.

Figure 3–4 depicts stimulus- and response-selection theories in terms of our overview model. If Broadbent or Treisman were asked to draw in their filter, they would place it between the sensory registers and access to long-term memory; thus, they would assume that recognition is influenced by selective attention. If Deutsch and Deutsch or Norman were asked to show where the filter should go, they would place it after access to long-term memory has taken place. By now you will have noticed that the overview model in Figure 1–2 is more consistent with response-selection theories. I have favored late selection, because several recent findings which we will discuss next suggest that considerable processing is carried out on unattended stimuli. These results have led most recent theorists to favor late selection.

Evidence for extensive processing of unattended stimuli.
The first kind of evidence was published by Lewis (1970). He presented his subjects with a dichotic listening task in which the subject heard a rapid sequence of simultaneous word pairs. The subject was

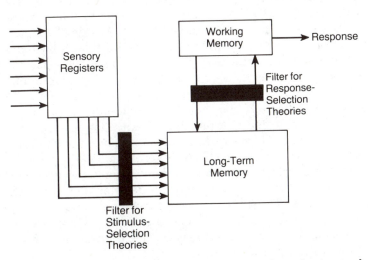

Figure 3–4. A diagram depicting where stimulus-selection and response-selection theories would place the filter in the overview model. Notice that stimulus-selection theories (e.g., Broadbent's) would place the filter prior to access to long-term memory, whereas response-selection theories (e.g., Norman's and Deutsch and Deutsch's) would place the filter after long-term memory has been contacted.

instructed to shadow each word in *one* of the channels immediately after it was presented. Sometimes the word in the rejected channel was unrelated to the simultaneous word to be shadowed, but other times the two words were related semantically (e.g., one was a synonym of the other). Lewis measured the reaction time of the shadowing response to words in the attended channel. If the meaning of the rejected words is not processed, then reaction time for shadowing an attended word should not be influenced by the meaning of the simultaneous unshadowed word. In fact, however, Lewis found that the meaning of the rejected word did influence reaction time. For example, the subject took longer to shadow the attended word *bad* if the simultaneous word on the rejected channel was *evil* than if it was *table*. Clearly, the meaning of the words in the rejected channel must have been processed.

A second phenomenon which suggests that the meaning of un-attended words is processed, is that words in a rejected message serve to disambiguate the meaning of an attended message (Mackay, 1973; Lackner & Garrett, 1973). In these studies subjects were presented with a dichotic listening task in which the message to be attended was always an ambiguous sentence, e.g., "They threw stones toward the bank today." The results revealed that words or sentences in the un-shadowed ear influenced the subject's interpretation of the ambiguous sentence. In the example presented here, if the rejected message con-tained the word *river* subjects were more likely to interpret the sen-tence as meaning "They threw stones toward the side of the river yes-terday" rather than "They threw stones toward the savings and loan association yesterday." However, if the unattended message contained the word *money*, subjects were more likely to adopt the *savings and loan* interpretation. This finding suggests that the meaning of the words in the rejected channel must have been determined, for it was this meaning that influenced interpretation of the attended sentence. It is of interest that subjects seemed completely unaware of the content of the nonshadowed message. They never accidentally included the words from the rejected channel in their shadowing, nor were they able to report any of the words from the rejected channel at the end of the experiment. Thus, the meaning of the unattended message was apparently processed, and it influenced interpretation of an attended message, despite the subject's apparent lack of awareness of the con-tent of the unattended material.

A third phenomenon is even more striking. In several studies (Corteen & Dunn, 1974; Corteen & Wood, 1972; Moray, 1970; von Wright, Anderson, & Stenman, 1975; Dawson & Schell, 1982) subjects first learned to associate certain words with the presence of a mild shock. After several pairings of a given word with shock, the word elicits a change in the subject's skin conductance, which is called a galvanic skin response (GSR). Thus, in this first part the GSR response was conditioned to certain words. In the second part of the study, subjects were given a difficult dichotic shadowing task in which the to-be-shadowed ear contained a passage from a Steinbeck novel for example, and the rejected ear contained a series of words. The experimenters recorded GSR's during shadowing. They found a reliable GSR when either the shock-associated words or words from the same category were presented in the rejected ear. Thus, if the words *Belfast, Moscow,* and *Sydney,* had been associated with shock in Part One of the experiment, both these words and semantically related words (such as *Zurich, London,* and *Dallas*) led to GSR's, whereas control words unrelated to the city names (e.g., *pencil, garbage, object*) did not. The fact that semantically related words led to a GSR indicates that the meaning of words in the rejected channel must have been processed. As in the studies we have just discussed, neither post-experimental questioning nor immediate tests provided any evidence that subjects were aware of the effect. In no case did the presence of the GSR interfere with the subject's ongoing shadowing performance.

All three of the phenomena we have just discussed suggest that far from being totally blocked out at an early stage of processing, at least some of the words presented to an unattended channel are analyzed for meaning, and this meaning influences other aspects of the person's performance, including stereotyped responses such as the GSR and the person's interpretation of attended material.

The finding that subjects seem unaware of the impact the unattended message is having on their performance is particularly intriguing, and a bit frightening for those who worry about their opinions and emotions being influenced without their awareness. Nonetheless, the conclusion that the effects we have just described are truly unconscious must be accepted only with caution. Awareness is, by definition, a subjective state, so the only way to determine whether or not someone is aware of something is to ask him and then to take him at his word (cf. Robinson, 1973). As we saw, when they are asked, subjects usually say they were unaware of the effects of the rejected message. For present purposes we will assume that subjects are doing their best to tell the truth. Even so, deciding whether or not you are conscious of something can be a surprisingly difficult task and answers are known to be influenced both by the way in which the question is phrased and by what the subject thinks the experimenter wants to hear. At this point, we have no clear criterion for telling us which is the most sensitive way to phrase our questions.

CAPACITY THEORIES OF ATTENTION: AUTOMATIC VS. CONTROLLED PROCESSING

The stimulus- and response-selection theories we have just discussed have at least two characteristics in common. First, both postulate the existence of a filter which protects a limited capacity processor from being overburdened with a deluge of stimuli to be processed. Second, neither provides a completely satisfactory explanation for all the phenomena we have discussed so far. We've already seen that placing the filter early in processing prior to recognition, as Broadbent and Treisman did, cannot account for the fact that the meaning of nonattended messages is frequently processed. The latter findings present no problem for theories which posit late selection after recognition has occurred. However, these response-selection theories assume that there is a severe limit on how many responses can be made at once. Contrary to this prediction, we've seen that at least one highly stereotyped response—the GSR—can occur during shadowing without providing any noticeable disruption in shadowing. In this case, then, two responses are occurring without interfering with each other, in direct conflict with the assumptions of response-selection theories. Indeed, two or more responses often occur simultaneously in daily life, as witnessed by the fact that most of us can walk and chew gum at the same time if we are so inclined.

Therefore, neither placement of the filter seems completely satisfactory, and this observation, among others to be discussed, has led recent theorists to question the value of positing any filter at all. This may strike you as the theory building analogy of closet cleaning; faced with a hockey stick that seems to fit neatly in none of your closets, you eliminate the difficulty by tossing out the offending possession. As a matter of fact, though, there is good basis for arguing that the postulation of a filter, and the subsequent attempts to locate its appropriate place in the sequence of processing, are hangovers from our acceptance of the passive view of human cognition—a view that was widely accepted during the decades of behaviorism, but that no longer fits with what we know about human perception.

A person needs a screen or filter to protect him from the environment only if he is the passive recipient (or victim) of stimuli that bombard him willy-nilly, regardless of his own actions. You need mosquito netting if you are to get any sleep when camped next to a swamp, for in this case environmental stimuli are particularly disturbing and unmanageable. In a similar fashion, the passive view of cognition we inherited from behaviorism suggested the necessity of postulating some sort of screen that would protect us from the deluge of otherwise unmanageable stimuli that impinge on our sensory organs at any given instant.

Notice how the situation changes however, if the individual is not passive, if instead perception is viewed as an active process during which the person uses past experience to choose and interpret external events. In this case, we don't need to postulate a filter to explain why people are aware of only a subset of all the items to which they are exposed. Neisser (1976) has offered the analogy of a person picking apples in an orchard. If we noticed that a man did not pick all the apples in the orchard (i.e., all the apples to which he was exposed), we would not deem it necessary to postulate that he has some filter which blocks certain apples. We would simply say that he didn't pick them. This follows because we view picking apples as an active event. The apples are there to be picked by the man; they are not attacking him.

Neisser argues that there are many similarities between perception and apple picking since both are processes in which the person actively selects certain stimuli for further processing. Neisser argues that searching for a filter implies a passive view of Man and a view of selective attention as a negative process (i.e., blocking out unwanted stimuli). He argues, rather, that Man is active and that selective attention should be viewed as a positive process.

At first this argument may sound like a discussion between an optimist and a pessimist arguing about the contents of a given bottle, with the former asserting that the bottle is half full and the other saying it is half empty. In fact, though, the choice of analogies affects the way in wich theories are built and the way in which we think about selective attention. In order to understand how discarding the search for a filter changes theories of attention, let us consider one recent *capacity theory* of attention proposed by Shiffrin and Schneider (1977). Their theory of attention is embedded in a general theory of information processing that is similar to the overview model we are discussing, so I will describe Shiffrin and Schneider's ideas in the context of our overview theory.

Shiffrin and Schneider assume that human cognition consists of two different kinds of processing—controlled processing and automatic processing. Controlled processing requires the use of a limited capacity processing mechanism whereas automatic processing does not. In our overview model, it is the working memory that has a limited capacity, so in terms of our model, controlled processing requires use of working memory whereas automatic processing does not. One example of controlled processing is rehearsing items to be maintained, such as a telephone number. An example of automatic processing would be holding an array in sensory storage. As we'll see later, most everyday activities such as walking and reading are assumed to be a mixture of both. We will now consider the characteristics of each kind of processing in more detail.

Controlled processing.   Since controlled processing requires use of a limited capacity processor, it follows that there will be a limit on the amount of controlled processing that can be done at once. Two or more controlled processes can be carried on at once without interfering with each other *only* if their combined processing demands do not exceed the capacity of the system. Therefore, most controlled processes will occur in sequence, one after the other, with the outcome of one process being used to help the person decide which process should be applied next. A familiar example would be the sequence of steps involved in problem solving. You attempt one particular strategy for solving the problem. Then you determine whether using this strategy has helped you move toward solution, and you decide what process to apply next depending on the outcome of that decision.

Furthermore, Shiffrin and Schneider assume that controlled processing can lead to permanent changes in long-term memory, i.e., it can lead to learning. Phrased in terms of our overview model, if any new experience is to be maintained permanently in long-term memory it must be processed by the limited capacity working memory.

Shiffrin and Schneider assume that there are two different kinds of controlled processes: (1) accessible controlled processes and (2) veiled processes. The former can be instituted and modified by instructions and they can usually be reported quite readily by the person. In other words, they seem accessible to conscious awareness. One such accessible controlled process is rehearsal. Veiled controlled processes, on the other hand, are difficult to modify through verbal instruction, and are outside the conscious awareness of the subject. One example of a veiled controlled process is searching for items in working memory, a topic we will consider in detail in the next chapter. Such searching can be demonstrated to require access to the limited capacity mechanism in that it interferes with other ongoing mental activity, but the process itself does not seem available to conscious awareness. Certain aspects of understanding language are also veiled controlled processes.

In summary, according to Shiffrin and Schneider's theory, the defining characteristic of controlled processing is that it requires access to a limited capacity processing mechanism, our working memory.

Automatic processing.   In contrast, Shiffrin and Schneider assume that automatic processing does not require access to working memory. Therefore, it should not interfere either with other ongoing automatic processing or even with simultaneous controlled process-ing. Furthermore, unlike controlled processes which usually occur se-quentially, one after the other, automatic processes often occur in par-allel (i.e., simultaneously)—a capability which is the result of the lack of interference. In a sense, then, automatic processing is assumed to be effortless, but this lack of effort is gained at cost, for automatic processes, once initiated, are assumed to continue to completion with-out control of the subject, whereas controlled processing may be ter-minated or modified at any point.

A final characteristic that distinguishes automatic from con-trolled processing in Shiffrin and Schneider's theory is that the former does not result in any permanent change in long-term memory, i.e., it cannot lead to learning about the processed material. Controlled pro-cessing, or attention, is required for learning to occur.

The nature of automatic processing is best understood by consid-ering a phenomenon that shows it in operation. In Figure 3–5 you will find a number of squares, each containing a certain number of a given digit. Begin in the upper left corner and call out the *number of digits* in each square as quickly as you can. Ignore the names of the digits themselves. Try that now before reading further.

You probably found the task surprisingly difficult. Most people have to fight the tendency to call out the names of the digits rather than the number of digits displayed. The problem seems to be that the meaning of the digits themselves conflicts with your ability to count

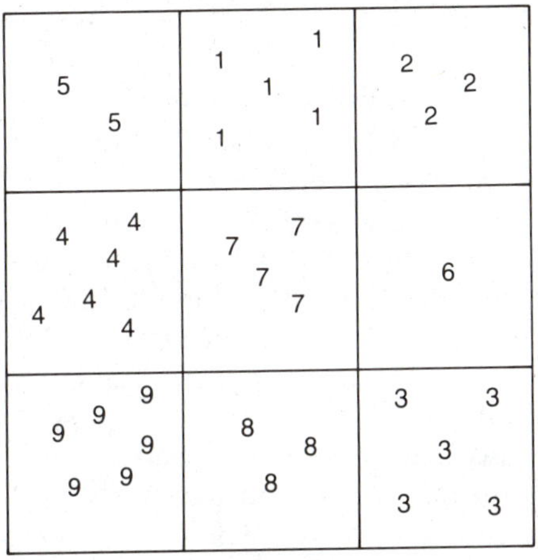

Figure 3–5. Sample stimuli from a modified Stroop task. Beginning in the upper left corner, call out the number of digits in each square, ignoring the names of the digits themselves.

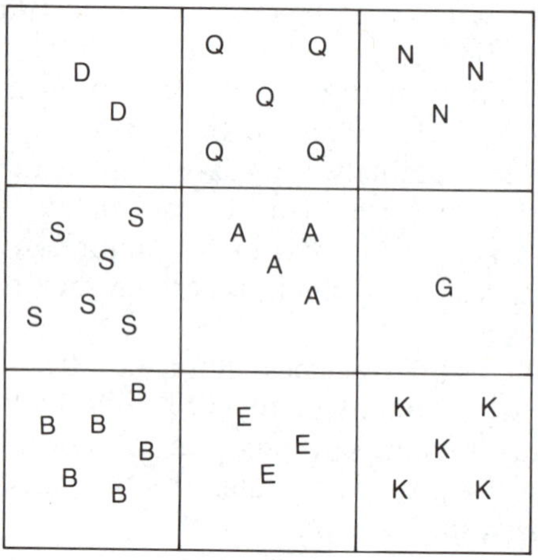

Figure 3–6. Sample stimuli from a control condition for the modified Stroop task. Beginning in the upper left corner, call out the number of letters in each square, ignoring the names of the letters themselves.

them, since both are numerical. To convince yourself that this is the difficulty, try the same task (calling out the number of items in each square) for Figure 3–6. This is usually much easier, because the meaning of the items being counted (the letters) doesn't conflict with the counting.

You have just experienced a modified version of the *Stroop effect* (Windes, 1968; Morton, 1969). In the original task, which was first described by Stroop (1935), subjects were presented with color words which were printed in a conflicting ink color (e.g., the word RED printed in blue ink). It is very difficult to call out the ink color, since the meaning of the printed word itself conflicts. People find it much easier to call out the ink color in which non-color words are printed (e.g., the word CAT printed in blue ink). Try this original color-word Stroop effect on yourself and on some friends.

Both versions of the Stroop effect reveal that even when you try to ignore the meaning of a digit or a word, you look up its meaning anyway. This processing is automatic in that it is outside your control. Thus, the sequence of events involved in looking up the word's or digit's meaning in long-term memory seems to be initiated automatically upon presentation of the item.

Distinguishing automatic processes from controlled processes. The definition of automatic and controlled processes we have adopted suggests an empirical means of determining whether a given task requires controlled processing. We can ask a person to perform two tasks at once (concurrently). We can then compare how well the person performs each of these tasks under this concurrent condition with how the person performs each task alone. If concurrent performance of the two tasks leads to a decrement in performance of either, then both must require access to the limited capacity mechanism, i.e., both must require controlled processing. (This is assuming, of course, that we've chosen our tasks in a way that precludes obvious response interference, e.g., the fact that you can't write and knit at the same time doesn't necessarily imply that both require access to a limited capacity central processor. It might simply reflect the fact that you have only two hands.) On the other hand, if concurrent performance of the two tasks leads to no decrement in performance of either task, then there are two possible interpretations. The first and most interesting is that at least one of these tasks requires only automatic processes; i.e., at least one does not require access to the limited capacity mechanism. The second possibility, however, is that one or both of the tasks require controlled processing, but that the combined demands of the two tasks do not exceed the capacity of working memory.

Therefore, the finding of no interference between two or more tasks must always be interpreted with some caution. Through additional research, however, it is often possible to distinguish between the two possibilities we have just described. We could try to make one or more of the tasks somewhat more difficult, thereby increasing the demands on processing capacity if the task does, indeed, require controlled processing. Alternatively, we might leave the two original tasks unaltered, but add a third task thought to require controlled processing. Under either of the latter conditions if the two original tasks were indeed automatic, then we should still witness no interference with either of them.

Such analyses of concurrent task performance, though reported at least as long ago as the late 1800's, are just beginning to be applied in the context of capacity theories of attention. Consider a couple of recent examples.

In our discussion of sensory storage we assumed that maintaining items in the sensory registers does not require access to the limited capacity central processor. If this assumption is accurate, then iconic and echoic storage should not be affected by the performance of concurrent activity. In fact, there is some evidence supporting this conclusion. Doost and Turvey (1971) had college students perform in a Sperling partial report study of the sort described in Chapter 2. At the same time, the subjects were required to hold a series of items in working memory. Doost and Turvey found that iconic storage and holding items in working memory did not interfere with each other. Subjects were just as good at performing both tasks together as they were at performing either alone. This finding is consistent with the conclusion that at least one of these tasks requires only automatic processing. Since there is good reason to believe that holding items in working memory requires processing capacity, it follows that iconic storage must be the task that does not. As we've indicated, it is possible, of course, that both tasks do require capacity, but that we simply have not exceeded the capacity limits, so further research is necessary. For example, see Chow and Murdock (1975; 1976).

A similar kind of analysis has been applied (Anderson & Craik, 1974) to an investigation of the extent to which echoic storage requires controlled processing. To understand their reasoning, consider again our discussion of the modality effect in immediate serial recall (Chapter 2). We argued there that the advantage of auditory over visual presentation in the recency portion of the serial position function reflects the operation of an auditory sensory register that outlasts the duration of visual sensory memory. Thus, we assume that all components of the serial position curve for visual presentation are due to processing that requires access to the limited capacity mechanism, but that the recency portion of the auditory curve reflects an automatic process (i.e., one that does not require the limited capacity mechanism). If this analysis is correct, then consider what should happen if we ask the subject to perform some concurrent task that is known to require controlled processing. Performing this concurrent task should interfere with all components of the visual serial position curve, and with all components of the auditory curve, *except* the recency portion. When Anderson and Craik performed such an experiment, their results were exactly as predicted. Furthermore, their study was particularly well done since they also varied the complexity of the concurrent task. This complexity affected how well the subject recalled all sections of the lists *except* for the recency portion of the auditory curve, an additional aspect of the results that is consistent with the analysis of echoic memory in the previous chapter.

The interaction of automatic and controlled processes. We indicated that most daily activities involve a combination of both automatic and controlled processing. Exactly how this interaction occurs is a topic we will take up when we discuss language comprehension and reading in a later section of the book. For now it is sufficient to note that automatic processes often direct attention. That is, the outcome of some automatic processing will cause the central processor to devote controlled processing to some stimulus or some internal representation.

This point is best illustrated by considering how the automatic vs. controlled processing distinction can be applied to the analysis of the selective listening studies discussed earlier. The subject is assumed to devote his controlled processing to the attended message. Throughout the task, however, automatic processing is occurring for the stimuli on the unattended channel. The Stroop phenomenon as well as the GSR and related evidence we discussed suggests that this automatic processing includes looking up at least some aspects of the individual word meanings in long-term memory. Most of the time this automatic processing goes on without affecting the task of shadowing, but sometimes the result of the automatic processing leads to an automatic attention response. In the selective listening task, this might occur when your own name is presented over the nonattended channel. The automatic processing detects the presence of your name, and this detection results in attention being shifted automatically to the rejected message.

The role of learning. Filter theories tended to treat selective attention as a process little influenced by learning. That is, the placement of the filter was assumed to be the same whether a person was engaged in a newly acquired skill or a highly practiced one. One advantage of the capacity theories is that they emphasize the influence of learning on attentional processes.

When the infant takes his first faltering step, it looks as though all the resources of body and mind have been called to the fore. Furthermore, as Jerome Bruner has demonstrated in a captivating film *From Cup to Lip*, getting a cup to her lips is no small feat for the seven-month-old infant. Yet a few short years later, eating with knife, fork, and spoon (or chopsticks, in some cultures), and running become activities that can be done without concentration and while doing other complex activities such as talking or reading. In other words, during the first few years of life, many activities that seemed initially to require attention (i.e., controlled processing) become automatic. Were it not so, our lives would be infinitely more difficult than they are. Consider what life would be like if every step required as much concentration as the first you took.

The switch from controlled processing to automaticity that we have just described is not limited to an individual's early development. In fact, the development of automaticity is a salient characteristic of most of the learning in which we engage throughout our lives. Complex motor skills are particularly obvious examples. For the adult, driving, typing, and playing tennis all require controlled processing at first try. Full attention must be brought to bear on the task, and any other attention demanding activity, such as talking, is impossible without serious disruption of the fledgling skill. After varying degrees of practice, many components of these skills seem to become automatic, with controlled processing being required only in unusual cases. For the person who has been driving for many years, it is easy to carry on conversation while driving as long as no emergencies arise. However, a child running across the street in front of the car leads to a necessary break in the conversation, while controlled processing is called into play for driving.

Such development of automaticity doesn't only occur for motor skills, as a consideration of reading reveals. Although reading never becomes completely automatic, at least for most of us, it is clear that some components of reading do. In particular, the Stroop effect indicates that for the skilled reader, fixating on a word results in the meaning of the word being looked up in long-term memory. As you would expect, this effect is less pronounced in beginning readers, for whom the meaning of a printed word is not automatically processed—a fact that is quite transparent to the teacher attempting to introduce a first-grader to the joy of the printed page.

The fact that automaticity develops even for extremely complex tasks renders it possible for people to perform astonishing feats. Indeed, it is safe to say that few people ever push themselves enough to realize their potential for doing several activities simultaneously. One such possibility for extending human limits led to some interest in the early part of this century. This is the case of so-called automatic writing (e.g., Solomons & Stein, 1896; Downey & Anderson, 1915). In 1896 Solomons and Stein reported a study in which they had acted as their own subjects. They practiced a series of concurrent tasks, with each pair being more difficult than the previous. Each pair of concurrent tasks was practiced over the course of months. The most difficult of these involved reading one story aloud while copying down another at dictation. They found that although difficult at first, after extended practice, the writing task became automatic. Unfortunately, the only measure of automaticity they had was their own introspection. At first they were conscious of both activities, but later they were conscious of only one.

Recently, Spelke, Hirst, and Neisser (1976) managed to induce two students, Diane and John, to attempt a replication and extension of these earlier findings. Diane and John participated in 5 one-hour sessions per week for about 17 weeks. Throughout the experiment their primary task was to read short stories. At the beginning of the experiment they were required to copy words at dictation. (This is a difficult task at first, as you will realize if you will take a few minutes to try it. Simply read a novel silently while a friend reads you a list of words to copy. The friend should read a new word the instant you finish writing the previous word.) By the end of the experiment Diane and John were required to categorize the dictated words for meaning, writing down not the word itself, but its category. (For example, if the dictation list contained the word *dog*, the subject was to write *ani-*

mal.) After several months of practice Diane and John were able to perform both tasks at once while reading at a rate and with as complete comprehension of the story as they would have without the concurrent dictation task. Thus, the writing and categorizing became automatic by our definition. Was the writing also unconscious? As is typically the case with subjective reports, they were quite unsatisfactory from the view of both experimenters and subjects. Sometimes Diane and John said the writing became almost unconscious, but other times they said they were aware of both reading and writing at once, and still other times they said they couldn't tell. Why not try such an experiment on yourself and examine your own introspections?

In this day of efficiency experts, I am surprised that there is not more interest in developing such dual processing skills. Think of how much more the government could accomplish if civil servants could read one report while writing another! In fact, the development of automaticity is a critical component of many occupations. It is not enough for the pilot to know how to land an airplane. He must be able to do so almost automatically so that in the stress of an emergency he will not need to rely upon executing the series of decisions required of controlled processing. Norman (1976) discusses the case of the scuba diver who finds his air tank and hose tangled in seaweed. If the diver does not panic, the situation is not desperate; all he need do is remove the tank and engage in one of several techniques for getting back to the surface without an air supply. What often happens, however, is that the diver is already tired and frightened and he panics, forgetting to pull the release cord. The best way to increase the likelihood that the diver will pull the cord in such an emergency is for him to practice such releasing again and again, until the action no longer requires the attention demanded of controlled processing, i.e., until it has become automatic.

We cannot yet provide a detailed theoretical account of exactly what changes occur when controlled processing becomes automatized, and this will surely be a direction for further theoretical development. From a practical standpoint, however, it is clear that the necessary component is *overlearning*. That is, a skill must be practiced again and again and again, typically long past the point of boredom, until your body seems to act without your being conscious of it. Keep this discussion in mind the next time you set out to learn such a skill and try to follow the changes in conscious awareness that accompany your growing expertise.

Before leaving discussion of the changes in automaticity that occur with practice, it is interesting to note that the direction of change is not always toward growing automaticity. One characteristic of some forms of mental pathology is that the normally automatic components of behaviors such as walking and sitting seem to require conscious attention. Consider the report of a schizophrenic patient quoted in McGhie's book, *Pathology of Attention:*

> I'm not sure of my own movements any more. It's very hard to describe this but at times I'm not sure about even simple actions like sitting down. It's not so much thinking out what to do it's the doing of it that sticks me. . . . I found recently that I was thinking of myself doing things before I would do them. If I'm going to sit down for example, I've got to think of myself and almost see myself sitting down before I do it. It's the same with other things like washing, eating, and even dressing—things that I have done at one time without even bothering or thinking about at all. . . . I take more time to do things because I am always conscious of what I am doing. If I could just stop noticing what I am doing, I would get things done a lot faster.
>
> I have to do everything step by step now, nothing is automatic. Everything has to be considered.

This patient's report, which is characteristic of many that McGhie obtained, would not have been of particular theoretical interest from the viewpoint of filter theories of attention. However, in light of capacity theories it suggests that one characteristic of schizophrenia is a breakdown of the automaticity which we have seen to be so important for normal functioning.

ATTENTION AND THE OVERVIEW MODEL

This chapter represents only the beginning of our study of attention, for the distinctions we have introduced here will be useful throughout our analysis of cognition. The distinction between controlled and automatic processing will be particularly important, so it is worth pausing here to consider more explicitly how this distinction might be built into our overview theory of human cognition.

It is helpful to think of both kinds of processes as being stored in long-term memory as procedures. Each such process, then, consists of a list of steps, or to use the computer analogy, a program. All of these programs reside in long-term memory. Controlled processes and automatic processes differ in whether or not they require access to the limited capacity central processor (working memory) for carrying them out. Programs that represent automatic processing (such as a skilled reader's finding the meaning of a word in long-term memory) do not require the use of working memory for execution. Thus, they do not interfere with other ongoing activity. Some such automatic processes may be built into the human information processing system. One possible example would be the automatic processes involved in holding items in sensory storage. Other automatic processes may have first been learned as controlled processes, but through overlearning have become automatized.

In contrast to programs that represent automatic processes, those that are controlled processes require use of the limited capacity working memory for their execution. Thus, executing two such programs at once will result in their interfering with each other if their combined demands exceed the limits of working memory. In the next chapter we will examine working memory, and hence controlled processing, in more detail.

CHAPTER SUMMARY

Contemporary experimental psychology emphasizes the importance of attention in cognition. Although Titchener proposed the Law of Prior Entry early in this century, American psychologists virtually ignored attention during the behavioristic decades of the 1930's and 1940's. In the early 1950's, Cherry's cocktail party experiments revived interest in selective attention. Cherry found that when people attempt to shadow and attend to one message, only the gross physical characteristics of a simultaneously presented unattended message are noticed and reported later.

In attempting to explain these facts, psychologists proposed filter theories of attention which assume that at some point in information processing there is a filter which may be tuned to accept certain stimuli (attended stimuli) and to reject others (unattended stimuli). Filter theories differ from each other concerning the point in processing at which the filter is assumed to operate. The first such theories were called stimulus-selection theories since they assumed that the filter operates early in processing, prior to the point at which the meaning of an item is determined. The original such theory was Broadbent's sensory-filter theory. However, several findings soon proved inconsistent with Broadbent's theory, since they suggested that the meaning of the unattended message was often processed. This led other theorists, such as Deutsch and Deutsch and Norman, to assume instead that the filter operates only after the meaning of the stimulus has been looked up in long-term memory. According to these so-called response-selection theories, the limit is not on how many stimuli can be recognized at once, but rather on how many stimuli can be responded to simultaneously.

The debate between stimulus- and response-selection theories has never been resolved, although several kinds of studies reveal that the meaning of unattended materials is often processed, leading most recent researchers to favor late selection over early. The debate has been productive in that it revealed important characteristics of selective attention, but more recently theorists have refocused their energies. Rather than attempting to locate a hypothetical filter at one point or another in processing, capacity theories have been proposed which emphasize the flexible nature of attention. These theories distinguish controlled processes, which require the use of a limited capacity processing mechanism, from automatic processes, which do not. In terms of our overview model, in order to be carried out controlled processes require use of the limited capacity working memory, whereas automatic processes do not. Experimental attempts to distinguish the two kinds of processes often involve the use of concurrent tasks, to determine whether or not the tasks interfere with each other. Most everyday activities such as walking, reading, and eating, consist of a combination of automatic and controlled processes.

The shift in emphasis from filter theories to capacity theories has led to a change in the kind of questions that researchers ask. Filter theories led to a focus on the fate of unattended information. That is, research focused on whether the meaning of unattended material was processed and whether there was any long-term memory for unattended material. One contribution of capacity theories is that they have led cognitive psychologists to be concerned with how learning influences the extent to which a given process demands attention. For example, when people learn to read, processes such as letter identification, which at first require controlled processing, later become automatic.

SUGGESTED READING

The best place to begin a more thorough study of attention is the second edition of Norman's brief text *Memory and Attention*. Chapters 2, 3, and 4 are particularly relevant and Norman suggests many additional readings at the end of Chapter 4. Keele's book *Attention and Human Performance* is also a good starting place, as is Chapter 6 of the text *Cognitive Psychology and Information Processing* by Lachman, Lachman, and Butterfield. In addition you will find it informative to read the classic papers and books by Broadbent, Treisman, and Norman that are referenced early in the current chapter, the book by Moray entitled *Attention*, and a recent review by Posner (1982).

Though I have opted for late selection over early in the overview model, the issue is far from resolved. An excellent place to read more about this controversy is an article by Egeth (1977) which reviews evidence that is inconsistent with late selection theories, and an article by Francolini and Egeth (1980). In contrast, Kellogg (1980) has presented interesting evidence for some long-term storage of unattended material.

The Shiffrin and Schneider (1977) theory discussed in this chapter is only one of a number of capacity theories. Kahneman's book *Attention and Effort* proposes another, and also provides an excellent review of the attention literature through 1973. Norman and Bobrow (1975) have introduced the distinction between data-limited and resource-limited processes. In a 1975 article Posner and Snyder propose a theory similar to that of Shiffrin and Schneider, and they provide a fascinating selective review of the literature. The Posner and Boies (1971) article "Components of Attention" is also informative, as is the review by Hasher and Zacks (1979). Lansman and Hunt (1982) have recently reported using concurrent task performance as a measure of individual differences.

I have included only the briefest of references to changes in attention that accompany mental pathologies. Norman (1976) provides a slightly more extended discussion, and the book by Reed entitled *The Psychology of Anomalous Experience: A Cognitive Approach* provides a thorough treatment of this topic.

Finally, conferences on Attention and Performance are held periodically and the proceedings published. For the more advanced student this series is a useful source of the latest research on attention. Eight volumes have been published so far, though Volume II is on reaction time, rather than attention. Volumes I and III were edited by Sanders (1967, 1970), Volume IV by Kornblum (1973), Volume V by Rabbitt and Dornic (1975), Volume VI by Dornic (1977), Volume VII by Requin (1978), and Volume VIII (1980) by Nickerson.

Working Memory

4

FOOD FOR THOUGHT

There is an interesting limit on the length of a series that can be repeated back for immediate serial recall without error, a limit which has been termed the *immediate memory span*. Try the following experiment on yourself. Have someone read each of the lists in Table 4–1 aloud to you, at the rate of about 2 items per second. (If no experimenter is available, then read the lists aloud to yourself.) Immediately after each list has been read, you should attempt to repeat the list in the order in which it was presented. Your immediate memory span for digits (sometimes called your *digit span*) is the longest list you can report perfectly. After doing the lists of digits, try the lists of letters, and the lists of words, determining your span of immediate memory for each. You might also try the same experiment on a few friends

TABLE 4–1.   Lists for Determining Your Memory Span.

9	2	5									
8	6	4	2								
3	7	6	5	4							
6	2	7	4	1	8						
0	4	0	1	4	7	3					
1	9	2	2	3	5	3	0				
4	8	6	8	5	4	3	3	2			
2	5	3	1	9	7	1	7	6	8		
8	5	1	2	9	6	1	9	4	5	0	
9	1	8	5	4	6	9	4	2	9	3	7

G	M	N									
S	L	R	R								
V	O	E	P	G							
X	W	D	X	Q	O						
E	P	H	H	J	A	E					
Z	D	O	F	W	D	S	V				
D	T	Y	N	R	H	E	H	Q			
K	H	W	D	A	G	R	O	F	Z		
U	D	F	F	W	H	D	Q	D	G	E	
Q	M	R	H	X	Z	D	P	R	R	E	H

CAT BOAT RUG
RUN BEACH PLANT LIGHT
SUIT WATCH CUT STAIRS CAR
JUNK LONE GAME CALL WOOD HEART
FRAME PATCH CROSS DRUG DESK HORSE LAW
CLOTHES CHOOSE GIFT DRIVE BOOK TREE HAIR THIS
DRESS CLERK FILM BASE SPEND SERVE BOOK LOW TIME
STONE ALL NAIL DOOR HOPE EARL BELL BUY COPE GRAPE
AGE SOFT FALL STORE PUT TRUE SMALL FREE CHECK STREET WHEEL
LOG DAY TIME CHESS LAKE CUT BIRD SHEET YOUR SEE MAIL LEAF

to determine whether there is any consistency across people and across types of items. It would be particularly interesting to test children of various ages to determine if there are age differences.

WORKING MEMORY

In this chapter we turn to the memory system which was the main focus of research on memory for 15 years or so. This system goes by several names which are often used interchangeably. Its most common names other than working memory are *primary memory, active memory, short-term store,* and the abbreviation STS. One usage can be confusing; the term *short-term memory* (or *STM*) is sometimes used to refer to a memory store, and, hence, as a synonym for working memory. Other times, however, it is used to refer to a kind of experimental task, namely any that requires the subject to remember items for only a very brief period, usually less than 1 minute. The distinction is important, because in many short-term memory *tasks* the subject is able to recall not only from working memory, but from other memory systems as well. For example, we saw in Chapter 2 that for the immediate serial recall task (which is usually called a short-term memory task) when the list is presented auditorily, subjects recall not only from working memory, but also from the auditory sensory store. Thus, although this is called a short-term memory task, it is not only tapping what is stored in the short-term store. We will see that many short-term memory tasks seem to call on material from long-term memory as well.

EVIDENCE FOR THE DICHOTOMY BETWEEN WORKING MEMORY AND LONG-TERM MEMORY

Memory theories like our overview theory are usually termed *dichotomous theories* or *multiple store theories* because they postulate that there are two or more functionally distinct kinds of memory systems. (When the term *dichotomous* is used, it refers to the working memory vs. long-term memory distinction. The sensory stores, being assumed by virtually all theories, are ignored.)

The notion that there are two different kinds of memory storage, one transitory and the other permanent, is perhaps the most ubiquitous assumption that has ever been made about memory. The assumption is usually preserved even in those theories which ostensibly oppose multiple-store models. For example, in 1972 Craik and Lockhart proposed that multiple-store models had outlived their usefulness, and Craik and Lockhart offered as an alternative framework a *levels of pro-*

cessing approach. In brief, this approach assumes that pattern recognition of a stimulus (e.g., the printed word *CAT*) proceeds through a series of stages of processing beginning with the physical characteristics (e.g., the lines and angles in the individual letters) and continuing through deeper and deeper levels (e.g., the identity of the letters, then the identity of the word, and finally its meaning). Each of these levels of processing is assumed to result in some form of memory trace and the durability of that trace is assumed to be dependent upon the depth of processing, with deeper levels of processing leading to more durable memory traces.

The levels of processing approach has led to important insights that we'll discuss later, but the point here is that even this alternative assumes a primary memory system of limited capacity, which functions in a way that is similar to the working memory of the overview model we are developing. Thus, even the most vocal contemporary advocates of an alternative framework have found it necessary to argue that there is a primary memory system. Why is the notion of a dichotomy of memory systems so prevalent? We'll consider four different kinds of evidence that have been particularly influential, though theorists have varied in the extent to which they have found each of these compelling.

Introspection. Thoughtful people, when reflecting on the nature of their own memories, have often been led to postulate a distinction between two different kinds of memory. The two most well-known of these thinkers are William James and Sigmund Freud. In his 1890 text *The Principles of Psychology*, James introduced the distinction between primary and secondary memory. In his terminology, secondary memory is "memory proper" in that it is memory for the distant past, which must be dredged up from among many other stored recollections. On the other hand, primary memory is equated with the current contents of consciousness. In James' words it is "the rearward portion of the present space of time."

Freud (1940) suggested a similar distinction when he discussed a "Mystic Writing Pad." He likened memory to the children's writing pads which consist of a wax substance under a thin sheet of waxed paper which, in turn, is under a transparent celluloid sheet. Writing on the celluloid sheet with a stylus makes the wax adhere to the middle layer, displaying whatever was drawn. The child can erase this drawing simply by lifting the two upper sheets, though the impression remains on the wax beneath. Freud argued that people have permanent memories which are like the wax pad and transient memories which are like the middle layer. The contents of this transient memory are the current contents of consciousness, according to Freud, just as the contents of the top two sheets of a pad are available to immediate view. The contents of consciousness may be erased from transient memory and replaced by new material, just as the drawings may be erased from view by lifting the upper layers of the writing pad.

Clinical cases. The second kind of evidence for a dichotomous view of memory comes from studying individuals who have suffered brain damage.

The most well-known pattern of loss was first reported in detail by Brenda Milner (1966). Milner worked with a patient HM who had undergone a brain operation (bilateral surgery on the temporal lobes and hippocampus) in an attempt to cure severe epileptic seizures. Although the operation cured the seizures, subsequent clinical testing revealed that HM suffered a dramatic pattern of memory loss. Some aspects of his memory were normal. He had no difficulty recalling his preoperative past, and his general IQ score remained unaffected. In addition, he had a normal span of immediate memory. For example, he could look up and remember a new telephone number long enough to dial it, as long as he was free to rehearse the number. On the other hand, HM was completely unable to learn and retain anything new. As soon as he was distracted he would forget the new material. For example, people whom HM first met after his operation had to be introduced anew each time they visited, for as soon as they left, HM forgot them. In a tragic sense, then, HM lived only in the past.

HM acts as though he has a normal working memory and a normal long-term memory, but that he has lost the ability to store new information in long-term memory (or, perhaps, to retrieve newly stored information from it). Unfortunately, this pattern of loss is not limited to patients who undergo brain surgery of a particular sort, but is also seen in patients suffering from Korsakov's syndrome—a disorder resulting from excessive drinking and inadequate diet. Such people, though able to remember the distant past and in possession of normal immediate memory span, have difficulty learning new material permanently. They remain unable to report the year, who is President, and so on (Zangwill, 1946).

There are many cases of such selective impairment of memory (see, for example, Shallice, 1979). Some patients perform normally on tasks thought to reflect working memory, but reveal gross impairments on tasks that call upon long-term memory. Others show the opposite pattern—apparently impaired working memory functioning, but normal long-term memory abilities. Such patterns of selective impairment are consistent with theories which propose two functionally distinct memory systems, and these clinical cases suggest that one of these systems may function more or less normally even though the other is impaired.

Analyses of the free recall serial position curve. In Chapter 2 we saw that the serial position curve from immediate serial recall tasks reveals evidence for the auditory sensory store. It turns out that a similar serial position function is obtained in a different memory task—the *free recall experiment*.

In the free recall task, the subject is presented with a long series of words (usually 20 or more) and later must attempt to recall as many as he can. It is called free because the subject is free to recall the words in any order he wishes, and a word is counted as correct regardless of whether or not it is recalled in the order in which it was presented. (This contrasts with immediate serial recall in that the latter requires that the original order be retained.) Since we will have occasion to consider free recall again in the future, it would be a good idea to try such an experiment now. Table 4–2 contains a list of items divided into 2 columns. Place a card over the entire list. Then slide the card down exposing each item in turn long enough to read it aloud. (First do one column, then the other.) When you have reached the end of the second column, immediately write down all the words from the list that you can recall, in any order you wish. The object is to report as many of them as possible. If you can find some volunteers, test them too. After the subject has finished recalling the list, circle those words on which he was correct.

You have just finished replicating an *immediate free recall* experiment. (The term *immediate* refers to the fact that recall took place immediately after presentation of the list.) When the per cent of correct recall is plotted as a function of the serial position in which an item was *presented*, the serial position function usually looks like that depicted in Figure 4–1. We see pronounced primacy and recency effects with poorer recall for items presented in the middle of each list. If you examine the data you have collected, you will probably find evidence for both of these effects, with your subjects being most

TABLE 4–2.   A List of Words for Free Recall.

SUMMER	ROAD
CLOSET	LINEN
ROBIN	BOX
FRIEND	MAPLE
DRESS	GLOBE
CRIME	SOLDIER
SQUIRREL	NURSE
TRAIN	CEILING
ROSE	COOKIE
PIANO	ARM
MEASLES	PRIEST
CARROT	GREEN
PENCIL	WRENCH
HOUSE	UNCLE
KITE	GLASS

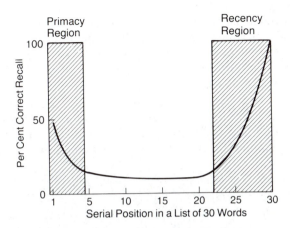

Figure 4–1. Idealized data depicting the serial
position function for immediate free recall.
The figure depicts the per cent correct recall as a function of the serial position in
which the word was presented. Notice that
recall is better for the primacy and recency
portions than for the central serial positions.

likely to recall items from either the beginning (e.g., the words SUM-
MER, CLOSET, ROBIN) or the end (e.g., the words WRENCH, UNCLE,
GLASS) of the list.

It is important to realize that in the case of the free recall experiment, the recency portion is not due solely to the contribution of the
auditory sensory store, because a strong recency effect is also obtained
even with visual presentation of the list to be recalled (a fact of which
you should convince yourself by testing a couple more volunteers).

Dichotomous theories of memory suggest an interpretation of the
free recall serial position function. The recency portion reflects the
contents of working memory. That is, the last five or so items are reported so accurately because at the time of testing they were still residing in working memory. This interpretation is strengthened by the
introspections of subjects as well as by the usual order of recall. Subjects usually write down the last few words they've been presented
with as soon as they are permitted to begin recalling, and when doing
so they scribble very quickly, later reporting that they wanted to pour
them out before the words were lost. On the other hand, the primacy
and center portions of the curve are thought to reflect recall from the
long-term memory. The finding that the first few positions yield better
recall than the middle ones is usually attributed to the fact that subjects were able to devote more time to committing them to long-term
memory in the absence of other material.

So far, our argument for the dichotomous stores interpretation of the free recall serial position curve is plausible, but not particularly compelling. For example, one could explain the same function by postulating that there is only one kind of memory system and that items are forgotten from this system because they are interfered with by adjacent items. According to such an interpretation, the serial position curve is obtained because the items in the center are interfered with both by preceding and following items, whereas the first items do not have any previous items to interfere with them and the latest have no following items.

Therefore, it is not the existence of the serial position curve per se that provides strong evidence for a dichotomous view. Rather, it is the set of predictions it makes regarding how certain variables should influence the different portions of the curve. According to the dichotomous view, the two portions of the serial position curve reflect the operation of two different memory systems. If this is the case, then it should be possible to alter one of these systems (and hence one portion of the curve) while leaving the other intact. Factors which are assumed to influence working memory should change only the recency portion of the curve, whereas factors assumed to influence long-term memory should change all but the recency portion.

Let's consider first a factor that should influence only working memory. Imagine that instead of permitting the subject to begin recall immediately after presentation of the list, we require him to delay recall for 2 minutes during which time he must do some attention-demanding task, such as counting backward by threes. According to a dichotomous theory, this activity should interfere with the words stored in working memory, thus decreasing the recency effect, but it should not influence the long-term components of the curve. The predicted pattern of results is displayed in Figure 4–2a. On the other hand, the dichotomous view predicts that the rate of presentation of a list should influence only the long-term components of the serial position curve. This is because fast rates of presentation allow the subject little time to commit each item to long-term memory, whereas slower presentation should result in more long-term storage. The predicted pattern of results when presentation rate is varied, then, is displayed in Figure 4–2b for the case in which immediate recall is permitted. In fact, when the experiments we've just outlined are carried out (Murdock, 1962; Postman & Phillips, 1965), the results are similar to those predicted in Figures 4–2a and 4–2b, thus providing support for the dichotomous model's interpretation of the free recall serial position curve.

You may already have thought of a way in which we could test our interpretation of both the clinical data discussed earlier and the serial position function. If amnesic patients like HM have normal short-

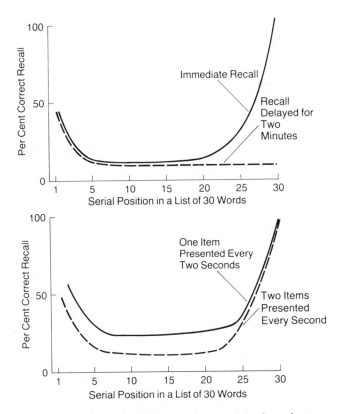

Figure 4–2. This figure depicts the pattern of results predicted by dichotomous memory theories. Figure 4–
2a shows how per cent correct recall should be affected by requiring the subject to delay recall (dotted line) for two minutes during which he counts
backward by threes. According to dichotomous theory, such a delay should influence only working
memory and, hence, the recency portion of the curve.
Figure 4–2b shows how recall should be affected by
varying the rate of presentation. According to dichotomous theory, this should influence only long-
term memory, so slow presentation (the solid line)
should be better than fast presentation (the dotted
line), but only for the primacy and central regions
of the curve.

term storage, but are deficient in storing and/or retrieving new material in long-term memory, then if we presented such patients with an
immediate free recall task, they should not differ from normals in the
recency portion of the curve, but should be poorer than normals for
the primacy and center portions, which are assumed to reflect long-
term memory. Baddeley and Warrington (1970) have reported such a

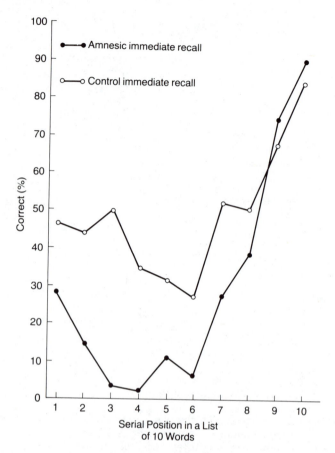

Figure 4–3. Immediate free recall serial position functions observed from amnesic and control patients.
Notice that the recency portion of the curve is the
same for both groups, but that the primacy and central portions are poorer for amnesic subjects (filled
circles) than for normals (open circles). (After Baddeley & Warrington, 1970. Copyright 1970 by Academic Press. Reprinted by permission.)

study and their results are depicted in Figure 4–3. You can see that
the results are as predicted, once again lending support to the dichotomous view of memory.

In fact, when people of different ages, levels of formal schooling,
and cultural backgrounds have been studied, the recency effect has
proven to be universal, but the primacy effect has not. For example,
five-year-olds in the United States show recency, but primacy effects
don't appear until children are in the later years of elementary school
(e.g., Hagen & Stanovich, 1977). Mentally retarded children usually

reveal recency, but not primacy, effects (e.g., Campione & Brown, 1977). Cross-cultural studies indicate that people reveal recency effects regardless of educational background, but only the older children and adults who have spent some time in formal schooling show primacy (e.g., Wagner, 1974; 1978). The fact that formal schooling influences primacy suggests that this effect may be due to some active memorization strategies that are encouraged in the formal educational setting. This hypothesis is consistent with the fact that when normal five-year-olds and mentally retarded children have been trained simple memorization strategies, this has resulted in their exhibiting primacy as well (cf. Campione & Brown, 1977; Kingsley & Hagen, 1969).

The fact that one part of the serial position curve (recency) is relatively invariant across individuals and cultures, while the other (primacy) is not, suggests that these different parts are reflecting the operation of different memory systems or processes.

Capacity limitations. This fourth kind of evidence for dichotomous theory has recently received increasing emphasis. For example, a set of three articles (Bjork, 1975; Craik & Jacoby, 1975; Shiffrin, 1975) written by leading students of memory is intriguing in that the authors have all reached similar conclusions; all argue that it is necessary to assume the existence of what we are calling a working memory system, because of the obvious limitations that seem to characterize human information processing. There is an apparent "bottleneck" in human thought. Though having a seemingly infinite capacity for permanent memory, there are obvious limits on the rate at which we can either place information in permanent memory or retrieve information from it. Furthermore, we can only think of a limited number of ideas simultaneously. These limits must be captured in any model of cognition, and these authors (along with Estes, 1976) argue that some sort of short-term store, working memory, or primary memory is a particularly inviting way of building such limitations into the human information-processing system. Thus, we are brought back to the topic of attention and limited processing capacity that occupied us in the last chapter.

CAPACITY OF WORKING MEMORY

Exactly how limited is the capacity of working memory? In order to discuss capacity, it is critical to have some unit of measurement that will enable the limits to be characterized in general terms. For example, we use the measurement unit of cubic centimeters to describe the capacity of a box. This unit is general in that the box can hold 3 cubic centimeters of anything, whether feathers, bricks, lead, or books. There are other units of measurement that could be used, but they would be of more limited generality. For example, the unit of pounds is inadequate because in order to specify the capacity in these terms we would have to specify the material to be placed in the box. Whereas the box might be able to contain 2 pounds of feathers, it might hold 25 pounds of lead.

What, then, is the unit of measurement that can be used to describe the capacity of working memory? As in the case of the box, we want to find a unit that will enable the limits to be described in general terms, i.e., terms which will apply to any material we might try to store there. George Miller addressed this problem in a well-known 1956 paper entitled "The Magical Number Seven, Plus or Minus Two: Some Limits on our Ability to Process Information."

Miller examined the possibility that psychology might borrow a unit developed in the new science of communication theory (Shannon & Weaver, 1949). Shannon and Weaver's work seemed relevant for psychology because they had proposed a general unit for measuring the amount of information contained in a given stimulus or event. In general, we judge events to be informative if they tell us something we don't already know. The more an event reduces our ignorance, the more informative it is. Shannon and Weaver proposed that the informativeness of an event be described by specifying exactly how much ignorance (or uncertainty) it reduces. In particular, they proposed the *bit* as the appropriate unit for measuring the amount of information. A bit is defined as the amount of information needed to distinguish between two equally likely alternatives. In general, n bits is the number of bits required to distinguish among 2^n equally likely alternatives.

For example, consider the amount of information conveyed by the toss of an unbiased coin. Before the coin is tossed, you know that there are two possible and equally likely outcomes—heads or tails. When the coin is actually tossed, the outcome provides you with exactly 1 bit of information, because it reduces your uncertainty from not knowing which of 2 alternatives would occur to knowing exactly which did occur. If, instead, I tell you that 1 of 8 different lights will come on, when one of the lights does come on your uncertainty has been reduced from not knowing which of 8 alternatives would occur to knowing exactly which occurred. Thus the light coming on provided you with 3 bits of information (it told you which of 2^3 equally likely alternatives had occurred). In sum, using the bit as a unit, it is possible to calculate the amount of information conveyed by an event.

George Miller suggested the hypothesis that since working memory can be thought of as containing information, it might be possible to define the capacity limits of working memory in terms of a certain number of bits. It is easy to demonstrate that there is a severe limit on the number of items that an individual can repeat back perfectly after one presentation. In fact, think back to the experiments you conducted at the beginning of this chapter. Considering only the data from the digit lists for the moment, you probably found that the *digit span* for your adult subjects was between 5 and 9 digits. Since people have little time to commit the list to long-term memory, most of the items being recalled in the digit span task may be assumed to be drawn from working memory. Therefore, the span of immediate memory task provides a rough indication of the capacity of working memory itself.

Using Shannon and Weaver's measure it is possible to calculate the number of bits of information people are holding when they correctly report 7 digits. Each digit has been drawn from 10 equally likely alternatives (i.e., the digits from 0 through 9), so doing a little arithmetic with logarithms, we can determine that each of the digits contains 3.32 bits of information ($2^{3.32} = 10$). Since people can recall 7 such digits, they have stored 7×3.32 or approximately 23 bits in working memory. Is this a general limit on the capacity of the short term store, in the sense that it can hold 23 bits regardless of the type of item?

If it is, then we should be able to predict exactly how many of each of a wide range of materials people can keep in working memory. We need only calculate how many bits of information each item contains and then determine how many such items will fit in the 23 bit capacity of the store. This point is illustrated in Table 4–3 which contains the predicted span of immediate memory for each of a number of kinds of materials. A moment's recollection of the results of your memory span experiment for words at the beginning of the chapter will convince you that the predictions depicted in Table 4–3 are not upheld. People usually are able to recall about 6 or so words correctly, far in excess of the 2.3 predicted by our hypothesis. Further-

TABLE 4–3. The Predicted Memory Span for 4 Kinds of Material If the Capacity of Working Memory Were 23 Bits.

Material to Be Remembered	Number of Alternatives Per Item	Number of Bits Per Item	Predicted Memory Span *
Digits from 0 through 9	10	3.32	6.9 items
Binary digits (0,1)	2	1	23 items
Monosyllabic English Words	1024 (approx)	10	2.3 items
Letters of the Alphabet	26	4.7	4.9 items

* 23 divided by the number of bits per item.

more, attempt to read the following string once and then repeat it back without error: 001011001010000101000010. You probably failed to do so, once again contrary to the predictions in Table 4–3; most people are able to report lists of no more than 8 or 9 such binary digits correctly. Miller concluded, therefore, that the limits of working memory cannot be characterized in terms of a constant number of bits. In fact, Miller observed that regardless of the number of bits per item, we seem able to hold between 5 and 9 of many different kinds of items in memory, leading him to propose the "magical" number of 7 plus or minus 2. That is, the immediate memory span is approximately 7 plus or minus 2 items whether people are asked to remember digits, letters, words, or familiar phrases (e.g., "A stitch in time saves nine," or "Early to bed, early to rise"), despite the fact that the number of bits varies widely in these cases.

Miller proposed, then, that since the bit will not work as a unit for measuring the capacity of working memory, psychologists must invent an appropriate unit. He proposed the *chunk*, admitting that one advantage of the term is that it sounds as vague as its definition. Any highly familiar unit seems capable of acting as a chunk, and therefore what acts as a chunk for one person may not be a chunk for another. For example, consider the following sequence of words: ATTENTION, COMPUTER, ESTABLISHMENT, VERBOSE, CALAMITY. If adults heard the sequence, they would probably be able to report all five of the words, since all are familiar units and each would probably be treated as one chunk. For the four-year-old, or the adult who does not speak English, however, the sequence might be treated as a list of nonsense syllables, and it is likely that he or she would be able to remember only a few syllables. Thus, for the person unfamiliar with the words, each syllable would act as a chunk, whereas for the person familiar with the words, each word would be a chunk.

This means that although the capacity of working memory is severely limited in the number of units or chunks that can be held simultaneously, it is possible to expand the total amount of information (defined in bits) by packing more and more information into each chunk. Imagine, for example, that you wish to impress others with feats of memory. You could appear to have a greater capacity working memory than other people by showing that you can repeat 18 binary digits after hearing the sequence only once. In fact, George Miller noted that it is quite easy to do this if you are familiar with the octal number system displayed in Table 4–4. As you listen to the first three digits of the to-be-remembered list, code them into the octal equivalent and store that one number as your first chunk, listen to the next three and recode them to the appropriate octal number, etc. Thus, by *recoding* you will have made the 18 digit sequence into 6 chunks. When you attempt to recall the list, you need only decode the numbers back to

TABLE 4–4.   The Octal Number System.

Binary Sequence	Octal Equivalent
000	0
001	1
010	2
011	3
100	4
101	5
110	6
111	7

binary again. Of course, for such a system to work, you must be very familiar with the recoding scheme so that it requires little time or effort to perform, or, in the terms introduced in the Attention chapter, so the recoding scheme is automatic in that it requires little if any of your processing capacity. Performing any recoding scheme that is not automatic or nearly so will take up valuable room (i.e., chunks) in working memory, thus detracting from the total amount of room available for the material you are trying to commit to memory.

It is important to realize that the definition of a chunk depends upon what is stored in long-term memory. Thus, permanent knowledge is a critical determinant of how much material an individual can keep in working memory at once. People engaged in a particular vocation or avocation often seem to have remarkably good memory for the components of their trade and perform feats of memory which startle the novice. One way in which such experts differ from novices is in the richness of the chunks they create. This has been demonstrated for many domains including chess players, bridge players, musicians, volleyball players, basketball players, electronics technicians and computer programmers (cf. Charness, 1981; McKeithen, Reitman, Rueter, & Hirtle, 1981).

The most carefully investigated example concerns master chess players. If an ordinary chess player is shown for 5 or 10 seconds a board of about 25 chess pieces representing a set of positions that might occur during a game, he can usually place about 6 of them correctly from memory. (Notice Miller's magical number again.) A chess master or grand master can usually replace all 25 pieces without error. These two groups obviously reveal dramatic differences in immediate memory in this situation, but the interesting question for the cognitive psychologist is: exactly how do the memory processes of these two groups differ? An answer is suggested by comparing the performance of the two groups when they are presented instead with a board containing 25 pieces placed randomly on the board (i.e., an arrangement that would be unlikely to occur in the course of a game).

In this case the novice and the master perform equivalently, both replacing about 6 pieces correctly (deGroot, 1966).

Apparently, then, the chess master's memory is superior only when he is able to use his knowledge of the rules of the game to help him chunk the pieces into meaningful units. Thus, he is remembering the same number of chunks as the novice, but for the meaningful chessboard configuration he is able to pack more pieces into each chunk. Simon and his colleagues (Simon, 1974; Simon & Chase, 1973) have attempted to find independent support for this interpretation by examining the pattern of pauses people make when they are placing recalled pieces on the board. In fact, chess masters group their recall of meaningful chess board configurations into about 6 or so units, placing about 4 pieces then pausing before placing 4 more, etc.

Though Simon and his colleagues have presented convincing evidence that the memory differences between chess novices and masters may be attributed to differences in the richness of the chunks employed, the extent to which individual differences in memory span are due to differences in the richness of chunks is unclear. For example, the digit span is known to increase systematically during early development, ranging from about 2 at the age of 2.5 years to 5 for the 7-year-old, to 8 for college students (Jacobs, 1887; Terman & Merrill, 1937). Does this increase reflect an increase in the number of chunks that can be held in working memory (i.e., a change in the capacity of working memory), or does it reflect an increase in the richness of the chunks the child uses? The first of these alternatives suggests that a structural change in the capacity of working memory occurs with development. The second possibility argues that the structural characteristics of working memory are constant, but that the child's increasing long-term knowledge results in a change in the automatic chunking that occurs. Whereas adults treat a digit (or, perhaps, sometimes a pair of digits) as a chunk, the young child who is less familiar with numbers may not do so.

As yet this question is unanswered. It is reasonable to conclude that at least some of the age difference is due to a change in chunking (Chi, 1976; Simon, 1972), for it is possible to increase a child's memory span by training him to use more effective control processes, such as chunking. However, even after such training children seldom reach the adult level of performance. The latter fact may be interpreted either as reflecting an additional structural limitation on young children's working memory capacity, or as showing that the training studies have not provided the child with enough extended practice to make the new recoding schemes automatic. As the automatic writing studies discussed in the Attention chapter suggested, quite extensive practice ranging over months is often necessary in order for processes to become automatic.

FORGETTING FROM WORKING MEMORY

In Chapter 2 we noted that people are unable to lengthen the time that an item is held in the sensory stores. Forgetting occurs when a new sensory input from the same modality displaces items already stored. In the absence of such a subsequent presentation, the sensory representation fades away within a second (visual) or several seconds (auditory and, perhaps, tactual). In sum, we are not able to prevent forgetting from the sensory stores. This is not true of working memory. As you might have noticed when looking up telephone numbers or trying to memorize lists for examinations, you can keep information in the short-term store indefinitely as long as two conditions are met. First, the number of chunks to be retained must not exceed the capacity of the store. Second, you must be able to repeat the items over and over to yourself, either aloud or silently. This overt or covert recycling of items through working memory is called *rehearsal*, and it prevents forgetting from this store.

What would happen, though, if a person were prevented from rehearsing a subspan set of items? Would there be a rapidly declining forgetting curve like that found with the sensory stores? In 1959 Peterson and Peterson at Indiana University reported an experiment which investigated this question, and their results inspired two decades of intensive research into the properties of working memory.

On each trial of the Peterson and Peterson experiment, the subject heard three consonants (often called a CCC or a *consonant trigram*). Then, after a retention interval ranging in duration from 0 to 18 seconds, at a signal from the experimenter the subject attempted to recall the CCC. As we've already discussed, if the subject were free to rehearse during the retention interval, he would recall perfectly since 3 letters are well within the capacity of the working memory. Therefore, Peterson and Peterson required their subjects to perform a *distractor task* during the retention interval: immediately after presentation of the CCC on each trial the subject heard a 3 digit number (such as 309). He was to repeat the number and then begin counting backward from it by threes, in time with a metronome ticking twice per second. Peterson and Peterson hoped this distractor task would prevent rehearsal.

The data of interest were per cent correct recall of the CCC's as a function of the length of the retention interval, and these data are shown in Figure 4-4. Notice that recall is almost perfect with an immediate test (0 second retention interval), indicating that the subjects were able to perceive all the letters initially, but after only 18 seconds of the distractor task the per cent correct is only about 10%. Thus, Peterson and Peterson's results indicated that if a person is prevented

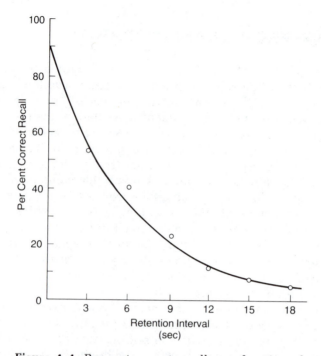

Figure 4–4. Per cent correct recall as a function of the duration of the retention interval in the Peterson and Peterson short-term memory task. Subjects were presented with a CCC which they attempted to recall after a retention interval filled with counting backward. Notice that the accuracy of recall declines rapidly as the retention interval is increased, and after a retention interval of only 18 seconds, recall is no better than 10% correct. (After Peterson & Peterson, 1959. Copyright 1959 by the American Psychological Association. Adapted by permission of the publisher and author.)

from rehearsing by counting backward, then a substantial amount of forgetting occurs in less than 18 seconds. This conclusion is straightforward and has met with little controversy. In fact, in the absence of rehearsal, forgetting may occur even more rapidly than Peterson and Peterson thought. Using a version of their task in which the subject does not expect a recall test, Muter (1980) found that forgetting was almost complete after only two seconds.

The fact that such rapid forgetting occurs has generated a second question that still puzzles students of memory. The controversy concerns the cause of the forgetting. Most explanations focus on one of two possibilities. The first alternative is *passive decay*. According to this hypothesis, without rehearsal items decay from working memory within 15 seconds or so even if no new information is placed in the store. The second possibility is *interference* or *displacement*. According to this alternative, forgetting from working memory is caused by other items in the store (such as the numbers in the counting backward task) interfering with (or displacing) those which are to be remembered. In the Peterson and Peterson task, the subject must remember not only the CCC, but also the current number. Furthermore, in order to subtract 3 from the current number he must call into play what he knows about the rules of subtraction. Doing all of this at once might tax the capacity limits of the store. Indeed, counting backward might displace the CCC items the subject is trying to remember, and as the retention interval increases there would be more and more opportunities for such displacement to occur. Thus, the precipitous forgetting curve Peterson and Peterson obtained could have been caused by either passive decay or by interference.

In principle, it is easy to describe the kind of task that would distinguish between these two possibilities. We need to prevent the subject from rehearsing during the retention interval, yet not require him to do anything that would demand access to the limited capacity working memory. Under such conditions passive decay theory predicts forgetting will occur, whereas interference predicts it will not.

The problem, of course, is that it is difficult to find a distractor task that meets these criteria. Now, after more than 20 years and several ingenious attempts to find such a distractor task (e.g., Reitman, 1971; Reitman, 1974; Shiffrin, 1973), it appears that both passive decay and interference (or displacement) cause forgetting from working memory. It is safe to say that in most daily circumstances it is interference that is the more important of the two causes of short-term forgetting, because there are few times when we are not processing other material in working memory. Unrehearsed material is seldom allowed to remain in working memory long enough to decay, because there is usually something else—if only some daydreaming—to be done with the limited capacity available. To convince yourself of this, try keeping your mind completely blank for 15 seconds.

FORM OF REPRESENTATION IN WORKING MEMORY

Articulatory-acoustic coding. Unlike the information held in the sensory stores, the information contained in working memory is often quite different in form from the external stimulus it represents. In fact, one kind of representation is particularly characteristic of working memory. When presented with material that can be labelled, people usually hold the label of the item in their working memory. This will not surprise you if you have done much thinking about your own memory. When you look up a telephone number, you don't feel as though you are storing away the visual images of the digits, rather you seem to be saying their names to yourself.

In 1964 R. Conrad published an important study in which he reported evidence supporting the validity of our introspections. Conrad gave his subjects an immediate serial recall task in which 6 letters are presented visually for immediate written recall. On each trial the six letters were drawn from the following 10: BCPTVFMNSX. Notice that the names of the first 5 letters all sound alike (all have a long e sound), whereas the names of the last 5 letters all have a short e sound.

Conrad's reasoning was simple and will be familiar from our discussion of the analysis of confusion errors in the sensory stores chapter. If subjects are storing the names of the letters, then if memory for an item begins to fade, resulting in an error, the person should mistakenly recall a letter that sounds similar to the correct one. Consider a trial on which the subject was presented with the list PFMSTX. If the subject forgets the M, he should substitute an F, N, S, or X rather than a B, C, P, T, or V. In fact, this is just the pattern Conrad found. Virtually all substitution errors were from the similar sounding set. This pattern of errors is particularly impressive because at no point in the experiment did subjects hear or speak the letter names. Nonetheless, the subjects apparently coded the items by their labels and used these for recall. Subsequent studies by other researchers (e.g., Wickelgren, 1965; 1966) have confirmed again and again that such acoustic confusions are particularly common in tasks that call on working memory.

Indeed, verbal coding is not limited to the case in which people are presented with letters and printed words (e.g., Conrad, 1971; Schiano & Watkins, 1981). Conrad (1971) has presented children with a series of pictures. On each trial the child was shown one picture after the other, with each being placed face down on a table. Then the child was presented with a duplicate set of pictures and asked to match them up with the face down items. On half of the trials the items pictured all had similar sounding names (e.g., mat, bat,) and on the other trials the items pictured all had different sounding names (e.g., fish, house). If children are using the names to help them remember the sequence, then the similar sounding names should get confused with each other and the children should make more errors on that list. On the other hand, if the children are simply remembering visual patterns, the names of the pictured items will not come into play at all, so the children should make the same number of errors on both sets. In fact, Conrad found that his 12-year-old subjects made many more errors on the similar than on the dissimilar sounding list, suggesting they used a verbal code, but the five-year-olds he tested made the same number of errors on his two types of lists, suggesting that they were not using the labels. Even though these youngest children were able to label the pictures correctly when asked to do so, they did not use the labels spontaneously as a code for remembering.

Let us look more closely at Conrad's findings, for we have not discussed an important question. His results are ambiguous regarding exactly what kind of code subjects are using. Subjects may be using an acoustic code (i.e., storing each item as a description of its sound) or an articulatory code (i.e., storing each item as a description of the way in which it is pronounced).

It is difficult to distinguish between these possibilities because most words or letters that sound similar are pronounced similarly as well. However, one way of investigating this question is to test congenitally deaf individuals who have learned to speak. If they reveal a pattern of errors that is similar to people with normal hearing, then since we cannot attribute the deaf people's confusions to acoustic similarity, we would have some evidence for the importance of articulatory coding. In 1970 Conrad reported just such an analysis of confusion errors in congenitally deaf subjects. He found that many of these people revealed the same pattern of errors as normal subjects, whereas others did not. Subsequent interviews with their teachers indicated that those deaf people who revealed evidence for articulatory coding were those who spoke most fluently. These findings suggest that articulatory codes can be held in working memory even in the absence of an acoustic code, and so they raise the possibility that the confusions observed in hearing people could be reflecting articulatory coding. Whether the confusions observed in those with normal hearing reflect *only* articulatory coding or both articulatory and acoustic coding is a question that has never been answered, and it is for this reason that the term *articulatory-acoustic* is usually used, thus reserving judgment.

Before leaving our discussion of articulatory-acoustic coding, it is important to stress that the prevalence of this kind of coding in working memory is of considerable importance for understanding human thought. Working memory operates as the working space for thinking. Thus, the finding that articulatory-acoustic coding is particularly prevalent in working memory implies not only that it is important for looking up telephone numbers, but also that it is important for thinking. Given anything that can be labelled, adults in our culture tend to generate the label in working memory. That this propensity seems to develop gradually suggests that with development language comes to play a more and more central role in the shaping of human thought, a hypothesis proposed by Bruner (1964) on the basis of his own work with children. Thus, Conrad's work with children and with deaf adults suggests that as they learn the language, at least in our highly literate society, individuals come to use that language not only to communicate with others, but also as a tool for remembering and thinking. Some cross cultural research by Kearins (1981), however, suggests that this predominance of articulatory-acoustic coding may not develop in individuals of all cultures. Kearins examined visual spatial memory in Australian Aboriginal adolescents who live in a desert region that requires accurate spatial memory for survival. These adolescents revealed superior spatial memory when compared with white Australian suburban children, but they gave no evidence of using articulatory-acoustic coding.

Semantic coding. Even in our culture, articulatory-acoustic coding is not the only form of representation used in working memory. In Chapter 7 we will focus on visual-spatial representation in working memory, but here we will be concerned with a third kind of code—semantic or meaning based representation.

The point of this section will be clearest if we first restate questions about representation in light of our overview model. According to our theory, when we discuss the nature of representation in working memory, we are asking what aspects or features of an item's representation in long-term memory are activated when it is copied into working memory. Conrad's work indicated that articulatory-acoustic features are usually activated, but we shall now see that at least some aspects of the meaning of the item are activated as well.

We will consider only the one most frequently cited kind of evidence for such semantic coding—work reported by Delos Wickens and his colleagues at the Ohio State University. Wickens used the Peterson and Peterson short-term memory paradigm we discussed earlier in this chapter. Recall that this involves presenting a person with a *CCC* (or some other small set of items). Then, after a retention interval of a few seconds during which the person engages in some attention demanding activity, the subject's ability to recall the *CCC* is tested. As Figure 4–4 depicts, Peterson and Peterson found that very rapid forgetting usually occurs, so that after a retention interval as brief as 18 seconds, there is almost no memory for the *CCC*.

As it turns out, however, soon after Peterson and Peterson reported their results, several researchers (e.g., Keppel & Underwood, 1962) showed that such precipitous forgetting does *not* occur on the very first trial in such an experiment. Rather, memory for that very first *CCC* is nearly perfect even after an 18 second retention interval. Performance worsens over the first several trials, however, reaching the low of 10% recall after 18 seconds only on the third or fourth trial. This decrease in performance over trials suggests that the earlier trials are interfering with the later, so this decline is usually referred to as a *buildup of proactive inhibition.* (Proactive inhibition refers to the fact that previously learned material interferes with, or inhibits, later learned material.)

The important point for present purposes is that Wickens and his colleagues (e.g., Wickens, 1972; Wickens, Born, & Allen, 1963) demonstrated that the extent to which such earlier trials interfere with later depends on how similar the items are from trial to trial. I suggest that you demonstrate this fact yourself by performing the following demonstration (which is similar to Wickens' study). Find a volunteer, and have your subject perform 4 trials using the Peterson and Peterson paradigm, with a retention interval of about 12 seconds on each trial. During the retention interval, require the subject to count backward by three's from some three-digit number. At a recall cue from you, the person should then attempt to recall the stimulus item. Thus, the first trial might go as follows:

Experimenter: "KXM, three hundred and eighty-one"

Subject: "Three hundred and eighty-one, three hundred and seventy-eight, three hundred and seventy-five," etc.

Experimenter (after waiting 12 sec): "Recall"

Subject: "KXM??"

Do two more such trials, using ZNW, *nine-hundred-fifty-four* on trial two, and *JQL, one-hundred-thirty two* on trial three. You will probably find that the person recalls the letters more accurately on the first trial than on later ones (i.e., the buildup of proactive inhibition). Finally, on trial 4, rather than giving the person 3 *letters* to remember, give him 3 *digits.* Thus, you might say FIVE, SEVEN, TWO, *four hundred eighty six.* Chances are that the person will recall FIVE, SEVEN, TWO quite accurately.

If you were to test many subjects in such an experiment, you would find the pattern of results shown by the filled circles in Figure 4–5. Performance declines steadily on the first three trials, all of which contain similar to-be-remembered items (this is called the buildup of proactive inhibition), but performance improves dramatically on the fourth trial when a different kind of stimulus (e.g., digits) is to be remembered (this is called release from proactive inhibition). Wickens and others have ruled out the possibility that people *always* improve on the fourth trial, regardless of the nature of the material, by testing a control group that is given the same kind of material (e.g., letters) on all four trials. As the open circles in Figure 4–5 show, this control group does *not* improve on trial 4.

This phenomenon of release from proactive inhibition (or release from PI, as it is frequently called) is important for understanding cod-

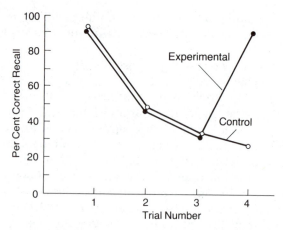

Figure 4–5. Idealized pattern of findings obtained in studies using the release from proactive inhibition (PI) technique developed by Wickens, Born, and Allen, 1963. The figure depicts the per cent correct recall as a function of trial number. For the control group (open circles) the to-be-remembered items are similar for all four trials (e.g., they are always letters). For the experimental group (filled circles) the to-be-remembered items are similar for the first three trials (e.g., they are letters), but are different for trial four (e.g., they are digits). Notice that for both groups, recall declines over the three trials on similar material. This is called the buildup of proactive inhibition (PI). The experimental group improves dramatically on the fourth trial when the type of material is switched. This improvement is called release from proactive inhibition.

ing in working memory, because Wickens (1972) and his colleagues have demonstrated that changes in the *meanings* of the to-be-remembered items lead to a release from PI. For example, imagine that on the first three trials a person is asked to recall triads of animal names (e.g., trial 1 = CAT, ELEPHANT, FROG; trial 2 = HORSE, RHINO, MOUSE; trial 3 = SQUIRREL, BIRD, GIRAFFE). On the fourth, however, he is given furniture names (e.g., CHAIR, COUCH, TABLE). There is usually a dramatic improvement on trial 4 , similar to that depicted for the experimental group in Figure 4–5. Now if holding an item in working memory resulted only in the articulatory-acoustic features of the item being activated, then such a change in the meaning of the to-be-remembered items should not influence performance at all. The fact that meaning does influence the pattern of errors indicates that at least some aspects of the word's meaning are looked up and activated from long-term storage. In fact, Wickens and others have subsequently shown that even more subtle aspects of a word's meaning are activated as well. For example, if the person experiences several trials on which words convey one sense impression (such as whiteness, e.g., SNOW, PAPER, CHALK) and then a trial on which the sense impression is different (such as blackness, e.g., COAL, DIRT, ASPHALT), there is a release from PI. In fact, this occurs even though the person often seems unaware of the nature of the change in the material.

There are two general points you should note about our discussion of release from PI. First, this phenomenon demonstrates that when a person attempts to hold an item in memory for a brief period, even though he is not *required* to note the meaning of the item, at least some components of the meaning are activated from permanent memory. Thus, at least some coding in working memory is semantic or meaning based. This phenomenon again shows the intimate connection between working and long-term memory. The working memory is *not* simply some brief duration way station through which unprocessed information passes on the way to more permanent storage. Rather, it acts as a working space for thinking and it can contain representations not only of the articulatory-acoustic form of an item, but of its meaning as well.

Second, the release from PI procedure is potentially a very useful technique for studying individual differences in the richness and automaticity of encoding. For example, we might expect the degree of release from PI that accompanies a shift in meaning to be related to the degree to which a person has become fluent in a second language. Since one concomitant of increased fluency should be that perceiving a word automatically elicits its meaning in memory, we might assess the effectiveness of various methods for teaching French by determining the extent to which students who have experienced the techniques reveal the typical pattern of release from PI when French words are used.

Though I am not aware of any such studies of second-language learning, the Wickens technique has been used to study the richness of coding that children exhibit during their learning of their native language. These studies show that although some aspects of a word's meaning lead to a release from PI even among preschool children, other aspects of the meaning do not seem to be activated automatically until later in elementary school at least (e.g., Kail & Siegel, 1977).

RETRIEVAL FROM WORKING MEMORY

The term *retrieval* refers to finding or locating information that is stored in memory. If you introspect you will notice that in contrast to retrieval from long-term memory, which often seems to require a great deal of time and effort, retrieval from working memory seems effortless and instantaneous. For example, hold the list *361* in memory and then decide as quickly as possible whether or not the list you are holding contains a *7*. That decision probably seemed instantaneous; indeed you may find it strange to refer to "retrieval" of the items since, as William James noted in 1890, it feels as though all items in working memory are in the present instant of consciousness. In 1966, however, Saul Sternberg of Bell Telephone Laboratories published several studies which suggest that our introspections are in error. We will spend some time analyzing the reasoning behind Sternberg's work, because it has had unusually broad impact on recent experimental analyses of many aspects of human cognition. In addition, the techniques Sternberg used promise to be useful for analyzing individual differences in mental processes and for studying the effects of drugs and alcohol on thinking.

Sternberg's memory search task. In order to study retrieval from working memory, Sternberg (1966; 1969) used the memory search task which is depicted in Figure 4–6. On each trial the subject was first given a *memory set* which consisted of a small number of items. Then he was presented with a test item which on half of the trials was a member of the memory set and on the other half was not. The subject was instructed to release a button labeled *yes* if the test item was a member of the memory set, and to release a button labeled *no* otherwise. Subjects were encouraged to respond as quickly as possible without making errors. Sternberg measured *reaction time* of the button release from onset of the test stimulus.

Sternberg assumed that this reaction time reflected the time taken to complete three stages of processing. In the first *encoding stage*, the subject places a representation of the test item in working memory. In the second, the *comparison stage*, the encoded test item is compared with the memory set items retrieved from working memory, and in the third stage, *response selection*, the subject decides whether to respond *yes* or *no*. Since Sternberg was interested in how information is retrieved from working memory, he focused on the comparison stage. Using a modification of reasoning introduced by Donders (1869) more than a century before, Sternberg argued that it should be possible to study this stage by finding some variable that would selectively influence only this stage. Sternberg reasoned that one variable that should meet this criterion is the size of the memory set. If the subject is hold-

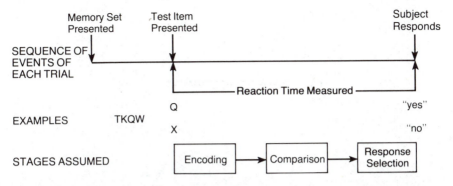

Figure 4–6. Sternberg's memory search task. The figure depicts the sequence of events that occurs on each trial, examples of trials on which the correct answer is either "yes" or "no," and the stages Sternberg assumes to intervene between onset of the test stimulus and the subject's response.

ing 4 rather than 2 items in working memory, this should not influence the encoding stage (there is only one test item to encode in either case), nor the response selection stage (there are only two possible responses in either case), but it might influence the comparision stage since 4 items must be retrieved and compared in one case, but only 2 in the other.

Sternberg reasoned that by examining how reaction time varies as the size of the memory set is increased, it should be possible to distinguish which of a number of possible retrieval processes occurs in working memory. Sternberg considered three such possibilities and the predictions each would make. The first possibility is that all items in working memory are available for comparison at once. This possibility, which Sternberg called *parallel scanning,* is most consistent with William James' introspections, since he argued that all information in primary memory is immediately available and need not be "fished up." If retrieval from working memory involves such parallel scanning of its contents, then Sternberg argued that reaction time should not be influenced by the size of the memory set, since all items can be examined at once. Therefore, the reaction time by set size function should be as depicted in Figure 4–7a.

A second possibility is that the items in working memory must be retrieved and compared with the test item in sequence one after the other. Sternberg referred to this possibility as *serial scanning.* For the moment, let's consider only the predictions for *no* responses, i.e., trials on which the test item is not contained in the memory set. If retrieving and comparing each memory set item takes a certain amount of time, then as the size of the memory set is increased reaction time should increase at a constant rate. Therefore, the function relating reaction time to set size should be a linear increasing function like that

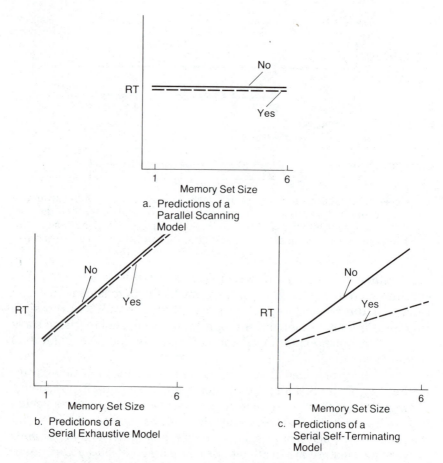

Figure 4–7. The reaction time predictions for Sternberg's memory search task for each of three possible kinds of retrieval process: (a.) the predictions of a parallel scanning model, (b.) the predictions of a serial-exhaustive model, and (c.) the predictions of a serial self-terminating model.

depicted in Figure 4–7b. The slope (rate of increase) of this function indicates how long it takes to retrieve and compare one memory set item with the test item. That is, the slope tells us how much additional time is required for each additional item in the memory set.

If you consider predictions for *yes* responses, you will realize that there are two possible serial scanning models. The first is a *serial exhaustive scanning* model which assumes that the subject searches through the entire list exhaustively comparing the test item to each of the memory set items in turn, continuing through the whole list *even after* he finds a match. This counterintuitive model would predict that the reaction time by memory set size functions for *yes* and *no* responses should be parallel, as depicted in Figure 4–7b, because for both *yes* and *no* responses the number of comparisons increases by exactly 1 each time an additional item is added to the memory set.

The third possible model is a *serial self-terminating* model. According to this model, the subject compares the test item with each of the memory set items in turn, until he either completes the list without finding a match, in which case he responds *no*, or until he finds a match, at which point he terminates the search and responds *yes*. According to this model, for a given memory set size the subject will usually have to do fewer retrievals and comparisons on *yes* trials than on *no* trials. This is because on *no* trials the subject will always have to search through the entire memory set (since he will never find a match), whereas on *yes* trials he will find a match and be able to avoid retrieving and comparing the remaining memory set items with the test item. More specifically, since on *yes* trials the test item will occur an equal number of times at each serial position, *on the average* the subject should have to search through about one-half of the list before finding the match. Therefore, the slope of the *yes* function should be exactly half that of the *no* function, as depicted in Figure 4–7c. Another way to think about this prediction is to realize that for the serial self-terminating model, every time the memory set size is increased by 1, for *no* trials the number of items to be searched is also increased by 1, whereas for *yes* trials the number of comparisons to be made increases by only one-half an item, on the average.

Once these predictions had been generated, all Sternberg needed to do was collect data to determine the actual pattern of reaction times. Sternberg's results were as depicted in Figure 4–8. There are two notable aspects of Sternberg's findings. First, the fact that the functions are increasing linearly and that the slopes for *yes* and *no* responses are equal suggests that subjects are engaging in a *serial exhaustive scan* of the items in working memory. Given our introspections, this result is surprising. Second, the slope of each function is approximately 38 msec. In other words, for each additional item which must be retrieved and searched, reaction time increases by 38 msec., suggesting that it takes 38 msec. for each such retrieval and comparison. Since there are 1,000 msec. in a second, this indicates that subjects must be able to examine items in working memory at the rate of about 25 items per second! It should be clear, then, why Sternberg termed the search process a *high speed* serial exhaustive scan. The rapidity with which items can be searched in working memory is particularly intriguing when compared with the rate at which covert verbal rehearsal seems to occur. Since most estimates (e.g., Landauer, 1962; Lovelace, Powell, & Brooks, 1973) suggest that the latter occurs no more rapidly than 8 items or so per second (try it yourself and see), Sternberg has argued that the representation through which subjects are searching in the memory search task is probably not an articula-

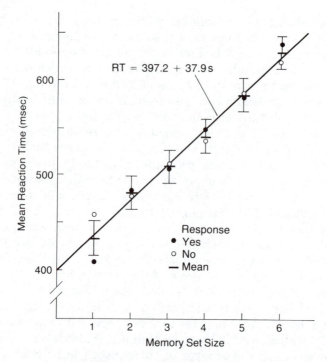

Figure 4–8. The results Sternberg obtained in his
memory search task. Reaction time is shown as a
function of the size of the memory set for *yes*
responses (filled circles) and *no* responses (open
circles). The line is the best-fitting straight line.
If you compare these findings with the predictions of the three models shown in Figure 4–7,
you will see that these results are most consistent with the predictions of the serial exhaustive
scanning model. (After Sternberg, 1966. Copyright 1966 by the American Association for the
Advancement of Science. Reprinted by permission.)

tory-acoustic one. In fact, Sternberg and others (e.g., Klatzky & Atkinson, 1971) have reported additional studies which suggest that subjects may be using a visual representation.

Kristofferson (1972) has shown that the pattern of results does
not change even when subjects are very highly practiced in the memory search task. She managed to get subjects to participate in 144
trials a day for 30 days. The slope of the reaction time function remained constant across days, with the only change being a decrease
in the y-intercept (i.e., the RT value at which the function crosses the
vertical axis). Thus, the rate of memory comparison remained constant with practice, although subjects improved at some other aspect

of the task—perhaps at encoding the test stimulus or at responding. This apparent invariance of search and retrieval with practice gives us more confidence in concluding that the phenomenon we are observing is not something that occurs only when a person is faced with an unfamiliar laboratory task. Furthermore, the general pattern of a linear increase in RT with increasing memory set size occurs for a wide range of material—not only for letters and digits, but for random forms, faces, geometric shapes, colors, and words (cf. Sternberg, 1975). This suggests that whenever we examine the contents of working memory, the same kind of retrieval processes are operating regardless of the nature of the material to be searched.

We have seen that the pattern of results Sternberg obtained led him to conclude that people engage in a high-speed exhaustive scan of working memory. This finding is troublesome, however, in that it does not fit with our introspections. If you were a subject in this experiment, you might be willing to believe that some sort of serial scan is occurring, but you would undoubtedly insist that it is self-terminating. You would feel as though you stopped scanning as soon as you found a match on *yes* trials. In addition, exhaustive scanning seems inefficient, since it involves continuing a search even after a match has been found.

Sternberg has offered a reply to the criticism that an exhaustive scanning process is inefficient. He has suggested that it is possible to construct a system in which an exhaustive search would, in fact, be most efficient. One such system would be composed of two main components. The first is a *comparator mechanism* which compares the test item with each of the memory set items in turn and sets a match register if a match is detected. (This match register could be thought of as a mental box into which a mental checkmark can be placed upon detection of a match.) The second component is a *response decision mechanism* which examines the contents of the match register and decides whether to respond *yes* or *no* on the basis of the contents. Sternberg argues that if only one of these mechanisms can operate at a time and if the time required to switch back and forth from comparator to response mechanism is long relative to the time required to perform comparisons, then the most efficient search process would be an exhaustive one in which the comparator first scans all items, followed by a switch to the response mechanism, which makes a response decision based on the contents of the register.

For example, consider what would happen if it takes the comparator 40 msec to make one comparison, and 100 msec to switch to the response mechanism. Imagine we present the list *538627* followed by the test item *8*. If the subject does an exhaustive search of the six-item list, then it would take 6 × 40 msec for the search, plus 100 msec to switch to the response decision mechanism, for a total of 340 msec.

(We are ignoring other times such as that required to make the response decision, execute the response, and encode the test stimulus.) On the other hand, if he were to attempt a self-terminating search, he would have to switch to the response decision mechanism after each comparison. Therefore, it would take 3 × 40 plus 3 × 100 or 420 msec for the self-terminating search, longer than the time required for an exhaustive search.

In fact, Sternberg (1975) has recently reported that he discussed the high-speed exhaustive scanning model with a group of engineers who design special purpose computers for telephone switching. Whereas most of his nonengineering audiences have been skeptical about the plausibility of exhaustive scanning, these engineers were not, for they told Sternberg that such scanning processes are often wired into computer hardware, because on the average they are faster than self-terminating scanning mechanisms.

Applications of Sternberg's analysis. It is obvious even to the casual observer that the time required to perform many tasks is affected by drugs and by various characteristics of the person, such as age and mental retardation. For both practical and theoretical reasons it is important to determine exactly what aspects of human performance are being affected. Is the slowing due simply to a slowing of the speed with which external responses can be made, or has the rate of mental processes such as retrieval from memory been affected?

One of the contributions of Sternberg's technique for decomposing reaction times is that it enables us to isolate the locus of these effects more precisely. Take the case of marihuana. If partaking of marihuana influences only the speed with which external responses can be made, then taking marihuana should not change the slope of the reaction time function, but should only increase the y-intercept. On the other hand, if taking marihuana slows down the rate of retrieval from working memory, then it should affect the slope of the function.

As yet only one study has attempted to distinguish these two possibilities. Darley, Tinklenberg, Hollister, and Atkinson (1973) tested subjects in a memory search task both before and after administration of either marihuana or a placebo. Their results are depicted in Figure 4–9. (The results for *yes* and *no* responses are averaged.) The placebo (depicted in the right panel) had no effect at all on reaction time; the before and after functions are superimposed. As the left panel shows, marihuana, on the other hand, had a significant effect on reaction time. Furthermore, notice that the effect is not on the comparison stage, for the slope is about 35 msec per item both before and after administration of the drug. According to Sternberg's analysis, then, marihuana is affecting some process other than memory retrieval and comparison. The most likely candidates are the time re-

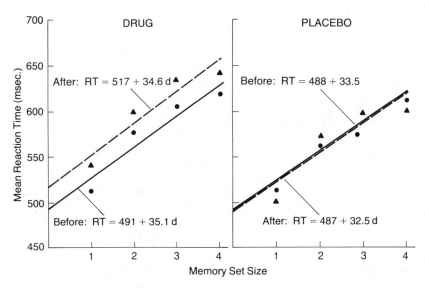

Figure 4–9. The effects of marihuana on retrieval from working memory. The right panel shows reaction time as a function of memory set size, before and after administration of a placebo. Notice that RT was not affected by the placebo. The left panel shows RT as a function of memory set size before and after administration of marihuana. Notice that marihuana has caused a slowing of overall RT, but it has not influenced the slope of the function. This suggests that marihuana does not affect the speed of retrieval from working memory, though it does slow down some other aspect of performance. (The data from *yes* and *no* responses have been combined.) (After Darley, Tinklenberg, Hollister, & Atkinson, 1973. Copyright 1973 by Springer-Verlag. Reprinted by permission.)

quired for a response decision or the time required to encode the test stimulus. Although the latter two possibilities cannot be differentiated with the data at hand, by doing more detailed analyses, it is possible to design experiments that would do so.

The extent to which long term conditions affect mental processes can also be investigated using Sternberg's analysis. In a preliminary study (unpublished work by Checkosky cited in Sternberg, 1975) Checkosky compared data from alcoholics and schizophrenics with data from normal college students. He found that the slopes of the reaction time functions did not differ among these groups, though the alcoholics and schizophrenics had much higher y-intercepts than normal college students. These findings, though highly tentative, suggest that neither schizophrenics nor alcoholics suffer from a slowing of retrieval from working memory.

Do not jump to the conclusion that the retrieval rate is constant across all individuals and conditions, however, for there is already

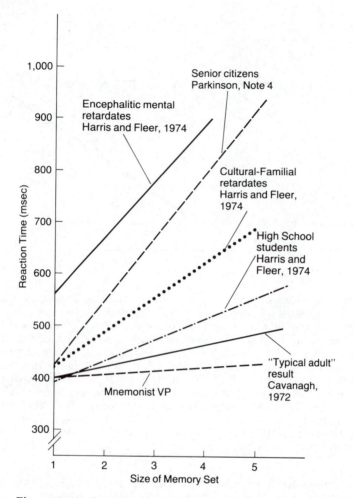

Figure 4–10. Reaction time by memory set size functions obtained in Sternberg's memory search task for widely differing groups of subjects. According to Sternberg's analyses, the slope of each function indicates the time required for the subject to retrieve one item in working memory. Therefore, this figure indicates that there are substantial group differences in the rate of memory search and retrieval. (From Hunt, 1978. Copyright 1978 by the American Psychological Association. Reprinted by permission of the publisher and author.)

evidence that this is not the case. Figure 4–10 summarizes the results from a number of studies in which subjects other than college students were tested. Notice, for example, that the slopes for mentally retarded individuals are considerably greater than for normal children

(Harris & Fleer, 1974). Furthermore, elderly individuals have significantly greater slopes than younger people, suggesting that the general slowing that accompanies old age may involve not only slower overt movements and sensory functioning, but slower mental comparisons as well (e.g., Anders, Fozard, & Lillyquist, 1972; Eriksen, Hamlin, & Daye, 1973; Salthouse & Somberg, 1982).

One other function in Figure 4–10 bears further scrutiny—the one at the bottom labeled *mnemonist VP*. This function is based on the performance of one rather remarkable individual, VP, who has been studied extensively by Hunt and Love (1972) at the University of Washington. VP came to the attention of Hunt and Love in 1971 when they heard that he gave exhibitions in which he played as many as seven simultaneous chess matches blindfolded. In fact, they later learned that VP could play as many as 60 correspondence games without consulting any written records at all! Upon further investigation, Hunt and Love found that VP's unusually accurate memory was not limited to the game of chess. For example, he is able to recall stories and conversations verbatim even after experiencing them only once. Hunt and Love have studied VP for several years attempting to determine how the information processing of a person with such unusually good memory differs from that of the more average individual. One of the tasks they gave VP was Sternberg's memory search task and, as Figure 4–10 reveals, they found that VP has a much more rapid search rate (i.e., a flatter slope) than average college students, suggesting that at least one aspect of VP's mental functioning is much more rapid than the average individual's. We will meet VP again later, so don't forget him!

I must emphasize that all of the results we have discussed in the last few paragraphs are tentative, for our conclusions are based on only one or two studies in each case. The reason for presenting them here is to illustrate that the reaction time analyses suggested by Sternberg have potential for enabling us to analyze exactly what components of thought are affected by drugs and various organismic conditions. In the future such analyses should help us to assess the dangers of certain drugs and to assess the effectiveness of training designed to remedy their effects.

WHAT IS WORKING MEMORY FOR?

We have been stressing that working memory is not simply a way station for new information on the way to more permanent storage, but it also acts as a limited capacity working space for information processing. How can we tell that this is so? Baddeley and Hitch (1974) reasoned that if working memory is used during thinking, then it should be possible to show that holding a list of items in working memory interferes with other aspects of thinking. You will recognize the reasoning from our discussion of attention. If two different tasks require access to the limited capacity work-space we call working memory, then they should interfere with each other. Baddeley and Hitch described a series of studies designed to test the role of working memory in reasoning, verbal comprehension, and free recall. We will consider each in turn.

Reasoning. One of the most widely used tasks for studying reasoning is the *sentence verification task*. In one version the person is presented with a sentence (e.g., "A precedes B") followed immediately by a pair of letters which is either in the order described by the sentence (i.e., *AB*) or the reverse order (i.e., *BA*). The subject is instructed to respond as quickly as possible by pressing one key labeled *true* if the letter pair is in the order described by the previous sentence, and to press a key labeled *false* if the letter pair is in the reverse order. The complexity of the sentence to be verified is varied by adding passives (e.g., "B is preceded by A"), negatives (e.g., "A does not precede B"), or both (e.g., "B is not preceded by A"). Although this task sounds simple and may be administered readily, it does seem to tap at least some components of reasoning. For example, Baddeley (1968) has shown that performance on this task is correlated with the person's intelligence level as measured by standardized IQ tests.

Baddeley and Hitch asked subjects to perform such a reasoning task while they held either 1, 2, or 6 digits simultaneously in working memory. The results revealed that holding 1 or 2 digits didn't affect either speed or accuracy of solving the sentence verification problems, but holding 6 items slowed down reasoning significantly, and the more difficult the sentence verification problems, the greater the effect of the 6 item memory load. These findings are just what would be expected if there is a limited capacity store which is called on both for holding items for short-term recall *and* for verbal reasoning. Holding only 1 or 2 items leaves plenty of capacity to be devoted to the reasoning task, but holding 6 items takes up almost all the capacity, cutting down the speed of reasoning considerably. In fact, it is particularly impressive that such slowing occurred since the reasoning problems were presented visually and remained in front of the subject until he made his response. Thus, the subject did not need to hold the reasoning problems in memory while solving them. Nonetheless, the reasoning task seemed to call upon the limited processing capacity of working memory.

We argued that one of the predominant means of coding in working memory is articulatory-acoustic. If working memory is the work-space for the sentence verification reasoning task, then we should find that articulatory-acoustic coding is used in the reasoning task. In order to test this prediction, Baddeley and Hitch gave their subjects the reasoning task just described, except that they varied the visual and acoustic similarity of the letter pairs used. Instead of the *AB* pairs, subjects saw pairs that were either of high acoustic and low visual similarity (e.g., TD, FS), high acoustic and high visual similarity (e.g., BP and MN), low acoustic and low visual similarity (e.g., MC and VF) or low acoustic and high visual similarity (e.g., OQ, XY). Given Conrad's findings, if the reasoning task requires working memory then we would expect high acoustic similarity to slow performance, whereas visual similarity should have no effect. This is exactly the pattern Baddeley and Hitch found. Notice that this finding is *despite* the fact that the reasoning task was always presented visually. Taken together then, these findings suggest that working memory is a working space for reasoning, and its characteristics, including the prevalence of articulatory-acoustic coding influence reasoning.

Language comprehension. In order to investigate whether working memory is required for language comprehension, Baddeley and Hitch had subjects *listen* to passages of prose, after which they were given a comprehension test to see how much they had understood of the story. While the subjects listened to the story, they were *shown* a series of digits. In one condition they were simply to copy down the digits as they appeared. Thus, at no point did the person need to hold more than 1 digit in working memory. In another condition, subjects were told to wait until they had seen 3 digits and then to write them all down. Thus, they had to hold 3 digits at a time in working memory. Finally, in a third condition subjects were to wait until they had seen 6 digits before writing them down—thus constituting a memory load of 6 digits during the language comprehension task.

Once again the results were as would be expected if comprehending prose requires access to a limited capacity working memory. Comprehension of the passages (as measured by 8 questions administered at the end of the passage) was as good in the memory load-3 condition as in the memory load-1 condition, but comprehension dropped significantly when the subjects were required to hold 6 items in memory while performing the comprehension task.

In a later study, Baddeley and Hitch sought to show that articulatory-acoustic coding was important in sentence comprehension as would be predicted if working memory is involved. They found that it took longer to comprehend sentences in which the words were acoustically similar (e.g., "The sad mad lad had a bad dad") as opposed to sentences in which the words were acoustically dissimilar (e.g., "The unhappy crazy boy had a wicked father") even though the two kinds of sentences could be read equally rapidly. Once again both series of studies on language comprehension suggested that comprehending prose requires use of a limited capacity working memory in which articulatory-acoustic coding predominates.

Long-term storage. One function of the short-term store has been stressed frequently since the early 1960's—maintaining an item in working memory is assumed to be a necessary prerequisite for long-term storage of the item. If this is the case, then simultaneously holding a near-capacity load of items in working memory should interfere with long-term memory for other material. Baddeley and Hitch tested this hypothesis by giving subjects a free recall task in which they listened to a series of unrelated words (which were later to be free recalled). At the same time, just as in the prose comprehension studies, subjects were asked to copy down visually presented digits, either 1 at a time (memory load 1), 3 at a time (memory load 3), or 6 at a time (memory load 6).

You should recall from the beginning of this chapter that the primacy and middle portions of the free recall serial position curve are usually interpreted as reflecting retrieval from long-term memory. Therefore, if long-term storage requires access to the limited capacity working memory, then holding the 6 items in memory should decrease these portions of the serial position curve when free recall of the words is examined. In fact, this is just what Baddeley and Hitch found, suggesting the importance of working memory for permanent learning.

It was particularly appropriate to discuss the work of Baddeley and Hitch at this point because it provides a link with both the preceding and following chapters. Their emphasis on the limited capacity nature of working memory harkens back to our discussion of attention in the last chapter, and we have seen them using concurrent tasks to examine capacity limitations. On the other hand, their work points forward to the topics we are to consider next, for they show that working memory functions as the work space for reasoning and language comprehension and as a crucial link in long-term storage.

CHAPTER SUMMARY

This chapter focused on working memory, which is also called the short-term store, primary memory, active memory, and the STS. Four kinds of evidence have led many theorists to propose such a memory system, which is functionally distinct from a more permanent, long-term memory. The evidence includes introspection, clinical cases, analyses of the serial position curve, and the capacity limitations that are apparent in human thinking.

For contemporary theories the most important characteristic of working memory is its limited capacity. Although early theorists attempted to describe this capacity in terms of a fixed number of bits, they were unsuccessful. This is because the number of bits we can hold in working memory depends upon our prior knowledge about the to-be-remembered material. Therefore, George Miller proposed the chunk as a unit, and argued that people can hold 7 plus or minus 2 chunks in working memory. A chunk may be thought of as anything that has a unitary representation in long-term memory. Thus, chunks vary from individual to individual, and at least some individual differences in the apparent capacity of working memory are due to the fact that some people build informationally richer chunks than others.

People can hold information in working memory indefinitely as long as the number of items does not exceed working memory capacity and as long as they are permitted to rehearse the items. However, if rehearsal is prevented, the material is forgotten from working memory within 18 seconds or so. There has been a great deal of debate regarding whether any of this forgetting is due to spontaneous decay, or whether it is due solely to new information displacing the to-be-remembered material. At present, it seems that displacement or interference is the most important mechanism of short-term forgetting, though some decay occurs as well.

When information is held in working memory it is often quite different in form from the external stimulus, for people exert a great deal of control over the form of representation. Among adults in our culture, at least, the most ubiquitous form of representation in working memory is articulatory-acoustic. That is, people tend to label the stimulus, and it is a representation of this label that is held in working memory. Although articulatory-acoustic coding is the most prevalent kind in working memory, both visual-spatial and semantic codes are used as well.

Introspectively it feels as though everything in working memory is available to consciousness at once, but Sternberg has performed detailed analyses of reaction times which lead him to conclude that people must, in fact, search through working memory in order to judge whether or not some information is currently stored there. Not only did Sternberg's analyses lead him to conclude that people engage in a high-speed serial exhaustive search of the contents of working memory, but they also provide important methods for studying the nature of individual differences in memory processes.

Working memory provides the work-space for thinking and comprehending language. Baddeley and Hitch have found that holding items in working memory interferes with concurrent thinking, language comprehension, and storage in permanent memory. Therefore, the characteristics of working memory that we have studied in this chapter—including its limited capacity and the ubiquity of articulatory-acoustic coding—will be critical for helping us to understand other aspects of cognition such as problem solving and understanding and producing language.

SUGGESTED READING

I recommend two general sources as good starting places for a more detailed investigation of the issues discussed in this chapter. Chapters 6, 7, and 8 of Baddeley's text are excellent and will send you to most of the important references through the early 1970's. The volume edited by Deutsch and Deutsch entitled *Short-Term Memory* contains articles on all aspects of short-term storage, including chapters focusing on the neuropsychology of memory.

Among the important issues that the serious student will want to pursue, the most central is the question of whether a separate short-term (or working) memory system exists. One of the most vocal opponents of the dichotomous view is Wickelgren, and he has summarized his arguments in two articles (1973; 1975). In addition, the levels-of-processing view is often thought of as being antagonistic to the dichotomous view, and many contemporary theorists think that the levels-of-processing view is replacing the multi-store view. The differences between the two views are not at all precise, however, since even the levels-of-processing approach assumes a primary memory system. Therefore, I have treated the levels-of-processing approach as supplementing multi-store theories rather than supplanting them. You might wish to become more familiar with the levels-of-processing approach and the arguments for and against it. Begin with the original article by Craik and Lockhart (1972) and then read the controversies it has spawned in Baddeley (1978) and the series of papers which contains a criticism of the levels approach by Eysenck (1978a), a reply to the criticisms by Lockhart and Craik (1978), and a rejoinder by Eysenck (1978b). The next chapter of the present book will send you to additional references as well, for the levels-of-processing approach has led to many important studies of long-term memory.

Another topic for further reading concerns Sternberg's work. His technique for using reaction time to make inferences about stages of processing has been extremely influential, and his RT findings discussed in this chapter have been replicated again and again in laboratories all around the world. Nonetheless, there is a great deal of controversy regarding exactly how the parallel, increasing set-size functions should be interpreted. Pages 141–150 of Baddeley's text contain a good overview of the alternative interpretations that have been suggested. These include parallel comparison models (e.g., Atkinson, Holmgren, & Juola, 1969), self-terminating search models (e.g., Theios et al., 1973), and trace strength discrimination models (Nickerson, 1972). Sternberg's (1975) article discusses evidence that he judges to favor his interpretation over these alternatives, and also provides an excellent summary of the recent findings using his technique.

There is a very interesting and important literature on the development and aging of working memory that we only touched on in this chapter. This includes some fascinating comparisons of mentally retarded children with their normal peers, and the discovery of some training techniques that lead retarded children to perform quite like normal children on some simple memory tasks. Two excellent sources on these topics are the brief, well-written book by Kail entitled *The Development of Memory in Children,* and at a slightly more advanced level, the book edited by Kail and Hagen entitled *Perspectives on the Development of Memory and Cognition.* An excellent source on the changes in memory that occur with aging is the book *New Directions in Memory and Aging* edited by Poon, Fozard, Cermak, Arenberg, and Thompson.

Baddeley has continued to develop his theory of working memory, and good sources on his latest thinking are his 1981 article in *Cognition* and a 1982 article by Salame and Baddeley. Baddeley and Hitch (1976) have presented evidence for a new interpretation of the recency portion of the free recall serial position curve, and Glenberg, Bradley, Stevenson, Kraus, Tkachuk, Gretz, Fish, and Turpin (1980) have reported supporting data.

Long-Term Memory: Remembering and Forgetting

5

APPLICATIONS TO STUDYING
CHAPTER SUMMARY
SUGGESTED READING

FOOD FOR THOUGHT

In contrast to the fleeting memories we have examined so far, this chapter focuses on learning, that is, on the question of how records of experience are stored so that they are available after days, weeks, or years have passed. In terms of the overview model, we will be investigating how information is placed in long-term memory, how it is retrieved at some later time, and how forgetting of previously stored material occurs.

It is best to begin by trying to commit some new experience to memory. Table 5–1 contains a list of 10 stimulus-response pairs. In each pair the stimulus is a number between 1 and 10 and the response is some common word. Beginning with the top pair, study each in turn for 5 seconds or less. After you have completed this study of the list, do something else for 10 minutes, i.e., read, solve arithmetic problems, or make a phone call. Then test yourself by attempting to write down the word that was paired with each of the following digits, in the order listed here: 4, 10, 1, 8, 2, 5, 7, 3, 9, 6. Count the number of pairs on which you were correct. Most people recall fewer than half of the pairs under these conditions.

Now, before you try to learn another such list, you should master a system for learning the pairs, called the *peg-word mnemonic*. The system requires that you commit the following rhyme to memory—a task you can accomplish easily by reading it through once or twice.

TABLE 5–1.   A List of Paired Associates.*

2 — tire
5 — pipe
8 — table
1 — kitchen
6 — camera
10 — necklace
7 — gun
3 — sandwich
9 — glasses
4 — kangaroo

* See the text for instructions.

one is a bun

two is a shoe

three is a tree

four is a door

five is a hive

six are sticks

seven is heaven

eight is a gate

nine is a line

ten is a hen

Having learned this rhyme (taken from Miller, Galanter, & Pribram, 1960) you now have a system of peg words (e.g., *bun*), each paired with a rhyming digit (e.g., *one*), and you can use the peg words to learn any new list of words to be paired with the digits. When you study a pair, simply recall the peg word for the digit. Then conjure up an image of the object named by the peg word interacting with the object named by the response word. Then move on to the next pair. For example, if the list with which you are presented contains the pair 4-horse, you should picture a door and a horse interacting in some way. The horse might be lifting his hoof to open the door, or he might have just charged through the door. Any image that comes to mind, no matter how ludicrous or improbable, is fine as long as the two objects are interacting in some way. Later when you try to recall, you need only recall the peg word (door) for the tested digit (4) and you will find that the correct word (e.g., *horse*) comes to mind effortlessly.

Now try to learn the list in Table 5–2 using the peg-word mne-

---

TABLE 5–2.   A Second List of Paired Associates.*

4 — tooth
1 — church
5 — typewriter
3 — bus
7 — bridge
9 — elephant
2 — television
6 — basket
8 — carpet
10 — hammer

---

* See text for instructions.

monic you just learned. In order to make study time for this list comparable to the first list you learned, be sure to allow yourself no more than 5 seconds to come up with each image. Again take a 10 minute break after you finish. Then test yourself by writing the correct word for each of the following numbers: 7, 2, 1, 5, 10, 9, 3, 6, 4, 8. You will probably remember almost all of the pairs. In fact, on several occasions I have asked my classes to learn a list using the peg-word system at the beginning of the semester. When I announced a surprise test on the list three months later, most of the students amazed themselves by remembering at least 8 of the pairs correctly, even though they hadn't thought of the pairs at all in the intervening months.

Using the peg-word mnemonic made it easy to learn and retain an arbitrary list of pairs, a task which is quite difficult (and dull) without such a system. If you found that the peg-word system helped your performance, compare this system with the strategy you used for the first list and try to propose hypotheses regarding why the peg-word mnemonic leads to superior long-term memory.

EBBINGHAUS AND NONSENSE SYLLABLES

In 1879 the German scholar Hermann Ebbinghaus began the first experimental investigations of long-term memory. Ebbinghaus realized that if he was to study the fate of memories over long periods, then he had to have control over the experiences of his subjects, and he had to be sure that subjects would be suitably motivated and available for subsequent tests—problems that are still bothersome to researchers 100 years later. Ebbinghaus hit upon an excellent, if somewhat self-sacrificing, solution—he would be his own subject!

At least two other problems remained, however, and Ebbinghaus' solution to each had tremendous impact on the direction experimental investigations of memory would take for the next century. First, Ebbinghaus wanted to study how new associations were learned and retained, but he was faced with the problem that previously learned associations might influence the learning of these new associations in unknown ways that he could not control. Therefore, he invented new materials to which he would have no old associations (i.e., materials that would be meaningless). Thus was born the *nonsense syllable*, the consonant-vowel-consonant (CVC) items such as TUZ, DAX, and SED which were to become the predominant stimuli for memory studies for decades to come. Ebbinghaus generated all possible CVC's and constructed lists of various lengths—over 1,200 lists in all.

Each day for several years Ebbinghaus attempted to learn several lists, using a method of *serial recall* in which he first read aloud the list at a rate of about 2 items per second, and then attempted to reproduce the list from memory. He repeated each list until he could reproduce the full list twice in succession in perfect serial order and without hesitation, and he recorded how many such repetitions were required to learn each list.

The only remaining challenge was that Ebbinghaus needed to develop a sensitive method for measuring retention of the lists. Since he wanted the technique to be capable of revealing even the most fragmentary memory, he developed the *savings* method; Ebbinghaus compared the time required to learn a list the first time with the time required to relearn the list after certain specified intervals. By subtracting relearning time from the original learning time and dividing the difference by original learning time, Ebbinghaus was able to measure the percentage of savings from the original learning experience, and, by inference, how much of the list must have been retained during the interval in question.

Ebbinghaus' contributions. Not only was Ebbinghaus responsible for many methodological innovations including the nonsense syllable, the serial learning procedure, and the savings method of measuring retention, but his careful studies of his own performance revealed several interesting phenomena. Two of his findings are particularly important for they have been replicated many times under a number of different conditions.

First, when Ebbinghaus investigated how the number of items in a list affected the number of repetitions required to commit the list to memory, he found the results depicted in Figure 5–1. There is a sharp discontinuity in the curve; lists containing 7 or fewer items require only one presentation, but for each additional item that is added to a list, one additional repetition is required. This discontinuity is consistent with theories that distinguish between short-term and long-term memories. According to such duplex theories, as long as the list has 7 or fewer items the capacity of working memory is not exceeded, so perfect recall is possible from working memory. Longer lists exceed working memory capacity, so at least part of the list must be committed to long-term memory, a process that requires additional time.

Ebbinghaus' second major finding was the *negatively accelerated forgetting curve*. When Ebbinghaus learned long lists and then relearned them either 20 minutes, 1 hour, 9 hours, 1 day, 2 days, 6 days or 31 days later, he found that the rate of forgetting was exceedingly rapid at first but then tapered off. The form of this forgetting curve is a very general phenomenon. The rate and/or total amount of forgetting depends on factors such as the type of material being remembered, the strategies the person adopts, and the kind of memory test, but the negatively accelerated form of this function almost always

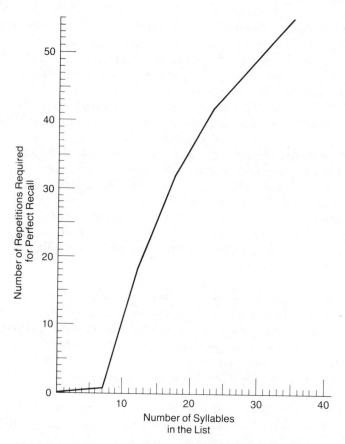

Figure 5–1. This figure is taken from Ebbinghaus' study in which he acted as his own subject. It shows how the number of repetitions necessary to learn the list varies as a function of the length of the list. Notice the discontinuity that occurs at list length 7. (After Ebbinghaus, 1964.)

holds. Remember that the forgetting curves obtained in studies of working memory have the same form (see Figure 4–4 again).

Criticisms of Ebbinghaus' work. Ebbinghaus took a domain that had seemed outside the realm of scientific inquiry and demonstrated that reliable, systematic relationships could be found. In this very important sense, then, he expanded the range of phenomena that could be addressed using the scientific method.

Nonetheless, Ebbinghaus' work has met with criticism. On the one hand, it is clear that his stimuli did not meet the ideal he had set for them. Nonsense syllables are not meaningless. People consistently rate some nonsense syllables, (e.g., WIS) as being more meaningful than others (e.g., GAX). When people are asked to free associate to nonsense syllables by saying as many words as they can think of for each, those syllables rated as more meaningful lead to a higher number of associations than those syllables judged to be less meaningful (Archer, 1960; Noble, 1961). Furthermore, McGeoch (1930) was the first to demonstrate the now accepted fact that the more meaningful nonsense syllables are learned more rapidly than less meaningful ones. In sum, one criticism of Ebbinghaus' work is that he did not fulfill his self-imposed goal of studying the rote learning of meaningless material.

A second criticism is more fundamental, for it calls into question the goal itself. Ebbinghaus proudly assures us that his data are unlikely to have been contaminated by the use of any plans for remembering of the sort you learned at the beginning of the chapter, for he notes,

> There was no attempt to connect the nonsense syllables by the invention of special associations of the mnemotechnik type; learning was carried on solely by the influence of the mere repetitions upon the natural memory. As I do not possess the least practical knowledge of the mnemotechnical devices, the fulfillment of this condition offered no difficulty to me. (1885, p. 25)

Thus, Ebbinghaus assumed that to study "natural memory" one must examine the acquisition of a meaningless string of items by a passive individual. However, this sort of passive learning is probably more unnatural than natural. Most of our memories are of meaningful material, and even when presented with nonsense to remember, instead of being passive, people go to amazing lengths to make it meaningful. Thus, by attempting to limit the scope of his inquiry primarily to the analysis of the passive acquisition of meaningless material, Ebbinghaus was eliminating from study the most important and intriguing aspects of human memory. Learning of the sort Ebbinghaus studied is only one kind of remembering, the kind that gets done when we tie the mind's hands, as it were.

HISTORY OF MNEMONIC TECHNIQUES

Ebbinghaus attempted to eliminate the use of mnemonic techniques so that he could study long-term memory. In this section we will take a very different approach; rather than banishing such systems for remembering we will exploit them. Over the centuries innumerable systems have been developed for improving memory and recent studies have confirmed the fact that, once mastered, they are quite effective. By analyzing some mnemonic systems, we will be able to discover characteristics they all share, providing us with a source of hypotheses regarding how long-term memory works.

Nowadays people often view mnemonic systems as the idiosyncratic tools of somewhat freakish stage performers who use them to impress us with elaborate feats of memory. We have printing presses, pencils, paper, typewriters, copy machines, and computer files, so few of us bother to cultivate mnemonic techniques. That this was not always the case is made clear in a delightful book by the English historian Frances B. Yates, entitled *The Art of Memory.* In tracing the origins and history of mnemonic techniques, Yates writes that in ancient times the ability to memorize was a much revered art. Indeed, the art of memory was assigned as one of the five parts of rhetoric, the art of public speaking, and rhetoric teachers taught mnemonic techniques to their students. Aristotle praised mnemonic systems and assigned them a role in thinking when he said, "these habits too will make a man readier in reasoning." Centuries later Shakespeare used mnemonic techniques, and it is said that Leibniz invented the calculus while he was searching for a mnemonic system to aid in memorizing numbers.

Thus, until the last century or so the ability to commit material to memory was viewed as an important component of thought rather than as its inferior cousin. Contemporary information-processing theories follow in this ancient tradition since they, too, view memory as a central component of thought.

Classical memory system: The method of loci. Cicero credited the fifth century Greek poet Simonides with the invention of the classical memory system which is called the *method of places and images,* or the *method of loci.* There is no doubt that Simonides was a gifted man (Yates notes that he is said to be the first to demand payment for his poetry, certainly a sign of a man ahead of his times), so Cicero may be correct in attributing Simonides with the invention of this method. It is equally likely, though, that the rules were derived from an earlier oral tradition that may have been Pythagorean or Egyptian. In any event, the first written descriptions of the method were apparently not prepared until around the time of the birth of Christ, and then they appeared in texts on Rhetoric.

The major steps in applying the system can be stated briefly. First, one must commit to memory a sequence of places or locations, so that the sequence of scenes is fixed in one's mind. For example, students were advised to memorize a sequence of locations in a familiar building. After learning this sequence, the student could use it to help him remember any series of items simply by picturing each item in turn at one of the memorized locations. Thus, the student of rhetoric "walked" through his mind depositing images on locations as he tried to commit a sequence to memory. Then, when he later wished to recall, he was simply to "walk" through the series of locations in his mind, examining each in turn and there he would find the images of the items to be recalled.

The next time you find it necessary to memorize a talk, or a list for an examination or a shopping trip, try to use this method. You will first have to commit a series of locations to memory—a task you will find easy if you deal with familiar areas, such as your university campus. Imagine you wish to memorize a speech favoring a particular piece of legislation. If the first topic to be discussed concerns the fact that passage of the bill will save the taxpayer's money, you might picture a dollar bill superimposed on your first location, perhaps the main gate to the campus. If the next point is that the bill will improve the quality of education, you might picture a mortarboard perched atop the next location, and so on. The technique is quite effective once you practice it a bit.

A particularly salient characteristic of the method of loci is its emphasis on visual imagery. Indeed, one anonymous rhetoric teacher writing in 85 BC (cited in Yates, 1966) provided his students with very detailed advice on the choice of locations and images. What is most interesting about this advice is the degree of visual precision that the teacher assumed the images to have. For example, in choosing locations, the student was advised to choose a deserted solitary place, because otherwise the people in the place would also be envisioned and might interfere with one's ability to "see" the item to be remembered. Furthermore, the student is advised that images containing activity are better than passive images, that comic, ornamental, extremely ugly or extremely beautiful images are more memorable than more common ones. Indeed, in one particularly gory passage our instructor indicates that it is often helpful to disfigure images by imagining them stained with blood or mud.

There is no doubting the effectiveness of the classical memory system (e.g., Bower, 1970a), although we are only beginning to investigate whether the detailed advice regarding the choice of images and places is valid. For example, is it really the case that memory will be more accurate if you imagine unusual bizarre images? The answer appears to be a qualified yes. When memory is tested immediately after learning, bizarre images are remembered no better than plausible ones, but if memory is tested three or more days later, bizarre images are remembered significantly better (O'Brien & Wolford, 1982).

Both the peg-word technique and method of loci rely upon visual imagery. Even though this is true of most memory systems (see, for example, Lorayne & Lucas's *The Memory Book*), a number of mnemonic systems do not involve visual imagery, and we turn now to one of these.

The method of analytic substitutions. As in the classical memory system, the origins of this method are obscure. It is usually credited to Stanislaus Mink von Wenussheim (usually known as Winckelmann, for obvious reasons) who described the method in 1648, but there is some evidence that it was developed slightly earlier in 1634 by a French mathematician Pietro Herigon.

The system was designed for remembering series of numbers, because series of abitrary digits are notoriously difficult to retain. The method involves changing the numbers to sounds, combining the sounds to form words, and the words to form a phrase. Thus a series of arbitrary and hard to remember digits is changed into an easy to remember, meaningful phrase.

Once again, the first step is to learn the system. This time you must learn a series of consonant sounds which can be substituted for each of the digits between 0 and 9. The exact translations to be used vary from one system to another, but we will adopt those of Loisette (reported in Norman, 1976), shown in Table 5–3. Once you have committed this list to memory, you can then translate any series of numbers you want to remember into a series of sounds, which can then be used to form a phrase. Later, when you wish to recall the numbers, you need only bring the phrase to mind, then decode it to its numbers.

If, for example, you wish to remember that the first laboratory of experimental psychology was founded in 1879, first do the conversion to sounds:

1 = t, th, or d
8 = f or v
7 = g (hard), k, c (hard), q, or ng
9 = b or p

then combine the sounds with vowels to form a meaningful phrase or sentence, such as "dof a cap." When you wish to recall the date in

TABLE 5–3. **Number and Sound Correspondences for the Method of Analytic Substitutions.**

0 = s, z, or c(soft)
1 = t, th, or d
2 = n
3 = m
4 = r
5 = l
6 = sh, j, ch, or g(soft)
7 = g(hard), k, c(hard), q, or ng
8 = f or v
9 = b or p

question, you need only recall "dof a cap" and then recode back to 1879, ignoring the vowel sounds. It is particularly helpful if you can manage to come up with a phrase that is related to the topic in some meaningful way, such as remembering the founding date of Harvard College (1636) with the phrase "*teach much.*" I think the method is also easier to practice if you use only the first consonant sound of each word, affording more flexibility so that it is easier to come up with phrases that are related to the item in a meaningful way. For example, to remember the founding year of Georgetown University (the first Roman Catholic university in the United States) you might learn "*the catholic fathers prayed*" or, since it was an all male institution at the time of its founding, "*the campus favored boys.*" Either would lead you to recall the correct date of 1789. Of course, at first this technique requires a lot of time and effort, but numerous writers over the centuries assure us that once learned and practiced regularly, the recoding can be done almost automatically, in the sense discussed previously in the Attention chapter.

It is amusing to apply this technique and it would be interesting to study your own ability to perform the translations more and more automatically. The major reason for describing the technique here, however, is to illustrate the fact that not all mnemonic systems include the use of visual images. Indeed, all of us employ other simpler mnemonics that do not require visual imagery. Rhymes such as "Thirty days hath September" or "All good boys do fine" are cases in point. So are various narrative chaining techniques (e.g., Bower & Winzenz, 1970) in which you commit an arbitrary list of words to memory by chaining them together in a meaningful sentence or story.

Common characteristics of mnemonic systems. Two commonalities among mnemonic systems are particularly important. First, *all systems,* whether based on visual imagery or verbal substitutions, *force the would-be memorizer to think about the material he is attempting to commit to memory.* That is, they force him to attend to it and act on it. Mnemonic systems require elaborating or enriching the material, so on the surface at least they seem to require the learner to recall *more,* rather than *less.* It is notable that in such cases having to remember more, far from detracting from memory, greatly enhances it.

A second commonality is that *all systems involve using some scheme for organizing the material to be remembered;* they provide a system to which new material can be related. In fact, using a mnemonic system to learn new material makes the task of memorizing into a thinking, problem solving activity. The memorizer uses a strategy for relating previously acquired knowledge to new experience.

STORING INFORMATION IN LONG-TERM MEMORY

The ancient orators had a practical problem; they needed to be able to commit large quantities of ordered information to memory so that they would be able to recall it later during delivery of a speech. Though we leave our orators for the time being to take up more contemporary analyses of memory, we will find that the techniques they developed will be relevant, for in this section we are concerned with exactly the problem they faced, though we will phrase it in terms of contemporary theory. We will examine the mental operations by which information is stored in long-term memory.

Savings, recognition, and recall. Most researchers have used one or more of three general types of test to study long-term memory. One is the *savings method,* a measure we already considered in our discussion of Ebbinghaus' work. In this technique the time required to relearn a particular set of items is compared with the time required to learn the set for the first time. Despite the systematic findings Ebbinghaus obtained, the savings measure has been used only infrequently during the last few decades. This neglect is unfortunate, because the few studies which have been reported (e.g., Nelson, 1971) have revealed potentially important properties of memory.

At present, the two most commonly used measures of memory are recognition and recall. There are many forms of each but the most important difference between them is that in the *recall* task the subject is expected to generate the answer from memory, whereas in *recognition* the subject is presented with one or more possible answers and is asked to judge which of these is correct (or, if only one is presented, whether or not the presented answer is correct). Thus, if the subject is asked, "Who was the first president of the United States?" he has been given a recall test. On the other hand, if he is asked either "Was Washington the first president of the United States?" or "Which of the following was the first president of the United States: Washington or Jefferson?" he has been given a recognition test.

It is important that different tests often yield very different assessments of the contents of long-term memory, a fact which will not surprise you. You have probably noticed that multiple choice and true-false tests (analogous to recognition tests) seem to tap different aspects of your knowledge than do fill-in-the-blanks and essay tests (analogous to recall tests). The differences between memory as measured by recognition and memory as measured by recall are of considerable theoretical interest, so we will have occasion to examine them again later in the chapter. For the moment, the important point is that since these various measures of memory often fail to agree with each other, it is always important to notice which kind of test has been used in a particular study.

Rehearsal and long-term storage. Our overview model assumes that in order for information to be stored in long-term memory, it must be attended to. That is, the information must be operated on in the limited capacity working memory from which it is then transferred (or, more accurately, recopied) into long-term memory. But exactly what operations, or control processes, are necessary during residence in working memory?

The first information-processing theories of memory (e.g., Waugh & Norman, 1965; Atkinson & Shiffrin, 1968; Norman & Rumelhart, 1970) assumed that the necessary control process was rehearsal. These theories assumed that such overt or covert repetition of an item has two functions. First, rehearsal maintains the item in the short-term store, and in that sense one rehearsal of an item is equivalent to a re-perception of the item. Second, rehearsal was assumed to result in the item being transferred to long-term memory. For example, Atkinson and Shiffrin assumed that for each period of time during which an item is maintained in working memory via rehearsal, there is a certain probability that information about the item will be transferred to long-term memory. Thus, the control process of rehearsal was assigned an important role in long-term memory.

Early research supported the assumption that rehearsal results in long-term recall. For example, Rundus (1971) instructed subjects to rehearse aloud during presentation of a free recall list, and he counted the number of repetitions (or rehearsals) produced for each word. As predicted, he found that the more times an item had been rehearsed, the more likely it was to be recalled during a later test. Despite this evidence for a correlation between number of rehearsals and recall from long-term memory, it soon became clear that this relation was not as simple as the early information processing theories proposed. The problem is that the number of rehearsals doesn't always predict long-term recall. Sometimes, as happens when mnemonic techniques are used, excellent long-term recall occurs with very little rehearsal. Other times, as we will see below, an item can be rehearsed many times, and yet not be recalled at all.

Maintenance versus elaborative rehearsal. The relation between long-term recall and rehearsal can be described more accurately if we adopt a distinction suggested by Craik and Lockhart (1972).

As mentioned in the previous chapter, Craik and Lockhart proposed what they called a *levels of processing* theory of memory. This approach assumes that the memorability of a stimulus is determined by the depth to which it is processed, or in terms suggested by Craik and Tulving (1975), by the degree to which the stimulus is elaborated. The more a stimulus is elaborated, the more likely it will be remembered later. For example, if you simply say a word to yourself after it is presented you have processed it less deeply than if you had tried to think of other words similar in meaning.

Craik and Lockhart proposed that it is necessary to distinguish between two different kinds of rehearsal. The first called *Type I* or *maintenance rehearsal* involves rote repetition of the item without attempting to process the stimulus more deeply, i.e., to relate it to other long-term knowledge. This type of rehearsal is assumed to maintain an item in primary memory, but not to affect the likelihood of recall from long-term memory. The second type of rehearsal, termed *Type II* or *elaborative rehearsal,* involves attempts to process the stimulus more deeply, i.e., to relate the material to long-term knowledge. According to Craik and Lockhart, it is the second type of rehearsal that not only keeps the information in working memory, but also increases the likelihood that it will be recalled after a delay. Since this distinction promises to be important in understanding both long-term remembering and long-term forgetting, let us examine each of these kinds of rehearsal in more detail.

Maintenance rehearsal. According to the Craik and Lockhart depth-of-processing view, maintenance rehearsal does not contribute to the long-term recall of an item; it simply maintains the item in working memory. In fact, it is quite difficult to test this hypothesis because few adults engage in pure maintenance rehearsal when they suspect that they will need to remember the material later. For example, the subjects in the Rundus (1971) experiment who were asked to rehearse aloud knew that they would have to recall each list. Rundus found that they frequently grouped related words together in their rehearsal, even though the words were not presented next to each other. Thus, if a subject happened to be rehearsing *dog, book, car* when presented with the word *cat* he would be likely to modify his rehearsal to *dog, cat, book, car* placing the related words next to each other. This pattern suggests that Rundus' subjects were engaging in elaboration of the material, not in pure maintenance rehearsal.

Given this tendency to use elaborative rehearsal, if we wish to study the effects of pure maintenance rehearsal on long-term recall, it is usually necessary to lead subjects to think that they will *not* be tested on the material later. Several studies in which this has been done indicate that, in keeping with Craik and Lockhart's distinction, the number of maintenance rehearsals does *not* affect the likelihood of recall from long-term memory. We will consider only two such studies.

The first of these was performed in 1966, prior to the proposal of the maintenance-elaborative distinction. Endel Tulving wanted to analyze the effect of rote repetition on memory. He presented two groups of subjects with several free recall trials on a list of 22 common English nouns. On each trial the subject listened to the list of 22 words and then attempted to recall as many of them as possible. The words were presented in a different order on each of the trials, and Tulving recorded the total number of words recalled after each trial. *Prior to* the 12 free recall trials just described, both groups of subjects read aloud a list of 22 words 6 times, ostensibly as a test of pronunciation. The only difference between the two groups of subjects was that for the experimental group this pronunciation list contained the same 22 words that would later be contained in the free recall lists, whereas for the control group the pronunciation list contained a different set of 22 words. Tulving's question was, would the 6 overt repetitions of the free recall list enable the experimental group to do better than the control group in the subsequent free recall test? The answer was a resounding *no*. The mean recall for subjects in the experimental group was 15.7 items, whereas the mean recall for subjects in the control group was 15.9. The 6 overt repetitions had apparently not aided long-term recall in the least.

The second procedure supporting the conclusion that maintenance rehearsal does not aid long-term recall was reported by Craik and Watkins (1973). These researchers induced their subjects to hold items in working memory for varying amounts of time by having them listen to a series of words on a tape. At the beginning of the series the subject was given a critical letter (e.g., *D*). He was told to monitor the list for a word that began with *D* and to hold that word in mind until another word beginning with *D* appeared, at which time he should then forget the previous D-word and hold the new one in memory. He was told to keep doing this until the experimenter signalled him, at which time he should report the *last* D-word he had heard. The subject was then presented with a new critical letter and a new series began. For example, a subject might hear the following sequence of words in a given series: DOG, BOOK, COFFEE, DRAGON, DOOR, BOX, PICTURE, TREE, SHOES, TABLE, DRUM, HOUSE. If the critical letter was *D*, he would keep DOG in mind until DRAGON occurred, at which time he would hold DRAGON until the next word DOOR, at which time he would discard DRAGON and hold DOOR. He would hold DOOR until DRUM occurred and then at the experimenter's signal following the word HOUSE, he would correctly respond DRUM. By planning the list carefully, Craik and Watkins could vary the length of time the subject would hold any given word in working memory. If the list was presented at the rate of one word per second, then the subject would have had to hold the word DOG for about 3 seconds, the word DRAGON for about 1 second, the word DOOR for 6 seconds, and the word DRUM for 2 seconds. If time in working memory determines the likelihood of recall from long-term memory, then DOOR (which was in working memory for 6 seconds) should be more likely to be recalled than DRAGON, which was in the working memory for only 1 second.

In order to test this prediction, Craik and Watkins surprised their subjects at the end of the experiment by asking them to report all the words they could recall from all the lists they had heard. (In order to eliminate recall from the working memory, subjects were engaged in about 2 minutes of conversation prior to this final surprise test.) Craik and Watkins examined the probability that a word would be recalled in this final recall test as a function of the amount of time the word had resided in working memory during the monitoring part of the experiment. Their results, which are depicted in Figure 5–2, were clear. Subjects were no more likely to recall an item that had been in the working memory for 13 seconds than one that had been there only 1 second. Apparently, then, in the Craik and Watkins study, longer residence in the working memory, and by inference, more maintenance rehearsals, did *not* increase the likelihood of recall from long-term memory.

All the results we have discussed in this section support the conclusion that rote, maintenance rehearsal does not increase the likeli-

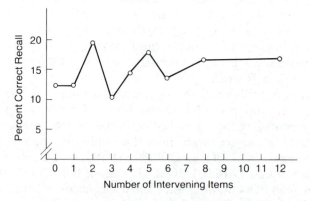

Figure 5–2. Percent correct recall on a delayed, unexpected test as a function of the number of intervening items in the Craik & Watkins (1973) experiment. The number of intervening items is assumed to indicate the amount of maintenance rehearsal. Notice that recall does *not* increase with increasing amounts of maintenance rehearsal. (Data from Craik & Watkins, 1973, Table 1.)

hood of recall from long-term memory. Does this conclusion mean that maintenance rehearsal does not lead to *any* information being transferred to long-term memory? The thoughtful reader will notice that so far we have talked about studies that test memory using recall tasks but we already noted earlier that recall tests are not always the most sensitive way of assessing the contents of the long-term memory. Does rote repetition aid recognition or savings? If it does, then we must conclude that such maintenance rehearsal does result in more information being recorded in long-term memory, but that the information is not of the sort that aids recall.

This question cannot yet be answered. The only studies that address this point using the savings measure would seem to be those of Ebbinghaus. Given his determination to avoid any sort of "unnatural" mnemonic schemes, we may assume that he tried not to use elaborative rehearsal. Since he did find that the more times he repeated a list, the more savings revealed later, his findings suggest the possibility that rote repetition might aid savings.

Several studies of recognition memory are relevant. Craik and Watkins (1973) examined recognition in an earlier experiment mentioned in the paper we discussed and found that number of repetitions did *not* increase recognition. However, in a study using a different technique Woodward, Bjork, and Jongeward (1973) found that it did. Thus, it is not clear whether rote repetition results in an item's being stored in long-term memory, but it is clear that any long-term storage that does result from rote repetition does little to aid recall.

Elaborative rehearsal. What about the other side of the rehearsal coin; is it possible to demonstrate that elaborative rehearsal is *sufficient* to store information in long-term memory?

We have already examined one kind of evidence for the usefulness of elaborative rehearsal in aiding long-term recall—the history of mnemonic techniques. These techniques are as interesting for the advice they don't offer as for the advice they do. As far as we know, no mnemonic system has ever proposed that you commit material to memory by reciting it over and over again. Woe be unto the orator who attempted to commit his speech to memory through rote repetition of the sounds of the items. Mnemonic systems involve one form or another of elaboration, either enriching the item to be remembered by imaging it (the peg-word system and method of loci) or by relating it to some verbal system (e.g., the method of analytic substitution). Thus, the wisdom of the ages suggests the value of elaboration.

A second form of evidence for the importance of elaborative rehearsal for long-term recall comes from studies of the role of organization in free recall. When college students are given a list of items in a free recall task, they tend to organize the items, and this organization is usually accompanied by increases in the accuracy of recall. Organization is usually measured in free recall tasks in one of two ways, both of which rely upon an analysis of the order in which items are recalled. The first measure is *clustering*. In this case subjects are presented with word lists that contain a given number of words from each of a set of categories. For example the subject might be presented with a 20-word list containing 4 animals, 4 kinds of clothing, 4 kinds of furniture, 4 color names, and 4 kinds of food. Numerous studies (e.g., Bousfield, 1953) have revealed that even when the list is presented in random order, subjects tend to group their recall by categories, a phenomenon called *categorical clustering*. Thus, the subject is likely to report all the clothes he can remember, then all the color names, and so on. In fact, the pattern of delays between responses is interesting as well, because subjects usually report a quick burst of items from a particular category, followed by a pause, then a quick burst of items from another category. Furthermore, if a subject is given repeated trials on the same list of items (presented in a different order each time) the amount of clustering increases over trials as does the total number of words recalled. Why not conduct a study of categorical clustering in free recall by testing a few friends?

Another way of examining organization in free recall is by measuring *subjective organization*. One drawback of the clustering analysis we have just described is that it is sensitive only to the kind of organization that the experimenter builds into the list. What happens when a subject is presented with a list that does not have such a built-in structure? In 1962 Tulving suggested a technique for finding out. He presented subjects with a series of trials on one free recall list of apparently unrelated items, with the list being presented in a different random order on each trial. Tulving recorded the order of report on each trial. He assumed that if subjects were imposing their own *subjective organization* on the list, then despite the fact that the list was presented in a different order on each trial, over the course of the experiment the subject should tend to report the items in a more and more fixed order. Based on this assumption, Tulving developed a measure of subjective organization that would reflect the degree of consistency in order of report of pairs of items. Again, as in the case of clustering, the degree of subjective organization was found to increase over the course of the free recall trials, and such increases in subjective organization were paralleled by an increase in the number of words recalled.

One reason subjective organization and clustering are so interesting to psychologists is that they demonstrate the extent to which people attempt to impose order on experience. This is particularly noticeable with the subjective organization task; given a list that was designed to have words as unrelated to each other as possible, the subject manages to impose some idiosyncratic organization over trials. It is interesting that both subjective organization and clustering are much more pronounced among college students than they are among elementary school children or the elderly in our culture (e.g., Moely, 1977; Hultsch, 1974; Smith, 1980), or among unschooled young adults in nonindustrialized cultures (e.g., Cole & Scribner, 1977). It is not the case that such individuals are *incapable* of clustering, for when they are induced to organize to-be-remembered material, their recall improves. Perhaps one effect of formal schooling is to lead the individual to adopt *spontaneously* strategies for intentional memorizing—an idea consistent with our discussion of the primacy effect in the previous chapter. (See Cole & Scribner, 1977, for further discussion of this point.)

The sort of organization college students seem to impose on the free recall task is one form of elaborative rehearsal, for the person is using knowledge of the words (usually their meaning) to enrich the arbitrary list he has been asked to commit to memory. The fact that increases in recall accompany increases in subjective organization and clustering is important in that it is consistent with the hypothesis that elaborative rehearsal is the control process necessary and sufficient for long-term recall. Nonetheless, it is important to keep in mind that a causal relation between organization and recall has not been demonstrated in these studies, for we have shown only that organization and recall are correlated with each other.

In order to demonstrate a causal relation, it is necessary to vary the degree of organization independently and then measure the resulting level of recall. In other words, it is necessary to do an experiment in which the degree of elaborative rehearsal is manipulated by the experimenter and the accuracy of recall from long-term memory is measured. Of course, the experimenter cannot manipulate mental processes such as rehearsal directly, but he can attempt to induce the subject to vary his strategies. The difficulty the experimenter faces is that studies of subjective organization and clustering indicate that if the subject knows that he is going to have to recall the item later, he is likely to attempt to impose some organization, i.e., some elaborative rehearsal on the list even if the experimenter instructs him not to. Therefore, the best way to study the effects of elaborative rehearsal on recall is to give the subject an *incidental memory task*. In such a task the subject is not told that he will have to remember the material with which he is being presented, so when we measure memory later, it is incidental memory rather than intentional.

One such study of particular interest was reported by Mandler in 1967. All of Mandler's subjects received 5 presentations of a list of 52 unrelated words, with the list being presented in a different order on each of the 5 presentations. All subjects received booklets with 5 pages with 7 columns on each page as well as a final blank page. The subject used one of the first 5 pages for each of the presentations of the list, writing down the words as they were read to him. The final blank page was used at the end of the experiment for a free-recall test during which the subject was to report as many of the 52 words as possible. One-half of the subjects in Mandler's experiment knew that they would be given a final recall test whereas the other half did not. Within each of these groups half of the subjects were instructed to categorize the items during presentation and the other half were not. In particular, subjects who were to categorize were told to write down the words as they were presented, grouping them in from 2 to 7 categories in any way they chose, but so that they would be able to use the same categorization each time the words were presented. Thus they were to attempt to construct a consistent categorization scheme. The subjects who did not receive the categorization instructions were instructed to write the first word they heard in the first column, the second in the second column, etc., placing the eighth word in the first column again, and so on with all the words.

In sum, there were four groups: Categorize-Intentional, Categorize-Incidental, Write-Intentional, Write-Incidental. Mandler's results are displayed in Table 5–4. As the table indicates, the only group that recalled significantly less than the others is the group that was not informed of the recall test and was not asked to organize. Comparing the two conditions in Column 1, notice that as long as subjects knew that recall would be tested, the directions to categorize did not aid recall. This result is consistent with our discussion of clustering and subjective organization, for we have already seen that when college students are told they will later have to recall a list they spontaneously organize the list anyway. Therefore, in Mandler's experiment, adding the instruction to categorize was superfluous for the group that knew they would have to recall later. The most important comparison in this study is that of the items in the top row of Table 5–4. As long as subjects were told to organize the list (i.e., to engage in a form of elaborative rehearsal) it did not matter whether they expected to be tested or not, for under categorization instructions Intentional and In-

TABLE 5–4. Mandler's (1967) Results Showing the Mean Number of Words Recalled (of 52).

	Intentional	Incidental
Categorize	31.4	32.9
Write	32.8	23.5

cidental subjects performed identically. This finding indicates that organization, even without the intent to memorize, is sufficient to facilitate recall from long-term memory.

Mandler's experiment suggests the hypothesis that memorability of a stimulus is determined by the nature of the mental operations performed on the stimulus, a point emphasized by Craik and Lockhart's levels-of-processing approach. This hypothesis also receives particularly strong support from studies in which the experimenter attempts to influence the mental operations performed on stimuli by requiring subjects to complete certain specified *orienting tasks* on each stimulus. Later, memory for the stimuli is examined to determine how the various kinds of orienting tasks affected memorability (e.g., Hyde & Jenkins, 1973). Consider, for example, a recent study by Craik and Tulving (1975) in which college students were presented with a series of 60 words. Before each word was presented, the subject was given one of three kinds of questions he was supposed to answer about the subsequent word. As soon as the word was presented the subject answered the question as rapidly as possible by pressing one of two response keys. The questions were chosen to require three different levels of processing, or degrees of semantic elaboration. The question designed to require the lowest degree of elaboration was the CASE question in which the subject had to decide whether the word was printed in upper or lower case. The next degree of elaboration was the RHYME question in which the subject was to answer whether or not the presented word rhymed with another word, and the question assumed to require most elaboration was the SENTENCE question in which the subject was to decide whether the word would fit into a particular sentence frame. Examples of the question types are displayed in Table 5–5.

After answering a question about each of the 60 words, the subjects were given a surprise final recognition test in which they were presented with 180 words, of which 60 were the items they had just

TABLE 5–5. Examples of the Question Types Used by Craik and Tulving (1975).

Question Type	Sample Question	Correct Answer Yes	No
CASE	Is the word in capital letters?	TABLE	table
RHYME	Does the word rhyme with WEIGHT?	crate	MARKET
SENTENCE	Would the word fit in the sentence: "He met a _____ on the street?"	FRIEND	cloud

After Craik & Tulving, 1975. Copyright 1975 by the American Psychological Association. Reprinted by permission of the publisher and author.

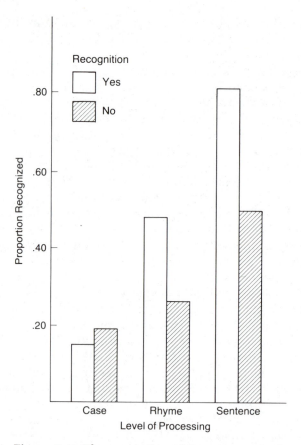

Figure 5–3. The proportion of items recognized, as a function of the type of processing for the Craik and Tulving (1975) study. Notice that recognition improves as the depth of processing that is required is increased. (From Craik & Tulving, 1975. Copyright 1975 by the American Psychological Association. Reprinted by permission of the publisher and author.)

seen, and they were asked to check all the words they recognized from the list. If degree of semantic elaboration affects memorability, then recognition probability should increase as the degree of elaboration given a particular word is increased. If you examine Figure 5–3, you will find that this is exactly the pattern obtained.

Other experiments revealed that the relation between degree of elaboration and memorability holds regardless of whether memory is tested by recall or recognition.

In sum, the Craik and Tulving (1975) studies suggest that the memorability of an event is determined by the nature of the operations performed at the time the event is perceived, independent of the intent to memorize. Operations that involve semantic elaboration of the stimulus facilitate both recall and recognition, and they do so whether or not the person intends to commit the stimulus to memory.

The careful reader will have noticed that there is an alternative interpretation of the results we have just discussed; the orienting tasks that require more semantic elaboration also require more time to complete. Therefore, it is possible that the factor determining memorability is not elaboration but rather length of processing time. Given the finding that maintenance rehearsal does not influence long-term recall, this alternative seems unlikely, however, and Craik and Tulving have offered additional evidence which rules out the processing time interpretation. First, they were able to demonstrate that within a given question type (e.g., SENTENCE questions), words that required longer to process (i.e., that required longer for the yes-no answer) were not better remembered than words that required a shorter answering time. Second, they devised an experiment that compared the effects of a time-consuming (mean response latency = 1.7 sec) structural question (e.g., a question about the pattern of vowels and consonants in the word) with a less time-consuming (mean response latency = .8 sec) question that required semantic elaboration (e.g., a question asking whether or not a word would fit in a simple sentence). The processing time interpretation predicts that in this task the structural orienting task should lead to better memory than the semantic orienting task, whereas the degree of elaboration hypothesis predicts the reverse pattern. The findings supported the elaboration hypothesis; even though subjects had spent less time studying each word under the semantic conditions, recall was substantially superior to the structural conditions. This finding is quite consistent with the conclusion we reached in our discussion of maintenance rehearsal. It is not the *time* devoted to processing an item that is important, it is the *nature* of the operations performed.

Summary. Early in this section we noted that information-processing theories of memory originally assumed that rehearsal serves the dual function of retaining information in some form of temporary storage (i.e., working memory) and of transferring information to a more permanent form of storage (i.e., long-term memory). However this assumption must be modified. One promising way of doing so is to distinguish between two forms of rehearsal, maintenance and elaborative. The rote repetition which characterizes the former is sufficient to hold information in temporary storage, but not to enable later recall. The degree of elaborative rehearsal, on the other hand, determines later recallability. The present results are equivocal regarding whether or not maintenance rehearsal leads to *any* storage in long-term memory, for some studies have suggested that increases in maintenance rehearsal do improve recognition performance whereas others have suggested it may not. This is a question for future research. In addition, the concept of elaborative rehearsal is an umbrella concept meant to include a number of very different kinds of control processes, their feature in common being that they involve enriching the material to be remembered by relating it to what is already stored in long-term memory. Future research must attempt to render this concept and the definition of depth of processing more precise. For the moment, we will be able to shed some light on the question of *why* elaboration aids recall by examining the causes of failures of long-term memory.

FORGETTING FROM LONG-TERM MEMORY

Decay versus interference.   Investigations of forgetting from the sensory stores and working memory began only recently, but the causes of forgetting over longer durations have been a topic of debate for centuries. The oldest theory of forgetting—that it is caused by passive decay which occurs automatically with the passage of time—was proposed by Aristotle. The *trace decay theory* was brought to the attention of experimental psychologists by E. L. Thorndike in 1914 when he proposed the *law of disuse*, which maintained that although practicing habits (i.e., using them) tends to strengthen them, the passage of time during which they are not practiced (i.e., disused) weakens them. Thus, a disuse or decay theory assumes that memories decay with the passage of time, much as does radioactive material (Reynolds & Flagg, 1977) or a mark in a pat of melting butter (Baddeley, 1976).

The major alternative is the *interference hypothesis* which postulates that forgetting occurs because memory is obliterated or masked by other events. According to this hypothesis, forgetting usually increases with the passage of time simply because there is more opportunity for other events to occur and interfere with the memory in question. We saw evidence for decay from the sensory registers and for both interference and decay from working memory, but what about memories that have been stored in long-term memory?

During the early part of this century evidence was collected which revealed that decay, if it occurred at all, could not be the only factor determining long-term forgetting. If decay were the only factor, then the amount of forgetting observed should depend only on the length of the retention interval and should be independent of the amount or kind of activity that takes place during the retention interval. A study published in 1924 by Jenkins and Dallenbach revealed that this prediction of decay theory was not upheld, for they showed that a subject who slept during the retention interval in a paired-associates task forgot much less than a subject who was awake during the retention interval. Assuming that the subject who was awake experienced more potentially interfering events, this finding suggests that at least some of long-term forgetting is due to interference.

Of course, demonstrating that interference is one factor in forgetting does not necessarily rule out the possibility that passive decay occurs as well. In discussing forgetting from working memory we already found that it is difficult to rule out the existence of decay, because in order to do so one would have to prevent the person from experiencing any potentially interfering experiences (including mental events) during the retention interval, and then demonstrate that there is no forgetting under such conditions. If this was a difficult situation to arrange when we were considering retention intervals of less than one minute, it is virtually impossible to do so when we wish to study retention over hours, days, weeks, and years.

Retroactive and proactive interference. In 1932 McGeoch published an influential paper in which he attacked decay theory on both logical and empirical grounds. McGeoch's arguments led to the development of a series of associative interference theories of forgetting which guided and dominated the study of memory from the 1930's through the 1960's (e.g., McGeoch, 1942; Melton & Irwin, 1940; Postman, Stark, & Fraser, 1968).

During three or four decades of research the associative interference theorists accumulated an impressive amount of data on the factors that influence forgetting, their most important contributions being the discovery and analysis of two different kinds of interference, retroactive and proactive. *Retroactive interference* or *retroactive inhibition* (often abbreviated RI) refers to the fact that material learned *after* learning of the to-be-remembered material interferes with memory for the to-be-remembered material. This phenomenon is usually studied using the RI design depicted in the top part of Table 5–6. Subjects first learn a list of paired associates usually designated the A-B list. Then the RI group learns a new list, termed the A-C list, because it consists of the same stimulus items as the first list but a new set of response items. Finally, following a retention interval, recall of the original A-B list is tested. The recall of the RI group on this final test is compared with that of a control group which differs only in that its members do not learn the A-C list; either they rest during that interval or they perform some unrelated task. Numerous studies have found that the RI group's recall of list A-B is inferior to that of the control.

The phenomenon of *proactive interference* or *proactive inhibition* (often abbreviated PI) refers to interference from material learned prior to learning of the to-be-remembered material. PI is studied using

TABLE 5–6. Designs to Study Two Different Kinds of Interference.

| | Retroactive Interference (RI) | | |
	Learn	Learn	Test
RI Group	A–B	A–C	A–B
Control Group	A–B		A–B

| | Proactive Interference (PI) | | |
	Learn	Learn	Test
PI Group	A–B	A–C	A–C
Control Group		A–C	A–C

the paradigm depicted at the bottom of Table 5–6. Subjects in the PI group first learn an A-B list. They then learn an A-C list, and following a retention interval, recall is tested on the A-C list. Their performance is compared with that of a control group that did not learn the A-B list. Numerous studies have revealed that the control group is more accurate than the PI group at recalling the A-C list, demonstrating the existence of PI.

Studies using the RI and PI paradigms have demonstrated unequivocally that old material interferes with memory for newly learned material (proactive inhibition) and new material interferes with memory for previously learned material (retroactive inhibition), so the phenomena of RI and PI have been well established.

Although the various versions of associative interference theories have differed from each other substantially, all have attempted to explain RI and PI in terms of automatic increases and decreases in the strength of associations. Thanks to the careful experimentation of the people who proposed these theories, it has become increasingly clear that none provides a completely satisfactory explanation of either RI or PI. For example, some associative interference theories (e.g., Melton & Irwin, 1940; Underwood, 1948) have assumed that a major cause of RI is the automatic unlearning or extinction of A-B associations during subsequent learning of the A-C list. This theory assumes, then, that the A-B associations are erased from memory by subsequent learning of the A-C list, and it predicts that even if memory for the A-B list were tested by recognition, RI would still be observed. Postman and Stark (1969) have demonstrated, however, that when memory of the A-B list is tested by recognition, no RI is found. That is, if the subject learned the pair 1-TUZ in the A-B list and then received the following test: "Pick which of the following four words was paired with 1: MIX, TUZ, ZEB, KUX?" he is equally accurate whether or not he has learned an A-C list in the interim. Apparently, then, the A-B pairs have not been unlearned, since the recognition test reveals they are still in memory.

Retrieval failure. It appears that most, if not all, forgetting from long-term memory is the result of failures to find information that is still stored there. To use the analogy of a library, it is not that the books have been removed from the library, but rather that they are still in the building but cannot be found. We refer to difficulties of finding information in memory as retrieval difficulties. In storage systems with very limited capacity, such as working memory, such retrieval difficulties should not be prevalent; one could examine the entire contents of the store in less than a second. However, retrieval difficulties are very likely to arise in storage systems so large that exhaustive examination of all the contents would be extremely time consuming.

Studies of long-term memory have revealed several kinds of evidence for the existence of retrieval difficulties. One phenomenon with which we are all familiar is the *tip-of-the-tongue* (TOT) phenomenon. This is experienced when you are sure that you know some fact but you cannot think of it at the moment. Several years ago Roger Brown and David McNeill (1966) made a systematic study of this phenomenon. They read a list of word definitions (e.g., "A navigational instrument used to determine the direction of the sun, moon, and stars at sea.") to college students, asking the students to try to report the word defined. Whenever any student reported being in a tip-of-the-tongue state, Brown and McNeill tried to determine just how much the person knew about the sought after word. They found that people in this state often could report the beginning letter of the word in question, the number of syllables, and the stressed syllable. Moreover, people who reported being in the TOT state were usually able to recognize the word when it was presented to them. The next time you encounter a TOT state in yourself or someone else, see if the person in this agonizing condition can report the above kinds of information.

Notice that the tip-of-the-tongue phenomenon suggests that we are able to judge that we know some material, even though we cannot report it. That such feelings of knowing are reliable was further confirmed by Hart (1967) in a series of studies in which he gave people a series of recall questions, similar to "trivia" kinds of questions. Whenever a person was unable to recall a particular answer, Hart asked him to rate how likely it was that he would be able to recognize the item. Finally, the subject was given a recognition test. Hart found that people were very accurate at predicting whether or not they would be able to recognize the answer. Thus, the TOT and feeling of knowing studies reveal not only that people suffer from retrieval difficulties, but that they are accurate at distinguishing a retrieval difficulty from a lack of knowledge.

Another kind of evidence for retrieval failures comes from studies in which cued and uncued recall are compared. Consider a study reported by Tulving and Pearlstone (1966). During acquisition the subjects were presented with a list consisting of blocks of words from given categories. Prior to each category block, the name of the category was listed, although subjects were told that they need not memorize the category name. Thus, the list words DOG, CAT, GIRAFFE, HORSE would be preceded by the category name ANIMAL. All subjects then received a free recall test. Half, the Uncued group, were presented with a blank piece of paper and asked to write down all the list items that they could remember. The remaining half of the subjects, the Cued group, were given the same instructions, except that in addition they were given a piece of paper containing the category names (e.g., ANIMAL). Not surprisingly, the Cued group recalled many more words than the Uncued group on this test. Of more interest, however, immediately following this recall all subjects were given a second recall trial, but this time all were given the category cues. On this second test the Cued group recalled as well as before, but in addition, the previously Uncued group recalled as many words as the group that had been Cued on both tests. Notice that the group of subjects who had previously received the Uncued test must have had more items stored than they were able to retrieve on the first test without the category name cues, providing additional evidence for retrieval failures.

Is information ever erased from long-term memory? Both research and introspection about daily experiences indicate that a great deal of forgetting from long-term memory can be attributed to retrieval failures. Indeed, some researchers have argued that once information is stored in long-term memory it is never erased, and thus, that all forgetting from long-term memory is due to retrieval failure. One such researcher, the neurosurgeon Penfield (1959), has electrically stimulated the brains of conscious patients who were undergoing surgery for the treatment of epilepsy. Penfield found that when certain parts of the brain were stimulated, these patients often reported vivid memories of events from their early childhood, events they said they'd not thought of for decades.

Penfield's findings are provocative, but they must be interpreted with caution. For one thing, it is difficult to verify whether the patient's reports are of events they actually experienced years before, or whether they are of events that the patient is unconsciously constructing at the time of electrical stimulation. Even if we assume that these are memories for previously experienced events, this does not imply that *all* previously stored memories are still present in long-term memory, only that *some* such memories are. Similarly, the fact that being hypnotized often leads people to recall many events from their childhood does not imply that all events that were stored in long-term memory are still there.

In fact, the question of whether or not all forgetting from long-term memory is due to retrieval failure can never be answered conclusively. We have just seen that one cannot *prove* the hypothesis, because even if you demonstrate that many past memories are still stored, the skeptic can always argue that at least some were erased. Furthermore, the hypothesis that information is never erased from long-term memory can, in principle, never be *disproven* either. In order to disprove the hypothesis you would have to demonstrate (1) that some information we will label *A* was once in long-term memory, but (2) that at some later time, *A* is no longer there. Demonstrating (1) is easy, since we need only establish that after some lengthy retention interval (such as several days) the person was able to produce *A* from memory. Since memory over such a long interval could not be attributed to recall from the other memory systems (such as sensory memory or working memory) we could infer that *A* was stored in long-term memory. The difficulty comes with (2). How can we prove that *A* is no longer in long-term memory? We have already seen abundant evidence for retrieval failures, so the fact that someone is unable to recall *A* does not mean that it has been erased. Even recognition and savings measures do not exhaust all the information that is stored. For example, people can sometimes recall information they could not recognize. And what we recognize on one day we may not recognize on another. In other words, it is always possible for the skeptic to argue that our failure to demonstrate memory for *A* is due to the insensitivity of our measure, not to the actual erasure of the information.

Given the fact that it will never be possible to prove that information is ever erased from the long-term memory, and given the abundant evidence that most forgetting is attributable to failures of retrieval, most contemporary theories of memory assume the following. Once stored in long-term memory, information remains there permanently, though it is often rendered irretrievable temporarily.

Encoding specificity. Many of the retrieval difficulties people encounter can be overcome by using appropriate retrieval cues. Sometimes these cues are presented by other people or by external events, as in the studies of cued recall in which the person who has failed to recall the word *dog* is given the cue *animal,* or when the sight of an old friend brings to mind some long-forgotten shared adventure. In *Remembrance of Things Past* Marcel Proust describes how tasting a little cake (*une petite madeleine*) brought to mind a seemingly forgotten childhood experience—another excellent example of the effectiveness of such externally provided retrieval cues.

At other times the person is able to jog his own memory with a skillfully chosen retrieval cue. For example, when an adult finds he has misplaced his keys, he often attempts to recall what he did with them by trying to reconstruct the events since the keys were last seen, hoping that this will bring to mind where he put them. In fact, young children do not generate effective retrieval cues of this sort spontaneously, so the ability to direct memory retrieval develops only gradually (e.g., Kobasigawa, 1977).

What, then, are the characteristics of a good retrieval cue? Tulving and Thomson (1973) proposed one answer to this question—the *encoding-specificity principle*. In their words (p. 369) this principle states that, "Specific encoding operations performed on what is perceived determine what is stored, and what is stored determines what retrieval cues are effective in providing access to what is stored." We have stressed the first half of this principle throughout the book. That is, we do not store away the stimulus itself, but rather some encoding or representation of it. Two people presented with identical stimuli, might store away very different encodings or representations of what happened, depending upon the way in which they interpreted the stimulus. We have not encountered the second half of the encoding-specificity principle before, however. It states that what determines the effectiveness of a retrieval cue is not the cue's relation to the to-be-remembered stimulus itself, but rather the cue's relation to the *representation* that the subject stored away. In other words, retrieval cues are most effective if they were encoded during initial storage of the to-be-remembered stimulus.

The encoding specificity principle will be clearest if we consider two kinds of evidence that support it. The first was reported by Thomson and Tulving (1970). They presented subjects with lists of words printed in capital letters. The subject was told that he should commit these words to memory since he would later be tested on them. Some of these words were accompanied by words printed in lower case letters. The subject was told that he need not remember the latter words, but that they should be used to help him commit the upper case words to memory. We will call these lower case words *cue words*. More specifically, during this acquisition phase some of the to-be-remembered words were accompanied by a cue word that was a high associate (e.g., hot-COLD), some were accompanied by low associate cues (e.g., blow-COLD), and some were accompanied by no cues at all (e.g., COLD). Thomson and Tulving tested recall for the to-be-remembered words in order to determine how effective the strong and weak associates were as recall cues. They considered a cue to be effective if it facilitated recall relative to a condition in which no cue at all was given during test. They found that a strong associate during testing (e.g., the cue *hot*) helped the subject to recall the word (e.g., COLD), regardless of whether the subject had been presented with hot-COLD or with COLD alone during acquisition of the list. However, presenting the strong associate at testing did not aid recall at all if the subject had originally studied the word with a weak associate (i.e., blow-COLD). In the latter case, only the low associate cue *blow* aided recall. Giving the cue *hot* led to no better performance than did providing no cue at all during the test phase!

This finding fits with the encoding-specificity principle, for it shows that what determines the effectiveness of a retrieval cue is not simply the relation between the to-be-recalled word and the cue (e.g., the fact that they are high associates of each other). Rather, what matters is the relation between the original encoding of the word and the encoding that the retrieval cue suggests.

This dependence between the conditions of encoding and retrieval is even more dramatically demonstrated in another kind of experiment reported by Tulving and Thomson (1973). There are three phases to this experiment. The first is an *acquisition phase* much like the preceding. That is, the subject is presented with a list of pairs, each containing one upper and one lower case word, and is instructed that he need only remember the upper case words, but that the lower case items might help him to commit the others to memory. Unlike the previous experiment, however, all the cue words are *weak* associates to the to-be-remembered words, e.g., blow-COLD. In the second phase of the experiment, called the *generation phase*, the subject is presented with a list of words that are *high* associates of the to-be-remembered words and is asked to write down words that the presented words bring to mind. For example, the subject would be presented with *hot* and asked to free-associate to that word by writing down any words that came to mind. As you would expect, almost everyone lists COLD to the stimulus *hot* during this generation phase. Finally, during the *recognition phase*, subjects are asked to look back over all the words they generated during the generation phase and circle those that they had learned during the acquisition phase. Thus, the subject should circle the word COLD, since he had experienced it during acquisition. Surprisingly, about 76% of the time, people fail to recognize acquisition words that they themselves have just generated.

Notice the similarity to the Thomson and Tulving findings in the previous experiment. Thomson and Tulving had shown that presenting a strong associate as a recall cue does not help if the person had encoded the to-be-recalled word in the context of a low associate. The present experiment makes the even stronger point that people often cannot even *recognize* a to-be-remembered word, *even when they have just produced and written the word themselves*, if they produced the word in the context of a strong associate, but studied it in the context of a weak associate. In fact, the last experiment provides a case in which recognition is actually poorer than recall. If people are presented with the original weak associate that they saw during acquisition (e.g., *blow*) they can recall the word, COLD about 63% of the time, whereas they are able to recognize the word in the context of a strong associate only about 24% of the time.

There have been many subsequent demonstrations of the encoding-specificity principle, all of which indicate the interdependence between encoding at acquisition and encoding at retrieval. One lesson to be derived from the encoding-specificity principle is that if you wish to maximize the likelihood that you will be able to remember something later, you had best encode the stimulus from a number of different viewpoints. You should try to relate it to other things you know, thereby setting up a variety of contexts, any of which if it later occurs, will bring to mind the to-be-remembered material. You might argue that you would be better off to determine the context in which you will later need to remember the stimulus and study it in that context only. The problem, however, is that for most important material, we can't predict all of the contexts in which we will need it. Therefore, the richer the connections to many potential retrieval cues, the more likely that you will be able to produce the material when you need it.

Elaborative rehearsal and retrieval difficulties. In our discussion of forgetting we have been stressing the importance of retrieval difficulties and we have shown that one important determinant of retrieval cue effectiveness is the extent to which the cue reinstates the context in which the sought after stimulus was encoded. These conclusions relate closely to our discussion of elaborative rehearsal. We found that if long-term recall is to be facilitated, it is not enough to engage simply in rote rehearsal. Rather, the individual must attempt to enrich the to-be-remembered material by relating it to what he already knows. The encoding-specificity principle suggests that such elaboration is so important because it greatly expands the number of kinds of retrieval cues that will later be effective in enabling recall. Thus the concepts of elaborative rehearsal and encoding-specificity are related closely.

APPLICATIONS TO STUDYING

It has probably occurred to you that, as a student, you have some of the same problems that faced the ancient Greek orators. You are frequently asked to commit large amounts of specific and ordered information to memory and then to produce that information when queried in various ways (e.g., multiple choice, essay, true-false, and other kinds of tests and papers). Of course, this requirement doesn't cease at the end of college or formal schooling, for virtually any job or hobby you undertake later in life will require committing new information (if only the names of acquaintances) to memory. Of course, unlike the Greek orators, you can write things down in readily available notebooks and look them up in books, but always having to rely on such external devices slows down your ability to get things done and can lead other people to believe (either correctly or incorrectly) that you don't know your job very well. An insurance agent who has to look up *everything* during a discussion with a potential client is not likely to engender confidence. Nor is he likely to sell the policy.

The insights provided by the research and theory we have discussed in this chapter should enable you to develop your skills for remembering. There are two different kinds of application I would like to bring to your attention. The first is that you will find it useful to master and practice frequently one or more of the mnemonic systems we discussed in this chapter. The one that will be most useful depends on your interests. For example, if you frequently need to learn dates or other arbitrary numbers—a task often confronted, for example, in history courses—you will find that the method of analytic substitutions makes such memorizing easier and more interesting.

On the other hand, a variation of the peg-word mnemonic called the *keyword technique* has proven helpful for learning the vocabulary of a foreign language (e.g., Raugh & Atkinson, 1975). Learning a vocabulary word using the keyword technique requires two steps. First, an acoustic link is formed in which you find some English word (assuming English is your native language) that *sounds like* the foreign word you are trying to learn. This English word is the keyword. In the second step, you generate in your mind a picture of the keyword's referent and the foreign word's referent *interacting* with each other. This is the imagery link.

For example, imagine that you wish to learn the Spanish word for DUCK which is PATO (pronounced *pot-o*). To form the acoustic link, you might choose the keyword POT. To form the imagery link you could picture a duck with his webbed feet stuck in a flower pot. Now, whenever you wish to recall the Spanish word for DUCK, you need only picture the duck, which will call to mind the interactive image and, hence, the word POT, which will then lead you to the Spanish word PATO. If, on the other hand, you were presented with the Spanish word PATO, you would go from it to the keyword POT, and from there to the image of the pot and the duck, and finally to the translation DUCK. As a second example, imagine that you wish to learn that CARTA (pronounced *car-ta*) is the Spanish word for LET-

TER. You could adopt CART as your keyword and then picture a letter perched in a shopping cart for your imagery link (example from Pressley, 1977).

This keyword technique may sound laborious, but in fact it is not at all difficult or time consuming to learn and use. It can be used by unpracticed college students (e.g., Atkinson & Raugh, 1975; Raugh & Atkinson, 1975) and even by second- and fifth-graders (Pressley, 1977) with dramatic results. In the Raugh and Atkinson study, for example, college students who used the technique were 88% correct on a vocabulary test, whereas students who did not use the technique were 28% correct after equivalent study time. Of course, you must choose your keywords carefully, but once you have done so, using this technique takes almost all of the misery out of memorizing a foreign language vocabulary. Try it!

The first application I suggest, then, is that you make it a habit to use one or more of the mnemonic systems we discussed. The second application is more general: when you are studying you should keep in mind the general characteristics of long-term remembering and forgetting introduced in this chapter. Three generalizations are particularly important. First, I remember from my undergraduate student days the frantic conversations that often took place a few minutes or hours before an examination. Students repeatedly asked each other "How many times did you get over the notes?" or "How many hours did you study?" As a professor, one of the most frequent laments I hear from students who have not done well on an examination is the statement, "but I studied for hours," or "but I went over both my book and my notes n times," where n is some number ranging from 3 through infinity.

The point of which this chapter should have made you aware, of course, is that the number of times you go over a set of notes or the number of hours you study is, within limits, irrelevant. It is possible to read over a set of notes passively without thinking about what they mean 100 times for eight consecutive hours, and still not remember them as well as someone who studied them thoughtfully for only an hour. The former is equivalent to maintenance rehearsal. While it will maintain severely limited amounts of information in working memory while you attend to it, maintenance rehearsal is of little, if any, use in facilitating long-term recall. Remember Tulving's subjects who read a list of 22 words aloud 6 times, yet subsequently learned the list no more rapidly than a group of control subjects who'd never seen the list before! The first principle to keep in mind, then, is that you should not aim for a certain number of repetitions or for a certain length of study time. What matters is the quality, not the quantity, of the effort you invest.

The second principle is that, for most studying, your goal should be to understand, not to memorize. There are, of course, some exceptions, such as learning a foreign language vocabulary, in which case you should attempt to apply one of the specialized mnemonic systems. In general, however, what usually happens is that if you work to understand the material, you remember it as a byproduct. This follows from the demonstrations we discussed earlier by Mandler and others which showed that the accuracy of memory is determined by the extent to which the individual imposes organization on the to-be-remembered material, not on whether or not he intends to commit the material to memory. Therefore, you should attempt to understand the material by outlining it, so that you can see how the parts relate to the wholes, and how theories relate to empirical observations. In essence, you should think as you study. Pose questions and try to anticipate the reading. Look for contradictions or for generalizations that the writer doesn't draw explicitly.

Third, keep in mind that many failures of long-term memory are retrieval difficulties, and that when you are studying you are attempting to build up paths for finding information. It is for this reason that organizing the material and relating it to what you already know is so important.

CHAPTER SUMMARY

We began our discussion of long-term memory by considering Ebbinghaus' pioneering studies of memory for nonsense syllables. Ebbinghaus reported a number of important phenomena, including the negatively accelerated forgetting function, and he introduced methodological innovations such as the nonsense syllable and the method of savings which are still used frequently. Nonetheless, since Ebbinghaus attempted to study memory in the absence of strategies for remembering, he ignored some of the most interesting aspects of human cognition. The important role strategies play in memory is particularly obvious when mnemonic systems developed over the centuries are examined. Both of the systems we examined in detail—the classical method of loci and the method of analytic substitutions—have at least two features in common. They force the would-be memorizer to think about the material to be remembered, and they involve using some scheme for organizing the material.

When we turned our attention to research on storing information in long-term memory, we found it important to distinguish among different measures of memory, including recall, recognition, and savings, since material which appears to be forgotten by one measure may not be when another measure is used. Although early information-processing theories assumed that holding an item in working memory by means of rote rehearsal was sufficient to enable long-term recall, this view has proven incorrect. It is necessary to distinguish between two very different kinds of rehearsal. The first, maintenance rehearsal, involves rote repetition of the material. Maintenance rehearsal keeps information in working memory, but does not contribute to long-term recall. Elaborative rehearsal, on the other hand, involves organizing the material and relating the to-be-remembered material to information already stored in long-term memory. Such elaborative rehearsal not only maintains material in working memory, but also enhances long-term recall. In fact, elaboration is equally effective whether or not the individual intends to memorize the material.

Long-term memory holds incredibly large amounts of information and most, if not all, forgetting from it is due to difficulties in finding or retrieving information, rather than to erasure. Cues which are either presented to the individual or produced by him at the time of attempted recall often help retrieval, and one important question concerns what characterizes an effective retrieval cue. The encoding-specificity principle states that the effectiveness of a retrieval cue depends upon the extent to which the retrieval cue reinstates the context in which the sought after stimulus was originally encoded.

It is likely, then, that elaborative rehearsal is critical for long-term recall because it leads the memorizer to establish a rich network of potential paths for later retrieval. Studying an item in isolation may lead to its being recorded in long-term memory, but since it leads to only minimal connections with other material, the item might never be found again. These characteristics of long-term remembering and forgetting have implications for study techniques, and some of these were outlined in the last section of the chapter.

SUGGESTED READING

There are a number of interesting sources on mnemonic systems. Norman's (1976) text is an excellent place to begin, particularly his Chapter 7 entitled "Mnemonics," as is Bower's (1970a) article in *American Scientist*. The history of mnemonic techniques published by the historian Yates is a book that no one should miss. If you wish to work more on improving your own mnemonic skills I suggest *The Memory Book* by Lorayne and Lucas, which is now available in paperback, the book *Improving your Memory* by the psychologist Laird Cermak, and the article "Improving Memory" by Bower.

Given the breadth of topics that might be subsumed under the current chapter title, I have of necessity ignored or considered only briefly some important topics. These include signal detection theories of recognition memory. Chapter 10 of Klatzky's text *Human Memory* contains an excellent introduction to such theories.

I have discussed the encoding-specificity principle in the text, but I did not indicate that there is considerable controversy between the proponents of that view and those who favor generation-recognition theories of retrieval. See, for example, the *Psychological Review* article by Flexser and Tulving (1978) and the comments on that article by Jones (1978) and Kintsch (1978).

I have given little attention to interference theory, despite its importance in the history of the study of memory, but Baddeley's (1976) text contains a clear presentation in Chapters 4 and 5. The topic of organization is of such central importance for the study of long-term memory that it bears further investigation. An excellent collection of papers is available in the book *Organization of Memory* edited by Tulving and Donaldson. Bower's 1970b article in *Cognitive Psychology* is also an important source.

The distinction between maintenance and elaborative rehearsal has some interesting implications for the effects of repetition in advertising. On this topic you might read articles by Bekerian and Baddeley (1980) and Thompson and Barnett (1981).

Long-Term Memory: The Structure of Knowledge

6

FOOD FOR THOUGHT

Take a few minutes now to try the memory task presented in Table 6–1. Instructions are included in the Table itself. *Do not read further until you have completed the test at the end of the Table.*

How many of the test sentences did you judge to be old? The correct answer is "none." All are different from the sentences you studied during the first phase. If you incorrectly "recognized" some of the test sentences, how can you account for this inaccuracy? In fact, large numbers of such false recognitions are the norm for this sort of task and this fact has played an important role in recent theories of long-term memory.

EPISODIC VERSUS SEMANTIC MEMORY

In 1972 Endel Tulving drew a distinction between two kinds of memory—episodic and semantic. Tulving defined *episodic memory* as memory for information that is associated with a particular time and/or place. Thus, episodic memories are often memories for personal experiences such as that you spent last Christmas in the Phillipines, that you saw an old friend at the airport, or that the answer to this exam question is on the upper left-hand corner of page 36 of the text. Notice that the studies of long-term memory we discussed in the last chapter all focused on episodic memory; the person was asked to commit to memory the fact that a particular word or sentence had occurred at a particular time and place (i.e., the list learned in the Psychology Laboratory). Indeed, studies of episodic memory had dominated the study of memory ever since Ebbinghaus' classic monograph discussed in the last chapter. In contrast, *semantic memory*, is knowledge of general concepts that are not specific to a particular time or place. As Tulving (1972, pp. 385,386) put it:

> Episodic memory receives and stores information about temporally dated episodes or events, and temporal-spatial relations among these

---

TABLE 6–1.

Sentence	Question
Acquisition sentences: Read each sentence, count to five, answer the question, go on to the next sentence.	
The girl broke the window on the porch.	Broke what?
The tree in the front yard shaded the man who was smoking his pipe.	Where?
The hill was steep.	What was?
The cat, running from the barking dog, jumped on the table.	From what?
The tree was tall.	Was what?
The old car climbed the hill.	What did?
The cat running from the dog jumped on the table.	Where?
The girl who lives next door broke the window on the porch.	Lives where?
The car pulled the trailer.	Did what?
The scared cat was running from the barking dog.	What was?
The girl lives next door.	Who does?
The tree shaded the man who was smoking his pipe.	What did?
The scared cat jumped on the table.	What did?
The girl who lives next door broke the large window.	Broke what?
The man was smoking his pipe.	Who was?
The old car climbed the steep hill	The what?
The large window was on the porch.	Where?
The tall tree was in the front yard.	What was?
The car pulling the trailer climbed the steep hill.	Did what?
The cat jumped on the table.	Where?
The tall tree in the front yard shaded the man.	Did what?
The car pulling the trailer climbed the hill.	Which car?
The dog was barking.	Was what?
The window was large.	What was?
STOP—Cover the preceding sentences. Now read each sentence below and decide if it is a sentence from the list given above.	
Test set. . . . How many are new?	
The car climbed the hill.	(old __, new __)
The girl who lives next door broke the window.	(old __, new __)
The old man who was smoking his pipe climbed the steep hill.	(old __, new __)
The tree was in the front yard.	(old __, new __)
The scared cat, running from the barking dog, jumped on the table.	(old __, new __)
The window was on the porch.	(old __, new __)
The barking dog jumped on the old car in the front yard.	(old __, new __)
The tree in the front yard shaded the man.	(old __, new __)
The cat was running from the dog.	(old __, new __)
The old car pulled the trailer.	(old __, new __)
The tall tree in the front yard shaded the old car.	(old __, new __)
The tall tree shaded the man who was smoking his pipe.	(old __, new __)

(continued on the next page)

TABLE 6–1. (continued)

Sentence	Question
The scared cat was running from the dog.	(old __, new __)
The old car, pulling the trailer, climbed the hill.	(old __, new __)
The girl who lives next door broke the large window on the porch.	(old __, new __)
The tall tree shaded the man.	(old __, new __)
The cat was running from the barking dog.	(old __, new __)
The car was old.	(old __, new __)
The girl broke the large window.	(old __, new __)
The scared cat ran from the barking dog that jumped on the table.	(old __, new __)
The scared cat, running from the dog, jumped on the table.	(old __, new __)
The old car pulling the trailer climbed the steep hill.	(old __, new __)
The girl broke the large window on the porch.	(old __, new __)
The scared cat which broke the window on the porch climbed the tree.	(old __, new __)
The tree shaded the man.	(old __, new __)
The car climbed the steep hill.	(old __, new __)
The girl broke the window.	(old __, new __)
The man who lives next door broke the large window on the porch.	(old __, new __)
The tall tree in the front yard shaded the man who was smoking his pipe.	(old __, new __)
The cat was scared.	(old __, new __)

STOP. Count the number of sentences judged "old." See
text for answer.

Taken from Jenkins, 1974. Copyright 1974 by the American Psychological Association. Reprinted by permission of the publisher and author.

events. . . . Semantic memory is the memory necessary for the use of language. It is a mental thesaurus, organized knowledge a person possesses about words and other verbal symbols, their meaning and referents, about relations among them, and about rules, formulas, and algorithms for the manipulation of these symbols, concepts, and relations.

Of course, the distinction between semantic and episodic memory is not always clearcut, since our general knowledge of concepts was gained through individual experiences that are often associated with a particular time and/or place. You should not think of episodic and semantic memory as being different memory systems in the sense that the sensory registers are distinct from working memory, for example. Rather, it is best to think of episodic and semantic memory as two kinds of information contained in long-term memory.

Ever since the late 1960's an increasing number of experimental psychologists have turned their energies from the study of episodic memory to that of semantic memory. This new emphasis is particularly important because it has brought the study of memory in closer contact with the study of language.

In this chapter we will focus on the kinds of theories which have been developed to account for the organization of knowledge in long-term memory. This chapter will form a link with earlier chapters in that the theories we will discuss attempt to encompass both episodic and semantic memory, even though they are usually called "semantic memory theories." This chapter will also form a link with later chapters, because in the Language section of the book we will elaborate on the theories proposed here to increase our understanding of how language is comprehended. The theories will be important for the Thinking section, too, for they offer insights on how memory and thinking are related.

CHARACTERISTICS OF LONG-TERM STORAGE TO BE EXPLAINED

The first detailed theory of semantic memory was not published until the late 1960's, but earlier studies and everyday experience suggested several characteristics of human memory which any theory should be able to explain. Let us consider three of these now.

The importance of meaning as a basis of organization. There are many kinds of evidence which suggest that meaning is the most important basis of organization in long-term memory. Some of the evidence comes from studies of episodic memory of the sort we considered in the previous chapter.

First, recall that the successful mnemonic techniques often involve relating the words or events to be remembered in some meaningful way. This suggests that the meaning provides a helpful clue for searching through memory. Second, studies of incidental memory revealed that semantic orienting tasks are the best facilitators of recall and recognition. Third, the studies of encoding specificity suggested that in episodic memory studies the subject stores information about the occurrence of a particular concept or meaning—not a word itself— since biasing a slightly different meaning at the time of recall or recognition greatly interferes with memory performance.

Fourth, when people are presented with a list of words to be remembered they tend to report semantically related words together (i.e., we observe categorical clustering). Seldom do adults reveal very much clustering based on the physical characteristics of the words themselves. That is, given a list which contained 50 words including ROBIN, SPARROW, BOBBIN, the person would be more likely to recall ROBIN and SPARROW near each other than ROBIN and BOBBIN. Apparently, then, when adults are given a list of words to remember, the meaning of the words is used spontaneously to organize the list.

A fifth kind of evidence for the importance of meaning as a basis for organization comes from studies of recognition memory for lists of words. Such studies of episodic memory usually reveal semantic confusions. That is, people often falsely recognize a word as having occurred in a list if that test word is semantically related to a word in the presentation list (e.g., Anisfeld & Knapp, 1968). For example, if you had been presented with a list of words that contained the item HAPPY, you would be more likely to falsely recognize the test item JOYFUL than either a semantically unrelated, physically dissimilar control word like PIGEON or an unrelated, but physically similar word like PAPPY. It appears that people store away the meaning of the to-be-remembered words, so semantically similar words are likely to be falsely recognized. It is of interest that such semantic confusions are less likely to occur in young children (Bach and Underwood, 1970).

Other kinds of evidence for the importance of meaning as a basis of organization of long-term memory come from studies that are more directly concerned with tapping the organization of material that the subject already knows, rather than with teaching the person lists. Consider *word association* studies, in which the person is simply presented with a series of words and asked, for each, to say the first word that comes to mind. Try those listed in Table 6–2.

Analyzing and explaining such free associations has fascinated a wide range of psychologists. Clinical psychologists often use such word associations to reveal the personality characteristics of individuals, but experimental psychologists have been more concerned with using word associations to reveal general properties of the organization of semantic memory. For present purposes the important fact is that such word associations are usually based on the meaning of the stimulus word, as opposed to the physical characteristics of the word

---

TABLE 6–2.   Free Word Associations.

For each word listed below, either write down or say the first word it brings to mind.

DOG
RUN
ROSE
PENCIL
LIBERTY
FOOD
LOVE
CHURCH

---

itself. Thus, given the word DOG you probably responded CAT or, perhaps, BARKS, not FOG or BOG. The only consistent exceptions to this rule are very young children and some individuals with brain damage who usually give response words that sound like the stimulus word.

The final evidence we will consider which suggests the importance of meaning comes from the results of studies which use the *lexical decision task*. The subject is presented with a series of letter strings, one such string at a time. For each string he is to release one of two buttons as quickly as possible—a button labeled *yes* if the string of letters (e.g., NURSE) is a word, and a button labeled *no* if the string of letters (e.g., NARSE) is not a word. Of course, there are few errors on such a simple task, and the measure of interest is the RT required for correct responses. For our purposes, we need only examine the pattern of results obtained on *yes* trials, i.e., trials on which the string of letters is, in fact, a word. As it happens, the meaning of the words influences the speed with which the response occurs. Most interestingly, if two semantically related words occur in sequence, the response to the second word occurs more rapidly than it would have if the two words were semantically unrelated (e.g., Meyer and Schvanveldt, 1971). For example, the fact that NURSE is a word can be reported faster if the previous string of letters was DOCTOR than if it was BUTTER. Apparently having just made a judgment about one word facilitates judgments about semantically related words, a phenomenon called *semantic priming*. On the other hand, judgments about physically similar words such as NURSE following PURSE are facilitated little if at all (Meyer, Schvanveldt, & Ruddy, 1974). The importance of meaning in this situation is particularly interesting because the subject was *not* asked to consider the meaning at all, only to make a decision about the lexical status of the tested string of letters. Nonetheless, meaning influences the speed with which the decision can be reported. Furthermore, at least some aspects of this facilitation seem to be unconscious and outside the control of the subject (e.g., Fischler, 1977). In fact, semantic priming occurs even when the first word of the pair is shown so briefly that the subject is unable to report it (Marcel & Patterson, 1978; Fowler, Wolford, Slade, & Tassinary, 1981).

All of the diverse observations we have just discussed indicate that the predominant basis of organization in long-term memory is meaning. This is not to say that meaning is the only possible basis of organization, for it is clear that you recall the physical characteristics of experiences. You are able to recognize faces and voices. Furthermore, the fact that you can label words and pictures implies that the physical features of the words and their referents are recorded in permanent memory. You can retrieve a word that sounds like CAT or a word that begins with B if asked to do so. Furthermore, Frost (1972) has demonstrated that if pictorial stimuli are presented in a free-recall task there is some clustering based on the visual features of the pictures as well as on the categories to which they belong. The point here is simply that the most salient basis of organization is meaning, and any theory of semantic memory should account for this fact.

Recall from long-term memory is abstractive and integrative.

Before going any further, please try the memory task described in Table 6–3.

The task you just experienced is a variation of one Jacqueline Sachs (1967) presented to her subjects in a classic study. Each college student heard a series of more than 20 passages, including the one you just read. Each paragraph had one critical sentence for which recognition memory was tested. In the passage you read, the critical sentence was "He sent a letter about it to Galileo, the great Italian scientist." After each passage one of four types of test sentence was presented. The subject was to judge whether or not the test sentence had occurred in the passage. Sometimes the test sentence was identical to the critical sentence, as is test item d in Table 6–3. Sometimes the test sentence was changed in meaning, as in example b. Sometimes an active critical sentence was changed to the passive form, as alternative c of the example, and sometimes the form of the test sentence was different though the meaning was the same as that of the critical sentence, as in example a of Table 6–3. In order to determine the effect of interpolated activity on the accuracy of recall, Sachs also varied the number of syllables that intervened between presentation of the critical sentence and presentation of the test sentence. Thus the test sentence occurred either 0, 80, or 160 syllables after the end of the critical sentence. (The paragraph you experienced in Table 6-3 contains 160 intervening syllables.)

Sachs found that subjects almost always detected a change in the meaning of the critical sentence, even when 160 syllables intervened between presentation and test. Thus, subjects almost never falsely recognized test sentences like example b. However, they only detected active/passive and formal changes when the test followed immediately after the critical sentence (with 0 intervening syllables). If testing was delayed for 80 or 160 syllables, subjects frequently "recognized" sentences such as a and c in the example.

These results suggest that people have detailed memory for the form of a sentence for only a very brief period after it has been heard. This detailed memory may reflect information residing in the auditory sensory store (Sachs' subjects listened to the passages) or in working memory. However, by the time 80 syllables have intervened, all that remains is memory for the meaning of the sentence.

TABLE 6–3.

Read the passage below at a comfortable pace, but without looking back. After you have finished reading, your memory for one of the sentences in the paragraph will be tested.

There is an interesting story about the telescope. In Holland, a man named Lippershey was an eye-glass maker. One day his children were playing with some lenses. They discovered that things seemed very close if two lenses were held about a foot apart. Lippershey began experimenting and his "spyglass" attracted much attention. He sent a letter about it to Galileo, the great Italian scientist. Galileo at once realized the importance of the discovery and set about to build an instrument of his own. He used an old organ pipe with one lens curved out and the other in. On the first clear night he pointed the glass toward the sky. He was amazed to find the empty dark spaces filled with brightly gleaming stars! Night after night Galileo climbed to a high tower, sweeping the sky with his telescope. One night he saw Jupiter, and to his great surprise discovered near it three bright stars, two to the east and one to the west. On the next night, however, all were to the west. A few nights later there were four little stars.

Now, without looking back, decide whether or not each of the following sentences occurred in the paragraph.

a. He sent Galileo, the great Italian scientist, a letter about it.
b. Galileo, the great Italian scientist, sent him a letter about it.
c. A letter about it was sent to Galileo, the great Italian scientist.
d. He sent a letter about it to Galileo, the great Italian scientist.

Check to see whether your answers were correct by referring back to the paragraph.

Sachs' (1967) study is one of a large number that have confirmed the conclusion suggested by everyday experience: when presented with prose passages people tend to remember the meaning or gist much more accurately than the form in which the sentences were presented. In fact, Sachs' study revealed that even when people know that they will be asked to detect changes in the form of a sentence, they still have difficulty doing so.

Not only do people abstract the meaning of individual sentences, but they integrate the information across sentences. In 1971 Bransford and Franks published the most well-known demonstration of this fact. Bransford and Franks constructed several complex ideas, including the following:

The ants in the kitchen ate the sweet jelly which was on the table.

Each complex idea was broken down into four simple ideas which could be expressed in four simple sentences. These sentences were called ONE'S, since each contained only one simple idea. Bransford and Franks also constructed TWO'S sentences by combining the ideas contained in pairs of the ONE'S sentences. THREE'S were constructed by combining the ideas in three of the ONE'S. The original complex idea sentence was termed a FOUR since it consisted of the combination of all four ONE'S. Table 6–4 demonstrates the ONE'S, TWO'S, THREE'S, and FOUR which made up one of the complex ideas.

Having constructed these stimuli, Bransford and Franks chose two of each of the ONE'S, TWO'S, and THREE'S from each of the complex idea sets and presented these to subjects in a fashion similar to that you experienced at the beginning of this chapter. Thus, subjects heard a series of sentences, and after each they were asked a simple question to make sure they had comprehended the meaning of the sentence. After this acquisition phase, Bransford and Franks tested recognition memory by presenting a list of test sentences from the idea sets they had generated. Some of these test sentences had been presented earlier (OLD sentences) and others had not (NEW sentences). For each sentence the subject was to decide whether or not he had experienced exactly that sentence during the acquisition phase, and in addition, to rate his confidence in the accuracy of his choice.

Bransford and Franks reported two important findings. First, subjects' recognition judgments were little affected by whether or not they had actually been presented with a sentence during acquisition. They were as likely to "recognize" a NEW sentence as an OLD one. You probably experienced this fact at the beginning of this chapter. This component of the Bransford and Franks results can be seen in

TABLE 6–4. Sentences for One Complex Idea in the Study by Bransford and Franks (1971).

FOUR: The ants in the kitchen ate the sweet jelly which was on the table.

THREE'S: The ants ate the sweet jelly which was on the table.
The ants in the kitchen ate the jelly which was on the table.
The ants in the kitchen ate the sweet jelly.

TWO'S: The ants in the kitchen ate the jelly.
The ants ate the sweet jelly.
The sweet jelly was on the table.
The ants ate the jelly which was on the table.

ONE'S: The ants were in the kitchen.
The jelly was on the table.
The jelly was sweet.
The ants ate the jelly.

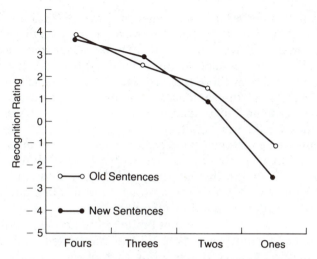

Figure 6–1. Results of Bransford and Franks' (1971)
study of semantic integration in memory. The
figure plots the mean recognition rating as a
function of the type of test sentence. Notice that
the functions for Old and New sentences are almost identical, indicating that subjects are just as
likely to "recognize" sentences they never saw
before as they are to recognize sentences that were
actually presented. (After Bransford & Franks,
1971. Copyright 1971 by Academic Press. Reprinted by permission.)

Figure 6–1 by comparing the recognition ratings for OLD and NEW
sentences; the functions are virtually identical.

The second important finding was that the likelihood of judging
a sentence to be OLD increased with the number of ideas it contained.
Regardless of whether the test sentences were OLD or NEW, ONE'S
were least likely to be judged OLD and FOUR'S most likely to be
judged OLD, while TWO'S and THREE'S were in between. This pattern of results, which Bransford and Franks termed the *linear effect*,
is also displayed in Figure 6–1. It is particularly striking that NEW
FOUR'S were more likely to be "recognized" (that is, judged to be
OLD) than were OLD THREE's, TWO'S, and ONE'S. Bransford and
Franks concluded that when people are presented with a series of sentences to be comprehended, they integrate the meanings of the various sentences to form a unified representation of each of the complex
ideas. This representation is stored in long-term memory. Then, when
the test sentences are presented, the subject compares them with this
abstract representation. The more similar the ideas conveyed in the
test sentence are to this abstraction the more likely the person is to

judge that he has experienced that sentence. Thus, ONE'S are least likely to be recognized because each represents only a small portion of the complex idea. FOUR'S are very likely to be recognized because they contain all the components of the complex idea. The fact that such integration occurs in the Bransford and Franks task is particularly impressive because the sentences presented during the acquisition phase were arranged in random order and the subject was not instructed to look for themes. The tendency to integrate such linguistic materials must be so strong that it occurs even under such nonoptimal conditions. In fact, similar studies with young children (e.g., Paris & Lindauer, 1977) and the elderly (e.g. Walsh & Baldwin, 1977) have indicated that this tendency to abstract out and integrate ideas begins very early in life and continues into old age.

Abstraction and integration are not limited to sentences and prose passages. Franks and Bransford (1971) have demonstrated similar results with geometric patterns. In designing each of these studies, the experimenters began with a prototype visual stimulus. See the example in Figure 6–2. This *prototype* was used to generate transformed visual patterns that differed from the prototype by different degrees. A subset of these deviations (but *not* the prototype itself) was presented during the acquisition phase. Then, during the test phase, subjects were asked to make judgments about a number of patterns, some of which they had previously seen and some which they had not. Franks and Bransford found that OLD patterns were no more likely to be recognized than NEW and that the more closely a test pattern matched the prototype, the more likely it was to be recognized. Thus, the prototype pattern itself was more likely to be "recognized" than any other, despite the fact that it was never displayed during the ac-

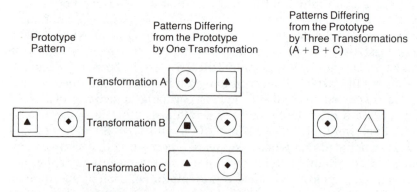

Figure 6–2. Sample stimuli from the Franks and Bransford (1971) study of the integration of visual patterns. (After Franks & Bransford, 1971. Copyright 1971 by the American Psychological Association. Reprinted by permission of the publisher and author.)

quisition phase. Just as in the case of sentences, subjects seem to have integrated the information across the various patterns presented to form some abstract representation of the prototype, and their recognition judgments were based on this abstract description.

We have noted in this section, then, that when people call on long-term memory, their judgments indicate that they have stored an abstract representation of experience. Details such as the form of individual sentences are lost and people remember the gist, or essence of meaning, of what has been experienced. Normal recollection from long-term memory often reveals omissions (e.g., of the form of individual sentences) and condensation (e.g., the meanings of a number of sentences or visual experiences are combined to form one condensed depiction of the meaning).

Recall from long-term memory is constructive. In 1932 Sir Frederic Bartlett published a volume entitled *Remembering* which reported a series of studies he had conducted almost two decades earlier. Barlett wanted to study memory for meaningful material (as opposed to the lists of nonsense syllables which Ebbinghaus had stressed), but like Ebbinghaus he wished to demonstrate that memory could be studied using the methods of experimental psychology. Bartlett presented his subjects with many different kinds of material including pictures, prose passages, and American Indian picture writing. He usually tested memory by the *method of serial reproduction*. That is, the subject would be asked to reproduce the material 15 minutes after presentation and then again (without additional presentations) at several longer intervals. In fact later tests occurred whenever Bartlett could induce the subject (frequently a friend) to attempt another recall. In at least one case Bartlett tested a person more than 6 years after the original presentation! Since each subject produced a series of reproductions of the original stimulus, Bartlett was able to study the nature of the progressive changes that occurred in individual subjects' depictions of the stimulus material.

Bartlett's most famous stimulus material was a North American folk tale entitled "The War of the Ghosts." The story itself is depicted in Table 6–5. Before you read further in this chapter, try reading through the story twice at your normal reading rate, as Bartlett's subjects did. Afterward, take a 15 minute study break and then, without looking back at the story, attempt to reproduce it in writing.

Compare the characteristics of your recall with the attempts of one of Bartlett's subjects depicted in Table 6–6. The most noticeable aspect of the reproductions Bartlett obtained reflects the characteristics of long-term memory we discussed in the previous section. There are many omissions of details (such as the names of the towns) resulting in increasingly condensed renderings of the story, and the word-

TABLE 6–5.

Read the following American Indian folk tale, take a 15 minute break, and then attempt to reproduce the story by writing it down from memory.

One night two young men from Egulac went down to the river to hunt seals, and while they were there it became foggy and calm. Then they heard war-cries, and they thought: "Maybe this is a war-party." They escaped to the shore, and hid behind a log. Now canoes came up, and they heard the noise of paddles, and saw one canoe coming up to them. There were five men in the canoe, and they said:

"What do you think? We wish to take you along. We are going up the river to make war on the people."

One of the young men said: "I have no arrows."

"Arrows are in the canoe," they said.

"I will not go along. I might be killed. My relatives do not know where I have gone. But you," he said turning to the other, "may go with them."

So one of the young men went, but the other returned home.

And the warriors went on up the river to a town on the other side of Kalama. The people came down to the water, and they began to fight, and many were killed. But presently the young man heard one of the warriors say: "Quick, let us go home: that Indian has been hit." Now he thought: "Oh, they are ghosts." He did not feel sick, but they said he had been shot.

So the canoes went back to Egulac, and the young man went ashore to his house, and made a fire. And he told everybody and said: "Behold I accompanied the ghosts, and we went to fight. Many of our fellows were killed, and many of those who attacked us were killed. They said I was hit, and I did not feel sick."

He told it all, and then he became quiet. When the sun rose he fell down. Something black came out of his mouth. His face became contorted. The people jumped up and cried.

He was dead.

Taken from Bartlett, 1932. Copyright 1932 by Cambridge University Press. Reprinted by permission.

ing of the reproductions is changed from the original, usually in the direction of modernization.

Even more interesting, however, are the *additions* that occur. For example, in both attempts at recalling the story included in Table 6–6 the person "recalls" that the war party tried to persuade the Indian to return with them after he had been wounded, whereas this fact was not contained in the original. Bartlett noted that many of these additions were rationalizations in that they rendered the story more coherent and rational than the original had been. For example, notice the way in which the protocols reported in Table 6–6 deal with the strange account of the ghosts. In the first reproduction the person "recalls" that the Indian only imagined seeing the ghosts and in the later recall, it is the villagers who imagine the ghost coming out of the mouth of the dying Indian. Such attempts to make sense of the story are seen

TABLE 6–6. Attempts by One of Bartlett's (1932) Subjects to Reproduce the "War of the Ghosts" Story.

First recall, attempted about 15 minutes after hearing the story:

Two young men from Egulac went out to hunt seals. They thought they heard war-cries, and a little later they heard the noise of the paddling of canoes. One of these canoes, in which there were five natives, came forward towards them. One of the natives shouted out: "Come with us: we are going to make war on some natives up the river." The two young men answered: "We have no arrows." "There are arrows in our canoes," came the reply. One of the young men then said: "My folk will not know where I have gone"; but, turning to the other, he said: "But you could go." So the one returned whilst the other joined the natives.

The party went up the river as far as a town opposite Kalama, where they got on land. The natives of that part came down to the river to meet them. There was some severe fighting, and many on both sides were slain. Then one of the natives that had made the expedition up the river shouted: "Let us return: the Indian has fallen." Then they endeavored to persuade the young man to return, telling him that he was sick, but he did not feel as if he were. Then he thought he saw ghosts all round him.

When they returned, the young man told all his friends of what had happened. He described how many had been slain on both sides.

It was nearly dawn when the young man became very ill; and at sunrise a black substance rushed out of his mouth, and the natives said one to another: "He is dead."

Second recall, attempted about 4 months later:

There were two men in a boat, sailing towards an island. When they approached the island, some natives came running towards them, and informed them that there was fighting going on on the island, and invited them to join. One said to the other: "You had better go. I cannot very well, because I have relatives expecting me, and they will not know what has become of me. But you have no one to expect you." So one accompanied the natives, but the other returned.

Here there is a part I can't remember. What I don't know is how the man got to the fight. However, anyhow the man was in the midst of the fighting, and was wounded. The natives endeavored to persuade the man to return, but he assured them that he had not been wounded.

I have an idea that his fighting won the admiration of the natives.

The wounded man ultimately fell unconscious. He was taken from the fighting by the natives.

Then, I think it is, the natives describe what happened, and they seem to have imagined seeing a ghost coming out of his mouth. Really it was a kind of materialisation of his breath. I know this phrase was not in the story, but that is the idea I have. Ultimately the man died at dawn the next day."

Taken from Bartlett, 1932. Copyright 1932 by Cambridge University Press. Reprinted by permission.

again and again in Bartlett's fascinating protocols, reflecting what he termed "an effort after meaning."

To explain his findings, Bartlett adopted the notion of a schema from the neurologist Sir Henry Head. According to Bartlett's definition, a *schema* is "an active organization of past reactions or past experiences." Bartlett argued that our knowledge consists of a set of schemata which are called into play in attempting to learn new material. If the new material conflicts with previously developed schemata, then the new material is often modified to fit the already existing schemata. Furthermore, at the time of recall, people do not simply "re-excite innumerable fixed, lifeless and fragmentary traces." (Bartlett, 1932, p. 213) Rather, Bartlett argues that people use what is retained of the original experience combined with the stored schemata to reconstruct a version of what they think they *must* have experienced.

Bartlett's findings, therefore, suggest that remembering is constructive. As C. S. Morgan (1917) put it, we fill in the lowlands of our memory with the highlands of our imaginations (cited in Loftus & Loftus, 1976). The importance of construction in memory is perhaps seen most clearly when people are asked questions such as the following: "What were you doing on Monday afternoon in the third week of September two years ago?"

Put your reading aside for a moment and try to answer that question. It is very unlikely that you will be able to answer it immediately, so don't just give up. Think about it for awhile, jotting down your thoughts as you work on it. After you have answered the question, or finally given up, compare your attempts with the protocol included in Table 6–7.

The illustrative protocol has a number of characteristics that are likely to be present in yours as well. The most important is that the person is not only calling upon remembered facts (such as that he was in high school in Pittsburgh), but also upon logical construction and inference. For example, in line 7, he does not seem to recall actually being in the chemistry lab, but he infers that since he had chemistry on Mondays and since this was a Monday, he *must* have been in the lab.

A second important characteristic of the protocol is that the person is turning what sounds like a rote memory question (i.e., "Where were you?") into a problem-solving task. That is, he seems to be breaking down the problem into a series of attempts. First, he uses the date to establish the general circumstances of his life at the queried time. These general characteristics are used to lead him to specifics. In fact, answering many questions from long-term memory seems to call upon such sophisticated strategies, demonstrating again the close relation between memory and thinking.

TABLE 6–7. A typical protocol produced when a person is asked the following question: WHAT WERE YOU DOING ON MONDAY AFTERNOON IN THE THIRD WEEK OF SEPTEMBER TWO YEARS AGO?

1. Come on. How should I know? (Experimenter: Just try it, anyhow.)
2. OK. Let's see: Two years ago. . . .
3. I would be in high school in Pittsburgh. . . .
4. That would be my senior year.
5. Third week in September—that's just after the summer—that would be the fall term. . . .
6. Let me see. I think I had chemistry lab on Mondays.
7. I don't know. I was probably in the chemistry lab. . . .
8. Wait a minute—that would be the second week of school. I remember he started off with the atomic table—a big, fancy chart. I thought he was crazy, trying to make us memorize that thing.
9. You know, I think I can remember sitting. . . .

Taken from Lindsay & Norman, 1977. Copyright 1977 by Academic Press. Reprinted by permission.

You probably were quite aware of the constructive nature of your recall as you went about answering the "September" question. In fact, in many daily situations you may find it quite easy to distinguish between what you remember and what you have constructed. Other times, however, you may find it hard to do so. Notice that the protocol in Table 6–7 contains at least one such questionable "memory" in Line 9. The subject "thinks" he can remember sitting, etc., but the "thinks" indicates that he is unsure whether he has recalled it or constructed it.

In fact, much of the construction in which we engage is unintentional, and we are often misled into thinking we remember something when, in fact, we have inferred that the event *must* have occurred. An experimental demonstration of this fact was reported by Bransford, Barclay, and Franks (1972) in an experiment on sentence memory. Subjects were presented with a list of unrelated sentences to be committed to memory. Later, memory was tested by presenting the subject with a series of test sentences and asking him to judge whether or not that sentence had been part of the to-be-memorized list. In fact, the sentences had been constructed very carefully to enable the experimenters to determine the extent to which subjects mistook material they had inferred, for material they had actually experienced. Consider Table 6–8 which depicts one sentence and how it might be presented and tested for two different subjects. For both Subjects A and B, the test sentence differs from the acquisition sentence in only one word. Therefore, for both subjects the correct response to the test sentence would be *no*. However, for Subject A, the acquisition sentence

TABLE 6–8.   Sample Sentences from the Bransford, Barclay, and Franks (1972) Study of Sentence Memory.

SUBJECT A:
> *Sentence Presented*
> Three turtles sat on a fallen log and a fish swam beneath them.
> *Sentence Tested*
> Three turtles sat on a fallen log and a fish swam beneath it.

SUBJECT B:
> *Sentence Presented*
> Three turtles sat beside a fallen log and a fish swam beneath them.
> *Sentence Tested*
> Three turtles sat beside a fallen log and a fish swam beneath it.

implies the test sentence to be true. That is, *if* the turtles are sitting on a log and a fish swims beneath them, *then* given what we know about spatial relations, we can infer that the fish must have swum beneath the log as well. On the other hand, the test sentence presented to Subject B is not implied by the acquisition sentence he heard. If turtles are sitting near a log and a fish swims beneath them, the fish did not necessarily swim beneath the log as well. Therefore, Bransford and his colleagues predicted that if people go beyond the information given to make inferences, and if they cannot distinguish these inferences from what was actually presented, then Subject A should be more likely to incorrectly recognize the test sentence than Subject B. This is exactly what happened. This finding is consistent with the general point of this section—that recall from memory is constructive—and it also indicates that people often have difficulty distinguishing between what they have inferred and what they experienced.

Implications for eyewitness testimony.   In general, the abstractive, integrative, and constructive characteristics of long-term memory are beneficial. We need not remember all the trivial experiences in our everyday lives. Instead, we can use our ability to reason to infer what must have happened. In fact, one of the main values of scientific theories is that they provide researchers and students with a way of organizing empirical facts and findings. For example, you need not memorize all of the conditions in which a partial report advantage is found and those in which it is not. Rather, you can simply remember that the pattern of results is consistent with the assumed sensory nature of iconic memory. I hope you have been putting theory to work in this fashion throughout your reading.

Nonetheless, our tendencies to abstract, integrate, and construct have drawbacks as well, for we often have difficulty distinguishing between what really happened and what we inferred. This fact has frightening implications for court cases in which the outcome relies heavily on the accounts of eyewitnesses. One of the first systematic investigations of the accuracy of eyewitness testimony was reported by Muensterburg (1908). Students in the Berlin classroom of the famous criminologist, Professor von Liszt, were listening to the lecture when a student shouted, "I wanted to throw light on the matter from the standpoint of Christian morality!" A second student shouted, "I cannot stand that!" The first replied "You have insulted me!" The second clenched his fist, shouting, "If you say another word . . ." at which point the first student pulled a gun out of his pocket and the second ran toward him. The Professor grasped the arm of the student with the gun and the gun went off. At this point, the Professor calmed his somewhat agitated class and asked them to write down exactly what they had observed.

Such highly realistic and emotionally charged demonstrations have been attempted more recently as well (e.g., Buckhout, 1974) with the added control that the entire episode was recorded on videotape as it happened, so that detailed comparisons could later be made between what actually happened and what the eyewitnesses reported.

As we would expect from the studies of Bartlett and Bransford, Barclay, and Franks, the "testimony" of the eyewitnesses was highly inaccurate in both studies. People omitted details and invented new "facts." Eyewitness reports of the same incident were vastly different. In the early study, Muensterburg found that the percentage of erroneous statements per witness was never lower than 26% and in some cases was as high as 80%. In the more recent study, people were asked to identify the perpetrator of the crime they witnessed. Only 40% were able to do so correctly. In fact, a full 25% "recognized" an innocent bystander as the criminal. The implications for the accuracy of identification from a police lineup are obvious and troublesome.

Some of the omissions and constructions which appear in eyewitness testimony are most likely the result of processing that occurs during initial perception and storage of the stimulus information. For example, in the chapter on Attention we noted how Titchener's Law of Prior Entry indicates that the direction of a person's attention during an episode might influence the order in which he perceives events to happen. Other distortions in recall are the result of processes that occur later when the information is retrieved. One particularly striking case of the latter is the use of leading questions, which are phrased so as to suggest the desired answer to an unsure witness. Loftus and Palmer (1974) have studied the influence of question wording on eyewitness answers. Subjects were shown a film of a traffic accident and then answered a series of questions about the incident. One half of the subjects were asked, "About how fast were the cars going when they hit each other?" while the others were asked, "About how fast were the cars going when they smashed into each other?" The subjects who were asked the second question ("smashed") gave higher estimates of the speed than those asked the first ("hit"). Since both groups saw exactly the same film and were asked the question only *after* the accident was over, the leading question must have influenced recall during retrieval rather than during initial storage of the experience.

Loftus and Palmer have demonstrated further, however, that such a leading question seems to change the nature of the subject's stored representation of the event as well. One week after the subjects had first been questioned about the accident, they were asked a series of questions without reviewing the film. Among these was the critical question, "Did you see any broken glass?" Subjects who had been asked the "smashed" question one week before were much more likely to answer "yes" than subjects who had been asked the "hit" question. These results suggest that the questions asked and/or the answers given during the first question session influenced the person's memory for the accident. During the later testing, the witnesses were unable to separate the original event from later alterations in the memory for that event which resulted from the questioning.

This discussion suggests, then, that eyewitness testimony must be used with great caution and that questions should be phrased in as neutral a fashion as possible. Even when people intend to be truthful, they often have difficulty distinguishing what actually happened from their interpretation of the event.

NETWORK THEORIES OF LONG-TERM MEMORY

Having discussed characteristics of long-term memory which theories of long-term memory must explain, it is now time to turn to the theories themselves. Since the late 1960's a number of semantic memory theories have been proposed. Though their emphases differ, they share the two broad goals of (1) specifying how long-term memory is structured or organized, and (2) specifying the processes which operate on this structure to enable such skills as memory storage and retrieval and language comprehension. In practice, these theories have often focused on the structures and processes that are called into play in *sentence verification* tasks, in which the subject is presented with a sentence (e.g., "All dogs are animals." or "A canary has fur.") and is asked to judge as rapidly as possible whether the sentence is true or false.

Though several kinds of semantic memory theories have been proposed, we will limit our discussion to so-called *network theories*. All network theories have several major features in common. The most important is that they assume the structure of long-term memory to consist of *a large set of nodes interconnected by relations.* Each *node* represents a concept and the *relations* which connect these nodes are special kinds of associations. Each node (i.e., concept) is defined by the network of relations attached to it.

The relations postulated by these theories differ from simple stimulus-response associations in two major ways. First, the relations are *labeled,* so there are different kinds of associations. Second, the relations are *directed* in that the direction in which an association is read influences its meaning. For example, as depicted in Figure 6–3, the nodes representing the concepts DOG and ANIMAL might be connected by an ISA relation, whereas the concepts for DOG and FUR might be connected by a HAS relation. The labels indicate that the association between DOG and ANIMAL is different in kind from that between DOG and FUR. Furthermore, the arrow on the association indicates that the label applies for that direction of the relation only. Thus, a dog is of necessity an animal, but an animal is not necessarily a dog. Similarly, a dog has fur, but fur does not have a dog. If the relation is read in the opposite direction from that indicated by the arrow the meaning is changed in a precise fashion. Thus, reading backwards, the relations indicate that one kind of an animal is a dog and one thing that has fur is a dog.

The second general characteristic of network theories is that *all assume that retrieving information from the memory network involves a search through the pathways (or relations), which leads the processor from one concept node to another.* The precise nature of the proposed processes varies from theory to theory, but for all, retrieval requires a "walk" through these hypothetical pathways of the mind.

A third characteristic is that *for all network theories, the nodes represent concepts, not words per se.* In referring to the nodes, we usually use the name associated with that node, but this is just for convenience of communication. The usual way of depicting the relation between a node and its name is to assume that there is a *mental dictionary* which stores the sounds and spelling for the words you know. Each of these dictionary units is connected by a NAME relation with one or more concept nodes in your memory. Consider the ex-

Figure 6–3. Examples of the labeled, directed links or relations postulated by network models of long-term memory. These links record A DOG IS AN ANIMAL AND A DOG HAS FUR.

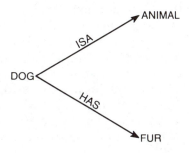

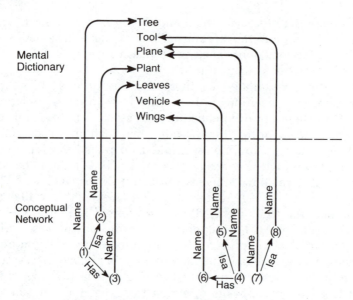

Figure 6–4. A depiction of how network models assume the mental dictionary and the conceptual network to be related. (The numbers are arbitrary in this and all later networks. They are included only so that I can refer you to specific nodes.)

ample in Figure 6–4. This depicts a mental dictionary containing the words TREE, PLANT, LEAVES, VEHICLE, WINGS, PLANE, and TOOL as well as *part of* the network structure defining the concepts associated with these words. Following the custom introduced by Rumelhart, Lindsay, and Norman (1972), numbered brackets in the semantic network are used to indicate the concept nodes. The numbers are arbitrary and are included here only so that I can refer to the figure.

Node 1 represents the concept that has the name TREE, whereas node 3 represents the concept named LEAVES, and the semantic network indicates that the two concepts are related by a "has" relation. It is important to realize that two different concepts (nodes) might share the same name, as in the case of homonyms (words with more than one meaning). Nodes 4 and 7 both have the name PLANE, but they stand for two different concepts. Node 4 represents the vehicle meaning of the word whereas node 7 represents the wood-working tool definition. Furthermore, though such an example is not shown, it would be possible to have concepts that have no NAME relation at all, since you have no name for them. Bower (1975) has suggested the example of "the person who stole my bike" as being a concept (i.e., a node) in his memory, for which he (unfortunately) has no name in his mental dictionary. Another possibility not illustrated in Figure 6–4 is that an individual concept might have two different names attached to it, if there are synonymous names for the concept.

You should examine Figure 6–4 very carefully, making sure that you understand it. For most of the rest of the book when networks are drawn, we will simply indicate the name of a node at the node itself, rather than drawing in the NAME links with the mental dictionary. This simplification makes the networks much easier to read. Nonetheless, you should always keep in mind that such networks are shorthand notations for the more complex networks shown in Figure 6–4.

A fourth general characteristic of all network models is that *they include some distinction between type and token nodes*. This distinction is critical if a semantic network is to be capable of representing both episodic and semantic information, and if it is to be capable of the sort of inference that is characteristic of human memory and language processing. To understand why, consider the kinds of information most of us have stored in memory. You might know that a dog is an animal who has legs, can bark, and so on (i.e., semantic memory). Furthermore, you may recall that one dog you knew was mean and spotty and another dog you knew had rabies.

In order to represent these diverse kinds of information in a network, theorists have come up with representations like the one in Figure 6–5. This figure distinguishes between type and token nodes. A *type* node is a definitional node which contains the definition of a concept. In our example it contains all the defining characteristics of dog, i.e., information that is, in general, true of all dogs. Hence the type node corresponds closely to the semantic memory component of long-term knowledge. There is assumed to be one and only one type node for each concept. In contrast, a *token* node represents a particular instance of the concept. Thus, there might be many token nodes for each concept. In Figure 6–5 there are two token nodes for DOG,

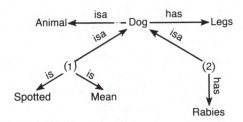

Figure 6–5. A network which demonstrates the distinction between type and token nodes. The node labeled "Dog" is a type node, whereas nodes (1) and (2) are token nodes.

one for each of the dogs the person recalls. Each token node has a pointer, i.e., a relation, with its type node, which indicates that the particular token node is an instance of (ISA) the general concept. Thus token nodes correspond to the episodic component of long-term recall.

The distinction between type and token nodes enables networks to represent the kind of information that is necessary for the sorts of inferences people make all the time. A person with the network depicted in Figure 6–5 has the information necessary to infer that the dog who was spotted and mean is an animal (since the node 1 concept is a member of the general class DOG and the general class DOG is an animal), but that the particular dog does not have rabies (since the token node 1 is *not* a subset of the token node 2).

In summary, all network theories of semantic memory share four general characteristics. (1) All depict the structure of long-term memory as consisting of a set of nodes interconnected by a set of labeled, directed relations. (2) All assume that retrieval from memory involves some form of search through the network. (3) All assume that nodes represent concepts, not words, so it is assumed that people can have concepts for which they have no names. (4) All distinguish between type and token nodes, in order to distinguish between semantic and episodic memories and to enable inference. Having considered these general shared features, we now turn to a consideration of two specific network models.

QUILLIAN'S TEACHABLE LANGUAGE COMPREHENDER (TLC)

In 1968 R. Quillian published a doctoral dissertation in which he proposed the first network model of semantic memory. His model, which was named TLC for the Teachable Language Comprehender, set an important precedent. Until this time most theorists had focused on explaining the processes involved in restricted laboratory tasks, such as the Peterson and Peterson short-term memory paradigm. Quillian instead set out to build a theory that would explain how people comprehend language. Furthermore, in order to test the sufficiency of his theory (i.e., to test whether or not it could in fact comprehend language) he wrote the theory in the form of a computer program. Quillian's TLC caught the interest of many cognitive psychologists for a couple of reasons. In the first place, his computer simulation was reasonably successful in that the theory was shown to be capable of some rudimentary language comprehension. This success suggested that TLC might be capturing some of the components of human language comprehension. Second, and of equal importance for memory theoreticians, he and Alan Collins (1969) showed that by making some simplifying assumptions, the theory made predictions that could be put to test by doing experiments.

Assumptions of TLC. TLC assumes that semantic memory is organized as depicted in Figure 6–6. According to TLC, each concept (i.e., node) is defined by two major kinds of relations: (1) a *superset relation* which specifies class membership, e.g., BIRD is a member of the class ANIMAL, and (2) one or more *property* relations, which define the properties of the concept, e.g., a BIRD can SING. (Of course, Figure 6–6 is greatly simplified, since like all network models, TLC incorporates a distinction between the mental dictionary and the semantic network, and between type and token nodes.)

As Figure 6–6 indicates, TLC assumes that semantic memory is structured in a logical, hierarchical fashion. That is, there is a logical nesting in which a category (such as CANARY) points to a higher level category of which it is a member (such as BIRD), which points to a still higher level category of which both are members (such as ANIMAL). Thus, the fact that a canary is an animal is not stored by

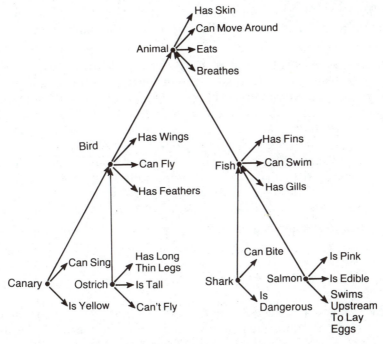

Figure 6–6. An illustration of the memory structure assumed by TLC. One part of the semantic network for animals is depicted. (After Collins & Quillian, 1969. Copyright 1969 by Academic Press. Reprinted by permission.)

one relation, but rather is stored indirectly by two relations, one between CANARY and BIRD and one between BIRD and ANIMAL.

Having specified the structures assumed by TLC, we turn now to its processes, since any theory of semantic memory must specify both. The most important process assumed by TLC is the *intersection search*. When comprehending a sentence, the network is contacted at all the concepts named in a particular sentence and a search then spreads out along *all* the paths from these concept nodes. This search is assumed to take place in parallel (i.e., to spread out along all the paths at the same time) and to have unlimited capacity (i.e., the rate of the search is not affected by the number of paths along which the search is spreading.) At each node reached by the intersection search, the processor leaves a marker or a tag indicating the node where the search originated. When an intersection is found, the path connecting the two originating nodes is checked.

Imagine that TLC is asked to verify the following sentence: "A canary is an animal." The intersection search will begin at CANARY and ANIMAL and will spread out along all relations from each of these nodes. Since the paths do intersect, TLC would use certain inference processes to determine whether the nature of the intersection indicates that the statement is true. In general, then, TLC verifies sentences by looking for and evaluating intersecting pathways.

Empirical predictions and findings of TLC. Collins and Quillian (1969) pointed out that if moving from one node to another is assumed to take time, then TLC will take longer to verify some kinds of sentences than others. If TLC is an accurate theory of how people go about verifying sentences, then people should show the same pattern of reaction times when they are asked to verify sentences. In particular, RT should increase as the number of nodes required to reach an intersection increases. Consider the following three sentences in light of the structure in Figure 6–6:

> S0: **A canary is a canary.**
>
> S1: **A canary is a bird.**
>
> S2: **A canary is an animal.**

According to TLC, people should verify sentence S0 faster than S1, since fewer relations must be traversed before an intersection is found in the case of S0. Similarly, S1 should take less time to verify than S2. A similar set of predictions can be made about the following three sentences:

P0: A canary is yellow.

P1: A canary can fly.

P2: A canary has skin.

P0 should be verified more rapidly than P1, which in turn should be verified more rapidly than P2.

Collins and Quillian tested these predictions by giving people a large number of sentences to verify, including an equal number of true and false sentences. Their results for the true sentences are shown in Figure 6–7. The figure indicates that the predictions of TLC were confirmed.

Criticisms of TLC.   Quillian's theory and the empirical research of Collins and Quillian generated research in many psychology laboratories across the country, and much of this research replicated and extended the findings we have just discussed. Nonetheless, some patterns did not, and it is three such findings to which we now turn.

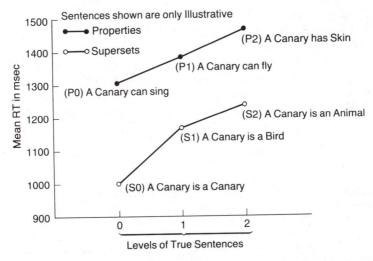

Figure 6–7. The results of Collins and Quillian's (1969) sentence verification experiment. The data depicted are for *true* responses only, showing mean RT as a function of the number of levels in the hierarchy that TLC assumes need to be searched. The sentences shown are only examples, since many sentences were used. Notice that RT increases systematically as the number of levels increases. (After Collins & Quillian, 1969. Copyright 1969 by Academic Press. Reprinted by permission.)

First, in some cases, class membership is judged more rapidly for superordinates than subordinates. Consider, for example, the following two sentences and attempt to verify each as rapidly as possible.

A dog is a mammal.

A dog is an animal.

The Collins and Quillian model would predict that you should be able to verify the "mammal" sentence faster than the "animal" sentence. This prediction follows from the assumption that the structure of memory consists of a set of logically nested concepts. In any logical nesting scheme, DOG would be nested within MAMMAL, which would in turn be nested within ANIMAL, so sentence 2 should require traversing two relations whereas sentence 1 should require only one. For the same reason, Collins and Quillian would predict that "A cantaloupe is a melon" would be verified more rapidly than "A cantaloupe is a fruit." As it turns out, however, these predictions are not upheld. In fact, people verify "A dog is an animal" faster than "A dog is a mammal," and they verify "A cantaloupe is a fruit" faster than "A cantaloupe is a melon" (Rips, Shoben, & Smith, 1973).

A second finding inconsistent with TLC is that *the typicality of category instances influences the speed of class membership judgments.* In order to understand this point it is necessary to consider typicality. Take a moment now to answer each of the three kinds of questions in Table 6–9. The answers to all of these kinds of questions yield very similar patterns of results (e.g., Battig & Montague, 1969; Rips, Shoben, & Smith, 1973; Rosch, 1975); they reveal that all mem-

---

TABLE 6–9.

Please answer each of the three kinds of questions below.

(1) Consider the meanings of the following word pairs. For each pair, indicate how similar the members of the pair are to each other, using a scale from 1 to 5 in which 1 indicates they are very dissimilar and 5 indicates they are very similar.

ANIMAL-HORSE
ANIMAL-ELK

(2) Allow yourself 30 seconds or so to list all the members you can think of for the category ANIMAL.

(3) Consider the following two instances of the category ANIMAL—ELK, HORSE. Which of these two would you judge to be the more representative animal?

---

bers of a category are *not* judged to be equally representative or equally *typical* of a category. People consistently judge some members to be more typical of the category than others. For question type 1 in Table 6–9, some members of a category are judged to be more similar to the category name than are others. For example, *horse* is judged to be more similar to *animal* than *elk* is to *animal*. Furthermore, when people are given the listing question (type 2 in the table), they tend to list first those cateogry members that other subjects had judged to be more similar to the category name (e.g., *horse* would be listed before *elk*). Finally, those examples of the category which people judge to be the "better" members of a category (Question type 3 in Table 6–9) are those likely to be listed first in response to Question 2 and to be judged similar to the category name in response to Question 1. The important point is that the RT required to verify category membership varies with the typicality of the category instance (e.g., Rosch, 1973, Wilkins, 1971;). For example, people verify the sentence "A horse is an animal" more rapidly than they verify "An elk is an animal." Notice that this effect of typicality would not be predicted by the Collins and Quillian model. Since all instances of a category are separated from the category node by the same number of levels, then RT should not vary with typicality according to the theory.

Third, *category-size effects occur in instances not predicted by Collins and Quillian's version of TLC.* A number of investigators (e.g., Landauer & Freedman, 1968; Landauer & Meyer, 1972; Meyer, 1970; Wilkins, 1971) have shown that the RT required to decide on class membership increases with the category size of the predicate concept. For example, subjects verify "A salmon is a fish" more quickly than "A salmon is an animal." In these two sentences, the predicate items are "fish" and "animal," respectively, and it is clear that the former category has fewer members than the second. Of course, TLC would predict this result in cases, such as the example, in which predicate size is varied by nesting the predicate categories. According to TLC, deciding that a salmon is a fish requires searching only one link, whereas deciding that a salmon is an animal would require that an additional link be traversed.

The problem for TLC, however, is that the category-size effect is obtained in two situations in which it is not predicted. For one thing, it occurs for false sentences as well as for true ones (e.g., Landauer & Freedman, 1968; Meyer, 1970). Thus, "A rose is a fish" is answered more quickly than "A rose is an animal." Furthermore, the category-size effect also occurs for nonwords (Meyer & Ellis, 1970). For example, if subjects are given a question such as "Is the following item a kind of fish?" followed by the test item "mafer," they will respond more quickly than if they had been asked "Is the following item a kind of animal?" Since the intersection search of TLC would never find an intersection in any of these cases, there is no ready way to explain these results within TLC.

TWO APPROACHES TO THEORIZING IN COGNITIVE PSYCHOLOGY

Let us step back and take stock of the last section, for we are now at an important choice point. We saw that Quillian's TLC theory had tremendous impact on cognitive psychology because it attempted, with some success, to specify how people comprehend language. Not only was the theory specified as a computer program so that its sufficiency could be determined, but, in addition, Collins and Quillian derived predictions from TLC so that some components of the theory could be tested through experimentation. Furthermore, one major prediction of the theory was upheld, for it was able to predict the pattern of RT's required to verify certain types of sentences. Nonetheless, in the latter part of the section we found that further experimentation has indicated that some of the detailed predictions of the theory are not upheld.

In short, then, we have a theory that seemed promising initially, but has now been shown to be inaccurate in at least some details. Of course, this sort of situation is one which every theoretician in every science confronts frequently, and the question that must always be asked is, "Where should I go from here?" The answer to this question has proven particularly elusive for those who would build theories of semantic memory, because the theories are so complex. Notice, for example, that TLC specifies not only a structure of long-term memory, but also a set of processes, including the intersection search and others. When the theory as stated originally cannot handle a particular pattern of findings, then it is difficult to decide which part (or parts) of the theory should be changed. Is the problem with the structure (and, if so, exactly what aspects of the structure) or with the processes (and, if so, exactly which processes should be changed)?

Faced with this dilemma, semantic memory theoreticians have taken one of two general directions. One group of theorists has argued that the best answer is to throw away TLC entirely, and indeed, to discard the whole network concept and to build instead a different kind of theory designed to account for the findings we discussed in the last section. Some such alternative theories are the set-theoretic model of Meyer (1970), the semantic-feature model of Smith, Shoben, and Rips (1974), and the category-search model of Landauer and Freedman (1968).

Each of these theories is able to account for at least some of the findings that were not consistent with Collins and Quillian's predictions from TLC. Nonetheless, they have done so at considerable cost, since these theories are much more restricted in scope than TLC and other network models. For example, these theories are designed to account for the patterns of results obtained in sentence verification studies, but none attempts to encompass more general aspects of language comprehension. Furthermore, since the theories are not written in the form of computer simulation programs it has been difficult to test their sufficiency, i.e., to see if the set of assumptions contained in the theories would be sufficient to actually answer sentence verification problems.

A second group of theoreticians has taken a different route, for they have chosen to maintain the network approach, but to alter the specific assumptions of the TLC theory (e.g., Collins & Loftus, 1975; Anderson & Bower, 1973; Anderson, 1976; Rumelhart, Lindsay, & Norman, 1972; Norman, Rumelhart, et al., 1975). For example, they have altered the assumption of a rigid, hierarchical structure that is logically nested, or they have changed the nature of the intersection search or decision processes. As we will see later in this section and in the chapters on language, a number of these newer network theories have met with some success in that they are capable of simulating some aspects of language processing (thus demonstrating their sufficiency) and they are able to account for most of the results that TLC had not predicted. Unfortunately, however, they have drawbacks as well, the most troublesome being that the theories are so general and so complex that we have no means for deciding among them.

The two different directions semantic memory theoreticians have adopted are important, for they represent the conflicting sides of a general debate regarding how best we can investigate the mind scientifically. Since we will see the influence of this debate again and again throughout the rest of the book, it is worth contrasting these two different approaches in a little more detail. Recently Laurence Miller (1978) of Harvard University suggested that these approaches be termed the Theory Demonstration versus the Theory Development approaches to cognitive science.

Theory Demonstration. Theorists who adopt this approach, according to Miller, attempt to design theories, usually stated in words, that will *explain performance in a particular task* or that will account for a *relatively limited aspect* of cognition. For example, the semantic memory theorists who abandoned the network concept and attempted to design theories of more limited scope to account for the pattern of RT's and errors obtained in the sentence verification task are representative of the Theory Demonstration view. Theorists who adopt this approach usually stress *parsimony,* in that they are concerned with proposing theories that make as few assumptions as possible. Furthermore, they design theories that lead directly to *experimental test*. That is, they expect their theories to generate predictions which enable each theory to be compared with opposing theories in the hope that through experimentation they will be able to decide upon the *unique* theory that is correct.

As these theoreticians view the world, the scientific endeavor works in the following manner. A particular aspect of cognitive processing would be investigated by proposing several theories all of which make predictions about experimental results. A period of experimental testing should follow in which these predictions are tested, and the correct theory identified. This process should be repeated for all the various aspects of cognition, and eventually all these mini-theories will be incorporated to form an overall theory of human cognition.

This Theory Demonstration approach is characteristic of most of experimental psychology and, in fact, of most of the work we have considered so far in our explorations of human memory. Miller's term *Theory Demonstration* derives from the fact that the emphasis of this approach is on *demonstrating* which of a number of competing theories is correct through the use of experimental tests. Such theorists believe that we already have too many theories in psychology and what we need are ways of eliminating those which are incorrect.

Theory Development. Theorists who take this approach, on the other hand, attempt to design theories, often in the form of computer programs, that will *explain wide-ranging aspects of cognition*, such as the understanding of language or general problem-solving strategies. Rather than emphasizing parsimony, such theorists are likely to stress *sufficiency* as a measure of the worth of a theory. That is, given the choice between two theories, they will emphasize that the important criterion for choosing among them is the question of which is sufficient to simulate the ability of interest. The developers of most network theories of semantic memory belong to this camp, and we find them concerned with whether the memory system and the processes proposed by a theory would be sufficient to actually remember and comprehend language. Since the emphasis is on sufficiency, such theories are not usually designed with experimental tests in mind. Rather, such theorists try first to develop theories that are sufficient. They believe that once such sufficiency has been determined, *then* we should turn our attention to the attempt to design experiments to test among two or more such sufficient theories. In the view of such theorists, if a theory is not sufficient, then whether or not it can predict the results of an experiment or two is of little consequence. Furthermore, unlike the Theory Demonstration approach, theorists of this camp tend not to be too upset if two theories exist for the same phenomenon. That is, they do not view the formulation of unique theories as essential.

Until high-speed computers made simulation of complex theories possible, the Theory Development approach was not feasible for scientific investigation. That is, if one wishes to argue that the major criterion for assessing a theory is whether or not its assumptions are sufficient to simulate the phenomenon of interest, then if the theory is to be tested, one must be able to have some way of assessing such sufficiency. However, as the complexity of the assumptions increases, it becomes more and more difficult for a human to work out the predictions of the theory by hand. Therefore, it is usually difficult to test the sufficiency of a theory of language comprehension, for example, unless the computer is used to simulate the theory.

Theory Demonstration versus Theory Development. Of course, both approaches have important points in common. Both emphasize the importance of theories and both are concerned with developing rigorous ways of testing theories of cognition, though they stress different techniques for testing (experimentation vs. simulation) and different criteria for judging the worth of a theory (parsimony vs. sufficiency). Furthermore, both have the goal of building theories which will eventually explain broad aspects of human cognition, though they differ regarding the order in which they believe such theorizing must proceed. The Theory Demonstration approach stresses the construction of mini-theories which will be combined to form higher-level theories, but the Theory Development approach stresses the development of global theories from the beginning.

The debate is a heated one and promises to continue in this vein. On the one hand, the Theory Demonstration theorists argue that computer simulation theories do not make enough contact with experiments and that these theories are so general that it is only possible to test small parts of them at a time. In fact, we saw the difficulty theorists encountered when some of the predictions of TLC failed to be upheld. On the other hand, the Theory Development theorists argue that Theory Demonstration attempts to do the impossible, that it will never be possible to build a general theory which will account for all of cognition by building theories to account for performance in isolated tasks. They argue that if we attempt to do so, we get lost in the details of experiments, and the performance observed in such experiments. Hence the theories developed to account for the performance may make little contact with daily cognitive activities.

Professor John Anderson has adopted a compromise between these two approaches in the hope of calling on the strengths of each. We will now consider the theory he has proposed in some detail, not only because it promises to become an influential theory of semantic memory, but also because it introduces a number of concepts that will provide a framework for thinking about both the kinds of episodic memory we talked about in the earlier chapters and about language and problem solving—topics that will occupy our attention for most of the rest of the book.

ANDERSON'S ACT THEORY

John R. Anderson, who is now at Carnegie-Mellon University, introduced his theory called ACT in a book entitled *Language, Memory, and Thought*. His goal was to develop a theory of long-term memory which would explain the structures and processes that underlie memory, inferential reasoning, language comprehension, and language acquisition. The ACT theory is specified in a set of assumptions which we will outline, but in addition Anderson has written computer programs to simulate individual parts of the theory to check for its sufficiency and internal consistency (i.e., to see if the parts work together).

A fundamental distinction in ACT is that between *declarative knowledge*, i.e., *knowing that*, and *procedural knowledge*, i.e., *knowing how*.

Declarative knowledge. Like TLC, ACT represents declarative knowledge as a conceptual network of nodes interconnected by labeled, directed links. In ACT, however, the central structure in long-term memory is the *proposition*. By definition, a proposition has three characteristics. First, it is *abstract*, in that it stands for an idea rather than a specific set of words or images. Second, a proposition is *rule-governed*, in that it must be constructed in keeping with a set of rules. Third, a proposition *can be assigned a truth value*.

In ACT a proposition *always* consists of a subject link (labeled S) and a predicate link (labeled P). Examples which illustrate the general form of ACT's propositions are displayed in Figure 6–8. The node at the peak of each representation is the *root node* and it stands for the proposition as a whole. Thus, the proposition takes the node (i.e., concept) pointed to by the predicate link and predicates it of the node pointed to by the subject link. For example, Figure 6–8a stands for the proposition "canaries are yellow," 6–8b for the proposition "Caesar is dead," 6–8c for the proposition "a dog is an animal." It will be helpful to keep in mind that a proposition states that the node pointed to by the subject link is a subset of the node pointed to by the predicate link. Thus, canaries form a subset of yellow things, Caesar is a subset (with one member) of the things that are dead, and the set of dogs is a subset of the set of animals

It is possible to *qualify* propositions and parts of complex prop-

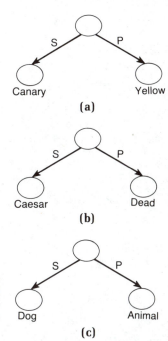

(a)

(b)

Figure 6–8. Illustrations of how propositions are depicted in ACT. These structures stand for: (a) CANARIES ARE YELLOW, (b) CAESAR IS DEAD, and (c) A DOG IS AN ANIMAL.

(c)

ositions. For example, it is possible to record that a proposition is true, or false, or fortunate. This ability to qualify propositions is necessary because ACT assumes that once a memory structure is formed in long-term memory, it is never erased. Imagine that you recorded in memory the proposition that an exam was easy. ACT assumes that your memory would represent that proposition as depicted in Figure 6–9a. Later, you store away the proposition that it is fortunate that the exam was easy (perhaps because you hadn't studied very much). ACT assumes that in order to represent this qualification, the original prop-

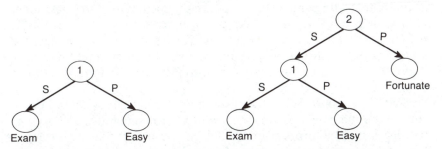

Figure 6–9. An illustration of how propositions can be qualified in ACT. (1) stands for THE EXAM WAS EASY, and (2) for IT IS FORTUNATE THAT THE EXAM WAS EASY.

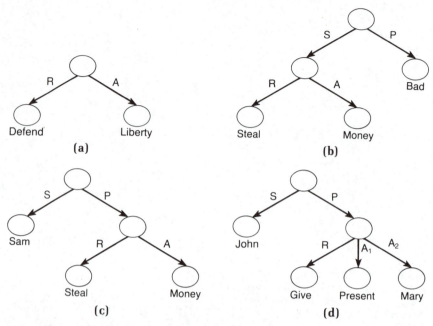

Figure 6–10. Illustrations of ACT's Relation-Argument structure. These structures depict: (a) DEFENDERS OF LIBERTY, (b) STEALING MONEY IS BAD, (c) SAM STEALS MONEY, and (d) JOHN GAVE MARY A PRESENT.

osition would be made the subject of a new proposition which points to the predicate FORTUNATE, as depicted in Figure 6–9b. Thus node 2 stands for the proposition "that the exam was easy is fortunate."

A second kind of structure in ACT is the *relation-argument* structure which enables concepts to be defined relationally. Consider, for example, the structures illustrated in Figure 6–10. The structure in Figure 6–10a stands for the concept "defenders of liberty."Relation-argument structures can form part of the subject of a proposition such as in Figure 6–10b which stands for the proposition that to steal money is bad, or part of the predicate of a proposition as in Figure 6–10c which stands for the proposition that Sam is a stealer of money. Relation-argument structures can have more than one argument as in Figure 6–10d, which represents the proposition that John gave Mary a present.

ACT can represent both episodic and semantic memory. For example, the meanings of concepts which form semantic memory can be represented as propositions, such as those depicted in the lower half of Figure 6–11. The propositions depicted here include (1) the proposition that canaries are a subset of the things that are yellow, (2) the proposition that canaries form a subset of birds, and (3) the proposition that canaries form a subset of the things for whom it is possible to fly (the qualifier POSSIBLE is included here because birds are not always flying). Recall from our earlier discussion of network theories that what we have just described is the *definitional* or *type* node for CANARY, i.e., it defines the concept.

ACT can also represent episodic memory by connecting token nodes (representing specific instances of the concept) to the definitional nodes through the proposition structure, in which the secondary node forms the subject and the primary definitional node forms the predicate. An example of an episode that might be stored in episodic memory is depicted in the top part of Figure 6-11. The episode has three propositions. The main one (4) indicates that a canary escaped from a cage. Two additional propositions indicate the time

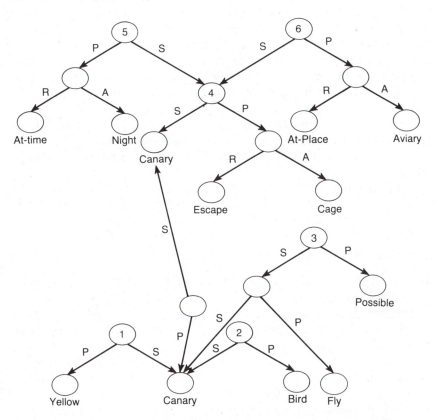

Figure 6–11. An illustration of how episodic and semantic memory are assumed to be related in ACT. The lower part of the figure represents the type node for the concept named *canary*. The upper part of the figure depicts a token node for *canary* (i.e., one particular canary) and an event in which it participates (i.e., escaping from its cage in the aviary at night).

(Proposition 5) and the place (Proposition 6) at which this event occurred.

In order to understand how the structure you have just learned is used and how it interacts with procedural knowledge, we must consider five additional assumptions ACT makes about declarative knowledge. First, the *strength* assumption is that each link coming out of a node has a certain strength, so some links will be stronger than others. The strength of a newly formed link is low, but is incremented each time the link is used.

Second, the *activation* assumption is that at any instant a small portion of the nodes in long-term memory are in an active state; all other nodes are not. Third, the *spread of activation* assumption states that activation spreads out from an active node to the passive nodes to which it is linked. It may help to think of this as a kind of domino effect. Furthermore, the stronger the link between two nodes, the more likely it is that the activation will spread along that link. This assumption about the spread of activation is similar to that proposed by TLC, but an important difference between TLC and ACT is that ACT assumes that the spread of activation has a limited capacity. That is, the more links that are being activated at once, the less activation will spread to any one.

Fourth, the *dampening* assumption is that periodically activation is dampened throughout the network, i.e., all nodes and links are deactivated. This is very similar to the notion of decay, since dampening is assumed to occur as a function of time.

Fifth, the *active list* asumption is that a maximum of 10 nodes can be kept on what is termed the Active List. This Active List is really ACT's working memory, which is assumed to contain 10 slots. Nodes that are on this limited capacity Active List are *not* dampened and they remain active as long as they are kept on the list.

Procedural knowledge. ACT's how-to knowledge consists of a *production system*, which is a set of productions. Each *production* has two parts: (1) a *condition* which specifies a set of features that must be true of memory, and (2) an *action* which specifies a sequence of changes which should be made to memory if the condition has been met. Thus, a production is an if-then pair; *if* a particular condition exists in memory, *then* perform the specified action. A *production system* is a set of such if-then, or condition-action pairs.

It is possible to write production systems which perform a wide range of tasks. In fact, production systems are playing an increasingly central role in theorizing about cognition, because they have proven useful for analyzing the sets of rules that underlie human language comprehension and problem solving. Production systems will come up again in later sections of the book, so you should understand some general characteristics of such systems. Consider the simple production system for crossing the street which is illustrated in Table 6-10. This table displays the form in which production systems are depicted. For each production in the system, the condition is written on the left side and the action on the right, with an arrow connecting them.

This example illustrates two characteristics of production systems that make them useful for theorizing about cognitive processes. First, the conditions of productions can refer to both external stimulus conditions that have just been registered in memory (e.g., just having perceived a red light) and to internal goals or states of mind (e.g., wishing to cross the street). In this example, the latter are indicated by assuming that the person has a memory location called STATE which contains a record of the person's current goal state. Since human thoughts and actions are a joint function of external stimuli and internal mental states, this first characteristic of production systems is necessary if they are to be useful for psychological theorizing. People do not always cross the street upon seeing a green light; they do so (under most conditions, at least) only if they wish to get to the other side.

A second characteristic of production systems is that the actions can be overt actions (such as walking) or covert mental actions (such as changing a goal state). In Production 2 of our example, seeing the green light when he has the goal of crossing the street leads the individual to take two actions, walking and then changing his current goal. This characteristic is also essential if production systems are to be used as models of thought processes, for people change their goals and these goals influence patterns of thought and behavior.

Now that you are familiar with production systems, we can complete our description of ACT's major assumptions. We have already listed five assumptions concerning declarative knowledge and we will now add two more concerning procedural knowledge. The sixth assumption is that *each production has some strength* associated with it. The strength of a production is assumed to be incremented every

TABLE 6–10. Production System for Crossing the Street.

Production Number	Condition		Action
P1	IF light is red AND (STATE = want to cross street)	$\longrightarrow$	Wait
P2	IF light is green AND (STATE = want to cross street)	$\longrightarrow$	Walk across street AND change STATE to (STATE = finished)

time the production is executed. Therefore, newly formed productions are of necessity weak (since they haven't been executed very much), but each time they are used they become stronger and stronger.

The seventh assumption concerns *how productions are chosen for execution*. The conditions of all productions are compared with active memory to see if their conditions are met, with the stronger productions being compared with active memory more quickly than the weaker productions. If the condition of a production is met, then it is executed (i.e., its action carried out). It is important that only the active portion of memory is compared to the production conditions, for this means that a production will be executed *only* if its condition is currently matched in the *active* portion of memory. Notice that this is ACT's way of focusing attention.

Summary of ACT's assumptions. All seven of these assumptions are listed in Table 6–11 for easy reference. Notice how ACT is related to the overview model we have been developing. ACT assumes that long-term memory contains two kinds of knowledge, declarative and procedural knowledge. Declarative knowledge consists of

TABLE 6–11. Assumptions of Anderson's ACT Theory.

Declarative Knowledge
1. Strength Assumption: Each link has a specified strength, and the strength of a newly formed link is low, but is incremented every time the link is used.
2. Activation Assumption: At any instant a small portion of the nodes in long-term memory are in an active state; all other nodes are not.
3. Spread of Activation Assumption: Activation spreads out from an active node to the passive nodes to which it is linked. The stronger the link between two nodes, the more likely it is that the activation will spread along that link. The spread of activation has a limited capacity, in that the more links that are being activated at once, the less activation will spread to any one.
4. Dampening Assumption: Periodically activation is dampened throughout the network, i.e., all nodes and links are deactivated.
5. Active List Assumption: A maximum of 10 nodes can be kept on the Active List (ACT's working memory). Nodes on this Active List are not dampened, so they remain active as long as they are kept on the list.

Procedural Knowledge
6. Strength Assumption: Each production has some strength associated with it, and the strength of a production is incremented everytime the production is executed.
7. Choice Assumption: The conditions of all productions are compared with active memory to see if their conditions are met. The stronger productions are compared with active memory more quickly than the weaker productions. If the condition of a production is met, then it is carried out.

a propositional network, only a small part of which is active at any one time. Part of this active portion of memory is in ACT's working memory (called the ACTIVE LIST), but the rest results from the spread of activation which occurs for a certain length of time before being dampened (a process similar to decaying). This spread of activation has limited capacity in that the more links being activated at any one time, the slower the spread will occur.

Procedural knowledge consists of a set of productions which specify what should be done if a given set of conditions become active. Thus ACT's productions represent the strategies the person has stored in long-term memory, strategies for remembering, for thinking, and for understanding and producing language. Some of these productions vary among persons depending upon individual experience, but others might be innate for all individuals.

An experimental test of ACT. Recall that Anderson wished to develop a network theory that would lead to empirically testable predictions. In his book he reported a number of experiments designed to test the theory, but we will consider only an experiment on fact retrieval. Anderson constructed sentences of the following general form: "A (person) is in the (location)." Examples are shown in the left column of Table 6–12. In the preliminary phases of the experiment, subjects were to learn the facts contained in the set of sentences, though they need not memorize the sentences verbatim. Then there was a study-test phase in which Anderson presented the subjects with questions such as, "Who is in the park?" or "Where are the hippies?"

TABLE 6–12. Examples of the Sentences Used in Anderson's Fact Retrieval Experiment.

Subject Studies	True Test Sentences
1. A hippie is in the park.	3-3 A hippie is in the park.
2. A hippie is in the church.	1-1 A lawyer is in the cave.
3. A hippie is in the bank.	1-2 A debutante is in the bank.
4. A captain is in the park.	
5. A captain is in the church.	**False Test Sentences**
6. A debutante is in the bank.	
7. A fireman is in the park.	3-1 A hippie is in the cave.
.	1-3 A lawyer is in the park.
.	1-1 A debutante is in the cave.
.	2-2 A captain is in the bank.
26. A lawyer is in the cave.	

From Anderson, 1976. Copyright 1976 by Lawrence Erlbaum Associates. Adapted by permission of the publisher and author.

If subjects made errors, then they were asked to study the set of sentences again. These preliminary phases were designed to ensure that the subjects had stored away all the facts contained in the sentences.

After Anderson was convinced that his subjects knew all the facts, the critical part of the experiment began. This was a fact recognition phase in which subjects were presented with test sentences of the sort shown in the second column of Table 6–12. They were to respond *true* or *false* by releasing an appropriate button as quickly as possible after each sentence had been presented. Anderson recorded the RT of each correct response.

The major variable in the experiment was the number of propositions in which each concept (i.e., each noun) in a given test sentence had occurred during the study phase. Anderson called this variable the *propositional fan*. Individual words had occurred in either one, two, or three of the study sentences. For example, in the same study set shown in Table 6–12 the word *lawyer* occurred in one proposition during study, the word *captain* occurred in two propositions, and the word *hippie* occurred in three. Therefore, a given test sentence could be classified as to how many propositions the subject and the predicate had occurred in during study. For example, the sentence, "A lawyer is in the park" would be classified as a 1-3 propositional fan, because its subject *lawyer* occurred in 1 study sentence and its predicate *park* occurred in 3 study sentences.

In order to see why Anderson was interested in the effects of propositional fan on RT, consider how ACT would assume these facts to be represented in memory. ACT would assume that during the study phase, the subject would build up a propositional network of the sort depicted in Figure 6–12. The node labeled 1 stands for the proposition, "The hippie is in the bank" (i.e., the hippie is a subset of the things that are in the bank). Similarly, the node labeled 2 stands for the proposition, "The hippie is in the church," and the node labeled 3 stands for the proposition, "The hippie is in the park." Nodes 4, 5, and 6 represent the propositions that the three propositions 1, 2, and 3, respectively, were contained in the list.

ACT assumes, in addition, that during the test phase the presentation of a test sentence, such as "A hippie is in the park" results in a chain of perceptual processes which leads to the string of words "A-hippie-is-in-the-park" being active. (You might think of this string as being an articulatory-acoustic code of the sort Conrad studied in working memory.)

We have now specified the form of representation of both the facts learned during study and of the test sentence, but before we can discuss ACT's predictions, we also need to specify the processes ACT assumes to operate in the fact retrieval experiment. As is always the case in ACT, the processes are specified in terms of a production sys-

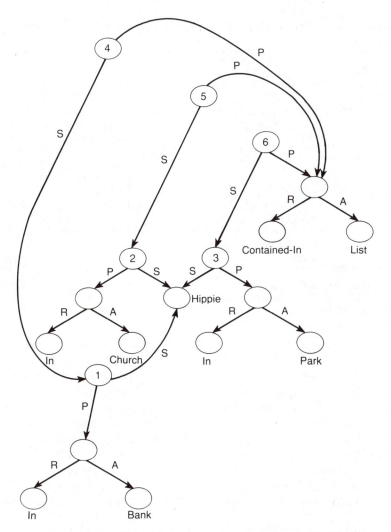

Figure 6–12. An illustration of how ACT assumes the memory structure to be organized for Anderson's fact retrieval experiment. (After Anderson, 1976. Copyright 1976 by Lawrence Erlbaum Associates. Adapted by permission of the publisher and author.)

tem. ACT assumes that as a function of the instructions and practice in the task, the subject adopts the production system depicted in Table 6–13. Anderson proposed this system, because he deemed it the simplest possible that would generate correct answers in the fact retrieval task.

The production system contains only four productions. P1 will

TABLE 6–13. **Production System for Anderson's Fact Retrieval Experiment.**

Production Number	Condition	Action
P1	(STATE = ready) AND A- $\longrightarrow$ VPER-IS-IN-THE-VLOC	(STATE = encode) AND rehearse VPER and VLOC
P2	(STATE = encode) AND $\longrightarrow$ VPER and VLOC	(STATE = test) AND retrieve concepts associated with VPER and VLOC and assign them to VIDEA1 and VIDEA2
P3	(STATE = test) AND (VIDEA1 $\longrightarrow$ and VIDEA2 intersect)	(STATE = ready) AND press true
P4	(STATE = test) AND (VIDEA1 $\longrightarrow$ and VIDEA2 don't intersect)	(STATE = ready) AND press false

After Anderson, 1976. Copyright 1976 by Lawrence Erlbaum Associates. Adapted by permission of the publisher and author.

be executed if the person's current state is READY *and* a string of the form A-VPER-IS-IN-THE-VLOC is in active memory. Notice that VPER and VLOC are variables that may take on, respectively, any name of a type of person and any name of a location. Thus the conditions of P1 will be filled if the subject is in the state READY and a string of words from a test sentence is in active memory. If these conditions are met, then two actions will be taken. The subject's internal state changes to ENCODE and the subject rehearses the two nouns for VPER and VLOC. Thus, if presented with the test sentence "The hippie is in the park," the subject would rehearse the words "hippie" and "park." Such rehearsal keeps the words on the ACTIVE LIST (i.e., in working memory).

After production P1 has been executed, the person will be in the ENCODE state, and the only production that could be fulfilled is P2. The conditions of P2 will be met if both the person is in state ENCODE *and* he is rehearsing some VPER and VLOC words. Both of these conditions having been met, the three actions of P2 will be taken. These include changing the internal state to TEST, retrieving the concepts associated with the words VPER and VLOC, and assigning these concepts to the variables VIDEA1 and VIDEA2. Thus for our example, these would be assigned the concepts associated with the words *hippie* and *park* respectively. Notice that after P2 has been executed (and the subject is therefore in the state TEST) either of two different productions could be executed since both productions P3 and P4 have, as part of their condition, that the internal state be TEST. Production

3 will be executed only if VIDEA1 and VIDEA2 intersect, in which case the internal state will be changed to READY and the subject will respond *true*. Production P4 will be executed only if the two do not intersect, in which case the state will again be changed to READY and subject will respond *false*. Thus, at the end of either production P3 or P4 the subject will again be in a state of readiness to respond to another test, but production P1 will not be executed until he has been presented with another test sentence.

Having specified both the structures and the processes ACT assumes for the fact retrieval task, it is possible to predict how the propositional fan variable should influence RT. First, consider *true* responses. According to the production system, this response cannot be initiated until an intersection between the two concepts named in the test sentence has been found. According to the spread of activation assumption (number 3 in Table 6–11), upon activation of a concept, activation fans out to all connected concepts, and the more such links there are, the less activation will spread to any one in a given instant of time. Therefore, ACT predicts that the greater the propositional fan of the concepts included in a test sentence, the longer it should take to find an intersection and thus the longer it should take before the condition for production P3 can be met. This leads ACT to predict that RT for *true* responses will increase as a function of propositional fan.

When Anderson conducted the fact retrieval experiment, he obtained the RT's displayed in Table 6–14 and, as you should verify for yourself, the RT's for *true* responses were as predicted. Notice that RT seems to depend upon the total propositional fan of the subject and predicate terms. For example propositional fan 1-2 and 2-1 have almost identical RT's (1167 and 1174 msec respectively) and both are shorter than conditions 2-3 and 3-2 (with RT's of 1233 and 1222 msec respectively).

Further examination of the results in Table 6–14 will reveal two important findings regarding *false* responses. First, for a given propositional fan, *false* responses are slower than *true* responses, and second, RT increases with the size of the propositional fan for *false* responses, just as it did for *true* responses. According to ACT's production system, a *false* response will be initiated (i.e., production P4 executed) only if an intersection is not found. Since the subject is responding to the *absence* of something, Anderson assumes that the subject waits for some period before he concludes that no intersection exists. Anderson argues that in order for this strategy to be successful, the subject must wait, on the average, past the time it would take to find an intersection. (Otherwise, the subject would often incorrectly respond *false* simply because he hadn't waited long enough to find the intersection.) This extended waiting time explains why RT is longer

TABLE 6–14.   Results from Anderson's Fact Retrieval Study.

	Propositional Fan	Reaction Time (msec)
True	1-1	1111
	1-2	1167
	1-3	1153
	2-1	1174
	2-2	1198
	2-3	1233
	3-1	1222
	3-2	1222
	3-3	1357
False	1-1	1197
	1-2	1250
	1-3	1262
	2-1	1221
	2-2	1356
	2-3	1471
	3-1	1264
	3-2	1291
	3-3	1465

After Anderson, 1976. Copyright 1976 by Lawrence Erlbaum Associates. Adapted by permission of the publisher and author.

for *false* than for *true* responses. In order to account for the fact that propositional fan affects *false* responses as well as *true*, Anderson assumes that as the propositional fan is increased (and activation takes longer) the subject waits longer before concluding that no intersection exists.

This extended discussion of ACT's assumptions and predictions about one experiment should illustrate how Anderson attempts to use his global model of long-term memory to make empirically verifiable predictions. This example should make clear that in order to make predictions about RT's (and errors) ACT combines a general structural model consisting of a propositional network, with a specific set of productions that are assumed to be used in the task at hand. These productions are essentially strategies. Notice that ACT assumes that the individual uses task-specific strategies. For example, in the fact retrieval task the assumed production system never actually comprehends the meaning of the sentence. This production system is adequate for the task at hand because the test sentences are always of the same form and the subject need not bother comprehending them.

ACT and the classic semantic memory findings. We have seen one example of how ACT generates predictions for novel experiments, but we have not yet compared ACT with TLC, the original network theory which also made some correct predictions, but ran into difficulty in accounting for later experimental results. We should indicate first that TLC would *not* have predicted the pattern of results Anderson obtained in the fact retrieval experiment. TLC assumes that the activation spreads at a rate that is *independent* of the number of paths that are activated, i.e., the activation process has unlimited capacity.

Not only does ACT predict the results of the fact retrieval experiment more accurately than TLC, but it is also able to account for the findings originally predicted by TLC; those in the sentence verification task in which the subject is asked to judge the truth or falsity of some proposition of the form "An S is a P" or "An S has P." ACT could assume a production system of the sort described for the fact retrieval task, with additional productions designed to check to see if the intersection obtained is of the sort specified by the test sentence. One way in which ACT could account for Collins and Quillian's findings depicted in Figure 6–7 would be to call upon its assumptions that the strengths of links vary depending upon how often the link has been traversed in the past (Assumption 1 of Table 6–11), and that the rate of the spread of activation along a link is determined by the strength of that link (Assumption 3). Therefore, ACT could explain the fact that "A canary is yellow" is verified more rapidly than "A canary has skin" by noting that the link between CANARY and YELLOW is usually stronger (because it has been traversed more often) than the link between CANARY and SKIN. Therefore, the intersection will be found more quickly.

Not only can ACT account for the findings predicted by TLC, but it is also capable of dealing with the phenomena that gave TLC difficulty. We listed three such phenomena earlier. The first was the finding that class membership is sometimes judged more rapidly for superordinates (e.g., "A dog is an animal") than it is judged for subordinates (e.g., "A dog is a mammal"), a finding contrary to what Collins and Quillian would predict. This finding provides no difficulty for ACT since it assumes that the time it takes to verify these sentences reflects the strength of the links between subject and predicate. Thus, the "animal" sentence is verified more rapidly than the "mammal" sentence, because the link between the nodes for DOG and ANIMAL is stronger (because it is activated more frequently) than the link between DOG and MAMMAL.

The second finding that TLC didn't predict was that the typicality of category instances influences the speed of class membership judgments. That is, people verify the sentence "A dog is an animal" faster than they verify "A lynx is an animal." Again, this fact is easily accounted for by ACT's strength of links assumption, since it need only be assumed that the link between DOG and ANIMAL is traversed more frequently, and hence is stronger, than the link between LYNX and ANIMAL.

The third finding problematic for TLC was that category size effects occurred for false sentences (e.g., "A rose is a fish" is judged faster than "A rose is an animal") and for nonwords (e.g., "A zork is a flower" is judged more rapidly than "A zork is a plant"). ACT can account for both these findings in the same way it accounted for the effect of propositional fan in Anderson's fact retrieval experiment. That is, the number of links emanating from a concept (the propositional fan) is greater for ANIMAL than for FISH, and greater for PLANT than for FLOWER. If the person waits an amount of time proportional to the propositional fan before deciding that there is no intersection, then he will wait longer to decide to respond *no* for the "animal" than for the "fish" question, and for the "plant" than for the "flower" question.

In sum, then, ACT is able to account for most of the classic semantic memory findings.

ACT and the general characteristics of long-term memory. It is particularly important that ACT, and indeed all network models of semantic memory, are consistent with the general characteristics of human long-term memory that we outlined at the beginning of the chapter. First, we discussed the many kinds of observations which indicate that the most important basis of organization of long-term memory is meaning. This, of course, is exactly the point of ACT's semantic network. Concepts are connected with other concepts that are semantically related. In this sense, then, concepts that are semantically similar are close together in that there are few links separating them.

ACT provides a useful framework for thinking about all of the phenomena we considered when we discussed the importance of meaning. For example, consider the findings from the lexical decision task. Recall that having just decided that one string of letters is a word facilitates the speed with which you can judge that a semantically related string of letters is also a word (e.g., you decide that DOG is a word more rapidly if you've just decided that CAT is a word than if you've just decided that FIG is a word). ACT suggests that we can attribute such semantic facilitation in lexical decisions to spreading activation in a semantic network. That is, having just activated the CAT node will result in activation spreading to related concepts (among them DOG) so that the DOG node will already be activated when the corresponding word has been presented for test. Similarly, according to ACT, people's word associations reflect the pathways of the mind that are activated spontaneously when a word is presented.

The second general characteristic of memory we discussed earlier is the fact that long-term memory is integrative and abstractive, in that we store the gist of a message rather than a verbatim account. Of course, this is exactly what ACT does when it represents sentences and events by abstract propostions. For example, if ACT experienced the sentence "Cats chase mice," it would build the same proposition it would build if it experienced the sentence "Mice are chased by cats." Later, then, ACT would not know which of the two sentences it had heard. It would only remember, just as we do, the underlying proposition.

The third characteristic of memory is the fact that long-term memory is constructive. We enrich experience automatically by making inferences. Then later we have difficulty distinguishing between what we actually experienced and what we inferred. Network models enable such inferences primarily because of the link between type and token nodes. Recall that every concept has one definitional (or type) node which records general information about the concept, and that whenever the individual experiences some particular instance of the concept, a token node is assumed to be established which is linked directly to the type node. Thus, experiencing a concept automatically activates some of your permanent knowledge about the concept which is stored at the type node. This information may then be incorporated into your memory (i.e., the new proposition that you store) for that particular event.

We have just seen, then, that ACT is able to explain the semantic memory findings and that, like other network models, it is consistent with the general characteristics of long-term memory. This is not to say that ACT is *the* correct theory of long-term memory. In fact, there are a number of other network models that, with appropriate assumptions, can also account for the findings we have discussed. The point, then, is not that ACT is the uniquely correct theory, but rather that it provides one promising way of conceptualizing the nature of long-term memory—a way that is consistent with both experimental findings and everyday observations about the quirks of our memory.

If you will think of long-term memory as consisting of a set of labeled, directed links connecting concept nodes, plus a set of procedures (or strategies for operating on the network), it will help you to conceptualize the characteristics of episodic long-term memory that we discussed in the previous chapter. For example, if long-term memory consists of such a complex network, then it makes sense that the major difficulty the memorizer encounters is in finding just the information he is seeking in this maze. Building up a rich network of links between his previous knowledge and the new propositions he is storing away—i.e., elaborative rehearsal—helps recall, because the more such relations he builds up, the more likely it is that he will be able to retrieve the sought after information later. That is, the more likely it is that the retrieval cues present when he wishes to recall the material will result in activation of the node he is seeking.

CHAPTER SUMMARY

Episodic memory is memory for material that is specific to a particular time and place, whereas semantic memory is knowledge of general concepts. Previous chapters have focused on episodic memories, but in this chapter we examined semantic memory theories. Such theories have been proposed to account for the structure of knowledge and the processes which enable us to use this knowledge in remembering, in speaking and listening, and in thinking.

There are three general characteristics of long-term memory that any theory of semantic memory must be able to encompass. These include the importance of meaning as the basis of organization, the fact that memory is abstractive and integrative, and the fact that memory is constructive. The latter two characteristics have important, often troublesome, implications for eyewitness testimony.

Of the many theories of semantic memory that have been proposed since the 1960's, we focused on network theories. All such theories have several features in common. First, they assume the structure of long-term memory to consist of a large set of nodes interconnected by labeled, directed associations, or relations. Second, all assume that retrieving information from the memory network involves a search through the pathways (or relations). Third, the nodes are assumed to represent, not words per se, but concepts. Fourth, all distinguish between type and token nodes in order to relate semantic and episodic memories and to enable inference.

The first network model was R. Quillian's Teachable Language Comprehender (TLC). Although early tests of TLC supported the theory, several phenomena were soon reported which it had not predicted. Faced with these conflicting findings, two general approaches to theorizing about semantic memory developed. One group of theorists retained the network approach, but modified the assumptions. Another group abandoned the idea of a network and proposed other, less all-encompassing theories which could account for the discrepant results. These two approaches to theorizing are examples of two different directions that research in cognitive psychology is taking—Theory Demonstration vs. Theory Development.

John Anderson has proposed the ACT theory of semantic memory which is a network theory similar to TLC. ACT assumes that long-term memory contains two kinds of knowledge, declarative and procedural knowledge. Declarative knowledge consists of a propositional network, only a small part of which is active at any one time. Part of this active portion of memory is in ACT's limited capacity working memory, but the rest results from the spread of activation which occurs for a certain length of time after a node has been activated. This spread of activation has a limited capacity in that the more links being activated at any one time, the slower the spread occurs along any one link. Procedural knowledge consists of a set of productions which correspond to strategies, and which specify what should be done if a given set of conditions becomes active.

Anderson has predicted successfully the results that should occur for a number of experiments, and he has also written computer programs to simulate parts of the theory. In addition, ACT is able to account for the earlier semantic memory findings, and it is consistent with the general characteristics of long-term memory discussed both in this and in the previous chapter. As we will discuss in the sections on language and thinking, semantic networks and production systems will be useful for helping us to conceptualize how people produce and comprehend language and how they go about reasoning and solving problems.

SUGGESTED READING

The issues we focused on in this chapter are attracting more current interest than any other single topic within the domain of memory. Therefore, the literature and the number of theories are growing at a staggering rate. Teaching semantic memory has convinced me that presenting students with brief vignettes of a number of widely different theories confuses rather than enlightens them, so I have focused on only one kind—the network approach. I chose this approach because it provides a useful conceptual framework for dealing with episodic memory, language, and thinking. In fact, I believe that the distinctions between network theories and other types (such as set-theoretic and feature theories) are more apparent than real. You should decide this issue for yourself, however, so I suggest the following sequence of reading. First, read the article by Smith, Shoben, and Rips (1974) in which they introduced the distinction between feature models and network models, and proposed their own feature model. Then read the comment on this article published by Hollan (1975) in which he argues that there is no fundamental distinction between feature and network models. Finally, read the reply to Hollan by Rips, Smith, and Shoben (1975) as well as the excellent article by Smith (1978). In the latter article, Smith not only comments further on the feature-network distinction, but also provides an excellent review of the semantic memory literature.

If you wish to read about some of the other theories of semantic memory that have been proposed, the best place to begin is probably the book *Organization of Memory* edited by Tulving and Donaldson. It was at the conference on which this book is based that several seminal theories were outlined. In particular, read the chapter by Rumelhart, Lindsay, and Norman which is the first published report of their model ELINOR, and the chapters by Kintsch, by Collins and Quillian, and by Tulving.

All of these theorists have continued to develop their ideas and theories since that conference. If you wish to learn about more recent developments of ELINOR, read the relevant chapters of the second edition of Lindsay and Norman's introductory text *Human Information Processing* and, for a more detailed and advanced treatment, *Explorations in Cognition* (1975) edited by Norman and Rumelhart. For Kintsch's more recent work consult his book *The Representation of Meaning in Memory*, and for a revision of TLC which accounts for most of the phenomena we discussed in this chapter, read Collins and Loftus (1975). For an example of how network theories can be used to understand the influence of emotions on learning, read Bower (1981) and Bower, Gilligan, and Monteiro (1981).

If you wish to read more directly about John Anderson's theory ACT, find his book *Language, Memory, and Thought,* and you may also be interested in an earlier book by Anderson and Bower (1973) entitled *Human Associative Memory.* The theory (called HAM) proposed in the latter book was the precursor of ACT, though it differed from ACT in some fundamental ways. See the article by Wexler for a critical assessment of ACT, and then read Anderson's reply in *Cognition.*

Early in the chapter we discussed briefly some implictions of the study of memory for eyewitness testimony. If you wish to pursue these topics further, I suggest the articles by Loftus (1979) and Loftus and Monahan (1980).

Imagery

7

FOOD FOR THOUGHT

Try to answer the following two questions. (1) How many windows are there in the house you lived in two houses ago? (taken from Norman, 1976), and (2) What was your phone number in that house? How do the processes you used to answer each of these questions seem to differ from each other, relative difficulty excluded?

THE HISTORICAL UPS AND DOWNS OF THE CONCEPT OF IMAGERY

We have now examined all the major memory components of the overview theory proposed in Chapter 1, and in the next chapter we will begin to discuss how such a theory might be elaborated to encompass the processing of language. Before doing so, however, it is important to consider a topic which cuts across all the memory components considered so far—the role of imagery in memory.

So far we have focused on propositional codes (in the TLC and ACT models in the last chapter) and on verbal codes (in the discussion of working memory). Nonetheless, most people report that they experience mental images often in dreaming, in thinking, and when trying to remember certain kinds of material, a case in point being the number of windows question.

As with so many interesting phenomena, although we find it easy to talk about mental imagery, it is difficult to define the term precisely. For the moment, we will adopt the following working definition paraphrased from Bower (1970a, p. 502): "A memory image of an object or event presents to the experiencing subject some of the same structural information as was presented in earlier perceptions of the object or event in question." Thus, experiencing an image is similar, subjectively, to experiencing the original object. When answering the windows question, people often report that they are "seeing" each room and scanning it to determine where the windows are. Though this chapter will focus on visual imagery, we experience imagery in other modalities as well. We can hear melodies in our minds, just as we seem to conjure up images of the smell of freshly cut grass and the softness of a baby's cheek.

Our subjective experiences of imagery are shared with centuries of people who preceded us. Indeed some of the earliest recorded ideas about the nature of memory and thought have asserted the importance of mental imagery. Consider Plato's (1963, p. 897) wax impression theory of memory:

> Imagine, then, for the sake of argument, that our minds contain a block
> of wax, which in this or that individual may be larger or smaller, and

composed of wax that is comparatively pure or muddy, and harder in some, softer in others, and sometimes of just the right consistency. . . . Whenever we wish to remember something we see or hear or conceive in our own minds, we hold this wax under the perceptions or ideas and imprint them on it as we might stamp the impression of a seal ring. Whatever is so imprinted we remember and know so long as the image remains, whatever is rubbed out or has not succeeded in leaving an impression we have forgotten and do not know.

Centuries of introspection notwithstanding, the notion that we think and remember in images has not been accepted without question. Indeed, Plato himself ultimately rejected the analogy quoted, and throughout the intervening centuries other scholars (e.g., Berkeley) have criticized theories that assume the existence of mental images.

The concept of imagery has suffered a particularly spotted history within the discipline of psychology. Early experimental psychologists designed experiments to investigate the role of imagery in thinking. For example, in the late 1800's German psychologists at the University of Wurzburg asked people to name the category to which a spoken word belonged, and to report whether or not they experienced an image of the spoken word's referent when doing so. Thus, when presented with the word *dress* the subject was to say *clothing* and to report whether or not he experienced a visual image of a dress in the course of producing his answer. (Do *you* experience an image when doing so??) As it happened, most observers reported that they did not. The failure of these early studies to reveal the importance of imagery did not discourage European psychologists (e.g., Bartlett, 1932) from studying mental imagery, but as radical behaviorism enveloped almost all of experimental psychology on this side of the Atlantic, mental imagery joined other mentalistic concepts in being considered outside the realm of scientific inquiry.

The recent rebirth of interest in human cognition has changed this picture dramatically. Questions concerning the nature and functions of mental images have captured the interest of experimental psychologists, and discussions of mental imagery once again are at the center of psychological inquiry. This new focus has come about in part because new experimental techniques promise to give intriguing glimpses into the inner world of images, and in part because information-processing theories offer more precise ways of conceptualizing the nature of mental representations.

FUNCTIONS OF IMAGERY

When experimental psychologists again began to study imagery in the late 1950's, they first focused on the functions of imagery. Several kinds of evidence soon emerged which suggested that mental imagery facilitates memory. We will consider only two of these. First, numerous studies (see Bower, 1972; Paivio, 1971) have revealed that when subjects are instructed to use images to commit a list of words to memory, recall is facilitated dramatically, relative to a condition in which subjects are left to their own devices. You have already experienced this phenomenon in our discussion of mnemonic techniques.

Second, the ease with which a word will be remembered is correlated with the rated imagery value of that word. Imagery (I) ratings are collected by presenting a group of subjects with a list of words and asking them to rate each word on how easily and quickly it arouses a mental image. (Paivio, Yuille, and Madigan, 1968, published the most widely used set of I ratings, but van der Veur, 1975, has more recently published ratings for 1,000 words.) When other subjects are asked to commit lists of words to memory (such as in a free recall task) those words which had been rated high in imagery value are much more likely to be recalled correctly than those rated low in imagery. In fact, many studies have shown that imagery rating is one of the best predictors of a word's memorability. It is more successful than ratings of the word's meaningfulness or the word's concreteness (cf. Bugelski, 1970; Paivio, 1971).

DUAL-CODING THEORY VERSUS PROPOSITIONAL THEORY

Paivio's dual-coding theory. The findings we have just discussed led Alan Paivio (1969, 1971, 1974) to propose a dual-coding theory of memory. According to this view, long-term memory contains two qualitatively different but interconnected systems of representation, or codes. One of these codes is verbal or linguistic, and is especially adapted for handling serially ordered information. The other is an imagery system that is specialized for representing spatial information. The two systems are connected in that the individual can produce a label given a picture and vice versa.

If it is assumed that information which is represented in both codes will be more likely to be recalled than information which is contained in only one of these codes, then the dual-coding theory can account for both the finding that imagery instructions aid recall and the finding that memorability is correlated with imagery value. It is argued that imagery instructions lead to improved recall since such instructions lead the person to encode the word in both the verbal and the imagery systems. Furthermore, words rated high in imagery are likely to be encoded in both systems, whereas words low in imagery value are likely to be encoded in only one.

Propositional theory. Dual-coding theory can account for the findings concerning the functions of imagery, and it is also quite consistent with introspective reports. Nonetheless, a number of theorists (e.g., Anderson & Bower, 1973; Pylyshyn, 1973) have argued for a very different kind of theory of long-term memory representation. According to the propositional viewpoint favored by these authors, all information in long-term memory is in the form of propositions which are abstract, i.e., neither imaginal nor linguistic. You are already familiar with two such propositional theories—TLC and ACT—for we discussed them in Chapter 6 and incorporated their major features into our overview theory.

Although propositional theorists offer a number of arguments against dual-coding theory (see Pylyshyn, 1973 for a detailed discussion), the single most important is that, in principle, a propositional format such as the networks of TLC and ACT can be used to represent all kinds of information, whether perceptual or linguistic (e.g., Cunningham, 1980). Indeed, the propositional theorists base this argument on the fact that computer simulation models of memory, pattern recognition, and language processing do just that. Propositional theorists go on to argue that since a propositional representation *could* represent all the various kinds of knowledge we possess, it is more parsimonious to assume that there is only one kind of underlying representation in long-term memory.

It is at this point in their argument that there is most room for debate. Just because it is theoretically *possible* to design a system which represents both perceptual and linguistic information in one abstract code does not necessarily mean that this is the way the human mind actually works. We saw in Chapter 1 that it is quite possible to design a system that solves problems, but does so using processes that are completely different from those involved in human problem solving.

Propositional theorists argue that propositional theory could account for the findings concerning the functions of imagery we have been discussing. The relation between *I* value and memorability could be accounted for by assuming that words that are high in *I* value are likely to have a richer network of propositions than words low in *I* value, because they have links to perceptual properties as well as to more abstract characteristics. Similarly, if subjects are instructed to use imagery to help them remember, they are likely to build up more detailed propositional networks.

According to propositional theorists, then, subjects who are given imagery instructions do not employ a qualitatively different kind of long-term memory representation from subjects who receive rehearsal instructions. It is just that the imagery instructions lead them to form more detailed propositional networks than the networks formed under verbal rehearsal instructions, and these more detailed networks facilitate recall.

Such an argument gains support from demonstrations showing that mnemonic systems that are not based on imagery also aid recall. For example, Bower and Winzenz (1970) found that when subjects were given a list of paired associates (e.g., CAT-TYPEWRITER) to remember, instructions to relate the two words in each pair by using a sentence (e.g., THE CAT SAT ON TOP OF THE TYPEWRITER.) were almost as effective in facilitating recall as were instructions to relate the two words using an image (e.g., imagining the cat sitting on the typewriter).

Of course, there is still one phenomenon which does not fit particularly neatly into a propositional theory—our introspections. Why is it that we feel as though some kinds of remembering and thinking require mental imagery whereas others require thinking in words or sentences? Propositional theorists argue that such introspective reports simply reflect the limitations on our ability to describe mental events; we have no way of expressing abstract propositions unless we talk about words or images.

We find ourselves, then, with two different theoretical accounts of mental representation, both of which can account for the findings on the functions of imagery we have been discussing. One theory postulates two different kinds of long-term codes, and a second postulates only one. This theoretical debate has been particularly productive, for it has led scientists to develop new techniques for investigating the nature of mental representation. In the next section, we will consider several kinds of evidence for dual-coding theory which these techniques have revealed.

EVIDENCE FOR SEPARATE VERBAL AND IMAGERY SYSTEMS

Patterns of errors. According to dual-coding theory's interpretation of the effects of imagery instructions on recall, subjects who are instructed to use visual imagery are using a qualitatively different kind of representation than subjects who are instructed to use rehearsal or other verbal strategies. If this is true then these two groups of subjects should make different kinds of errors.

In fact, analyses of error patterns have revealed some evidence for dual-coding theory. For example, in a study reported by Peterson (1975), all the subjects were presented with 12 letters and later tested for recall. Subjects differed, however, in the conditions of presentation of the 12 letters. The visual presentation group saw the letters arranged in a 4 × 4 matrix as shown in Figure 7–1 (4 cells were blank).

G	R	I	A
	F		V
K	B		M
D		Q	P

Figure 7–1. An example of a stimulus array used in the Visual Presentation condition of Peterson's (1975) study of seen and imagined matrices.

The Auditory Sequential group heard the list read aloud sequentially. The third group, termed the Auditory Sequential-Visualize group, was identical to the Auditory Sequential group except that as they heard the letters they were instructed to *imagine* them being placed in the 4 × 4 array. Thus, the latter group was instructed to construct mentally a grid like that actually seen by the Visual Presentation group.

Peterson examined the subject's recall for serial position effects, to see which positions led to the best recall. As you would expect from our earlier discussions, the Auditory Sequential group showed the usual primacy and recency effects obtained in free-recall experiments. In contrast, the group that saw the 4 × 4 grid made a different pattern of errors; they were most accurate on the letters located in the four corners of the visual grid, next most accurate on all the items around the edges of the grid, and least accurate on the items in the center of the grid. The condition of most interest is the group presented with the list sequentially, but instructed to imagine the matrix in their minds. If the image does contain some of the structural properties of the external matrix, then the pattern of errors should be like that obtained for visual presentation, because subjects in both conditions should be holding a similar spatial array in memory. In fact, that is what Peterson found, suggesting a similarity between external visual scenes and spatial scenes constructed by the mind's eye.

Hemispheric differences in processing imagery and verbal codes. It has been known for at least a century that the two hemispheres of the human brain are asymmetrical in function. Although we will reserve detailed discussion of this topic for the chapters on language, it is important to know now that in general, the left hemisphere is the more important for language and the right hemisphere is specialized for spatially organized tasks. For example, Milner (1971) has reported analyses of people who have suffered brain damage. She found that temporal lobe lesions in the left hemisphere were usually accompanied by impaired verbal memory, whereas temporal lobe lesions in the right hemisphere result in impaired visual memory, e.g., for geometric designs or faces. If the hemispheric differences in memory reported by Milner and others reflect the operation of the two coding systems proposed by dual-coding theory, then changes from one coding system to another should be accompanied by a corresponding shift in the hemisphere that is most important for processing.

A study by Seamon and Gazzaniga (1973) tested this hypothesis and also provides an example of how hemispheric differences can be studied in normal subjects using only behavioral measures. Seamon and Gazzaniga took advantage of the following characteristic of the visual system. If a subject is required to fixate on a point, then the neural outcome of any stimulus which is flashed to the left of that point will arrive at the right hemisphere before it arrives at the left. Similarly, any stimulus which is flashed to the right of the fixation point (i.e., the right visual field) will arrive at the left hemisphere first. This fact enables an experimenter to direct a test stimulus to one or the other hemisphere. Of course, since the two hemispheres are connected in normal subjects, information about each stimulus will eventually reach both hemispheres regardless of the visual field to which it is presented.

On each trial of the Seamon and Gazzaniga experiment the following sequence of events occurred, an example of which is depicted in Figure 7–2. The subject was shown a pair of words for several seconds, followed by a fixation point (which the subject was instructed to stare at), and finally by a test stimulus. The test stimulus was a picture, and the subject was to respond by pushing a button labeled *yes* if the item pictured had the same name as one of the two words he was trying to remember, and to push a button labeled *no* otherwise. Of course, errors were few, and the measure of interest was the

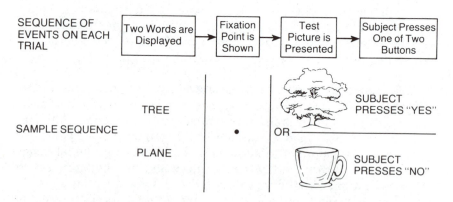

Figure 7–2. This figure illustrates the sequence of events which occurred on each trial of the Seamon and Gazzaniga (1973) experiment. Reaction time was measured from onset of the test picture until the subject pressed the correct button. As the sample sequence indicates, the subject was to respond *yes* if the test picture depicted one of the words the subject was remembering and to respond *no* otherwise.

reaction time required to make the response, timed from onset of the test picture until the subject pushed the correct button.

Seamon and Gazzaniga varied two factors. First, on a given day one-half of the subjects were instructed to remember the two words by forming an interactive image of the objects named by the words. Thus, given the pair BOOK-SHOE, the subject might construct an image of a book sticking out of the top of a shoe. The other half of the subjects were instructed to remember the two words on each trial by rehearsing the names over and over again. The second factor varied was whether the test picture was presented to the right of the fixation point (thus arriving first at the left hemisphere) or to the left of the fixation point (thus arriving first at the right hemisphere). The side varied from trial to trial, so the subject could not predict where the test would appear. From now on we will refer to this variable as Hemisphere Tested.

Consider the predictions the dual-coding hypothesis would make. When subjects are given imagery instructions, the right hemisphere should be more important than the left, so reaction times should be faster for right hemisphere tests than for left. On the other hand, when subjects are given rehearsal instructions, the opposite pattern should obtain, i.e., tests presented to the left hemisphere first should be faster. The results Seamon and Gazzaniga obtained were consistent with this prediction. When subjects had been instructed to use an imagery code, reaction time was 24 msec faster on right hemisphere tests than on left, whereas when subjects had been instructed to use rehearsal, reaction time was 25 msec faster on the left hemisphere tests than on the right.

These results are particularly important because they show that the hemispheric advantage follows the subject's strategies, suggesting that the pattern of hemispheric advantage is determined at least in part by the control process the subject adopts. The actual test item presented was *always* a picture, but whether the memory comparison could be completed most rapidly in the right or left hemisphere was dependent upon the *coding strategy* the subject adopted.

Speeded matching. In 1967 Posner and Keele published an important paper in *Science*. The experiment presented the subject with a simple letter-matching task. On each of a series of trials, the subject was first shown a letter and then, following an interstimulus interval which ranged from 0 to 2 seconds in length, a second letter was presented. The subject's task was to respond as quickly as possible by releasing one key if the second letter had the same name as the first and a different key if the second letter had a different name. The data of most interest were the reaction times of the responses, timed from onset of the second letter. The case (upper or lower) in which the letters were presented was also varied. Thus, on "same" trials the two letters on a trial were sometimes physically identical (e.g., *A-A* or *a-a*), but other times they were not (e.g., *A-a* or *a-A*). Posner and Keele termed the former "physical matches" and the latter "name matches."

The results revealed that when the interval between the stimuli was 1.5 seconds or less, physical matches were completed more rapidly than name matches, but at longer interstimulus intervals name matches and physical matches took equivalent amounts of time. This pattern of RT's suggests that at interstimulus intervals of 1.5 seconds or less, the subjects still had a memory for the visual form of the letter. If memory for the first letter had consisted of a verbal code or a more abstract propositional code, the fact that the test letters matched in case should have been unimportant, since the case of the first letter would not be held in memory. The fact that physical and name matches are equally rapid with interstimulus intervals greater than 1.5 seconds suggests that by that time the subject may be using an articulatory-acoustic record of the letter name.

Thus, Posner and Keele interpret their results to mean that the subject uses a visual code of the first stimulus for approximately 1.5 seconds and then switches to a verbal code. Notice that this interpretation makes a straightforward prediction about the pattern of hemispheric lateralization that should be seen in the Posner and Keele task. Wilkins and Stewart (1974) reported a study which used the Posner and Keele letter matching task, with one important exception—they varied the visual field to which the second letter was presented, thereby varying the hemisphere which would process the test stimulus first. These researchers found that at short interstimulus intervals (which yielded faster physical than name matches), test stimuli flashed first to the right hemisphere were responded to more quickly than those flashed first to the left hemisphere—a pattern of hemispheric advantages that suggests visual coding. Furthermore, at the long interstimulus intervals which yielded equally fast name and physical matches, test stimuli flashed to the left hemisphere were responded to more rapidly than right hemisphere tests—a pattern suggesting verbal coding. This study by Wilkins and Stewart is a particularly good example of how different techniques for assessing mental representations can help to test interpretations of results.

By now you might have noticed that given the evidence we have discussed so far, the visual memory revealed in the Posner and Keele letter matching studies might simply reflect the operation of the visual sensory register. In fact, in a later study Posner and his colleagues (Posner, Boies, Eichelman & Taylor, 1969) reported several findings which contradict this interpretation. First, they found that the visual memory important in the letter matching task is not disturbed by filling the interstimulus interval with a visual patterned mask. Visual sensory storage, on the other hand, would be affected by such a mask. Second, they found that the capacity of the visual memory in the letter matching task is very small—not more than three items—whereas the capacity of the visual sensory register is known to be very large. Third, when Posner and his colleagues gave subjects a concurrent task to complete during the interstimulus interval, this interfered with maintenance of the visual memory, suggesting that such maintenance calls on a limited capacity processing system (controlled processing), whereas we saw in Chapter 3 that maintaining items in sensory storage does not. Furthermore, other studies reveal a fourth property which distinguishes this visual memory from visual sensory storage. Whether or not a visual code is used is *not* tied to the mode of presentation. That is, subjects can generate a visual representation, even though given a verbal one (e.g., Tversky, 1969). Recall that this is very different from sensory storage which maintains a veridical visual record of whatever stimulus is presented—the coding being automatic and outside the individual's control.

Selective interference. The following reasoning underlies a series of selective-interference studies: if there are two different coding systems, then it should be possible to selectively interfere with one or the other. In one such study, Brooks (1968) reasoned that if visual imagery involves the visual system, then doing some other task with the visual system should interfere with the ability to generate or remember visual images. The activity of the "external" eye should interfere with the mind's eye, as it were. Brooks' main task involved asking the subject to imagine a line drawing of a letter (e.g., the letter F displayed in Figure 7-3). The experimenter would then say either "top-bottom" or "right-left." In the former case the subject was to begin at the point containing the asterisk and, moving clockwise around the letter, make a series of judgments about whether or not each point was at the extreme top or bottom (in which case he should report "yes") or not (in which case he should report "no"). If the experimenter said "right-left", the subject should do the same thing, except that he should report "yes" if each point was at the extreme right or left of the figure, and "no" otherwise. Thus, if told "top-bottom" the subject should report "yes, yes, yes, no, no, no, no, no, no, yes."

The important variable was the way in which the subject was to report the series of judgments. Sometimes he was simply to say the sequence aloud. On other trials, he was to point to a series of Y's and N's arranged on a page in front of him as displayed in Figure 7–3. It is important to realize that the letter was not physically present while the subject made his judgments, so he had to make judgments from a remembered record of the letter in question. Brooks timed how long it took subjects to complete the series of judgments in each case.

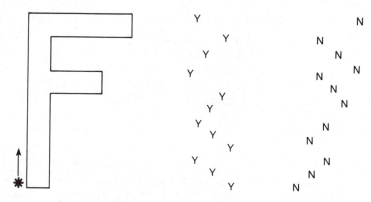

Figure 7–3. An example of one of the block letters Brooks (1968) used in his study of mental imagery is shown on the left. The asterisk indicates the starting point, and the arrow indicates the direction in which the points of the letter should be reported. On the right is a sample response sheet for the pointing mode of response. Notice that the Y's and N's are staggered on the page so that careful spatial and visual tracking is required.

Brooks reasoned that if the subject was using a visual image of the letter and making his judgments by "scanning" this mental image, then having to respond by pointing to a series of staggered letters should interfere more with making the judgments than should saying a series of "yes" and "no" responses, because both visual imagery and visually guided pointing should require the same limited capacity visual processing system, whereas saying the responses should not involve this system. Brooks' results from the two conditions just described are displayed in the first row of Table 7–1. In keeping with his prediction, pointing takes more than twice as long as speaking the response. The effect is so strong that you can *feel* the difference in difficulty if you try the task yourself. Prepare a response sheet, similar to that shown in Figure 7–6. Commit the letter to memory. Now, using the speaking mode of response, make a series of top-bottom judgments as quickly as possible, using your memory of the letter. Now, do the same thing, but point out your responses on the response sheet instead. You will probably notice that the pointing mode of responding is much more difficult than the speaking mode.

Consider Table 7–1 again. So far we have discussed the two conditions depicted on the first row of that table. If those were the only two conditions Brooks had tested, we would not be able to conclude that the relative difficulty of the two tasks is due to the fact that the pointing task *selectively* interferes with mental imagery. One could argue, instead, that the relative difficulty simply reflects the fact that overall it is harder to point than to speak; the former is certainly much

TABLE 7–1.   Time (sec) Required to Complete
Each Condition in Brooks' Study of Selective
Interference

| | Mode of Response | |
Kind of Material	Speaking	Pointing
Letter	11.3	28.2
Sentence	13.8	9.8

After Brooks, 1968.

less highly practiced than the latter. Therefore, Brooks gave the subjects a second kind of judgment task in which they were asked to
commit a sentence to memory (e.g., "A bird in the hand is worth two
in the bush.") The subject was to hold this information in memory
and, beginning at the first word in each sentence, make a series of
yes-no judgments. Either he was told "articles" in which case he
should report "yes" if each word was an article and "no" if it was
not, or he was told "nouns" in which case he should report "yes" if
each word was a noun, and "no" if it was not. Thus, for the *article*
decision in the given sentence, he should report "yes, no, no, yes, no,
no, no, no, no, yes, no." As in the case of the sentence judgments, on
some trials he had to report by saying a series of *yes*'s and *no*'s,
whereas on others he had to point out his answers. Again try this
yourself. Using the sentence given, first report on *nouns* using the
speaking method of responding and then do the same thing using the
pointing method. You will probably find, as Brooks did, that in this
case it is slightly easier to *point* your answer than it is to speak it.
Brooks' results are shown in the bottom row of Table 7–1.

Therefore, the overall difficulty interpretation can be ruled out.
Pointing is only more difficult when you are trying to make spatial
judgments about a mentally imagined letter. Thus, the critical feature
of selective interference studies is that they show that certain kinds of
tasks interfere *selectively* with imagery as opposed to verbal codes. In
fact, a number of other studies, often using very different kinds of
tasks from that Brooks developed, have also revealed evidence for such
selective interference (e.g., Brooks, 1967; den Heyer & Barrett, 1971;
Segal & Fusella, 1970).

One interesting implication of Brooks' results is that the modality in which information is presented might influence the ease with
which a person would be able to generate mental images. In fact, if
you are studying a poem in which the author attempts to evoke images in the mind of the reader, you would be advised to listen to the
poem rather than read it, because the act of scanning your eyes across

the page might interfere with your ability to conjure up the images. You may have noticed that when people try to conjure up a mental image, they often stare blankly at some unpatterned surface, like a ceiling, wall, or floor, or they close their eyes, presumably because past experience has led them to sense that they will be able to generate the mental image more easily if they don't try to process external visual stimuli at the same time.

We have now considered four kinds of evidence which provide support for dual-coding theory. These findings suggest that a number of measurable aspects of performance depend upon whether the person is using an image code or a verbal-linguistic code. These aspects of performance include the patterns of errors observed, the pattern of hemispheric advantages obtained, the patterns of reaction times revealed in speeded matching, and the patterns of interference observed when subjects are asked to perform two tasks at once.

EVIDENCE FOR PROPOSITIONAL THEORY

All of this evidence might seem to rule out propositional theory, but it does not. It is true, of course, that in almost all cases the experiments were planned with the dual-coding theory in mind, and the results were predicted by that theory. Nonetheless, propositional theory could be modified to account for most of these findings. For example, consider the selective-interference phenomena we just discussed. Propositional theorists (cf. Anderson, 1978) argue that in Brooks' study, both the letter and the sentence involve the same abstract propositional code, but the pattern of selective interference obtained reflects the fact that the propositions used to encode the letter are likely to be more similar to the propositions that would be activated in the pointing task than they are to the propositions that would be activated during the speaking task. That is, propositions describing the letter would be likely to contain information about spatial relations, whereas the speaking task does not. Thus, the selective interference results would be explained by postulating different degrees of interference due, not to qualitatively different codes, but rather to differences in the degree of similarity between the contents of the propositional representations involved. In fact, the only one of the four phenomena we discussed which seems to present severe difficulties for propositional theory is hemispheric lateralization.

Not only can propositional theories be modified to account for most of the findings favoring dual-coding theory, but in addition there are some findings that seem more consistent with propositional theories than with dual-coding. We will consider only one example here, a study reported in *Nature* by Potter and Faulconer (1975). First, Potter and Faulconer replicated an earlier finding—that people can report the name of a printed word about 250 msec more quickly than they can report the name of a picture. Thus, people say *dog* more quickly when presented with the printed letters DOG than they do when presented with a picture of a dog. Having completed this preliminary study, Potter and Faulconer gave their subjects a task reminiscent of those of the Wurzburg school in the nineteenth century. On each of a series of trials, the subject was presented with a category name, e.g., ANIMAL followed by presentation of a test item which was either a word or a picture. The subject was to respond "yes" as quickly as possible if the test item was a member of the category and "no" otherwise. Thus, presented with the category name ANIMAL if the subject subsequently saw either a picture of a dog or the word DOG he was to respond "yes," but if presented with either a picture of a car or the word CAR he was to respond "no." Dual-coding theory would predict that subjects would be able to judge the category membership of words prior to that of pictures, because such theories assume that knowledge about category membership is stored in the verbal system. Therefore, category judgments about words involve only one system, whereas in order to judge the category of a picture, one would first have to find its label in the verbal system (a relatively slow task given the fact that it takes longer to label a picture than a word), and then find out the category membership. Potter and Faulconer's results, to the contrary, revealed that category membership was judged 50 msec *faster* for pictures than for words. Potter and Faulconer concluded that it is difficult to reconcile this finding with dual-coding theory.

PROPOSITIONAL VERSUS DUAL-CODING THEORY REVISITED: A WORKING HYPOTHESIS

We seem to be in a quandry, for the discussion reveals some evidence for the dual-coding formulation and some for the propositional theory. One way to resolve this apparent standoff is to call upon the distinction between the working and long-term memory systems. A working hypothesis proposed recently by several authors (e.g., Peterson, Rawlings, & Cohen, 1977; Baddeley, 1976, 1981; Baddeley & Lieberman, 1980) is that long-term memory contains only one abstract propositional form of representation like the networks discussed in the last chapter; all information stored there, whether of perceptual or linguistic features or the meaning of stimuli, is stored in this same form. This hypothesis states, however, that there are two distinct short-term or working memory systems—one visual-spatial, the other verbal-linguistic.

This hypothesis that there is only one form of propositional representation in long-term memory, but two distinct kinds of working memory activation of that information is particularly inviting, because if you will think back over the patterns of results supporting dual-coding as opposed to propositional theories, you will notice that the tasks which suggest two qualitatively distinct kinds of codes are tasks that would call primarily on short-term (i.e., working memory) activation, whereas the findings supporting propositional theory seem to be calling upon the structure of long-term memory.

The studies discussed suggest several characteristics of the working memory systems. First, the selective interference studies suggest that the two can operate relatively independently in that simultaneous tasks that involve different systems can be performed much more efficiently than simultaneous tasks that call on the same system. Indeed, Peterson, et al. (1977) have argued that each of these systems seems to have a capacity of about 7 plus or minus 2 chunks, even when both are being used at once, so that the overall capacity of working memory may be underestimated when we consider retention that calls on only one of these systems.

Second, the findings of Peterson with the imagined matrices of letters, of Seamon and Gazzaniga with hemispheric differences, and the facilatory effects of imagery instructions on recall, all suggest that the person can exert control over which of these systems is used for a given task. That is, the person may use the abstract information stored in long-term memory to construct either an image or a verbal-linguistic code in working memory. Indeed, as we'll see, certain individuals may be prone to use one of these working memory systems more than the other. Third, the hemispheric lateralization finding of Seamon and Gazzaniga suggests that these two working memory systems may each call primarily on a different hemisphere, with the right being specialized for generating and manipulating spatial activations from long-term memory, and the left for generating and manipulating verbal-linguistic activations.

Kosslyn and Schwartz (1977; see also Kosslyn, 1978, 1980, 1981) have formulated a computer simulation theory of imagery based on the working hypothesis discussed here, and you may find the analogy they propose helpful. Kosslyn and Schwartz liken images generated in working memory to the array of dots which is displayed on a cathode ray display (similar to a television screen) by a computer. Though these are visual-spatial arrays, in the long-term memory of the computer the information used to generate these displays is contained in an abstract propositional format, not unlike that used to store verbal-linguistic information. Kosslyn and Schwartz argue that, far from being epiphenomena, the images generated from the underlying abstract propositional base are critical for thinking, for the person can then perform manipulations on the image and make judgments that would be difficult, if not impossible, if the images were not available.

THE NATURE OF MENTAL IMAGERY

If we adopt the hypothesis that there are two distinct working memory systems, each employing a qualitatively different kind of code, then it is of interest to explore the properties of the imagery system more carefully. We begin our quest here by recalling again the definition of imagery adopted at the beginning of the chapter: the image presents to the experiencing subject some of the same structural information as does immediate perceptual experience. This definition suggests that the structural information contained in mental images should influence judgments about mental images in the same way it influences judgments about objects in the external world. This line of thinking has led to a number of attempts to understand the nature of images.

Rotating and folding images. Look at Figure 7–4 and judge whether each of the items, if upright, would be a letter of the alphabet or whether it would be a mirror image of the letter. What processes seemed involved in making the decision? Most people report rotating each letter mentally until it is upright and then looking at the rotated image to determine whether the letter was mirror-imaged or not. Is there any objective evidence to support this feeling?

Roger Shepard and his colleagues at Stanford University have performed a series of studies using RT measures to find out. Let's consider their studies of the operations people perform on three dimensional objects of the sort displayed in Figure 7–5. In one experiment (Shepard & Metzler, 1971) subjects were presented with a series of such pairs and in each case asked to respond as quickly as possible whether the two objects pictured were identical or mirror images. Subjects were told to ignore differences in orientation. Shepard varied the degrees of difference between the two stimuli in the pair. For each pair, the stimulus on the right was rotated from 0 to 180 degrees clockwise from the picture on the left, either in the picture plane (a sample pair differing by 80 degrees is illustrated in the top pair in

Figure 7–4. For each letter, decide whether or not it would be oriented correctly if it were upright.

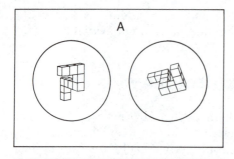

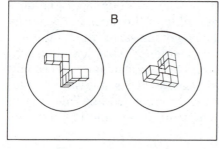

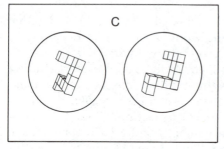

Figure 7–5. Samples of the three-dimensional stimulus pairs Shepard and Metzler used in their study of mental rotation. The top panel (A) shows a pair differing by an 80 degree rotation in the picture plane. The middle panel (B) shows a pair differing by an 80 degree rotation in the depth plane. The bottom panel (C) shows a pair that differs by a reflection as well as a rotation. The subject was to respond *same* to pairs like *A* and *B*, and *different* to pairs like *C*. (After Shepard & Metzler, 1971. Copyright 1971 by the American Association for the Advancement of Science. Reprinted by permission.)

Figure 7–5) or in the depth plane (a sample pair differing by 80 degrees is illustrated in the middle of Figure 7–5). The experimenter measured the reaction time of correct decisions from onset of the test pair.

If people are rotating mental images in a manner analogous to rotating objects in the external world, then the greater the difference in orientation between the two stimuli in a pair, the longer it should take to rotate them into congruence so that they can be compared. If people rotate at a constant rate then each time there is an additional degree to be rotated, there should be a uniform increment in reaction time, reflecting the time it took to rotate that extra degree. In other words, adopting the logic discussed in the context of Sternberg's memory search task (Chapter 4), the slope of the RT by degrees of rotation function should indicate the rate of mental rotation.

Shepard and Metzler's results for trials on which the correct re-

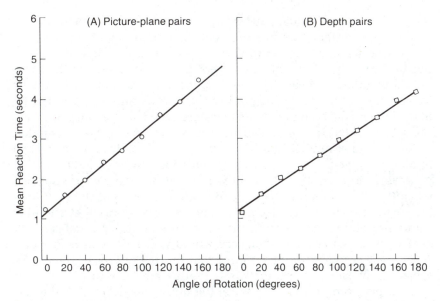

Figure 7–6. These are the data from the Shepard and Metzler study of mental rotation. They depict the mean RT to determine that two objects have the same three-dimensional shape, as a function of the angular difference in their portrayed orientations, plotted separately for pairs differing by a rotation in the picture plane (circles) and by a rotation in depth (squares). Notice that the slopes for these two kinds of rotation are identical. (After Shepard & Metzler, 1971. Copyright 1971 by the American Association for the Advancement of Science. Reprinted by permission.)

sponse is *same* are displayed in Figure 7–6. As you can see, they found strikingly linear functions relating RT to degrees of rotation, both for rotations in the picture plane and in the depth plane. Furthermore, the slope for both of these functions was 17.5 msec/degree. Shepard and Metzler concluded that subjects are performing mental operations which are analogous to rotating one image into congruence with the other and that they are able to perform this rotation at the rate of about 55–60 degrees per second (i.e., 1,000 msec / 17.5 msec per degree) for three dimensional stimuli of the sort used in their study. In addition, they noted that since subjects performed the rotation as quickly in the depth plane as in the picture plane, the images they are dealing with are best thought of as being analogous to three-dimensional objects rather than two-dimensional pictures. Otherwise, picture plane rotation would be faster than depth plane rotation.

Shepard and his colleagues have done additional studies in order to test the validity of their interpretation (cf. Metzler & Shepard, 1974). For example, if subjects are performing mental operations analogous to rotation, then it should be possible to determine the rate of rotation for an individual subject (by determining the slope of his RT by degrees of orientation function) and then to anticipate the orientation of his/her image at given times. In order to test this prediction, the two stimuli to be compared were presented one after the other with a delay in between. The duration of this delay varied from trial to trial depending on the degrees of rotation required for that particular trial; i.e., the second stimulus was presented after a delay at which the subject should have rotated the first stimulus into the orientation of the second stimulus. Consider, for example, a subject whose slope in Shepard's typical simultaneous presentation condition indicated that he rotates images at the rate of 60 degrees per second. For this subject, when the second stimulus was rotated 60 degrees from the first, Shepard would wait exactly 1 second after presenting the first stimulus before presenting the second. If the second stimulus was rotated 120 degrees from the first, then Shepard would wait 2 seconds before presenting the second stimulus. Notice that in each of these cases, if the subject is in fact rotating the first stimulus mentally at a rate of 60 degrees per second, then the second stimulus should match the orientation of his image precisely and he should be able to respond quickly without any further mental rotation. That is, RT should not increase with degrees of rotation. In fact, this is what Shepard found. Apparently, then, Shepard was able to predict the orientation of the subject's mental image, adding additional credibility to the conclusion that subjects actually are engaging in mental rotation that occurs at a fixed rate.

Shepard and his colleagues have gone on to study other mental operations in the imagery system. For example, Shepard and Feng (1972) reported a study of mental paper folding. Examine the problems in Figure 7–7. In each case, keeping the shaded portion as a stationary base, judge whether the two arrows would be pointing directly at each other if the box were folded up. In doing this task most people judge that they are folding a mental image of the box. Shepard and Feng found some evidence consistent with these introspections; as the number of folds required to make the judgment increased they found an accompanying increase in reaction time.

Is the imagery system visual? The mental rotation and paper folding studies we have just discussed suggest that operations on mental images are similar to the operations performed during perception of external objects. Is it possible to specify the nature of images more precisely? For example, the introspections reported in the kinds of tasks we have just described suggest that visual arrays are involved. People often report "seeing pictures" in their minds when they are performing these tasks. Is it safe to conclude that this imagery system

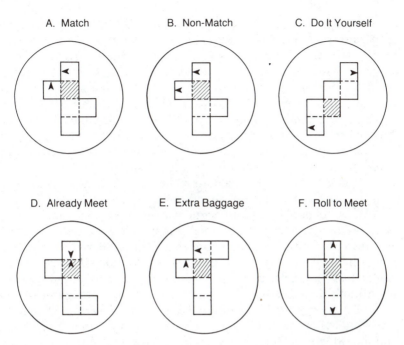

Figure 7–7. Six illustrative mental-paper-folding problems from the Shepard and Feng study. Try each of them yourself. (From Shepard & Feng, 1972. Copyright 1972 by Academic Press. Reprinted by permission.)

is visual? No. In fact, recent studies suggest that the system is better characterized as spatial than as visual.

Consider a series of studies by Baddeley and Lieberman which are cited in Baddeley, 1976. Recall Brooks' selective interference study in which he found that making judgments about an imagined letter is rendered more difficult when the subject must point his responses than when he must say them. Baddeley and Lieberman noticed that the interference with imagining the letter might come from either or both of two characteristics of the pointing response. For one thing, the response requires visual monitoring and it may be the visual nature of this response that causes the selective interference with mental imagery. This possibility is in keeping with the notion that imaging the letter requires part of the visual perceptual system. On the other hand, the pointing response also requires spatial monitoring, since the Y's and N's are scattered, and it might be that the spatial organization required by the response is interfering with the spatial relations in the image.

In order to decide between these possibilities, Baddeley and Lieberman examined the effects of two different kinds of interfering tasks on performance in Brooks' visual and sentence tasks. One of the interfering tasks was designed to provide visual, but not spatial, interference. This was accomplished by asking subjects to make judgments about the brightness of a series of blank stimulus slides that could have one of two levels of brightness. The second interfering task was designed to provide spatial, but not visual, interference. In this case, the subject was blindfolded and given a flashlight with which he was to track a swinging pendulum. The pendulum was equipped with a photosensor, so that whenever the subject shined the flashlight beam on the pendulum he heard a sound. The subject's task, then, was to keep the sound on continuously.

When Baddeley and Lieberman examined how much each of these tasks interfered with Brooks' sentence task (which presumably requires verbal coding), they found that both interfered equally. However, when subjects were asked to perform Brooks' imagery task, the spatial task of tracking the pendulum while blindfolded interfered much more than did the visual task of monitoring brightness. Thus, the selective interference studies we considered earlier, though still providing evidence that the imagery system is distinct from the verbal, should not be interpreted to mean that this imagery system is visual—in the sense of being a mental picture of the object imaged. The fact that a nonvisual spatial task interferes with imagery so much suggests that the structural characteristic that visual imagery has in common with visual perception is the fact that both rely upon spatial organization.

Another line of evidence suggesting that the imagery system is not necessarily visual comes from studies of individuals who have been blind from birth. If the imagery system is visual, then such people should be lacking this system, or, at least it should operate in a fashion different from that of the sighted person. It would be helpful to have a series of systematic investigations comparing the blind and sighted on tasks that seem to require imagery, but so far we only have isolated studies. Two of these are particularly interesting. First, it has been shown that people who have been blind since birth benefit just as much from instructions to use imagery as do sighted people, and in addition, such individuals remember concrete words better than abstract words, just as sighted people do (Jonides, Kahn, & Rozin, 1975). These findings suggest, then, that whatever is the cause of the memorial advantage conferred by imagery, it does not require that the visual system ever have processed external stimuli.

In another study (Marmor & Zaback, 1976) a haptic version of Shepard's mental rotation task was given to three groups of subjects, one sighted, one blind either from birth or before the age of 5 (early blind), and one blinded later in life (late blind). In this task, people had to feel two stationary objects to decide whether they were identical or mirror images of each other, and the experimenters varied the degrees difference in orientation between the stimuli to be compared. The most striking characteristic of the results was that all three groups, whether sighted or not, showed a linear increase in RT as the number of degrees of rotation was increased, suggesting that all three groups are using some internal rotation process that is analogous to the operation of rotating the objects. The major difference among the groups was in the rate of mental rotation (inferred from the slopes of the functions). Whereas the sighted rotate at the rapid rate of 233 degrees/second, the early blind group only rotates at the rate of approximately 60 degrees/second, and the late blind group falls somewhere in between. Since people who have never had any visual experience reveal a pattern of RT's so similar to that of sighted individuals, both groups may be engaging in a similar mental process. Since this process cannot be visual for the blind people, these findings are most consistent with the hypothesis that the imagery system does not consist of mental pictures.

DIFFERENCES AMONG INDIVIDUALS

In the late 1800's Sir Francis Galton (1883) distributed an imagery questionnaire to 100 people, many of whom were learned scientists and scholars. Each respondent was asked to call to mind his breakfast table from that morning and answer a series of questions about the images this brought forth. Galton found enormous differences among individuals. Some reported vivid images which preserved detailed information, whereas others insisted that they could not conjure up any image at all. If you will question friends, I suspect you will find as much variation among individuals as Galton did.

You might think that people who report vivid visual imagery would have more accurate memory for visual scenes and would gain more benefit from using imagery mnemonics than subjects who report little or no visual imagery. Nonetheless, there is no evidence that this is the case (e.g., Sheehan & Neisser, 1969; Bartlett, 1932). For example, Bartlett classified his subjects into verbalizers (who reported using words to remember) and visualizers (who reported using visual images to remember). He found that the visualizers were more confident in their own accuracy of recall than the verbalizers, but the groups, in fact, recalled equally well.

Although subjectively rated vividness of mental imagery is not a reliable predictor of individual differences in memory accuracy, it is clear that there are substantial and reliable differences in the speed and accuracy with which people operate on mental images. For example, the mental rotation task developed by Shepard and his colleagues is especially revealing. They have found substantial differences among individuals in the rate at which images can be rotated (e.g., Metzler & Shepard, 1974). (Recall that this rate is inferred from the slope of the RT by degrees of rotation function.) Furthermore, these differences in speed are correlated with measures of spatial reasoning that are often included in standardized tests of IQ (cf. Snyder, 1972). That is, people who are slow at rotating mental images in Shepard's task are poor at solving more complicated spatial reasoning problems, suggesting that the slope obtained in Shepard's studies is tapping the processes involved in spatial thinking. It is also of interest that Shepard and his colleagues have found that women tend to have steeper slopes (i.e., rotate more slowly than men), a finding in keeping with the fact that women usually score more poorly than men in standardized tests of spatial reasoning.

We have seen then that for reasons as yet unknown, some individuals are more skilled at manipulating mental images than others. We have seen, too, that people differ from one another in the extent to which they report visual imagery, but that as yet there is no evidence that such reports predict the accuracy of memory. People who report being visualizers remember no better than people who report being verbalizers. There are at least two possible explanations for the lack of correlation. One is simply that being asked to rate the vividness of your imagery is a very strange task, since you are being asked implicitly to compare the vividness of your own images with those of others. Since you cannot experience someone else's images, such ratings of imagery vividness may have little meaning.

The alternative possibility is more interesting. Perhaps people who report vivid mental images *do* rely more upon such images than people who report that they do not use images. (In terms of our overview theory, the former group relies more upon visual working memory than the latter.) However, such reports may not correlate with the accuracy of memory, because either visualizing or verbalizing can be used for effective recall. We saw in an earlier chapter that though most mnemonic techniques have employed mental imagery, some very effective ones have not (e.g., the method of analytic substitutions). Some evidence in keeping with this alternative is particularly fascinating, for it comes from examining two extraordinary mnemonists.

The first is S, a mnemonist who was studied by A. R. Luria in the Soviet Union prior to World War II. Luria's account of S is contained in a wonderful book entitled *The Mind of a Mnemonist*. The second is VP, a man who has been studied by Earl Hunt and his colleagues at the University of Washington since 1971. We already mentioned VP briefly in our discussion of Sternberg's research.

Both S and VP have remarkable memories. As adults, for example, both could remember conversations verbatim that took place years before. In fact, both S and VP earned at least part of their living by performing memory feats. VP was tested quite recently, since the development of many of the theories and techniques we have discussed, so we have very detailed information on his skills. For example, he reveals no forgetting in the Peterson and Peterson short-term memory paradigm. He recalls Bartlett's stories almost verbatim. Like most master chess players he remembers the placement of chess pieces extremely accurately, but unlike them, he remembers illegal combinations as accurately as legal combinations, as long as he is given additional time to study the illegal combinations.

Despite their shared feats of memory, closer examination of S and VP indicates that they use very different kinds of strategies, differences which parallel the distinction between visual-spatial and verbal-linguistic codes that we have stressed throughout this chapter. S reported imagery so vivid that it was actually troubling. He could not read poetry since it immediately brought to mind vivid visual images which he could not control. This imagery was helpful, though, when he needed to learn long lists of arbitrary items for his memory performances. He often used the method of loci to perform these feats. The few errors he made on such occasions, he said, were due to having constructed images that were of poor visual quality. For example, once he had pictured an egg on a white background. Later when he tried to recall it he could not "see" the egg in his mind because it faded into the background. It is clear from Luria's studies that S had unusually accurate visual imagery which he used almost to the exclusion of any kind of semantic coding. Once, for example, S was given the matrix below to remember:

```
1  2  3  4
2  3  4  5
3  4  5  6
4  5  6  7
```

He learned it no faster than he would have learned a randomly arranged set. In fact, he commented later that if he were given the letters of the alphabet in order, he probably wouldn't notice the fact!

In contrast, VP reports no strong visual imagery at all. Instead, he says he uses verbal recoding schemes, often relying on the fact that he knows many languages. Therefore, even if he must try to remember arbitrary sequences of letters, it is usually the case that he knows a word in some language that is similar to that sequence. Hunt and Love's (1972) studies of VP confirm his reports. There is no evidence that he has unusually accurate visual imagery. When he is given standardized IQ tests, in fact, his lowest scores are on visual-spatial tasks such as object assembly, picture completion, and picture arrangement.

When he is given free recall tasks in which it would be possible to cluster by both visual characteristics and meaning (e.g., Frost's 1972 study described in Chapter 6), he clusters only on the basis of meaning, despite the fact that most college students use both visual characteristics and meaning. This suggests that, if anything, VP uses imagery less often than the rest of us.

Comparing S and VP, then, indicates that individuals who have remarkably good memories do not necessarily rely upon the same kinds of strategies and codes. We should not find it too surprising, then, that among more normally fallible individuals, reports of the vividness of imagery are not correlated with the accuracy of recall. It is possible that people are accurate at reporting whether or not they use imagery to represent to-be-remembered material, but that people who are not using imagery are employing equally effective verbal-linguistic or semantic codes. Of course, if this is the case, then future studies should reveal that reports of the vividness of imagery are correlated, not with overall accuracy of recall, but with other more analytic measures such as patterns of errors or reaction time. To use just one example, recall Peterson's study of memory for seen versus mentally constructed matrices. People who report vivid mental imagery would be expected to show more similarity in error patterns on the seen and imagined matrices than people who do not report vivid mental imagery. Thus, by using some of the more analytic techniques we have discussed so far it may be possible to gain a better understanding of how individuals differ from each other, and how these differences influence other aspects of thinking.

CHAPTER SUMMARY

This chapter has explored the functions and nature of mental imagery. Theorists may be divided into two major camps: the propositional theorists and the dual-coding theorists. We saw that there are findings which support both approaches, and we suggested that the best working hypothesis is that there is only one underlying propositional code in long-term memory—a code which is neither verbal nor imagery based, but is more abstract than either. Propositional networks of the sort proposed by Anderson's ACT model provide promising models of the organization of this knowledge. All long-term knowledge, including knowledge about the perceptual characteristics of experiences is stored in this underlying propositional network. In addition, we postulate at least two different working memory systems which operate relatively independently, one of which is spatial-imagery and the other verbal-linguistic. People can exert at least some control over which of these systems will be used. The nature of the imagery system must be investigated further, because there are reasons to doubt that it is actually visual in nature.

SUGGESTED READING

You will find good general discussions of the topics considered in this chapter in Chapter 9 of Baddeley's text *The Psychology of Memory,* in Chapter 8 of Norman's *Memory and Attention* (1976) which also includes many references for further reading, in Neisser's (1972) article, "Changing conceptions of imagery," in Paivio's book *Imagery and Verbal Processes,* in Block's edited volume, and in Kosslyn's book.

The debate between the propositional and dual-coding views is particularly important and interesting. You would best begin by reading Pylyshyn's article, "What the mind's eye tells the mind's brain: A critique of mental imagery." All later articles reference this one, since Pylyshyn outlined the important issues so well. Then read the recent articles by Anderson (1978) and Kosslyn and Pomerantz (1977). The article by Shepard and Podgorny (1978) also contains a wealth of thought-provoking ideas. Palmer (1978) presents an excellent discussion of the general problem of mental representation.

The mental rotation studies by Shepard and his colleagues have captured a great deal of interest, for they promise to provide us with a way of examining the operations of the mind's eye using reliable measures such as RT. I particularly recommend the review articles by Metzler and Shepard (1974) and Shepard (1975).

For want of space, I have omitted the interesting work on the so-called symbolic distance effect; I suggest articles by Moyer and Bayer (1976), Banks (1977), Kerst and Howard (1977), and Banks and Flora (1977). You might also be interested in recent work on the acuity of mental images by Finke and Kurtzman (1981) and Finke and Kosslyn (1980).

The accounts of individuals with extraordinary memories are always inherently interesting. Everyone should have the joy of reading Luria's book *The Mind of a Mnemonist.* For accounts of more modern day mnemonists, consult Hunt and Love's (1972) article and Chapter 14 of Baddeley's text. The latter contains brief accounts of several other mnemonists as well.

Language THREE

Language as the Linguist Sees It

FOOD FOR THOUGHT

Begin by answering two questions:

1. Is the following string of words grammatical?

COLORLESS GREEN IDEAS SLEEP FURIOUSLY

2. Is the following string of symbols grammatical? That is, does it conform to the rules of arithmetic?

$32 \times 483 = 15,456$

Now, try to explain how you decided the answer to each. Is it easier to provide this explanation for one of these questions than for the other? Why? What does this suggest about the differences between the rules that underlie language and those that underlie arithmetic?

LINGUISTICS AND PSYCHOLOGY

So far we have talked about language only incidentally. We examined how people remember and forget linguistic units such as words, sentences, or paragraphs, but we were not concerned with the processes by which we perceive the sounds of speech or comprehend the meaning of stories and conversations. Our emphasis is about to change, for in this and the following three chapters we are going to focus on a branch of cognitive psychology called *psycholinguistics*. As its name implies, psycholinguistics is a hybrid discipline that unites the psychologist's study of mental processes and structures with the linguist's study of language. The goal of the psycholinguist, then, is to specify the mental processes and structures that underlie our ability to produce and comprehend language.

For the most part, people take language for granted. In everyday conversation language is a *tool* through which ideas are communicated, so there is no reason it should be the center of focus. Furthermore, language is a common part of our everyday lives and a skill which virtually all humans master, and all of us tend to take the commonplace for granted.

One of the best things about studying psycholinguistics is that you will gain new respect and admiration for the linguistic abilities we all share. The major goal of the next few chapters will be to help you appreciate more fully the remarkable complexity and subtlety of language, and to make you aware of the mysteries of language that still remain to be explained.

In the three chapters following this one, we will consider how the information-processing model we have been developing can be expanded to capture what psycholinguists have learned about language comprehension and production. In the present chapter, however, we will examine language as the linguist sees it. Why this foray into the domain of linguistics? First, since linguists have attempted to specify precisely the nature of language itself, the terms and theories they introduced have been important tools for *psycho*linguists, who seek to specify how people go about using language.

Second, linguistics provided one major impetus for the cognitive revolution in psychology. In the first chapter I indicated that the arguments put forth by the linguist Chomsky led many psychologists to see the inadequacy of traditional behavioristic approaches. Furthermore, these arguments led other psychologists to study how children acquire language. When they did so they became even more disenchanted with behavioristic theories, because a number of phenomena appeared that could not be explained in any obvious way within the confines of behaviorism. In this chapter you will learn exactly what arguments Chomsky put forth, and you will become familiar with some characteristics of language acquisition that seem incompatible with behavioristic accounts of language.

COMPETENCE AND PERFORMANCE

When they are first confronted with linguistics, many students of psychology are confused, because the linguist is likely to ask different questions than the cognitive psychologist. When psychologists study language, they are usually concerned with understanding the series of mental processes and structures that are called into play when a person attempts to comprehend or to produce a statement. Psychologists take into account various characteristics of human cognition, such as memory and information processing limitations. Another way to put it is that the psychologist wishes to specify the strategies (or, to use the program analogy, the set of programs) that the person uses when understanding and planning utterances. In these senses, then, the psychologist is interested in linguistic *performance*.

The linguist, on the other hand, usually has a more abstract goal in mind. Linguists wish to outline the system of rules that would be sufficient to describe the person's knowledge of the structure of his language. This system of rules is called a *descriptive grammar*. Thus, the linguist focuses not on performance, but on linguistic *competence*, or linguistic knowledge. The linguist does *not* claim that this set of rules describes the sequence of steps involved in actually producing or understanding an utterance, only that this set of rules is adequate to describe the structure of language. In sum, the linguist's focus is on the abstract system of language, whereas the psychologist's stress is on how people use language.

Of course, the distinction between competence and performance is not clear cut, and in fact, the two are intimately related. Two different analogies may help here. One way to think about competence and performance is to think of the distinction between definitional and calculational formulae in the domain of mathematics. For example, there is both a definitional formula and a computational formula for the standard deviation. The former is best if you wish to define the nature of the standard deviation, but it is a rather cumbersome formula to use if you wish to compute a given value. For the latter task, the computational formula is more appropriate. Thus, although people know both formulae, it is usually only the computational formula that is brought into play when people solve problems. Notice, however, that the two formulae are equivalent in the sense that either of them would lead to the same answer for a given set of scores. The grammar the linguist seeks is analogous to the definitional formula (i.e., linguistic competence), whereas the performance theory the psychologist seeks is analogous to the computational formula.

A second analogy has been suggested by Slobin (1979) in which the model of competence is likened to a map of language, and the model of performance is likened to a set of rules for using the map.

Both of these analogies show that it would be foolish to study either competence or performance in isolation. If we wish to specify the set of strategies that underlies performance, it is helpful to have a theory of competence. Furthermore, they illustrate that adopting a particular theory of competence puts *some* limits on the nature of the theory of performance, but for a given theory of competence, there might be a number of alternative models of performance. That is, given a particular definitional formula in mathematics, it is possible for there to be a number of different computational formulae, all of which yield the same answer, though by markedly different routes.

In this chapter, then, we will examine the grammars (i.e., models of competence) that linguists have developed, and in the remaining chapters of this section we will attempt to incorporate these models into our information-processing theory in order to explain linguistic performance.

Explicit and implicit rules. The single most important point that we can gain from the linguists' study of competence is that language users know a set of rules. This is clear, the linguists note, because language is *productive*. That is, native speakers of a language are able to produce and comprehend an infinite number of sentences, many of which they have never heard before.

Of course, language is not the only rule-governed, productive system that we possess. Another is arithmetic, and it is instructive to analyze the similarities and differences between these two rule-governed systems. Arithmetic, like language, enables you to deal with an infinite number of novel problems. You were able to answer the second question posed at the beginning of this chapter because you were able to apply the rules of arithmetic in analyzing it. It is highly unlikely that you remembered the answer to that particular problem. Similarly, you were able to judge that Chomsky's famous string of words in the first question (COLORLESS GREEN IDEAS SLEEP FURIOUSLY) is grammatical, not because you have heard that particular string before, but because it seems to conform to the rules of English, even though it doesn't make much sense.

Thus, both arithmetic and language are rule-governed, productive systems, but there are at least two important differences between these two rule systems. First, the rules of arithmetic were probably taught to you quite intentionally. For the most part, children who are not taught arithmetic do not learn it. In contrast, as we will see later in this chapter, children seem to acquire knowledge of the rules of language without such intentional teaching, merely through exposure to the language, during the first four years or so of life.

The second, and related, difference is that you probably find it easy to describe the rules of arithmetic, whereas you find it difficult to describe the rules of language. Thus, in the case of the multiplication question at the beginning of the chapter, you were probably able to describe the sequence of steps involved in determining the answer. In contrast, you probably had more difficulty justifying your answer to the COLORLESS GREEN string. Most people report that it just "sounds" grammatical, in much the same way that THE TWO RED BRICKS sounds right, whereas THE RED TWO BRICKS sounds wrong.

Given these differences, the rules of arithmetic are often called *explicit rules*, because the user can state them readily and learns them through explicit teaching. The rules of language are termed *implicit rules*, because the language user cannot state them readily and they are learned without explicit tuition. The linguists have set themselves the task of specifying what this elusive set of rules must be, and we turn to that attempt now.

LINGUISTIC INTUITIONS

Remember that when we attempted to develop a theory of the structure of long-term memory in Chapter 6 we began by determining what phenomena the model should be able to explain. Linguists have adopted a similar approach when they have attempted to write descriptive grammars. That is, they have noted that the native speakers of a language have certain *linguistic intuitions*, and that if a descriptive grammar is to be an adequate competence theory, it must be able to account for these. Let us consider four such intuitions now.

Grammaticality. First, the speakers of a language are able to judge whether or not a given string of words is grammatical, i.e., they have intuitions about *grammaticality*. You would judge (1) following to be a grammatical English sentence, whereas (2) is not, even though both strings consist of the same four words.

(1) All politicians kiss babies

(2) Kiss politicians babies all

Furthermore, these judgments of grammaticality are not simply judgments of whether or not a string "makes sense" as Chomsky's COLORLESS GREEN sentence demonstrates. These intuitions suggest that you know, albeit implicitly, a set of rules which specifies the constraints to which a string of words must conform in order for it to be grammatical. The linguist attempts to write a descriptive grammar that makes these rules explicit.

Grammatical relations. Second, the speakers of any language have intuitions about *grammatical relations*; presented with a grammatical string of words, people are able to report the relations among them. For example, in sentence (1), people agree that POLITICIANS is the subject of the sentence, BABIES is the object, KISS the action, and ALL modifies POLITICIANS, not BABIES. You might argue that these intuitions are learned in school, since children are taught to assign the labels *subject, verb, object*, etc. This is not the whole story, though, because even if he/she didn't know the labels we used, any native speaker would be able to answer correctly such questions as, "Who is doing the kissing?" and "Who is being kissed?"

Chomsky noted that people have very subtle intuitions about these things. Despite the fact that (3) and (4) following have very similar word order, people understand intuitively that the relations among the words in the two sentences are different.

(3) John is eager to please

(4) John is easy to please

You will realize this if you ask yourself who is doing the pleasing in each sentence. Clearly, the answer is "John" in (3), and "someone else" in (4). Apparently, you have a set of rules that specifies the grammatical relations. Any grammar proposed by the linguist should be able to account for these intuitions.

Sentence relations. Third, the speakers of a language have intuitions about *sentence relations*. That is, people will usually agree that, despite apparent differences among the following sentences, they are all closely related to each other.

(5) **The gorilla chased the orangutang.**

(6) **The orangutang was chased by the gorilla.**

(7) **The gorilla did not chase the orangutang.**

(8) **The orangutang was not chased by the gorilla.**

(9) **Did the gorilla chase the orangutang?**

(10) **Was the orangutang chased by the gorilla?**

(11) **What chased the orangutang?**

(12) **What did the gorilla chase?**

If the linguist's grammar is to capture the knowledge the native speaker possesses, it must account for those perceived relations among sentences.

Ambiguity. Fourth, native speakers of a language have intuitions about *ambiguity*. Upon examination of strings of words like (13) and (14) following, they are able to realize that each string is ambiguous in that it has more than one possible meaning.

(13) **They are eating apples.**

(14) **Visiting relatives can be a nuisance.**

Sentence (13) could refer to people who are eating apples or to a group of eating, as opposed to cooking, apples. Sentence (14) could be paraphrased either as "It is a nuisance to visit relatives," or "Relatives who visit are a nuisance." On the other hand, you know that (15) and (16) are not ambiguous.

(15) **They are eating pie.**

(16) **Visiting relatives is a nuisance.**

In writing a descriptive grammar, then, the linguist will insist that it account for the knowledge that underlies these intuitions about ambiguity.

Of course, we have many other intuitions about language, but we will concentrate on the preceding four because these were the intuitions on which Chomsky focused when he advanced his arguments against behavioristic theories.

THREE KINDS OF GRAMMAR: CHOMSKY'S ANALYSIS

In his 1957 book *Syntactic Structures*, Chomsky examined three different kinds of grammars, and it was his criticisms of the first two that were to have so much impact on the scientific revolution in psychology. We will examine each kind of grammar in turn.

Left-to-right grammar. In this first kind of grammar, *the occurrence of each word is determined by the immediately preceding word or series of words.* According to this kind of grammar, then, linguistic competence can be reduced to a set of probabilities that one word or string of words will follow another, and the native speaker's knowledge of his language can be expressed as a large set of such probabilities. As Chomsky noted, such a left-to-right grammar has been assumed (either implicitly or explicitly) by most stimulus-response and behavioristic theorists.

As an example, imagine an organism (or a machine) with a very limited vocabulary consisting only of the set of words depicted in Figure 8–1. One possible left-to-right grammar describing how those words could be combined is shown in the figure. The grammar depicts links between words, and each link has associated with it some probability that the pointed-to word will follow the word preceding it. Thus, according to this grammar, if the word THE is produced, the grammar records that the next word in the sentence will be YOUNG with probability .6, OLD with probability .2, and INTELLIGENT with probability .2.

According to this kind of grammar, then, judgments of grammaticality reflect the probability that a particular string of words could

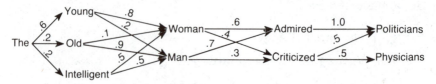

Figure 8–1. An example of a left-to-right grammar. The values next to each link refer to the probability of the linked words occurring next to each other.

occur. Grammatical strings are those with high probabilities of occurrence. For example, the string THE YOUNG WOMAN ADMIRED POLITICIANS is grammatical, according to the grammar in Figure 8–1, but the string THE YOUNG ADMIRED INTELLIGENT is not, since there is no path in the grammar corresponding to the latter string.

This example should clarify why this form of grammar is so attractive to stimulus-response theorists. Sentences are viewed simply as stimulus-response chains, with each word acting both as a response to the preceding word and as a stimulus for the next. Thus, sentences are assumed to be organized in a left-to-right fashion. Furthermore, this kind of grammar does not require that any abstract unobservables be postulated. It simply requires the assumption that people store records of past sequences of events, i.e., the relative frequency with which an individual word or series of words has occurred in a particular sequence in the past.

As Chomsky argued in 1957, though, language cannot be explained so simply. In fact, several years before Chomsky published his criticisms, the great neuropsychologist Karl Lashley (1951) published a paper entitled "The Problem of Serial Order in Behavior," in which he anticipated many of the inadequacies Chomsky highlighted. We will draw on both Lashley's and Chomsky's criticisms in marshalling evidence for the inadequacy of this kind of grammar.

First, left-to-right grammars are not capable of accounting for *any* of the linguistic intuitions outlined. They cannot account for our intuitions about grammaticality, because our judgments are not determined by the past frequency with which given pairs of words have occurred together. Consider again Chomsky's COLORLESS GREEN sentence, which most people judge to be grammatical. It seems very unlikely that most of us have been exposed to numerous occurrences of the pairs COLORLESS GREEN, GREEN IDEAS, IDEAS SLEEP, or SLEEP FURIOUSLY. On the other hand, it is possible to take a string of words which consists of very high frequency pairs, yet is judged to be ungrammatical. Number (17) following, taken from Miller and Selfridge (1950) is a case in point.

(17) Was he went to the newspaper is in deep end

Clearly, then, contrary to the assumptions of left-to-right grammars, judgments of grammaticality are *independent* of the past probabilities of word-to-word pairs.

Left-to-right theories fare no better with the other intuitions. A machine or a person that possessed only a grammar of the sort depicted in Figure 8–1 would have no basis for knowing about grammatical relations, sentence relations, or ambiguity. In the case of the latter, for example, if the grammar records only the probability of word-to-word pairs, then there is no way for the grammar to distinguish strings of words that are ambiguous from those that aren't.

A second problem of left-to-right grammars is that they display only very limited creativity or productivity, because the only strings that will be judged grammatical are those containing word-to-word pairs experienced in the past. An individual whose linguistic knowledge consisted of such a grammar could produce (and comprehend) only those strings he had experienced before.

A third inadequacy is the fact that left-to-right grammars are unable to account for many of the slips of the tongue and typographical errors that people make when speaking and writing. One of the most interesting kinds of slips of the tongue is *reversals*, which are also called *Spoonerisms*, after William A. Spooner, an English clergyman who made such slips quite frequently. Some of his most notable slips were the following. Instead of "You have missed all my history lectures", he complained, "You have hissed all my mystery lectures." On what must have been a particularly tongue-tied day, he stated, "Take the flea of my cat and heave it at the louse of my mother-in-law," rather than the intended (??), "Take the key of my flat and leave it at the house of my mother-in-law." Other mistakes, in which the intended words are more obvious, include, "Easier for a camel to go through the knee of an idol" and "The Lord is a shoving leopard to his flock." As these examples reveal, a Spoonerism is an error in which two segments are interchanged. Such slips of the tongue are frequent, and I suggest that you take particular note of them from now on. As you will notice, the resulting errors sometimes lead to words, as in the preceding examples, but this is not always the case. For example, Fromkin (1973), who has recorded and analyzed many slips of the tongue, reported the phrase "glear plue sky" was produced instead of "clear blue sky."

Spoonerisms and other types of speech errors are important here, because of the fact that the reversals often bridge several words in an utterance, e.g., "*h*eave it at the *l*ouse," "*k*nee of an *i*dol," and the usher's infamous statement "let me *s*ew you to your *sh*eet." The point is that left-to-right grammars which propose that each word is the stimulus for the immediately following word cannot account for such errors. In order for someone mistakenly to say "heave it at the louse", he must have had the anticipated word *house* in mind at the time he tried to say *leave*, contrary to the left-to-right grammar's assumptions.

There is a fourth inadequacy of left-to-right grammar, which was noted most graphically by Miller, Galanter, and Pribram (1960, pp. 146–147). If we only learned such associative strings, no one would live long enough to acquire language! Miller, Galanter, and Pribram estimate that each of us would have to hear a minimum of 10^{30} sentences just to be able to produce all possible sentences of 20 words or less!

In summary, then, the probabilistic, left-to-right kind of grammar that is implicit in behavioristic and stimulus-response accounts of language fails on at least four counts. (1) It fails to account for our intuitions concerning grammaticality, grammatical relations, sentence relations, and ambiguity. (2) It does not display creativity. (3) It cannot account for the patterns of speech and typing errors that are observed. (4) It cannot explain how we learn language in a lifetime, let alone the few years that most children require.

Phrase structure grammar. The problems we have just described led Chomsky to conclude that left-to-right grammars are inadequate to describe linguistic competence, so he examined a second kind of grammar—phrase structure grammar—that is radically different. The most important difference is that whereas left-to-right grammars assume sentences to be structured in the form of a left-to-right chain, phrase structure grammars propose a hierarchical structure. They employ a *constituent analysis* in which the sentence is divided into several *constituents* or parts at several levels. Consider, for example, sentence (18).

(18) The terrier tormented the turtle.

If you were asked to divide the sentence into two parts at the most sensible place, where would you put the division? Most people choose the following: (THE TERRIER) (TORMENTED THE TURTLE). Each of these parts is termed a *constituent*. Each constituent can be broken down further to produce constituents at another level. The first, of course, can be broken down into (THE) (TERRIER), and the second into (TORMENTED) (THE TURTLE). The constituent (THE TURTLE) can then be broken down into two more constituents (THE) (TURTLE). We have just divided the sentence into a hierarchy of constituents—a fact that is particularly obvious in the tree diagram depicted in Figure 8–2. Such tree diagrams are called *phrase markers*.

Phrase structure grammars explain our ability to divide sentences into such hierarchically organized constituents by assuming that we have the psychological equivalent of a grammar which contains three kinds of components: (1) a set of *constituent symbols*, such as ARTICLE, NOUN, VERB, NOUN PHRASE, VERB PHRASE, each of which stands for a unit or constituent of the sentence, (2) a set of phrase structure *rules* of the form $X \rightarrow Y$, which stands for "X may be rewritten as Y." These rules specify how one constituent may be replaced by another, and (3) a set of *terminal elements* (usually words),

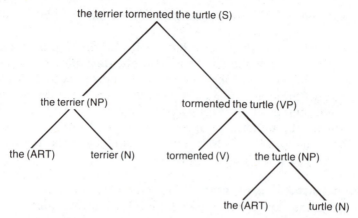

Figure 8–2. A phrase marker for a sample English sentence. The letters in parentheses refer to sentence constituents described in the text and in Figure 8–3.

which are so-called because they cannot be rewritten. That is, they can only appear to the right of the arrow in a phrase structure rule.

The linguist's goal is to propose a set of constituent symbols, phrase structure rules, and terminal elements that will *generate* all the grammatical sequences in a language, but none of the ungrammatical. Thus, phrase structure grammars are one kind of *generative grammar*, in that they attempt to specify a finite set of rules which, if fed into a machine would enable the machine to generate all and only the grammatical sentences in a language. Do not be confused by the term *generative*. Phrase structure grammars do *not* claim that this set of rules specifies how people actually plan and produce sentences, only that the set of rules is sufficient to *characterize* or to *describe the constituent structure* of all possible sentences in a language.

Consider Figure 8–3 which contains an example of a phrase structure grammar that could account for a small sample of English. This example contains each of the three components described. There are constituent symbols; in this case S (for SENTENCE), NP (for NOUN PHRASE), VP (for VERB PHRASE), ART (for ARTICLE), ADJ (for ADJECTIVE), N (for NOUN), V (for VERB). There are terminal elements; in this case *a, an, the, tiny, terrible, terrier, turtle, tormented, teased, tortured.* Finally, there are phrase structure rules describing how grammatical sentences may be derived by beginning with the highest level constituent (S) and progressively applying rules until all constituent symbols have been replaced by terminal symbols.

Consider each of the rules in Figure 8–3 in turn. Rule 1 states that the constituent S may be rewritten as (i.e., may be replaced by) a NOUN PHRASE followed by a VERB PHRASE. Rule 2 states that a

Rule 1	S	$\longrightarrow$ NP + VP
Rule 2	NP	$\longrightarrow$ ART + (ADJ) + N
Rule 3	VP	$\longrightarrow$ V + NP
Rule 4	ART	$\longrightarrow$ { a / an / the }
Rule 5	ADJ	$\longrightarrow$ { tiny / terrible }
Rule 6	N	$\longrightarrow$ { terrier / turtle }
Rule 7	V	$\longrightarrow$ { tormented / teased / tortured }

Figure 8–3. A sample phrase structure grammar.

NOUN PHRASE may be replaced by an ARTICLE, followed by an AD-JECTIVE, followed by a NOUN. The constituent ADJ is placed in parentheses by convention, to indicate that it is optional; i.e., a NOUN PHRASE may or may not include the ADJECTIVE constituent. Rule 3 states that a VERB PHRASE may be replaced by a VERB plus a NOUN PHRASE. The last four rewrite rules specify which terminal elements can replace which constituents. For example, Rule 4 states that the constituent ART may be rewritten as either (the brackets stand for *either*) A, AN, or THE.

Figure 8–4 depicts how the grammar in Figure 8–3 would generate the string THE TERRIER TEASED THE TERRIBLE TURTLE. We begin, as always, by applying Rule 1 which tells us to rewrite the constituent S as NP + VP. We then apply Rule 2, rewriting the NP as

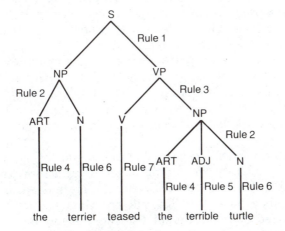

Figure 8–4. An illustration of how a sentence would be generated using the phrase structure grammar of Figure 8–3.

ART + N. Next we apply Rules 4 and 6, inserting the terminal elements *the* and *terrier*. These cannot be rewritten further, so we then apply Rule 3, rewriting the VP as V + NP. Applying Rule 7, we replace V with the terminal element *teased*. We then apply Rule 2 to the remaining NP, replacing it with ART + ADJ + N. Finally, we apply the rules that enable us to fill in the remaining terminal elements.

Notice that the grammar depicted in Figure 8–3 would classify THE TERRIER TORTURED THE TERRIBLE TURTLE as grammatical, because it can generate this sentence using its rules. On the other hand, this particular grammar would classify the string TERRIER TINY TURTLE THE TEASED as ungrammatical, because it could not generate this string. Strings which lack such a constituent structure are ungrammatical.

You should realize how radically different phrase structure grammars are from the left-to-right grammars we considered earlier. First, they assume sentences are organized *hierarchically,* with constituents lodged within other constituents, rather than being a string of responses. Second, they posit a *finite set of rules* that is assumed to underlie the native speaker's linguistic competence, rather than a simple record of all the sequences that have been heard in the past. Finally, they add a level of *abstraction* to language. That is, the constituent symbols and the rewrite rules are never observed directly, rather they are *inferred*.

These changes enable phrase structure grammars to overcome many of the inadequacies of the left-to-right grammars. A first advantage of phrase structure grammars is that they are able to account for several of the linguistic intuitions outlined earlier. They can account for judgments of grammaticality: sentences are judged to be grammatical if they could have been generated by the set of rewrite rules contained in the grammar, regardless of whether or not that particular string of words has ever been encountered before.

Another intuition for which phrase structure grammars can account is our understanding of the grammatical relations among the words within a sentence. According to phrase structure grammars, our ability to decide "who did what to whom" after hearing a sentence reflects the underlying rules that enable us to divide the sentence into constituents.

Phrase structure grammars are also able to account for many of our intuitions about ambiguity. According to phrase structure grammars, sentences like THEY ARE EATING APPLES are judged to be ambiguous because they have two different constituent structures; they could be generated by two different sequences of rewrite rules. To convince yourself that this sentence can be broken down in two different ways, try placing parentheses in the sentence to divide it into constituents, first for one of the possible meanings, and then for the other. You should come up with the following:

((they)((are eating)(apples)))

((they)((are)(eating apples)))

According to phrase structure grammars, then, strings of words for which the grammar specifies no constituent analysis are ungrammatical. Strings for which the grammar specifies a single constituent analysis are grammatical and unambiguous. Strings for which the grammar specifies two or more constituent structures are grammatical, but ambiguous.

A second advantage of phrase structure grammars is that they are capable of displaying unlimited creativity or productivity. The individual who possessed such a grammar could produce, and find constituent analyses for, sentences he had never heard before, as long as the sentences conformed to the rules.

A third advantage of phrase structure grammars is that they are not foiled by the fact that typographical errors and slips of the tongue often bridge several words. This is because they assume sentences to be organized hierarchically, so that two non-contiguous words in the sentence might be related closely at a higher level in the phrase maker.

Fourth, language learning becomes a more manageable task if we assume a phrase structure grammar. Children need not hear and remember all possible grammatical strings of words in order to be fluent. Rather, they need learn a set of phrase structure rules plus a vocabulary organized by form class (e.g., noun, verb, etc.). To be precise, rather than saying that language learning becomes more manageable, perhaps I should say that it becomes different in nature. Fewer strings need be memorized, but the child must acquire something that is never observed directly—phrase structure rules.

Despite these advantages, there are a few inadequacies of left-to-right grammars that phrase structure grammars do not overcome. We will consider three which troubled Chomsky.

First, there are some kinds of ambiguity that phrase structure rules cannot explain. Consider, for example, the ambiguous sentence VISITING RELATIVES CAN BE A NUISANCE. Try dividing it up into constituents for each of the meanings. You will find that both meanings have exactly the same breakdown:

((visiting relatives)((can be)(a nuisance)))

Thus, according to a phrase structure grammar, the sentence is not ambiguous, since it has only one constituent structure.

Second, phrase structure grammars cannot account for our intuitions about sentence relations. As far as such grammars are concerned, the sentences THE DOGS CHASED THE CATS and THE CATS WERE CHASED BY THE DOGS are unrelated. They were generated using two different sets of rules. Therefore, phrase structure grammars cannot explain why we judge these sentences to be related. Furthermore, we know that the JOHN IS EASY TO PLEASE and JOHN IS EAGER TO PLEASE sentences are quite different from each other, yet phrase structure grammars would classify them as closely related, because both sentences were generated using the same rewrite rules (except for inserting EAGER instead of EASY). Thus, phrase structure grammars cannot capture our intuitions about sentence relations.

Third, Chomsky noted that in order for a phrase structure grammar to account for all the linguistic knowledge of the native speaker, it would have to contain a very large number of rules. For example, separate sets of rewrite rules would be needed for generating passive sentences, questions, negatives, and so on. Chomsky proposed an alternative, transformational grammar, in an attempt to overcome these remaining inadequacies.

Transformational grammar. Transformational grammars incorporate phrase structure grammars, but they add a new distinction and a new set of rules.

The inadequacies of the first two grammars we discussed have in common the fact that native speakers of a language have intuitions about sentences that go beyond the strings of words themselves. For example, two strings can look and sound similar (or even identical, in the case of ambiguous sentences), yet people who know the language know that they have different meanings. Furthermore, we know that strings that look and sound quite different, such as THE ELEPHANT ATE THE MOUSE and THE MOUSE WAS EATEN BY THE ELEPHANT are very similar in meaning, nonetheless.

Chomsky attempted to account for these facts by postulating that every possible sentence consists of two levels: a *surface structure* and a *deep structure*. The surface structure is closely related to the string of words we hear or see, whereas the deep structure is closely related to the underlying meaning of the sentence. Thus, we judge JOHN IS EASY TO PLEASE and JOHN IS EAGER TO PLEASE as being quite different in meaning because they have different underlying deep structures despite their similar surface structures. Furthermore, we judge THE ELEPHANT ATE THE MOUSE and THE MOUSE WAS EATEN BY THE ELEPHANT to be similar because they have the same underlying deep structure despite their dissimilar surface structures.

To go along with this new distinction between the surface and deep structure levels of language, Chomsky proposed a new set of

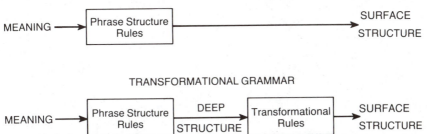

Figure 8–5. An illustration of the levels of sentence structure assumed by phrase structure and transformational grammars.

rules called *transformational rules,* that generate surface structures from underlying deep structures. Transformational rules differ from phrase structure rules in that the latter specify how an individual constituent (e.g., NP) can be rewritten, whereas transformational rules specify how sequences of constituents can be rearranged. For example, transformational rules often include such operations as substitution (stating that one element or set of elements should be substituted for another), displacement (stating that an element should be moved from one place in the deep structure to another), and permutation (stating that two or more elements should be switched with each other, or permuted).

The relation between phrase structure grammars and transformational grammars is illustrated in Figure 8–5, which shows, in somewhat simplified form, the levels of language and the kinds of rules assumed by each kind. Phrase structure grammars assume that there is a level of meaning and a level of surface structure, and that phrase structure rules connect the two. Transformational grammars, on the other hand, assume an additional level of structure and an additional set of rules. They assume that a set of phrase structure rules enables the generation of deep structures, and a set of transformational rules enables surface structures to be generated from deep structures.

We need not go into the details of transformational grammars, but we need to consider at least the outlines of a derivation in order for you to understand this abstract discussion. Figure 8–6 shows an outline of the steps a transformational grammar would take to generate the surface structures THE TERRIER TEASED THE TURTLE, WHAT TEASED THE TURTLE, and THE TURTLE WAS TEASED BY THE TERRIER. The generation of all three sentences would begin by applying the same set of phrase structure rules to generate the deep structure depicted in the figure. This phrase marker represents the deep

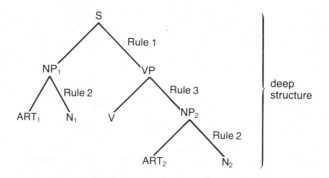

To generate surface structure: THE TERRIER TEASED THE TURTLE.

Substitute terminal elements in the deep structure $((ART_1 + N_1) + (V + (ART_2 + N_2)))$.

To generate surface structure: WHAT TEASED THE TURTLE?

Change $((ART_1 + N_1) + (V + (ART_2 + N_2)))$ to $(("What") + (V + (ART_2 + N_2)))$.
Then insert terminal elements.

To generate surface structure: THE TURTLE WAS TEASED BY THE TERRIER.

Change $((ART_1 + N_1) + (V + (ART_2 + N_2)))$ to $((ART_2 + N_2) + ((AUX + Past Participle of V) + (ART_1 + N_1)))$.
Then insert terminal elements.

Figure 8–6. An illustration of the steps a transformational grammar would assume to underlie three sentences. Note that the sentences have the same deep structure (i.e., the same phrase marker) but different surface structures (i.e., different transformational rules have been applied to the deep structure). The rules refer to those in Figure 8–3. The subscripts differentiate among parts of the deep structure. For example, NP_1 is the first noun phrase in the deep structure, and NP_2 is the second.

structure for all three of the sentences we are discussing. In order to generate the surface structure THE TERRIER TEASED THE TURTLE, we need only insert the appropriate terminal elements (i.e., words). However, in order to generate the surface structure WHAT TEASED THE TURTLE, we need first to apply a transformational rule which specifies that the element WHAT be substituted for the first NP. Alternatively, in order to generate the surface structure THE TURTLE WAS TEASED BY THE TERRIER, a different transformational rule would be applied to the deep structure. This rule would state that the V in the deep structure must be replaced by an auxiliary + the verb in the past participle form, and that the two NP's must be permuted.

Chomsky argued that transformational grammars overcome the inadequacies of phrase structure grammars. First, they are capable of accounting for native speakers' intuitions about the relations among sentences. According to transformational grammar, you know that sentences (5) through (12) are related, because they were all generated with the same set of phrase structure rules and thus they all share the same deep structure. Similarly, you know that the JOHN IS EAGER TO PLEASE and JOHN IS EASY TO PLEASE sentences are different in meaning, because they have been generated using two different sets of phrase structure rules, and thus they have two different deep structures. For the EAGER sentence, JOHN was in the left-most NP in the deep structure (i.e., he was the subject), whereas for the EASY sentence JOHN was in the right-most NP in the deep structure (i.e., he was the object of the action). The superficial surface structure similarity between the two came about because a transformation was applied to the EASY sentence which made the resulting sequence of words similar to those in the EAGER sentence.

Second, transformational grammars can account for the intuitions about ambiguity that foiled phrase structure grammars. According to transformational grammars, sentences such as VISITING RELATIVES CAN BE A NUISANCE are ambiguous because they have two different deep structures, i.e., they could have been generated by either of two different sets of phrase structure rules. In one of these deep structures the relatives are the underlying subject (since they are doing the visiting), and in the other deep structure the speaker is the underlying subject (since the speaker is doing the visiting).

A third advantage of transformational grammars is that they are more parsimonious than phrase structure grammars. Transformational grammars assume a relatively small number of phrase structure rules which generate all deep structures, and a set of transformational rules which enable one deep structure to underlie many different surface structures, including active and passive sentences, negatives, questions, and so on. The total number of rules required is much smaller than the number that would be required if only phrase structure rules were used.

Implications for psychology. Neither linguistics nor psychology has ever been the same since Chomsky's criticisms of left-to-right and phrase structure grammars. At the time of Chomsky's 1957 book, most psychological theories of language acquisition and language use were behavioristic, but Chomsky's (and Lashley's) arguments indicated that two of the basic assumptions of behaviorism were incorrect. In the first place, behavioristic theories (such as B. F. Skinner's) assume language to consist of a chain of responses, not different in principle from the chains of responses that rats can be conditioned to make in a Skinner box. Chomsky's analyses of our linguistic intuitions and Lashley's analyses of slips of the tongue showed, however, that sentences are not simply chains, but rather have hierarchical structure.

In the second place, behavioristic theories assume that behavior can be explained without postulating any abstract unobservables. Yet Chomsky demonstrated that if we are to account for linguistic intuitions and all the other phenomena we outlined, then we *must* postulate a system of rules and an abstract level of language (deep structure) that is not observable. Thus, Chomsky's arguments forced psychologists to view language in a new light, and helped to usher in the cognitive revolution we discussed in the first chapter.

RECENT DEVELOPMENTS IN LINGUISTICS: THE EMPHASIS ON SEMANTICS

It was Chomsky's arguments that first drew linguistics and psychology closer together, but linguistics has continued to change in the past two decades. The overall character of this change is important, since it has influenced psychology.

Chomsky's transformational grammar focused on *syntax*, defined as the *rules for combining* words and parts of words to form sentences. Recently, many linguists have argued that more emphasis must be placed upon *semantics*, defined as the *meanings* underlying words and sentences.

Linguists have argued that semantically focused theories are superior to Chomsky's purely syntactic theory for the same reason that transformational grammar is superior to phrase structure grammar— because semantically based theories can account for a greater number of the native speaker's linguistic intuitions. Consider, for example, the following six sentences:

(19) **Mary broke the bottle.**

(20) **The bottle was broken by Mary.**

(21) **Mary broke the bottle with a hammer.**

(22) **The bottle was broken by Mary with a hammer.**

(23) **The hammer broke the bottle.**

(24) **The bottle broke.**

You would probably agree that all six are very closely related. However, the transformational grammar we outlined cannot account for this intuition. Now it is true that according to Chomsky's grammar (19) and (20) have identical deep structures, that (21) and (22) have identical deep structures, and that the deep structure of (19) and (20) is very similar to that of (21) and (22). But what about (23) and (24)?

Transformational grammar assigns a completely different deep structure to these. For example, the deep structure subject of (23) is HAMMER, and the deep structure subject of (24) is BOTTLE.

Case grammar. Grammatical theories that emphasize semantics are able to account for the relations among these sentences. One such theory is *case grammar*, which was proposed originally by Fillmore (1968). Case grammar is, in fact, a kind of transformational grammar in that it assumes that each sentence has both a deep structure and a surface structure, and that a set of transformational rules relates the two levels. The major difference between case grammar and Chomsky's original transformational grammar is in the nature of the deep structure.

Chomsky's deep structure was organized into a set of syntactic constituents (such as NP), but Fillmore's is organized as a set of semantic relations called *cases*. These *cases* are semantic relations that hold between the verb and each of the noun phrases of the sentence. Fillmore argued that the underlying propositions expressed in all languages can be described by a small, fixed set of universal cases, such as AGENTIVE (the case of the animate instigator of the action), INSTRUMENTAL (the case of the inanimate force or object which causes the action), LOCATIVE, OBJECTIVE, and TEMPORAL. For all of sentences (19) through (24), MARY is the AGENT (though in sentences (23) and (24) she is the implicit agent since she is not named), BOTTLE is the OBJECT, and HAMMER the INSTRUMENT (though unnamed in (24)). Their surface structure differences are assumed to be due to the fact that different sets of transformational rules were applied to the deep structure to yield the surface structures.

The difference between Chomsky's original transformational grammar and Fillmore's case grammar is highlighted in Figure 8–7, which shows the deep structures each would assume to underlie sentence (21). Fillmore assumes the deep structure of each sentence to be composed of a MODALITY (which describes the general mood of the sentence, such as its tense, whether it is a negative or a question, etc.) plus some PROPOSITION. The PROPOSITION is composed of a VERB plus one or more cases, such as AGENTIVE (A). According to both Chomsky's transformational grammar and Fillmore's case grammar, the different surface structures in sentences 19 through 22 are the result of applying different sets of transformational rules.

Advantages of case grammar. Case grammar has two advantages over Chomsky's original transformational grammar. We have already noted the first, i.e., that it describes relations among sentences that were not explained in Chomsky's original formulation. A second advantage is that case grammars have been particularly useful for re-

CHOMSKY'S TRANSFORMATIONAL GRAMMAR

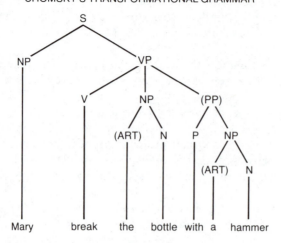

FILLMORE'S CASE GRAMMAR

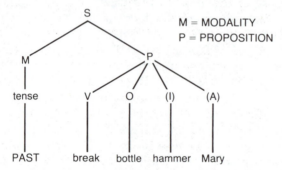

M = MODALITY
P = PROPOSITION

Figure 8–7. A comparison of the kind of deep structures assumed by Chomsky's transformational grammar and Fillmore's case grammar, for the sentence MARY BROKE THE BOTTLE WITH A HAMMER.

cent psychological theorizing, since they stress the centrality of the underlying propositions sentences convey. Recall, for example, that Anderson's ACT theory of long-term memory, which captured many important features of our memory for linguistic materials, incorporated a semantic representation similar to the deep structures postulated by case grammar. Recall that ACT, too, assumed that the sentence must be broken down into a set of propositions.

We have seen, then, that linguistic theories continue to change and that these changes bring with them new insights into the nuances of language—nuances we usually take for granted in our day-to-day use of language. Nonetheless you should remember that these recent developments do *not* change the central message Chomsky presented in 1957—that there is more to language than meets the eye or ear, and that in order to account for linguistic competence and performance, we must postulate unobservable levels of organization and unobservable rules.

LANGUAGE ACQUISITION

Few psychologists still subscribe to a left-to-right conception of language. Some were convinced by Chomsky's arguments that *in principle* no left-to-right theory could account for the characteristics of language, such as ambiguity and productivity. Nonetheless, there were other psychologists who remained unconvinced. You will understand why if you consider the distinction between the Theory Development and Theory Demonstration approaches we discussed in Chapter 6. Remember that the Theory Demonstration approach is the one that most experimental psychologists advocated. That is, experimental psychologists often demand that experiments be designed to test opposing theories. They have been quite skeptical of introspection and naturalistic observation, when employed in the absence of corroborating experiments. Chomsky's arguments did not rest on the results of any experiments. Rather, he relied upon his own and other linguists' intuitions. Some psychologists argued that Chomsky's intuitions might not be the same as the average person's. For example, perhaps only Chomsky and other linguists judge COLORLESS GREEN IDEAS SLEEP FURIOUSLY to be grammatical. Many of these skeptics later became convinced of the inadequacy of left-to-right approaches, though, when empirical evidence accumulated from a related source—detailed analyses of the characteristics of language acquisition.

It is a remarkable fact that children around the world gain fluency in their native languages within the first five years or so of life. In the decades before Chomsky's work came to the attention of psychologists, the acquisition of language was usually explained in behavioristic, stimulus-response terms. It was assumed that the child learned language through reinforcement, imitation, and classical conditioning. Of course, theories differed on the relative weighting they gave to each of these mechanisms, but in general they argued that with development, the child's language comes more and more to mirror that of the adult, and that this occurs because the child is reinforced for speaking grammatically. For example, it was argued that parents and other adults shape the child's speech to be more grammatical by withholding reinforcement (such as a requested cookie) until the child rephrases the statement more grammatically. Furthermore, it was argued that children imitate the speech of the adults around them, and that they are more likely to be reinforced if their imitation is accurate.

Though stimulus-response theories of language acquisition differed, all had at least two points in common. First, they assumed that the child is born without any innate knowledge of language and without any innate tendency to learn it. Second, all such theories predict that with development the child's language will gradually come to mirror the adult's more accurately. Thus, child language should be an unstructured, poor version of adult language. This view of language development follows directly from a left-to-right conception of language. If you assume that sentences are chains of responses, then it seems reasonable to propose that children learn such chains through reinforcement and imitation. In fact, try asking people who have never studied linguistics or cognitive psychology how children go about acquiring language. You will probably find that the accounts they offer are much like the one just outlined.

Chomsky's arguments against left-to-right grammars call the preceding account into question. If linguistic competence consists of an abstract set of rules, and if there are levels of linguistic structure (e.g., deep structure) that are unobservable, then the child is not learning chains of responses. He must acquire rules which are never explicitly presented to him. In fact, Chomsky argued that the child is born with an innate knowledge of language, or at least, with an innate set of rules for processing linguistic stimuli. According to this view, the child need not learn all of language from scratch. Chomsky suggested that components of the deep structure might be innate and that the child's task was then to learn which of the possible sets of rules his particular linguistic community used. Chomsky and other psycholinguists after him argued that there must be some such innate knowledge since children all around the world learn to talk, just as they learn to walk, seemingly without explicit teaching. This is despite the fact that linguistic analyses suggest that learning to talk and comprehend involves mastering a set of abstract rules.

In sum, Chomsky's account of language acquisition differed from the stimulus-response version on two counts. First, he argued that children have some innate knowledge of language at birth. Second, unlike the behaviorists who predicted that child language would be unsystematic, and come gradually to mirror that of the adult, Chomsky's view held that language would be rule governed from the beginning, though the rules might be different from those of the adult community. To some extent, then, child speech should be independent of adult speech.

Of course, Chomsky's proposals flew against both stimulus-response theories and common sense, and the lines of battle were drawn. The conflicting viewpoints and predictions suggested a host of interesting questions to ask about the characteristics of language acquisition, and the 1960's and 1970's saw a previously unheard of number of psychologists doing detailed studies of child language. A number of the characteristics they uncovered were incompatible with the behavioristic view.

Characteristics of language acquisition. First, *children seem geared to learn rules.* One kind of evidence of this is that *children are able to deal with novel sequences in a systematic way.* For example, Berko (1958) studied children's understanding of how words are pluralized. In her procedure, she would present a picture of some object and give it a nonsense name. For example, she showed a child a picture of a birdlike creature and said, "This is a wug." She then presented a picture of two such creatures and primed the child by saying, "Now there are two _____?" The child readily replied "wugs!". This kind of response cannot be explained by arguing that the child had simply remembered what he heard, for it is unlikely that the child had ever heard the word "wugs" before. Clearly, the child had learned a rule for pluralizing.

An even more impressive kind of evidence that children are geared to learn rules is that *overregularization or overgeneralization is rampant in child speech.* Overregularization means that the child applies a rule to an instance which would be an exception in adult speech. Consider, for example, the development of the past tense word ending. The following developmental pattern is usually observed. The first past tenses to appear in the child's speech are typically those of the irregular verbs, such as CAME, WENT, and DID. At this same time the child does *not* use the past tense of most regular verbs, such as WALKED; when such regular verbs are used, they are always in the present tense (e.g., WALK). Later in development, however, the child comes to use the past tense for regular verbs such as WALKED, at which point he also overregularizes this ending to irregular verbs. Thus, the child who was saying CAME, WENT, and DID now begins saying COMED, GOED, and DOED. Such overregularizations sometimes occur for a year or more, before the child learns the exceptions (Ervin, 1964).

This pattern is incomprehensible from the behavioristic perspective. The child had used the correct forms CAME, WENT and DID, presumably being reinforced for them for several months, yet he gave them up to use a form that most parents would never produce themselves, let alone reinforce.

From the cognitive perspective, however, this sequence makes sense, as long as it is assumed that the child attempts to impose organization on experience. Presumably he used CAME, WENT, DID at first because irregular verbs are more frequent than regular. Thus, he learned them by rote memorization. However, when he discovered the rule for making the past tense (i.e., adding the -ed ending), he tried to make order out of the chaos by applying the rule to all verbs. Apparently this striving for order is so strong that he persists for some time despite evidence to the contrary. According to the cognitive view, then, the regression (or step backward) that the child *seems* to make when he switches from CAME to COMED is, in fact, an advance, signalling the fact that he has constructed a rule.

A second fascinating characteristic of child language is that *children around the world make similar patterns of errors, despite the fact that they are exposed to very different languages.* For example, children around the world overregularize. Another example comes from an analysis of the errors children make as they are acquiring the ability to negate sentences. In English, for example, the earliest form of negation is termed *extrasentential negation* in that the child places the negative element (e.g., *no* or *not*) at the beginning (or sometimes the end) of the sentence to be negated, e.g., NO GO HOME or ME FALL NO. In fact, this is the case in all languages that have been studied so far (e.g., Slobin, 1973), despite the fact that none of the languages studied uses this simple form in the adult language. These universals of language development again reveal that the child's language is often quite different from the adult's, but different in a systematic way.

A third characteristic of language development is that *the child's imitations are usually not progressive.* That is, when the child attempts to imitate the adult (which he admittedly does quite frequently) he usually changes the adult utterance to fit with his current level of development (i.e., his current set of rules), rather than mimicking the adult exactly. In fact, observant parents often notice that even when they try to teach the child a new linguistic form, the offspring insists on imitating according to his own rules, not those of the frustrated parent. Amusing examples of such exchanges are frequent in the literature on child development. One particularly famous one was cited by David McNeill (1966, p. 69) taken from the transcripts collected by Roger Brown.

Child: Nobody don't like me.

Mother: No, say "nobody likes me."

Child: Nobody don't like me.

(*Eight* repetitions of this dialogue follow.)

Mother: No, now listen carefully; say "nobody likes me."

Child: Oh! Nobody don't *likes* me.

But my favorite is the following incident reported by the psycholinguist Martin Braine (1971, pp. 160–161):

> I have occasionally made an extensive effort to change the syntax of
> my two children through correction. One case was the use by my two-
> and-a-half-year-old daughter of *other one* as a noun modifier. . . . I re-
> peatedly but fruitlessly tried to persuade her to substitute *other* + N
> for *other one* + N . . . the interchange went somewhat as follows:
> "Want other one spoon, Daddy"—"You mean, you want THE OTHER
> SPOON"—"Yes, I want other one spoon, please, Daddy"—"Can you
> say 'the other spoon'?"—"Other . . . one . . . spoon"—"Say . . .
> other"—"Other"—"Spoon"—"Spoon"—"Other . . . spoon"—"Other
> spoon. Now give me other one spoon." Further tuition is ruled out by
> her protest, vigorously supported by my wife.

In addition to being amusing, these anecdotes (and more controlled
studies examining children's imitations, e.g., Ammon and Ammon,
1971) cast serious doubt on the notion that imitation enables the child
to learn the syntax of his native language. If the child is learning new
forms through imitating what he hears, then his imitations should
contain those new forms. Yet it has been shown again and again that
the child omits those forms that he doesn't use in his spontaneous
speech and, in fact, reformulates the utterance to use his old (and, by
adult standards, incorrect) forms.

A fourth characteristic that has emerged from careful analyses of
spontaneous parent-child interactions is that *there is no evidence that
parents differentially reinforce grammatically correct statements.* The
most oft-cited evidence for this statement is taken from the records
Brown and his colleagues collected by recording parent-child conversations for several children from the ages of one to four-and-one-half
years. Of course, these are just the years during which the most dramatic syntactic development occurs; the average one-year-old makes
only one-word statements, whereas the four-and-one-half-year-old
seems to have mastered most of the rudiments of his language and is
able to converse quite well. If we are to explain language development
by calling upon the concept of differential reinforcement of grammatical statements, then surely we must find evidence that parents are
more likely to reinforce grammatical than ungrammatical statements
during these critical years. When these parent-child interactions were
analyzed extensively, however, there was no evidence for such differential reinforcement. As the authors summarized their findings (Brown,
Cazden, & Bellugi, 1969, pp. 70–71):

> What circumstances did govern approval and disapproval directed
> at child utterances by parents? Gross errors of word choice were some-
> times corrected, as when Eve said *What the guy idea.* Once in a while
> an error in pronunciation was noticed and corrected. Most commonly,
> however, the grounds on which an utterance was approved or disap-
> proved . . . were not strictly linguistic at all. When Eve expressed the

opinion that her mother was a girl by saying *He a girl* mother answered *That's right*. The child's utterance was ungrammatical but mother did not respond to the fact; instead she responded to the truth value of the proposition the child intended to express. In general the parents fit propositions to the child's utterances, however incomplete or distorted the utterances, and then approved or not, according to the correspondence between proposition and reality. Thus *Her curl my hair* was approved because mother was, in fact, curling Eve's hair. However, Sarah's grammatically impeccable *There's the animal farmhouse* was disapproved because the building was a lighthouse and Adam's *Walt Disney comes on, on Tuesday* was disapproved because Walt Disney comes on, on some other day. It seems then, to be truth value rather than syntactic well-formedness that chiefly governs explicit verbal reinforcement by parents. Which renders mildly paradoxical the fact that the usual product of such a training schedule is an adult whose speech is highly grammatical but not notably truthful.

You should notice that this fourth characteristic is more tentative than the others I've cited, because it is based on a *lack* of a finding. The skeptic could quite correctly argue that perhaps the authors simply didn't define reinforcement appropriately or look for it carefully enough. If you are such a skeptic, why not try an informal study yourself if you have any opportunity to observe parents and toddlers talking. If your observations agree with mine, I suspect that your findings will correspond with those of Brown and his colleagues. Of course, middle-class parents try valiantly to alter the speech of the school child or the adolescent who says "ain't" or "me and John," so casual observation suggests that parents *do* try differential reinforcement on their older children. But the major part of language acquisition has occurred much earlier, before the age of five, and it is during these very years that adoring parents seem to provide so little explicit guidance.

Implications.   The characteristics we have just outlined convinced many former stimulus-response theorists (e.g., Palermo, 1970) of the inadequacy of such accounts of language acquisition.

Of course, this is not to say that the child is born knowing language. No one would deny that children acquire the language to which they are exposed. The conclusion we are drawing here is *not* that experience is unimportant, but rather that each new generation of children uses this experience to *construct* language anew. Children do seem to have innate tendencies to process language in certain ways. For example, they all seem to assume that it will be systematic. The fascinating task that is now occupying developmental psycholinguists is that of determining exactly what assumptions are innate and how this innate component enables the child to construct the rules of language using the data provided by experience.

CHAPTER SUMMARY

In this chapter we began our discussion of psycholinguistics, the hybrid discipline that examines the mental processes and structures which underlie our ability to produce and comprehend language. For the most part the current chapter focused on the contributions of linguistics. Linguists stress the distinction between competence (knowledge) and performance, and they usually focus on competence. They attempt to write descriptive grammars, i.e., systems of rules that are sufficient to describe the person's knowledge of the structure of language. When linguists write descriptive grammars, they attempt to propose a set of rules that can account for the linguistic intuitions of the language user.

Chomsky altered the assumptions of both psychology and linguistics in the late 1950's by examining the strengths and weaknesses of three kinds of grammar, including left-to-right (assumed by stimulus-response theories), phrase structure, and transformational grammar. Chomsky's arguments concerning the inadequacies of the first two types of grammar convinced many psychologists that traditional stimulus-response theories are in principle inadequate to account for language, and led psychologists to view language in a new light. The discipline of linguistics has continued to change since Chomsky's writings. More recent linguistic theories (e.g., Fillmore's case grammar) stress meaning, or semantics, more than Chomsky had.

Many psychologists who had previously been behaviorists were convinced by Chomsky's linguistic arguments, and the great majority of the remaining skeptics were won over by the accumulating data from studies of language acquisition in children. A number of the characteristics that have emerged from such empirical observations are totally inconsistent with behavioristic views of language and language acquisition. In particular, (1) children seem geared to learn rules from the very beginning, (2) there are remarkable cross-language similarities in the patterns of language acquisition, (3) imitations are not progressive, and (4) there is no convincing evidence that grammatical statements are differentially reinforced during the preschool years.

SUGGESTED READING

Excellent introductions to linguistic theory can be found in the text by Fromkin and Rodman entitled *An Introduction to Language* and the text by Bolinger called *Aspects of Language*. If you would like to read Chomsky himself, I suggest you begin with *Language and Mind* (1968). This book is more recent than the work discussed in this chapter, but it is easier to follow than the earlier, more technical presentations and it presents an account of Chomsky's views on the relation between linguistics and psychology.

Language acquisition is one of the most fascinating topics in all of psychology, and our account has been very brief. If you wish to read more, you might begin by reading the fine chapters on acquisition in *Psycholinguistics* by Slobin (Chapter 4) and *Psychology and Language* by Clark and Clark (Chapters 8, 9, 10). If you want to delve into the topic in more detail, find the textbook *Language Development* by Dale or *Language Acquisition* by deVilliers and deVilliers. For a thorough bibliography on the topic, containing annotated references to most of the important papers and books published through 1976, turn to Abrahamsen's *Child Language: An Interdisciplinary Guide to Theory and Research.*

As I mentioned in this chapter, most people are unaware of the complexity of everyday language usage, and it is true that linguistics and psycholinguistics texts are often technical. If you would like to recommend engaging, nontechnical books to friends or relatives who've never studied psychology or linguistics, or if you'd like some light, but educational reading yourself, I have two suggestions. Read Jean Aitchison's *The Articulate Mammal* for an account of psycholinguistics and, even better, Peter Farb's *Word Play*, which contains fascinating discussions on wide-ranging aspects of language and its use.

Language Comprehension

FOOD FOR THOUGHT

Here are two different kinds of questions to ponder. First, consider the following two sentences: (1) THE OLD MAN THE BOATS. (2) THE MAN JUDGED THE WINNER BOWED. Why are these sentences difficult and what does their difficulty suggest about the processes underlying language comprehension?

Second, consider the following telephone conversation between a mother and her college student daughter (from Winograd, 1977).

> *Mother:* **Where will your boyfriend sleep?**
>
> *Daughter:* **We have a couch in the living room.**

Assume, for the moment, that the daughter does *not* plan to have her visitor sleep on the couch. Exactly how has she used language to mislead her mother without actually stating an untruth? What does this suggest about the assumptions listeners (in this case the mother) make about communication?

THE PROBLEM OF COMPREHENSION

In the previous chapter we focused on language as a system, but now we return to psychological questions. In particular, we will consider how people comprehend spoken and written language. In this chapter we will examine the processes and structures that are thought to be the same for both language by ear (i.e., listening) and language by eye (i.e., reading and sign language). Then, in the next two chapters we will consider how language processing is influenced by these different modalities.

Throughout this set of chapters, it is important to keep in mind that, for the most part, language is used as a tool for communicating. In most acts of communication, the speaker (or writer) has some idea which he wishes to convey to one or more listeners (or readers). In terms of our overview model, the speaker has some particular set of propositions in long-term memory (i.e., some part of his semantic network) which he wishes to convey to the listener. The only way the speaker can accomplish this is to translate this set of propositions (i.e., this portion of his memory network) into a string of words that the listener can use to construct the appropriate propositional network.

This state of affairs is depicted in Figure 9–1. The diagram is meant to convey the notion that before the conversation began, both the speaker and listener had nodes in semantic memory referring to Sam and to Fred (i.e., both participants in the conversation already

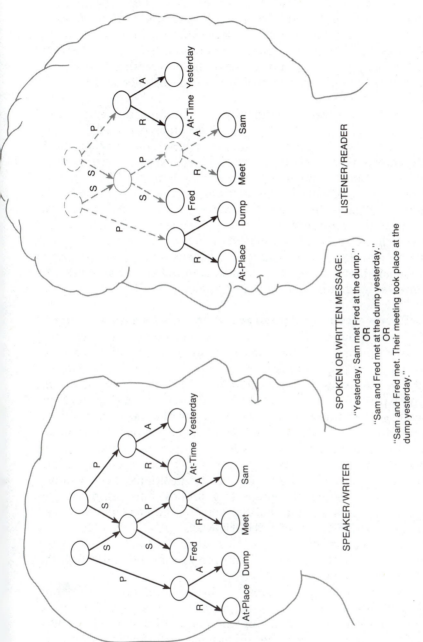

Figure 9–1. A depiction of a successful act of communication. The speaker or writer converts a set of propositions he has in mind into one of a number of alternative strings of words which leads the listener/reader to construct an equivalent set of propositions. In the figure, the solid lines stand for nodes and links that existed in the minds of the participants prior to the speaker's statement, whereas the dashed lines stand for nodes and links that the listener constructed after he heard the speaker's statement.

know Sam and Fred) and both had semantic memory nodes defining the concepts of DUMP and YESTERDAY (though, in the interest of clarity, the diagram does not show these definitions). However, prior to the conversation only the speaker knew that SAM and FRED had met at the dump yesterday, a proposition he now wishes to convey to his listener. If he does so effectively, then the listener will be led to construct the appropriate new links or relations in his own memory.

Framed in this way, the difficulty of communication emphasized by Wundt (1912, cited in Slobin, 1979) becomes particularly apparent—the parts of an idea exist simultaneously with each other, but in order to convey them to someone else, the speaker or writer must order the components sequentially. Then the listener, in turn, must use this sequence to reconstruct the relations among the parts again. As Figure 9–1 indicates, there are always many different strings that the speaker or writer could use to convey a given set of propositions.

Even though communication is a two-way street involving both production and comprehension, we will focus almost exclusively on comprehension. We do so, not because comprehension is inherently more interesting, but because more is known about it.

Propositions as the end-product of comprehension. I argued that if we adopt our overview model, one end-product of a successful act of communication is the construction of a proposition, or set of propositions, in the comprehender's memory network. Notice two important characteristics of this assumption. First, it is consistent with what you have already learned about long-term memory, since it claims that people store away the meaning or gist of the message. Humans, as we saw in Chapter 6, are notably poor tape recorders, but remarkably good meaning-extractors. The second important characteristic of the present assumption is that it proposes that people store away the meaning in a *particular* form, i.e., as propositions. For example, adopting ACT's method of representing propositions (introduced in Chapter 6), we are assuming that the person who has comprehended the sentence GEESE CROSSED THE HORIZON AS WIND SHUFFLED THE CLOUDS has stored away the two propositions (1 and 2) shown in Figure 9–2, plus the superordinate proposition (3) indicating the relation between the two.

Of course, we can never hope to see such structures in the mind directly, but how might we test the propositional assumption by examining performance? A number of techniques for doing so have been developed, all relying upon the following fact: propositional theory assumes that the concepts contained within the same proposition are closer together in the memory network than the concepts contained in different propositions. Thus, according to propositional theory, for our sample sentence, the nodes corresponding to the concepts GEESE

PROPOSITIONAL STRUCTURE

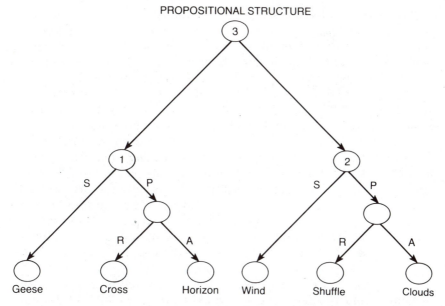

Figure 9–2. A depiction of the propositions contained in a sample sentence
from Ratcliff and McKoon's (1978) study of priming.

and HORIZON are closer together in the memory representation of
that sentence than those corresponding to WIND and HORIZON, because the former is a within-proposition pair and the latter a between-
proposition pair. Propositional theory predicts, then, that these different distances in memory will be reflected in performance.

We will consider only one of the experiments designed to test
this prediction, a study conducted by Roger Ratcliff and Gail McKoon
(1978). Ratcliff and McKoon's study relied upon the phenomenon of
priming, which is defined as the facilitation of response to one test
item when it is preceded by another. You have already learned about
semantic priming in the chapter on the structure of long-term memory. Recall that the time required to make a lexical decision about the
word NURSE, for example, is faster following the semantically related
word DOCTOR than following the unrelated word BUTTER, i.e., DOC-
TOR primes NURSE. According to network theories, this semantic
priming reflects the spread of activation that accompanies looking up
a word in memory. The degree of priming between two words provides a measure of the distance between their concept nodes in
memory.

Ratcliff and McKoon used priming to reveal the memory structure of newly learned sentences. They presented their subjects with a
list of sentences to memorize, including the sample sentence shown

in Figure 9–2. After the subject had demonstrated that he had committed the sentences to memory, a 20-minute retention interval occurred, followed by a word recognition test. In this test the person saw a series of words, some of which had occurred in the sentences he had just memorized (i.e., old words) and some of which had not (i.e., new words). For each, the person was to judge as quickly as possible whether the word was old or new. The major dependent variable was how long it took to make the recognition response.

Network theories make two important predictions. First, words from the same sentence should prime each other. Thus, for our example sentence, subjects should respond "old" more quickly to the test item HORIZON when it immediately follows the test stimulus GEESE (from the same acquisition sentence) than when it follows the test item DRIVER (a word from a different acquisition sentence). This prediction was confirmed; the former primed responses were about 130 msec faster than the unprimed responses. This indicates that words from the same sentence are stored near each other in memory.

Propositional theory makes a second important prediction; pairs of words from the same proposition should prime each other more than pairs of words from different propositions. For example, the test stimulus HORIZON should be recognized more quickly following the word GEESE than following the word WIND. In fact, this is exactly what Ratcliff and McKoon found; within-proposition pairs (GEESE-HORIZON) yielded significantly more priming than between-proposition parts (WIND-HORIZON). This difference between within- and between-proposition priming cannot be attributed to distance in the surface structure of the sentence. GEESE and HORIZON are two words apart in the surface structure (i.e., CROSSED THE occurs between them), whereas only one word (AS) separates WIND and HORIZON. Nonetheless, it is the GEESE-HORIZON pair that reveals most priming.

The fact that within-proposition primes are more effective than between-proposition primes, then, is consistent with the assumption that when people store away sentences, they store away sets of propositions. Other techniques have also revealed evidence for the propositional nature of memory for linguistic materials (e.g., Kintsch & Glass, 1974; Kintsch & Keenan, 1974; Wanner, 1975), so we will view propositions as the end-product of comprehension.

From word strings to propositions. How, then, do we convert the speaker's string of words into a set of propositions? It is clear that we must identify the meanings of the words in the string, but that is not enough. As anyone who has tried to translate a passage from one language to another has learned, looking up each of the words in a dictionary does not reveal the meaning of the sentences. This is because the underlying propositions are signaled through grammatical devices, such as word order and word endings, some of which we discussed in the previous chapter. The listener who hears MAN BITES DOG should construct one proposition, whereas the listener who hears DOG BITES MAN should construct another. When we listen or read, then, we call upon our knowledge of word meanings and syntax to convert strings of words into propositions. For the rest of the chapter, we'll study how we do so.

TWO THEMES: THE PROBLEM OF AMBIGUITY AND THE IMPORTANCE OF EXPECTATIONS

Psycholinguistics is an exciting field, but it is often a confusing and argumentative one as well, not only because the processes being studied are so complex and elusive, but also because current research and theory derive from at least three different disciplines, those of psychology, linguistics, and artificial intelligence. These disciplines often use different techniques, propose different kinds of theories, and ask different questions. Nonetheless, there are certain themes that emerge from all of them, and keeping two of these in mind will provide a framework for our discussion of language comprehension.

The problem of ambiguity.   If there is a central puzzle in psycholinguistics, it is this: how do people comprehend language so quickly and so effortlessly, given that the majority of words and sentences are potentially ambiguous?

People can listen to 250 words per minute with good comprehension, and most college students read approximately 280 words per minute (although very skilled readers often read at 600 words per minute or more). Thus, even the average among us is able to process more than four words per second. This speed is particularly impressive when you realize that most words have more than one meaning and can be members of more than one grammatical class. For example, the simple word PLANT can be either a noun or a verb and for each of these grammatical classes it has several different meanings. Not only do individual words have more than one meaning, but many sentences are ambiguous syntactically as we saw in the previous chapter (recall VISITING RELATIVES CAN BE A NUISANCE).

Language would not necessarily have to work this way. Consider how you might structure a language if you were designing one. You could make sure that each word had one and only one meaning and could be a member of one and only one form class. Furthermore, you could devise a very simple grammar in which a given word order *always* indicates a given underlying proposition. For example, you could design a language in which the word order noun-verb-noun always referred to actor-action-object. It would be easy to write a computer program that could comprehend such a language. On the surface, it would seem that this kind of language would be much easier to process and to learn than our ambiguous mother tongue.

It is of no small interest, therefore, that *no* natural language of the world has this simple form. All are replete with potentially ambiguous words and sentence structures. The closest human languages come to being simple and unambiguous are the *pidgin* languages, which are languages that develop when two groups who speak different native languages come into infrequent, but important contact. Often this occurs in the context of trading.

Slobin (1979) has described one such pidgin, Russenorsk, which was a trade language combining Russian and Norwegian vocabulary. It was used prior to the Russian revolution of 1917, when Norwegian fishermen traded their fish for Russian agricultural products. Since this trading only occurred during brief yearly thaws, the groups only needed a language sufficient to discuss the rudiments of trading, and so Russenorsk developed. The syntax of Russenorsk is appealingly simple. First, there is a simple word-order rule: any noun-verb-noun sequence should be interpreted as a subject-verb-object. Second, there is no ambiguity about which words are verbs, because any word being used as a verb contains a particular grammatical marker—the ending *-om* (e.g., CAPTAIN SAIL-OM SHIP). Third, if two nouns occur together, *without* the preposition *po*, then the first noun is the possessor and the second the thing possessed. Fourth, if two nouns occur together, *with* the preposition *"po"* between them, then the phrase should be interpreted in any way that makes sense, with the exception of possession. Thus, CAPTAIN PO CABIN means CAPTAIN IN THE CABIN whereas CAPTAIN PO SHIP means CAPTAIN ON THE SHIP, and CAPTAIN CABIN means CAPTAIN'S CABIN. With the addition of rules about intonation (e.g., a statement with a rising intonation pattern is interpreted as a question), the Russenorsk grammar is more or less complete.

The speaker of Russenorsk could not make a complicated sentence like THE CAPTAIN SAILING THE SHIP DRANK TEA, although something similar could be conveyed by a couple of simple sentences: CAPTAIN SAIL-OM SHIP, CAPTAIN DRINK-OM TEA. Of course, the Russenorsk version misses some of the nuances of the syntactically more complex English construction, but then Russenorsk avoids the potential syntactic ambiguities that come about when languages have more complicated rules.

Simple and unambiguous languages such as Russenorsk appear to be unsatisfactory as the primary language of human communities. Whenever contact between linguistic communities expands so that interaction is frequent and varied in content (not only for trading, but for governing, marrying and so on), then the pidgin, if it survives at all, expands to include a more complicated syntax and vocabulary. The fact that all human languages have evolved to include lexical and syntactic ambiguities, and that the speakers of a language usually are little troubled by these, suggests that the information-processing system has special characteristics that enable it to deal with ambiguity.

Linguists have been aware of the problem of ambiguity for a long time, but the difficulties such ambiguity creates for a processing system became particularly obvious when artificial intelligence researchers first attempted to write computer programs to comprehend language. Whether or not the computer program exhibits comprehension is usually assessed by determining whether the computer program can convert an input string of words into a set of underlying propositions that is sufficient to enable the computer to produce either a paraphrase of the input string, or to answer questions about the string. (Note that this is the way we assess the level of human comprehension as well. For example, you receive an input string consisting of the words in a textbook, and then the professor assesses your comprehension by asking you to state the argument in your own words, or by asking you a series of questions about the contents.)

When people attempted to write programs that would comprehend natural language, they found it very difficult to avoid having the program get hopelessly bogged down in ambiguities. For example, consider what would happen if the computer was given the sentence THE WOMEN LIGHT THE CANDLES. This, of course, is an extremely simple sentence for humans to understand, and the fact that the word LIGHT could be either a noun or a verb is usually never even noticed, since in the context of the sentence, we know it must be a verb. But exactly what strategies would you build into the computer program so that it could know this as well? Furthermore, how would you program the computer to be able to make the appropriate distinctions between the underlying relations in I SAW THE COW GRAZING IN THE PASTURE and I SAW THE GRAND CANYON FLYING TO NEW YORK? (Sentences from Rumelhart, 1977.) The solution that the artificial intelligence researchers proposed brings us to the next major theme of the chapter—the importance of expectations for language comprehension.

The importance of expectations. At first thought, most people assume that we comprehend language in a *bottom-up* or *stimulus-driven* fashion. That is, each word is identified first and its various possible meanings and syntactic roles looked up, and then, when some appropriate set of words has been identified (perhaps all those in a clause or a sentence), the words are assigned to grammatical categories, and the set of underlying propositions is constructed. According to this view, analysis of the sentence is always driven by the stimulus in that the stimulus is the sole determinant of what will be identified.

When people tried to program computers to comprehend language, however, they found that ambiguous words present a problem for such a processor, because it must consider all possible interpretations of each word. Given that any representative sample of vocabulary items and sentences would have many ambiguous words, this slows down processing considerably.

It turns out that the problem of ambiguity can be overcome at least in part, by combining such bottom-up, stimulus-driven processes, with what have come to be called *top-down or conceptually-driven* processes. Top-down processing is guided by *expectations* about what the incoming stimulus is likely to be, given the context in which it occurs. A system that includes top-down processing is actively looking for certain items in certain contexts. Consider again the simple sentence THE WOMEN LIGHT THE CANDLES. A top-down system could be programmed to expect a verb to follow the article-noun construction, so after THE WOMEN occurred, the system would expect the next word to be a verb. A top-down process, then, would look in memory to see whether or not LIGHT could be a verb and, since it can, would not need to determine what else it could be.

In sum, then, a bottom-up processor looks at each stimulus and asks, "Now what could this be?", whereas a top-down processor looks at each stimulus and asks, "Could this be a _____?" Theoreticians have found that in order to build computer programs that are capable of the rudiments of language comprehension, it is necessary to include both bottom-up and top-down processes. This suggests that human language comprehension might also rely upon a combination of these kinds of processes, and we will find evidence that this is the case throughout this and the next two chapters.

LANGUAGE PROCESSING: LEXICAL LOOKUP AND SYNTACTIC PROCESSING

We still do not understand exactly how people comprehend language, but thanks to two decades of research in psycholinguistics, we are making progress. We will now outline the major components of a theory of language processing, and consider the kind of evidence that has led many psycholinguists to adopt this view.

Access to the lexicon.   Most contemporary theories of language processing assume that our knowledge of words and word meanings (i.e., our lexicon) consists of two interrelated parts: a semantic network and a mental dictionary. We have already discussed these in

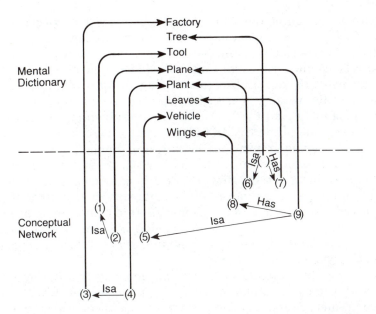

Figure 9–3. An illustration of how network models assume the mental dictionary and conceptual network to be related. The links between the mental dictionary and the conceptual network are NAME relations.

Chapter 6. Recall that the semantic (conceptual) network consists of a large set of concept nodes interconnected with each other by labeled, directed associations. This network is abstract in that the nodes stand for concepts, not for words. All adults and children who have begun to learn language are assumed to also possess a mental dictionary. This dictionary has an entry for each word the person knows; the entry for a given word contains information about the way the word sounds and looks (if the person knows how to read). Most importantly, each such dictionary entry also has a pointer (or pointers) to the appropriate concept node(s) in the semantic network, i.e., to the meaning of the word. An example is shown in Figure 9–3.

According to this theoretical framework, when a word is processed, the dictionary unit corresponding to this word is activated, and this activation spreads along the NAME link to the concept node corresponding to the meaning of the word. Furthermore, as you learned earlier, this activation of the concept node spreads in the semantic network, so that nearby related concept nodes are also activated temporarily. According to this theory, then, as you process a sentence, each word you encounter leads to temporary activation of a portion of your semantic memory.

One of the central questions that psychologists have raised about lexical access concerns what happens when ambiguous words are encountered. Look again at Figure 9–3. An ambiguous word (e.g., PLANE or PLANT) would have more than one NAME link pointing to the semantic network, one link corresponding to each of the possible meanings of the word. When such a word is encountered, does activation spread along all the NAME links corresponding to that word, or only along one of the NAME links? Notice we are asking how our language processing systems deal with lexical ambiguity. Do we look up only one meaning of an ambiguous word, or do we look up all possible meanings? The question we are asking here does not concern whether or not people are *aware* of the ambiguity, but whether or not alternative meanings of an ambiguous word are activated in memory when a word is processed. In order to find out, we need a way of tapping the patterns of memory activation that occur during language comprehension.

One way of doing so is to use the *phoneme-monitoring technique*. In this often-used procedure, the subject is presented with tape-recorded sentences and asked to perform two tasks at once: (1) to comprehend the sentence, and (2) to monitor the sentence for a word beginning with some target phoneme (e.g., the sound *d*). When the subject detects the target phoneme, he is to press a button as rapidly as possible. The major dependent variable is the time required to detect the phoneme, measured from onset of the target phoneme until the subject presses the button. The reasoning behind the phoneme-monitoring task should be familiar to you from our discussion in the attention chapter. The time required to detect the phoneme provides a measure of the difficulty of comprehension at the point in the sentence at which the target phoneme occurs. If comprehending the sentence is requiring little mental effort (i.e., processing capacity), then reaction time to the phoneme should be fast, but if comprehending the sentence is requiring most of the person's processing capacity, then reaction time to the phoneme should be slower.

Consider a study by Swinney and Hakes (1976). Their subjects performed phoneme monitoring for sentences drawn from a set of sentence pairs. Within each sentence pair, the sentences were identical except that one contained an ambiguous word (e.g., BUGS) and the other contained an unambiguous word (e.g., INSECTS). Swinney and Hakes reasoned that if people process only one meaning of an ambiguous word, then the ambiguous word should not take up any more processing capacity than the unambiguous word, so phoneme-monitoring speed should be equal for the two sentences. On the other hand, if all meanings of an ambiguous word are activated momentarily and if this requires additional processing capacity, then phoneme monitoring should be slower after the ambiguous word, as opposed to the unambiguous word.

TABLE 9–1.

Sample sentences used in Swinney and Hakes' (1976) study of the processing of ambiguous words. The subject was instructed to monitor the sentence for the target phoneme hard-c. The critical word for each sentence is shown in upper-case.

	Ambiguous Critical Word	Unambiguous Critical Word
Neutral Context	Rumor had it that, for years, the government building had been plagued with problems. The man was not surprised when he found several BUGS in the corner of his room.	Rumor had it that, for years, the government building had been plagued with problems. The man was not surprised when he found several INSECTS in the corner of his room.
Biased Context	Rumor had it that for years, the government building had been plagued with problems. The man was not surprised when he found several spiders, roaches, and other BUGS in the corner of his room.	Rumor had it that for years, the government building had been plagued with problems. The man was not surprised when he found several spiders, roaches, and other INSECTS in the corner of his room.

After Swinney and Hakes, 1976. Copyright 1976 by Academic Press. Reprinted by permission.

First, Swinney and Hakes investigated sentence pairs in which the context did not bias the subject toward either of the possible interpretations of the ambiguous word. The first row of Table 9–1 shows a sample comparison pair. The subject was to monitor for a word beginning with the hard-c sound, so he/she should have pushed the button upon detection of the word CORNER.

Swinney and Hakes found that their subjects took significantly longer to respond to CORNER in the sentences containing the ambiguous word (e.g., BUGS) than in the sentences containing the unambiguous words (e.g., INSECTS). This finding suggests that the ambiguity of the word is making language comprehension harder, and that when ambiguous words are presented in a context in which either of their meanings would be appropriate, both meanings are activated or looked up.

Swinney and Hakes (1976) went on to ask another question: are both meanings of an ambiguous word activated even when the context rules out one of the possible meanings? This, of course, is the more usual situation in everyday conversation, since either the sentence itself or the context in which it is spoken usually rules out all but one meaning. Therefore, Swinney and Hakes also compared phoneme monitoring following ambiguous and unambiguous words when they occurred in a context that biased one meaning. Sample sentences are shown in the second row of Table 9–1. Swinney and Hakes reasoned that if such a biasing context leads the person to activate only the one appropriate meaning of an ambiguous word, then the difference in phoneme monitoring between the sentences within a pair should disappear.

In fact, this biasing context did erase the difference between sentences containing ambiguous vs. unambiguous words. For the biased context, the phoneme was detected just as quickly in the BUG sentence as it was in the INSECT sentence. This would seem to suggest, then, that only the appropriate concept node is activated when the prior context is consistent with only one meaning.

There is an alternative interpretation of these data, though, which illustrates a general point you should keep in mind when interpreting studies of language processing. People comprehend language with remarkable speed, so the underlying processes must occur very quickly. Therfore, if we wish to assess the mental effort required by processing one word as opposed to another (e.g., an ambiguous word vs. an unambiguous word), we must assess this effort as soon as possible following presentation of the critical word. In the Swinney and Hakes study, the capacity required for processing the critical words (e.g., BUG versus INSECT) was not assessed until three syllables following the word (i.e., the target phoneme occurred three syllables after the critical word). It is possible that the subject had looked up both meanings of BUG initially even in the condition that biased only one meaning, but that by the time the phoneme target occurred three syllables later, the subject had eliminated all meanings but the contextually appropriate one.

Swinney (1979) tested this possibility using a different kind of secondary task. Again subjects attempted to comprehend spoken sentences chosen from pairs like those in Table 9–1, but instead of monitoring for phonemes, they performed a simultaneous visual lexical decision task. A letter string was presented visually either *immediately* upon offset of the critical word *or* three syllables later in the sentence. The subject was asked to push a button labeled *yes* if the visually presented string was a word and *no* otherwise. We will consider only those trials on which the correct answer was *yes*. As the samples shown in Table 9–2 demonstrate, the important variable was that the lexical decision word was related to either (1) the meaning of the word that is appropriate in context (i.e., ANT in the sample sentence), (2) the meaning of the word that is inappropriate in context (i.e., SPY in the sample sentence), or (3) a control word unrelated to either (i.e., SEW).

We can measure the degree to which the critical word (e.g., BUG)

TABLE 9–2.

Sample sentences used in Swinney's (1979) study of the processing of ambiguous words. Subjects listened to the sentences and made lexical decisions about visually presented words which occurred at the point indicated by the "▲."

	Ambiguous Critical Word	Unambiguous Critical Word
Immediate Lexical Decision	Rumor had it that for years the government building had been plagued with problems. The man was not surprised when he found several spiders, roaches, and other BUGS▲ in the corner of his room.	Rumor had it that for years the government building had been plagued with problems. The man was not surprised when he found several spiders, roaches, and other INSECTS in the corner of his room.▲
Delayed Lexical Decision	Rumor had it that for years the government building had been plagued with problems. The man was not surprised when he found several spiders, roaches, and other BUGS in the corner of his room. ▲	Rumor had it that for years the government building had been plagued with problems. The man was not surprised when he found several spiders, roaches, and other INSECTS in the corner of his room. ▲

> **Lexical Decision Words:** ANT (contextually appropriate)
> SPY (contextually inappropriate)
> SEW (control)

After Swinney, 1979. Copyright 1979 by Academic Press. Reprinted by permission.

primes the visually presented word by comparing response time on lexical decisions for the related as opposed to the control words. If the context leads the person to process only the "little beasties" meaning of the word BUG, then the time to respond to ANT should be faster than that to either SEW (the control word) or SPY. However, if both meanings of the word are looked up despite the context, then BUG should also prime SPY (i.e., lexical decisions to both BUG and SPY should be faster than those to the control SEW).

Swinney's results were straightforward. When the lexical decision word was not tested until three syllables following the ambiguous word, then response time was fast only for ANT, and response times to SPY and SEW were equal to each other. This finding, of course, is consistent with Swinney and Hakes' phoneme-monitoring results. More interesting, however, was the fact that when the lexical decision word was presented *immediately* upon offset of the ambiguous word BUG, the lexical decision response was equally fast for ANT and SPY, both of which were faster than responses to the unrelated control word SEW.

When the data from the phoneme-monitoring study (Swinney & Hakes, 1976) are combined with those from the lexical decision study (Swinney, 1979), we find a consistent picture of the way in which ambiguous words are accessed. Upon presentation, activation spreads along the NAME links to all possible meanings of the word, regardless of whether or not the context biases one particular meaning. Thus, this is a bottom-up process in that the activation depends only upon the presence of a certain stimulus. This activation of more than one meaning lasts during the processing of several subsequent syllables if the context does not bias a single meaning, but the activation of the inappropriate meaning fades very quickly if the context favors only one meaning (based on the findings of the lexical decision study). That is, top-down, conceptually driven processes operate to limit the activation of inappropriate concept nodes.

Since most of the words we encounter are potentially ambiguous, these conclusions tell us a great deal about lexical access during everyday language processing. They indicate that even though we are usually unaware of the potential ambiguity of individual words, all potential meanings are processed briefly. Context can be brought to bear very quickly to limit the potential interpretations, however, and within a few syllables only the context-appropriate meaning is still being considered.

The Moses illusion discussed in Chapter 1 also reflects the interaction of top-down and bottom-up processes in lexical access. The fact that we are *not* fooled by semantically unrelated substitutions (e.g., NIXON for NOAH) indicates that at least part of the meaning of the presented word is looked up (bottom-up processing), but the fact that we *are* fooled by semantically related substitutions (e.g., MOSES for NOAH) suggests that we forego complete identification, relying upon our expectations about what the word should be (top-down processing). (Read Erickson and Mattson, 1981, for a more specific explanation of the causes of the illusion.)

We have found, then, that lexical access involves both bottom-up stimulus-driven processes and top-down conceptually-driven processes. Thanks to these top-down processes, and the fact that context usually favors one interpretation of each word, it is likely that our information-processing systems usually have to deal with multiple possible interpretations of words for only a very brief time.

Syntactic processing: Constituent analysis. Activating word meanings in memory is not sufficient for comprehension, for we must be able to use what we know of the syntax of language to discover the underlying propositions conveyed by a string of words. Several kinds of evidence suggest that people actively divide up the sentence into clauses (i.e., phrases that correspond to underlying propositions) even as they are hearing or reading it. That is, people break down sentences into constituents of the sort discussed in the preceding chapter.

The most well-known such evidence comes from the *click perception studies* conducted by Fodor, Bever, and Garrett at MIT (Fodor & Bever, 1965; Garrett, Bever, & Fodor, 1966). Fodor and his colleagues presented subjects with sentences, and a click occurred sometime during each sentence. The subject's task was to write down the sentence and then to mark where the click had occurred. Fodor and his colleagues were interested in how the subject's placement of the click was related to the constituent structure of the sentence. A sample sentence follows, with asterisks indicating the possible places at which the click could occur.

As a result of their invention's influence/the company was given an award
                                             *   *

Fodor made two assumptions, the first of which should be very familiar by now. He assumed (1) that processing language and detecting clicks both draw upon our limited processing capacity, so they should influence each other, and (2) that perceptual units tend to preserve their integrity by resisting interruptions, an assumption borrowed from Gestalt psychology. These assumptions led Fodor and colleagues to argue that if people are dividing the sentence into constituents as they process the sentence, then each clause should be a perceptual unit. Since such units resist interruption, subjects should perceive the click as having occurred *between* clauses even when the click in fact occurred within a clause. Thus, in the sample sentence the break between clauses is between INFLUENCE and WAS, so subjects should think they heard the click there even when it occurred elsewhere. This is exactly what Fodor, Bever, and Garrett found; the subjects' click placements indicated that perceptually the click had "migrated" toward the clause boundary. In order to make sure that this migration wasn't due simply to a pause in the acoustic signal itself, Fodor and his colleagues compared click migration in the sentence we have just discussed with that in the following sentence:

The chairman whose methods still influence the company/was given an award.
                                               *   *

The underlined words in both sentences were taken from an identical tape, so the pause patterns had to be exactly the same for both. On the other hand, the underlying constituent structure for the two sentences is quite different, as the slash placed at the major boundary of each sentence indicates. If the click migration finding is due to pauses in the acoustic signal, then the pattern of click migration should be identical for both of the sentences, but if click migration is due to subjects *imposing* constituent structure on the sentence, then the clicks should migrate toward the boundary between INFLUENCE and THE for the first sentence, and the boundary between COMPANY and WAS for the second. In fact, the results conformed to the second pattern, suggesting that the click migration effect is due to an active segmentation imposed by the subject. Thus, people appear to "hear" clicks in linguistically convenient places. The person who did not know a language would presumably place the clicks differently from one who knew the syntax of the language in question.

If you recall the lesson from the lexical access section, you might be skeptical of this conclusion, since subjects did not place the click until *after* they heard and wrote down the entire sentence. This means that the segmenting might have occurred later in memory, not during actual presentation of the sentence. Fortunately, there is other evidence which suggests that the segmentation is indeed occurring as the subject perceives the sentence. For example, Abrams and Bever (1969) required people to press a button as soon as they detected the click. The pattern of reaction times they found was consistent with the idea that the person actively imposes constituent structure on the sentence as he hears it.

If people "unpack" strings of words into underlying constituent structures as they perceive sentences, then this should influence the availability of words in working memory. That is, while a person is hearing (or reading) a clause, the words in that clause should be readily available in working memory, since the person has not yet completed all processing of the underlying proposition. However, the words in already ended clauses should be less available in working memory, since the person has finished assigning a propositional structure to them. Caplan (1972) tested this prediction using a probe word technique. Subjects listened to sentences and attempted to comprehend them. At the end of the sentence, a probe word was presented, and the subject responded as quickly as possible whether or not the probe word had been in the immediately preceding sentence. Consider, for example, the following two sentences.

Whenever one telephones at night / rates are lower
Make your calls after six / because night rates are lower

Caplan used the same taped sequence for the underlined sections, so those are known to be identical acoustically. The probe word for each of these sentences was NIGHT. In both sentences there are exactly three words following NIGHT, so the number of words intervening between presentation and test is identical. However, if the most recent clause is in a state of activation in working memory, then we would expect response time to the probe word NIGHT to be faster in the second sentence than in the first. This is exactly what Caplan found. Again, then, we have evidence that people actively segment sentences into constituents as they hear them.

Do these constituents people are constructing correspond to the underlying propositions in the sentence? If so, then what the person is holding in working memory should correspond more closely to the underlying deep structure of the sentence than it does to the surface structure word order. The probe word technique has been used to test this prediction. Walker, Gough, and Wall (1968) presented subjects with a task in which two probe words followed each sentence. The subject was to respond "yes" only if both probes were from the sentence. For example, subjects might be presented with the sentence shown followed by one of the two probe pairs shown:

The scouts the Indians saw killed a buffalo

Probe: scouts killed

Probe: Indians killed

The members of the pair SCOUTS KILLED are further apart in the surface structure of the sentence than the members of the pair INDIANS KILLED. Therefore, if subjects are holding a surface structure in working memory, they should respond more quickly to the INDIANS KILLED probe than the SCOUTS KILLED probe. On the other hand, in the underlying propositional structure of the sentence, SCOUTS and KILLED are part of the same underlying proposition, whereas INDIANS and KILLED come from two different propositions. Therefore, if subjects are holding a representation of the underlying propositions in memory, then they should respond more quickly to SCOUTS KILLED than to INDIANS KILLED. The latter pattern is, in fact, what Walker and colleagues found.

This finding supplements the Ratcliff and McKoon study of priming that we discussed at the beginning of the chapter. They had found that in long-term memory, people store away propositions. The present findings indicate that this propositional structure is established in working memory while the person is processing the sentence, not during some later extended retention interval.

Syntactic processing: The derivational theory of complexity. All the research we have just cited suggests that people are constructing underlying propositional structures when they comprehend sentences, but how do they go about doing so? What are the rules people use to convert strings of words (i.e., surface structures) into the appropriate underlying propositions?

In the early 1960's, the first psycholinguists were intrigued with Chomsky's notion that surface structures may be generated from deep structures by applying a set of transformational rules. These psychologists proposed that in comprehending a sentence (in Chomsky's terms, moving from surface structure to deep structure), people might go through these transformational rules in reverse order. (Chomsky himself had not made this claim.)

If people do process sentences by taking the surface structure and applying transformational rules in reverse to get back to the deep structure, then sentences that are derivationally more complex in Chomsky's theory (in that they require more transformations) should also be more complex psychologically (i.e., harder to comprehend). This has come to be called the *derivational theory of complexity*, and it initiated a decade of psycholinguistic research aimed at determining whether derivational complexity predicted psychological complexity.

The first set of such studies seemed to confirm the predictions of the derivational theory of complexity. For example, since passive sentences require more transformations than active sentences according to the linguistic model, then passive sentences should take longer to comprehend than active sentences. This proved to be the case in several studies (e.g., McMahon, 1963). People comprehend THE BOY KISSED THE GIRL more quickly than they comprehend THE GIRL WAS KISSED BY THE BOY. These were ecstatic days among psycholinguists, because it appeared that the linguists had done all their theoretical work for them; it appeared that psycholinguists could adopt linguistic competence models as models of performance as well.

As studies progressed, however, it became clear that the early findings were subject to other interpretations. We will consider only one of a number of problems that arose. In most of the early studies, derivational complexity was confounded with the number of words in the sentence. For example, not only is THE GIRL WAS KISSED BY THE BOY derivationally more complex than its active counterpart, but it also contains more words. Therefore, the passive might take longer to comprehend simply because it takes longer to read or hear it. Fortunately, transformational grammar makes other predictions that enable us to unconfound sentence length and derivational complexity to see which is important in predicting psychological complexity. Two examples (taken from Fodor, Bever, & Garrett, 1974) will suffice. According to transformational theory THE BOY LOOKED THE NUMBER UP is derivationally more complex than THE BOY LOOKED UP THE NUMBER, because the former requires a particle-movement transformation (i.e., moving the particle UP from the position next to LOOK to the end of the sentence). Both sentences have exactly the same number of words, however, so length and derivational complexity are not confounded. It turns out that when psychological measures of complexity are collected (such as measuring how long it takes to comprehend the sentences), the two are of equal psychological complexity—contrary to the predictions of the derivational theory of complexity. A second blow comes from a comparison of the sentences JIM DANCES MORE THAN FRED versus JIM DANCES MORE THAN FRED DANCES. According to transformational theory the former (shorter) sentence is derivationally more complex than the latter (longer) sentence, since the shorter sentence would be generated through applying a comparative-deletion transformation. When psychological complexity is assessed, however, the shorter but derivationally more complex sentence is actually *easier* to comprehend, contrary to the derivational theory of complexity. Many other disconfirming studies followed (for a discussion of these, see pp. 320–328 of Fodor, Bever, & Garrett, 1974). In sum, more recent research has failed to confirm the derivational theory of complexity.

With the wisdom afforded by hindsight, we can now see that we should never have expected the linguist's models to provide accurate theories of performance, because language is processed word by word. Note in contrast how the derivational theory of complexity views comprehension. The person is assumed to have the surface structure of the entire sentence in memory and then to go in reverse order through the steps that would have been required to derive the sentence. Thus, the sentence is analyzed as a unit. Yet the findings we discussed in the preceding section suggest that we do not wait until the end of the sentence to begin assigning it a grammatical structure. The best way to become aware of this subjectively is to consider sentences that mislead you, such as THE OLD MAN THE BOATS. Chances are that on first reading of that sentence in the Food for Thought section, you assumed the subject of the sentence to be MAN. You only realized that the subject was OLD and the verb MAN after reading the entire sentence. Thus, you did a doubletake. If you were waiting to assign words to grammatical categories until you reached the end of the sentence, no such doubletake would have been required. Thus, in building a model of the psychological processes involved in comprehension, we must build a model of how language is processed word by word, as it is encountered. Transformational grammar will not suffice.

This is not to say, of course, that psychological research disproved linguisitc theory in general or transformational grammar in particular, but only that linguistic theories cannot be adopted unaltered as models of linguisitc performance.

Syntactic and semantic processing: Processing strate-gies. Drawing a distinction between algorithms and heuristics will be helpful at this point. Whereas algorithms are rules that always lead to a solution (though sometimes by a long and circuitous route), heuristics are shortcut rules of thumb that often lead to quick solutions, but sometimes fail to yield any solution at all. When linguists write generative grammars of the sort we talked about in the last chapter, they are seeking algorithms for generating structural descriptions for all the possible grammatical sequences in the language. Therefore, when psychologists attempted to apply such linguistic theories to performance, they were attempting to find algorithms that people use to move from the surface structure of a sentence to the underlying deep structure relations. The failure of the derivational theory of complexity indicates that such approaches have not worked.

Recently, psycholinguists have tried a different approach. They have argued that perhaps language comprehension is more accurately viewed as involving a set of heuristics, i.e., a set of rules of thumb that provide guidelines for uncovering the propositions encoded in the string of words. These heuristics are often called *processing strategies*. A number of psychologists in different laboratories (e.g., Bever, 1970; Carroll & Bever, 1976; Clark and Clark, 1977) are attempting to specify a set of such strategies that will be consistent with the patterns of human performance, and their progress to date has been promising. We will consider just three such strategies to illustrate the nature of these heuristics and the kinds of evidence psycholinguists are seeking to test the reality of these strategies.

A number of these strategies involve word order. The most often-cited word order strategy is the following.

> **WORD ORDER STRATEGY: When a noun-verb-noun sequence is encountered, assume that the first noun is the agent of the action coded by the verb and that the second noun is the object of the action.**

This strategy is consistent with a number of aspects of the performance of English speakers. For example, people usually are slower at comprehending passive sentences than active sentences. The word order processing strategy accounts for this pattern; the N-V-N equals actor-action-object strategy works correctly for active sentences, but not for passive. Therefore, for passive sentences the person must go back and reassign the cases. This strategy also accounts for the difficulty people have with some short, but nonetheless misleading sentences. Consider again the following sentence.

The horse raced past the finish line won

According to the processing strategy notion, people have difficulty with this sentence because they apply the preceding word order strategy to it at first, thus assuming that RACED is the main verb of the sentence. This assignment works well until the end of the sentence, at which point the person finds himself with an extra verb, so he must go back and construct a new interpretation.

Other sentence processing strategies that have been proposed rely upon the existence of certain cue words in a sentence. For example, consider the following strategy (taken from Clark and Clark, 1977, p. 59).

> **CUE WORD STRATEGY: Whenever you find a relative pronoun (that, which, who, whom) begin a new clause.**

This strategy assumes that people monitor sentences for such cue words, and then use these to help them divide up the sentence into constituents. If people do use the cue word strategy, then sentences that contain relative clauses, but do not contain these cue words should be harder to process than those that contain the cues. Consider again the sentence THE HORSE RACED PAST THE FINISH LINE WON. We saw that the word order strategy would lead to a misassignment on the first reading of the sentence. However, if the word THAT had been included after HORSE, thereby enabling the subject to use the cue word strategy, then the misassignment would have been prevented.

A number of studies have revealed experimental evidence for the relative pronoun strategy. Consider, for example, a phoneme-monitoring study by Hakes (1972). Hakes presented subjects with sentences like the following.

> **The blind student felt (that) the material in the art course would be too difficult for him to understand**

> **Everyone who was at the party saw (that) Ann's date had made a complete fool of himself**

Subjects were to monitor each sentence for the phoneme underlined. Half of the subjects heard a given sentence *with* the relative pronoun THAT and half without. If subjects are using the preceding strategy, then phoneme detection should be faster in sentences containing THAT than in those that do not, since THAT clears up an ambiguity thereby lessening processing demands for the words following the verb. This is exactly what Hakes found.

The strategies discussed so far have relied upon word order and the presence of certain cue words, but another class of strategies has also been proposed. These rely upon the person's knowledge of word meanings and of the semantic roles (i.e., cases) various words can take on. For example, Clark and Clark (1977, p. 64) have proposed the following strategy.

> **SEMANTIC STRATEGY: After encountering a verb, look for the number and kind of cases appropriate for that verb.**

Such strategies assume that semantic memory contains information concerning the cases various verbs require and the kinds of words that can fill these cases, and, furthermore, that people use this knowledge to anticipate the roles that words will play in the underlying structure of the sentence. For example, it is assumed that people know that the action described by the verb EAT requires an animate agent, so that when the person encounters the verb EAT he will expect to find an animate agent.

One kind of evidence that people do indeed rely upon strategies that take into account the semantic properties of the words in the sentence comes from looking again at passive and active sentences. We mentioned that passive sentences usually take longer to comprehend than active ones. However, this is the case *only* for reversible passives, which are defined as passives in which it would be logically possible for the roles of agent and object to be reversed.

Thus THE BOY WAS KISSED BY THE GIRL, is a reversible passive, since it would be logically possible for the nouns BOY and GIRL to be reversed, rendering the equally sensible sentence THE GIRL WAS KISSED BY THE BOY. On the other hand, for irreversible passives in which switching the nouns would lead to a nonsensical sentence (e.g., THE TOMATO WAS EATEN BY THE MAN), passive sentences are comprehended just as quickly as actives (e.g., THE MAN ATE THE TOMATO) (e.g., Slobin, 1966). According to the processing strategy proposed, this is because when the person encounters the verb EAT he knows immediately that TOMATO cannot be the agent, and he uses this semantic information to cue him to look for a different agent.

Other techniques (such as phoneme-monitoring) have also provided evidence consistent with the conclusion that people are sensitive to the semantic characteristics of the words in the sentence and that these properties guide the person in "unpacking" the sentence into its underlying propositional structure.

At present, then, the most promising kind of theory of language comprehension assumes that people use a set of heuristics called processing strategies to discover the underlying propositions contained in a sequence of words. We said earlier that this processing strategy approach differs from the derivational theory of complexity in that processing strategy theory assumes that people use heuristics rather than algorithms during language comprehension. The kinds of theories differ in another way as well. Whereas the derivational theory of complexity posits syntactic processes (e.g., transformational rules) that are largely independent of semantic strategies, the processing strategy approach assumes that both syntactic cues (such as word order) *and* semantic information (such as word meaning) are used throughout the processing of a sentence.

Processing strategies as production systems. Processing strategy models are still in their infancy. The goal of such models is to specify precisely a set of strategies that is sufficient to describe all the characteristics of human comprehension, and to specify how these strategies operate together. The latter problem is particularly important. Consider, for example, that the three strategies we stated must be combined in some way. In many cases they suggest that contradictory interpretations be placed on some input sentence. For example, for the sentence THE HOUSE WAS BUILT BY THE CARPENTER, the word order strategy would suggest that HOUSE is the agent of the sentence, but the semantic strategy would suggest that HOUSE should be the object (since BUILT requires an animate agent). How is this discrepancy resolved? Are the processing strategies always attempted in a given order, e.g., is the word order strategy used before the semantic strategy? Or does the person attempt to apply all at once? We do not know.

The main drawbacks of processing strategy models so far, then, are that (1) we still have not outlined a precise set of strategies that are known to be sufficient for language comprehension, and (2) we have not yet described exactly how these strategies interact with each other. Thus, further development of processing strategy models will require that the strategies be stated more precisely.

As we saw in earlier chapters, one of the best ways of making a processing theory more precise is to attempt to state it in terms of a computer program, i.e., to attempt computer simulation of the human skill being studied. The challenge then is to state a set of processing strategies that is precise enough to program into a computer, and that will enable the computer to take sentences as input and to produce the appropriate underlying propositions as output. A number of computer scientists, psychologists, and linguists (e.g., Anderson, 1976; Kaplan, 1972; Rumelhart, 1977; Wanner and Maratsos, 1978) are attempting to do just that.

For example, consider Anderson's ACT system again. Recall that procedural knowledge is assumed to consist of a set of production systems. In fact, as Anderson (1976) has shown in his book, the processing strategies we have described can be developed into production systems, i.e., sets of condition-action pairs. For example, IF the current word is a verb and it calls for an animate agent, THEN look for an animate agent. You can find details of how this can be done in Anderson's own work (e.g., Anderson, 1976; Anderson, Kline, & Lewis, 1977). The important point here is that the writing of such production systems and their implementation on a computer makes it possible to determine whether or not the strategies are sufficient to enable the underlying propositions of sentences to be discovered.

The speed of syntactic and semantic analysis. We have been arguing that as people take in sentences, they use processing strategies to unpack the sentence as they go. We assume, then, that language comprehension occurs "on-line" (in the words of Marslen-Wilson and others, e.g., Marslen-Wilson & Tyler, 1980). Listeners use their knowledge of the syntactic and semantic constraints of the language to assign functions (e.g., agent, object) to words that have already occurred and to anticipate what is likely to follow. But how quickly can we use syntactic and semantic constraints? For example, does such analysis occur so quickly that the characteristics of a given word can be used to predict characteristics of the very next word in the sentence? A number of phenomena indicate that the answer is "yes."

Marslen-Wilson (1973), for example, has examined the constructive errors made by fast-shadowers, i.e., by people who are able to shadow (i.e., repeat aloud) an auditory message at a delay of only 250 msec behind the message itself. Such people are little more than a syllable behind the material they are hearing. Marslen-Wilson noticed that when such people make constructive errors (i.e., when they add or change words or parts of words), these errors are almost always consistent both syntactically and semantically with the preceding context. In many cases these errors were apparently determined by the immediately preceding word. For example, in the sentence IT WAS BEGINNING TO BE LIGHT ENOUGH SO I COULD SEE, people inserted a THAT following SO. In the sentence HE HAD HEARD AT THE BRIGADE, people changed it to be HE HAD HEARD THAT THE BRIGADE. What is striking is that in order to change AT to THAT, the person must have already processed the *immediately* preceding word HEARD and computed what words were likely to follow it.

Other findings also point to a very rapid analysis of the semantic and syntactic constraints imposed by words. Cole and Jakimik (1978) had subjects listen to sentences which contained a few mispronunciations. Subjects were to press a button as soon as they detected a mispronunication. Cole and Jakimik assumed that the time required to detect a mispronunication of a word depends upon the time required to look up the word in memory, since you cannot detect that something has been *mis*pronunced unless you have determined how it *should* be pronounced. Cole and Jakimik constructed pairs of sentences that were identical except for the word that immediately preceded the mispronounced word.

He noticed that a green *rag* garpet covered the hallway

He noticed that a green *shag* garpet covered the hallway

In the second sentence, the occurrence of the word SHAG renders CARPET very predictable, whereas in the first sentence the word RAG does not. If people can use the semantic information contained in the immediately preceding word to limit their expectations for the next, then people should detect the mispronunciation GARPET more rapidly in the SHAG sentence than in the RAG one. This is exactly what happened. Since *only* the immediately preceding word could have caused this difference (the sentences are otherwise identical), the person must have already looked up the word SHAG by the time GARPET appeared.

Finally, Tyler and Marslen-Wilson (1977) wondered just how quickly context can be used to disambiguate a sentence that is ambiguous at the level of deep structure (see again our discussion of ambiguity in the previous chapter). A sample pair of sentence fragments is displayed in Table 9–3. Each sentence fragment contains the potentially ambiguous phrase LANDING PLANES, but in each sentence the immediately preceding clause disambiguates it, i.e., renders one meaning more likely than the other. The table displays what would seem to be appropriate continuations for each sentence.

Tyler and Marslen-Wilson presented subjects with one or the other of the sentence fragments in Table 9–3 through headphones. At the offset of the final word (PLANES), a visual word appeared on the screen, and the subject was simply to pronounce this word as quickly as possible. The word was always either ARE or IS. Tyler and Marslen-Wilson reasoned that if people have already chosen the appropriate interpretation of the sentence, and if they are using this knowledge to anticipate what will follow, then the appropriate verb should be pronounced more quickly than the inappropriate. Thus for the first sentence (WALK TOO NEAR THE RUNWAY), ARE should be pronounced faster than IS, since ARE is an appropriate continuation, but for the other sentence fragment, IS should be pronounced faster than ARE. This is exactly what Tyler and Marslen-Wilson found. In fact, the difference between pronunciation times for the appropriate versus inappropriate continuations for the fragments containing poten-

TABLE 9–3.   Sentence Fragments Used in Tyler and Marslen-Wilson's (1977) Study of the Speed of Semantic Processing.

Fragment: If you walk too near the runway, landing planes . . .
APPROPRIATE CONTINUATION: ARE likely to hit you.

Fragment: If you've been trained as a pilot, landing planes . . .
APPROPRIATE CONTINUATION: IS easy.

tially ambiguous phrases was just as large as the difference for those following sentences that contained no ambiguous phrases, e.g., IF YOU'VE STUDIED FOR YEARS TO BE A DENTIST, CLEANING TEETH . . . This suggests that the immediately preceding context was so effective in establishing an interpretation that the subject anticipated just as effectively for the potentially ambiguous as for the unambiguous phrases.

All of these findings, then, suggest that language comprehension occurs word by word, and exceedingly quickly. The syntactic and semantic characteristics of each word influence the perception of the word which immediately follows. Such top-down analysis is a critical part of language comprehension.

THE ROLE OF INFERENCE IN LANGUAGE COMPREHENSION

We have seen that when people comprehend sentences, they call upon their knowledge of word meanings and syntax, and they use this knowledge not only to interpret what they have already seen or heard, but also to anticipate what is to follow. Psycholinguists have recently come to realize, however, that if people only had a lexicon and a knowledge of syntax, they would not be able to comprehend language in the usual sense of the term. At least two other kinds of knowledge come into play: knowledge about the properties of the physical and social world (often called *world knowledge*) and knowledge about the implicit rules of conversation. As we participate in conversation (or read and write) we draw on these knowledge sources to make inferences.

Since we are usually unaware of having drawn these inferences, it was easy for psychologists and linguists to overlook their importance in language comprehension. Ironically, it was the artificial intelligence researchers who brought our attention to the importance of inference. When these computer scientists tried to write computer programs that would comprehend language, one of the first things they learned was that it proved impossible to get a computer to give acceptable evidence of comprehension unless the computer was programmed, not only with a lexicon and a set of syntactic and semantic processing strategies, but also with some extra-linguistic knowledge about the world and with the ability to draw inferences. Thus, artificial intelligence researchers argued that the human tendency to go beyond the information given (which we discussed in Chapter 6) is not an unfortunate human quirk, but rather an essential part of language comprehension. This point becomes clearest when viewed in light of a general problem—the problem of reference.

The problem of reference. It is not enough to convert a string of words into an underlying proposition or set of propositions. The listener must also determine the intended referent of the speaker's words. Consider this problem of reference in terms of a network model of long-term memory; the listener must figure out how the new propositional structure the speaker is conveying relates to information already in the listener's memory, so that he can add this information at the appropriate node. The problem of reference, then, is the problem of insuring that the speaker and listener are referring to the same concept or event.

For example, if you are told "The senator died," you do not have enough information to enable you to place this new proposition at the appropriate node in semantic memory unless you know to which senator the speaker refers. Taken out of context, most sentences are ambiguous regarding the exact referent. I say "taken out of context" because most of the time we are able to infer the intended referent either from the conversation itself (for example, a sentence preceding the one above might have concerned a particular senator) or from general information (the speaker and you might both work for a given congressman). Thus, the problem of reference is but another example of the potential ambiguity in language.

Consider, for example, how the problem of reference comes into play in interpreting the following simple children's story taken from Charniak (1972).

> **Janet wanted a nickel. The piggy bank was in her room, so she went there and got it. "I will get that nickel," she said. She shook the piggy bank very hard. Finally it came out.**

Notice that the pronoun IT occurred twice. To what concept does each IT refer? You probably responded without any hesitation, that the first refers to the piggy bank whereas the second refers to the nickel. But how did you know this so readily? More specifically, can you state a precise set of rules that would enable a non-native speaker (or a computer) to come up with the proper assignment of reference for each IT? Although we are still not in a position to do this, it is clear that any such set of rules will call upon at least two kinds of knowledge: knowledge of the properties of the world and knowledge of the rules of conversation. We will consider each in turn.

World knowledge. Roger Schank and Robert Abelson at Yale University have been developing a computer program called SAM (Schank and Abelson, 1977). For a limited domain of topics, SAM is able to receive printed stories as input and either generate paraphrases as output or answer simple questions about the stories. Table 9–4 dis-

TABLE 9–4.   A Sample Story Presented to Schank and Abelson's SAM (Script Applier Mechanism) Program, and an Elaborated Paraphrase Produced by SAM.

Story: John went to a restaurant. The hostess seated John. The hostess gave John a menu. John ordered lobster. He was served quickly. He left a large tip. He left the restaurant.

Sam's Elaborated Paraphrase: John decided he was going to go to a restaurant. He went to one. He asked the hostess for a table. She told him he could go to it. He went to it. She went to it. He sat down in a chair. He got a menu from her. He read it. A waiter saw John at the table. The waiter went to it. John ordered lobster. A chef cooked it. The waiter got it from the chef. The waiter served it quickly to John. He ate it. He asked the waiter for a check. John got it from the waiter. John remembered the waiter had served him quickly. John left the waiter a large tip. John paid the check. He left the restaurant.

From Schank et al., 1975.

plays a sample story SAM was given as input, and the extended paraphrase SAM produced as output. Despite SAM's rather uninspiring style, it has produced an extended, appropriate paraphrase which includes information that was not stated explicitly, but seems reasonable.

What enables SAM to achieve such success? SAM, of course, has been programmed with some elementary syntactic processing strategies and with a rather sophisticated semantic base, but the important point for our purposes is that Schank and Abelson found it impossible to program SAM to paraphrase and answer questions without giving him a substantial set of knowledge about the properties of the physical and social world.

To understand this point, consider again the piggy bank story. If SAM were given this story and later asked some questions about it, such as, "What did Janet get in her room?" or "What came out of the piggy bank?" he would only be able to answer the questions correctly if he was able to determine the referent of each of the IT's in the sentence. However, solving this problem of reference is not possible using simple word order rules or word definitions. People are able to tell what each IT refers to because of their knowledge about the properties of piggy banks (i.e., that one can get things out of them by turning them over and shaking them) and rooms (i.e., they are not the sorts of things little girls carry around).

Consider a couple of other examples taken from Schank and Abelson (1977). The first (from their page 9) is: THE POLICEMAN HELD UP HIS HAND AND STOPPED THE CAR. You know that the policeman did not stop the car with the sheer force of his hand. Rather, given what you know about the actions of policemen, cars, and drivers, you infer that the policeman's action led the driver to put on the brakes, which in turn stopped the car. If you had not drawn this inference, you wouldn't have been able to make sense of the sentence. The same holds for the following sentence (from Schank & Abelson, 1977, p. 23): JOHN BURNED HIS HAND BECAUSE HE FORGOT THE STOVE WAS ON. Humans, even very young ones, have no difficulty interpreting this sentence even though it is preposterous if interpreted literally. If you knew only the definitions of each word in the sentence and the syntactic structure of the sentence, you would not be able to make any sense out of the fact that the act of forgetting (a mental event) resulted in a charred extremity. The sentence is not at all strange to you, however, because you make the seemingly effortless inference that John touched the stove (having forgotten it was on) and this touching of a red-hot object caused the burn.

It is easy to overlook the importance of such drawing of inferences as long as we consider only human comprehension, because the inferences are so easy for us to draw. Yet, as Schank and Abelson (1977) learned in creating SAM, it has proven impossible to program computers to paraphrase or answer questions about even simple stories unless they are programmed with some extra-linguistic knowledge and the ability to draw inferences. We still do not understand the processes by which people draw such inferences. At present the most promising kind of theory is *schema theory*, which has been adopted by a number of different theorists (e.g., Minsky, 1975; Rumelhart & Ortony, 1977; Schank & Abelson, 1977). Of course, the term *schema* is not a new one; Bartlett used this concept to explain the constructive errors people made in recalling a story. A *schema* is simply generalized knowledge about a sequence of events. Schema theory assumes that people have schemata for a large number of familiar events (e.g., going to a restaurant, applying for college, going to a party, getting up in the morning), and they call upon these schemata to help them to fill in the gaps in stories and conversations.

Consider, for example, the way in which Schank and Abelson's SAM uses such schemata to paraphrase and answer questions about stories. Schank and Abelson call their schemata *scripts* (in fact, SAM stands for Script Applier Mechanism). SAM has a number of scripts including a restaurant script. The main features of this script are illustrated in Table 9–5. This script, as all scripts, consists of the name of the script, a cast of characters, and several scenes that make up the schema. When SAM is presented with a story, such as the one in Table 9–4, he searches memory for a script that is appropriate. In this case, the story should lead him directly to the restaurant schema, since the first sentence mentions a restaurant. SAM then proceeds to match

TABLE 9–5. A Sample Script from Schank and Abelson's (1977) SAM Program.

Script: restaurant
Characters: customer, hostess, waiter, chef, cashier
Scene 1: *entering*
  customer goes into restaurant
  customer finds a place to sit
    he may find it by himself
    he may be seated by a hostess
      he asks the hostess for a table
      she gives him permission to go to the table
  customer goes and sits at the table
Scene 2: *ordering*
  customer receives a menu
  customer reads it
  customer decides what to order
  waiter takes the order
    waiter sees the customer
    waiter goes to the customer
    customer orders what he wants
  chef cooks the meal
Scene 3: *eating*
  after some time the waiter brings the meal from the chef
  customer eats the meal
Scene 4: *exiting*
  customer asks the waiter for the check
  waiter gives the check to the customer
  customer leaves a tip
    the size of the tip depends on the goodness of the service
  customer pays the cashier
  customer leaves the restaurant

After Rumelhart, 1977. Copyright 1977 by John Wiley. Reprinted by permission.

up the incidents and people described in the story with the characters and events contained in the script. Thus, the script provides SAM with a context in which to interpret the rather disjointed events in the story. As SAM's paraphrase in Table 9–4 indicates, when SAM states the story in his own words, he uses the information contained in the script to fill in what likely happened, but was not stated explicitly.

Whether or not schema theory will prove to be an accurate account of the processes and structures that enable people to make inferences during language comprehension is still unclear, but it is impressive that including such schemata in computer programs enables them to simulate at least some characteristics of human paraphrasing and human question answering. Notice again that schema theory assumes a combination of top-down and bottom-up processes. Bottom-up processes come into play in locating the script, since the word RESTAURANT leads SAM to the appropriate script. On the other hand, having found the restaurant script gives SAM a host of expectations that lead him to look for certain things in the story (for example, he expects to find a customer and a waiter or waitress).

Conversational postulates. There is yet another kind of knowledge a person must have in order to comprehend language—knowledge of the rules of conversation. Grice (1967) pointed out that there is a set of conventions accepted implicitly by all speakers and listeners (and all readers and writers), though we are usually unaware of these conventions. Grice called these global rules of conversation *conversational postulates.* All of them, he argued, derive from the *cooperation principle,* which states that the speaker and listener agree that the speaker should form every aspect of his/her statement so as to maximally facilitate the agreed upon aims of the conversation. Some specific conversational postulates cited by Grice are the following.

> **(1) QUANTITY: Make your contribution as informative as possible. Do not be more informative than required.**

> **(2) QUALITY: Do not say what you believe to be false, or that for which you lack sufficient evidence.**

> **(3) RELATION: Be relevant.**

> **(4) MANNER: Avoid obscurity and ambiguity. Be brief, orderly, and polite.**

These conversational postulates come into play when we determine reference, at least in some contexts. If someone pointed to a house and said DO YOU SEE THAT WHITE HOUSE WITH THE ORNATE DOOR? WHAT COLOR IS IT?, you would probably reply with the color of the door. On the other hand, if they said DO YOU SEE THAT HOUSE WITH THE ORNATE GOLD DOOR? WHAT COLOR IS IT?, you would probably reply with the color of the house. That is, you would have assumed that IT referred to the door in the first case, but to the house in the second. Why? You have assigned reference in this fashion because you assume (implicitly) that the speaker is not being superfluous. Since, in the first case, he told you the color of the house, he could not possibly have been asking its color.

Similarly, if a classmate walks up to you, glances at the watch on your arm, and asks CAN YOU TELL ME THE TIME?, you are likely to assume that since he has seen your watch, he knows that you *can* tell him the time. Therefore, since you assume that he is obeying the cooperation principle, he must be asking something else, i.e., that you tell him the time. In fact, we often understand indirect requests (e.g., Can you open the window?) by invoking conversational postulates.

When the speaker intentionally (or unintentionally) violates these unspoken rules of conversation, misinterpretations are likely to occur. For example, imagine the following conversation (taken from Clark & Clark, 1977, p. 122).

> *Steven:* **Wilfred is meeting a woman for dinner tonight.**
>
> *Susan:* **Does his wife know about it?**
>
> *Steven:* **Of course she does. The woman he is meeting is his wife.**

Steven's initial statement violated the maxim of quantity, since it was less informative than it could have been.

Speakers sometimes violate conversational postulates in a way that will be obvious to the listener and, in so doing, convey some overriding message. For example, consider the sarcasm implicit in MISS X PRODUCED A SERIES OF SOUNDS WHICH CORRESPONDED CLOSELY WITH THE SCORE FOR "HOME SWEET HOME." In violating the maxim of manner by being unnecessarily wordy, the speaker has conveyed the notion that whatever Miss X was doing should not be called singing (Grice, 1967).

Speakers can also violate a maxim intentionally in the hope that the listener will not notice the violation, thereby getting away with an implicit lie. This is just what has happened in the conversation between mother and daughter in the Food for Thought section. If the boyfriend does not sleep on the couch, then the daughter will not have lied (at least in the strict sense). Rather, she will have violated the maxim of relevance, hoping that her mother will assume that she has obeyed it.

Clark and Haviland (1977) have discussed a particularly important conversational postulate called the *given-new contract*. This is, in fact, a special case of the maxim of manner. According to the given-new contract:

> **the speaker agrees to provide information he thinks the listener already knows as *given* and information he thinks the listener doesn't know as *new*. The listener agrees to assume that the speaker is trying to provide, to the best of his ability, given and new information.**

Phrased in terms of network models, both speaker and listener assume that the speaker attempts to construct his message so that the given information will send the listener to the relevant concept node in long-term memory, and the *new* information will provide him with some new information about this node. Thus the speaker treats the given information as an address to information already in memory, and then integrates the new information into memory at that node. If speakers don't provide any given information at all, then it is impossible for the listener to relate the new information to his previous knowledge.

It is remarkable that as speakers we usually do a reasonably good job of tailoring our statements so as to make given and new information distinct. Furthermore, we usually do it without being consciously aware of planning our utterances carefully. The speaker signals the distinction between given and new information by using one or more of a number of syntactical devices, including the following three.

(1) The definite article *the* usually signals *given* information.

Thus, the statement THE WOMAN BECAME ANGRY assumes that the listener already knows which woman the speaker is discussing (i.e., this is given information), whereas the sentence A WOMAN BECAME ANGRY signals the listener that some new (previously undiscussed woman) is now being introduced into the conversation. Notice, then, that although articles often seem to be unnecessary redundancies, they do convey information to the listener regarding the referent, and they make it possible for the people conversing to become aware of failures to communicate. When presented with an uninterpretable THE SENATOR IS ANGRY, the listener can ask quickly WHAT SENATOR?, since it is clear that the speaker has assumed (incorrectly) that the listener has a particular senator in mind.

> **(2) Restrictive relative clauses in the initial part of a sentence signal *given* information. (e.g., THE JOKES HORACE TELLS ARE AWFUL. *Given:* Horace tells jokes. *New:* They are awful.)**

> **(3) The cleft construction (*it is*) signals *new* information. (e.g. IT IS HORACE WHO TELLS HORRIBLE JOKES. *Given:* Someone tells horrible jokes. *New:* It is Horace.)**

Although the two HORACE sentences describe the same propositions, they differ regarding what the speaker assumes the listener to know already, and what the speaker wants to convey.

In order to comprehend, then, listeners (or readers) must find appropriate antecedents (i.e., appropriate information in memory) for what the speaker marks as *given*. Sometimes the speaker makes this quite easy for the listener by making the referent obvious. For example,

We got some beer out of the trunk.

The beer was warm.

In this set of sentences, it is easy to find the antecedent for THE BEER in the second sentence, since SOME BEER was introduced in the immediately preceding sentence. Other times, however, the listener's task is more difficult, since he must infer the antecedent, as in

We checked the picnic supplies.

The beer was warm.

In order to find the antecedent for THE BEER in this case, the listener must infer that the beer was among the picnic supplies. That is, the listener must use his knowledge about picnic supplies and beer to *construct* a link between the two sentences. Clark has called this construction of a link *bridging*.

Haviland and Clark (1974) have demonstrated that this bridging takes time. They presented subjects with pairs of sentences including the BEER sentences and asked them to press a button when they had comprehended the sentences. Subjects took almost 200 msec longer to comprehend sentence pairs in which the link had to be constructed.

The dangers of inference. The main point of this section is, of course, that inference is a necessary part of language comprehension. Much of the message a sentence is meant to convey is not stated explicitly (probably because if we stated everything explicitly, we would never have enough time or energy to get anything said), but must be added by the listener/reader. People use their knowledge of the world and of conversational postulates to relate the new information the speaker is providing with the appropriate old information in memory.

Though drawing such inferences is essential for language comprehension, our tendency to draw them so readily and unconsciously makes us subject to certain dangers. Here we will consider how such inference makes us susceptible to (1) lying, (2) leading questions, and (3) misleading advertising.

We have already seen that the clever speaker (e.g., the coed with the inquisitive mother, visiting boyfriend, and couch) can surreptitiously break a maxim of conversation which leads the listener to draw an inference which the speaker intended the listener to draw, but which the speaker knows to be untrue. (Confusing, isn't it?) In this case, then, the speaker has not uttered a lie. Rather, the speaker has only broken a conversational postulate (presumably a less serious offense) which has led the listener to infer an untruth.

If the speaker is willing to lie outright, he can also use the conversational postulates to make it less likely that his lie will be noticed. In particular, the given-new contract leads the listener to expect that the given information will be true and, indeed, focuses his attention on the new information. Therefore, listeners are probably less likely to scrutinize the truthfulness of given than of new information.

Hornby (1974) tested this hypothesis by presenting subjects with a sentence-picture verification task in which the subject heard a sentence and then, one second later, saw a picture which lasted for only 50 msec. The subject was to judge whether or not the sentence accurately described the subsequent picture. Consider, for example, trials on which the following sentence was presented:

It is the girl that is petting the cat

In this sentence the given information is that someone petted the cat, whereas the new information is that the girl is doing the petting. Now compare two pictures that might be presented, both of which are *not*, in fact, true of the sentence: (1) a picture of a boy petting a cat, and (2) a picture of a girl petting a dog. Notice that (1) is incorrect because the new information is violated, whereas (2) is incorrect because the given information is violated. Hornby found that people were more likely to pick up the inconsistency (i.e., "the lie") for picture (1) than for picture (2). This suggests that people are less likely to examine the truth or falsity of given information than they are that of new information. Therefore, liars are more likely to get away with their untruths if they mark the lie syntactically as given information, because listeners implicitly assume the given-new contract.

So-called leading questions also often capitalize upon the listener's implicit acceptance of conversational postulates. Consider, for example, the little noticed, but very important determinate and indeterminate articles THE and A. We said that THE is used to direct the listener to some specific old information in memory, whereas A is often used to introduce new information. This suggests, then, that a lawyer would be more likely to get "yes" as a reply from a witness if he asked DID YOU SEE THE BROKEN HEADLIGHT? rather than DID YOU SEE A BROKEN HEADLIGHT? The former suggests subtly to the listener that there was indeed a broken headlight. Loftus and Zanni (1975) have, in fact, demonstrated this bias in the laboratory.

The fact that people go beyond the information stated explicitly is probably misused more often in advertising than in any other single domain. As we have seen earlier, people often draw *pragmatic implications*, i.e., conclusions that are neither explicitly stated nor logically implied by a given statement. For example, for most listeners THE HUNGRY PYTHON CAUGHT THE MOUSE pragmatically implies that the python ate the mouse, even though this is not necessarily the case. Presumably, we draw this inference because of our general knowledge about the propensities of pythons.

If people draw such pragmatic implications, and later cannot distinguish what they heard from what they inferred, then advertisers need not make false claims explicitly when they write commercials; they need only lead the consumer to draw his own pragmatic inferences. Consider the following examples which, like the python sentence, are drawn from Harris (1977). Advertisers can pragmatically imply a false claim by inserting hedges, such as ZAP PILLS MAY HELP RELIEVE PAIN. Of course, this statement does not say that Zap pills *will* relieve pain (one could just as truthfully say that taking sugar water *may* relieve pain—since, then again, it may not), but people are likely to draw the inference that Zap pills are effective pain relievers. Professor Earl Hunt has pointed out a similar example from an actual ad: THIS DIET ALLOWS YOU TO LOSE UP TO TEN POUNDS IN TWO WEEKS WITHOUT STARVATION. Using comparative adjectives without stating the comparison is another such technique. CHORE GIVES YOU A WHITER WASH usually leads the listener to conclude that CHORE gives you whiter washes than other laundry detergents do, but the sentence, of course, does not say this explicitly. The advertiser might have had in mind the deleted phrase THAN WASHING WITH COAL DUST.

Harris (1977) set out to determine just how serious a problem such misleading statements might be. He presented college students with commercial excerpts and then with test sentences concerning the contents of the commercial. Sample commercial excerpts and the paired test sentences are shown in Table 9–6. For a given commercial

TABLE 9–6.   Sample Commercials and Test Sentence from Harris' (1977) Study of Pragmatic Implications in Advertising.

Assertion Commercial	Implication Commercial	Test Sentence
Aren't you tired of the sniffles and runny noses all winter? Tired of always feeling less than your best? Taking Eradicold Pills as directed will get you through a whole winter without colds.	Aren't you tired of sniffles and runny noses all winter? Tired of always feeling less than your best? Get through a whole winter without colds. Take Eradicold Pills as directed.	If you take Eradicold pills as directed, you will not have any colds this winter.

After Harris, 1977. Copyright 1977 by American Psychological Association. Reprinted by permission of the publisher and author.

(e.g., the ERADICOLD commercial), some subjects were presented with the assertion version and others with the implication version. In the assertion version, the commercial explicitly asserts the test sentence, whereas in the implication version the commercial only pragmatically implies the test sentence. When asked immediately after presentation of the commercial excerpts whether the commercial had asserted the test sentence, subjects who heard the assertion version were only slightly more likely to say "yes" than were subjects who heard the implication version. Furthermore, if testing was delayed until subjects had heard all 20 commercials, then people were just as likely to say "yes" following an implication passage as following an assertion passage. These findings suggest that even when people are tested immediately after they have heard a commercial, they have difficulty discriminating what the commercial actually claimed from what they constructed. Furthermore, if testing is delayed for a few minutes, people do not discriminate at all between what was asserted and what was pragmatically implied. Harris was also able to show that this tendency to go beyond the specific assertions is present even when subjects have been warned ahead of time that they should try hard to differentiate what the commercial actually claims from what it might lead the person to infer.

The implications of this and related work are important for those who make legislation concerning false advertising. If people treat asserted and pragmatically implied information as equivalent, even when they have been encouraged to make the distinction, then should companies be held legally accountable not only for what their commercials assert, but also for what their commercials pragmatically imply? If the latter, then on what basis should we determine what the commercial pragmatically implies?

It is clear, then, that going beyond the information stated explicitly is a necessary part of language comprehension, but that such unconscious inference makes us prey to lying, leading questions, and misleading advertising. The best way to minimize these pitfalls is to be aware of their existence, and to be aware of the subtle ways in which the messages implicit in language are conveyed.

CHAPTER SUMMARY

We viewed language comprehension as the task of taking strings of words and using them to construct a set of underlying propositions, and we investigated the processes people use to make this conversion. The insights we have gained from the disciplines of psychology, linguistics, and artificial intelligence share two general themes. First, words and sentences are potentially ambiguous at many different levels, yet this ambiguity usually goes unnoticed by speakers, listeners, writers, and readers. All three disciplines seek to explain how people deal with this potential ambiguity. Second, it appears that any answer to this puzzle must consider the importance of expectations. Therefore, contemporary theories assume that language comprehension requires both bottom-up (i.e., stimulus-driven) and top-down (i.e., conceptually-driven or expectation-driven) processes.

In constructing underlying propositions from strings of words, people call upon their knowledge of word meanings and upon their knowledge of syntax. Studies using a number of different techniques (including lexical decisions and phoneme-monitoring) suggest that all possible meanings of each word are looked up or activated briefly, but the semantic and syntactic context is used quickly to eliminate all but the contextually appropriate interpretation. Furthermore, as people take in sentences, they process the sentence word by word, breaking the sentence down into underlying constituents as they go. Currently, the most promising theories of how this constituent analysis proceeds assume that people use a set of heuristics called processing strategies, which embody the person's expectations regarding the syntactic and semantic properties of sentences. These processing strategies can be specified more precisely in the form of production systems.

Complete comprehension requires even more than knowledge of word meanings and syntax, however. For example, in order to comprehend a story or a conversation, people must solve the problem of reference, i.e., they must determine the concepts to which the speaker is referring, so that the new information provided by the speaker can be related to what the listener already knows. In many cases the appropriate referent must be inferred by the listener, using not only his knowledge of word meanings, but also his knowledge of the properties of the physical and social world, and his knowledge of the implicit rules of conversation, called conversational postulates.

The fact that human listeners and readers draw such inferences unconsciously is to be celebrated, since, the inferences make communication possible. Nonetheless, this propensity for going beyond the information explicitly stated makes humans susceptible to certain forms of lying, leading questions, and misleading advertising.

SUGGESTED READING

If you would like to learn what is known (and what is not known) about how people plan and produce language, it would be best to begin with Chapters 6 and 7 of Clark and Clark's text *Psychology and Language* or with Chapters 6 and 7 (is this a magic number for chapters on language production??) of Foss and Hakes' text *Psycholinguis-*

tics. A more advanced discussion is contained in a chapter by Mac-Neilage and Ladefoged entitled "The production of language."

The importance of inference for language comprehension is a fascinating topic, particularly because it leads you to become more aware of the usually unnoticed wonders of our linguistic abilities. General discussion of this topic can be found in Winograd's chapter entitled "A framework for understanding discourse" and in Bransford's text *Human Cognition.* The book by Schank and Abelson entitled *Scripts, Plans, Goals and Understanding* provides abundant examples of the ubiquity of inference as well as a computer simulation theory of how inference is used in language comprehension. If you wish to read more about the *dangers* of such inference, you might begin with a 1978 article by Harris and Monaco entitled "Psychology of pragmatic implication: Information processing between the lines."

We only discussed a very few processing strategies in the present chapter, but you will find more complete discussions in Slobin's textbook *Psycholinguistics,* Clark and Clark's textbook *Psychology and Language,* in Bever's chapter entitled "Cognitive basis for linguistic structures," and in a chapter by Carroll and Bever entitled "Sentence comprehension: A case study in the relation of knowledge and perception."

As I indicated, one promising way in which processing strategy theory is being made more explicit (and hence more testable) is through the development of computer simulation theories in which the processing strategies are stated in terms of computer programs. The two most well-known such approaches are production systems and augmented transition networks. I mentioned the production systems approach as it is embodied in Anderson's ACT theory. The best place to read more about the way in which production systems can be used to model processing strategies is in the chapter by Anderson, Kline, and Lewis entitled "A production system model of language comprehension." The augmented transition network (ATN) approach is best understood by beginning with Chapter 3 of Rumelhart's text *An Introduction to Human Information Processing,* and then by reading Wanner and Maratsos' chapter in a book entitled *Linguistic Theory and Psychological Reality.* If this reading whets your appetite for ATNs, then turn to a debate that is underway in the pages of the journal *Cognition.* In 1978 Frazier and Fodor had published an article there entitled "The sausage machine: A new two-stage parsing model," in which they proposed a theory they argued to be superior to ATN theory. Two years later in a 1980 issue, Wanner (one of the developers of ATN theory) wrote a reply with the tantalizing title "The ATN and the sausage machine: Which one is baloney?" Fodor and Frazier replied to Wanner's reply in a later 1980 issue! This debate would make a good, thought provoking term paper topic.

There is a more general debate that would also merit further reading and thinking—the question of whether artificial intelligence will ever teach us anything about human language comprehension. This debate is part of the general debate between the Theory Development and Theory Demonstration views we discussed in Chapter 6. I have argued that attempts to write computer programs that comprehend language are useful both because they help us to become aware of the complexity of processes we often take for granted and because they provide a way of making theories more explicit. Nonetheless, there are those who argue that artificial intelligence is of little or no use for psychological analyses of language comprehension. For a heated debate of this question, look back to the 1976 and 1977 volumes of the journal *Cognition*. In 1976 Dresher and Hornstein published an article that began the argument, an article entitled "On some supposed contributions of artificial intelligence to the scientific study of language." The term *supposed* tells you the side of the argument they took, and among the work they criticized sharply was that of Schank (which we discussed briefly in this chapter) and that of Winograd. Schank and Wilensky replied in the pages of the journal in 1977, and Dresher and Hornstein replied to the reply in the same issue. Then Winograd (1977) joined the fray by defending himself and the artificial intelligence approach, leading Dresher and Hornstein to reply again. Needless to say, the issue was not resolved to the satisfaction of either side; you might write a critical analysis of the debate for a term paper.

Finally, I suggest another topic for those who like to wrestle with the puzzle of how we can study mental processes (in this case the processes underlying language comprehension) using empirical methods. Any time we try to make inferences from experimental findings to mental processes, we are making an inferential leap, so it is always necessary to look carefully for alternative interpretations of particular results. A general discussion of methods in psycholinguistics is included in a chapter by Olson and Clark in the *Handbook of Perception, Vol. VII.* One particular example of potential difficulties concerns the phoneme-monitoring technique we discussed. For a number of years, this was the major task used to study language processing, but in 1978 two articles (one by Mehler, Segui, and Carey and one by Newman and Dell) were published in *Journal of Verbal Learning and Verbal Behavior.* These articles demonstrated that a number of the most oft-cited studies of phoneme-monitoring (though not the ones we discussed in this chapter) contained confounds which rendered the findings uninterpretable. Reading these 1978 articles provides a case study of the difficulties inherent in empirical studies of language comprehension.

Language by Ear: Speech Perception

10

FOOD FOR THOUGHT

Recall the last time you listened to someone speaking in an unfamiliar foreign language. Could you tell where one word left off and another began? What does this suggest about the processes underlying speech perception?

Now try a very different demonstration. Find a volunteer who is willing to have you use your finger to trace out letters on his/her back. Can the person tell you which letter you have printed? Now switch roles. Can you tell which letters are being printed? Is it difficult to do so? What does this suggest about your knowledge of letters?

THE PROBLEM OF PATTERN RECOGNITION

In the previous chapter we studied how people convert strings of words into their underlying propositions, and how they relate these conveyed propositions to their previous knowledge. We found that such language comprehension requires both top-down and bottom-up processes, and that it calls upon a number of different kinds of knowledge including knowledge of syntax (exemplified in processing strategies), of word meanings (which can be conceptualized as network structures), of the characteristics of the physical and social world (which may be thought of as schemata), and of conversational postulates.

In that chapter we overlooked one of the major puzzles in the study of linguistic abilities: how do we convert the stream of sound that reaches our ears into words? On first encounter with this question, most people fail to see the mystery. The sounds of speech do not seem particularly special. The proverbial person on the street assumes that perceiving speech sounds is not qualitatively different from perceiving other kinds of sounds. In this chapter, we will find that many psychologists and linguists disagree.

Speech perception as an example of pattern recognition. In this chapter we will explore how people identify speech sounds, e.g., how they recognize one acoustic pattern as the sound *ba* as in *bad* and another as the sound *da* as in *dad*. Speech perception is one kind of *pattern recognition*, but there are many other kinds of pattern recognition as well. For example, people recognize patterns of lines as certain letters, patterns of musical notes as melodies, patterns of facial features as particular individuals.

In the overview model in Figure 1–2, we defined pattern recognition as the process by which the sensory input in sensory memory contacts the location in long-term memory where information about that stimulus is stored. The puzzle that intrigues psychologists can be put simply: how do people recognize patterns despite the fact that each individual instance of a pattern differs from others? In terms of our overview model: how is it that many different sensory stimuli all result in the same long-term memory location being contacted? For example, if you see a picture of John Doe when he is smiling, you recognize him the next time you see his face, even though on this second presentation his face is sad. You have, in other words, extracted some pattern that enables you to recognize John Doe (i.e., to activate the appropriate concept node in long-term memory) despite irrelevant changes in his expression. A similar phenomenon occurs with handwritten or printed letters; you are able to recognize an *A* even when it is printed in a sloppy fashion and even when it is inverted or written sideways. In fact, as the demonstration in the Food for Thought section makes clear, you are able to recognize an *A* even when it occurs in a completely different modality (touch) from that in which it is usually experienced. These observations suggest that whatever it is you know about a given pattern is quite general; this knowledge is abstract enough to enable you to recognize the pattern despite irrelevant changes in its appearance.

A couple of decades ago computer scientists began the task of writing computer programs that would convert speech *sounds* into written language, i.e., computer programs that would take dictation. This task has practical importance, since such programs would enable computers to "hear" for deaf individuals. Now, after more than two decades of work, such programs are still far less than adequate at what humans find to be a boringly simple task (cf. Reddy, 1976; 1980). Similarly, though it was not difficult to program computers to read the stylized numbers and letters you see printed at the bottom of your bank checks, it proved extremely difficult to program computers to read handwriting. The difficulty in designing pattern recognition programs for both listening and seeing, of course, is that it is necessary to figure out exactly how people distinguish relevant from irrelevant features of a pattern, so that we can tell the computer how to do so as well. Once again, then, attempts at computer simulation of a human ability led us, not to lessen the stature of Man, but to wonder anew at the complexity of the tasks that he performs apparently effortlessly.

In this chapter we will examine one particular kind of pattern recognition in some detail. As we shall see, speech seems special in several ways, and the puzzles it presents are even more perplexing than they are in the case of other kinds of pattern recognition. Nonetheless, throughout our discussion, you should keep in mind that speech is acting for us as a case study of the more general problem of how people recognize patterns.

THE STIMULUS FOR SPEECH PERCEPTION

If we are to examine how people recognize patterns, the first step is to specify the stimulus precisely. The smallest unit of speech is the *phone* or *phonetic segment*. Linguists have developed an International Phonetic Alphabet that consists of a listing of all the different phones that occur in the languages of the world. By convention, each such phone is indicated in brackets. Thus, the spoken English word *keep* consists of three phones: [k] [i] [p].

Linguists also noted, however, that the languages of the world differ in the extent to which two different phones (i.e., sounds) are distinguished from each other. Linguists adopted the term *phoneme* to refer to the shortest element of speech that makes a difference in meaning for a given language. A *phoneme* refers to a set of phones that are treated as equivalent within a given language. To distinguish them from phones, phonemes are usually indicated by slashes. Thus, in English the word KEEP would be said to consist of the three phonemes: /k/ /i/ /p/.

To understand the distinction between phones and phonemes, say aloud the two words *keep* and *cool*. Most English speakers judge the initial sounds of these two words to be identical, i.e., in English, both words begin with the same phoneme /k/. In fact, however, the two sounds are different, i.e., *keep* begins with one phonetic segment [k] and *cool* begins with another [q]. The two sounds are formed differently by the speaker (try saying each several times and analyzing how you arrange your tongue and lips for each) and the acoustic signals they produce are noticeably different for the members of some linguistic communities. In Arabic, for example, these two phonetic segments belong to two different phonemes. A word beginning with the phone [k] has a meaning different from an otherwise identical word beginning with the phone [q]; /kalb/ means DOG and /qalb/ means HEART. If an English speaker wants to learn Arabic, then, he must learn to hear the differences between the phones [k] and [q], or he will have difficulty conversing about dogs and/or hearts.

There are many other examples of how different linguistic communities group phones into phonemes differently. Therefore, a phoneme is an abstract concept in that it stands for a set of different sounds (phones) which are treated as equivalent by the speakers of a given language.

Phones can be described in two different ways, in terms of the positions and movements of our vocal apparatus when they are produced (i.e., articulatory terms), or in terms of the resulting sounds (i.e., acoustic terms).

Articulatory features. Each phone may be differentiated from all other phones by a set of articulatory *distinctive features*. We will consider only two of a number of such features: place of articulation and voicing. The *place of articulation* specifies the place in the mouth at which constriction of the vocal tract occurs. Pronounce the words *pat* and *bat*. In producing the initial phone of both words, you close your lips, so both [p] and [b] are called bilabial phones. Now pronounce the words *dad* and *tad*. In producing these, you touch your tongue to the roof of your mouth, so [d] and [t] are referred to as apical phones. Finally, try saying *gad* and *kad*. You will find that you constrict your vocal tract still further back; [g] and [k] are called velar consonants.

The sounds [b], [p], [d], [t], [g], and [k] can also be contrasted on a different articulatory distinctive feature which is called *voicing*. Voicing refers to the relation between the time at which the vocal cords start vibrating and the time at which the constriction of the vocal tract is released. *Voiced consonants* are defined as those in which the vocal cords start vibrating immediately after the closure is released, whereas *unvoiced consonants* are those in which the vocal cords do not start vibrating until some brief time after the closure has been released. Thus, [b], [d], and [g] are voiced consonants, whereas [p], [t], and [k] are unvoiced. The best way to experience this distinction is to hold your hand lightly on your Adam's apple and repeat *ba* and *pa* several times. You can feel the vibration of your vocal cords more quickly when you say *ba* than when you say *pa*. Try this contrast for the other two pairs as well (i.e., [d] versus [t] and [g] versus [k]).

As Table 10–1 illustrates, then, the six consonants we have just discussed can be differentiated on the basis of the two distinctive features of place of articulation and voicing.

Acoustic characteristics. Although each phone can be characterized by a unique combination of a set of articulatory features, such a description alone is not adequate if we wish to understand how people go about perceiving speech sounds. The stimulus that impinges on the listener's ears is not a set of articulatory features, but a sound pattern.

All sounds, including speech sounds, are simply pressure variations transmitted through some vibratory medium, such as air. For example, a pure tone can be generated by striking a tuning fork. If

TABLE 10–1. Classification of Six Stop Consonants Along Two Articulatory Features

Voicing	Place of Articulation		
	Bilabial	Apical	Velar
Voiced	[b]	[d]	[g]
Unvoiced	[p]	[t]	[k]

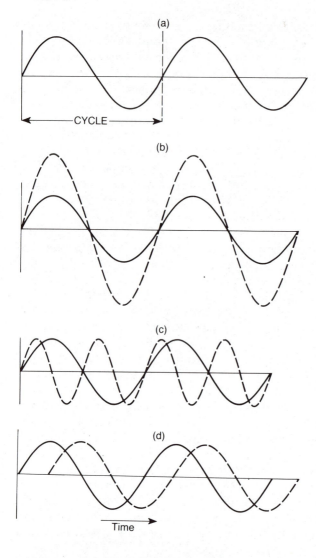

Figure 10–1. Illustrations of the characteristics of sound. Part *a* depicts a simple sine wave underlying a pure tone. Part *b* depicts two waves differing only in amplitude, *c* depicts two waves differing only in frequency, and *d* depicts two waves differing only in phase.

you were able to see the perturbation of the air caused by this vibration, it would look like the simple wave shown in Figure 10–1a. Note how the fork would displace the air in one direction and then in another again and again over the time period shown. As the figure shows, a *cycle* is defined as one complete vibration of the tuning fork. Any given simple wave of this sort can be defined in terms of three characteristics: its amplitude, frequency, and phase.

The *amplitude* depends upon the degree of displacement of the air caused by the wave. Figure 10–1b depicts two waves which differ only in amplitude. Perceptually, tones of higher amplitude are heard as being louder than tones of lower amplitude. Waves can also differ in their *frequency*, i.e., in the number of cycles that occur per second. Figure 10–1c depicts two waves that differ only in frequency. Perceptually, waves of higher frequency are heard as higher pitched than waves of lower frequency. Finally, waves can differ in *phase*, defined as the beginning point of the wave's cycle. The waves depicted in Figure 10–1d differ only in phase.

Each of the waves illustrated in Figure 10–1 depicts a pure tone. However, most sounds we hear, including speech sounds, are made up of many such waves of different frequencies, amplitudes, and phases, all occurring simultaneously. In the case of speech sounds, the most important kinds of variation are changes in frequency over time. Therefore, the development of an instrument called the *sound spectrograph* was a particularly important advance, since it converts a stream of sound into a visual picture of how frequency varies as a function of time. Figure 10–2 demonstrates in outline form how a sound spectrograph works. Notice (at the left of the figure) that a roll of paper is turned at a specified rate. When a person speaks into the microphone displayed at the right, the sound is fed through a bank of filters, each of which allows only a certain small range of frequencies to pass through. Each filter is also attached to a writing device. If a large amount of energy at a particular frequency is contained in the sound at a given instant, then a dark mark is made on the paper, and the greater the amount of energy, the darker the line. Since the paper moves along at a fixed rate, the result is a picture of how frequency varied as a function of time, i.e., a picture of the speech signal. This picture is called a *sound spectrogram*.

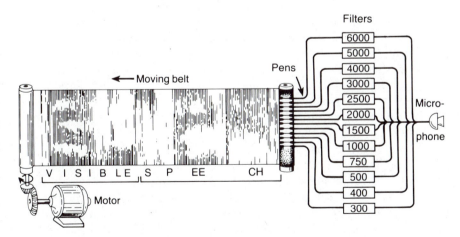

Figure 10–2. An illustration of how a sound spectrograph operates. (After Potter, Kopp and Kopp, 1966. Copyright 1966 by Dover Publications, Inc. Reprinted by permission of the publisher.)

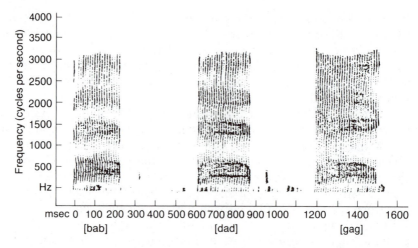

Figure 10–3. A spectrogram of the words [bab], [dad], and [gag]. (From A COURSE IN PHONETICS by Peter Ladefoged, © 1975 by Harcourt Brace Jovanovich, Inc. Reprinted by permission of the publisher.)

The sound spectrogram produced when a speaker said the syllables [bab], [dad], and [gag] is depicted in Figure 10–3. This figure illustrates two important characteristics of most speech signals. First, there are certain frequency ranges at which a great deal of energy is concentrated. These frequency bands of concentrated energy are called *formants*. For example, each of the syllables in the figure contains four such formants, formant 1 (the lowest formant is always designated the first formant) is centered at 500 cycles/sec, the second at 1,500 cycles/sec, the third at 2,000 cycles/sec, and the fourth at 3,000 cycles/sec. The second characteristic is that most speech signals consist of some time segments during which the formants remain constant, and other time segments during which the frequencies in a formant change rapidly. The former are called *steady state* components of the signal, and the latter are called *transients*. For example, the early and final portions of each of the syllables in Figure 10–3 are the transient portions of the signal, and the middle parts of the signal are the steady state portions.

You might be wondering exactly what parts of the signal are critical for having someone perceive these sounds as [bab], [dad], and [gag]. That is, must the entire signal be presented just as it is shown, or can only certain frequencies be produced with the same perceptual result? It is possible to answer this question, thanks to the development of a device that does the reverse of the sound spectrograph. Instead of converting sounds into pictures, the *speech synthesizer* converts pictures into sounds. Therefore, it is possible to paint a particular

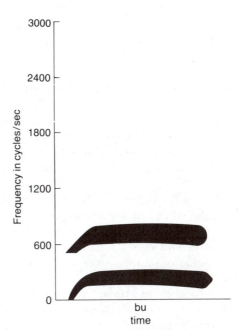

Figure 10–4. Schematized sound spectrogram of [bu]. (After Delattre, Liberman, & Cooper, 1955. Copyright 1955 by the Acoustical Society of America. Reprinted by permission.)

set of formants, and feed them through the speech synthesizer. The synthesized speech sounds can then be played to human listeners who are asked to say what sound they heard. For example, researchers have found that if only the two formants depicted in Figure 10–4 are synthesized and played to human listeners, most report hearing the speech sound [bu]. Apparently, then, these two formants are *sufficient* stimuli for the perception of this sound.

It would be impossible to overestimate the importance of the sound spectrograph and speech synthesizer for helping us to study how people perceive sounds, for these devices enable us to specify the stimulus precisely and to see how perception changes systematically as a function of specified changes in the acoustic signal.

BOTTOM-UP THEORIES OF PATTERN RECOGNITION

Imagine now that you wish to build a computerized pattern recognition device that will convert a spoken acoustic input into a string of phones. Notice that your device need not actually *comprehend* the words spoken, i.e., the computer need *not* output a set of propositions underlying the acoustic input. It need simply provide a printed copy of the string of phones spoken into it. How would you go about programming the computer to do this pattern recognition feat?

Chances are that you will come up with an approach that corresponds to one of two traditional theories of pattern recognition, either a template-matching theory or a feature-detection theory.

Template matching. One solution you might have proposed is to store away in the computer's memory a copy (i.e., a *template*) of the sound spectrogram pattern that corresponds to each possible phone, and you could equip the computer with a sound spectrograph which would convert incoming speech into a sound spectrogram. The computer could then be programmed to recognize the sounds by having it compare each incoming acoustic pattern with all possible templates. The acoustic pattern would then be identified as being an exemplar of the phone corresponding to whichever template it matched best. This is a *template-matching* theory of speech perception. Of course, you could also propose template-matching theories for other domains of pattern recognition as well.

Feature detection. You might have proposed a slightly different, but related kind of theory. Instead of storing away a template for each phone in memory, you might store a list of acoustic features that characterize each phone. Sample features might be, for example, a rising first formant, simultaneous onset of first and second formants, etc. According to such a *feature-detection* theory of pattern recognition, the incoming acoustic pattern could again be converted to a sound spectrogram and then the spectrogram would be analyzed into a set of features. This feature list for the presented stimulus would be compared with the stored feature lists for all possible phones. The stimulus would be recognized as the phone whose feature set it matched most closely.

Template-matching and feature-detection theories are quite similar to each other. For example, a list of features can be viewed simply as a list of templates for *parts* of the stimulus. The major difference between the two is that template theories treat each stimulus as an unanalyzed, unique whole, whereas feature-detection theories define each category in terms of a small set of features chosen from a larger set. For example, the feature of a rising first formant would be part of the description of a number of different phones.

Most contemporary theories assume that feature detection plays an important role in pattern recognition. This is because there is empirical evidence for the existence of feature detector mechanisms. We will have reason to discuss other kinds of evidence later in the chapter, but here we will mention only neurophysiological data. A couple of decades ago techniques were developed that enabled scientists to record the responses of individual nerve cells, so the firing of a single cell could be studied as different stimuli were presented to the organism. They found cells in the visual system of the frog and the cat that fired *only* when a particular pattern of visual stimulation (i.e., a particular feature) occurred (e.g., Hubel & Wiesel, 1962; Lettvin, Maturana, McCulloch, & Pitts, 1959). For example, there were cells that fired only when vertical lines were presented, other cells that fired only when horizontal lines were presented, etc. The discovery of such cells had tremendous impact on the study of pattern recognition, because it suggested the possibility that similar feature-detection mechanisms might be present in the human visual system, and perhaps in other sensory modalities as well.

Despite the fact that feature detectors appear to play some role in pattern recognition, it is now clear that neither feature detection nor the closely related template theories will be adequate for explaining all of pattern recognition. The main difficulty is that both are purely bottom-up, stimulus-driven theories. They assume that pattern recognition relies solely upon a match between information extracted from the stimulus and some previously stored description. When computers have been programmed with programs of this sort, they have been able to recognize patterns accurately only in highly artificial situations. For example, a template-matching or feature-detection method enables computers to identify the stylized letters and numbers printed on bank checks, but it does not enable them to recognize human handwritten letters accurately. Since humans can recognize the often sloppy handwriting of their peers with much higher accuracy, this suggests that the processes humans use are not limited to template matching and feature detection.

Ambiguity and expectations again. Bottom-up theories are inadequate for all but the very simplest kinds of pattern recognition. They have particular difficulty in accounting for human speech perception, because they fail to explain a number of its most interesting characteristics. We will turn to these characteristics next, and as we do so the themes of ambiguity and expectations that we stressed in the previous chapter will appear again. We will find that the acoustic signal is ambiguous in a number of ways, and psychologists are trying to understand how people manage to overcome this ambiguity with so little apparent difficulty. Furthermore, we will find that just as expectations are critical for enabling us to convert strings of words into propositions, they are also critical if we are to convert an acoustic signal into a sequence of phonemes.

CHARACTERISTICS OF SPEECH PERCEPTION

We will now consider five salient characteristics of speech perception. These are of particular interest both because they place constraints on the kind of theory that might account for human speech perception, and because they have suggested to many psychologists and linguists that at some level of information processing, speech sounds are processed differently from other sounds.

Phoneme restoration. If speech perception involved only bottom-up processes, then we should hear only sounds that are actually present in the acoustic signal. However, people often hear phonemes even when the part of the acoustic signal that carried that phoneme has been removed. For example, Warren (1970) tape recorded sentences such as "THE STATE GOVERNORS MET WITH THEIR RESPECTIVE LEGISLATURES CONVENING IN THE CAPITAL CITY." Then he removed the part of the acoustic signal that carried the acoustic cues for the first [s] in LEGISLATURES, and he replaced this segment of the tape with a cough. When this doctored-up tape recording was presented to listeners, Warren found that his subjects were unable to tell that the [s] was missing. In fact, even when they were told ahead of time that the [s] had been removed, and even though they listened to the sentence repeatedly, subjects still insisted that they *heard* the [s]. This phenomenon of hearing phonemes that would be contextually appropriate, but are not present is called *phoneme restoration*, and it suggests that speech perception is, at least in part, a process of construction.

Lack of segmentation in the acoustic signal. When you listen to someone speaking English, the acoustic stream seems to consist of a series of isolated words. You usually have little difficulty determining where one lets off and another begins. In fact, however, this segmentation into words is not present in the acoustic signal itself, a fact which becomes obvious when you examine sound spectrograms of fluent speech. Consider Figure 10–5, which shows the sound spectrogram for the spoken phrase "to catch pink salmon." Although there are pauses in the acoustic signal (i.e., places where there is no energy at any frequency), these do not always correspond to breaks between words. This is because your mouth does not return to some starting position between words. Rather, your lips and tongue slide from the movements needed to produce one word to those needed to produce the next. The remarkable fact about speech perception is that your listener manages, with little apparent effort, to decode that continuous stream of sound back into the series of discrete words you had in mind.

It is possible to become aware of this lack of segmentation by listening to a language you do not know. It is impossible to determine where one word ends and another begins. Newcomers to a given language usually find it harder to listen to the language than to read it. In part, this is because it is only in reading that the units are well

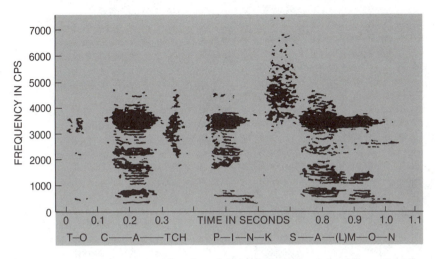

Figure 10–5. A spectrogram for the phrase, "to catch pink salmon." (After Liberman, Mattingly, and Turvey, 1972. Copyright 1972 by Hemisphere Publishing Corporation. Reprinted by permission of the publisher and author.)

marked, with spaces separating words and periods separating sentences.

This lack of segmentation in the acoustic signal means that a given acoustic segment can usually be divided into words in more than one way. Cole and Jakimik (1980, p. 138) offer the following examples. The same acoustic signal that can be heard as "more rice" can also be heard as "more ice," "some more" as "some ore," "fresh shout" as "fresh out," "real love" as "reel of," and "grew wise" as "grew eyes." Usually people have no difficulty "hearing" the appropriate division into words, because context makes one of the interpretations reasonable and the other nonsensical.

So far we have talked about the acoustic signal lacking one kind of segmentation, segmentation into words, but the acoustic signal also lacks segmentation into phones. Instead, in fluent speech every segment of the acoustic signal carries information about more than one phone at once; in other words there is *parallel transmission* of phones. Contrast listening with reading again. In the case of reading from the printed page, the letters are distinct from each other; the word BAG obviously consists of the three separate letters B, A, and G arranged in serial order. We can change the word to BEG by changing only one of the elements. If the *spoken* word *bag* worked the same way, then the acoustic signal for BAG could be broken down into three separate parts, one standing for each of the phones [b], [ae], [g]. Figure 10–6 demonstrates that this is not the case. This figure depicts idealized

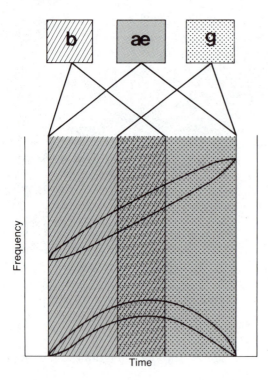

Figure 10–6. A schematic sound spectrogram of the syllable [baeg], demonstrating the phenomenon of parallel transmission of phones. (After Liberman, Mattingly, and Turvey, 1972. Copyright 1972 by Hemisphere Publishing Corporation. Reprinted by permission of the publisher and author.)

formants that when played through a speech synthesizer are heard as the word *bag*. As the figure shows, however, the phones overlap in the acoustic signal. For example, if we wished to change *bag* to *nag*, we would have to change more than the first half of the signal, not just the first third. If we wished to change the word to *beg* the whole syllable would have to be changed, since information about the vowel is distributed across the entire syllable.

In summary, the acoustic signal itself is not segmented into either words or phonemes, yet under most conditions we cannot help but hear a series of words, and when asked, we are able to break the series down into phonemes. This lack of segmentation creates special difficulties for any bottom-up theory of pattern recognition. For example, if you wished to program a computer to convert an acoustic signal into a string of phones and subsequently into a string of words, not only must you find a set of acoustic features that would distinguish one phone from another, but you must program the computer with rules for dividing up the acoustic stream into the appropriate units.

Context-conditioned variation. The phonemenon of parallel transmission leads to another characteristic that is equally challenging for bottom-up theories—context-conditioned variation. Those who study speech perception have been unable to find invariant acoustic cues for most phones. Rather, they find that the particular acoustic form of a given phone depends upon the surrounding context. This *context-conditioned variation* means, then, that there are marked discrepancies between the actual acoustic signal and our perception of it. Some speech sounds that are quite different acoustically are perceived as being identical, whereas other speech sounds that are identical acoustically are perceived as being different.

First, we will consider an instance in which we hear similarities that are not present in the acoustic signal itself. Consider the following syllables: [di] as in *deed*, [de] as in *date*, [dɛ] as in *dim*, [da] as in *dam*, [də] as in *daughter*, [do] as in *dote*, and [du] as in *due*. All begin with the same phone [d]. Therefore, if you looked at a sound spectrogram of all these syllables, you might expect to find that their first segments are all identical acoustically. However, examine Figure 10–7, which shows the sets of formats that are perceived as each of these syllables respectively. The initial transient part of each of these spectrograms is quite different, yet the initial parts of the syllables *sound* alike. Thus, there is no simple correspondence between the similarities we hear and the similarities in the acoustic stimulus. The particular acoustic signal that will be perceived as [d] depends on the vowel with which the consonant is paired. In other words, there is context-conditioned variation in the acoustic signal that corresponds to the phone [d]. This context-conditioned variation is true for all consonants.

The similarities we perceive among speech sounds are more closely tied to the ways in which the sounds are *articulated* than to the actual acoustic signals. Consider Figure 10–7 again. We know that the beginning parts of all these acoustically different signals are perceived to be similar, and all are *produced* in a similar fashion, i.e., all are voiced, apical consonants. Thus, when processing speech, we *perceive* two acoustic signals to be similar if they were *articulated* simi-

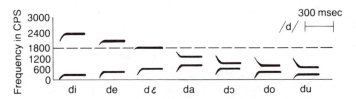

Figure 10–7. Schematic sound spectrograms for the phone [d] before different vowels, illustrating the phenomenon of context-conditioned variation. (After Liberman, 1957. Copyright 1957 by the Acoustical Society of America. Reprinted by permission.)

larly, even though the acoustic stimuli themselves are quite different. This fact suggests that our perception of speech depends upon our knowledge of how speech sounds are produced. It is as if our speech perception mechanisms, when confronted with the signals in Figure 10–7 say, "Even though the initial parts are acoustically different, given what I know about the properties of the human vocal tract, I know they were all made in a similar fashion." It seems likely, then, (though this is still just a guess), that your pet dog does not hear the initial parts of the signals in Figure 10–7 as being similar. Whereas you treat them as *speech* sounds (i.e., as sounds produced by a human vocal tract with certain properties) thus hearing the sounds in terms of how they were articulated, your dog (presumably lacking implicit knowledge about the properties of the human vocal tract) hears them as purely acoustic events.

Not only do people perceive similarities that are not present in the acoustic signals underlying speech, but they often perceive *differences* between two acoustically identical signals. Ladefoged and Broadbent (1957) reported an intriguing demonstration of this phenomenon. Listeners were presented with a tape recording of the sentence "Please say what this word is" followed by a single spoken word. The sentence was spoken by one of two different speakers, but the single spoken word that followed was always acoustically identical since it was spliced onto both tapes. Listeners, however, identified the single word as "bet" when it followed one speaker's voice and as "bit" when it followed another. This demonstration is one example of the general phenomenon that listeners unconsciously adjust their perceptions to take into account the way in which individual speakers produce sounds. Of course, it is absolutely necessary that we make such adjustments, because there is considerable variation among speakers in both the size and shape of the vocal tract and, hence, in the resulting speech sounds. The puzzle for psychologists is *how* we are able to make such adjustments in our perceptions, and how we do it so very quickly (in Ladefoged and Broadbent's study after hearing only a few words). Here again we are finding that the way in which we perceive speech seems tied closely to our implicit knowledge about human vocal tracts, and the way in which they articulate sounds.

Usually we are completely unaware of making allowances for individual speakers. However, you might have noticed this phenomenon when listening to someone who has a foreign accent. At first, it is quite difficult to understand the person, but after a few minutes of conversation you find it more and more easy to follow. You are adjusting your perceptual processes to take into account the unaccustomed way in which the individual produces sounds.

We have seen that the relation between acoustic signal and perception is not a simple one-to-one correspondence in which a particular acoustic segment is always perceived as a particular phone. Rather, the way in which a particular acoustic segment is perceived depends upon the acoustic context in which it occurs or, put another way, the particular acoustic signal that will be perceived as a [p], for example, will vary depending on the context in which the phone occurs. Such context-conditioned variation presents formidable problems for feature-detection and template-matching theories, since both require that there be some invariant acoustic properties which can be used to define and identify each phone.

Categorical perception. Human perception of some speech sounds is categorical, a mode of perception in which two stimuli are judged to be different from each other (i.e., are discriminated) only if they belong to different categories. This mode of perception is different from the more usual case of *noncategorical perception* in which people are able to discriminate among different stimuli even though those stimuli all belong to the same category. In the case of noncategorical perception, then, discrimination is more sensitive than categorization, but in the case of categorical perception, discrimination is no more sensitive than categorization.

An example of noncategorical perception occurs in the case of colors. If asked to label the color of all the objects in a room, you might assign the label *green* to several objects, but you would have no trouble deciding that the green of the plant was different from the green of the table. Thus, your ability to discriminate exceeds your ability to categorize. Most nonspeech sounds operate in a similar fashion. Many speech sounds are different, however, in that if the two sounds belong to the same category, people do not discriminate between them, even though they are different acoustically.

We will consider categorical perception of voicing. The difference between voiced consonants (e.g., [b]) and unvoiced (e.g., [p]) corresponds to an acoustic dimension which is called *voice-onset-time*, abbreviated VOT. In articulatory terms, VOT is defined as the delay between release of the consonant and pulsing of the vocal cords. In acoustic terms, VOT corresponds to the difference in time of onset between the first and second formants of the sounds. This is illustrated in Figure 10–8. Synthetic signals that would be perceived as the voiced phones [ba], [da], and [ga] are shown at the top, and synthetic signals that would be perceived as the unvoiced [pa], [ta], and [ka] are shown at the bottom. For the voiced consonants, the first and second formants start simultaneously (thus these are 0 VOT stimuli), whereas for the unvoiced phones, the first formant starts approximately 40 msec after the second (thus this is a 40 msec VOT stimulus).

Lisker and Abramson (1970) presented subjects with synthetic

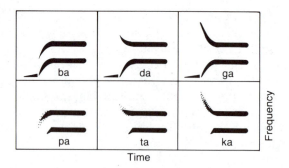

Figure 10–8. Schematic sound spectrograms for three voiced (upper panel) and three unvoiced (lower panel) consonants, demonstrating that the time difference between onset of the first and second formants, called voice onset time (VOT), distinguishes voiced from unvoiced consonants. (From Liberman, Ingemann, Lisker, Delattre, and Cooper, 1959. Copyright 1959 by the Acoustical Society of America. Reprinted by permission.)

speech syllables that were all identical, except that they varied in 10 msec steps ranging from −150 msec VOT to +150 msec VOT. These 31 stimuli were presented in random order, and for each the person was asked to categorize the stimulus as either *ba* or *pa*. The different values of VOT that were presented are shown on the horizontal axis of Figure 10–9, and the percentage of times the subject identified each of these stimuli as *ba* or *pa* is shown on the vertical axis. The functions plotted in Figure 10–9 are called *categorization functions*, since they depict how the person's categorization of speech sounds varies as a function of some acoustic variable (in this case VOT).

These categorization functions make an abrupt change at about 25 msec VOT; stimuli with VOT's of 20 msec or lower are almost always identified as *ba*, whereas stimuli with VOT's of 30 msec or greater are always heard as *pa*. This break in the categorization function at 25 msec VOT is called the *phonetic boundary*, since stimuli on one side of this boundary are heard as one phone and stimuli on the other side as another.

In order to study categorical perception, it is necessary to collect discrimination data from the same individuals. Stimulus pairs are presented and the person is asked to report whether the members of the pair are identical acoustically (in which case he would say "same"). On each trial the stimuli are either identical acoustically (e.g., two 20

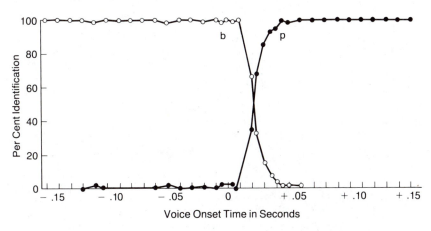

Figure 10–9. Categorization functions for synthetic stimuli varying from [b] to [p]. The open circles indicate the per cent of times that each stimulus was perceived as [b], and the filled circles indicate the percentage of times each stimulus was perceived as [p]. (After Lisker and Abramson, 1970. Copyright 1970 by Academia. Reprinted by permission.)

msec VOT stimuli), or they differ by 20 msec (e.g., a 20 VOT stimulus is paired with a 40 VOT stimulus). The per cent of times the person is correct for each comparison can then be plotted, yielding a *discrimination function*. When discrimination functions are collected for speech continua such as VOT, the usual finding is that people are only able to discriminate two stimuli reliably if they are from opposite sides of the phonetic boundary. For example, subjects readily judge a 20 msec VOT stimulus to be different from a 40 msec VOT stimulus, but they don't discriminate a 0 msec VOT from a 20 msec VOT stimulus, or a 40 msec from a 60. This fact that discrimination is no more sensitive than categorization is called *categorical perception*. An idealized form of categorical perception is shown in Figure 10–10.

Early studies of categorical perception had suggested that it was impossible for people to discriminate within a phonetic boundary. However, more recent research (cf. Carney, Widin & Viemeister, 1977; Strange & Jenkins, 1978) suggests that if extensive training is given it is sometimes possible for people to learn to make within-category discriminations. Nonetheless, it is clear that people have a strong tendency to perceive many speech sounds categorically.

Like our tendency to make inferences during language comprehension, our tendency to perceive certain speech sounds categorically is not an unfortunate quirk of human information processing. In trying to comprehend what someone is saying to you, you need to notice those acoustic differences that make a difference in meaning. If you

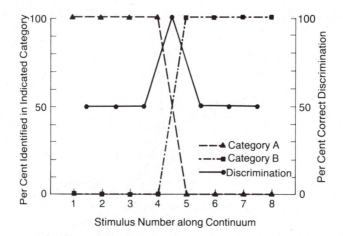

Figure 10–10. Idealized form of categorical perception showing the categorization function (left ordinate) and the discrimination function (right ordinate). (From Studdert-Kennedy, Liberman, Harris, & Cooper, 1970. Copyright 1970 by the American Psychological Association. Reprinted by permission of the publisher and author.)

always distinguished subtle differences among the sounds within a phonetic category, the task of speech perception would be impossible or, at least, much more difficult.

You might not be very surprised at the phenomenon of categorical perception, for you might think that during early development people simply learn which distinctions matter in their language. According to this *learned equivalence* explanation, at birth we are able to discriminate equally well at all points along a given sensory continuum (e.g., the VOT continuum), but gradually we learn to discriminate only between items that bridge a phonetic boundary. One way in which to test the adequacy of this explanation is to ask infants to discriminate among speech sounds. According to the learned equivalence explanation, one-month-old infants, for example, should reveal very different discrimination functions from adults, since they have not yet learned the phonetic boundaries. Eimas, Siqueland, Jusczyk, & Vigorito (1971) studied categorical perception in one-month-olds by taking advantage of some characteristics of the infant's response to the world. Earlier studies of human infants had shown that they will suck a nipple that provides no food (a non-nutritive nipple), if every suck is followed by some interesting event, such as a sound or a picture. After a while, however, the infant appears to tire of the formerly interesting event, since his rate of sucking declines. This decrease in response that follows repeated presentation of the same stimulus is called *habituation*. If after habituation has occurred, the nature of the stimulus is changed, the infant's rate of sucking increases again. This increase in response that follows a detectable change in the stimulus is called *dishabituation*.

Eimas and his colleagues used dishabituation to infer which speech sounds the infants judged to be alike and which to be different; dishabituation is the infant's way of responding "these stimuli are different." Eimas and his colleagues found that the one-month-old's pattern of dishabituation is remarkably similar to the discrimination function generated by the adult. This fact is depicted in Figure 10–11, which shows the results they obtained. If the first stimulus (to

[handwritten margin notes: "✓ V, grad", "But see GELFAND p 337. Chinchillas Can do this!"]

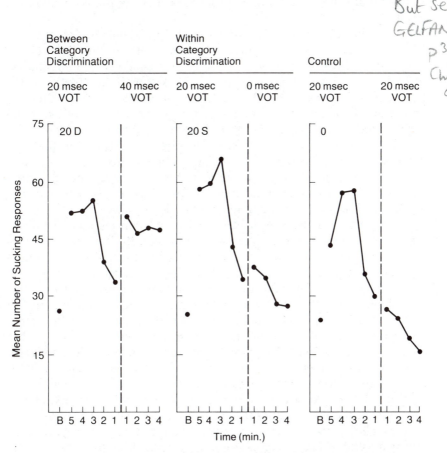

Figure 10–11. The data from the Eimas, Siqueland, Jusczyk, and Vigorito (1971) study of categorical perception in infants. Notice that the infant dishabituates only when the second stimulus is from a different phonetic category from the original stimulus. (After Eimas, Siqueland, Jusczyk, and Vigorito, 1971. Copyright 1971 by the American Association for the Advancement of Science. Reprinted by permission.)

which the infant has become habituated) is a 20 msec VOT, then the infant does not dishabituate to a 0 msec VOT (the middle panel of the figure), but he does dishabituate to a 40 msec VOT stimulus (the first panel of the figure). The infant is telling us that he can discriminate between the 20 and 40 msec VOT sounds, but that the 0 and 20 msec VOT stimuli either sound identical to him or sound so similar that the change isn't big enough to rekindle his interest. Though we can't be sure which of the latter he means, the important point is that there is a remarkable degree of consistency between the distinctions the newborn finds to be important and those the adult detects. This suggests that the discontinuities in the VOT domain are not simply learned, but reflect some innate propensities of the human perceptual system.

We should not abandon the learned equivalence notion entirely, however, because recent experiments have indicated that infants can make some discriminations that adults do not. For example, studies of both Spanish infants (Lasky, Syrdal-Lasky, & Klein, 1975) and Kikuyu infants (Streeter, 1976) reveal that the discrimination functions of young infants have not one, but two, phonetic boundaries along the voicing dimension. One is at the 25 msec VOT value we described, but the other is at approximately −40 msec VOT (i.e., the first formant begins 40 msec before the second). When adults from these same linguistic communities are examined, however, only the 25 msec boundary is distinguished by Spanish speaking people, whereas neither of the boundaries is distinguished by Kikuyu adults.

The fact that the speech discrimination abilities among the infants of the world are more similar that those of the adults is reminiscent of the fact (Chapter 8) that children around the world make amazingly similar patterns of errors when they are acquiring language. These cross-cultural similarities among infants suggest that the phonetic boundaries to which they respond are innately present in the human species, i.e., that people are born with the ability to detect distinctions only at certain places along speech continua. The fact that adults do not make all the distinctions that newborns make suggests that experience operates to teach the infant that only some of these innately present distinctions really matter. In the case of speech perception, at least, experience influences the infant's discrimination, but only within the limits imposed by his innate perceptual abilities.

Psychologists and linguists once thought that categorical perception occurs only for speech sounds. It is now clear, however, that it does occur for some other sounds as well, particularly those that, like speech, are highly complex and involve categorization. For example, musical sounds that vary in rise-time (i.e., the rate at which the transient parts of the formants rise) and can be categorized as a "pluck" (e.g., a guitar sound) or a "bow" (e.g. a violin sound) are perceived categorically (cf. Cutting & Rosner, 1974).

We still do not know why some sounds are perceived categorically and others are not, but it appears that categorical perception may result in part from our limited memory capacity. Notice that judgements about whether or not two sounds are identical must always involve comparing memory representations of the sounds, since the first sound terminated before the second began. For stimuli that can be labeled, these discrimination judgements, then, might be based upon either information taken from auditory sensory memory or on information stored in working memory, most likely the label of the stimulus. As it happens, the acoustic cues that distinguish among voiced and unvoiced consonants (and other categorically perceived sounds, such as pluck and bow sounds) are of very short duration and are embedded in the midst of other complex sounds. Therefore, we would expect their representations in auditory sensory memory to be rather poor and difficult to distinguish from each other. Thus, people would be likely to rely upon comparing the labels of those stimuli stored in working memory. In fact, there is some experimental evidence that such memory difficulties do contribute to categorical perception. For example, Hanson (1977) has shown that the longer the delay between two speech sounds to be discriminated (and hence, the more opportunity for the auditory sensory memory to deteriorate), the more likely it is that categorical perception will be observed.

We have seen, then, that people perceive certain speech sounds in a categorical manner. Such categorical perception appears to reflect some innate perceptual tuning, though infants around the world respond to some distinctions that adults ignore, and with extensive training adults can be trained to make at least some within-category discriminations. This very useful tendency to perceive categorically occurs not only for some speech sounds, but also for other sounds that are complex and readily labeled. Though we do not yet understand the processes underlying categorical perception, it is likely that it is due in part to characteristics of human memory.

Hemispheric specialization. The final characteristic of speech perception we will consider is the fact that one hemisphere of the brain is specialized for perceiving the sounds of speech. It has been clear for some time that such *hemispheric specialization* (which is also called *hemispheric lateralization* or *cerebral dominance*) occurs for processing meaningful language (e.g., words and sentences), but recent research has shown lateralization of function for processing the *sounds of speech*, even when they occur in meaningless syllables such as *ba* or *tuz*.

It has been known for more than a century that the two hemispheres of the human brain are not equally important for language. Reflecting the respect we have for language, the hemisphere specialized for language is usually termed the *dominant hemisphere*. Among right handers, approximately 97% are left-hemisphere dominant (and right handers make up about 90% of the population). Less is known about dominance among left-handers, but it is thought that a significant proportion are either right dominant or of mixed dominance. Although it is clear that some lateralization is present in human infants (e.g., Glanville, Best, & Levenson, 1977; Witelson & Pallie, 1973), it appears to become more pronounced with development.

If you wish to determine your dominant hemisphere, administer the following test to yourself. Keeping both eyes open, line up your index finger with some vertical line a few feet or yards away (the edge of the window will do). Now without moving, close your left eye and note whether or not your finger still appears to be lined up perfectly with the vertical target. Now, still without moving, open your left eye and close your right, and again note whether finger and vertical target are still in perfect alignment. You are right eyed if the alignment remains perfect only with the right eye open, and left eyed if the alignment remains perfect only with the left open. Furthermore, your dominant hemisphere is the one *contra*lateral (i.e., on the opposite side) to the preferred eye. Therefore, most of you will probably find that you are right eyed and, hence, left-hemisphere dominant.

By now you should be wondering what kind of evidence exists for hemisphereic lateralization—how can we tell which hemisphere of the brain is more important for language processing? There are several kinds of evidence for hemispheric lateralization. These include (1) analyses of aphasia patients, (2) studies of split-brain patients, (3) results of the Wada test, (4) patterns of evoked potentials in the brain, and (5) behavioral evidence for hemisphere advantages.

Aphasia is a general term which indicates a disturbance of language and/or speech caused by brain damage. Of 100 people who suffer permanent aphasia following brain damage, 97 of these people will have suffered damage in the left hemisphere (Geschwind, 1972). The fact that language disturbances rarely follow right hemisphere damage, but frequently follow left-hemisphere damage, is one kind of evidence that the left hemisphere is more important for language processing than the right.

The second kind of evidence for hemispheric lateralization comes from the dramatic reports of *split-brain* patients studied by Gazzaniga and Sperry (1967) and Gazzaniga (1970). Split-brain patients are individuals who have had the corpus callosum severed. (The corpus callosum is the main bundle of nerve fibers connecting the two hemispheres of the brain.) Such a drastic operation is sometimes undertaken in order to control severe epilepsy. In the person who has an intact corpus collosum it is very difficult to separate the functions of the two hemispheres, because virtually every stimulus event that impinges on the individual's senses is conveyed to both hemispheres. A stimulus presented in the right visual field projects directly to the left (i.e., contralateral) hemisphere, but the information is then transferred to the right hemisphere as well, via the corpus callosum. The converse holds for stimuli presented to the left visual field.

For split-brain patients, however, since the corpus callosum is cut, a stimulus presented in the right visual field goes *only* to the left hemisphere. Gazzaniga and Sperry (1967) found that when a familiar object (such as a cup) is presented to the right visual field (hence the left hemisphere), the split-brain patient usually names the object with little difficulty. However, if the object is presented to the left visual field (hence the right hemisphere) the person usually reports that he sees nothing! It is clear that the right hemisphere's difficulty is linguistic, not visual; although the patient cannot *name* the object presented to his right hemisphere, he can use his left hand (which is controlled by the right hemisphere) to pick out the cup from a group of other objects all of which are hidden behind a screen. Although there is still debate concerning the degree of language function of which the right hemisphere is capable, it is clear from the split-brain studies that the linguistic functions of the left hemisphere are much more extensive than those of the right.

The third kind of evidence for hemispheric lateralization comes from the results of the so-called *Wada test*, which can be administered to any individual to determine his/her linguistically dominant hemisphere. The test involves injecting sodium amytal (which is a nerve depressant) into one carotid artery at a time. If the person's left hemisphere is specialized for language, then a left carotid artery injection will result in a temporary disturbance of his speech. For example, the person will have difficulty naming objects, and will talk nonsense. The Wada test is particularly useful for clinical purposes. If a surgeon is considering brain surgery on a particular patient, perhaps to treat severe epilepsy, then it is important to determine which hemisphere is dominant since surgery on the dominant hemisphere runs the risk of damaging, perhaps permanently, the person's ability to communicate. Despite its clinical usefulness, however, the Wada test is not appropriate for most research purposes, since the test itself is risky and disturbing for the person tested.

A fourth kind of evidence for hemispheric lateralization is that the brain wave patterns evoked during speech processing are different for the right and left hemispheres. If electrodes are placed at appropriate locations on the surface of the skull, it is possible to measure the *average evoked potential* (AEP) that occurs in each hemisphere during processing of a given stimulus. Consider, for example, a pioneering study conducted by Wood, Goff, and Day (1971). Each of their subjects performed two simple auditory identification tasks, one a speech task and the other a nonspeech task, and the experimenters measured the pattern of AEP's in the left as opposed to the right hemisphere.

On each trial of both tasks the subject heard one of two possible stimuli, played through a set of headphones to both ears. For both the speech and nonspeech tasks, one of the possible stimuli was a synthetically produced low-pitched *ba* sound, and the subject was to press a button with his right index finger only when he heard this particular stimulus. The difference between the speech and nonspeech tasks was in the other possible stimulus that the subject might hear. For the nonspeech task, this alternative stimulus was a high-pitched *ba* sound, identical to the low-pitched *ba* in every way except that all the formants were shifted to a higher frequency. Thus the subject's discrimination here was to be based on a nonlinguistic attribute of the sound, its overall pitch. For the speech task, the alternative stimulus was a low-pitched *da*. Thus, both sounds were of the same overall pitch, but the subject was required to make a linguistic discrimination between two different phones. [d] and [b].

Wood and his colleagues found that for the *nonspeech task* the averaged evoked potentials were the same in the left as in the right hemisphere. This suggests that for the nonspeech decision, both hemispheres were functioning similarly. However, for the *speech* discrimination task, the averaged evoked potentials were different in the left and right hemispheres. This suggests that the two hemispheres perform different functions when phonetic discrimination is required.

Notice two important points about this finding. First, hemisphere differences were observed in the present speech task, even though it only involved differentiating between two relatively meaningless *ba* and *da* sounds. Thus, the special functions of the left hemisphere are called into play, not only during language comprehension, but also any time a person must discriminate speech sounds. Second, whether or not there is a difference between the evoked responses of the left and right hemispheres depends, not on the stimulus per se, but rather on the particular kind of processing (i.e., the kind of decision) the person attempts to perform on the stimulus. In the Wood, Goff, and Day study, the target stimulus (i.e., a low-pitched *ba*) is the same for both the speech and nonspeech tasks. The hemispheric differences in brain responses were observed, however, only when the discrimination to be made was linguistic, i.e., concerned the phonemic identity of the sound. This conclusion is reminiscent of the findings of Seamon and Gazzaniga (1973) reported in Chapter 7. They found that whether there would be a right- or a left-hemisphere advantage for visual tests in a memory task depended not on the stimulus per se, but on whether the subject was using a verbal or imagery memory code.

The fifth kind of evidence for hemispheric lateralization is that under conditions of dichotic presentation, there is a *right-ear advantage* for processing language and speech, whereas nonlinguistic auditory processing usually reveals either no ear advantage at all or a very slight left-ear advantage.

Under normal conditions a sound presented to the right ear, for example, is sent to both the ipsilateral (same side) and contralateral (other side) hemispheres. However, when stimuli are presented dichotically (i.e., one stimulus to one ear and a different stimulus simultaneously to the other ear), the activity of the ipsilateral pathway is suppressed. Therefore, if two different stimuli are presented simultaneously, then each stimulus is sent first to the contralateral hemisphere. Of course, due to the presence of the corpus callosum, the information can subsequently be sent to the ipsilateral hemisphere as well. However, such neural transmission takes time, so the arrival of the information at the ipsilateral hemisphere is delayed.

Doreen Kimura (1961; 1967) was the first to demonstrate that when the dichotically presented stimuli are linguistic materials (such as digits or words), stimuli presented to the right ear are reported more accurately than those presented to the left (i.e., there is a right-ear advantage). Since stimuli presented to the right ear go first to the left hemisphere under such dichotic conditions, the right-ear advantage for language processing indicates a left-hemisphere advantage. It is important that we do not find a left-hemisphere advantage for *all* auditory processing; in fact, Kimura found a left-ear (right-hemisphere) advantage for processing musical tones.

A right-ear advantage occurs not only for processing meaningful linguistic stimuli such as words and sentences, but also for processing isolated, relatively meaningless syllables, such as [ba] and [da]. For example, if [ba] is presented to one ear and [da] simultaneously to the other, people who are asked to judge which occurred first will usually perceive the stimulus presented to the right ear as the one that occurred first (Day and Bartlett, 1972). If they are asked to report both stimuli, people usually are more accurate at the stimulus presented to the right ear (Studdert-Kennedy & Shankweiler, 1970). Again, then, as we found with evoked responses, the left hemisphere appears specialized, not only for processing meaningful linguistic stimuli, but also for differentiating among speech sounds.

Although there is a great deal of evidence that the left hemisphere is more important for speech processing than the right, we still do not understand what differentiates those tasks on which there is a right-ear advantage from those on which there is a left-ear advantage. This is because there are some instances in which the processing of nonlinguistic stimuli shows a right-ear advantage. A particularly interesting example was presented by Bever and Chiarello (1974). These researchers demonstrated that although people with little knowledge of music usually show a left-ear advantage for music, moderately skilled musicians reveal a right-ear advantage for musical stimuli. Apparently then, the musician processes music differently from the novice, and the processes the musician calls upon seem to depend more on the left hemisphere. This suggests the intriguing, though largely untested hypothesis, that the dominant hemisphere is called upon to the extent that the person has a set of analytical rules (i.e., a syntax) for the task at hand.

ANALYSIS-BY-SYNTHESIS THEORY

General assumptions. The characteristics we have just discussed have led most contemporary theorists to argue for some form of analysis-by-synthesis theory. Although there are a number of different versions, all such theories have three major points in common. First, all include not only bottom-up (analytic), but also top-down (synthetic) processes. The latter conceptually-driven processes appear necessary, because the phenomena of phoneme restoration, listener imposed segmentation, and context-conditioned variation indicate that what we hear is not simply a function of the acoustic signal itself, but also a function of our expectations based on our knowledge about speech and language.

Second, analysis-by-synthesis theorists assume that perceiving speech requires a specialized mode of auditory processing. This follows in part from the fact that unlike most other sounds, many speech sounds are perceived categorically. Additional support comes from the fact that phonetic discriminations, unlike most other acoustic discriminations, appear to call more upon the language dominant hemisphere than upon the nondominant hemisphere. Third, they assume that this special mode of perception shares some of the same processes as speech production. This derives from the fact that the similarities that we hear among speech sounds are more closely related to the way in which the sounds are articulated than to the acoustic signals themselves.

An analysis-by-synthesis theory. Figure 10–12 outlines a representative theory which incorporates the salient characteristics of the original analysis-by-synthesis theory proposed by Halle and Stevens (1964) as well as more recent "on-line" theories (e.g., Cole & Jakimik, 1980; Cutler & Norris, 1979; Dell & Newman, 1980; Foss & Blank, 1980; Marslen-Wilson & Welsh, 1978).

As we examine the theory, keep in mind that the figure depicts a set of processes that are assumed to occur during speech processing, not a series of memory stores or structures. The theory is meant to

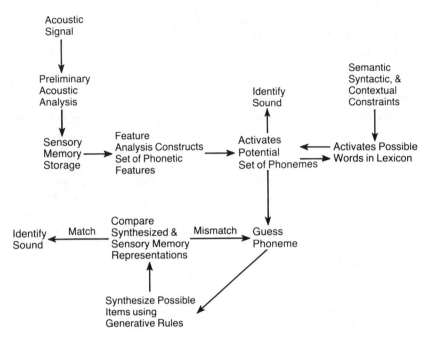

Figure 10–12. An analysis-by-synthesis theory of speech perception.

encompass both the perception of isolated speech sounds (such as in a discrimination or recognition experiment) and the perception of sounds in fluent speech (such as during everyday conversation).

It is assumed that the acoustic signal first undergoes some preliminary acoustic analysis which is the same for all sounds regardless of whether they are human speech or other environmental sounds. The resulting representation is stored in the short-lived auditory sensory memory we studied in Chapter 2, and a set of feature detectors analyzes the signal for the presence of certain distinctive features that have invariant acoustic cues. We are assuming that there are at least *some* invariant acoustic features that signal the possible presence of certain phonemes. For example, voicing is cued by a certain time difference between the onset of the first and second formants, so we assume a feature-detector which fires only when a certain such VOT is present in the acoustic signal.

So far we have outlined only bottom-up (analytic) processes; the preceding feature analysis occurs regardless of the person's expectations and depends only on the acoustic signal itself. However, from the next stage of processing on, both top-down and bottom-up processes are assumed to interact. After feature detection has occurred, we assume that the memory representations of a potential set of phonemes are activated. The phonemes that are activated will be a joint function of (1) the features that were detected in the signal, a bottom-up process, and (2) the person's expectations as to what phonemes are likely in context, a top-down process.

For example, imagine that the feature-detection process has detected the feature *voiced*. This would lead the phonemes /b/, /d/, and /g/ to be activated. If the sound had occurred in isolation and if the person has been given no information as to which sounds might occur, then there will be no additional activation from top-down sources, and further processing of the sort we'll discuss soon must occur. However, if the person had been asked, "Which sound occurred /b/ or /p/?", note that he now has enough information to make a decision about the sound. The bottom-up information has limited the set to /b/, /d/, and /g/, and the top-down limits it further to only /b/. Under this condition, then, the sound could be identified without further processing.

Top-down processes often limit the possible phonemes during conversation as well. For example, imagine that the person has just heard the sequence, "Last night I was kept awake by a barking . . ." Given the person's knowledge about the syntax of his language, he expects a noun to occur next, and his knowledge about the properties of various creatures leads him to expect a particular word and hence a particular phoneme to occur next. This top-down expectation, then, combined with the potential set /b/, /d/, and /g/ suggested by the bottom-up feature detection, would enable the person to identify the current phoneme without going further. Note, in addition, that this identification enables the listener to generate still further expectations for the following acoustic signal. He expects the phonemes /o/ and /g/ to follow, and then he expects the next phoneme to begin a new word. Thus, he establishes expectations not only about the identities of phonemes, but also about where new words will begin, helping him to segment the continuous acoustic signal. The phonemic restoration effect suggests that sometimes the activation from top-down sources alone is sufficient to enable a person to identify a phoneme that was not presented at all.

Although the combination of information from feature detection and expectations sometimes enables us to come up with only one possible phonemic identification, quite often these two sources of information still leave us with more than one possible phoneme. This is because (1) context-conditioned variation limits the extent to which feature detection can cut down the possible set of phonemes, and (2) even though some words are highly predictable in certain positions, the context more often only places limits on the kind of word that is likely to occur. We assume, then, that when there is still uncertainty, further processing of the acoustic segment must take place.

In such cases we assume that the person then makes a guess as to which phoneme has just occurred (perhaps by choosing that phoneme in the activated set with the highest activation). The listener then uses his knowledge of how sounds are produced to generate (or synthesize) a mental representation of the phoneme he has just guessed. In generating this internal representation, the listener takes into account the inferred characteristics of the speaker's vocal tract. This synthesized mental representation is then compared with the record of the acoustic signal stored in sensory memory to see whether or not they match each other. If they do, then the guess is confirmed and the sound has been identified. If they do not, then another guess is generated and they are compared again. Note that in essence, the listener checks to see whether the phoneme he has guessed could have the acoustic form of the signal stored in memory. Thus, this guessing loop enables the listener to make adjustments for the ways in which individual speakers make sounds and for the surrounding context in which a phoneme occurs. It is as if the listener's speech perception system is saying, "From the earlier sounds this person has produced, I have some knowledge of the properties of his vocal tract, and I have some general knowledge of how sounds are produced. Given this knowledge, could the sound I have stored in my sensory memory have resulted from that particular vocal tract having tried to produce the phoneme I've just guessed?"

One criticism that is frequently leveled at analysis-by-synthesis theory is that speech perception occurs too rapidly for all this guessing and matching to be going on. However, as we have learned more about the importance of top-down processes for language comprehension and speech perception, this argument has lost some of its force. It seems likely that the guess-synthesize-match loop might often be bypassed entirely (because feature detection and context have limited the possibilities to only one phoneme) or, at least, to be passed only once per phoneme (because the first guess proved accurate).

TESTS OF ANALYSIS-BY-SYNTHESIS THEORY: THE METHOD OF SELECTIVE ADAPTATION

Like most theories that attempt to account for complex cognitive processes, analysis-by-synthesis theories are difficult to test. It would be ridiculous to attempt to come up with a single experiment that would test the theory. The theory makes many different assumptions and it is usually possible to test only one or two of these at a time. Rather than consider all the possible ways in which analysis-by-synthesis theory has been tested to date, we will focus here on two different aspects of the theory that have been tested using one method—that of selective adaptation. Selective adaptation has been used to test: (1) the assumption that there are feature detectors for certain invariant acoustic features, and (2) the assumption that there is a close tie between the processes involved in perceiving and producing speech.

Feature detectors for speech. The analysis-by-synthesis theory outlined in Figure 10–12 assumes that there are feature detectors, each of which is tuned to detect restricted ranges of acoustic information that signal certain phonetic features. For example, we assume that the voicing feature detection system consists of two detectors—one for voiced and one for unvoiced—each differentially sensitive to the most frequent VOT value for that value of voicing. The closer to this modal value a given stimulus is, then the more the detector fires. This state of affairs is illustrated in Figure 10–13. The acoustic signal is assumed to impinge on both detectors, one of which is particularly sensitive to short VOT (voiced) stimuli and the other to long VOT (unvoiced) stimuli. Furthermore, both of these detectors feed into a decision component which can report either one of two classifications—voiced or unvoiced. If the short VOT detector fired more than the long, then the decision component would report VOICED, whereas if the long VOT detector fired more than the short, then the decision component would report UNVOICED. We assume that only the output of the decision component is available to the listener. Note that such a feature detec-

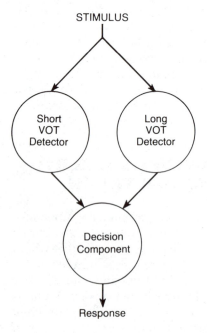

Figure 10–13. A diagram of a possible feature-detection system for registering VOT. Each detector is assumed to fire only when it detects a certain range of VOT values.

tor system accounts neatly for the phenomenon of categorical perception. People find it difficult to distinguish between two different short VOT stimuli, because both lead the decision component to output the same judgment.

How can we look for evidence for the existence of such feature detectors? Clearly, we don't want to insert electrodes into the brains of humans for the sole purpose of searching blindly for feature detectors, and using animals as our subjects (as has been done in the case of visual feature detectors) won't help, since it is quite likely that if auditory feature detectors for speech exist they are unique to humans—perhaps a property of our hemispheric lateralization for language processing.

In 1973 Peter Eimas and John Corbit of Brown University introduced an ingenious method for studying feature detectors for speech. Eimas and Corbit took advantage of a general property of feature detectors. With repeated stimulation, and hence repeated firing, individual detectors became fatigued and decrease their rate of firing, i.e., they adapt. Eimas and Corbit reasoned that if there are feature-detection systems of the sort outlined in Figure 10–13, then it should be possible to selectively adapt one or the other of the detectors by stimulating it repeatedly. Furthermore, such adaptation of only one of the two detectors should result in a measurable shift in the category boundary. That is, the usual (unadapted) phonetic boundary is located at that VOT value to which both detectors fire equally. Imagine, however, that we attempt to adapt (i.e., fatigue) the short VOT detector by repeatedly presenting a short VOT stimulus. If the rate of firing of the short VOT detector slows down overall, then for VOT values at the old phonetic boundary, in this fatigued state the long VOT detector will be firing more rapidly than the short VOT detector. Therefore stimuli that had formerly been at the boundary would now be judged as being long VOT stimuli (i.e., unvoiced).

To test this prediction, Eimas and Corbit first collected unadapted identification functions for college students who were presented with synthetic speech stimuli ranging in VOT from − 10 to 60 msec, and which were heard as [ba] or [pa]. These unadapted identification functions are shown in Figure 10–14a by the solid line function. Thus, at short VOT's people judged the stimulus to be [ba] and at long to be [pa]. *Adapted* identification functions were then collected from the same students, one function for trials on which a short VOT stimulus ([ba]) served as the adapting stimulus, and a second function for trials on which a long VOT stimulus ([pa]) served as the adapting stimulus. These adaptation functions were collected by presenting the adapting stimulus repeatedly (150 times to be exact) to the subject, and then presenting one test stimulus to be identified as [ba]

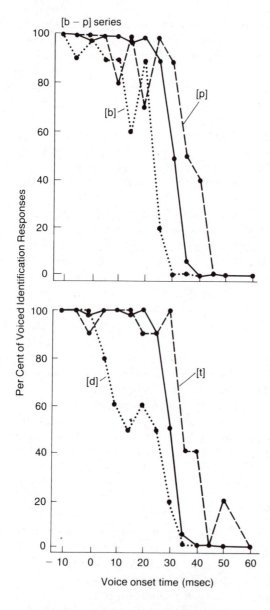

Figure 10–14. The classification data for ba-pa stimuli from the selective adaptation study of Eimas and Corbit, 1973. The dark line functions depict the classification functions in the unadapted state. The other functions depict classification functions after adaptation with the phone indicated. (After Eimas and Corbit, 1973. Copyright 1973 by Academic Press. Reprinted by permission.)

or [pa]. Then the adapting stimulus was presented for 150 times again, followed by a second test stimulus to be identified. This whole procedure was repeated again and again.

The results under both conditions of adaptation are shown in Figure 10–14a as well. The results are as predicted by the feature detection model; the category boundary shifts in the predicted direction after each kind of adaptation. For example, note that when the subject made his identification judgments after having been adapted with [ba], the same 30 msec VOT stimuli that had been heard as [ba] in the unadapted state were now judged to be [pa]. On the other hand, presenting [pa] repeatedly as the adapting stimulus moved the category boundary in the opposite direction.

If we only had the findings described so far, the shift in the identification boundary might simply be a shift in the person's response criterion. For example, having heard [ba] 150 times, the person gets sick of hearing [ba], and so is less likely to judge the test item to be a [ba]. Eimas and Corbit (1973) reported two kinds of data that argue against this response criterion explanation. First, they demonstrated that cross-adaptation occurs. They kept the same [ba]-[pa] test series, but adapted with either the adapting stimulus [da] (voiced) or [ta] (unvoiced). If the shift reflects simply a shift in response criterion, then there is no reason that repeatedly hearing the stimulus [da] should make you any less likely to say [ba], so the boundary shift should not occur. On the other hand, the feature detection explanation of the data assumes that repeated presentation of [da] should adapt the short VOT detector which is also used for detecting [ba], so it predicts that we should observe a boundary shift. As the data shown in Figure 10–14b indicate, the boundary shift did occur, in keeping with the feature-detector explanation.

Second, Eimas and Corbit showed that repeated presentation of a stimulus shifts not only the classification function, but also the discriminability function. This is exactly the finding we would expect from a feature-detection theory. Recall from our discussion of categorical perception that for stop consonants, at least, two stimuli are usually discriminated only if they bridge a phonetic boundary. In other words, there is a peak in the discriminability function at the phonetic boundary. If categorical perception is reflecting the output of the decision component of a feature-detection system (as depicted in Figure 10–13), then when adaptation leads to a shift in the identification boundary, the peak in the discriminability function should change as well. This shift in discriminability would not be predicted by a simple change in response criterion explanation, since the discrimination task does not involve responding with a stimulus name at all.

Many fascinating studies of selective adaptation have been conducted in an attempt to specify more precisely the nature, locus and function of feature detectors. For example, evidence has been reported for detectors for other features such as place of articulation (cf. Cooper, 1979). Furthermore, there is evidence that feature detectors are most likely operating at some point in information processing after information from the two ears has been combined, since presenting an adapting stimulus to one ear and the test stimulus to the other ear also results in phonetic boundary shifts (e.g., Sawusch, 1977).

A link between perception and production. A second central tenet of most contemporary and ancient accounts of speech perception is that at some level of processing speech perception and production share common mechanisms. In a fascinating series of studies, William Cooper (1979) has begun to test this assumption by employing a variation of selective adaptation. The central notion behind these studies is that if perceiving speech calls upon some of the same processes and structures as producing speech, then we might find perceptual-motor adaptation and motor-perceptual adaptation as well as the perceptual-perceptual adaptation we discussed. (The Eimas and Corbit (1973) study is said to involve perceptual-perceptual adaptation in that both the adapting stimulus and the test stimulus are to be perceived.) In the case of *perceptual-motor adaptation*, the adapting stimulus is perceptual (e.g., the subject *listens* to a repeatedly presented [pa]), but the test stimulus is to be *spoken* by the subject (e.g., after having listened to the [pa], the subject attempts to produce a [pa] or, for cross-adaptation, a [ta]). In this case the dependent variable would be the VOT value *produced* by the subject. Cooper has shown that the VOT value the subject produces after perceptual adaptation is systematically different from the VOT value he produces in an unadapted state. Thus, listening to a sound influences the way in which the subject produces other sounds involving the same feature.

In the case of *motor-perceptual adaptation*, the subject is instructed to *produce* a given stimulus such as [pa] repeatedly (while noise is played through earphones to prevent him from hearing himself), and then to identify a subsequent auditory stimulus. Again, Cooper finds that producing a sound repeatedly affects the way in which a subsequent sound is heard. That is, motor adaptation produces a shift in the perceived phonetic boundary. We still do not understand exactly how perception and production are related, but Cooper's work promises to help us examine this relation more carefully in the future.

CHAPTER SUMMARY

Having focused in the previous chapter on how people comprehend language, in this chapter we asked how people perceive the sounds of speech. Speech perception is one kind of pattern recognition, which is the process by which sensory input contacts the appropriate long-term memory location where information about that stimulus is stored. Explaining pattern recognition is a challenge for psychologists, because people routinely recognize patterns despite the fact that each individual instance of a pattern differs from others.

In order to explain how people perceive the sounds of speech, a theory must specify how the listener recognizes acoustic patterns as being instances of particular phonemes. When psychologists and computer scientists first attempted to understand speech perception, they usually proposed either feature-detection or template-matching theories, both of which postulate only bottom-up, stimulus-driven processes.

The inadequacies of pure bottom-up theories of speech perception become particularly apparent when some of the major characteristics of human speech perception are examined. First, the phenomenon of phoneme restoration indicates that people report hearing phonemes that were not actually present in the acoustic signal. Second, the acoustic signal itself is not segmented into either words or phonemes, yet under most conditions people cannot help but hear a series of separate words and, when asked to do so, they are able to break the sequence into a series of phonemes. Third, speech perception is characterized by context-conditioned variation in that there are not invariant acoustic patterns for most phones. Instead, the particular acoustic form that will be heard as a given phone depends upon the surrounding context. Fourth, unlike most domains of perception, many speech sounds are perceived categorically in that people discriminate between two speech sounds only if the sounds belong to different phonetic categories. Fifth, there is hemispheric specialization for processing not only meaningful language, but also the sounds of speech.

These characteristics have led most contemporary theorists to argue for one form or another of analysis-by-synthesis theory, all of which have several points in common. First, all include not only bottom-up (analytic), but also top-down (synthetic) processes. Second, all assume that there is a speech processing mode that is a specialized form of auditory processing. Third, all assume that the processes involved in perceiving speech are related to those involved in producing it. The representative analysis-by-synthesis theory we outlined is consistent with the known characteristics of speech perception, though the details of the theory are still being worked out. Experiments using the method of selective adaptation have provided insights on two major components of analysis-by-synthesis theory, including feature detection and the assumed tie between perception and production.

SUGGESTED READING

If you would like to learn more about other kinds of pattern recognition, I suggest that you begin by reading either Chapter 3 of the Reynolds and Flagg (1977) text *Cognitive Psychology* or Chapters 6 and 7 of Lindsay and Norman's (1977) text *Human Information Processing.* Neisser's (1967) Chapter 3 does an excellent job of introducing the problem of pattern recognition.

There are several general reviews of speech perception including chapters by Darwin (1976), Pisoni (1978), and Studdert-Kennedy (1976). Two additional excellent general sources are the collections of original articles edited by Cole (1980) and by Eimas and Miller (1981).

A number of specific topics bear further investigation. The extensive and fascinating work on selective adaptation and feature detectors for speech is reviewed in the chapters by Eimas and Miller (1978) and Cooper (1975) and in Cooper's (1979) book entitled *Speech Perception and Production: Studies in Selective Adaptation.* For a critical view of feature detectors read Remez (1979; 1980). Good sources on hemispheric specialization include the book by Gazzaniga and LeDoux (1978) and by Springer and Deutsch (1981), as well as the review article by Studdert-Kennedy and Shankweiler (1970). If you would like to learn more about the study of infant speech perception, then you should find reviews by Eimas (1975; 1978), by Morse (1974), and by Jusczyk (1981). Though little is known so far about how other animals perceive human speech sounds, you will find some interesting beginnings in the chapter by Morse (1977) and the articles by Kuhl and Miller (1975) and Morse and Snowden (1975). Reviews of the literature on computer pattern recognition may be found in Reddy (1976; 1980).

In addition, there are two topics we didn't touch on directly in this chapter, but that you might investigate on your own. First, Lieberman (1973) has offered some fascinating and highly controversial arguments regarding what speech perception can tell us about the evolution of human language. Second, there has been some controversy as to whether or not phonemes are perceived at all when we are listening to fluent speech. That is, it has been argued that the units of perception might be larger (i.e., syllables or words). Dell and Newman (1980) have presented interesting data which suggest that phonemes are indeed processed during the perception of fluent speech. Their article would be an excellent place to begin an investigation of this topic.

Language by Eye: Reading and Sign Language

FOOD FOR THOUGHT

Take a few minutes to try two different tasks. First, turn back to Table 6–5 and read through Bartlett's passage again rapidly, putting a slash through every instance of the letter e that you find. Do not read any further until you have completed that task. After you have finished, look at Table 11–1 which contains a duplicate of the passage in Table 6–5, but this time with all the e's indicated. Note that silent e's are shown by a slash and spoken e's by a circle. Check your performance by tabulating the number of each type you failed to detect. Most people miss a higher percentage of the silent than the spoken e's. What does this phenomenon suggest about the processes involved in reading?

    Second, consider a different kind of language by eye—the sign language that is used by the deaf community. Given what you have learned so far about language and memory, how would you expect the processing of sign language to differ from spoken language?

EYE VERSUS EAR

In the previous chapter we considered language by ear, and indeed this is the most frequently used modality for language. For the overwhelming majority of us, in fact, audition is the modality through which we first learned language. Nonetheless, from the age of five years onward, we also encounter a significant proportion of language by eye, through reading. Furthermore, there is one population, the profoundly deaf, for whom language is almost exclusively visual.

    As we noted in the chapter on language comprehension, in a successful act of communication, the listener (or reader) is led to construct a set of propositions which corresponds to the propositions the speaker (or writer or signer) had in mind. There is some empirical evidence that reading and listening result in similar, if not identical propositional structures (e.g. Kintsch and Kozminsky, 1977). Therefore, throughout our discussion of language by eye, we will assume

TABLE 11–1.

Use this paragraph to check your performance on the Food for Thought demonstration. Silent e's are marked with a slash and pronounced e's with a circle.
(The e's in "the" are not marked at all and you should ignore them when
counting your errors). The passage contains a total of 63 silent and 91 pronounced e's. Figure out the percentage of each kind that you missed.

One night two young men from Egulac went down to the river to hunt
seals, and while they were there it became foggy and calm. Then they
heard war-cries, and they thought: "Maybe this is a war-party." They
escaped to the shore, and hid behind a log. Now canoes came up, and they
heard the noise of paddles, and saw one canoe coming up to them. There
were five men in the canoe, and they said:

"What do you think? We wish to take you along. We are going up the
river to make war on the people."

One of the young men said: "I have no arrows."

"Arrows are in the canoe," they said.

"I will not go along. I might be killed. My relatives do not know where
I have gone. But you," he said turning to the other, "may go with them."

So one of the young men went, but the other returned home.

And the warriors went on up the river to a town on the other side of
Kalama. The people came down to the water, and they began to fight,
and many were killed. But presently the young man heard one of the
warriors say: "Quick, let us go home: that Indian has been hit." Now he
thought: "Oh, they are ghosts." He did not feel sick, but they said he
had been shot.

So the canoes went back to Egulac, and the young man went ashore to
his house, and made a fire. And he told everybody and said: "Behold I
accompanied the ghosts, and we went to fight. Many of our fellows were
killed, and many of those who attacked us were killed. They said I was hit,
and I did not feel sick."

He told it all, and then he became quiet. When the sun rose he
fell down. Something black came out of his mouth. His face became contorted. The people jumped up and cried.

He was dead.

---

that the end product of successful communication is the same, regardless of the modality through which language is conveyed.

How, then, does the modality in which language is presented
influence its processing? We will examine this question in the present
chapter by studying two very different kinds of visual language—the
printed word and sign language.

READING: SPEECH RECODING

Reading is the focus of a great deal of contemporary research in experimental psychology, in part because society has discovered that
many of our high school graduates (and some college graduates as

well) are functionally illiterate. The psychological literature on reading has focused on many interesting questions and several lively controversies, but in this chapter we will focus on only two of these. The first concerns the role that speech plays in reading, and the second, to which we'll turn in the next major section, concerns individual differences in reading ability.

The tie between speech and reading. Most of us feel that there is a close connection between speech and reading. Particularly when reading difficult material, it often feels as though we are speaking in our minds. In fact, there is some basis for this introspection, because most of us were taught to read by learning how to *pronounce* the strange black inscriptions. Although the goal of reading instruction is to teach the child to derive *meaning* from the printed page, we usually teach him first how to derive speech from it, assuming that the phonemes will then take him to the meaning of the word stored in memory.

The hypothesis that speech plays a role in reading was important in the earliest psychological theorizing. In 1908, Huey wrote the following in his classic text on reading:

> Although it is a foreshortened and incomplete speech to most of us,
> . . . it is perfectly certain that the inner hearing or pronouncing, or
> both, of what is read, is a constituent part of the reading (of) by far the
> most people, as they ordinarily and actually read.

But are our introspections accurate in this case, and if they are, exactly what role does speech play in the reading of adults?

Let us begin by specifying what we mean by *speech* in this context. It is quite clear that reading does *not* necessarily involve literal talking under the breath or subvocalizing, although people certainly do this on occasion. For one thing, it takes longer to initiate a vocal response (roughly 525 msec for a three-letter word according to Cosky, 1975) than it does to understand a word (we can access the lexicon within 200 msec according to Sabol and DeRosa, 1976). Therefore, we can hardly argue that making a silent vocal response is a necessary step in comprehending a word. Furthermore, the rate of silent reading is much faster than the rate at which we can speak (Kolers, 1970).

In the rest of our discussion then, when we refer to speech recoding we will not be talking about subvocal speech. Rather we will follow Kleiman (1975) and use the term *speech recoding* as a general term for "the transformation of printed words into any type of speech based code, whether it is articulatory, acoustic, auditory imagery, or a more abstract code." Thus, we will use the term speech recoding just as we used the term articulatory-acoustic coding in the chapter on

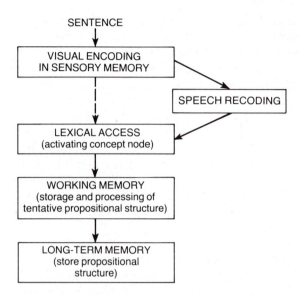

Figure 11–1. A simplified view of the processes
involved in reading. The dotted line depicts
a direct visual access route. (After Kleiman,
1975. Copyright 1975 by Academic Press.
Reprinted by permission.)

working memory. The question that concerns us, then, is what role if
any does such speech recoding play in reading?

The best way to consider the alternatives is to refer to Figure 11–
1, which depicts a simplified view of the major processes involved in
reading. We assume that a visually presented sentence first undergoes
visual encoding into sensory memory (as we discussed in Chapter 2).
During subsequent lexical access, these codes in sensory memory activate the appropriate conceptual node in semantic memory, thereby
retrieving the meaning of the word and its syntactic properties. Subsequently, the activated word and other words in the sentence are
held in working memory where the person constructs a tentative
propositional structure for the input string. Finally, this propositional
structure is stored in long-term memory, and/or it leads the person to
make some overt response. You should recognize, of course, that this
view of reading is oversimplified. As we have argued again and again
in the last two chapters, language comprehension involves not only
the bottom-up, data-driven processes depicted here, but also top-down,
conceptually-driven processes. This simplification will be adequate for
current purposes, though, since it enables us to contrast various views
on the role of speech recoding in reading.

The alternate routes from visual encoding to lexical access shown in Figure 11–1 depict the two major alternative hypotheses concerning the role of speech in reading. Note that one of these alternative routes (depicted with solid line arrows) assumes that a speech recoding stage occurs prior to lexical access. According to this *speech recoding access hypothesis,* this is the *only* route through which a word may contact its conceptual node. This hypothesis assumes, then, that not only do we learn to read by converting a printed word to a string of phonemes and using that phonemic code to access meaning, but we continue to use this speech recoding route throughout our lives. According to the alternative *direct visual access hypothesis,* on the other hand, skilled readers are able to go directly from printed word to concept node (as indicated by the dotted line in Figure 11–1). In sum, these two hypotheses disagree upon the existence of the route depicted by the dotted arrow.

Evidence for the speech recoding access hypothesis.   What is perhaps the oldest kind of evidence favoring the speech recoding view comes from EMG (electromyographic recordings) taken from the speech musculature. As early as 1900 Curtis reported that *EMG's reveal muscle movement of the vocal apparatus during silent reading.* Such demonstrations have continued to the present (and are summarized by McGuigan, 1970). Nonetheless, such EMG evidence alone is not particularly convincing. The fact that such movement occurs under some conditions certainly does not imply that it is *necessary* or even, for that matter, that it is helpful. Furthermore, if we conducted an experiment in which we found no EMG activity in the speech muscles, this would not prove the absence of speech recoding, since as we stressed, the speech recoding view does not assume the presence of muscle movement or implicit speech. Rather it posits an abstract transformation of information from a visual code to a phonemic one. Thus, not only are the EMG data questionable, but the technique itself seems to hold little promise for revealing very much about the speech recoding access hypothesis.

Stronger evidence for speech recoding comes from the patterns of reaction times obtained in the lexical decision task, which requires that the person judge whether or not strings of letters are words. This task is particularly appropriate for asking questions about lexical access, because making a correct judgment requires that the concept node of the word be looked up (since in these experiments the only characteristic differentiating words from nonwords is that the former have concept nodes). Thus, we can be reasonably sure that the word has been looked up in memory. However, since the task does not require that the person hold the words in working memory or relate them to previous words, it is likely that the working memory and later stages depicted in Figure 11–1 play only a minimal role in this task. Thus, we would seem to have a reasonably pure measure of lexical access.

The important evidence for the speech recoding access hypothesis is the finding that *phonemic similarity affects lexical decision reaction times.* Rubenstein, Lewis, and Rubenstein (1971) showed that it takes people longer to say "no" to pseudohomophone nonwords like BRANE than to other nonwords like MELP. This suggests that people are being slowed by the phonemic similarity between BRANE and BRAIN. In a different lexical decision study, Meyer, Schvaneveldt, and Ruddy (1974) demonstrated that people respond "yes" more quickly to phonemically similar pairs like SET-WET than to phonemically dissimilar pairs like FEW-SEW. The degree of graphemic (i.e., visual) similarity is the same for both pairs, so it must be the phonemic similarity that is speeding the SET-WET response.

A third kind of evidence for the speech recoding access hypothesis is that the *errors made during letter search and proofreading are influenced by phonemic factors.* In the late 1960's, Corcoran and his colleagues (Corcoran, 1966; 1967; Corcoran & Weening, 1968) reported the patterns of errors people made on two different kinds of tasks. In the proofreading task, people were asked to search prose for misspelled words. They found that proofreaders are more likely to detect misspellings that are phonetically incompatible with the correct word (e.g., BORST for BURST) than they are to detect phonetically compatible misspellings (e.g., HURD for HEARD). In their letter search task, people searched passages for a designated letter (just as you did in the Food for Thought section). Their subjects more often missed silent than spoken letters. Thus, if searching for the letter *k*, subjects were more likely to miss it in KNITTING than in KEEPING. Not only does this suggest that people are using speech recoding, but it indicates that they do so even when the recoding actually *hurts* performance. This is consistent with the hypothesis that such encoding is automatic.

Evidence for the direct visual access hypothesis.   Although the lexical decision and proofreading data we've just described provide strong evidence that speech recoding is sometimes used for lexical access, they do not prove that speech recoding is *necessary*, i.e., they do not prove the absence of the direct visual access route. Furthermore, there are several kinds of evidence that argue strongly for the existence of direct visual access.

First, *the profoundly deaf are capable of learning to read, and they do not appear to use phonemic recoding during reading.* It is true that the deaf have extreme difficulty in learning to read and most never become as skilled as hearing individuals. For example, the reading of 15-year-old deaf children is usually at the third grade level for individuals educated either in the United States or Great Britain (Conrad, 1977). Whether the reading difficulties of the deaf are due directly to the lack of acoustic input, or whether they are due to more general environmental restriction (i.e., less experience with language and communication in general) is unclear. What is important for our purposes is the fact that the deaf readers who have been studied do *not* appear to rely upon speech recoding.

For example, Locke (1978) studied a group of deaf and hearing children on a letter search task similar to the one you completed in the Food for Thought section (though the passages she used were adjusted to the more elementary reading levels of her subjects). Both her deaf and hearing subjects performed quite adequately. Both groups comprehended the paragraphs they read, witnessed by the fact that they were equally good at answering questions about the paragraphs, and both groups detected about the same number of target letters. However, the pattern of detection errors was completely different. The hearing children, just like Corcoran's adults, were more likely to detect letters in what Locke called "modal" phonemic form (e.g., *rag*, *rage*) than in "nonmodal" form (e.g., *rough*, *right*) suggesting speech recoding, but the deaf children made equal numbers of errors for both. This finding is particularly interesting since the deaf children with whom Locke worked were in an "oral" school. That is, lip reading and speaking were taught and the children were encouraged to use oral means of communication. The fact that they were able to comprehend the passages and yet give no evidence of phonemic effects indicates that reading comprehension is possible without speech recoding (contrary to the speech recoding access hypothesis).

A second kind of evidence for direct visual access comes from studies of a different abnormal population, patients who have acquired phonemic dyslexia as a result of damage to the left cerebral hemisphere (Marcel and Patterson, 1978). Such *acquired dyslexic patients are capable of reading silently for meaning, but they have severe difficulty with phonemic recoding.* For example, such patients cannot read aloud orthographically regular nonwords (e.g., WIDGE). The problem is not articulatory, since they can repeat such nonwords if they hear them; rather the difficulty seems to be in converting the printed letters into sounds. Particularly striking is the fact that deep dyslexic patients often make semantic errors when attempting to pronounce familiar words. For example, when presented with the string DREAM, the patient might pronounce *sleep*. Clearly, he managed to go from the printed word to its meaning; however, since he could not pronounce the word, it is unlikely that he used a speech recoding route.

In keeping with the conclusion that phonemic dyslexics do not use speech recoding for lexical access are some findings Marcel and Patterson (1978) obtained when they presented such patients with a lexical decision task. The dyslexic patients performed the lexical decisions accurately, indicating that they must have looked up the letter strings in memory. Unlike the normal subjects of Rubenstein et al., however, who were slower at responding "no" to pseudohomophones (such as BRANE), the dyslexic patients responded "no" just as quickly to pseudohomophones as to other nonwords. This pattern suggests that the dyslexic patients are not using speech recoding to access memory.

A third kind of evidence for direct visual access is the finding that among normal individuals, *semantic decisions about individual words are unaffected by phonemic factors*. Two kinds of studies have contributed relevant evidence. Both Green and Shallice (1976) and Klapp, Anderson, and Berrian (1973) presented subjects with a category name followed by an exemplar. The task was to respond "yes" if the exemplar was a member of the category (e.g., OCCUPATION-CLERK) AND "no" if it was not (e.g., OCCUPATION-SQUASH). Thus, the task required that the person judge the category membership of the second word, a decision clearly requiring access to the lexicon. The phonemic variable of interest was the number of syllables in the exemplar word. Sometimes the exemplar contained only one syllable (CLERK), whereas other times it contained several syllables (SECRE-TARY). Previous research has demonstrated that it takes subjects longer to initiate pronunciation of words with more syllables (e.g., Eriksen, Pollack, & Montague, 1970). Therefore, the experimenters reasoned that if subjects must look up the pronunciation of the exemplar in order to get to its meaning, then the number of syllables should influence the time to make the category membership decision as well. In both experiments, however, the result was that decisions were made just as quickly for long exemplars as for short, suggesting that subjects did not engage in speech recoding.

The other kind of evidence that semantic decisions are unaffected by phonemic factors comes from a study by Kleiman (1975). Kleiman used a disruption technique, which assumes that speaking some irrelevant material aloud interferes with or disrupts speech recoding. Thus, the extent to which such articulating interferes with a concurrent reading task provides a measure of how important speech recoding is for the reading task at hand. Kleiman asked subjects to make one of three kinds of judgments about pairs of words which were presented tachistoscopically. The different kinds of judgments are displayed in Table 11–2. For one-third of the experiment, the subject was to make a graphemic decision for each pair. That is, he was to respond "yes" if both items in the pair were spelled identically after the first letter. Thus, for graphemic decisions the subject should respond "yes" to HEARD-BEARD but "no" to GRACE-PRICE. On another third of the trials, the subject was to make a phonemic decision, saying "yes" if the words in the pair rhymed (e.g., TICKLE-PICKLE) and "no" if they did not (e.g., LEMON-DEMON). Finally on the remaining trials, the subject was to make a semantic decision, respond ing "yes" if the two words had approximately the same meaning (e.g., MOURN-GRIEVE) and "no" otherwise (e.g., BRAVERY-QUANTITY). On half the trials of each decision type, the subject was required si-multaneously to shadow aloud a series of digits. Kleiman assumed that the shadowing should interfere with speech recoding, so the mea-sure of interest was the extent to which shadowing disrupted perfor-mance of each kind of decision.

The graphemic and phonemic tasks were meant to provide base-line measures of disruption, to which the synonymy task could be compared. The graphemic task requires no speech recoding at all, by any theory, since it relies only upon a visual judgment which does not require lexical access. Therefore, the degree to which shadowing increases response times for this decision type should provide a mea-sure of the general disruption caused by shadowing. On the other hand, the phonemic task must require speech recoding by any theory, since the person must determine how the words are pronounced in order to make the judgment. Thus, the shadowing task should greatly disrupt performance on this task, if shadowing is disrupting speech recoding. As the far right column of Table 11–2 indicates, the degree of disrup-tion caused by shadowing was indeed much greater for the phonemic judgments (response times 372 msec longer during shadowing) than for the graphemic judgments (response times 125 msec longer during shadowing). The critical question, then, concerns the semantic syn-onymy task. If looking up the word's meaning does not require speech recoding, then shadowing should lead only to general disruption (as it did for the graphemic task) so the degree of disruption should be similar to that seen for the graphemic task. However, if looking up the

TABLE 11–2. Stimuli from Kleiman's (1975) Experiment. The Right Columns Show Mean Reaction Times (in msec) and Percentage of Errors.[a]

Type of Decision	True		False		Without Shadowing	Increase with Shadowing
Graphemic	HEARD NASTY	BEARD HASTY	GRACE SHADOW	PRICE FALLOW	970(4.5)	125(0.4)
Phonemic	TICKLE BLAME	PICKLE FLAME	LEMON ROUGH	DEMON DOUGH	1137(8.3)	372(7.7)
Synonymy	MOURN INSTANCE	GRIEVE EXAMPLE	BRAVERY DEPART	QUANTITY COUPLE	1118(4.2)	120(3.8)

[a] In parentheses.

From Kleiman, 1975. Copyright 1975 by Academic Press. Reprinted by permission.

meaning of a word requires speech recoding, then the degree of disruption caused by shadowing should be similar to that seen in the phonemic task. As Table 11–2 shows, the results supported the direct access hypothesis. The synonymity task was no more disrupted by shadowing than was the graphemic task.

Lexical access: Speech recoding and direct access revisited. The data we have discussed so far fit best with the visual access hypothesis. Most theorists now agree that although the speech recoding route in Figure 11–1 is available, and perhaps even necessary during the early stages of learning to read, direct visual access to word meaning is also possible. In fact, the most useful working hypothesis at the moment is a horse-race type model which states that both lexical access routes are not only possible, but actually operate in parallel during reading (Coltheart, 1978). Lexical access to the meaning of any particular word occurs via whichever route happens to be traversed more quickly. For the average skilled reader, the faster route is most likely the visual one, so this route is probably the more important under most circumstances.

If speech recoding is unnecessary for lexical access, does this mean that it plays no important role in skilled reading? No, because lexical access is only part of what is required in order to comprehend written (or spoken) language. As we discussed in the chapter on language comprehension, the reader or listener must use knowledge of syntax, semantics, and the properties of the physical and social world to construct the appropriate underlying set of propositions. It is possible, then, that these higher-level aspects of language comprehension either require, or are facilitated by, speech recoding. One particularly likely role of speech recoding is that it might facilitate working memory storage and/or processing.

Working memory hypothesis. In Chapter 4, we assumed that working memory acts not only as a storage buffer for newly presented and/or newly retrieved material, but also as a working space for thinking and language processing. In the language comprehension chapter we proposed that working memory is used for constructing tentative propositional structures during the interpretation of a sentence or story. In Chapter 4 we also stressed that among adults, at least, working memory relies heavily, though not exclusively, upon articulatory-acoustic (i.e., phonemic) encoding. This fact has led theorists (e.g., Baddeley, 1979; Kleiman, 1975) to propose the *working memory hypothesis* which states that speech recoding plays an important role in skilled reading because it facilitates storage and processing in working memory.

This working memory hypothesis predicts that speech recoding will be particularly important for comprehending difficult sentences and passages (since such material requires the holding of more complex propositional structures and/or the use of more complex syntactic rules), and in situations in which memory for the material read is to be tested.

In fact, the working memory hypothesis is compatible with the findings to date. A few years ago Hardyck and Petrinovitch (1970) found that if people were forced to suppress lip movements during silent reading, this had a detrimental effect on the comprehension of difficult but not easy material, in keeping with the working memory hypothesis.

Kleiman (1975) has also reported supportive data using his shadowing disruption technique discussed previously. In this experiment, Kleiman again asked subjects to make a number of different kinds of judgments and compared the speed with which they were made with and without the concurrent shadowing task. However, in this case strings of words (instead of word pairs) were presented, and a fourth kind of decision was also required. The various trial types are displayed in Table 11–3. For the graphemic, phonemic, and category judgments, the display contained a target word above a string of five words. In the graphemic task the subject was to respond "true" if the word string contained a word identical in spelling to the target except for the first letter. For the phonemic task, he was to respond "true" if the word string contained a word rhyming with the target, and for the category decision, the subject was to respond "true" if the word string contained an exemplar of the target category. For the fourth type of judgment, the acceptability judgment, the subject was to respond true if the five words, in the order written, formed a semantically acceptable sentence. According to the working memory hypothesis, the acceptability judgment (unlike the category judgment) should be highly disrupted by the concurrent shadowing, because it requires the use of working memory to construct an interpretation of the sentence. The results are also shown in Table 11–3.

The graphemic condition yields a low level of disruption, fitting with the assumption that it requires only direct visual matching. The phonemic task yields a great deal of disruption, presumably since it requires phonemic recoding. The category judgment reveals little disruption indicating that it does not call upon speech recoding. This finding is in keeping with the working memory hypothesis, since comprehension of the sentence is not required and all the words are displayed in front of the subject thereby calling little upon working memory capacity. Finally, the acceptability task is greatly disrupted by the shadowing, suggesting that speech recoding is important for this task, just as the working memory hypothesis would predict. In fact Levy (1977) has shown a similar pattern of results using not only iso-

TABLE 11–3. Stimuli from Kleiman's (1975) Experiment. The Right Columns Show Mean Reaction Times (in msec) and Percentage of Errors.[a]

Type of Decision	Examples of Stimuli	Without Shadowing	Change With Shadowing
Graphemic	BURY YESTERDAY THE GRAND JURY ADJOURNED (True) GATHER RUNNING FURTHER WAS TED'S MOTHER (False)	1557(6.3)	140(2.0)
Phonemic	CREAM HE AWAKENED FROM THE DREAM (True) SOUL THE REFEREE CALLED A FOUL (False)	1401(6.8)	312(2.1)
Category	GAMES EVERYONE AT HOME PLAYED MONOPOLY (True) SPORTS HIS FAVORITE HOBBY IS CARPENTRY (False)	1596(9.9)	78(−2.6)
Acceptability	NOISY PARTIES DISTURB SLEEPING NEIGHBORS (True) PIZZAS HAVE BEEN EATING JERRY (False)	1431(7.3)	394(2.6)

[a]In parentheses.
From Kleiman, 1975. Copyright 1975 by Academic Press. Reprinted by permission.

lated sentences, but also paragraphs. This finding suggests that speech recoding is just as important when reading connected prose as it is for less semantically rich tasks.

A very different kind of evidence that is consistent with the working memory hypothesis comes from studying reading in a non-alphabetic writing system. Note first that English is an *alphabetic* system in that there is a limited number of visual symbols that stand for phonetic units, so there is a systematic relation between visual symbol and sound. Thus, during the course of learning to read, we learn spelling-to-sound correspondence rules that enable us to "sound out" unfamiliar printed words. In contrast are *ideographic* systems in which there is a very large number of visual symbols, each of which represents a semantic unit. There is a close relation between visual symbol and meaning, but the visual form of an unfamiliar ideogram does not provide clues as to how the word should be pronounced. We might expect that such different kinds of systems would involve different kinds of processing, and, in particular, that speech recoding might be less important for processing an ideographic language. In fact, there is some evidence consistent with this hunch. Dyslexia appears to be much less common in Japan, where a partially ideographic system is used (Makita, 1968), and there is some evidence that English dyslexics are more successful at learning to read Chinese than English (Rozin, Poritsky, & Sotsky, 1971). In fact, Japanese is particularly interesting in that two types of writing symbols (one type phonetic and the other ideographic) are used in combination. Evidence that these two kinds of symbols involve different kinds of processing is found in the fact that when a Japanese person acquires dyslexia, one of these systems (usually the phonetic one) often is affected, while the other remains intact.

Given these differences among alphabetic and ideographic orthography, then, it is particularly interesting that speech recoding is used during the processing of ideographic as well as alphabetic systems. For example, Tzeng, Hung, and Wang (1977) gave Chinese graduate students two different kinds of tasks in which the stimuli were printed Chinese characters. In the short-term memory experiment, they used a retroactive interference paradigm in which subjects saw four Chinese characters (the memory list), then shadowed some auditorily presented words (the interference list) and finally attempted to write down the four characters they had seen in the memory list. The experiments varied the degree of phonemic similarity between the memory list and the interference list. If people do *not* use phonemic recoding when reading ideographs, then phonemic similarity between the visually presented memory list and the interference list should not influence performance. In fact, however, the data revealed that phonemic factors did influence the accuracy of written recall. Just as for

English speakers (Conrad, 1964), subjects recalled the memory list of ideographs more poorly when it was followed by a phonemically similar list than when it was followed by a phonemically dissimilar list. This suggests that the Chinese readers were engaging in speech recoding.

Tzeng et al. were particularly interested in the role speech recoding plays in actual reading (as opposed to memorizing lists of words). Therefore, in a second experiment they presented Chinese subjects with a sentence comprehension task similar to one conducted by Baddeley and Hitch (1974) with English speaking subjects. People were presented with single sentences and asked to judge as rapidly as possible whether or not each sentence made sense. The dependent variable of interest was the time required to make the judgment, and the major independent variable was phonemic similarity of the words within a sentence. On half of the trials the visually presented sentences contained many phonemically similar words, whereas on the other half the sentences contained phonemically dissimilar words. If in making their judgment about the sense of the sentence, Chinese readers do not use speech recoding, then they should take an equal amount of time to respond to each of the sentence types. However, if they do engage in speech encoding, then they should take longer to make the decision about the phonemically similar sentences. In fact, the phonemically similar sentences yielded longer response times, indicating that the Chinese readers, just as Baddeley and Hitch's readers of English, were engaging in speech recoding.

When readers of an ideographic language attempt to remember or comprehend written material, then, they appear to engage in speech recoding just as do readers of alphabetic systems. Since ideographic systems are characterized by a direct link between visual symbol and meaning, it is unlikely that the speech recoding is favoring lexical access. Rather, the human tendency to recode printed material into a phonemically (articulatory-acoustic) based code suggests that a universal property of information processing is a working memory that is important for reading and that favors articulatory-acoustic coding.

Summary: Speech recoding in reading. We have found, then, that the evidence to date suggests that speech recoding plays at least two roles in reading. As Figure 11–1 shows, one role is in lexical access. Under some conditions, particularly when learning how to read or when dealing with an unfamiliar word, the reader converts the visual symbol into a phonemically encoded form, which is then used to address the appropriate concept node in long-term memory. Such speech recoding is not necessary for lexical access among skilled readers, however, and it may play a rather minor role during most reading, since the direct visual access route is faster. The second role of speech encoding is more important, and apparently more universal, for speech recoding facilitates working memory storage and/or processing, thereby enabling the reader to integrate the presented ideas more readily. The small amount of cross cultural work to date suggests that this speech recoding may be a universal tendency of humans, reflecting the properties of a working memory that favors articulatory-acoustic coding.

READING: INDIVIDUAL DIFFERENCES

There are obvious differences among individuals in both the speed of reading and in the quality of comprehension; verbal SAT scores attempt to assign a numerical value to such skill. In information processing terms, what differentiates the good reader from the average or poor one? This question is of theoretical interest since learning about the correlates of successful reading would help to isolate the processes that play a prominant role in all reading. Questions about individual differences are of practical importance as well, because isolating those processes that differentiate skilled from unskilled readers might help us to design more effective training programs.

Experimental psychologists have only begun to investigate individual differences in reading using the tools of information-processing psychology, so we can only make some tentative statements here. So far, research suggests three major processing differences between good and poor readers: (1) the use of phonemic coding in working memory, (2) the capacity of working memory, and (3) the speed of encoding letters.

Phonemic coding in working memory.   A number of studies indicate that among children learning to read, the good readers use phonemic coding *more* than the poor readers. Phonemic factors influence the memory of good readers more than poor, regardless of whether the stimuli to be remembered are letter strings (Liberman, Shankweiler, Liberman, Fowler, & Fischer, 1977; Shankweiler & Liberman, 1976), word strings (e.g., Byrne & Shea, 1979; Mark, Shankweiler, Liberman, & Fowler, 1977), or sentences (Mann, Liberman, & Shankweiler, 1980). This effect occurs whether the stimuli are presented in written or spoken form.

Consider, for example, the study by Mann, et al. (1980). Second graders were classified as either good or poor readers using their teachers' assessments and standardized reading tests. Children of both groups then listened to sentences or word strings and attempted to repeat the stimulus strings in correct order immediately after the last item. The most important variable was whether or not the items within

TABLE 11–4. Sample Stimuli from the Short-Term Memory Study of Phonemic Coding in Good and Poor Readers by Mann, Liberman, & Shankweiler (1980).

Stimulus Type	Sample Nonrhyming Sentences	Sample Rhyming Sentences
Meaningful Sentences	Tom and Bill piled books on the chair in front of the door	Jack and Mack stacked sacks on the track in back of the shack
Meaningless sentences	Sam and Chuck fried words on the leaf inside of the month	Fred and Ed read sleds on the thread instead of the bed
Word Strings	Sells duck sand good green	Red dead Ted thread bread

a string rhymed with each other (i.e., were phonemically confusable). Table 11–4 contains sample stimuli for all the possible conditions in the experiment. Figure 11–2 shows the results Mann and her colleagues obtained. Note that for all three kinds of stimuli (meaningless sentences, meaningful sentences, and word strings), the poor readers make the same number of errors on rhyming and nonrhyming versions, suggesting that they are not using phonemic coding. On the other hand, good readers make more errors on rhyming than on nonrhyming materials, indicating that they rely upon phonemic coding.

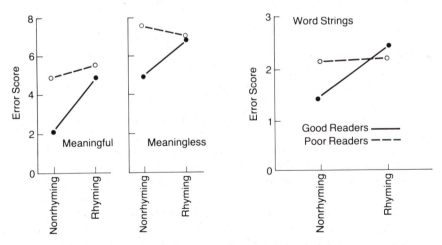

Figure 11–2. Good and poor readers' mean error scores on meaningful sentences, meaningless sentences, and word strings, in rhyming and nonrhyming conditions. (After Mann, Liberman, & Shankweiler, 1980. Copyright 1980 by the Psychonomic Society. Reprinted by permission.)

Thus, good beginning readers rely upon articulatory-acoustic coding more than poor beginning readers, a finding that is consistent with the argument in the previous section that speech recoding facilitates reading. Of course, we do not know yet whether this relation between phonemic coding and reading skill holds only for the initial stages of learning to read, or whether it also holds for adults. As we saw in the chapter on working memory, this tendency to use phonemic coding develops, appearing first at about the age of 5 (Conrad, 1971), which is also the age at which teachers usually judge children to be able to learn to read. This suggests the possibility (Conrad, 1972) that one of the skills underlying "reading readiness" is the development of the tendency to use phonemic coding.

Working memory capacity. Several studies of college students indicate that good readers have greater working memory capacity than poorer readers. For example, Daneman and Carpenter (1980) studied a group of college students at Carnegie-Mellon University in Pittsburgh. In order to assess each student's working memory capacity, they administered a reading span task. The span task required the student to read aloud a series of sentences. After the series, he/she attempted to recall the final word of all the sentences. The reading span was defined as the number of final words the subject was able to recall. Among the students they tested, this span ranged from 2 to 5. In order to assess reading comprehension, students were required to read passages silently, after which they were asked questions designed to assess their memory for specific facts in the stories (fact questions) and their understanding of the referents of specific pronouns in the story.

The important finding was that subjects' reading span scores (assumed to assess working memory capacity) were highly correlated with their reading comprehension scores, suggesting that the more skilled readers among these college students have greater working memory capacity. In fact, the experimenters found that the span score was also highly correlated with the verbal SAT score, and with measures of *listening* comprehension. This finding that good readers (and good listeners) have larger working memory capacity than average readers is also consistent with the findings of Hunt and his colleagues at the University of Washington (e.g., Hunt, Luneborg, & Lewis, 1975; Hunt, 1978).

The correlation between working memory capacity and reading comprehension is also apparent from studies of developmental dyslexia. Critchley (1970) has defined developmental dyslexics as children "who despite conventional classroom experience, fail to attain the language skills of reading, writing, and spelling commensurate with their intellectual abilities." The dyslexia these children suffer does not seem to be a defect in visual perception. Dyslexic children perform as well as normals at scanning a row of letters for the presence or absence of a target letter (Katz & Wicklund, 1972), and they are as good as normals at reporting visual information as long as they are tested within 300 msec of stimulus offset (Morrison, Giordani, & Nagy, 1977). This finding suggests that the dyslexic child does not have deficient sensory storage. In contrast, a number of authors have noted (cf. Jorm, 1979), however, that dyslexic children have impaired performance on digit span tasks and on tests of visual short-term memory, suggesting that they suffer from deficient working memory processes.

We have seen, then, that there is a correlation between the capacity of working memory and what is often called verbal ability (i.e., reading and spoken language comprehension). Of course, this correlation raises many interesting and unanswered questions about exactly how the working memory of skilled readers differs from that of less skilled. Is it, for example, that the skilled reader's working memory has more capacity in terms of storage room (e.g., number of storage slots) or is it that the skilled reader's working memory performs processes more quickly and efficiently, thereby enabling the person to use the same amount of space more effectively? As yet, we cannot tell.

Speed of encoding letters.   Several researchers have reported that among college students, skilled readers look up letters in long-term memory (i.e., encode letters) more rapidly than average readers (e.g., Graesser, Hoffman, & Clark, 1980; Hunt, Lunneborg, & Lewis, 1975; Jackson & McClelland, 1979; Perfetti & Lesgold, 1977). For example, Jackson and McClelland (1979) compared fast and average readers on a number of sensory processing and reaction time tasks. They found that the speed and accuracy of sensory perception did not distinguish good from average readers, but that the speed of encoding letters did.

This conclusion was based primarily on the results of a number of same-different matching tests of the sort introduced by Posner and his colleagues (Posner, Boies, Eichelman, & Taylor, 1969). For all tasks two stimuli were presented simultaneously, and the time required for the subject to indicate a match or mismatch was recorded. Three of the matching tasks are shown in Figure 11–3. For the letter name task, the subject was to respond "same" if the two letters had the same name and "different" otherwise, so a correct response requires that the subject access the name of the letter from long-term memory. For the dot-pattern task, the subject was to respond "same" if the two patterns were physically identical, so careful perceptual processing, but no long-term memory access, is required. Finally, for the homophone task, subjects were to respond "same" only if the two nonsense syllables sounded identical. Therefore, for this task the subject must

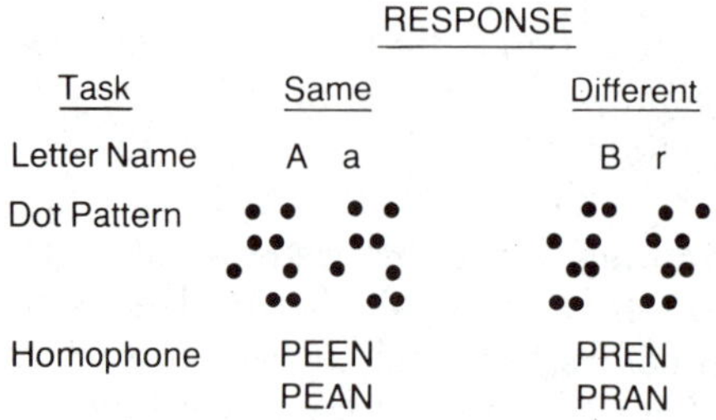

RESPONSE

Task	Same	Different
Letter Name	A a	B r
Dot Pattern		
Homophone	PEEN PEAN	PREN PRAN

Figure 11–3. Examples of a same and different stimulus pair for each reaction time task included in the Jackson and McClelland (1979) study. (From Jackson & McClelland, 1979. Copyright 1979 by the American Psychological Association. Reprinted by permission of the publisher and author.)

not only look up individual letters in memory, but also use his knowledge of letter-sound rules to generate a pronunciation.

When Jackson and McClelland compared the performance of fast and average readers on each of these three tasks, they found that fast readers were quicker than average readers at both tasks that required long-term memory access, but they were *not* faster at the dot-pattern task that relied only upon perceptual matching. This pattern of results is important since it indicates that the difference between good and average readers on the letter matching task is not due to a difference in general speed of perceptual processing, but rather to the speed of long-term memory access.

Summary: Individual differences.   Current research suggests that skilled readers differ from less skilled on three components of information processing: use of phonemic encoding, working memory capacity, and the speed of encoding letters. Cognitive research on individual differences is only beginning, however, as the recency of most of the previous references indicates. It is particularly important that you be aware of a couple of the limitations on our current knowledge. First, although we have talked about three components of information processing, these might all be reflecting one underlying common process. For example, one person's working memory capacity might be greater than another's precisely because he uses phonemic coding, and he may use phonemic coding because he has such rapid access to phonemic codes in long-term memory.

The second limitation is that we do not know that these differences in working memory, encoding speed, and phonemic coding are the *causes* of differences in reading skill. The studies cited demonstrate only a *correlation*. One way in which we might investigate causal relations in this case is to attempt to train a particular skill (e.g., train children to use phonemic coding) and then determine whether that training results in improved reading skill.

Finally, it is important to stress that the studies of individual differences in reading skill point to a common core of language comprehension ability that encompasses both language by eye (reading) and language by ear (listening). Several of the researchers we discussed have reported that people who are skilled readers tend to be good at comprehending spoken language as well. Thus, we are led again to stress the close connections between reading and listening.

SIGN LANGUAGE

We turn now to a very different kind of language by eye—American Sign Language. American Sign Language (ASL) is a language of hand signs that was developed among the deaf people of the United States, and has been in use since the early 1800's. ASL, in fact, is the native language of many deaf children born to deaf parents. People who are unfamiliar with ASL often have a number of misconceptions about it (cf. Bellugi & Klima, 1978), so it is important that we begin by clarifying some things that ASL is *not*. For one thing, ASL is *not* a derivative or degenerate or gestural form of English. It has separate historical roots (going back to French sign language, in fact) and is a completely separate language from spoken English. Second, ASL is *not* finger spelling. In finger spelling, there is a sign for each letter of the alphabet and the speaker literally writes English words in space. In ASL there is a sign for each concept, so signs are analogous not to letters, but to words. Third, ASL is *not* a universal language of pantomime. For example, American Sign Language differs greatly from British Sign Language and, for the most part, people who only know one of these cannot understand signing in the other. Fourth, American Sign Language is *not* limited to expressing only concrete ideas. There are vocabulary items dealing with religion, politics, ethics, and history, for example, and ASL (just as spoken language) continually adds new signs to adapt to changes in the world (e.g., names for technological advances).

ASL is fascinating in itself, but the main reason for including it here is that it offers an ideal medium for asking how deeply language structures are rooted in the human mind. That is, in the last few chapters we have considered many characteristics of spoken language. To what extent are these characteristics determined by the auditory modality in which most of us learn and experience language, and to what extent by underlying cognitive capacities and processes that hold regardless of modality? American Sign Language provides an ideal test case. During the last few years several islands of research on ASL have sprung up around the country, particularly at the Salk Institute in San Diego, at Northeastern University in Boston, and at Gallaudet College in Washington, D.C., the latter being a college for deaf and hearing-impaired individuals in which classes are conducted in ASL. The psychologists and linguists at these and other universities have already provided fascinating accounts of ASL, and in doing so they have given us new insight on spoken language and on the universal properties of human cognition. There is already evidence for a number of notable similarities between ASL and spoken languages. We will consider these now.

Individual signs have internal structure.   As you have already learned, all spoken languages are structured hierarchically. Each sentence may be broken into constituents, each constituent into still smaller constituents, and eventually into words. Each word consists of phonemes, and each phoneme can be described in terms of a set of features. Furthermore, there are rules (often known only implicitly by users of the language) which specify allowable combinations at each level of this hierarchy. Thus, it is through rule-governed combination of a set of finite elements that language makes possible the expression of an infinite number of potential messages. The study of ASL has made it clear that this hierarchical structure is not limited to oral languages.

Casual observers usually think that each sign of ASL is an unanalyzable, iconic whole, much like gestures in pantomime. However, linguistic analyses (e.g., Stokoe, Casterline, & Croneberg, 1965; Klima & Bellugi, 1979) have demonstrated that individual signs have an internal structure. Each sign can be described in terms of a set of *formational parameters* that are analogous to the features we used to describe phones. Any given sign can be specified in terms of four formational parameters: hand configuration, place of articulation, orientation, and movement. Figure 11–4 shows examples of pairs of signs that differ along each of these parameters. Thus, in ASL HOME and YESTERDAY differ in only one feature, just as in spoken language [b] and [p] differ in only one.

For each formational parameter, furthermore, there is a finite set of possible elements or *primes*. For example, possible hand configurations include the closed fist, the pointing index hand, the /V/ hand, and so forth. There are also rules which restrict the combinations that may occur. These are analogous to the rules in spoken language which specify that while both *block* and *brock* could be English words, *bnock* could not. Signs are further constrained in that among adult signers, at least, most are formed within a specified area known as the signing space, which is illustrated in Figure 11–5.

We are arguing, then, that individual signs are not unanalyzable wholes, but rather, like words and phonemes consist of rule-governed combinations of elements. You might wonder, however, whether such an analysis isn't simply a form of organization superimposed on signs by linguists (who are notorious for finding order in almost anything).

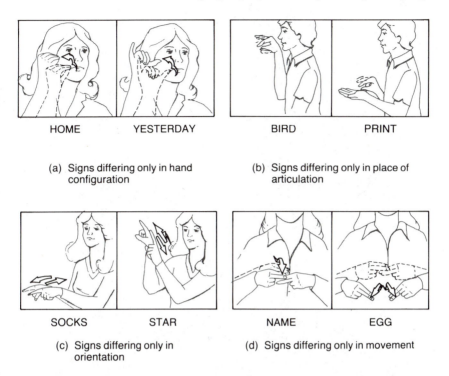

HOME   YESTERDAY   BIRD   PRINT

(a) Signs differing only in hand configuration

(b) Signs differing only in place of articulation

SOCKS   STAR   NAME   EGG

(c) Signs differing only in orientation

(d) Signs differing only in movement

Figure 11–4. Sample pairs of ASL signs differing on each of the formational parameters. (After Bellugi & Klima, 1978. Copyright 1978 by Academic Press. Reprinted by permission.)

That is, you may wonder about the psychological reality of these parameters for the user of sign language.

One kind of evidence for the psychological reality of formational parameters comes from studies of short-term memory for signs. If people use and remember signs as unanalyzable wholes, then when they forget a sign in a short-term memory task, they should forget it as a unit. However, this is not what happens. Bellugi, Klima, and Siple (1975) used videotape to present lists of three to seven signs to deaf subjects for whom ASL was their native language. Immediately after presentation of the lists, the subjects attempted to write down their English equivalents. The experimenters found that when subjects misrecalled a sign, they usually (two-thirds of the time, in fact) substituted a word whose sign equivalent differed in only one of the formational parameters. For example, when a subject was presented with the sign for HOME, he might later misrecall it as the word YESTERDAY, a sign differing from the one for HOME in only one formational parameter (even though he correctly perceived it as HOME initially.)

Figure 11–5. A depiction of the normal signing space in ASL. (After Klima & Bellugi, 1979. Copyright 1979 by Harvard University Press. Reprinted by permission.)

In fact, the sign pairs illustrated in Figure 11–4 represent sign-error pairs that Bellugi et al. obtained in their experiment. This pattern of errors provides strong evidence for the psychological reality of the parameters, for it suggests that a sign is stored as a bundle of formational parameters which may be forgotten independently from each other.

Other evidence for the psychological reality of the formational parameters comes from analyses of *slips of the hand,* the sign language equivalent of the slips of the tongue that we discussed in Chapter 8. Like slips of the tongue, not only do slips of the hand occur frequently, but they are usually systematic (Klima & Bellugi, 1979). Recall that slips of the tongue usually result in sound combinations that are acceptable in the speaker's language. For example, a slip of the tongue rarely results in an English speaker producing a "word" like TLIP, though it might result in his producing a "word" like MIP. Similarly, a slip of the hand rarely results in the signer producing a combination of movements that violates the rules of combination for signs. Frequently, one prime from a sign is mistakenly placed in another sign. For example, the movement of one sign may persevere into the following sign, the place of articulation of a following sign may be anticipated in the preceding sign, or the configuration of two signs may be switched. Again, then, as in the case of short-term memory intrusions, in slips of the hand formational parameters are switched independently of each other, providing strong evidence of their psychological reality for the signer.

Additional evidence for this psychological reality comes from analyses of historical change in ASL. Bellugi and Klima have obtained information on changes in ASL signs that have occurred during the last 50 years. Among their sources for this study were some films of elderly fluent signers produced in 1913, a book describing signs published in 1918, and interviews with elderly deaf couples. They have found that the historical changes that have occurred in ASL can be characterized as a shift from iconicity toward arbitrariness and systematization. That is, when individual signs were first introduced into ASL, they were usually iconic (in that the sign resembled some property of the intended referent) and they sometimes violated the usual formational rules for signs. For example, the original sign might have contained a unique hand configuration or be produced outside the regular signing space. However, during the ensuing years as the sign was passed on within the signing community, it tended to become less and less iconic and, in addition, to conform to the set of primes of which most signs are composed. An example is the sign for SWEETHEART. In the early 1900's it used to be made over the heart, touching the body, with the two hands together only at the little fingers (presumably depicting the point of a Valentine heart). Now, however, the sign is made near the midline without touching the body and with the two hands in full contact. Unlike the original iconic sign, this more recent one contains primes that are characteristic of many other signs.

At first it might seem surprising that during generations of usage signs tend to become *less* iconic. One might have guessed that it would be easier to learn and remember signs that resemble their meaning, and that this would tend to preserve their iconicity. Why, then, have signs evolved into more arbitrary, conventional forms? One possible explanation is that if a language is to be acquired and used effectively by the human mind, and if it is to have the potential for conveying an infinite set of messages, then the language system *must* be hierarchically structured and based on a systematic recombination of arbitrary elements. Thus, we are suggesting that the historical change toward abstract, conventionalized signs in ASL reflects the joint demands of communication and the structure of the human mind.

Sequences of signs have grammatical structure. Not only do individual signs have an internal structure, but signs are combined and modified in rule-governed ways in order to convey propositions.

It is clear now that ASL has a grammer of its own, though the exact nature of this grammar remains to be worked out in detail.

The spoken languages of the world differ in the extent to which they use a fixed word order to convey semantic relations, though English relies upon word order quite heavily. There is still some debate as to whether the grammar of ASL restricts the order in which signs are permitted to occur (cf. Stokoe, 1972; Tervoort, 1968), but there is some recent psychological evidence that word order is important for signers. Tweney, Heiman, and Hoemann (1977) studied how well people could perceive sequences of signs that were disrupted visually (the visual analogue of listening to speech in a background of static). Native deaf users of ASL watched sequences of five signs and then attempted to reproduce the series immediately. On some of the trials the sign sequence consisted of a sequence of signs that other ASL users had judged to be grammatical (Grammatical Strings), whereas on other trials the signs from such grammatical strings were presented in a scrambled order (Scrambled Strings).

Tweney and his colleagues found that people perceived the Grammatical Strings more accurately than the Scrambled Strings. Furthermore, when reproducing the Scrambled Strings, they tended to reorder the signs into their grammatical order. Thus, this study demonstrates that sign order does matter in ASL, just as it does in most spoken languages.

Though word order does seem to play a role in the grammar of sign language, inflections are even more important. This emphasis on inflections is characteristic of many spoken languages as well. Just as inflections in spoken language involve modifying the form of the spoken word (e.g., RUN is changed to RUNNING, HOUSE to HOUSES) in some systematic way, inflections in sign language involve modifying the form of the sign systematically. For example, there is an inflection that changes a sign for transitory states or actions into a sign for permanent characteristics or dispositions (i.e., TENDS TO BE or PRONE TO BE). The inflection requires making the original sign with two hands instead of one and alternating them in repeated smooth circular movements. Three applications of this inflection are shown in Figure 11–6.

ASL is extremely rich in inflections, much richer than English. It is particularly important that inflections are systematic and rule-governed in ASL. In fact, the rule-governed obligatory manner in which inflections are applied often overrides the iconic properties of a given sign. For instance, in order to intensify the meaning of a sign, one inflects the sign by making it with a very rapid, tense movement. Thus, QUICKLY is changed to VERY QUICKLY by making the sign for QUICKLY in a rapid, tense movement. In this case the changed visual nature of the sign is, of course, quite consistent with the new mean-

WRONG   ERROR-PRONE

DIRTY   DIRT-PRONE

QUIET   TACITURN or RESERVED

Figure 11–6. Three ASL signs and their inflected forms using a modulation that adds the general meaning of "prone to be" or "tends to be" to the sign. (After Bellugi & Klima, 1978. Copyright 1978 by Academic Press. Reprinted by permission.)

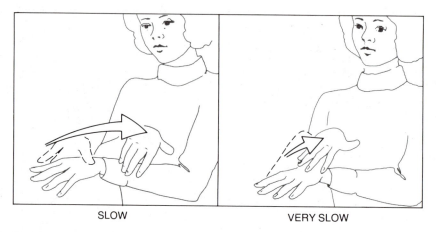

SLOW   VERY SLOW

Figure 11–7. The suppression of iconicity under regular operations on signs. (After Klima & Bellugi, 1979. Copyright 1979 by Harvard University Press. Reprinted by permission.)

ing. However, in order to change the sign for SLOW to VERY SLOW, the signer must make the SLOW sign more rapidly and tensely (as Figure 11–7 attempts to depict). If one were using iconic means to convey the notion of VERY SLOWLY, of course, you would make the sign for SLOWLY even more slowly and in a more elongated fashion than usual. Yet we see that the tendency for rule-governed modulation of signs is so strong that (as in the case of historical change) the rules take precedence over iconic considerations.

Similarities in acquisition.   In our discussion of language acquisition, we indicated that children around the world acquire their native spoken language with little apparent teaching. Furthermore, they learn at similar rates and they make remarkably similar errors. There is a small population of deaf infants—the 10% of the deaf population born to deaf parents—for whom the native language is ASL. Just as hearing infants are surrounded daily by the spoken language of their community, such deaf infants are cared for by individuals who communicate with each other through ASL.

We know much less about the acquisition of sign than of speech, but what we have learned so far indicates that there are remarkable similarities between the two. When infants (either deaf or hearing) are exposed regularly to sign language they pick it up as readily as children learn spoken language. In fact, a number of studies (e.g., Schlesinger and Meadow, 1972) indicate that the first sign usually occurs at about the age of 5–6 months and the first two-sign combinations appear at 14 months. This is a timetable that is about six months ahead of what is observed for spoken languages. One possible explanation for the difference is that speaking must await further maturation of the vocal apparatus, whereas signing need not.

Among children learning spoken language, there is a steady increase in the average length of their utterances with development, and this occurs during the acquisition of sign language as well. The rate of increase in the size of the vocabulary also seems to be roughly similar for language acquisition in the two modalities. Even more striking is the fact that children learning sign make some of the same kinds of errors as children learning spoken language. For example, children acquiring sign language *overgeneralize* rules, applying them to what would be exceptions in adult ASL. In ASL, for example, there are verbs such as SEE and GIVE for which the direction of the motion can be varied to convey meaning. To convey I SEE YOU the sign is made in a direction outward from the speaker, but to convey YOU SEE ME, the direction of movement is reversed. However, there are verbs to which this inflection cannot be applied, according to the adult grammar. The sign for SPELL is one such exception, and adults always make it with the palm facing out from the signer with the fingers wiggling. Nonetheless, Bellugi and Klima (1972) report one of the children they observed overregularizing by turning her hand with fingers wiggling toward herself, thereby trying to convey to her mother YOU SPELL ME, that is, "finger spell to me."

Apparently, then, the child's tendency to impose a consistent organization on language (which even encompasses what adults consider to be exceptions) is just as strong when the child learns a visual language as when he learns an auditory one.

It is hard to read the literature on the acquisition of ASL without gaining the impression that children are predisposed to learn language. If exposed to *any* rule-governed communication system, whether visual or auditory, they seem to discover its properties and use them spontaneously to communicate with others. Goldin-Meadow and Feldman (1977) observed deaf children of hearing parents, ranging in age from 1½ to 4 years of age. Since the parents did not know ASL, the children had never been exposed to sign language. Goldin-Meadow and Feldman found that the children spontaneously created rudimentary sign languages of their own. Each of the children created a vocabulary of manual signs to stand for actions, objects, and attributes, and the children combined these signs in systematic, apparently rule-governed ways. It would be hard to find more dramatic evidence that the human mind is predisposed to acquire language, regardless of modality. In the absence of a language model, children are capable of inventing their own.

Hemispheric specialization. We saw earlier that the left hemisphere is specialized for speech processing, but is it also specialized for processing sign language? This question is important because the answer might help us to specify more precisely what differentiates left hemisphere functions from right. We usually think of the right hemisphere as being specialized for holistic, visual-spatial processing and the left hemisphere as specialized for analytic processing of rule-governed sequences. Sign language presents an interesting contrast in that it is visual-spatial (suggesting right hemisphere specialization), but highly structured and rule-governed (suggesting left hemisphere specialization).

Most of the research to date indicates that cerebral specialization is similar for deaf signers and hearing speakers. Consider, for example, a recent study by Virostek and Cutting (1979) who presented signers (both deaf and hearing) and nonsigners (i.e., people who did not know sign language) with a simple matching task. The stimuli used in the experiment were of the four types shown in Figure 11–8. The alphabetical group of signs in the upper left is the most important group, for this is a set of handshapes that are used in ASL. These handshapes, then, have linguistic significance only for signers. The set in the upper right also contains legitimate signs in ASL, but they might also have meaning for nonsigners, since they have numerical significance. The third set (in the lower left) is a set of linear figures that should have no linguistic significance for either group. The fourth set consists of handshapes that are not legitimate in ASL. Thus, this set should have no linguistic significance for either group.

Virostek and Cutting presented each subject with a series of trials. On each, stimuli from only one of the sets appeared. One stimulus from the set was presented for 100 msec, followed by a 100 msec blank field, followed by a second stimulus from the same set. The subject then wrote either SAME or DIFFERENT on a piece of paper (depending on whether or not the two stimuli were identical) and then the next trial began. On each trial the second stimulus was always presented at the center of the display (thus to both visual fields), but the first stimulus was presented from either the right or the left visual field on each trial. The data of interest, then, were per cent correct judgments for the right and left visual field presentations, and these scores are shown in Figure 11–9.

Look first at the data for the alphabetical handshapes. Recall that this is the only set which should have linguistic significance for the signers, but not the nonsigners. In fact, the groups have opposite patterns of lateralization for this set. In particular, the nonsigners show a slight left visual field (right-hemisphere) advantage, typical of nonlinguistic spatial processing, whereas the signers show a right visual field (left-hemisphere) advantage, typical of linguistic processing. On the basis of this set of stimuli alone, however, one might be led to conclude that the deaf would show a left-hemisphere advantage for all

LEGITIMATE HANDSHAPES

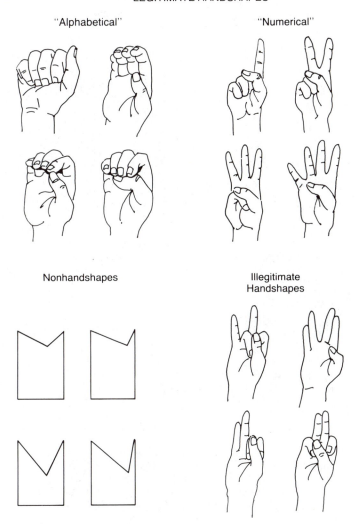

Figure 11–8. The stimuli from the study of cerebral lateralization conducted by Virostek and Cutting, 1979. (After Virostek & Cutting, 1979. Copyright 1979 by the Psychonomic Society. Reprinted by permission.)

visually presented stimuli. The other three sets of stimuli show that this is not the case. For the three remaining sets the signers and non-signers show equivalent patterns of performance. In the case of the non-handshapes, both groups show a left visual field (right-hemisphere) advantage as is typical for spatial processing, and on the other two sets, neither group of subjects reveals significant lateralization.

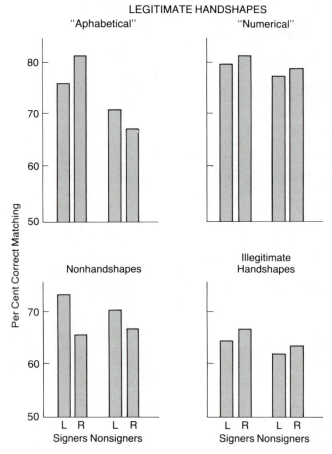

Figure 11–9. Per cent correct matching for signers and nonsigners for right and left visual field presentations for the four different stimulus sets in Figure 11–8. (After Virostek & Cutting, 1979. Copyright 1979 by the Psychonomic Society. Reprinted by permission.)

This pattern of findings suggests that left-hemisphere dominance reflects a property of linguistic processing per se, not a property of the modality in which language is processed.

Similar rate of expression of propositions. The aim of language is to express propositions, and it is of interest to determine the relative efficiency of sign and spoken language in this regard. Bellugi and Fischer (1972) did so by asking three hearing sons and daughters of deaf parents, who were fluent in both sign and speech, to tell a personal anecdote or story, first in one language, then in the other.

TABLE 11–5.   Comparisons of the Rates of Speaking and Signing.

a. The rate of producing individual words or signs

	Mean Words Per Second	**Mean Signs Per Second**
Subject A	4.0	2.3
Subject B	4.9	2.3
Subject C	5.2	2.5
Deaf Signers		1.7–2.1

b. The rate of producing propositions

	Mean Seconds Per Proposition **Speaking**	**Signing**
Subject A	1.6	2.0
Subject B	1.2	1.4
Subject C	1.0	1.0
Deaf Signers		1.3–1.7

From Bellugi & Fischer, 1972.

These stories were tape-recorded and videotaped. Bellugi and Fischer first analyzed the number of words or signs produced per second. The results depicted in Table 11–5a indicate that words are conveyed much more rapidly than signs. Though you might think that deaf signers would be more skilled at signing than these hearing subjects, when Bellugi and Fischer tested an additional group of three deaf signers they found an equivalent rate of signing, as the last row of Table 11–5a indicates. Subsequent studies (e.g., Grosjean, 1977) have confirmed that, in general the average duration of a sign is twice that of a word.

In contrast, when Bellugi and Fischer went on to compute the mean number of seconds it took to convey a proposition, they found that the two forms of communication were identical. These values are displayed in Table 11–5b both for the original three hearing subjects, and for the additional three deaf signers. Thus, despite the dramatic differences in element (word or sign) duration and in modality of presentation, the rate at which sign and speech convey ideas is equivalent. This suggests the possibility that this rate reflects some level of optimum cognitive processing. Perhaps Bellugi and Fischer have discovered a "magical propositional rate" to go with Miller's magical number.

You may be wondering how sign language manages to convey propositions as quickly as speech, when it conveys only half as many signs per second. Bellugi and Fischer argue that sign does so in several ways. First, of course, it simply condenses, using fewer signs per idea. For example, when signers were asked to translate the English sentence "It's against the law to drive on the left side," they translated it into a sequence of four signs: ILLEGAL DRIVE LEFT SIDE. Fortunately, ASL is able to enrich each sign so that it conveys more information. One way in which it does so is through the structured use of space. When signers talk about objects and people, they usually establish a series of loci for each the first time the object or person is mentioned. Later references to that particular object or person are made simply by signing the appropriate action or descriptor sign toward the object's particular imagined location. Thus, if I wish to convey that a boy chased his dog. I might sign BOY facing in one location and DOG in a different location. Then later, in order to convey that the dog was happy, I need only sign HAPPY toward the dog's place. This elaborate and structured use of space cuts down on the need for repetition of subjects, objects and pronouns, but without sacrificing clarity.

Another way in which sign language packs extra meaning into each sign is through the use of inflections of the sort we discussed earlier. Instead of needing two signs to convey VERY SLOWLY, for example, the signer simply makes the appropriate rule-governed change in the sign for SLOWLY.

Finally, facial signals are extremely important in ASL. In fact, as they talk, signers typically fixate, not on each other's hands, but on their faces. Of course, facial expressions are important in speaking as well, but their usage in sign is more intentional and much more systematic. Signs can be negated through a facial gesture alone, changing the sign for FRIENDLY into a sign for UNFRIENDLY, for example. Furthermore, there are certain well-defined, restricted facial gestures that serve as signals for clausal embedding of signs (Liddell, 1977 cited in Klima & Bellugi, 1979). That is, a particular facial gesture accompanying the signs for MAN and HAPPY can convey the idea that "who is happy" is an embedded clause in the sign equivalent of the statement "The man who was happy left."

In summary, then, individual signs take longer to produce than individual words, probably reflecting the relatively large muscle movements and large spaces involved. Nonetheless, sign manages to convey propositions just as quickly as does spoken language by taking advantage of some of the unique properties of the visual mode. In particular, space is used in a structured way, signs are modulated in rule-governed ways to convey differences in meaning, and facial expressions are used systematically as an integral part of the message.

Tool for memory. In our discussion of memory among hearing persons, we found that coding in working memory is predominantly articulatory-acoustic. Even when presented with visual stimuli, people usually encode them in terms of their labels. Evidence for this comes from the fact that the errors usually reflect articulatory-acoustic confusions. On the other hand, such articulatory-acoustic coding appears to play little role in long-term memory, which is characterized more by semantic coding. For example, if hearing adults are given a list of words to free recall, they always show categorical clustering based on the meaning of the words, but they rarely group the words on the basis of articulatory-acoustic similarity (Dolinsky, 1972). Thus, for the hearing individual, speech seems to play a special role as a tool for working memory, but not for long-term memory.

Locke and Locke (1971) studied deaf signers' short-term memory for letter strings and Bellugi and Siple (1974) studied deaf signers' short-term memory for printed words. Both found that the signers' memory errors reflected formational parameters of signs. Typically the incorrect item recalled differed from the sign for the original item in just one formational parameter. In other words, even though the stimuli in these studies were letters and printed words, the error patterns were based on the similarity of the corresponding signs, suggesting that the deaf had used the formational parameters as a working memory code.

What about long-term memory among the deaf? Liben, Nowell, and Posnansky (1978) presented deaf subjects with a list of 16 signs which they were later to free recall. The lists were constructed so that there were four sets of four signs that had very similar formational properties. Liben and her colleagues reasoned that if formational properties of the sign are used to organize long-term memory, then signs of similar form should be clustered together in recall. In fact, Liben et al. found no evidence of spontaneous clustering on the basis of formational parameters. To the contrary, the signers clustered together items with similar *meaning*. This, of course, is exactly the pattern we see with hearing individuals.

These studies suggest, then, that language plays a remarkably similar role in memory, regardless of whether the language is auditory or visual. In both cases, the articulatory features of the language serve as the major means of encoding in working memory, but such surface features are of little importance in the organization of long-term memory which relies heavily upon semantic coding.

The heightened use of sign. Although language most frequently serves very pragmatic functions, a universal characteristic of spoken language is that it serves other, lighter yet higher purposes as well. We play with language, as it were, in both wit and poetry. Klima and Bellugi (1979) have termed this the "heightened use of language."

They point out that in wit and poetry we exploit the regularities of form, function, and meaning to create expressions with multiple levels of meaning. As they put it (1979, p. 318):

> To be significant and meaningful, such artful manipulations and distortions must stand out against a background of recognized regularities. Thus, how language is used in wit and poetry can inform us about the psychological reality of abstract linguistic constructs and about the awareness, on the part of language users, of regularities in the language.

Bellugi and Klima have noted that both wit and poetry occur in sign language, just as in spoken, though their exact form is modified by the modality. Consider wit. In spoken language, plays on words and puns call upon the *sound* of the language. Plays on signs call upon the *visual form* of the language. Such plays on signs abound and often evoke laughter in the signing participants. Just as hearing persons enjoy constructing tongue-twisters, so deaf persons have their finger-fumblers. Puns occur in sign language, but not as frequently as in spoken, probably because there are fewer signs than words that have more than one meaning. One frequent kind of word play involves the blending of signs to form new name signs for individuals. Usually name signs are coined within a group by taking the handshape corresponding to the initial of the person's name in English and arbitrarily choosing a movement and location for the handshape. However, sometimes epithets are formed by combining the letter handshape with a sign referring to some special characteristic of the person. For example, even before the Watergate scandal, deaf people had a name sign for Nixon, consisting of the letter N made across the chin with a brushing motion. The latter corresponds to the ASL sign for LIAR. Thus the deaf had their own way of calling the former president "Tricky Dick." (Klima & Bellugi, 1979, p. 331).

Poetry in sign language must, of course, take a different form than it takes in spoken language, but the principles are the same. The equivalent to June, moon, and croon can be seen in the development of patterned occurrences of signs with similar hand configurations or other parameters. In fact, the members of the National Theater of the Deaf are developing Art Sign, a special form of signing in which the hands simultaneously create signs and designs in space, much like a visual analogue of song. Figure 11–10 shows Bernard Bragg who is a deaf master signer with the National Theater of the Deaf, signing a line from E. E. Cummings, "since feeling is first." In the top strip of the figure Bragg uses regular ASL, but in the bottom strip he uses poetic ASL or Art Sign. The Art Sign version employs repetitive movements and patterned spatial effects that are reminiscent of the rhyming and alliteration we find in spoken poetry.

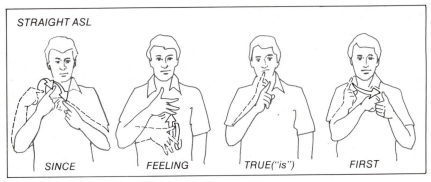

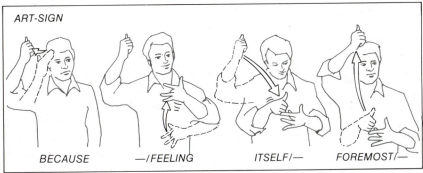

Figure 11–10. A comparison of straight ASL and Art-Sign versions of E. E. Cummings' line "since feeling is first." (After Klima & Bellugi, 1979. Copyright 1979 by Harvard University Press. Reprinted by permission.)

Thus, not only does sign language serve the pragmatic functions of communication and remembering, just as does speech, but it is also used in a playful, language-conscious manner by its users. Its form and function become objects of play and of heightened expression. The wit and poetry humans produce is not tied to a particular sensory modality.

Summary: Sign language. The similarities between spoken and sign language are remarkable. Both are structured, acquired with little necessity for teaching, and exhibit left-hemisphere dominance. Further both serve similar functions in that they convey propositions at equivalent rates, serve similar roles in working memory, and serve as the basis for wit and poetry. These similarities suggest that the characteristics of language reflect some underlying properties of the human mind that are universal for any medium of communication.

CHAPTER SUMMARY

This chapter studied two kinds of language by eye, the printed word, which is derived from oral language, and ASL an independent visual-gestural language. We examined two issues about reading. The first concerned the role of speech recoding, defined as the transformation of printed words into any type of speech based code. According to the speech recoding access hypothesis, speech recoding is necessary in order for a word to access its conceptual node in long-term memory, whereas the alternative direct visual access hypothesis proposes that a direct visual route to the lexicon is available, though speech encoding is sometimes used. The evidence we considered indicates that speech recoding is not necessary for lexical access, but it may be important in reading because it facilitates working memory processing.

The second issue about reading concerned the nature of individual differences in information processing that distinguish good from poor readers. We found that so far, research has suggested three aspects of information processing that differentiate these groups. First, among young children learning to read, the more skilled readers are more likely to use phonemic coding in working memory. Second, college students who are superior readers have larger working memory capacity than average readers. Third, college students who are good readers are faster at encoding letters than are slower readers. We do not yet understand the relations among these three differences, nor do we know whether they cause the observed differences in reading skill.

Analyses of American Sign Language are particularly important because they provide an opportunity to ask: to what extent are the characteristics of spoken language due simply to the modality in which it is processed, and to what extent are they due instead to underlying cognitive processes that are independent of modality? The similarities between sign language and oral languages are extensive. Individual signs (like words and phonemes) have internal structure and sequences of signs, like spoken sentences, have grammatical structure. Thus, sign language, like spoken language, is organized hierarchically. Furthermore, sign language acquisition is similar to the acquisition of oral language, and both appear to be processed primarily in the left cerebral hemisphere. Sign language also serves functions similar to spoken language in that it conveys propositions at a similar rate, serves as a tool for working memory, and is used in heightened ways including wit and poetry.

SUGGESTED READING

We have considered only a small corner of the extensive literature on reading. The best place to begin further study would be the text by

Gibson and Levin (1975) entitled *The Psychology of Reading*. There are also a number of recent edited volumes that contain articles on many different topics. These include *Basic Processes in Reading: Perception and Comprehension* edited by LaBerge and Samuels (1977), *Cognitive Processes in Comprehension* edited by Just and Carpenter (1977), and *Toward a Psychology of Reading* edited by Reber and Scarborough (1977). There are also many review articles in journals that concern themselves with specific topics. You might look up articles by Bradshaw (1975) on several issues, Baron (1978) on the word-superiority effect, Coltheart (1978) on lexical access, Jorm (1979) on dyslexia, and Kintsch and Van Dijk (1978) on text comprehension.

A few years ago it was difficult to find any information at all on the psychological aspects of sign language, but now there are a number of excellent and fascinating sources. The best general source is the wonderful book by Klima and Bellugi (1979) entitled *The Signs of Language*. This book contains both new material and republications of a number of previous articles. Harlan Lane has published a fascinating account of the history of the education of the deaf and of sign language in his book *The Wild Boy of Aveyron*. A number of recent edited volumes contain interesting papers on a wide range of topics within sign language. These include the book edited by Friedman (1977) entitled *On the Other Hand: New Perspectives on American Sign Language* which focuses on linguistic concerns, the book edited by Liben (1978) entitled *Deaf Children: Developmental Perspectives,* the book by Kavanagh and Cutting (1975) called *The Role of Speech in Language,* and the volume edited by Siple (1978) called *Understanding Language Through Sign Language Research*. Finally, almost everyone has heard of the recent attempts to teach chimps gestures similar to those used in ASL. It would be difficult to find a topic in which there is a more heated debate. On the one side are those (including the Gardners) who argue that the chimps are learning at least the rudiments of a language, and on the other are those (such as Terrace, Petitto, and Seidenberg) who argue that the chimps have not yet demonstrated behavior that should be termed linguistic. The recent volume edited by Peng (1978) entitled *Sign Language and Language Acquisition in Man and Ape* has a number of articles that stress the similarities between chimp and human signing, whereas the review articles by Petitto and Seidenberg (1979) and Seidenberg and Petitto (1979) present cogent criticisms of the chimp research. Try reading some of this literature to see which argument you find more convincing.

Thought FOUR

Problem Solving

12

FOOD FOR THOUGHT

Begin by trying to solve the recreational problems contained in Table 12–1. As you work on them, take special notice of the strategies you use. If possible, give a few of the problems to a friend or two and ask them to talk aloud as they work. Did they approach the problems in the same way you did?

THINKING: PROBLEM SOLVING, REASONING, AND CONCEPTUAL THINKING

How does *thinking*, the topic that will occupy us in this last section of the book, differ from the topics of *remembering* and *comprehending language* that formed the focus of the earlier sections? The person who has never studied cognitive psychology is likely to think that the distinctions are clear; remembering and comprehending seem to be more passive than those activities we usually call "thinking." Remembering appears to involve only storing away something that has been experienced and then reproducing it upon later demand. Comprehending language appears to require taking in that which is heard or read, and looking up its meaning in memory. In contrast, the activities we term thinking seem to require that the thinker go beyond the information given, i.e, that the thinker create or discover a novel solution.

Yet, if we define thinking as "going beyond the information given," then one of the major points of this book has been that both remembering and comprehending language involve a great deal of thinking. We saw that remembering involves construction, some of it intentional (as when you try to figure out what you must have been doing on a particular day several years ago), but much of it unintentional (as when you try to recall exactly what you saw during an accident or what was said in a conversation). Similarly, we saw that the person attempting to comprehend language must make inferences about the speaker's meanings, indeed even about the particular sounds the speaker produced, since there is a great deal of ambiguity in the acoustic string itself. Thus, the earlier chapters should have convinced you that both remembering and comprehending language involve thinking, or going beyond the information given. On the other hand, thinking would be impossible without memory. If we lacked working memory, then we would not be able to hold a problem in mind long enough to solve it. If we lacked long-term memory, then we would not have the record of past experience which forms the basis for solving our current problems.

Given these intimate relations among memory, language, and thought, you should keep in mind that this section does not represent a major break from the earlier sections. We will find that theories of thinking are similar to the theories of memory and language we have discussed previously. The same characteristics of human cognition that we have stressed in earlier chapters, such as our limited capacity working memory and our difficulties in retrieving information from long-term memory, are reflected in thinking.

Within cognitive psychology, it is customary to break down the topic of thinking into three closely related areas: problem solving, reasoning, and conceptual thinking. We will follow this organization here, concentrating in this chapter on the more general topic of problem solving and then turning in the next chapters to the more specific kinds of problem solving reflected in logical reasoning and conceptual thinking.

PROBLEMS

There are many different kinds of problems, including many kinds of recreational problems of the sort contained in Table 12–1, career and school oriented problems (such as the problem of how to get promoted or the problem of how to study for a test), personal problems (such as the problem of who to marry or whether to have a child), and scientific problems (such as how to find a cure for cancer or how to prove a particular theorem). Though there are important differences among these problems, there are three characteristics that hold in all cases in which a person is faced with what we would call a *problem*. First, there is some *initial state* in which the person begins. Second, there is some *goal state* that is *different from the initial state* and which the person wishes to achieve. Third, the actions that are necessary to convert the initial state into the goal state are *not immediately obvious.*

If all three of these conditions are present, then we would usually judge that the person is faced with a problem, but if only a subset of the conditions are present we would not. For example, consider the case of a person who wishes to move from his present position in a room (initial state) to the other side of the room (goal state). Even though there are initial and goal states which are different from each other, and even though the person wishes to achieve the goal, we would not judge that a problem exists because one defining condition for a problem is lacking; the means of getting from the initial state to the goal state is obvious, so no problem exists. Of course, under unusual circumstances such a state of affairs might represent a true problem. For example, the person in question might be unable to walk

TABLE 12–1.   Problems to Solve.

1. *Notched-checkerboard problem.* You are given a checkerboard and 32 dominoes. Each domino covers exactly two adjacent squares on the board. Thus, the 32 dominoes can cover all 64 squares of the checkerboard. Now suppose two squares are cut off at diagonally opposite corners of the board (see the diagram below). Is it possible to place 31 dominoes on the board so that all of the 62 remaining squares are covered? If so, show how it can be done. If not prove it impossible.

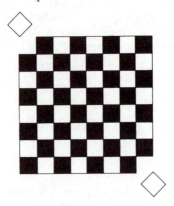

2. *Six-arrow problem.* You are given six arrows in a row, the left three pointing up, and the right three pointing down. The goal is to transform these arrows into an alternating sequence such that the left-most arrow points up, the next arrow to it points down, the next up, then down, then up, and then down. The actions allowed are to simultaneously invert (turn upside down) any two adjacent arrows. Note that you cannot invert one arrow at a time but must invert two arrows at a time, and the two arrows must be adjacent. The given and goal states are illustrated below. Achieve the solution using the minimum number of actions (inversions of adjacent pairs).

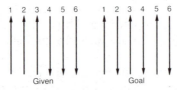

3. *Men-boys-raft problem.* Nine men and two boys want to cross a river, using an inflatable raft that will carry either one man or the two boys. How many times must the boat cross the river in order to accomplish this goal? (A round trip equals two crossings.)

4. *Bowling-pin-reversal problem.* Six-year-old Heather Phillips set up the ten pins for her bowling game at the end of the hall in a manner exactly opposite to the correct configuration. Although Heather is given to childish reversal errors of this sort when she forgets to put on her thinking cap, she is actually a budding mathematical genius. So, upon being informed of her error, Heather ran down the hall, and, by moving just three pins, was able to reverse the configuration from the given state to the goal state, as illustrated following. How did she do it? (The exact placement of the pins on

TABLE 12–1. Problems to Solve. (Continued)

the floor is not important, so long as the relative placement of the pins with respect to each other is correct.)

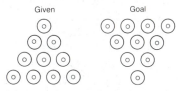

5. *Nim-game problem.* Fifteen pennies are placed on a table in front of two players. Each player is allowed to remove at least one penny but not more than five pennies at his turn. The players alternate turns, each removing from one to five pennies n number of turns, until one player takes the last penny on the table, and wins all 15 pennies. Is there a method of play that will guarantee victory? If so, what is it?

6. *Coin-rearrangement problem.* You are given six coins arranged in two rows as shown below on the left, so that each coin touches the coins immediately above or below it and to the left or right of it. Specify a procedure for moving exactly two coins so as to achieve the hexagonal arrangement shown below on the right.

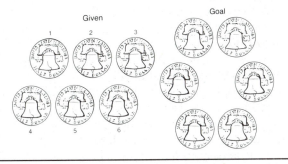

From HOW TO SOLVE PROBLEMS: ELEMENTS OF A THEORY OF PROBLEMS AND PROBLEM SOLVING by Wayne A. Wickelgren. W. H. Freeman and Company. Copyright © 1974.

across the room either because of a physical handicap or because the floor between the initial and goal states is covered with wet wax.

Well-defined and ill-defined problems. It is helpful to think of all possible problems as occupying some point on a continuum. At one end of this continuum are well-defined problems and at the other end are ill-defined problems. The problems contained in Table 12–1 are all toward the well-defined end of this continuum, whereas many scientific, personal, and artistic problems are ill-defined. Well-defined problems differ from ill-defined ones in at least two important ways. First, for well-defined problems the criteria that should be used to decide whether or not the goal has been attained are specified clearly, whereas in ill-defined problems the goal is often vague. Second, for well-defined problems the information necessary to solve the problem is usually specified precisely in the statement of the problem, whereas for ill-defined problems it is often unclear exactly what kind of information is relevant to the problem at hand.

The problems in Table 12–1 are well-defined by both of these criteria. The goal states are defined clearly for each problem, so that it is easy to tell whether or not you have attained them, and the critical information that is needed to solve the problem is contained in the statement of the problem. Contrast these problems with the ill-defined problem of how to decide on the best career for you. There is no clearly specified way to decide whether or not you have hit upon the best solution. Furthermore, it isn't even clear what kind of additional information you need to collect in order for you to solve the problem. In fact, in this and many other cases of real-life dilemmas, part of the problem is that of specifying the goal state more precisely and determining what kind of additional information you need. For example, you must decide what you mean by the "best career." Is it the one that will bring you the most wealth, or the one that will give you plenty of time to pursue other interests such as raising a family? Having settled on the criteria you judge to be important, you will be in a better position to seek out the kind of information you need in order to enable you to attain a solution.

When psychologists have studied problem solving, they have almost always used well-defined problems, primarily because they are easier to study objectively. For well-defined problems, it is possible to figure out an optimal strategy and to determine whether individuals discover it, and it is easy to determine whether or not the person has solved the problem. Psychologists usually assume that the major characteristics of problem solving will be the same for both well- and ill-defined problems, since the same limitations and strengths of the human information processing system must come to bear on both (Simon, 1973). Nonetheless, this assumption remains to be tested empirically.

STAGES OF PROBLEM SOLVING

We all spend a great deal of time solving, or attempting to solve, problems. This is particularly true for scientists, mathematicians, and artists, who spend virtually all their working hours trying to come up with novel solutions to vexing questions. Over the ages, many scientists and mathematicians have become so fascinated with the mental processes involved in problem solving that they have written articles and books describing their introspections. It is remarkable that the introspections of all these authors have a great deal in common. One striking commonality is that most great thinkers argue that solving a problem involves a series of *stages*.

Polya's stages and our overview theory. We will consider the series of four stages described by the mathematics teacher Polya in his classic book *How to Solve It* (1957), but we will translate them into the framework of the overview theory. The advantage of doing this translation is that it shows how problem solving is related closely to both memory and to language comprehension. Therefore, we will find that what we have already learned about how people remember and how they process language has important implications for how they go about solving problems. This translation is illustrated in Figure 12–1.

In terms of our overview theory, Polya's first stage of *understanding the problem* corresponds to *encoding the problem in working memory*. That is, the person reads or listens to the problem and converts it into a set of propositions to be held in working memory. The problem is translated from its verbatim form to a statement of "I know ..., and I want to find out ..., and I am only allowed to use the following actions ..." Of course, since working memory has a severely limited capacity, if the problem solver must rely solely upon memory while solving the problem, then he/she is in danger of only remembering part of the problem, thereby leading to errors in problem solv-

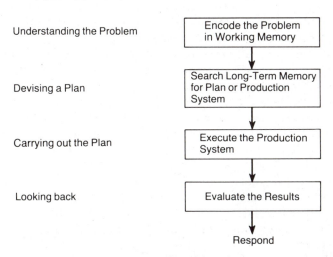

POLYA'S STAGES   INFORMATION PROCESSING TRANSLATION

Understanding the Problem — Encode the Problem in Working Memory

Devising a Plan — Search Long-Term Memory for Plan or Production System

Carrying out the Plan — Execute the Production System

Looking back — Evaluate the Results

Respond

Figure 12–1. Polya's (1957) four stages of problem solving viewed from the perspective of our overview theory.

ing. However, even if the person is allowed to rely upon paper and pencil throughout problem solving, the limits of working memory capacity still place constraints on solution. In order to think about something, we need to activate its representation in working memory. Therefore, even though we may be able to store a large amount of information about the problem on a piece of paper in front of us, we can still only think simultaneously about a very small fraction of that information (i.e., a few chunks). Thus, working memory places constraints on human problem solving.

Even though the focus in this first stage of problem solving is on encoding the problem in working memory, long-term memory (and hence the person's past experience) comes into play as well. As the overview model in Figure 1–2 depicts, encoding in working memory requires that the information be looked up in long-term memory. In fact, since many problems are presented linguistically, this stage of problem solving often involves language comprehension. As we saw in Chapter 9, this means that the person often draws inferences in constructing the working memory encoding. The point, then, is that even in this initial stage of problem solving, the contents of long-term memory influence the encoding of the problem, and this influence is often not obvious to the person who is solving the problem.

In our overview model, Polya's second stage entitled *devising a plan* is one in which the person *searches long-term memory* for a plan for solution, or to find information that will help him construct a plan for solution. This plan may be thought of as a production system of the sort we discussed in Chapter 6. Unlike the previous stage in which the role of long-term memory is largely unconscious and automatic, in this stage the person consciously attempts to retrieve potentially useful information. Sometimes this search will lead the person to find a very similar problem he solved in the past, in which case he might try to use the same production system that succeeded before. In other cases, it may be necessary to construct a new production system. Viewing this planning stage in light of our overview model suggests that what we have learned about long-term memory in earlier chapters is likely to influence problem solving as well. All of us have long-term memories that store an essentially infinite amount of information, only a small part of which is relevant for any given problem. The problem solver's task is to use the representation he has constructed in working memory to provide retrieval cues to help him find relevant stored experiences and knowledge. We would expect to find, then, that people often fail to retrieve the information that will help them solve a given problem, even though this information is stored in long-term memory.

In our overview model, Polya's third stage of *carrying out the plan* can be viewed as *executing the production system* which the person found or developed in Stage 3. If the production system has few steps and is worked out in detail, then this stage can be completed quickly and with few errors. However, if the production system involves a large number of steps, or if it leaves the actions to be taken under certain conditions vague, then this stage can be both time consuming and error prone.

Finally, in our overview model, Polya's fourth stage of *looking back* can be thought of as a stage of *evaluating the results,* in which the problem solver compares the solution with the representation of the problem in working memory. He asks whether he has gotten from the initial state to the goal state using the actions that were specified as legal. In addition, the problem solver may search long-term memory to see if the production system used to solve this problem might be useful for others as well. If so, the person may store away retrieval cues that will enable him to find this production system for future similar problems. Of course, sometimes the evaluation stage leads the person to conclude that he has not solved the problem adequately. Then he must go back to an earlier stage, and it is likely that the stage to which he returns will depend upon what he judges to be the source of the inadequacy.

All four of the stages probably come into play any time someone solves a problem, but their relative importance varies with the type of problem and with the previous experience of the problem solver.

PHENOMENA OF PROBLEM SOLVING

As you might suspect, it is extremely difficult to make broad statements about the characteristics of problem solving, because individuals vary widely in the skill with which they solve problems and, to complicate matters further, problems themselves vary greatly. Nonetheless, over the last century or so analyses of problem solving have revealed that there are a number of phenomena which virtually all problem solvers exhibit at one time or another. We will consider three of the more important of these. First, however, take a few minutes to try to solve the following problems. The first is one of Luchins' (1942) classic water-pitcher problems:

> **Your goal is to measure out exactly 100 units of water from an unlimited source of water. The only tools you have to do this are three pitchers, Pitcher A which will hold 21 units of water, Pitcher B which holds 127 units, and Pitcher C which holds 3 units of water. Describe the sequence of filling and pouring that would be necessary in order to measure out the goal amount.**

Problem	Pitcher A	Pitcher B	Pitcher C	Goal
1	21	127	3	100
2	14	46	5	22
3	18	43	10	5
4	7	42	6	23
5	20	57	4	29
6	23	49	3	20
7	15	39	3	18

Figure 12–2. Luchins' (1942) water-pitcher problems.

After you have solved this problem, then attempt to solve the additional Luchins problems shown in Figure 12–2. You have alreaey solved Problem 1 in that figure, so you should now solve Problems 2 through 7 in turn, jotting down your solution to each as you go. We'll discuss the solutions in a few minutes.

Now try a different, also classic problem, studied first by Duncker (1945). Imagine that you are presented with the objects depicted in the picture in Figure 12–3. Your goal is to mount the candle vertically on a nearby plywood wall, so that it will act as a lamp. How could you do so, using only the materials shown in the picture? Work on this problem for a while. If you cannot solve it in its present form, turn to Figure 12–4. Can you solve the problem now?

Rigidity. Both of these problems illustrate different forms of the first phenomenon of problem solving we will discuss, that of rigidity. This refers to the fact that people often fail to see adequate solutions for problems, because they fixate on only one way of viewing the prob-

Figure 12–3. One version of Duncker's (1945) famous problem. Figure out how to mount the candle vertically on a plywood wall, so that it will act as a lamp.

lem. One kind of rigidity occurs when we continue to use (or attempt to use) a method of solution that has worked in the past, even though there is a better way of solving the problem. This kind of rigidity is often called *response set*, since it involves continuing to use a response that worked in other situations. When we exhibit such response set, then, we are the victims of habit.

Consider the series of water-pitcher problems you solved a few minutes ago. The best solution to Problem 1, as you probably figured out, is that you should first fill Pitcher B (127 units). Then, using the water in Pitcher B, fill Pitcher A once (21 units) discarding that amount. Then using the remaining water in Pitcher B (now $127 - 21 = 106$ units), fill and discard the contents of Pitcher C (which holds 3 units) twice. This leaves $106 - 3 - 3 = 100$ units, or the goal amount, in Pitcher B. You probably found that this same pattern of $B - A - 2C$ works equally well for the next few problems, and in fact, most people continue to use it throughout all 7 problems. If you continued to do so even for Problems 6 and 7, though, you actually used an inefficient method for these problems, for they are much simpler. Both can be solved using only A and C. Virtually everyone notices the simple solution for Problems 6 and 7 if these problems are presented first (as you can verify by presenting these to a friend), but the previous experience with the more complicated problems often blinds people to this simple solution. We all find ourselves victims of such rigidity at one time or another. I have noticed it particularly when I am doing computer programming. Having developed a technique for performing some operation in one program, I then use it again in later programs. More than once an alert assistant has pointed out a simpler method that works for the problem at hand.

A different kind of rigidity is often referred to as *perceptual set*, since it refers to a tendency to perceive or encode a problem from only one perspective. One kind of perceptual set often appears when people try to solve Duncker's (1945) candle problem in Figure 12–3. The correct solution to this problem is to empty the box containing the tacks, then use a couple of tacks to attach the box to the wall to form a platform. The candle can then be burned to form a few drops of wax which can be used to affix the candle firmly to the platform. As presented in Figure 12–3, this problem is often quite difficult to solve. The major difficulty seems to be that people fail to see the box as having a possible function other than the one it is already serving (i.e., that of a container for the tacks). Evidence that this is the difficulty comes from the fact that people usually solve the problem much more readily when presented with the problem in the form shown in Figure 12–4 (Duncker, 1945; Adamson, 1952). Here the box is not serving any particular function, and people have less difficulty generating novel functions for the box, in this case as a platform.

Figure 12–4. A second version of Duncker's (1945)
famous problem, designed to help the problem solver overcome functional fixity.

Duncker (1945) termed this tendency to perceive objects as having only their most common or most recent function *functional fixedness*. Another classic problem which reveals it is one in which the
person must attempt to tie together two strings which are hanging
from the ceiling, but are too far apart to be grasped simultaneously
(Maier, 1930; 1931; Birch & Rabinowitz, 1951). The correct solution is
to tie a set of pliers that is also in the room to the end of one of the
strings, forming a pendulum, and then to swing the pendulum over
to the other string. Again most people have difficulty divorcing the
pliers from their usual function and seeing them as a pendulum weight.

Given what we learned about memory and language comprehension in earlier chapters, it is not surprising that people demonstrate
functional fixedness. Recall that when an object or a word is perceived and activated in working memory, at least some components
of the meaning of the item are looked up and activated automatically.
Thus, the encoding of a word is likely to bring to mind its most salient typical characteristics. Seeing a pair of pliers would lead to activation of the concept node corresponding to pliers, and through spreading activation, this is likely to activate memory about habitual uses of
the tool, but unlikely to lead to such novel uses as a pendulum weight.

Functional fixedness is not the only kind of perceptual set people exhibit. In fact, it is quite common for people to encode a problem
in one way, and to persist in viewing the problem in this way even
though a slightly different encoding might enable immediate solution.
Try to solve the following verbal problem taken from Posner's text
(1973, p. 150):

Two train stations are fifty miles apart. At 2PM one Saturday afternoon two trains start toward each other, one from each station. Just as the trains pull out of the stations, a bird springs into the air in front of the first train and flies ahead to the front of the second train. When the bird reaches the second train it turns back and flies toward the first train. The bird continues to do this until the trains meet.

If both trains travel at the rate of twenty-five miles per hour and the bird flies at a hundred miles per hour, how many miles will the bird have flown before the trains meet?

If you encode this problem in terms of the bird's flight, then it is a very difficult problem indeed, for you need to figure out a way of calculating how far the bird flies on each of his trips. On the other hand, the problem becomes trivial if you focus on the *time* the bird will by flying. Since it will take the trains one hour to meet each other, the bird will be flying exactly one hour or one hundred miles.

Now try the visual problem shown in Figure 12–5, also presented in Posner (1973, p. 151), though it originally appeared in Kohler (1969). This problem is difficult as long as you focus on using the triangle *d, x, l* to calculate *l*. However, it is very easy if instead you look for another line that is equal in length to *l*. You will notice immediately that if *d* and *x* are viewed as the sides of a rectangle and *l* as one of the diagonals in the rectangle, then the other diagonal in the rectangle must be the same length as *l*, and this new diagonal is also the radius of the circle. The problem is now solved, since you know the radius of the circle already.

Of course, the two problems were set up deliberately to lead you to encode the problem in the least useful way. The point is, however, that people tend to adopt one encoding and they then have difficulty seeing the problem in a different way.

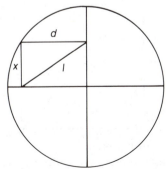

Determine the Length of *l* given the Radius of the Circle

Figure 12–5. Kohler's (1969) problem.

We have seen, then, that one of the major phenomena of human problem solving is *rigidity*—the tendency to adopt one mode of approach to a problem and to persist with this approach even though it is inefficient or fails to lead to a solution. Rigidity reflects two general characteristics of human cognition which we have stressed again and again throughout the book. These are our limited working memory capacity and our tendency to go beyond the information given. Our limited working memory capacity leads us to focus on viewing the problem one way at a time. This tendency to see the world from only one angle at once has an analogy in the domain of reversible perceptual illusions. Three classics are shown in Figure 12–6. Most people

Figure 12–6. Three classic reversible figures, exemplifying our tendency to view the world from only one perspective at a time. Illusion (a) can be seen as either a young woman or an old one, (b) as either a vase or two profiles, and (c) is the famous reversible Necker cube.

can see each of these in only one way at a time, and having established one view, it is often hard to switch back again.

Rigidity also reflects our ubiquitous tendency to go beyond the information given. Although precategorical, uninterpreted information may reside in sensory storage for a second or so, at all later stages of information processing, present stimulation is interpreted in light of past experience, even though we are often not aware of it. We saw that the meaning of words and objects is activated automatically when the items are encoded into working memory. In addition, we saw both in our discussion of long-term memory and in our consideration of language comprehension, that people draw implicit assumptions and that the drawing of such inferences is absolutely necessary if communication is to proceed. Nonetheless, this tendency to draw implicit inferences can lead to the manifestations of rigidity we see. For example, recall that in order to interpret the speech of others we must assume certain conversational postulates, e.g., that the speaker is being relevant and concise. Of course, it is this very assumption that enables us to be fooled by the superfluous information in the bird flying problem. We unconsciously assume that all the information presented is relevant, thereby leading us to incorporate it in our representation of the problem. Even when we expect to be tricked, it is often difficult to overcome our tendency to make implicit assumptions.

It is important to realize that our tendency toward rigidity in problem solving has, for the most part, more positive than negative consequences. Usually the responses we have used to solve similar problems in the past, and the initial way in which we encode the stimulus situation are the best, in that they lead to the most rapid solution with the least effort. Our tendency to be rigid is only problematic when we are faced with problems that require novel, insightful solutions. When we attempt to solve such problems, we need to be aware of our tendency to be rigid and we need to devise ways of overcoming this rigidity. We will discuss how to do so in the last section of this chapter.

Incubation and insight. We use the term *incubation* to refer to the increase in likelihood of solving a problem that results from placing a delay or rest interval between two periods of intense work on the problem. Everyone has experienced at least one form of incubation—that which often accompanies the tip-of-the-tongue phenomenon we discussed earlier in the book. People often struggle to find the sought after name or fact, finally give up in frustration, and then a few minutes (or sometimes hours) later, the elusive information pops into consciousness. In fact, just about everyone has noticed this kind of incubation, for people often say, "Oh well, it'll come to me if I think about something else."

If you have ever had occasion to work on difficult problems, either of the recreational or real-life kind, you have probably experienced at least a few instances of incubation. Scientists, inventors, mathematicians, and artists often report instances of incubation (cf. Koestler, 1964). One well-known account comes from the mathematician Poincaire, who described how he came to one of his important discoveries. In 1929, Poincaire wrote:

> Then I turned my attention to the study of some arithmetical questions apparently without much success and without a suspicion of any connection with my preceding researches. Disgusted with my failure, I went to spend a few days at the seaside, and thought of something else. One morning, walking on the bluff, the idea came to me, with just the same characteristics of brevity, suddenness, and immediate certainty, that the arithmetic transformations of indeterminate ternary quadratic forms were identical with those of non-Euclidean geometry. (p. 388) . . . It never happens that the unconscious work gives us the result of a somewhat long calculation all *made*, where we have only to apply fixed rules. . . . All one may hope from these inspirations, fruits of unconscious work, is a point of departure for such calculations. As for the calculations themselves, they must be made in the second period of conscious work, that which follows the inspiration, that in which one verifies the results of this inspiration and deduces their consequences. The rules of these calculations are strict and complicated. They require discipline, attention, will, and therefore consciousness. (p. 394)

Poincaire's account includes several observations that are common to most reported instances of incubation. First, it makes clear that incubation occurs *only after* the thinker has already devoted considerable time and mental effort to the problem at hand. In terms of our information processing model in Figure 12–1, the person has already struggled with Stages 1 and 2, attempting to come up with a way of representing the problem and searching again and again for an algorithm or heuristic for solving the problem. A second general characteristic described in Poincaire's account is that incubation almost always involves an "aha" kind of feeling, a sudden burst of insight which is accompanied by a feeling of certainty that this new idea is correct. The third and final point to note in Poincaire's description is that, for complex problems at least, after the moment of insight there is usually still a great deal of work to be done. In terms of the four stage model, the insight gained following incubation has offered us a new way of representing the problem (Stage 1) or perhaps a plan for solution (Stage 2), but usually the steps of carrying out the solution (Stage 3) and verification of the solution (Stage 4) remain to be done.

Intuitively, then, incubation is a salient phenomenon of problem solving. Nonetheless, incubation rests upon much more shakey ground than does the phenomenon of rigidity. That is, virtually all psychologists who have studied thinking will agree that rigidity is a well-documented phenomenon. It is easy to demonstrate it in the laboratory, and, in fact, to study the kinds of conditions that make it more or less likely to occur. In contrast, incubation has been extremely difficult to demonstrate unequivocally under the controlled conditions of the laboratory, although a few brave psychologists have attempted to do so (e.g., Dominowski & Jenrick, 1972; Fulgosi & Guildford, 1968; Murray & Denny, 1969; Silveira, 1971). Some of these attempts have revealed evidence for incubation and some have not. Of course, the failures to demonstrate incubation do *not* prove that it doesn't exist. It is just as likely that incubation does occur, but that the conditions of the experiments were not sufficient or appropriate for producing it. It is difficult to set up in the laboratory the kind of intense, almost driven work on a particular problem that usually characterizes the instances of incubation as reported by scientists and inventors.

You might ask, then, why is it necessary to demonstrate incubation in the laboratory at all? The reason is that if we cannot do so, we can never be sure that our introspections are correct. As the definition at the beginning of this discussion indicates, the notion of incubation implies that we are *more* likely to solve a problem after a rest period than after continued work on the problem. Unfortunately, in anecdotal accounts of incubation we can never be sure that the solution would not have occurred to the person even if he had continued to work on the problem. Would Poincaire, for example, have had his flash of insight even if he had continued to work instead of going to the shore? In addition to this nagging question about the reality of incubation, the other reason for wishing to induce it in the laboratory is that we could then study more carefully the conditions under which it is most likely to occur. Then we will be able to explain it theoretically and to help people to induce it when they are trying to solve problems.

Fortunately, there is at least some evidence that incubation can be induced in the laboratory. The most convincing comes from a doctoral dissertation which was conducted at the University of Oregon by Silveira (1971). Silveira presented her subjects with the popular (and difficult) cheap necklace problem that follows:

> **A man had 4 chains, each 3 links long. He wanted to join the 4 chains into a single closed chain. Having a link opened cost 2 cents and having a link closed cost 3 cents. The man had his chains joined into a closed chain for 15 cents. How did he do it?**

Silveira had a control group of subjects work on this problem for about one-half hour and found that only half of that group solved the problem. There were four experimental groups in addition. For the first two experimental groups, a brief period of working on the problem was followed by a break of either one-half hour (short delay) or four hours (long delay). For the second two groups, a longer period of working on the problem was allowed before the short or long delay. If incubation occurred, then the experimental groups should have shown a higher probability of solving the problem than the control group. Silveira found that the two experimental groups who had only worked on the problem briefly before the delay period showed no evidence of incubation, but both groups who had worked on the problem more extensively prior to the break showed clear evidence of enhanced problem solving. Thus, Silveira's results agree with intuition in indicating that incubation occurs *only* following an extended period of working on a problem. *Lesson:* don't count on incubation to enable you to fashion a brilliant term paper if you haven't done the groundwork first.

There are a couple of other things to note about Silveira's results. For one thing, when questioned, her subjects did not report having worked on the problem during the rest period, suggesting (though not establishing beyond the shadow of a doubt) that conscious work on the problem during the rest period is not necessary for incubation to occur. Another aspect of Silveira's findings, however, leads us to wonder whether the incubation she observed in the laboratory is qualitatively different from that observed in anecdotal reports. Silveira asked her subjects to talk aloud as they worked on the problems, and she noticed that the subjects in the groups that showed incubation did not return after the break with a solution in mind. They began much as they had left off, though during the course of this second work period they were quite likely to think of the correct solution. Thus, the sudden "aha" of insight accompanied by a feeling of certainty was lacking in this experiment. We do not know why.

Although we need more demonstrations of incubation under controlled laboratory settings, it is likely that the phenomenon occurs. The final question to be asked about incubation now, then, is what causes it? The first thought you might have is a simple fatigue explanation. That is, pure fatigue might be preventing the person from coming up with a solution and the rest period simply provides a time for rest, so that the individual returns to the problem in a more alert state. Though this explanation undoubtedly has some truth to it, it does not seem adequate in and of itself. In Silveira's experiment both experimental groups that had the four hour break must have been equally rested, yet only one of them (the one that had already put extensive work into the problem) demonstrated incubation.

A definitive explanation of incubation must await further research on the conditions under which it occurs, but the most promising explanation at the moment can be phrased in terms of our overview model and the four stages of problem solving depicted in Figure 12–1. When the person first encounters a difficult problem, he attempts to come up with a useful representation of the problem in working memory, and he then uses this to search for a potential solution, or plan for solution, in long-term memory. This conscious search of long-term memory is guided by the particular retrieval cues suggested by the representation that he has adopted in working memory. If this first representation fails to lead to a solution, the person may attempt to go back and frame the problem in a different way and then to search for clues in long-term memory again. As long as the person concentrates his attention on the problem, however, it is quite likely that each subsequent way in which he views the problem will be constrained by the earlier ways in which he viewed it. If instead, the person attends to something else, an unconscious search and activation of the paths of long-term memory may continue. Since this search is not so constrained by the items in the person's limited attention span, it may be more likely to touch upon promising, but remote paths of memory. In fact, it is possible that sometimes this search is influenced (unbeknownst to the problem solver) by some external event that happens during the incubation period. For example, Maier (1931) demonstrated that subjects often hit upon an insightful "aha" type of solution to the two strings problem we discussed if they are exposed to the experimenter accidentally brushing one of the strings and setting it in motion. It is particularly interesting that most of the people seemed unaware of the fact that this hint helped them. It is possible that many instances of insight are similarly inspired by unconsciously perceived events that happen to occur during the incubation period.

In summary, our overview model suggests that incubation can be explained by postulating that an unconscious search and activation of the pathways continue during the rest period, and since this search is less likely to be constrained by the set the person had developed during the work period, it has a greater chance of leading to a novel insight. This hypothesis remains to be tested rigorously.

Satisficing. There are, of course, many decision points in problem solving. During the stage of encoding, for example, the solver must decide upon an apropriate form of representation. During the search stage he must attempt to develop or find a search plan and when one is found he must decide whether it is adequate for the task at hand. During the looking back or evaluation stage, the person must decide whether the solution he has completed is adequate, or whether he needs to begin all over again.

Herbert A. Simon, of Carnegie Mellon University, has made the important observation that when people make such decisions, they *satisfice* rather than maximize or optimize (cf. Simon 1956; 1979). That is, people accept a choice that is good enough, rather than continuing to search for one that is the best possible. For example, when playing chess, a player satisfices in that he sets some acceptance level as the criterion which a move must meet in order for it to be acceptable, and then he takes the first move that meets this criterion. Our player might decide, for example, that he must find a move that will win at least one pawn. He examines moves until he finds one that will do this, and he then performs the move. Note that he might have found another move that would have had even better results, but he did not attempt to find it. He chose a move that was good enough. Similarly, when making decisions in the practical world, the businessman might decide to make a change in the corporate organization that will yield at least x dollars of profit, and he then searches until he finds such a change, rather than examining all possible changes and then choosing the one that is likely to lead to the greatest increase in profit.

One of the reasons that Simon won the Nobel prize in economics is that he noted that economic theories usually fail to take this human tendency into account. Rather, they assume that humans have a greater capacity than they do for obtaining information from the environment and for performing computations. That is, economic theories have usually assumed erroneously that people (and hence corporations) are optimizers or maximizers when they go about making decisions.

We should not be surprised to find that people tend to be satisficers. Most real world problems have many possible solutions, i.e., there are many different ways in which a term paper could be organized, a marriage partner chosen, or a child raised. In order to find the best possible solution, it would be necessary to consider all such possibilities and to have some reliable way of comparing the relative acceptability of each. This would take so long that we would probably be frozen in indecision forever. In fact, I think the tendency many of us have to put off writing papers (or in my case book chapters) reflects not only laziness, but also a futile attempt at optimizing. I always have the notion that I want to find the *best* organization possible, and I think that if I procrastinate long enough I will have more time to come up with the optimal organization rather than one that is simply satisfactory. Of course, this usually isn't true and, given the existence of deadlines, this kind of procrastination can simply lead to a product that is worse than it would have been had the writer simply looked for an organization that met certain criteria and then plowed ahead working on it carefully.

One reason for our tendency to satisfice, then, is the essentially infinite set of possible solutions that characterizes so many real world problems. Even in the case of simpler problems such as those recreational problems you dealt with at the beginning of the chapter, however, the characteristics of information processing we have discussed throughout the book lead people to satisfice rather than optimize. We have a large, essentially infinite amount of information stored in long-term memory, and the retrieval difficulties that occur so frequently make it difficult to retrieve the most optimal solutions under many circumstances. In addition, we have a limited capacity for processing information, so that we cannot hold many possibilities in mind at once. Therefore, we are well designed to be satisficers, but poorly designed to be maximizers.

Like rigidity, then, we should not view our human tendency to satisfice as a negative characteristic. It is a reasonable trait to possess in the face of an environment with infinite possibilities coupled with a limited capacity attention and working memory span and a large, sometimes unwieldy store of information, some of which may be difficult to retrieve at any given time. Our tendency to satisfice enables us to set up reasonable criteria for making decisions and to avoid being mired forever in the throes of indecision. Simon has referred to our tendency to satisfice as a form of *bounded rationality*, a topic we will explore in more detail in the next chapter on reasoning.

COMPUTER SIMULATION THEORIES OF PROBLEM SOLVING

So far we have seen that introspection and experiments have revealed some general characteristics of problem solving, namely that it may be divided into a series of stages, that people are prone to rigidity, they benefit from incubation, and they tend to satisfice rather than maximize. Further, we have seen how these characteristics may be viewed in light of the information processing system we have studied throughout the book. The characteristics of human cognition that are particularly relevant for understanding problem solving are the capacity limitations of working memory, the storage and retrieval difficulties characteristic of long-term memory, and our ubiquitous tendency to draw inferences, i.e., to go beyond the information given.

We have seen, then, how problem solving fits into the framework of our overview model. Nonetheless, we haven't proposed a specific theory of problem solving. We would like to be able to describe the exact sequence of processes that occurs from the time a problem is presented until the person produces a solution. It is very difficult to do this because people and problems differ so greatly that we cannot hope to predict exactly how an individual will solve a novel problem. Furthermore, problem solving is a complex cognitive activity, so when we theorize about it, it is particularly important that the theory be specified precisely so that it can be disproven if it is incorrect and so we can test whether or not the theory is sufficient to explain problem solving.

As in the case of language comprehension, the most promising kind of theory in the early 1980's involves computer simulation. In the last couple of decades a number of computer simulation theories of problem solving have been published, but we will deal only with one illustrative example, the General Problem Solver (GPS for short) developed by Newell, Shaw, and Simon (1958) at Carnegie Mellon University. I have chosen it because it set the stage for all other computer simulation theories of problem solving and it introduced a way of looking at problem solving which has influenced virtually all problem solving theories since.

The General Problem Solver (GPS) theory. Newell, Shaw, and Simon's GPS theory was first reported in 1958 and a fuller description of the theory and further developments were published in a lengthy book written by Newell and Simon in 1972. Newell, Shaw and Simon attempted to write a computer program that would be capable of solving problems using the same strategies people use. Therefore, in writing their program they took into account what was known about human cognition, and they did not include any strategies or operations that would be possible for the computer, but outside the abilities of the human. In particular, their program was equipped with the equivalent of (1) a limited capacity working memory characterized by rapid storage and retrieval, (2) a large capacity long-term memory characterized by relatively slow storage and retrieval, (3) a serial processor that performs one operation at a time, and (4) a reliance upon heuristics, rather than on algorithms that would require a large number of high speed calculations.

Having decided that they wanted to write a program that would use the heuristics people use, the theorists' next task, of course, was to discover exactly what these heuristics were. In order to do so, Newell and his colleagues collected *verbal protocols,* i.e., they kept records of people talking aloud as they solved problems. Then they transcribed these lengthy records carefully to see if they could find general heuristics that emerged. Thus, rather than conducting experiments in which the number of errors or the time required for solution was the dependent variable, Newell and his colleagues chose verbal reports of problem solvers' on-the-spot introspections. They chose such verbal protocols—an almost unheard of practice in the 1950's—because they believed that they provided more insight into strategies than could the more traditional measures. Newell and his colleagues admitted that people might not be capable of describing everything they do when they solve problems, but they argued it seems reasonable to assume that people can describe at least *some* of the steps they are using, and that their descriptions of these steps can provide clues as to their general strategies.

The GPS program that Newell and his colleagues developed introduced a way of conceptualizing problems that is adopted in most contemporary theories of problem solving. The GPS assumes that the problem solver represents a problem as a *problem space* which consists of a set of nodes, each node corresponding to a *state of knowledge* about the problem. Each *state of knowledge* represents what is known about the solution at a given point in solving the problem. The problem solver begins at some initial state of knowledge which contains what is known about the solution at the beginning, and the solver seeks to convert this initial state into the goal state, which is the state that must be reached in order to solve the problem. The problem solver moves from one state of knowledge to the other by applying *operators*, which are actions that are permitted in order to move from one state to another. Thus, according to GPS, problem solving involves moving through a series of states of knowledge by applying operators. Problem solving, then, requires a constructive search during which the solver builds up a problem space, which leads from the initial to the goal state using a set of allowed operators.

What strategies or heuristics do people use when deciding which operators to apply? On the basis of their verbal protocols, Newell and his colleagues argued that a general problem solving heuristic that people use is *means-end analysis*. Means-end analysis involves a search for operations that will reduce the difference between the present state of knowledge and the goal state. In particular, means-end analysis involves the following series of steps: (1) set up a goal, (2) look for a difference between the current state and the goal state, (3) look for a method to decrease or eliminate the difference, (4) set as a subgoal the application of that method, and (5) if necessary, apply means-end analysis to get to the subgoal. The method is most clearly illustrated in the following quote from Newell and Simon (1972).

> I want to take my son to nursery school. What's the difference between what I have and what I want? One of distance. What changes distance? My automobile. My automobile won't work. What is needed to make it work? A new battery. What has new batteries? An auto repair shop. I want the repair shop to put in a new battery; but the shop doesn't know I need one. What is the difficulty? One of communication. What allows communication? A telephone . . . and so on.

Thus, the main heuristic used in GPS involves setting up goals and subgoals. In fact, this strategy can be expressed very precisely as a production system, i.e. as a set of if-then pairs of the sort we discussed in Anderson's ACT model in Chapter 6. GPS's strategies, like those of most contemporary theories of problem solving are stored in the computer's memory as productions.

The best way to consider how GPS operates is to consider a specific example. One kind of problem that GPS can solve is the hobbits and orcs (sometimes called the missionaries and cannibals) problem. Work on it yourself for a few minutes now.

> **There are three hobbits and three orcs on one side of a river, and you wish to transport them all to the other side. They have a boat that is capable of carrying a total of two hobbits and/or orcs at one time. Since orcs eat hobbits, it is critical that hobbits never be outnumbered by orcs at any time, on either side of the river. Describe a sequence of crossings that will transport all six individuals across the river without endangering the hobbits.**

In order to convey this (or any other problem) to the GPS, it is necessary to provide it with four kinds of information. First, the program must be provided with information regarding the *general form of the problem states*. In the case of the hobbits and orcs problem, each state can be fully specified by indicating the number of hobbits on each bank, the number of orcs on each bank, and the location of the boat. If, instead, the problem was cryptarithmetic, the general form of the problem states would consist of a statement of all the letter-digit assignments known to date (e.g., $D = 5$) as well as any known constraints (e.g., K must be an even number). Thus, GPS must be told how it should represent the problem states in its memory.

The second kind of information that must be given GPS is the *initial problem state*. In the case of hobbits and orcs, this might be stated as 3 hobbits, 3 orcs, and the boat on the left bank of the river. The third kind of information to be given to GPS is the *desired goal state*. For the hobbits and orcs problem, this would be 3 hobbits, 3 orcs, and the boat on the right side of the river. Fourth, and finally, GPS must be provided with a set of *operators* that may be used, including a statement of the conditions under which these operators may be applied. For the hobbits and orcs problem, the operator which is permitted is that of *moving x hobbits and y orcs to a given river bank*, and the only conditions under which this operator can be applied is if (a) the total of x hobbits and y orcs is either 1 or 2 (an empty boat can't cross the river), *and* (b) at both banks the number of orcs is either zero or less than the number of hobbits, *and* (3) the boat must be on the same side of the river as the hobbits and orcs to be moved.

Having been presented with this problem, GPS then goes about applying means-end analysis to solving the problem, presenting an

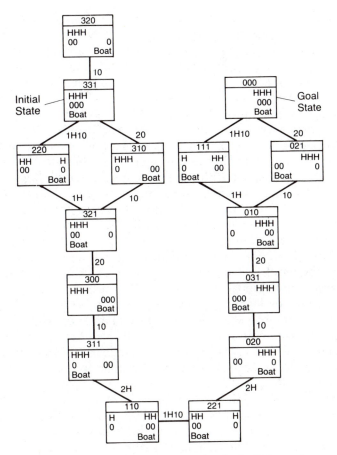

Figure 12–7. The problem space for the hobbits and orcs
problem. Each problem state is labeled with a three-
digit number, with the first digit indicating the
number of hobbits, the second the number of orcs,
and the third the number of boats, to the left of the
river. (After Thomas, 1974. Copyright 1974 by Academic Press. Reprinted by permission.)

output that describes each of the successive problem states it reaches.
In order to see better how this works, it will help to refer frequently
to Figure 12–7 which shows the possible problem states that could be
reached legally (i.e., without killing off any hobbits) in the course of
solution. For ease of reference, each problem state is referred to by a
three-digit number, with the first digit indicating the number of hobbits to the left of the river, the second indicating the number of orcs
to the left of the river, and the third indicating the number of boats
(only 0 to 1) to the left of the river. Thus the initial state is labelled

331 and the goal state 000. If you tried solving the problem yourself a few minutes ago, you were probably unaware of how simple the problem is, simple in the sense that there are only a few possible ways in which you can go wrong (i.e., deadends that you can encounter) if you stick to legal moves in this problem. For example, in the initial state 331, there are only three possible legal moves; one of these (to 320) leads to a deadend, since all you can do next is to bring the boat back with one orc, ending up where you started. On the other hand, the other two legal moves (i.e., to 220 or to 310) are equally useful, and regardless of which you choose you can only get to state 321 next.

When GPS is presented with the problem, it sets up a hierarchy of goals and, if necessary, subgoals, using the principles of means-end analysis. For example, the initial goal would be to transform state 331 to state 000. Having established this goal, it attempts to specify the nature of the difference between these two states and to find some way of reducing this difference. In this case, the difference is in the number of hobbits and orcs on the left bank. This difference can be reduced by applying the move operation, so GPS searches for a particular move that will be legal (i.e., meet the specified conditions) and that will enable it to move some orcs and/or hobbits to the right bank. Sometimes, of course, there is no legal move that will reduce the difference immediately, so GPS has to set up a subgoal that must be met before it goes back to fulfill the main goal. Consider, for example, state 110. When it is in this problem state, GPS set up the goal of getting the hobbit and orc on the left bank to the right bank. However, there is no move that will enable GPS to fulfill that goal directly since the condition of the boat being on their side of the river is not met. In this case, GPS must first set up the subgoal of getting the boat onto the left side of the river before it can go back to fulfilling the current goal.

Testing GPS. When GPS is presented with the hobbits and orcs problem, it is able to solve it. In addition, it is also able to solve a range of other problems including cryptarithmetic, chess, and proving logic theorems. Thus, it is clear that the GPS theory provides a *sufficient* description of the way in which problem states are constructed during problem solving. This is no small feat in the way of theorizing, then, because we have at last demonstrated a heuristic (i.e., means-end analysis) that enables solution of a variety of problems.

As we indicated in the first chapter of the book, though, from the psychologist's perspective it is not enough that a computer simulation theory be sufficient to perform the task at hand. We want to know, in addition, whether or not the strategies the computer program incorporates are the same as the strategies that people use. In order to find out, it is necessary to apply Turings' test, which we discussed in the first chapter. That is, we need to find out whether the performance of the computer program can be distinguished from that of a human.

So far, there have been few tests of GPS and other computer simulation models in which careful comparisons between human and computer performance are made. However, one excellent example will illustrate how this might be done.

In 1974 Thomas reported a study of the points at which people have difficulty in solving the hobbits and orcs problem. He used two measures of difficulty—the number of errors (illegal moves) people made at each problem state and the time it took them to decide on a move at each problem state. He found that people had particular difficulty in deciding where to go from two problem states: 321 and 110. Although Thomas did not have decisive evidence to determine exactly why these states are difficult, it is likely that getting out of state 321 is difficult for people because it is the only state at which it is possible to make a legal move that takes you backward, but does not return you to the state you just left. For example, if you'd been in state 310 and moved 1 orc to get you to state 321, it would be possible to now send 1 hobbit across taking you to state 220. This does not get you closer to the goal, but you might not recognize that immediately since you have never been in this particular state before. The reason for the difficulty people often have in getting out of state 110 is not as clear, but this is the only place in problem solution when it is necessary to bring *two* individuals back across the river. This move apparently troubles people, even though they have no legal alternative, because it seems to them that they have reached a dead end or are moving backward.

If GPS is using the same strategies that people use, then it ought to have difficulty at the same places. Greeno (1974) investigated whether or not this was the case by counting the number of operations GPS tried at each problem state. He found that GPS had difficulty at problem states that were different from those that troubled humans. In particular, GPS took longest to choose a legal move at states 221 and 021. Both of these are very simple states for people, particularly state 021 at which point people realize the problem is virtually solved.

Why, then, does GPS have difficulty at these states? At both of these GPS runs into a *looping problem* because of the rigid way in which it nests subgoals within goals. This is best illustrated for state 021. When it was at state 010, with only one orc remaining on the wrong side of the river, GPS assessed the difference between the present state and the goal state and set up the goal of moving 1 orc to the right of the river. When it attempted to do so, however, it found that it could not because there was no boat on that side. Therefore, GPS then set up the *subgoal* of getting the boat. It accomplished this subgoal by having either one orc or one hobbit take the boat back, resulting in either state 021 or state 111. At this point, having fulfilled the *subgoal* of getting the boat, GPS now reverts back to the *goal* it had set up before—getting *one orc* across the river. Of course, this is inefficient, since it is now appropriate instead to modify that original goal and substitute the goal of taking *two* orcs (if in state 021) or an orc *and* a hobbit (if in state 111) across the river, thereby attaining the goal state. People see this immediately, but because of the rigid way in which GPS sets up and attempts to carry out hierarchies of goals and subgoals, it does not discover this immediately.

We have seen, then, that applying Turings' test reveals an important difference between the performance of GPS and the performance of people. Therefore, we know that there is at least *something* wrong with GPS as a theory of human problem solving. We can only establish exactly what is wrong about GPS by modifying the theory and comparing the new version to human performance. One possibility, for example, is that the assumption that people do indeed use means-end analysis, is correct, but that they use it more flexibly than GPS does. Though they build up goals and subgoals as GPS does, they might always check to see whether the successful completion of the subgoal now makes a new goal more appropriate. We can test this hypothesis by modifying GPS so that it conducts such a flexible means-end analysis and see whether it now exhibits behavior more similar to that of humans.

At the beginning of this discussion, I indicated that computer simulation theories, such as GPS, are the most promising theories of problem solving we have at present. Yet, I have just shown that GPS is inaccurate in at least one respect; though it is capable of solving the hobbits and orcs problem, it exhibits a different pattern of difficulties from people. Why, then, is GPS so promising? First, computer simulation theories of problem solving are the first for which *sufficiency* tests can be applied. For the first time, we can at least demonstrate that we have come up with a set of strategies that if programmed into a machine enables the machine to solve problems. As long as theories were stated only in words, this was not possible. Second, the exercise of writing computer programs that solve problems has suggested several *general and powerful* problem solving heuristics, such as means-end analysis. The fact that such heuristics are general means that they can be used to solve a wide range of problems, including not only those solved by GPS, but also many other classic problems such as the water pitchers problem we talked about (Atwood and Polson, 1976). Thus, we have been led to discover some general strategies that can, at least in principle, be used for problems that initially seemed quite different. This imposes an order on the study of problem solving that had previously been lacking. In addition, these general problem solving methods can be taught to people in order to help them improve their problem solving abilities—a topic we will turn to in the final section of this chapter. Third, as we indicated in the first chapter of this book, one important characteristic a theory needs to have if it is to further science is that it must be specific enough to be capable of being disproven. We have shown, using Greeno (1974) and Thomas's (1974) work that GPS meets this criterion. Furthermore, the discrepancies between GPS and human performance that were revealed were specific enough that they lead to testable hypotheses about how GPS must be modified to more closely approximate human performance.

Questions and extensions of GPS. I have stressed the promise of models like GPS, but before leaving this discussion it is important to suggest two points the skeptic should keep in mind. First, if you will refer back again to Figure 12–1 which displays our four stages of problem solving, you will notice that GPS does not, in fact, deal with Stage 1, that of coming up with a representation for the problem. Instead, the person presenting GPS with the problem must tell it how it should represent the problem by specifying the general form of the problem state, the initial and goal states, and a list of operations with limiting conditions. Thus, GPS focuses on Stages 2 and 3 as we have outlined them, and it provides little insight into what is most likely the most important single stage in problem solving. Thus, GPS provides a model of only part of problem solving.

This limitation is being overcome, however, by extensions of GPS. For example, Hayes and Simon (1974) have been developing a program called UNDERSTAND which is designed to simulate Stage 1 of problem solving. UNDERSTAND contains two major components, a language comprehension component which interprets the language of the instructions using a grammar like the case grammars we discussed in Chapter 8, and a construction component which accepts the sentence-by-sentence information from the language comprehension component and builds a representation of the problem which contains information concerning the general form of problem states, the initial and goal states, and the operations that are permitted. Thus when the UNDERSTAND and GPS programs are combined, it becomes possible to present a problem to the programs in English and have it construct a representation and then go about searching for a solution. UNDERSTAND and other programs like it promise to help us build precise models of the earliest stage of problem solving. Such efforts must be closely allied with work on language comprehension and inference.

The second caveat that should be stressed about GPS is that we must wonder whether the particular view of problem solving it adopts is in part, at least, an artifact of the kind of data on which it is based.

The verbal protocols Newell and his colleagues collected led them to conclude that problem solving involves only serial processes. Therefore, they did not include any parallel processes in GPS. However, whenever a person is talking aloud about his problem solving, it is physically possible to describe only one action or decision at a time. Therefore, verbal protocols force the person to report in a serial fashion. It is possible, however, that a number of mental processes occur in parallel during at least some stages of problem solving. For example, it is possible that long-term memory is searched in a number of different directions at once in the form of spreading activation that we have discussed previously. We must recognize, then, that the assumption that problem solving involves only serial processes is simply that—an assumption, and one that is quite possibly incorrect.

IMPROVING PROBLEM SOLVING

We turn now to a practical question: how can individuals improve their problem solving ability? If you wish to improve your ability to solve problems in a particular domain (e.g., chess, conducting proofs in geometry, or anagrams), then it is clear that your best bet is to learn more about that domain and to practice solving many, many problems in it. Not only can learning about the subject domain improve your ability to chunk the information, but you can often learn "tricks of the trade" that represent particular strategies that usually work for the kind of problem in the domain in question.

But what if you want to improve your general problem solving ability, so that you will be able to approach *any* kind of problem more systematically? As we just saw, attempts to write computer programs that solve a range of problems have suggested that there may be general problem solving heuristics that people might adopt. So far there has been little attempt to apply these heuristics to the task of teaching people to solve problems. The notable exception to this neglect, however, is Wayne Wickelgren, who in 1974 published a wonderful paperback book called *How to Solve Problems*. A number of years ago Professor Wickelgren decided to take the insights psychologists had gained from years of studying problem solving and use these to develop a course that would teach general problem solving methods. At the time Wickelgren was a professor at MIT, so he hoped to teach problem solving methods that would help students to improve their ability at solving elementary mathematics, science and engineering problems. During this semester-long course Wickelgren taught the students seven general problem solving methods and they practiced these methods by using simple recreational problems, some of which you tried to solve in Table 12–1. Wickelgren's course was greeted enthusiastically and in three years, the enrollment grew from 20 to more than 80 students. Ever since I discovered Wickelgren's book, I have devoted a few sessions of my cognitive psychology classes to teaching these methods and working on sample problems, and I have also found that students find the methods helpful. For the rest of this chapter, we will discuss Wickelgren's general problem solving strategies and illustrate how they can be applied to selected problems. Even this brief exposure should help you to approach all kinds of problems more systematically, but if you are majoring in a scientific discipline or if you enjoy confronting recreational problems, you should be sure to get Wickelgren's book and work your way through it.

Before considering the problem solving techniques, it is important to adopt Wickelgren's view of problem solving, which is, in fact, based upon information processing theories such as GPS. That is, he assumes that a formal problem contains three types of information: (1) a statement of the initial (or given) state, (2) a description of the goal state, and (3) a description of a set of operations (or transformations), which are actions one can perform to get from state to state. A solution, then, consists of a sequence of allowable actions (or states) that leads from the initial, given state to the goal state. Although the solution can be defined as either a sequence of actions or as a sequence of states, it helps to represent both in a diagram he calls a *state action tree*. A schematic of such a state action tree is shown in Figure 12–8. The *nodes* or branch points on the tree represent all the *possibly* different problem states that could result from all the different action sequences. Therefore, two different nodes on the tree might represent the same state of knowledge; they differ in the route (i.e., sequence of actions or states) by which the problem solver arrived at the node. The *branches* on the tree represent the possible actions that could be made at that particular state of knowledge. The given state is represented by the single node at the top level (level 0) of the state action tree, and the goal state is represented by the indicated node in the lowest level of the tree. For this schematic tree, we assume that from the goal state there are only two possible actions that the person can take, one of which starts the person on the path toward the goal, the other of which does not. Having chosen one of these (thereby leading the person to state level 1), the person is then faced with a new set of possible actions. Here, we arbitrarily assume that there are three possible actions that could be taken at either of the state level 1 nodes. This successive making of choices goes on and on until the person either reaches the goal state or finds himself at a dead end. The main lesson to be gained from thinking about state action trees is the fact that as you get further and further into a problem (i.e., lower and lower levels in the tree) the number of possible action sequences increases rapidly. The problem solver's task is to find the correct action se-

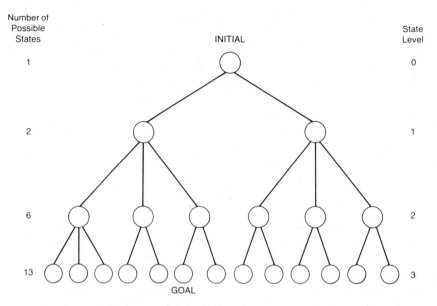

Figure 12–8. A schematic state action tree. The nodes represent all the potential problem states that could result from all possible action sequences. The branches represent the possible actions that could be taken at each state. (Adapted from HOW TO SOLVE PROBLEMS: ELEMENTS OF A THEORY OF PROBLEMS AND PROBLEM SOLVING by Wayne A. Wickelgren. W. H. Freeman and Company. Copyright © 1974.)

quence out of all of these possibilities. Wickelgren argues that his purpose is to teach people methods for pruning this tree, i.e., for seeking out the correct action sequence. The untrained person, Wickelgren notes, often approaches problems with a trial and error type approach in which he retries the same action sequence (i.e., the same branch of the tree) several times. Wickelgren argues that the seven general problem solving techniques which follow give the problem solver a more systematic set of techniques for searching the state action tree.

Inference. The first general problem solving technique Wickelgren suggests is *inference*: draw inferences from the explicitly stated goals, givens, and operations stated in the problem. That is, ask, "what else do I know?" We have argued that people draw some inferences automatically and that problems (particularly recreational and test problems) are often set up so that these automatically drawn inferences will mislead the problem solver. Further, the person may then tend to rigidly stick with those unconscious assumptions he has inferred, to the detriment of his performance. Wickelgren's suggestion here is that you should try consciously to draw as many inferences as possible

from the goals, givens, and operations stated in the problem, and that you should apply this method first when solving a problem. By forcing yourself to generate as many inferences as possible, you are doing a kind of one-person brainstorming that may keep you from being overcome by the tendency to view a problem from only one perspective.

The first problem in Table 12–1 illustrates the usefulness of this technique of drawing inferences. If you didn't solve the notched checkerboard problem previously, try drawing some inferences now based on the given information. For example, ask yourself what are the properties of dominoes and checkerboards? One useful property is that the domino covers two adjacent squares of the checkerboard. What are the properties of any two squares covered by a domino? Quit reading now and try to use these inferences to help you solve the problem.

If these inferences don't lead you to the solution, note that one property of the two squares covered by a domino is that they are always of two different colors. Got it yet? Note further that the two squares that are cut off are both of the same color. Therefore, it will be impossible for the remaining 62 squares to be covered by only 31 dominoes, because 32 of the squares will be black and only 30 will be white. Since two black squares never occur adjacent to each other, one of the black squares must remain uncovered if there are only 31 dominoes. Note that the critical information for solving this problem was an inference derived from the given information.

Wickelgren suggests, then, that the very first general problem solving method you should use when you encounter a new problem is to try to draw as many inferences as you can from the givens, the goal, and the operations stated in the problem. Though some of these inferences will prove fruitless, others will often lead to insights that will make the solution easier or obvious.

Classification of action sequences. Wickelgren notes that some problems must involve a certain amount of trial and error, but that the purpose of general problem solving techniques is to replace *random* trial and error with *systematic* trial and error. Systematic trial and error prevents the solver from going in circles and can be accomplished by (1) recording or remembering the operations you have already tried, so you will know where you have been in the state action tree, and (2) having a system for generating sequences of operations or actions, so that you can keep track of where you are going. One way in which to make trial and error systematic, rather than random, then, is to attempt to organize possible sequences of actions (or operations) that are equivalent as far as the problem is concerned. Wickelgren calls these *equivalence classes.* Two kinds of equivalence are

particularly useful: actions that are *commutative*, in that the order in which they are performed makes no difference, and actions that are the *inverse* of each other, in that performing the two in succession leaves you right back where you started.

You will see how useful it can be to recognize commutative and inverse actions by considering again Problem 2 in Table 12–1, the six-arrow problem. If you use the method of classification of action sequences, virtually no trial and error is involved. Note first that there are exactly 5 possible actions—flipping pair 1-2, pair 2-3, pair 3-4, pair 4-5, pair 5-6. Note further that all 5 actions are commutative; that is, if you flip pair 4-5 followed by pair 5-6, you end up with the same arrangement as if you had flipped pair 5-6 followed by pair 4-5. This tells you, then, that you need not worry about the order in which the five actions occur—all are equivalent. Furthermore, flipping a pair twice leads you right back to where you started, i.e., the second flip is the inverse of the first. Therefore, you should never make any of the five actions more than once. Furthermore, you can note from looking at the goal state that you will never want to flip pair 1-2, since it puts arrow 1 in the wrong position, and, for the same reason, you will never want to flip pair 5-6. This eliminates all possible actions except flipping pairs 2-3, 3-4, and 4-5. You will find that by performing these three actions you convert the goal into the given and that you have done so in the minimum number of steps (since none of the few possible shorter sequences is sufficient).

Taking time to notice sequences of actions that are equivalent changed what appeared to be an infinite number of possible actions into a very small number. Whenever you are faced with a problem of any kind you should always notice whether or not some of the possible sequences are equivalent. If they are, you will have pruned the state action tree considerably.

State evaluation and hill-climbing. This method provides a specific means of helping you to decide which possible action you should choose as you reach each node in a state action tree. The method has two parts: (1) *state evaluation* which involves defining a quantitative evaluation function that can be calculated for all possible problem states, and (2) *hill-climbing* which, at any given problem state, involves choosing the action to be taken next that will have an evaluation that is closest to the goal. We will use the six-arrow problem again to illustrate possible evaluation functions you might adopt. One possibility would be to count, for each possible state, the number of arrows that are in the same position as they are in the goal state. Count for yourself to demonstrate that the value of this function is 4 for the initial state and 6 for the goal state. Figure 12–9 shows the values that would be assigned to the initial node and to the nodes at the next

(a) Evaluation function: count the number of arrows in the same position as the goal state. Initial state value = 4. Goal state value = 6.

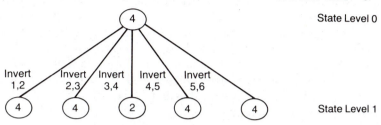

(b) Evaluation function: count the number of runs of arrows in one direction. Initial state value = 2. Goal state value = 6.

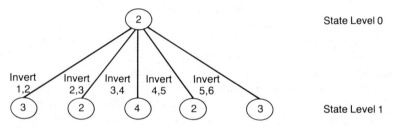

Figure 12–9. An illustration of two possible evaluation functions for the six-arrow problem. For each function (a) and (b), the figure displays the values that would be assigned to the initial node and to the nodes at the next level for each of the five possible actions.

level for each of the five possible actions. Notice that this particular evaluation function doesn't look particularly useful, since four of the five possibilities have the same value (4), and there is no basis for choosing among them. Another possible evaluation function for the six-arrow problem would be to count the number of runs of items in the same direction at each state. Using this function, the initial state would be given a value of 2 and the goal state a value of 6. Figure 12–9b illustrates the values for each of the five possible initial actions that might be taken. This evaluation function is more useful than the first, since the nodes vary in value and there is one that is clearly the best choice (the one with a value of 4). Other evaluation functions could be developed for this same problem, and the solver's goal is to find the one that seems most useful.

Since this and all other general problem solving methods we are presenting are heuristics, not algorithms, they are not guaranteed to lead us to solution. Therefore, it is quite possible that hill-climbing will not lead to the correct solution at least on the first try. If this happens, then, the solver has a number of options open to him. He might go back to the beginning and choose the second best option at some point. Another option the solver might try would be to consider using a different evaluation function. Notice that even if the hill-climbing doesn't work on the first try, the problem solver has learned something about the problem as long as he keeps a record of where he went in the tree, for he knows now that one particular path does not work, and he need not try it again. Again, then, state evaluation and hill-climbing is a heuristic that helps the problem solver engage in a systematic, rather than a random trial and error search.

Subgoals. A fourth general problem solving method described by Wickelgren is searching for *subgoals*. Unlike the previous method, this is one most people have already learned—indeed it is incorporated within the means-end heuristic we discussed. That is, when the problem solver can't figure out a way of getting from the initial to the goal state, he may at least be able to find a way of getting to some intermediate state. This technique is particularly useful for multi-step problems such as the men-boys-raft problem in Table 12–1. For this problem, you can set a subgoal of calculating how many crossings will be necessary in order to get *one* man across. You will find that this requires exactly 4 crossings. First, the two boys cross in the raft. Second, one boy returns with the boat. Third, the boy gets out on the original side and one man gets into the boat, crosses the river, and gets out. Fourth, the boy on the right bank gets in the boat to return it. Thus, four such crossings will be required to get each of the nine men across, leading to a total of 36 crossings to transport the men. This will leave the two boys on the original bank, and one more crossing, for a total of 37, will get them to the goal side.

What seemed like a long and tedious problem became quite simple when broken down into subgoals. This is true of many personal, scientific, and recreational problems.

Contradiction. Using the method of contradiction, you try to derive some inference from the givens that is inconsistent with the goal state. This method is particularly useful if the problem asks whether some goal is possible, or when there is a limited number of possibilities and you know that one and only one is correct (e.g., multiple choice tests).

The usefulness of this method is illustrated by the bowling-pin-reversal problem in Table 12–1. This problem becomes much easier if you first adopt a subgoal (note the last general problem-solving method we discussed) of figuring out where the row of 4 pins will be in the goal state. There are six possibilities—it could be above the present top row of the given state, at the top row of the given state, at the second row of the given state, at the third row of the given state, at the fourth row of the given state, or below the fourth row of the given state. You are required to get to the goal configuration by moving no more than 3 pins. It is now possible to consider each of the six possible final locations of the goal configuration to see if any of them could *not* be accomplished with only three moves. Note that you can eliminate the possibility that the four pin row will be either above or below the present given configuration, because either of these would require *at least* the movement of four pins. It is also possible to contradict the possibility that the row of four pins will be in row 1 of the initial state. This is because you would have to move at least three pins to get a total of four into that row, yet this would have used up all your moves without reaching the goal state, since the other rows are still wrong. By considering each of the three remaining possibilities in turn, you will find that the only one that is feasible is that row 2 of the initial array will become the four-pin row in the goal configuration. This can be accomplished by moving each of the outer items in the bottom row of the given state up to the second row of the given state, and then moving the item in row 1 to the position at the very bottom of the given state.

Thus, the method of contradiction helped to narrow down the state action tree in a systematic fashion by eliminating possibilities that could not possibly work. This problem also demonstrates how it is often useful to combine general problem solving methods—in this case we combined subgoals and the method of contradiction.

Working backward. As the name implies, Wickelgren's sixth general problem solving method is one in which you begin at the goal state and try to work backward from it. This can be a very useful heuristic, particularly for problems that contain a uniquely specified goal state and a vague statement of the initial state. One problem which lends itself particularly well to working backward is the nim problem in Table 12–1. In fact, you will probably want to master this one since you can earn a little extra spending money by playing a few nim games with unsuspecting friends. There is a method of play that guarantees victory, and you can discover it if you work backward. In order to be able to win, you must find yourself at your last turn with from 1 to 5 pennies in front of you; this is your goal state. Now your problem becomes, how do I make sure that my opponent will be forced to leave me with from 1 to 5 pennies? The answer, of course, is that you must confront your opponent with exactly 6 pennies. Then, no matter how many pennies he removes (he must remove from 1 to 5) he is forced to leave you in the goal state of having 1 to 5 left. Of course, you won't be able to leave your opponent with exactly 6 pennies after your very first move, since you cannot remove more than 5 of the original 15 pennies. Therefore, you must work backward still further to figure out how many pennies you should leave after your first move so that you will be able to face your opponent with exactly 6 pennies on the following move. This is possible if you leave your opponent with exactly 12 pennies after your first move. Then, regardless of how many pennies he removes next, you are sure to be able to leave him with exactly 6 on your next move. Working backward from the goal state, then, has enabled us to discover a guaranteed victory strategy: work to leave your opponent with 12 pennies and then 6 pennies, and you are guaranteed to win.

Finding relations between problems. Wickelgren's final general problem solving strategy suggests that the solver always attempt to find relations between the new problems and problems he/she has solved previously. In this way we use past experience to advantage, though it is always important to make sure that the new and old problems are similar in more than just a superficial way.

Consider the coin rearrangement problem in Table 12–1. If you think back to problems you solved earlier in this chapter, you will be able to solve it quite readily. Try to do so now.

You should have noticed the similarity to the bowling pin reversal problem. Recall that it was solved readily by trying to ascertain which items would remain in the same position in the goal state as they were in the initial state. If you look at the current problem with this in mind, you will probably be able to see immediately that 1, 3, 5, and 6 are in exactly the position they need to be for the goal state, so only 2 and 4 need to be moved up to form the appropriate configuration. Alternately, you might leave 1, 2, 4, and 6 in their original positions and move 3 and 5 to the bottom of the array. In either case, you will have solved the problem.

General comments on Wickelgren's problem solving methods. Wickelgren has offered a set of very general heuristics which the problem solver can use to help generate systematic searches for problem solution. These methods are general in that they can be applied to problems of all kinds, and they are heuristics in that they do not guarantee solution. By keeping such a set in mind and using it, you will find that you are able to avoid blind trial and error when dealing with problems.

CHAPTER SUMMARY

In this chapter we began the study of thinking by examining problem solving. Problems are characterized by an initial state, a goal state and a situation in which the actions necessary to convert the initial state into the goal state are not immediately obvious. Both experimental studies and the introspections of scientists, mathematicians, and inventors suggest that problem solving consists of a series of stages of processing. These usually include the stages of (1) understanding the problem, or encoding it in working memory, (2) devising a plan, or searching long-term memory for a solution plan (3) carrying out, or executing, the plan, and (4) looking back, or evaluating the results. Analyses of problem solving have revealed several phenomena that all problem solvers exhibit at one time or another. The first, rigidity, is that people often fixate on only one way of viewing a problem. The second phenomenon is incubation, which refers to an increase in likelihood of solving a problem that results from placing a delay or rest interval between two periods of intense work on the problem. The third phenomenon is satisficing, or the tendency to seek a solution that is good enough, rather than continuing to search for the best possible solution.

The most promising current theories of problem solving are those based on computer simulation. One such theory, the General Problem Solver (GPS), introduced important principles that have been incorporated into most subsequent theories. GPS assumes that the problem solver represents a problem as a problem space, which consists of a set of states of knowledge about the problem. The problem solver moves from one state of knowledge to another by applying operators. GPS has been able to solve a wide range of problems, and it is precise enough to be put to empirical test. So far the few comparisons of human and GPS performance that have been conducted have revealed some interesting differences which suggest that GPS would need to be modified if it is to provide a more accurate account of human problem solving.

Wickelgren has noted that the information processing approach suggests some general heuristics people can learn to improve their general problem solving ability. The goal of all of these general heuristics is to help the problem solver engage in a systematic, rather than a random search for a solution.

SUGGESTED READING

The best place to begin more in-depth reading on problem solving would be in the appropriate section of *Thinking*, a book of readings edited by Johnson-Laird and Wason (1977). The readings they have selected range from early studies of problem solving by the Gestalt psychologists to descriptions of computer simulation. Their introduction to the readings is very useful. You will find other classic articles reprinted in their earlier book of readings entitled *Thinking and Rea-*

soning (Wason & Johnson-Laird, 1968). Greeno's review article, "Natures of problem solving abilities" in the Handbook edited by Estes (1978) is also a helpful source of ideas and references, though it is a difficult article.

If you would like to learn more about the General Problem Solver, turn to Newell and Simon's lengthy book *Human Problem Solving* (1972). Herbert Simon's influential ideas on problem solving, computer simulation, and their implications for economics and other disciplines can be found in *Models of Thought* (1979), a collection of his earlier writings, and also in his (1981) article in the *American Scientist*.

For advice and exercises on how to improve your problem solving ability, the best source is Wickelgren's *How to Solve Problems: Elements of a Theory of Problems and Problem Solving* (1974). You will also profit from Polya's (1957) classic *How to Solve It*.

If you would like to investigate age differences in problem solving—an excellent topic for a term paper—the recent article by Klahr and Robinson (1981) and the chapter by Young (1978) present interesting examples of research with children and provide references to the earlier literature. For a review of aging and problem solving, read the chapter by Rabbitt in Birren and Schaie's (1977) *Handbook of the Psychology of Aging*. Charness (1981) presents an interesting analysis of changes in chess playing skill during aging.

Reasoning

FOOD FOR THOUGHT

Several reasoning problems are presented in Table 13–1. Take a few minutes now to answer each of these, making sure to write down your answers for later reference. How do these problems seem to differ from the problems you confronted in the previous chapter?

TABLE 13–1. Reasoning Problems.

Below are several reasoning problems. Solve each, being sure to write down your answers for later reference. As you solve these problems, keep in mind that the term "Some" should be interpreted as meaning "Some and possibly all" and that "Some are not" should be interpreted as meaning "Some are not and possibly all are not."

1. All A are B
   Some B are C
   What conclusion follows logically from the premises above the line?
   (a) All A are C
   (b) Some A are C
   (c) No A are C
   (d) Some A are not C
   (e) None of the foregoing is proven
2. All A are B
   All C are B
   What conclusion follows logically from the premises above the line?
   (a) All A are C
   (b) Some A are C
   (c) No A are C
   (d) Some A are not C
   (e) None of the foregoing is proven
3. Some B are A
   Some C are not B
   What conclusion follows logically from the premises above the line?
   (a) All A are C
   (b) Some A are C
   (c) No A are C
   (d) Some A are not C
   (e) None of the foregoing is proven
4. All Russians are Bolsheviks
   Some Bolsheviks are undemocratic people
   What conclusion follows logically from the premises above the line?
   (a) All undemocratic people are Russian
   (b) Some undemocratic people are Russian
   (c) No undemocratic people are Russian
   (d) Some undemocratic people are not Russian
   (e) None of the foregoing is proven

TABLE 13–1. (Continued)

For each of problems 5 through 8, answer *yes* if the conclusion follows logically from the premises and *no* if it does not.

5. If the object is green, then it is rectangular.
   The object is green.
   Therefore, it is rectangular.
6. If the box is large, then it is orange.
   The box is not orange.
   Therefore, it is not large.
7. If the object is square, then it is purple.
   The object is not square.
   Therefore, it is not purple.
8. If the square is large, then it is blue.
   The square is blue.
   Therefore, it is large.

9. [E]   [F]   [4]   [7]

   Assume that each of the above squares is a card which has a letter on one side and a number on the other. Thus, the E and F cards have some number on the back and the 4 and 7 cards have letters. Here is a rule that might apply to the cards: *If a card has a vowel on one side, then it has an even number on the other side.* What cards would you need to turn over in order to find out whether the rule is true or false? Be sure to turn over only the card(s) that are necessary to test the rule.

REASONING AS PROBLEM SOLVING

Reasoning, the kind of deductive thinking that will concern us in this chapter, is a special kind of problem solving, so the general characteristics of problem solving we discussed in the previous chapter are relevant here as well. In most of the tasks that we discussed in the problem solving chapter, however, the focus was on *discovering* some novel solution. You will find that this is also the case with the kinds of tasks that we will discuss in the next chapter on conceptual thinking. In contrast, when we use the term *reasoning* we are concerned with the thinking involved in determining whether or not one proposition follows logically from another. When we reason we are attempting to determine the validity of an argument or an idea.

There are many different kinds of reasoning, and the problems in Table 13–1 tap only a few of these. Although you rarely confront problems exactly like those in Table 13–1, the kind of deductive reasoning that they require plays an important role not only in scientific thinking, but also in everyday life. Every time you judge the implications of an "if . . . then" statement or judge the validity of an argument, you are engaging in deductive reasoning.

IS HUMAN REASONING INHERENTLY LOGICAL?

Philosophers have studied reasoning for centuries, ever since Aristotle invented the syllogism. *Logic* is the branch of philosophy which is concerned with specifying rules of inference that yield valid arguments, regardless of the particular content of the arguments. Logic tells us how we *ought* to reason.

The relation between logic and the psychology of reasoning is similar to that between linguistics and the psychology of language. As we saw in Chapter 8, linguistics specifies a set of rules that differentiates grammatical from ungrammatical sentences, whereas psychology attempts to ascertain the rules that people actually use when they produce and comprehend language. Similarly, logic specifies rules of inference that will differentiate valid from invalid arguments, whereas psychology attempts to specify the rules people actually use when drawing inferences.

The central question in the psychology of reasoning, and the question that will form the major theme of this chapter is: To what extent is human reasoning inherently logical? That is, do the rules of logic describe the reasoning of people untrained in formal logic, or are humans capable of such logical reasoning only after careful training? Writers in the nineteenth century (e.g., Kant, 1885; J. S. Mill, 1874; Boole, 1854) usually viewed the laws of logic as the laws of thought, but philosophers and psychologists in the first half of this century (e.g., Cohen, 1944; Nagel, 1956; Dollard & Miller, 1950; Morgan & Morton, 1944) have often viewed human reasoning as inherently illogical.

This question has remained unsettled for so long, because it is easy to find evidence supportive of either view. Those who view human thought as inherently rational (e.g., Henle, 1962) point out that if most people were unable to reason logically, then given the same premises, people would usually draw radically different conclusions. Under such conditions, it is difficult to see how people could follow each other's thinking, reach common decisions, or work together—all functions which are critical for even the most primitive society to exist. In contrast, those who view human reasoning as inherently illogical call upon the indisputable fact that people often make errors in reasoning, both in everyday life and in the laboratory. In fact, for many of the problems presented in Table 13–1, the most frequent response produced by college students is logically incorrect.

Reasoning and the stages of problem solving.   The difference between the two views concerning the relation between logic and thought becomes clearer if we think of reasoning in light of the four stages of problem solving we outlined in Figure 12–1. In the first stage the reasoner encodes or represents the problem in working memory, and in the remaining three stages the reasoner either develops or retrieves some set of rules that is used to decide whether an argument is valid or invalid.

The two views regarding the relation between logic and thinking disagree concerning what happens during these last three stages. Those who view reasoning as logical believe that long-term memory contains a set of rules of inference that are functionally equivalent to the rules specified by formal logic. They are functionally equivalent in that arguments that are judged to be valid by formal logic are also judged to be valid by these inference rules. (This relation is similar to that between formal grammars and linguistic processing strategies that we discussed in the section on language.) According to this view, then, when people make illogical judgments, they do so either because they encoded the problem incorrectly during the first, encoding stage, or because during the later stages they failed to call upon these inference rules, and instead responded on some other basis. In contrast, those who believe human reasoning is fundamentally illogical or irrational argue that humans usually do not possess such inference rules unless they are trained formally in the rules of logic.

In this chapter we will discuss this debate by considering two kinds of deductive reasoning: categorical syllogisms and conditional reasoning.

CATEGORICAL SYLLOGISMS

Logical analysis. The reasoning task that has been studied most extensively by logicians and psychologists is also one of the most ancient. Called the *categorical syllogism*, the *formal syllogism,* or the *Aristotelian syllogism*, it is an argument which has the following form: two propositions called *premises* are followed by one proposition called the *conclusion*. A *valid syllogism* is one in which the conclusion necessarily follows logically from the premises. Logicians have specified rules for differentiating valid from invalid syllogisms, and in psychological experiments human subjects are usually either presented with syllogisms and asked to judge their validity or, less frequently, they are presented with two premises and asked to draw a valid conclusion from them.

An example of a categorical syllogism is shown in Table 13–2a. Each proposition in a syllogism describes a relation between two terms. The *major premise* states a relation between the predicate (P) of the conclusion and another middle term (M). The *minor premise* states a relation between the subject (S) of the conclusion and the middle term (M). As shown in Table 13–2b, a syllogism can be presented in one of

TABLE 13–2.   Possible Categorical Syllogisms.

(a) *An example of a categorical syllogism*

MAJOR PREMISE	All *M* are *P*	All scientists are honest
MINOR PREMISE	All *S* are *M*	All women are scientists
CONCLUSION	All *S* are *P*	All women are honest

(b) *Possible figures of a categorical syllogism*

Figure 1	Figure 2	Figure 3	Figure 4
M-P	P-M	M-P	P-M
S-M	S-M	M-S	M-S
S-P	S-P	S-P	S-P

(c) *Possible sentence types in a syllogism (determines mood of the syllogism)*

Affirmative-Universal (A)	All *S* are *P*	All students are intelligent
Negative-Universal (E)	No *S* are *P*	No children are unruly
Affirmative-Particular (I)	Some *S* are *P*	Some politicians are truthful
Negative-Particular (O)	Some *S* are not *P*	Some millionaires are not greedy

four possible *figures* or forms. The figures differ in the order of the terms within each of the two premises. By agreement, logicians have given each of the four combinations a numerical designation. Thus, the sample premise in Table 13–2a is a Figure 1 syllogism.

Another way in which syllogisms vary is in the sentence types they contain. Each of the premises and the conclusion can be one of the four types shown in Table 13–2c. Logicians have given each type a letter designation, either A, E, I, or O. Though this labeling looks completely arbitrary at first, the labels are easy to remember if you know that they were drawn from the first two vowels in the Latin verbs *affirmo* (to affirm) and *nego* (to deny). Thus, affirmative propositions are labeled *A* if they are universal (All) and *I* if they are particular (Some). Similarly negative propositions are called *E* if they are universal (No) and *O* if they are particular (Some . . . are not). The *mood* of a syllogism describes the sentence types it contains. For example, a syllogism with the mood AEI would have *All* in its major premise, *No* in its minor premise, and *Some* in its conclusion.

In order to be sure that you understand these designations, stop reading for a moment and determine the figure and mood of the following syllogism:

No zebs are dwecks

All dwecks are mubs

Some mubs are not zebs

Given the possible variations in mood and figure, there are a total of 256 possible kinds of categorical syllogism, i.e., 4 possible figures times 4 possible moods for the major premise times 4 possible moods for the minor premise times 4 possible moods for the conclusion. Courses in formal logic teach rules for sorting valid from invalid syllogisms; of the 256 possible syllogisms, only 24 (6 for each figure) are valid arguments. *Note:* The previous syllogism is in the fourth figure and the EAO mood.

You may be thinking that although categorical syllogisms fascinate logicians, they never appear in everyday life, so why study how people process them. In fact, though they rarely appear in exactly these forms, Henle (1962) has noted that syllogistic reasoning is implicit, though unnoticed, in the real world. She offers several examples, including the following: "I do not want to wear the same dress two days in succession. I wore this dress yesterday, so I do not want to wear this dress today."

Traditional views on the sources of error: Human reasoning is not logical. Even college students accept many invalid syllogisms as being valid. Young children and unschooled people in traditional, nonindustrialized societies perform even more poorly. Prior to the cognitive revolution, psychological studies in the first half of this century focused on two particular sources of error.

The first, called the *atmosphere effect* was proposed by Sells (1936) and Woodworth and Sells (1935), who tested subjects on a wide range of syllogisms. They noticed that for syllogisms that had no valid conclusion, the mood of the premises influenced the kind of conclusion the subject was most likely to judge to be valid. Therefore, Woodworth and Sells argued that the mood of the premises creates an atmosphere which leads people to accept a conclusion that is consistent with this atmosphere. As Begg and Denny (1969) have pointed out, the atmosphere effect encompasses two basic principles: (1) whenever at least one premise is negative, the most frequently accepted conclusion is also negative; otherwise it is affirmative, and (2) whenever at least one premise is particular (i.e., contains *Some*), the most frequently accepted conclusion is also particular; otherwise it is universal. In fact, the errors college students make usually agree quite well with the predictions of the atmosphere hypothesis.

In order to see whether your reasoning reveals an atmosphere effect, consider your responses to Problems 1 through 3 in Table 13–1. In all three cases, the correct conclusion is (e) *None*. The atmosphere hypothesis predicts that if you make an error, you will choose the (b) choice of *Some* for Problem 1, the (a) choice of *All* for Problem 2, and the (d) choice of "Some are not" for Problem 3.

The atmosphere hypothesis assumes that reasoning is irrational. Rather than possessing inference rules, people simply make responses in keeping with the general mood of the syllogism. Even though the atmosphere hypothesis makes reasonably accurate predictions about the kinds of errors people make on syllogisms that are logically invalid (i.e., that must logically be answered "Can't say"), the hypothesis fails to account for important aspects of human reasoning. The most important is that people perform more accurately on valid syllogisms (i.e., those which logically lead to a conclusion) than on invalid syllogisms (e.g., Ceraso & Provitera, 1971). This is inconsistent with the atmosphere hypothesis which assumes that people do not differentiate between valid and invalid syllogisms at all—all are responded to simply on the basis of their premise moods.

In summary, then, the atmosphere hypothesis is useful in that it predicts the most frequent error that people will make on invalid syllogisms, but it is inadequate in that it does not explain the fact that people are sensitive to the validity of syllogisms.

The second source of error that was revealed in early studies of syllogistic reasoning was *content*. Many studies (e.g., Lefford, 1946; McGuire, 1960; Morgan & Morton, 1944) found that the contents of the conclusion influenced the reasoner's assessment of the validity of a syllogistic argument. When faced with syllogisms that contain emotionally laden premises and conclusions, people's judgments appeared to be based on the believability of the conclusion, rather than on the logical form of the argument. Consider, for example, problem number 4 in Table 13–1 (taken from Revlin, Leirer, Yopp, & Yopp, 1980). The correct answer is (e), but students often accept (b) instead. You might think that this is just another example of the atmosphere effect, but the early studies revealed that this error is much more likely when the syllogism contains emotionally laden material than when it contains abstract material such as letters. These findings led early researchers to argue that rather than using inference rules, people simply base their decisions about the validity of an argument on their biases and beliefs. Again, then, human reasoning is viewed as being illogical or irrational.

As in the case of the atmosphere hypothesis, however, this argument fails to explain why people perform more accurately on valid than on invalid syllogisms, and it fails to offer any explanation at all of how people decide to respond to abstract syllogisms containing conclusions such as "All A are B." It is highly unlikely that people have any strong beliefs about the truthfulness of such conclusions. These early psychological studies of human performance made important contributions, for they illustrated that in some ways, at least, human performance on reasoning tasks deviates systematically from what would be predicted if people followed the proscriptions of logic.

Contemporary views on the sources of error: Human reasoning is logical, but fallible. The information processing approach has led contemporary cognitive psychologists to return to a view of human reasoning that is closer to that of the nineteenth century philosophers. That is, information processing theories view human thought as rule governed. Rather than assuming that errors reflect a lack of rational ability on the part of logically untrained individuals, information processing theories propose that all people have logical competence (e.g., their long-term memories contain production systems that embody logical inference rules). In searching for the sources of error in syllogistic reasoning, then, information processing theorists have tried to isolate the stages of thinking at which errors come into play. Recent research has suggested several such sources of error, and we will consider four of these now.

The first source of error is a *failure to accept the logical task* (Henle, 1962). The categorical syllogisms you attempted to solve in Table 13–1 are special in that these and other deductive reasoning tasks require that you ignore the actual accuracy of the premises and conclusions—that you set aside all you know about the real world outside the syllogism—and that, instead, you reason within the syllogism itself. That is, you are asked to ignore the empirical truth value of the premises and conclusions and to make your judgment based solely on the validity of the argument contained in the syllogism. Thus, you are required to approach the syllogism as a *theoretical* task rather than an *empirical* one.

In an influential paper Henle (1962) reported findings from a study in which 46 graduate students (who had no formal training in logic) were asked to evaluate the logical adequacy of deductions that were presented in the context of everyday problems. Rather than focusing on the number of errors the students made, however, Henle analyzed the nature of the thinking that was revealed by the students' explanations of their answers. Here is one of Henle's problems. Take a few minutes now to solve the problem before reading further.

> **A group of women were discussing their household problems. Mrs. Shivers broke the ice by saying: "I'm so glad we're talking about these problems. It's so important to talk about things that are in our minds. We spend so much of our time in the kitchen that of course household problems are in our minds. So it is important to talk about them." (Does it follow that it is important to talk about them? Give your reasoning.)**

If you approach the problem as a task in logical reasoning, you can cast it into the following syllogism:

> **It is important to talk about things that are in our minds.**
>
> **Household problems are in our minds.**
> _____
>
> **It is important to talk about household problems.**

Therefore, the logically correct answer is that given Mrs. Shivers' premises her conclusion does follow logically.

Henle (1962) found that some students on some such problems, however, treated the task as an empirical rather than a theoretical one. They set out to evaluate the actual truth of the premises or the conclusion, rather than the logical form of the argument. Some sample empirical responses follow, some of which happened to lead to an incorrect choice (that of "No, it doesn't follow"), and some of which happened to lead to a correct one (that of "Yes, it does follow").

> *Incorrect empirical responses:*
> "The women must talk about household problems because it is important to talk about their problems, not because the problem is in their minds."
> "No. Just because one spends so much time in the kitchen it does not necessarily follow that household problems are 'in our minds.' "
>
> *Correct empirical responses:*
> "Yes. It seems obvious that problems which are in the forefront of one's mind bring more consideration to them and possibly newer aspects when they are discussed with another. Two heads may be better than one."
> "Yes, it does. By talking about household problems, a problem can be solved or worked through."

These protocols emphasize the value of asking not only for a yes-no answer, but also for an explanation of the reasoning underlying it. If we only had the yes-no answers we would have judged the first two people to have failed the logical task and the second two people to have passed it. However, examination of their reasoning reveals that none of them approached it as a logical task at all. Thus, all four people have made an error in encoding the *nature* of the problem. Rather than accepting the premises as givens and asking whether the conclusion follows logically from them, they have given their opinions on the empirical truth or falsity of the propositions contained in the premises and/or conclusion.

Since these people did not encode the task as a logical one, we cannot say anything about whether or not they are capable of logical thinking. That is, in searching long-term memory for a solution plan, these subjects would not have called upon any logical reasoning rules they might possess; as the subject has encoded the task, such rules are simply not relevant. In fact, there is some evidence that these subjects do have logical inference rules, because virtually all the subjects in the experiment approached at least one of the problems with which they were presented theoretically (rather than empirically) and when they did so they produced the logically correct response.

Failure to accept the logical task offers some insight into the nature of cross-cultural and developmental differences in logical reasoning. Scribner (1977) has summarized the results of many studies of syllogistic reasoning conducted not only on children and college students in this country, but also on schooled and unschooled members of isolated, nonindustrialized societies around the world. She makes two major conclusions. First, the overall accuracy with which people respond correctly to syllogisms is much higher among industrialized than nonindustrialized peoples, though this difference in performance is apparently due to differences in schooling, rather than in culture per se. In all societies the schooled members perform much more accurately than the unschooled members. In fact, when individuals with a few years of schooling are compared, there are few cultural differences.

Such findings have led earlier psychologists and anthropologists to argue that the unschooled lack the ability to reason logically, and that logical inference rules must be taught in school. Scribner's results suggest a different interpretation however, for her second major conclusion is that when their protocols are examined more closely, the main difference between schooled and unschooled individuals is in the degree to which they accept the task as a logical (as opposed to empirical) one.

Following is a sample protocol included in Scribner (1977), which is taken from an unschooled man of the Kpelle tribe, a rice farming tribal people in Liberia West Africa.

E: All Kpelle men are rice farmers.
Mr. Smith is not a rice farmer.
Is he a Kpelle man?
S: I don't know the man in person. I have not laid eyes on the man himself.
E: Just think about the statement.
S: If I know him in person, I can answer that question, but since I do not know him in person I cannot answer that question.
E: Try and answer from your Kpelle sense. (Note: This is a Kpelle expression)
S: If you know a person, if a question comes up about him you are able to answer. But if you do not know the person, if a question comes up about him, it's harder for you to answer it.

As Scribner noted, it is not that unschooled people are incapable of logical reasoning. For one thing, these people often used logical if-then arguments in their answers, as is evidenced in the transcript from the Kpelle man. In fact, every time I read that transcript I have the impression that the Kpelle man must think that the *experimenter* has difficulty with logical reasoning, since the experimenter cannot seem to follow his completely logical if-then argument! A second kind of evidence that unschooled people are capable of logical reasoning is that virtually every such person tested gave at least one theoretical response (i.e., accepted the task as a logical one), and when we look only at such protocols, we find that they then produced the logically correct answers.

The studies analyzed by Scribner suggest, then, that schooling doesn't teach us *how* to reason, it teaches us *when* to reason. That is, both schooled and unschooled people appear to possess rules for logical inference, but schooling teaches people to treat syllogisms as theoretical, isolated problems in which they should rely only upon these rules of logical inference, ignoring the real world truth value of the premises and conclusions. As Henle's data show, even American college students sometimes fail to treat reasoning tasks in this theoretical fashion. Thus, at least one source of errors in syllogistic reasoning is encoding the *nature of the problem* as being empirical rather than theoretical.

A second source of errors which has been noted by a number of researchers (e.g., Henle, 1962; Revlis, 1975b; Braine, 1978) is a *failure to discriminate between information given in the premises and information retrieved from long-term memory.* This is a different kind of encoding failure. Here, the person accepts the task as a logical one, and so does call upon rules of inference. However, when the premises are encoded into working memory, the person unintentionally supplements the premises with information from long-term memory. For example, in encoding the premise "Some men are honest," the person might supplement it with "but some are not"—information stored in long-term memory from long experience. This inadvertent translation could of course lead to apparent errors in reasoning, because the person is now reasoning with premises that are different from those presented. (That is, in formal logic "Some men are honest" might mean "All men are honest", but because of having supplemented the premise with information from long-term memory, the reasoner has failed to consider this interpretation.)

Of course, this source of error reflects a natural and necessary characteristic of language processing—the automatic drawing of implicit inferences that we saw earlier is essential for daily language comprehension. In most of daily conversation, we expect our listeners to draw upon long-term memory to supplement what is stated explicitly. However, when people are attempting to evaluate the validity of a syllogistic argument, they need to suspend such drawing of inferences. It is not surprising that it is often difficult to do so.

A third source of errors, *incorrect conversion of premises*, is closely related to the second. A number of researchers (e.g., Chapman & Chapman, 1959; Ceraso & Provitera, 1971; Revlis, 1975; Revlin & Leirer, 1980) have reported that people tend to convert the premises that are presented to them. In particular, they seem to assume symmetry (Tsal, 1977). That is, they tend to convert "All *A* are *B*" to "All *A* are *B* and All *B* are *A*". They convert "Some *A* are *B*" to "Some *A* are *B* and Some *B* are *A*." They convert "Some *A* are not *B*" to "Some *A* are not *B* and Some *B* are not *A*" and they convert "No *A* are *B*" into "No *B* are *A*." Revlin and Leirer (1980) have presented evidence for such conversions among college students and Bucci (1978) and Neimark and Chapman (1975) have shown that such conversions are even more prevalent among young children.

In all but the case of *No* statements, such conversion is illicit in that it leads the subject to fail to consider some of the possible meanings of the premise. It is easiest to appreciate that this is the case by examining Figure 13–1, which shows possible interpretations of the premises using Venn diagrams. Notice that "All *A* are *B*" can logically have one of two interpretations, either *A* is a proper subset of *B* or sets *A* and *B* are identical. The conversion to "All *A* are *B* and All *B* are *A*" results in the person considering only the second possible

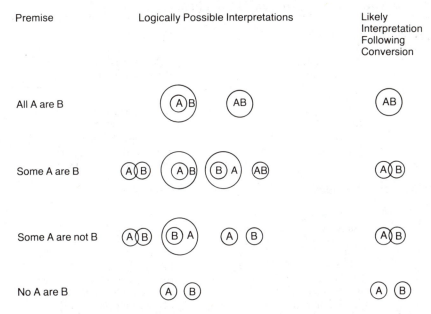

Figure 13–1. Venn diagram representations of premises. The left column depicts all logically possible interpretations of each premise. The right column depicts the interpretations subjects would adopt by converting the premises as described in the text.

interpretation. "Some A are B" could logically have any of the four interpretations diagrammed in the figure, yet the conversion based on an assumption of symmetry is likely to lead the subject to consider only the partially overlapping sets interpretation. "Some A are not B" has three logically possible interpretations, yet the conversion is likely to lead the person to only the partially overlapping sets interpretation. This tendency toward conversion thus leads the person to (incorrectly) treat "Some A are B" and "Some A are not B" as equivalent. Finally, the conversion of "No A are B" is not illicit, since there is only one logically correct interpretation of this statement and its interpretation remains unchanged in the conversion.

Conversions of the sort we have just described do serve to simplify the task, since they narrow down the number of possible interpretations (and thereby possible combinations) of the premises. This might, in fact, be why people often seem to adopt them, given our limited capacity working memory. Unfortunately since such conversions are usually illicit they often, though not always, lead to incorrect deductions. This point is illustrated in Table 13–3. Syllogism A in that table is one in which the converted premises lead to a different

TABLE 13–3. Syllogisms in Which Premise Conversion Either Does or Does Not Alter the Logically Valid Conclusion.

Syllogism A:	*Presented*	*Converted*
	All P are M	All M are P
	Some M are S	Some S are M
	Therefore:	Therefore:
	(a) All S are P	(a) All S are P
	(b) No S are P	(b) No S are P
	(c) Some S are P	*(c) Some S are P
	(d) Some S are not P	(d) Some S are not P
	*(e) None of the above is proven	(e) None of the above is proven
Syllogism B:	*Presented*	*Converted*
	No P are M	No M are P
	Some M are S	Some S are M
	Therefore:	Therefore:
	(a) All S are P	(a) All S are P
	(b) No S are P	(b) No S are P
	(c) Some S are P	(c) Some S are P
	*(d) Some S are not P	*(d) Some S are not P
	(e) None of the above is proven	(e) None of the above is proven

* Indicates the logically correct conclusion.
Examples taken from Revlin, Leirer, Yopp, and Yopp, 1980.

logically correct conclusion than do the unconverted premises. Whereas the logically correct conclusion to the presented syllogism is (e), the logically correct conclusion to the converted premises (shown on the right) is (c). Thus, for this problem conversion leads to an error. In contrast Syllogism B in the table is one in which the converted premises lead to the same conclusion (d) as the presented premises. Therefore, for this problem conversion does not lead to an error.

If such premise conversion is indeed a source of errors, then we would expect to find that students are more often correct on syllogisms like B in the table (in which the conversion does not change the logically valid conclusion) than they are on syllogisms like A (in which the conversion does change the valid conclusion). In fact, several studies have shown that this is the case (e.g., Revlin, Leirer, Yopp, & Yopp, 1980; Revlis, 1975b).

Researchers have also shown that when the reasoner's knowledge of the external world blocks illicit conversions, then performance improves (e.g., Revlis, 1975a). For example, if Syllogism A in Table 13–3 were changed to

All dogs are animals

Some animals are mean

the reasoner's knowledge of the relation between dogs and animals would prevent him from making the illicit conversion to "All animals are dogs." Therefore, if illicit conversions are contributing to erroneous judgments, people should be much less likely to incorrectly choose the (c) answer (i.e., Some mean things are dogs) in this concrete version of the syllogism than they are in the more abstract version. In fact, this is exactly what happens.

One study (Revlin, Leirer, Yopp, & Yopp, 1980) has demonstrated that conversion of premises can account for many errors that were traditionally thought to reflect illogical reasoning with emotionally laden material. Recall that earlier work had shown that people are more likely to accept a conclusion as being valid if the conclusion agrees with their own beliefs. Revlin and his colleagues pointed out that there is another possible interpretation of these findings, since in most early experiments not only the conclusion, but also the premises, consisted of emotionally laden material. Revlin noted that the individual's beliefs might be influencing the way in which the premises are encoded (e.g., whether or not they are converted), after which reasoning proceeds logically, largely uninfluenced by whether or not the subject believes the conclusion.

Revlin and his colleagues tested this hypothesis in two experiments. In the first, college students were given syllogisms which contained controversial premises and neutral conclusions. An example of one of their problems is the following:

No Republicans in Newton are residents of Sea Side.

All Republicans in Newton are upper class people.

(a) **All upper class people in Newton are residents of Sea Side**

(b) **No upper class people in Newton are residents of Sea Side**

(c) **Some upper class people in Newton are residents of Sea Side**

(d) **Some upper class people in Newton are not residents of Sea Side**

(e) **None of the foregoing is proven**

The second premise is potentially belief laden in that people might have preconceived notions about the extent to which republicans are upper class and the extent to which upper class people are republicans. On the other hand all of the possible conclusions are neutral in that there is no reason to think that people would have preconceptions about the residents of the hypothetical town of Newton and its section called Sea Side.

Either prior to or after answering all the syllogisms, each person was asked questions about the potentially belief-laden premises, in order to determine whether the subject judged the premise to be reversible. For example, people were asked, "What percentage of upper class people are republican?" Revlin and his colleagues reasoned that if a person's beliefs influence whether or not he converts the premises, then people who believe the converse of the controversial premise to be true will be likely to convert it to "All upper class people in Newton are republicans", and then reasoning logically from this converted premise will conclude that (b) is true. (Work this out so you understand why they would be led to this conclusion. Using the Venn diagrams as we did in Figure 13–1 should help.) On the other hand, people who do not believe the converse of the controversial premise are unlikely to convert it, and reasoning logically from the unconverted premises will conclude (correctly) that (d) is the correct answer. (Again, figure out why this is the correct answer.)

In fact, the findings were as predicted. People who believed the converse of the controversial premise usually chose (b), whereas those who did not believe the converse of the controversial premise usually chose (d). This finding demonstrated, then, that the subjects' beliefs influenced the way in which they interpreted the controversial premise. However, subjects clearly were capable of thinking logically, since the conclusions they drew followed logically from the premises *as the subjects had encoded them.*

In their second experiment, Revlin and his colleagues investigated syllogisms in which the conclusions themselves were belief laden. People were presented with syllogisms in which conversion of the premises would not influence which conclusion was logically correct (i.e., syllogisms like Syllogism B in Table 13–3). Therefore premise conversion could not influence the results. The important variable in this experiment was whether the logically correct conclusion was also empirically correct or whether it was not. In the former case, logic agrees with belief, so these are termed LA syllogisms. In the latter case logic conflicts with belief, so these are termed LC syllogisms. Examples of each kind are shown in Table 13–4. For the LA problem, the logically correct conclusion is (d), and this conclusion is also true empirically, since we all know that some US senators aren't women. Therefore, belief and logic agree. (You might also notice that choice (c) is empirically correct, but this doesn't prove to be a problem since only 3% of the subjects chose it.) In contrast, for the LC syllogism the logically correct conclusion is (d), but the empirically correct conclusion is (b). Thus, belief and logic conflict.

TABLE 13–4. Categorical Syllogisms in Which the Logically Correct Conclusion Either Agrees or Conflicts with Empirical Truth.

Logic Agrees with Belief Syllogism LA

No members of the ad hoc committee are women
Some US senators are members of the ad hoc committee
Therefore:
    (a) All US senators are women
    (b) No US senators are women
Empirically true   (c) Some US senators are women
Logically correct   (d) Some US senators are not women
    (e) None of the above is proven

Logic Conflicts with Belief Syllogism LC

No US governors are members of the Harem club
Some Arabian sheiks are members of the Harem club
Therefore:
    (a) All Arabian sheiks are US governors
Empirically true   (b) No Arabian sheiks are US governors
    (c) Some Arabian sheiks are US governors
Logically correct   (d) Some Arabian sheiks are not US governors
    (e) None of the above is proven

Examples taken from Revlin, Leirer, Yopp, & Yopp, 1980.

Revlin reasoned that if people are not engaging in logical reasoning at all, but are simply responding on the basis of their beliefs, then they should always be correct on LA syllogisms, and never be correct on LC syllogisms. In contrast, the conversion hypothesis predicts that people should be equally accurate on LA and LC problems, because in neither case does conversion influence the logically correct conclusion. In fact, Revlin's results revealed that there was some tendency for subjects to be more accurate on LA syllogisms (83% correct) than on LC syllogisms (67% correct), but this tendency was not particularly strong, since people were correct well over half of the time even on LC syllogisms. Furthermore, when Revlin looked more carefully at the choices people made on LC trials, he found that they were not simply choosing the empirically true statement. Instead, when belief and logic conflicted, they usually opted for the "none is proven" conclusion. Thus, they were sensitive to both the logical form of the argument *and* the real-world truth value of the conclusion. When the two conflicted, they often refused to choose between them.

The important conclusion from Revlin's experiments, then, is that the influence of content on reasoning does not indicate that people are incapable of logical inference. Rather, our beliefs influence the way in which we interpret premises, but we are then capable of reasoning quite logically from the premises *as we interpreted them*.

A fourth source of errors in syllogistic reasoning is *forgetting of the premises*. Given the capacity limits of working memory, it is reasonable to expect that even if someone does encode individual premises correctly, he/she might sometimes forget them, again resulting in the reasoner operating on premises that are different from those intended. Sylvia Scribner (1975) demonstrated that this is indeed the case in a cross-cultural study in which she tested Kpelle nonliterates, Kpelle junior college students, and American college students on problems of the following form:

Some kwi (western) people are wealthy

All wealthy people are powerful

Are some kwi people powerful?

The following sequence of events happened for each syllogism. First, the experimenter read it aloud to the subject. Then, the subject provided an answer to the syllogism and a reason for his choice. Next, the subject attempted to repeat the syllogism (first repetition). Then the experimenter reread the problem again slowly, after which the subject again attempted to repeat it (second repetition).

The results on the reasoning judgments were in agreement with those we discussed earlier. The nonliterate Kpelle were much less likely to make the correct choice (they were only 53% correct, which is chance performance) than either the Kpelle students (80% correct) or the United States students (90% correct). Also as before, the non-literate Kpelle usually offered empirical reasons for their answers (68% of the time), indicating they hadn't tried to solve the problem as a logical task, whereas the Kpelle and American students usually gave theoretical reasons (75% and 82% of the time respectively) indicating they had accepted the logical task.

More important for the present discussion are the findings concerning recall accuracy. Scribner measured recall accuracy by determining whether or not the subject's repetition preserved the meaning of each of the three propositions in the syllogism. She found that people in all groups made a large number of recall errors, even on the second repetition which was attempted immediately after the experimenter finished reading the syllogism. Furthermore, recall errors were particularly prevalent among the nonliterate Kpelle. Fully 75% of such villagers were incorrect on some aspect of recall of each problem, whereas this occurred for 50% of the Kpelle students and 33% of the American students. Scribner found that across all the groups three types of recall errors were particularly prevalent. People omitted a premise, they displaced terms from one premise to another, and they changed the quantifiers in the premises (e.g., from Some to All).

Once again, then, we find that people often are operating on premises that are different from those presented to them. Many apparent deficiencies in logical reasoning may be due to the forgetting of premises. For example, Trabasso and his colleagues have studied young children's ability to make transitive inferences. For example, children might be told that the red stick is taller than the green stick and that the green stick is taller than the blue stick. When asked to decide which is taller, the red or the blue stick, children often fail to draw the correct conclusion. Their failure has usually been blamed on a lack of logical ability (Piaget, 1928; Piaget, Inhelder, & Szeminska, 1960). However, Trabasso and his colleagues have shown that children often forget the premises in such problems, and when learning and memory of the premises is insured, they found that even very young children make logical inferences (Bryant & Trabasso, 1971; Trabasso, Riley, & Wilson, 1975).

Models of syllogistic reasoning. Most contemporary researchers and theoreticians agree that human reasoning is characterized by a kind of *bounded rationality* (a term you should recall from our discussion of Simon's concept of satisficing in the problem solving chapter). Individuals untrained in logic are capable of reasoning logically; they have production systems that enable them to make logical judgments about the validity of arguments. However, people often fail to reveal their logical competence, drawing invalid conclusions from a set of premises, either because they fail to treat the task as one in logical reasoning, or because they are operating on premises that are different from those presented. As we have just discussed, several factors can lead to this alteration in premises, including a failure to distinguish material presented in the premises from information drawn from long-term memory, illicit premise conversion, and forgetting.

In recent years, a number of specific theories of syllogistic reasoning have been proposed, which attempt to outline more precisely the series of steps people use when they solve categorical syllogisms (e.g., Braine, 1978; Erickson, 1974; 1978; Johnson-Laird & Steedman, 1978; Revlis, 1975). Although all these theories share the view of bounded rationality, they differ regarding such points as the nature of the representation people adopt when solving syllogisms, and the form of the logical rules people use to draw conclusions. At the moment, there are no compelling reasons to favor one of these theories over the other. Indeed, it is likely that no one of them will provide a satisfactory account of reasoning that will apply to all individuals, since it appears that different people adopt different modes of representation, for example. All of the theories are able to account for the general characteristics of performance that we have discussed, e.g., the atmosphere and conversion errors that often appear.

The existence of such theories has already helped to increase our knowledge about human reasoning. This is because the attempt to find evidence that would support one theory while refuting others has encouraged more careful experiments on reasoning, and these have already revealed new information about the characteristics of human inference. We will consider one such example now.

One of the most convincing and influential theories of syllogistic reasoning is the *set analysis theory* proposed by Erickson (1974; 1978). This theory assumes that syllogistic reasoning involves three stages. Each of these stages is illustrated in Table 13-5, which shows how a conclusion would be drawn on a correct trial. In the first stage, the reasoner represents each of the premises in turn as one or more Venn diagrams. For each of the premises in the example in Table 13–5, there are two possible Venn diagram representations, representing the subset and the set identity interpretations of each premise. As we have discussed earlier, one potential source of error, then, would enter here if the subject failed to consider both interpretations of each of the premises. In the second stage, the reasoner attempts to combine the Venn diagrams from the two premises. As the table reveals, several combinations are usually possible, so another potential source of error is that the person might fail to generate all possible combinations. Finally, during the third stage, the reasoner prepares verbal labels (i.e., conclusions) that are consistent with each of the possible combinations produced in the second stage, and then produces the conclusion that holds for all possible combinations. This provides another potential source of errors, since subjects might either label the combinations incorrectly or fail to make sure that the one they have chosen is consistent with *all* possible combinations.

Erickson's theory has intuitive appeal, since many of us feel as though we use Venn diagram representations to solve syllogisms, and in addition, the theory is able to account for many aspects of human performance. Nonetheless, a recent study by Johnson-Laird and Steedman (1978) revealed results which cannot be accounted for by Set

---

TABLE 13–5. Set Analysis Theory of Reasoning.

Analysis of Problem of Drawing a Conclusion from Premises in a Syllogism

Task: Draw a conclusion from premises (or state that no conclusion is logical)

All P are M	Major Premise
All M are S	Minor Premise
? ? ?	Conclusion

Stage I: Interpretation of premises

Possible Interpretations

All P are M   1   2

((P)   M)   or   (PM)

All M are S   3   4

((M)   S)   or   (MS)

Stage II: Combination of interpreted premises

Possible Combinations

1 and 3   1 and 4   2 and 3   2 and 4

((P) M S)   (P (MS))   ((PM) S)   (PMS)

Stage III: Labeling of set relation of S to P

Possible Labels

1 and 3	1 and 4
Some S are P	Some S are P
or	or
Some S are not P	All S are P
2 and 3	2 and 4
Some S are P	All S are P
or	or
Some S are not P	Some S are P

Logical Conclusion: Some S are P

TABLE 13–6. The Eight Possible Figures of the Syllogism When Premise Order Is Varied.

	Figure 1	Figure 2	Figure 3	Figure 4
Traditional Premise Order	M-P S-M	P-M S-M	M-P M-S	P-M M-S

	Figure 1'	Figure 2'	Figure 3'	Figure 4'
Reversed Premise Order	S-M M-P	S-M P-M	M-S M-P	M-S P-M

Analysis Theory, at least in its present form. These new results came about because Johnson-Laird and Steedman examined performance on syllogistic figures that had never been studied before. They noted that traditional logic only distinguishes among the four figures shown at the top of Table 13–6. That is, the major premise connecting the M and P terms is always presented first. However, it is quite possible to reverse the order of presenting the major and minor premises, resulting in the four additional figures we have shown as 1' through 4' at the bottom of the table. Thus, there are in fact 512 different syllogisms possible, not only the 256 that are normally considered.

Johnson-Laird and Steedman presented examples of all possible combinations of figure, premise order, and mood to college students, requiring them to generate conclusions that were consistent with the premises. They found that figure, premise order, and mood all interacted to influence the kind of decision that the subject was most likely to produce. For example, they found that when Figure 1' was presented (i.e., S-M, M-P), subjects usually (about 85% of the time) produced conclusions of the form S-P, rather than those of the form P-S. In contrast when Figure 4' was presented (i.e., M-S, P-M), subjects usually (about 86% of the time) produced conclusions of the form P-S, rather than S-P. The following specific examples illustrate this *figural effect*. The syllogism

Some of the parents are scientists.

All of the scientists are drivers.

yields the conclusion "Some of the parents are drivers" rather than the equally valid "Some of the drivers are parents." In contrast, the syllogism

All of the scientists are parents.

Some of the drivers are scientists.

yields the conclusion "Some of the drivers are parents" rather than the equally valid "Some of the parents are drivers."

This figural effect is important because it cannot be accounted for readily by Set Analysis Theory. This is because any Venn diagram that can be labeled as "Some *A* are *B*" could also be labeled "Some *B* are *A*." (You can convince yourself of this by examining the Venn diagrams illustrated in the second stage of Erickson's model in Table 13–5. Note that he has labeled them all with "Some *S* are *P*", yet each could also be labeled "Some *P* are *S*".) Erickson's theory cannot explain why subjects prefer one statement after some figures and the other statement after other figures.

The finding of this figural effect led Johnson-Laird and Steedman (1978) to propose what they call an analogical theory of syllogistic reasoning. Their theory assumes that people represent the premises using an analogic form of representation that preserves the order in which premises and terms within the premises are presented. Therefore, their theory is able to account readily for the figural effect. Of course, it would also be possible to attempt to modify Set Analysis Theory to account for the figural effect, and as yet it is not clear which approach makes more sense.

The important point here, however, is that theories of human reasoning have been proposed which are specific enough to test, and attempts to determine which of these theories is to be preferred are leading to new insights into human reasoning.

CONDITIONAL REASONING AND THE DEDUCTIVE TESTING OF HYPOTHESES

Logical analysis. Conditional reasoning is particularly important in scientific fields, but it is also prevalent in everyday experience. For example, a student is told "If you do well on the final, then you will get an *A*." A lover is told, "If you loved me, then you would marry me," and a child is promised, "If you eat all your dinner, then you may have dessert."

Conditional or *hypothetical syllogisms* consist of (1) a statement of a conditional rule, stating that if one proposition is true then a second is true, followed by (2) a statement concerning the truth or falsity of one of the propositions. The reasoner must decide what follows regarding the truth or falsity of the other proposition. For example,

If you eat all your dinner, you may have dessert (If p, then q)

You ate all your dinner (p is true)

May you have your dessert? (Is q true?)

Propositional calculus specifies the conclusion which follows logically from a given conditional syllogism. There are four major forms in which conditional syllogisms may appear, two of which are valid arguments and two of which are invalid. These four forms are illustrated in Table 13–7. In conditional syllogisms, the first proposition in the rule (p) is called the *antecedent* and the second proposition (q) is called the *consequent*. Notice that the two invalid inferences (or fallacies) are named after their second premise, not after the invalid conclusion. Denying the antecedent is a fallacy since the first premise leaves the possibility that q might be true even if p is not true. Affirming the consequent is a fallacy, since the first premise leaves the possibility that p might be false even if q is true.

TABLE 13–7. Conditional Syllogisms.

Form	Name	Example
If p, then q p ——— Therefore q	*modus ponens* (Valid inference)	If the object is square, then it is blue The object is square ——— The object is blue
If p, then q not q ——— Therefore not p	*modus tollendo tollens* (Valid inference)	If the object is square, then it is blue The object is not blue ——— The object is not square
If p, then q not p ——— Therefore not q	denying the antecedent (Invalid inference)	If the object is square, then it is blue The object is not square ——— The object is not blue
If p, then q q ——— Therefore p	affirming the consequent (Invalid inference)	If the object is square, then it is blue The object is blue ——— The object is square

Errors on conditional syllogisms. Are people logical, in that they successfully draw the two kinds of valid inferences and avoid the fallacies? To find out, Shapiro (cited in Wason and Johnson-Laird, 1972, pp. 43–44) gave 20 college students two problems of each type, using fairly abstract materials such as the examples shown in Table 13–7. People were asked to read each problem and then to judge whether the argument it contained was valid or invalid. Shapiro found that there were marked differences in difficulty for the various forms. The fewest errors occurred with *modus ponens* which people failed to judge as valid only 5% of the time. The highest percent of errors (52.5%) occurred on *modus tollendo tollens*. Thus, people often failed to appreciate that this is a valid inference. The two fallacies were between these two extremes in difficulty, with people incorrectly affirming the consequent about 20% of the time and incorrectly denying the antecedent about 25% of the time. You were presented with a problem of each type in Table 13–1. How did you do? You might also test a number of friends to see whether or not their pattern of difficulty is the same as that Shapiro's subjects displayed.

It appears, then, that *modus ponens* (If p then q; p; therefore q) is a natural rule of inference that is used readily by college students. Indeed Hill (1961 discussed in Wason & Johnson-Laird, 1972) found that even six-year-olds make *modus ponens* inferences with ease. In contrast, people have a great deal of difficulty with *modus tollendo tollens* (If p then q; not q; therefore not p). At least part of this difficulty is probably attributable to the fact that it contains a negative premise (not q). We know from many other tasks (e.g., Chase & Clark, 1972; Clark, 1969) that negative sentences are more difficult to interpret and reason with than positive sentences.

Testing hypotheses: A bias toward confirmation. A conditional statement, such as "If p, then q" proposes a hypothesis about the existence of a relation between p and q. For example, you might hold the hypothesis (prejudice?) that "If someone is poor, then he/she is stupid." Indeed, as this example indicates, our beliefs and prejudices about the world can be expressed as conditional statements. How do people go about evaluating such hypotheses? What evidence do people believe they need to collect in order to evaluate the truth or falsity of a given hypothesis?

Wason and Johnson-Laird have developed several ingenious tasks for investigating this question. You have already attempted one of these, their *selection task* in Table 13–1. Table 13–8 again displays the four cards from which you were to make your selection, as well as the hypothesis that you were to test, i.e., If the letter is a vowel (p), then the number is even (q). Note that using more general designations, the E (vowel) card is the p card, the F (consonant) card is the

TABLE 13–8. The Selection Task and the Percentage of Subjects Making Various Choices.

E	F	4	7
p	not-p	q	not-q

Rule: If the letter is a vowel (p), then the number is even (q).

Choice	Per Cent Choosing
p & q	46%
p	33%
p, q, & not-q	7%
*p & not-q	4%
others	10%

* indicates the correct choice.
Data taken from Wason and Johnson-Laird (1972, p. 182).

not-p card, the 4 (even) card is the q card, and the 7 (odd) card is the not-q card. The lower part of the Table shows the percentage of subjects who make each kind of selection. The great majority choose either the p card alone (i.e., the E) or the p and q cards (i.e., the E and the 4), even though the logically correct response is p and not-q—a combination chosen by only 4% of all college students. Which did you choose? Before considering what this pattern of errors suggests, we should first make sure that you understand why p and not-q are the logically correct choices. As most subjects notice, the E card *must* contain an even number in order for the hypothesis to be true, but as most subjects don't notice, the 7 card must *not* contain a vowel. If it did, then a vowel would be paired with an odd number in violation of the rule. The remaining two cards are irrelevant, since regardless of what occurred on the other side of these cards, the rule would not be falsified.

We see then, that in this deceptively simple looking selection task, people choose to examine a card (p) which could confirm the hypothesis, but they almost always fail to examine a card (not-q) which could falsify the hypothesis. This suggests that we are biased to seek to confirm, rather than to falsify, our hypotheses. In fact, people seem to fail to appreciate the value of attempting to falsify a hypothesis. This failure to appreciate the importance of the not-q card while recognizing the importance of the p card, is another example of the relative difficulty of *modus tollendo tollens* inferences compared to *modus ponens*.

The difficulty people have in realizing the necessity of testing the not-q card is particularly striking because on the surface, at least, the task appears to be so simple. Nonetheless, Wason and Johnson-Laird (1972, p. 173) report that even logicians often fail to choose the not-q card, much to their later embarrassment. Why not try giving the selection task to a variety of friends, including those who have taken courses in logic, to see how they do on it?

Not only do few subjects make the logical choice of p and not-q cards spontaneously, but Wason (1977) has shown that even when people are shown that the not-q card could falsify the rule, they *still* often fail to understand its importance. Wason demonstrated this by introducing an additional task to the experiment. Immediately after students had made their choices, if they failed to choose the correct (p and not-q cards), these two cards were turned over. In keeping with the rule, the p card contained a q on its other side, but in violation of the rule the not-q card contained a p on its reverse side. The subjects were asked about the implications of these two exposed cards and asked if they wished to alter their initial choices. Wason found that even in light of this contradiction of the rule, almost three-quarters of his college students *still* failed to alter their choice to include the not-q card.

Wason and Johnson-Laird, as well as other researchers, have given subjects the selection task in a variety of guises and under a variety of conditions in an attempt to find out if any such variations make it easier. The only major variation which seems to help is a variation in content. If the task is made more concrete, performance improves substantially. For example, Johnson-Laird, Legrenzi, and Legrenzi (1972) gave two selection tasks, one concrete and the other abstract, to a group of college students. Some received the concrete task first and others received the abstract task first. For the concrete task, they were asked to imagine that they were postal workers sorting letters. Their task was to determine whether the following rule had been violated: If a letter is sealed, then it has a 5d stamp on it. Rather than being cards, the material consisted of the four envelopes shown in the top half of Figure 13–2: the back of a sealed envelope (p), the back of an unsealed envelope (not-p), the front of an envelope with a 5d stamp on it (q), and the front of an envelope with a 4d stamp on it (not-q). The subjects were told "select just those letters that you definitely need to turn over to find out whether or not they violate the rule." For the abstract condition, the rule was: "If a letter has a D on one side, then it has a 5 on the other side." The bottom half of Figure 13–2 shows the materials used for this abstract task. Otherwise the procedure for the abstract task was the same as that for the concrete. The experimenters found that under the abstract condition only 2 of 24 subjects were correct, whereas under the concrete task condition 21 of the 24 correctly chose the p and not-q envelopes.

Wason and Shapiro (1971) and Gilhooly and Falconer (1974)

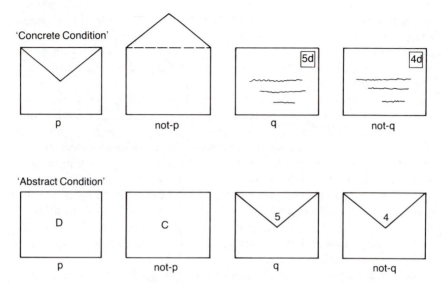

Figure 13–2. Stimuli used in the concrete and abstract conditions of the "envelope" selection experiment conducted by Johnson-Laird, Legrenzi, and Legrenzi (1972). (After Wason & Johnson-Laird, 1972. Copyright 1972 by B. T. Batsford, Ltd. Reprinted by permission.)

have also demonstrated that making the problem more concrete facilitates reasoning in this task, though the improvement they found was not nearly as dramatic as that obtained in this envelope experiment. These studies do demonstrate that concrete content makes it more likely that people will spontaneously use *modus tollendo tollens,* i.e., that they will attempt to disconfirm a rule. Again, then, as in the case of reasoning with categorical syllogisms, the *content* of the logical problem does influence human performance.

Our bias toward attempting to confirm rather than falsify hypotheses is also seen clearly in the so called *2-4-6 experiments* of Wason and Johnson-Laird (1972). Try this simple task on several friends. Subjects are given the series "2-4-6" and told that it conforms to a simple rule that the experimenter has in mind. The subject's task is to discover this rule by generating series of his/her own. After each, the experimenter will indicate whether or not the series the subject has generated also conforms to the rule. The subject is instructed that *only* after he/she has collected enough evidence to be sure of the correct rule, should the rule be announced to the experimenter. In order to facilitate later interpretation of the data, the subject is asked to write down each series generated and the reason for this choice on a record sheet. The experiment continues either until the person states the correct rule or until the experimenter or subject gives up in frustration.

Before you read further, write down the first series you would generate if you were a subject in the task, and also jot down your reason for choosing it.

The rule the experimenter has in mind is "numbers in increasing order of magnitude." What is of primary interest in this task is not whether or not the subject discovers the correct rule. Instead, we are interested in the way in which the person goes about testing his hypotheses. For example, many came up with the hypothesis "numbers increasing by 2." Notice that in order to test this hypothesis you could either attempt to confirm it by generating a series consistent with the rule (e.g., 5-7-9), or you could attempt to disconfirm it by generating a series inconsistent with your hypothesis (e.g., 5-6-7). The striking phenomenon that is observed with this task is that people rarely, if ever, attempt to disconfirm their hypotheses; they only seek to confirm them. Then after generating a number of series and collecting a number of such confirmations, subjects gain enough confidence in the current hypothesis to offer it to the experimenter as a solution. Given the generality of the correct rule the experimenter had in mind, this confirmation strategy rarely leads to discovery of the correct rule. Nonetheless, even after repeated wrong guesses of the hypothesis, most subjects continued to plow ahead without attempting to falsify their rule. This, of course, is extremely frustrating, since the person receives a series of confirmations, yet is repeatedly told that he hasn't found the rule. In fact, Wason (1968) reported that one subject was so frustrated with this experiment that he developed psychotic symptoms in the middle of the experiment and had to be removed by ambulance. Wason hastens to assure us that nothing similar has occurred with any other subject before or since.

The results of the 2-4-6 task are so important because, together with the selection task, they highlight a general property of human thinking. Whenever we have a hypothesis, we have a strong bias to seek confirmations, rather than disconfirmations. This is despite the fact that, logically speaking, one disconfirmation is much more informative than a confirmation. That is, only one disconfirmation is necessary to prove that a hypothesis is incorrect, but countless confirmations cannot prove that a hypothesis is correct.

This confirmations bias is particularly noteworthy, because people have a strong bias toward developing hypotheses in the first place, a fact that will become particularly apparent in the next chapter on conceptual thinking. This, of course, is in keeping with the cognitive view of the human as an individual that seeks to organize experience. Thus, on the basis of one or a very few observations of related events, we develop all-encompassing hypotheses, which we then seek to confirm. This tendency to develop hypotheses and the bias to seek only confirmation of them is apparently a very general property of human thought that holds across a range of tasks and subject populations. For example, it is even observed in very young children. Karmiloff-Smith and Inhelder (1977) presented a task with toy blocks to children and found that even the seven-year-olds tended to develop hypotheses which often led them to fail to notice important properties of the blocks that didn't fit with their hypotheses. Furthermore, they exhibited the confirmation bias just as adults do. Mynatt, Doherty, and Tweney (1977) have shown a confirmation bias in a study of college students in which a more realistic, simulated research environment was used, and Mitroff (1974), in an observational study, reported many examples of confirmation bias in the daily conversation and scientific work of NASA scientists. In fact, Mahoney (1976), testing the reasoning skills of physicists, psychologists, and Protestant ministers, found that the scientists were more likely than the ministers to develop theories on the basis of only scanty evidence and then to continue to hold the theories even in the face of contradictory evidence.

Of course, our tendency to hypothesize and then attempt only to confirm the hypothesis has advantages. It helps us to organize and simplify experience, thereby lessening the burdens on our limited processing capacity. And, as we have noted often throughout the book, it is often useful to keep a theory (particularly a scientific theory) even when we know of some disconfirming evidence, simply because lacking a better theory, the old one helps to organize and remember individual findings. Nonetheless, our tendency to seek only confirmation of our own hypotheses does have the distinct disadvantage of contributing to false beliefs and prejudice. Given a prejudice regarding a group of people, for example, we are likely to seek out only evidence confirming it—a phenomenon witnessed repeatedly in daily life.

HUMAN REASONING: LOGICAL OR ILLOGICAL?

Throughout this chapter we have seen that those uneducated in formal logic (and, indeed, even those educated in it) often fail to make judgments that are consistent with the canons of formal logic. We make atmosphere errors, we are often influenced by the contents of arguments rather than their logical structure, we often fail to use *modus tollendo tollens,* and we have a bias to seek only confirmation of our hypotheses. Yet we are not completely illogical, either. Most of the errors people make on categorical syllogisms are due to a misinterpretation of the task or the premises, rather than to a lack of logical ability per se, and the logic of *modus ponens* is used readily by virtually everyone, including young children. Thus, human reasoning is best described as a *bounded rationality* in that all humans are capable of at least the rudiments of logical deduction, but we often fail to call upon this logical ability.

Implications for Piaget's theory of the development of logical thinking. That great developmental psychologist, the late Jean Piaget, did more than any other individual to reveal the mysteries of children's thinking. In fact, virtually all studies of logical reasoning in children owe a debt to Piaget's keen observations of children. Nonetheless, the findings we have discussed in this chapter cast doubt upon some of Piaget's most basic assumptions.

As most people who have taken introductory psychology courses know, Piaget assumes that during the course of development the child constructs a series of stages. Very young children in the early sensory-motor and preoperational stages are incapable of logical thinking, because they have not yet constructed a set of logical operations (which are analogous to production systems for performing logical tasks, in information processing terminology). In later childhood (during the concrete operational stage), the child possesses such logical operations, but is only able to apply them to concrete tasks, not to abstract ones. Finally, during the stage of formal operations which is usually reached during early adolescence, the individual develops the ability to apply the logical operations to all kinds of problems, either concrete or abstract, independent of content. Indeed, in this final stage of development, Piaget argues that the person's logical competence can be modelled by propositional calculus.

Thus, according to Piaget, we develop from individuals who are incapable of logical thought into individuals who are completely logical, and whose logical reasoning ability is applied equally regardless of the contents about which we are reasoning. What we have learned in this chapter calls into question two major aspects of this theory. First, even very young children are capable of logical reasoning, their failures often being due to such factors as failing to accept the logical task or forgetting the premises, rather than to a lack of logical ability per se. Therefore, Piaget may have underestimated the logical abilities of young children. Second, even as adults, our reasoning is influenced by the contents about which we are reasoning. Thus, Piaget may have overestimated the logical abilities of adults. In fact, Piaget seems to have come to the latter conclusion himself in at least one of his later writings (Piaget, 1972).

IMPROVING YOUR REASONING ABILITY

Perhaps the best way to improve your own reasoning skills is to be aware of the biases we have discussed in this chapter, and in so doing you may be able to avoid their negative effects. For example, be sure to consider all possible interpretations of a premise when you attempt to judge the validity of an argument, and when you hold a hypothesis, remember to seek out disconfirming as well as confirming evidence. That such simple awareness of our biases can improve reasoning has, in fact, been demonstrated in several experiments. For example, subjects who are warned to avoid the atmosphere effect show a rapid improvement in judgments of categorical syllogisms (Simpson & Johnson, 1966), as do subjects who are warned to avoid conversion errors (Dickstein, 1975).

CHAPTER SUMMARY

Reasoning is a form of problem solving in which we attempt to determine whether or not one proposition follows logically from another. The major issue in the study of reasoning concerns the relation between the laws of formal logic and the laws of human thinking. To what extent do the laws of logic describe the thinking of people untrained in formal logic? We examined this question by considering two kinds of logical tasks: categorical syllogisms and conditional reasoning.

A categorical syllogism is an argument which contains two propositions called premises followed by a conclusion. People often make errors on categorical syllogisms and their accuracy varies with the mood, figure, and contents of the syllogism. Early psychological studies stressed two sources of error—atmosphere and content. These early studies suggested that human reasoning is illogical. More recent psychological research has suggested that logically untrained people are capable of logical inference, but that they often fail to use their logical competence because of errors that appear in one or more stages of processing. Four such sources of error are: (1) failure to encode the task as a logical problem, (2) failure to discriminate between information stated in the premises and information retrieved from long-term memory, (3) premise conversion, and (4) forgetting of premises. Thus, human reasoning is best characterized as possessing a bounded rationality. Several information processing models of reasoning have been proposed which assume such bounded rationality.

Conditional reasoning involves determining what follows logically from "If-then" statements. When presented with conditional syllogisms, people make predictable patterns of errors. Although they are very likely to make *modus ponens* (i.e., If p then q; p; therefore q) inferences, they usually fail to make *modus tollendo tollens* (i.e., If p then q; not q; therefore not p) inferences. In addition, people often incorrectly judge two kinds of fallacies to be valid. When people attempt to test hypotheses, they have a strong bias to seek to confirm rather than falsify them. Thus, analyses of conditional reasoning also suggest that human reasoning is characterized by bounded rationality, a conclusion which calls into question some major assumptions of Piaget's influential theory of the development of logical reasoning.

SUGGESTED READING

There are four edited volumes that contain many of the most important articles on reasoning. Two of these were already suggested in the problem solving chapter. These are Johnson-Laird and Wason's (1977) collection called *Thinking* (which contains several of the original articles on confirmation bias) and the 1968 volume edited by Wason and Johnson-Laird entitled *Thinking and Reasoning* (which contains a number of classic articles, including Henle's 1962 paper). The other two edited volumes, which focus on more recent work are Falmagne's (1975) *Reasoning: Representation and Process,* which also contains articles on developmental and cross-cultural research, and Revlin and Mayer's *Human Reasoning* (1978). In addition, Wason and Johnson-Laird provide an integrated account of their own work in their excellent volume *Psychology of Reasoning* (1972).

Psychologists have studied many kinds of reasoning that we have not considered at all in this chapter, including sentence-picture verification, linear syllogistic reasoning, and analogical reasoning. You might wish to focus on any one of these as a term paper topic. Sentence-picture verification research has been concerned with specifying the series of operations people use to make speeded judgments about whether or not a sentence (e.g., The star is above the plus) describes a picture (e.g., $\overset{*}{+}$). Some very simple but powerful theories have been developed to account for patterns of response times in such studies. The article by Carpenter and Just (1975) is a good starting place and it will send you to the earlier references (e.g., Chase and Clark, 1972). In addition, Hunt and his colleagues have recently published fascinating work on individual differences in this task (MacLeod, Hunt, & Mathews, 1978; Mathews, Hunt, & MacLeod, 1980).

Research on linear syllogistic reasoning asks how people solve syllogisms such as "If Pete is taller than Fred and Fred is shorter than Allen, then who is tallest?". In the late 1960's two theories were proposed, one of which (Huttenlocher, 1968) assumed that people use imagery to solve such syllogisms, and the other of which (Clark, 1969) assumed they used a verbal code. A heated debate followed in the pages of the *Psychological Review*. After reading these articles, turn to more recent articles (e.g., R. Sternberg, 1980; Shaver, Pierson, & Lang, 1974/5) which suggest how the two views might be reconciled.

Analogical reasoning research is concerned with how people solve problems such as "*A* is to *B* as *C* is to what?" A good place to begin reading on this topic would be R. Sternberg's (1977) article. An article on aptness in metaphor by Tourangeau and Sternberg (1981) will also be of interest.

Conceptual Thinking

FOOD FOR THOUGHT

Begin by doing the task described in Table 14–1, and *do not read further until you have completed that experiment.*

In order to find out how well you did, consult the answer key contained in Table 14–3. How many of the test items did you answer correctly?

If you had learned nothing at all about the rules during the initial part of the task, then you could have guessed correctly only about 50% of the time, so you would have been correct on approximately 25 of the 50 test strings. You probably did better than this, suggesting that you did pick up something about the rules. Are you surprised at this? Did you feel certain of your answers during the testing? What does this suggest about our ability to learn unconsciously about regularities in the environment?

Now try a very different kind of concept learning task, by following the instructions contained in Figure 14–1. Do not read further until you have completed the experiment. Now try a little introspection. How did you go about solving the problem? Describe in as much detail as possible how you decided to make your choice in each case and how you incorporated the feedback you were given into your decision. Compare and contrast the ways in which you attempted to deal with each of the problems you just solved.

THE IMPORTANCE OF CONCEPTUAL THINKING

The world we live in is characterized by infinite variation. Each person differs from every other and the same can be said, though perhaps to a lesser degree, of trees, animals, books, and events. If we always noticed this variation, if we treated every single person and object as a brand new experience, then we would be faced with a task of phenomenal proportion. We would be unable to use what we had learned about earlier objects and events to deal with this new one. We would have to discover anew each time that this particular fire, for example, has the characteristic of inducing pain if touched, just as the earlier fires we have experienced. In order to deal with this infinite variation, we must segment the world into *conceptual classes* within which nonidentical stimuli are treated as equivalent. Then new events, objects, and people can be identified as members of these classes and assumed to have the properties of these classes.

Of course, each object, event, or person can be classified in a number of different ways, and the classification we choose influences the assumptions we will make about the individual. For example, I might be classified as a university professor, a woman, a daughter, a

TABLE 14–1.

Use a card or piece of paper to cover over all the lists below except the first one. Read the list silently to yourself, then cover it over and write down the list from memory in the blank provided to the right. Then move your card down to reveal the second list and do the same for it, continuing in this manner until you have read and written down all 40 lists.

1. TPTXVPS	_____
2. VVPXXVS	_____
3. TPTS	_____
4. VXXVS	_____
5. TPPTXXVS	_____
6. VXXVPS	_____
7. VVPXVPS	_____
8. TTS	_____
9. VVPXXXVS	_____
10. TTXVS	_____
11. TTXXXVS	_____
12. VXXXXXVS	_____
13. VVPS	_____
14. TPPPPPTS	_____
15. VXVPXVPS	_____
16. VXVPXVS	_____
17. TTXVPXVS	_____
18. TPTXXVPS	_____
19. VVS	_____
20. TPPPTS	_____
21. VXXVS	_____
22. TTXXXVS	_____
23. VVPS	_____
24. TPPPPPTS	_____
25. TPTXVPS	_____
26. VVS	_____
27. TPPPTS	_____
28. TTXVPXVS	_____
29. TPTS	_____
30. VVPXVPS	_____
31. VXVPXVPS	_____
32. TTXVS	_____
33. VVPXXXVS	_____
34. VVPXXVS	_____
35. TPTXXVPS	_____
36. TTS	_____
37. VXXXXXVS	_____
38. VXVPXVS	_____
39. TPPTXXVS	_____
40. VXXVPS	_____

Now please turn to Table 14–2 and follow the instructions there.

TABLE 14–2.

The lists you saw in Table 14–1 were all constructed by using a rather complex set of rules. The rules only allowed certain letters to follow other letters. Now, in order to find out whether or not you learned anything about those rules, please look at each of the 50 test lists below and decide whether or not it conforms to the same set of rules as the lists you saw in Table 14–1. Take a guess at each one even if you think you don't know the answer. Use the space provided to the right of each list to write "yes" if you think the list conforms to the rules and "no" if you think it doesn't.

1. TPPTS	_____	26. TTXVPS	_____
2. TPPPXS	_____	27. VXTPS	_____
3. TPPSXVS	_____	28. TTXXXVPS	_____
4. TPTXVS	_____	29. VVPXVS	_____
5. PXXXXVPS	_____	30. SVXXPVV	_____
6. VVPS	_____	31. VXXXVPS	_____
7. TVXXXVPS	_____	32. VXVV	_____
8. TPTXXXVS	_____	33. VVPXXVPS	_____
9. VXXXXVS	_____	34. VPVPXVS	_____
10. PPTS	_____	35. VXVS	_____
11. TPPTX	_____	36. TSXXXXVS	_____
12. XTXXVPS	_____	37. TPPTXXVS	_____
13. TPPPPTS	_____	38. VVPXPS	_____
14. TPPPTXSS	_____	39. VXVPXVPP	_____
15. TPTXXVS	_____	40. TTXVS	_____
16. TPPPTXVS	_____	41. VVPXXVXS	_____
17. SXXVS	_____	42. TTXXXXVS	_____
18. VXXVPXVS	_____	43. VXVPXXVS	_____
19. SPVXXTPT	_____	44. TXXXVS	_____
20. VXVPS	_____	45. TPTXVPS	_____
21. TTXXXVP	_____	46. SPVXTT	_____
22. VPXVPXVS	_____	47. VVPXVVS	_____
23. VXXXVT	_____	48. TPPTXVS	_____
24. TPPTXVPS	_____	49. STXVPXVS	_____
25. VXXVPS	_____	50. VXXXVS	_____

The correct answers are shown in Table 14–3.

mother, a wife, or a person. Each such classification is likely to suggest different characteristics. This fact demonstrates that our tendency to categorize has negative consequences as well, for it means that we have a propensity to impose a classification on new events, people, and objects, thereby bringing to mind a set of expectations about this new experience—expectations which may or may not turn out to be true. Thus, we are likely to approach new experiences with a certain amount of prejudice acquired from earlier experiences (or perhaps from hearsay) with members of the same class.

Experimental psychologists have been fascinated with the question of how people acquire and use concepts, because such conceptual thinking seems to form so central a part of human cognition. Much of the child's cognitive and social development consists of learning the classifications used by his/her society, and learning the words that should be attached to these concepts. Thus, the child must learn the range of visual experience to which the name red should be applied and the range of auditory experience to which the name music should be applied. As the latter example makes clear, the criteria that should be adopted for such classification may vary depending upon the group doing the socializing. Even after we have attained adulthood, concept acquisition continues; as we learn about new disciplines and new skills, we must learn new sets of concepts and their corresponding labels. Indeed, learning an academic discipline consists in large part of learning a new vocabulary and a new set of criteria for classifying instances.

In this chapter, we will focus on what psychologists have learned about conceptual thinking. This is certainly not the first time we have been concerned with concepts. Viewed from the perspective of our overview theory we will be concerned in this chapter with semantic memory. We argued earlier that semantic memory may be viewed as a network of concept nodes interconnected by labeled, directed associations, and we distinguished primary definitional nodes, which contain a description of the general class, from secondary nodes, which record specific examples of the class. We will be concerned in this chapter with specifying more precisely how primary definitional nodes are constructed. We will be trying to figure out the strategies (i.e., the set of production systems) people have for learning and using concepts.

Explicit and implicit concept learning. Psychologists have studied two different kinds of concept acquisition, explicit and implicit. You experienced both kinds in the Food for Thought section. Explicit and implicit concepts differ in two ways: (1) in the extent to which they are learned intentionally, and (2) in the extent to which the learner can describe the concept accurately after having learned it. The second problem you solved (with the triangles, circles, etc.) is an example of explicit concept learning, in that you set out to discover the concept and at the end of learning you were probably able to describe the defining criteria without any difficulty (e.g., all members of the class had two figures). On the other hand, the first task was an example of implicit concept acquisition. That is, the problem was disguised as a simple memory problem so you probably did not set out to discover a concept, and once you had completed the task, you probably still found it difficult to describe the defining criteria even though you probably performed at better than a chance level.

In this chapter we will consider each of these kinds of concept

TABLE 14–3.

Answers for the test items in Table 14–2.

1.	yes	26.	yes
2.	no	27.	no
3.	no	28.	yes
4.	yes	29.	yes
5.	no	30.	no
6.	yes	31.	yes
7.	no	32.	no
8.	yes	33.	yes
9.	yes	34.	no
10.	no	35.	yes
11.	no	36.	no
12.	no	37.	yes
13.	yes	38.	no
14.	no	39.	no
15.	yes	40.	yes
16.	yes	41.	no
17.	no	42.	yes
18.	yes	43.	yes
19.	no	44.	no
20.	yes	45.	yes
21.	no	46.	no
22.	no	47.	no
23.	no	48.	yes
24.	yes	49.	no
25.	yes	50.	yes

acquisition in turn, and then we will examine what they might tell us about how people learn and use the concepts underlying language.

EXPLICIT CONCEPTS: HYPOTHESIS TESTING

Consider an example of explicit concept acquisition presented by Bruner, Goodnow, and Austin (1956) in their classic book *A Study of Thinking*. Imagine the problem facing a foreigner who has just arrived in town and is being introduced around to the residents by a trusted friend. After each meeting, the friend tells the foreigner either that the resident is influential in the town or that he is not influential. The foreigner, trusting the judgment of his friend and wishing to be in the know about such things, attempts to figure out exactly what features differentiate influential people from noninfluential. The problem, of course, is that people differ in many characteristics (including gender, friendliness, degree of wealth, years of education, etc.) and only some of these are relevant to the person's degree of influence in the community. How then, does our foreigner go about discovering the critical characteristics?

Concept identification tasks. It is difficult to study how people go about attaining concepts in daily life, so psychologists developed the *concept identification task* which seems to reproduce the critical features of concept attainment, but in a controlled experimental setting. You have already attempted to solve one such concept identification problem in the second problem in the Food for Thought section. The best way to understand the general characteristics of the concept identification task is to consider an example. We will use the classic study by Bruner, Goodnow, and Austin (1956). Bruner and his colleagues began by constructing a set of stimulus items that varied along four *attributes* or *dimensions*—in this case the attributes of form, color, number of forms, and border type. In addition, each of these attributes could take on one of three values. The form in each stimulus could be either a cross, a circle, or a square. The color could be either green, red, or black. The number of forms could be either one, two or three, and the border type could contain either one, two, or three lines. The set of all possible stimuli that can be constructed by combining the three values of these four attributes is displayed in Figure 14–2. The stimuli you saw in the Food for Thought problem were chosen from this set.

Having chosen a set of attributes and values for the experiment, the experimenter then arbitrarily chooses a concept that the subject must attempt to discover. This concept consists of one or more values and a rule for combining them. For example in the task you solved earlier, the concept you were to discover was *two figures*. In order for a stimulus to be a member of the class the experimenter had in mind, it had to consist of two figures. Thus, the attribute of number of figures was *relevant* in that the value of this dimension determined class membership, whereas the other three dimensions were *irrelevant*, since the value along them did not determine class membership. Of course, it is possible for the experimenter to choose two relevant dimensions and then it is necessary to specify a rule for combining them. For example, the experimenter might designate the attributes of color and figure as relevant, with the positive values of red and cross. The concept might consist of a conjunctive rule, which states that in order for a stimulus to be an exemplar of the concept it must be *both* red and a cross. Alternatively, if a disjunctive rule were used for combining the values, in order for a stimulus to be a member of the class, it would have to be *either* red *or* a cross.

Having chosen a set of stimuli and a concept, the experimenter still has another option in constructing a concept identification prob-

Thought

Before you read further, place a piece of paper over the column below labeled "Feedback", so that you cannot see the feedback listed. Your task in this experiment is to discover a concept I have in mind. We will go through a series of trials. On each you will look at a stimulus that will have a certain geometric form (square, circle, cross), a certain pattern (cross-hatched, black, white), a certain number of forms (one, two, three), and a certain number of borders (one, two, three). If you think that the stimulus on a given trial exemplifies the concept I have in mind, then write down "member" in the column labeled "Response". If you think it does not, then write down "nonmember". After you have written your response, you may uncover the feedback for that trial to see whether you were correct or not. Then move on to the next trial. You should keep in mind that the concept I have in mind is either square, circle, cross, cross-hatched, black, white, one form, two forms, three forms, one border, two borders, or three borders. Remember, I have exactly *one* of these concepts in mind and you should attempt to discover it by paying careful attention to which stimuli are members of the concept and which are not. Keep going through the trials either until you have completed them all or until you have predicted the feedback correctly 5 times in a row.

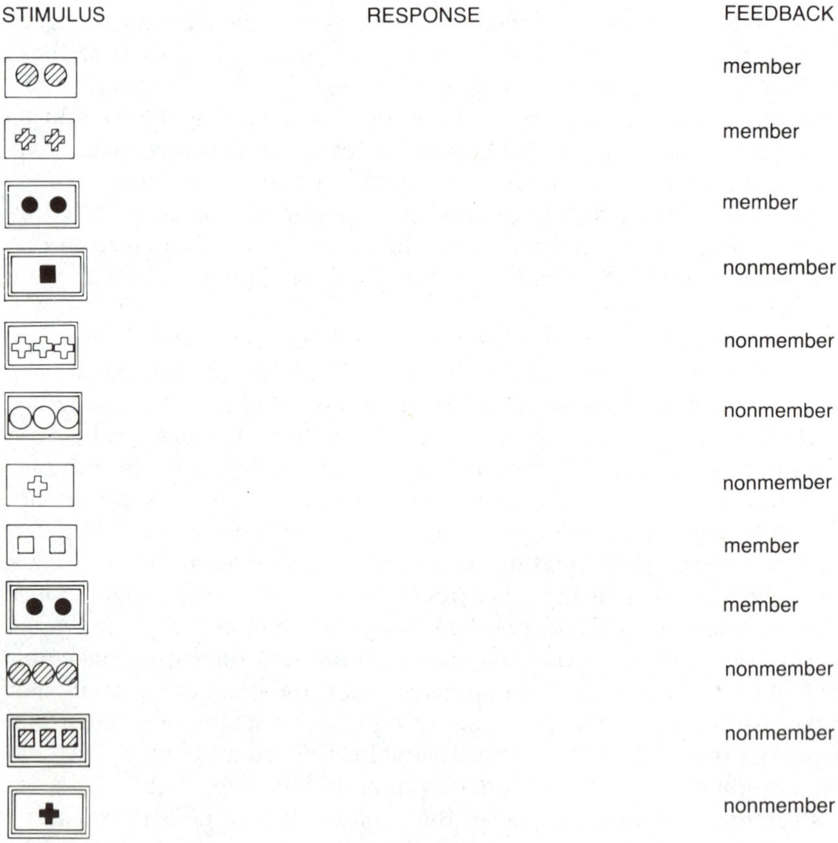

STIMULUS	RESPONSE	FEEDBACK
		member
		member
		member
		nonmember
		nonmember
		nonmember
		nonmember
		member
		member
		nonmember
		nonmember
		nonmember

Figure 14–1. A concept identification problem.

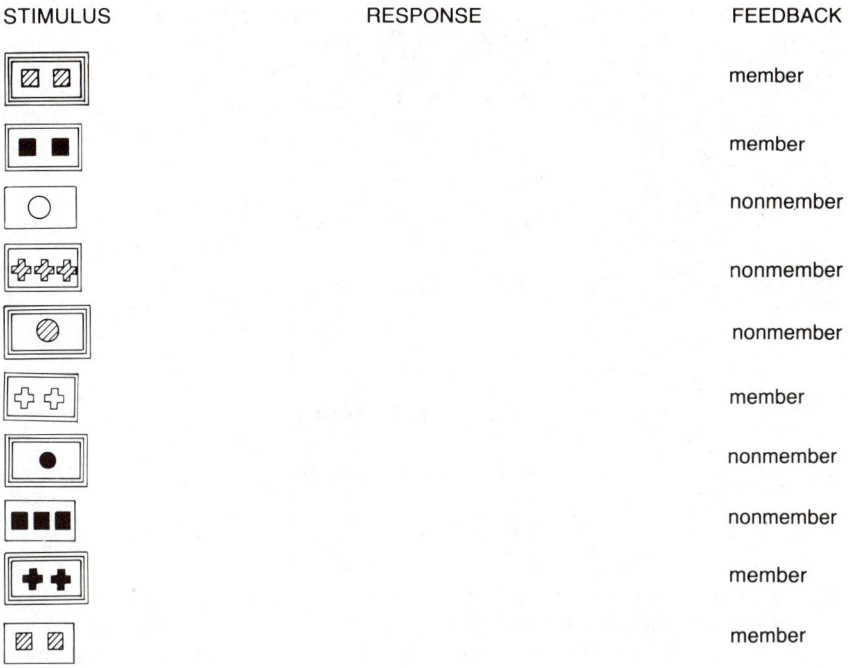

STIMULUS	RESPONSE	FEEDBACK
		member
		member
		nonmember
		nonmember
		nonmember
		member
		nonmember
		nonmember
		member
		member

Figure 14–1. (Continued)

lem. He must decide how the stimuli will be presented to the subject. The most important decision is whether to use a reception or a selection problem. The *reception* problem is so-called because the subject receives stimuli in the order chosen by the experimenter. You experienced a reception procedure, since you had to make a judgement about the stimuli in the order in which they were presented to you. In the *selection* procedure, on the other hand, the subject is allowed to choose the stimulus order. For example, you might be shown the whole array in Figure 14–2 and allowed to point to a stimulus and make a guess about its category membership. Then, after receiving feedback as to your correctness, you could point to another stimulus of your choice and make a guess, continuing until you had solved the problem.

Regardless of whether the reception or selection procedure is used, the experimenter usually measures how many trials the person requires to solve the concept. Sometimes the person is asked to guess at the solution on each trial, and the experimenter assumes that he has solved the concept as soon as he states it correctly (e.g., "the concept is all stimuli that are red crosses"). Other times (particularly when working with young children) the subject is simply required to make a *yes-no* judgement as you were, and the experimenter assumes the

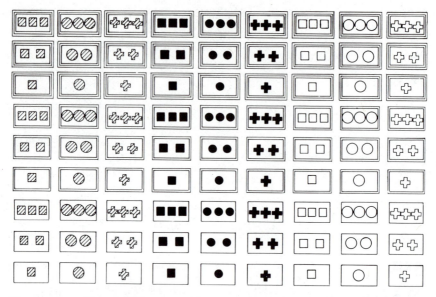

Figure 14–2. The stimulus set used in Bruner, Goodnow, and Austin's (1956) study of concept identification. (Cross-hatched items were green, filled were black, and open were red.) The stimuli in Figure 14–1 were drawn from this set. (From Bruner, Goodnow, & Austin, 1956. Copyright 1956 by Wiley. Reprinted by permission.)

person has discovered the concept when he makes a criterion number of correct choices (say 10 in a row).

In summary, then, explicit concept formation problems typically involve a set of stimuli that consist of all possible combinations of a specified set of attributes and a specified array of values of each attribute. The concept is chosen arbitrarily by the experimenter to consist of some value or values and some rule of combination. People are presented with stimuli chosen from the set of possible stimuli until they give evidence of having discovered the concept, and the experimenter's primary measure is the number of trials it takes the person to discover the concept.

Of course, there are countless possible variations. For example, the experimenter might study how such factors as the number of relevant dimensions, the number of irrelevant dimensions, and the kinds of rules influence problem solution.

Wholist and partist strategies. By now hundreds of studies of explicit concept formation have been completed and they reveal that the great majority of adults solve such problems by forming and testing *hypotheses*. That is, the person forms a hypothesis or a guess based on the first instance of the concept, and then retains or modifies this hypothesis in light of later experience. People differ not so much in their tendency to engage in such hypothesis testing, but rather in the kinds of hypotheses they form and in the efficiency with which they use subsequent information to modify them.

Strategies of hypothesis testing in concept identification were first studied systematically by Bruner, Goodnow, and Austin using the stimulus set shown in Figure 14–2. When they employed their reception procedure, Bruner and his colleagues required their subject to guess the solution after each trial. This enabled Bruner, et al. to study the kinds of hypotheses people adopted and how these were modified as they went along. Bruner found that most subjects engaged in either a *partist* or a *wholist* strategy. Subjects who adopted the *wholist* strategy took all the values displayed in the first instance as their initial hypothesis and then used later feedback to omit those attributes that proved to be irrelevant. In contrast, *partists* adopted only one (or some subset) of the original values as their initial hypothesis and kept this hypothesis until they encountered contradictory evidence, at which point they adopted a new hypothesis consistent with all the past instances they could remember. Each type of strategy is illustrated in Figure 14–3. In the left column of the figure, you see a series of stimuli that might be presented to the subject. The next column contains a record of the feedback the person was given, and the next two columns show hypothetical series of hypotheses generated by a wholist and a partist. Notice that the wholist begins by adopting a hypothesis consisting of all the values present in the instance. The member presented on the next trial demonstrates that a single border is not necessary (since this instance contains a double border), so he eliminates the "one border" part of his hypothesis. On Trial 3 he is presented with an instance that is not a member of the concept. Since this non-

Stimulus Presented	Feedback Given	Wholist Hypotheses	Partist Hypotheses
 ⬜ • •	Member	one-border, two, black, circle	black, circle
 ⬜ • •	Member	two, black, circle	same as above
 ⬜ □□□	Not Member	same as above	same as above
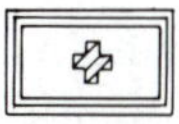 ⬜ ✧	Not Member	same as above	same as above
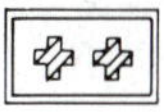 ⬜ ✧ ✧	Member	two	must eliminate black and circle. What to choose???

Figure 14–3. An example of wholist and partist strategies in concept identification.

member has neither black, nor circle, nor two forms it does not falsify his hypothesis, so he keeps the current hypothesis. Again on Trial 4, the person is confronted with a nonmember that contains none of the values of his hypothesis, so he keeps the current hypothesis since it is consistent with this feedback. Finally on Trial 5, the person, is confronted with a member that is neither black nor contains circles. Thus, the old hypothesis must be modified. Therefore, our wholist discards both black and circles from his hypothesis leaving him only with the hypothesis *two* which is consistent with all previous feedback.

Contrast this approach with the partist who is shown in the right column. He begins with a hypothesis based on only a subset of the present values; in this case he choses black and circles. The information he encounters on the next three trials is all consistent with this hypothesis, so he keeps it. However, when he encounters Trial 5 he is faced with a concept member that is neither black nor contains a circle. Thus, logically he must discard his old hypothesis, but he is now faced with the question of which hypothesis should be adopted next. He could, of course, simply choose randomly from the attributes of the current stimulus, perhaps adopting the hypothesis *double border* or the hypothesis *two*. If he has good memory for the past trials, he might in fact be able to eliminate the double border hypothesis since he might recall that some members did not have double borders. If he does not remember the earlier instances well, though, he might adopt this incorrect hypothesis. Thus, the person using the partist strategy faces a more difficult problem when the feedback forces him to discard his current hypothesis.

Bruner and his colleagues found that most of their college student subjects adopted the wholist strategy and that people who adopted this strategy were usually faster at discovering the correct concepts. Why is this strategy more efficient? In the wholist strategy the current hypothesis acts as a memory that cumulates all information encountered to date. The person need not recall anything at all about individual past instances. As long as he remembers his current hypothesis, he can modify it so that it is consistent with all information encountered so far. On the other hand, the partist is often forced to rely upon a memory for individual past instances when he is forced to eliminate his current hypothesis. Given what we have learned about the limited capacity of working memory, it is not surprising that such precise memory for instances is usually not very good. Thus, the wholist strategy is usually more effective than the partist because it helps to overcome memory limitations.

A method for inferring hypotheses. Bruner, Goodnow, and Austin's book was published in the mid-1950's just at the time when the cognitive revolution we discussed in Chapter 1 was beginning.

Their book was so influential because it was the first to analyze systematically the *strategies* people use during concept discovery. The findings led to the development of a number of hypothesis-testing theories (e.g., Levine, 1966; Restle, 1962; Trabasso & Bower, 1963). All hypothesis-testing theories share several important assumptions. First, all assume that the person establishes a pool of potential hypotheses at the beginning of a problem. If the experimenter tells the person the possible solutions at the beginning of the problem, then it seems reasonable to assume that the initial hypothesis pool consists of the set specified by the experimenter. If the experimenter does not specify the possibilities precisely, then the person must call upon past experience to come up with a set of likely possibilities. Second, hypothesis-testing theories assume that the person samples one or more hypotheses from the set and responds on that basis. Third, the theories assume that if the hypothesis leads him to make a correct classification of the current stimulus then he keeps it, but if the hypothesis leads him to make an incorrect classification he discards it and samples a new hypothesis from the set. This process continues until the person samples the correct hypothesis (i.e., the one that always leads him to a correct solution). Despite these three similarities, hypothesis-testing theories differ from one another regarding the assumptions they make concerning the details of hypothesis testing. For example, some theories assume that previously tested hypotheses are thrown back into the pool, so that they have some chance of being sampled again (the so-called "no-memory" assumption), whereas others assume that once a hypothesis is tested and found to be incorrect it does not reenter the pool.

How can we test the three common assumptions of hypothesis-testing theories, and how can we decide among them when they make different assumptions? The problem we encounter should be familiar by now. Hypotheses are not observable, nor are hypothesis pools or sampling. What we need then is some way of inferring hypotheses by examining behavior. Recall that Bruner, Goodnow, and Austin (1956) did this by asking their subjects to verbalize a hypothesis (or a guess) for each trial. They did find systematic patterns as we saw, but their method has the drawback that it might lead people to engage in hypothesis testing even though they would not do so otherwise, simply because the procedure forces them to state a hypothesis on each trial. Even if the person would have tested hypotheses without the verbalization requirement, the possibility remains that engaging in the verbalization changes the efficiency with which people adopt and modify hypotheses. Furthermore, it is difficult to use this kind of procedure to study explicit concept acquisition in young children who are notoriously poor at verbalizing, and it is impossible to use this procedure with other animals.

What we need, then, is a method for inferring hypotheses without asking the person to describe them aloud. Several such procedures have been adopted, but the most influential is the *blank trials method* introduced by Levine (1966). Levine uses the reception procedure. The subject is given a series of concept identification problems. In each he is told that he will see two stimuli on each trial and that one of these will exemplify a concept the experimenter has in mind. The subject is asked to discover this concept by choosing the stimulus in each pair that he thinks exemplifies the concept. Then the experimenter will tell him whether or not he has chosen correctly and he will then be presented with another pair. The subject is further told that the concept will be one of the following: black, white, X, T, large,

Number	Stimulus Array	Response left right	Feedback Provided	Logically Correct Hypotheses After Feedback*
1	T x	right	correct	small, white, x, right
2	X T	right		
3	x T	left		
4	T X	left		
5	T x	right		
6	T X	left	incorrect	x, right
7	x T	left		
8	T x	right		
9	X T	left		
10	T X	right		
11	x T	left	correct	x
12	x T	left		
13	T X	right		
14	T x	right		
15	X T	left		
16	T X	right	correct	x

* If the subject remembers all information from earlier trials

Figure 14–4. An illustration of a concept identification problem using Levine's (1966) blank trials procedure.

small, right, or left. The "stimulus" column in Figure 14–4 shows a possible sequence of trials. On each the subject need simply point to the left or the right stimulus; he need say nothing.

How, then, can Levine determine anything about the person's hypotheses? He accomplished this by inserting sequences of trials on which no feedback is given (called blank trials) and arranging the stimulus arrays on such blank trial series so that the hypothesis being tested could be inferred from the pattern of choices. To understand how this was done, look again at the sample trial sequence in Figure 14–4. Imagine that on the first trial, the subject chooses the stimulus on the right and is told "correct." In order to find out what hypothesis (if any) the subject had adopted, Levine inserts a series of four blank trials next. These trials are depicted again in Figure 14–5 which demonstrates that each of the simple hypotheses corresponds to a unique pattern of choices. For example, if the hypothesis guiding the subject's choices is X then he will respond *left, left, right, right* on Trials 2 through 5, tracking the X. Each blank trial sequence in Levine's task is set up so that the sequence of choices reveals the hypothesis the person must be using. Notice that the problem in Figure 14–4 contains three blank trial sequences (Trials 2 through 5, Trials 7 through 10, and Trials 12 through 15). Column 3 of the figure indicates the response pattern of a hypothetical subject. Take a minute now to test your understanding of Levine's procedure. For each blank trial sequence, determine which hypothesis was guiding the person's response.

Given Levine's procedure we can ask a number of questions about

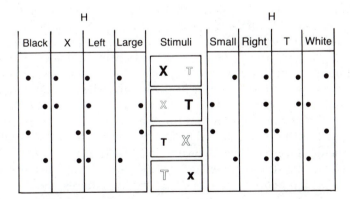

Figure 14–5. A depiction of the blank trials response pattern that would be produced by using each of the simple hypotheses in part of one of Levine's problems. (After Levine, 1966. Copyright 1966 by the American Psychological Association. Reprinted by permission of the publisher and author.)

hypothesis testing. First, do people test simple hypotheses at all during blank trial sequences or do they simply respond haphazardly? For a set of 4 blank trials, there are 16 possible left-right patterns of response. As shown in Figure 14–5, only 8 (i.e., 50%) of these correspond to simple hypotheses. Therefore, if people responded randomly on blank trials, then only about 50% of their blank trial sequences should correspond to one of the simple hypotheses. In fact, Levine and others have found that among college students more than 90% of all blank trial sequences correspond to simple hypotheses. This suggests that people do adopt a hypothesis which guides their choices in such a task, and they do so even when they are not required to verbalize the hypothesis.

A second question we can investigate using Levine's procedure concerns what people do with their current hypothesis in the face of feedback information. Recall that hypothesis-testing theories assume that people keep a hypothesis until it leads them to make an incorrect choice, at which point they discard the hypothesis and sample a new one. This is often termed a win-stay, lose-shift strategy, since as long as they are winning, people stay with a hypothesis, but as soon as they lose, they shift to a new one. We can find out whether people use a win-stay, lose-shift strategy by comparing the hypothesis used before and after each feedback trial. Consider our hypothetical subject in Figure 14–4. On Trials 2 through 5, we found his hypothesis seems to be *small* (since his choices tracked the small letter). Then on Trial 6 he was told that his choice on that trial was incorrect. If he is using a lose-shift strategy, we should find him using a different hypothesis on Trials 7 through 10. As you can see, our subject did switch hypotheses on these trials, since he now seems to be tracking the x. Notice that on Trial 11, our subject was told that he was correct. If he is using a win-stay strategy, then he should retain the hypothesis x for Trials 12 through 15. His pattern of responses indicates that he did so. Thus, our subject seems to be using the win-stay, lose-shift strategy postulated by most hypothesis testing theories. In fact, Levine has found that the people he has tested retain a hypothesis after making a correct choice on about 95% of the trials (i.e., they use win-stay about 95% of the time) and that they throw away a hypothesis after they have made an error (i.e., they use lose-shift) about 98% of the time. Therefore, this strategy seems to provide an accurate description of the way in which people retain and discard hypotheses on the basis of feedback.

One other major question we can investigate using Levine's procedure concerns the extent to which people use information from earlier feedback trials to reduce the pool of possible hypotheses. Recall that hypothesis-testing theories differ from each other on this point. Let us consider the two possible extremes. First, there is the so-called no-memory assumption which holds that whenever the person is told he is incorrect, he throws the hypothesis back into the pool and samples again, i.e., he forgets which hypotheses he has tested and all previous information. If a person operated in this manner, then throughout one of Levine's problems he would have a pool of about 8 hypotheses from which to sample each time he made an error. This extreme no-memory possibility is represented by the top line in Figure 14–6 which shows how hypothesis pool size would vary as a function of the number of feedback trials the person has received in Levine's task. At the other extreme would be the perfect focussing described by Bruner and his colleagues, in which the subject uses all information from previous feedback trials to reduce the pool of hypotheses from which he is sampling. In order to see how such a person would perform in Levine's task, consider again our hypothetical subject in Figure 14–4. Although at the very beginning of the task, there were 8 hypotheses that could have been correct, the first feedback reduces this set to only 4 hypotheses, as shown in the right hand column. That is, the person chose the stimulus on the right and was told he was correct, so logically, this limits the pool of potentially correct hypotheses to *small, x, white,* and *right*. The next feedback (on Trial 6) tells the person that the correct choice was the *black, large, x* on the right. Combining this information with the information he gained on the first feedback trial enables the person, *if* he remembers all the information and reasons logically, to eliminate not only his current hypothesis *small* (which had guided his responses during the

Figure 14–6. The hypothesis pool size as a function of number of feedback trials in a blank trials task. The top function depicts the performance expected under the "no memory" sampling with replacement assumption, the bottom function depicts the performance expected under the "perfect focussing" assumption, and the middle function depicts the actual performance of Levine's college student subjects. (From Levine, 1966. Copyright 1966 by the American Psychological Association. Reprinted by permission of the publisher and author.)

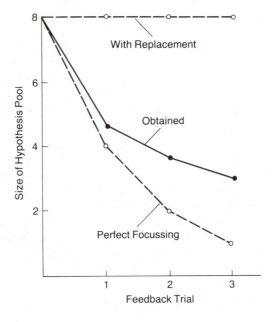

set of 4 blank trials just completed), but also the hypothesis *white*. Thus, if the person is remembering all the information and using it logically, he can now reduce his hypothesis to *x* and *right*. Notice that our hypothetical subject does, in fact, respond consistent with all this previous information, since the next hypothesis he adopts (on Trials 7 through 10) is *x*. Finally, then, on Trial 11, the subject is told his choice of a small, black *x* on the left is correct. This feedback combined with the hypothesis set of *x* and *right* would enable a perfectly focussing subject to limit the pool to the one hypothesis of *x*. Note that our hypothetical subject does use this hypothesis on the last set of blank trials (Trials 12–15). The bottom function in Figure 14–6, then depicts the size of the hypothesis pool in Levine's task for such a perfectly focussing subject.

Fortunately, it is possible to estimate the size of a person's hypothesis pool after any feedback trial by examining the proportion of trials on which the subject's hypothesis is consistent with all earlier feedback. The question then, is which of these two extremes more accurately matches the performance of actual people? The middle curve in Figure 14–6 reveals that Levine's college students fell somewhere between the two extremes. They appear to be focussing, but not perfectly. Why don't people focus perfectly? Perfect performance requires not only that the person be able to reason logically about current feedback, but also that he/she remember the information from previous trials. It is likely that among young adults, at least, the problem is a memory one, since conditions that reduce memory load usually lead to more perfect focusing (cf. Bruner, Goodnow, and Austin, 1956).

The development of explicit concept acquisition. We have seen then that college students, when faced with problems in concept acquisition, propose and test hypotheses in a highly logical fashion. How do young children perform in explicit concept identification tasks? This question is particularly important, because children, even more than adults, are engaged in learning new concepts every day.

Eimas (1969) and Gholson, Levine, and Phillips (1972) have studied people ranging in age from 7 through the early 20's using Levine's blank trials procedure. They found that even the youngest children tested hypotheses, although they did so less efficiently than adults. For example, they were less sensitive to feedback information and less likely to focus perfectly. In fact, one study using a different procedure (Offenbach, 1974) has found that elderly adults have similar difficulties, suggesting the possibility that the logical hypothesis testing strategies young adults use may not be universal.

What is the nature of the difficulty that young children experience in explicit concept acquisition tasks? Is it that they lack the logical abilities required, or is it a memory problem? Recall from our discussion of working memory that children usually reveal poorer digit span than adults. There is some important evidence which suggests that the difficulties young children face in explicit concept identification tasks are due largely to memory. Eimas (1970) presented Levine problems of the sort depicted in Figure 14–4 to young children, but rather than allowing them to see only the current stimulus pair on each trial, he left all previous feedback trials and feedback information in front of the children throughout the problem, thereby providing an external memory aid. Under such memory aid conditions, the second graders he tested performed as efficiently as college students.

Ubiquity of hypothesis testing.   The most important point of the work on explicit concept acquisition is that when people are presented with explicit concept identification problems, they formulate and test hypotheses in an attempt to come up with attributes that distinguish members from nonmembers. We have seen that even children engage in such hypothesis testing, though not as efficiently as young adults. As we noted in the previous chapter, this tendency to formulate and test hypotheses is a salient feature of human performance, reflecting our inherent propensities to organize and impose regularity upon experience. In fact, people engage in such hypothesis testing even in tasks in which the stimuli are not rule-governed at all. One favorite of psychologists has been the so-called probability learning task. The subject sees a sequence of events and is asked to predict which will occur next. For example, he might be faced with two light bulbs. On a series of trials, one or the other of these lights is flashed on. After watching such a series the person is asked to predict which bulb will flash on next. In fact, this is determined randomly, but in their attempts to make accurate predictions, subjects develop hypotheses, often becoming more and more elaborate (e.g., Feldman, 1963).

This strong propensity to formulate and test hypotheses is useful, but it is not an unmixed blessing. Dogged persistence with incorrect hypotheses can prevent us from discovering actual regularities in the world, as we have seen frequently in our discussion of reasoning and problem solving. The difficulty, of course, is that the hypotheses we adopt influence the direction of our attention and what we remember, so an incorrect hypothesis or an inadequate hypothesis pool may prevent us from finding an adequate solution. Levine (1971) demonstrated this fact by presenting two groups with a simple concept identification problem in which they were presented with a large or a small circle on each trial. They were always told they were correct if they chose the large circle and incorrect if they chose the small. This, of course, is usually a very simple problem, and indeed the group which was given this problem first solved it within a very few trials. How-ever, the second group was first given a series of problems involving complex sequences. For example, the person had to choose the stim-ulus on the right for three trials and the stimulus on the left for two trials. People with such experience at difficult sequences failed to solve the simple small-large problem even after 100 trials. Apparently, their hypothesis pool did not contain the simple small-large hypotheses, so they were unable to discover the solution. In fact, all of us have no-ticed how we can become bogged down in simple problems by per-sisting with complicated hypotheses that blind us to the elegant and obvious solution.

In summary, then, when people are presented with explicit con-cept identification problems, they formulate and test hypotheses. This tendency is so strong that people engage in such hypothesis testing even when they are faced with stimuli that are not rule-governed. Al-though this tendency to engage in hypothesis testing helps us to find regularities, it can blind us to alternative solutions if our original hy-pothesis pool is inadequate.

IMPLICIT CONCEPTS: ABSTRACTION OF PROTOTYPES AND ANALOGIC PROCESSES

So far we have talked only about situations in which people con-sciously try to abstract a concept. However, people also pick up reg-ularities which they can later use to classify events, even when they are not trying to do so, and even though they may not be able to state the exact nature of the regularities they are using.

Learning about prototypes. People are sensitive to the regulari-ties among class members, even when there is no defining attribute for the class. Consider, for example, a series of studies conducted by Posner and Keele (1968, 1970). Posner and Keele studied the acquisi-tion of concepts in which class membership was defined, not by a common shared attribute, but rather by overall similarity to a basic pattern called a *prototype*. Samples of Posner and Keele's stimuli are shown in Figure 14–7.

When constructing these stimuli, Posner and Keele began with a set of prototypes, each consisting of 9 dots arranged in a random pat-tern. Three sample prototypes are shown in the top row of Figure 14–7. Then, for each prototype, the experimenters generated other pat-terns which were distortions of these prototypes, which were formed by moving one or more of the dots slightly, sometimes in one direc-tion and sometimes in another. The best way to understand this is to see what happens to a prototype of a triangle, which is shown in Fig-

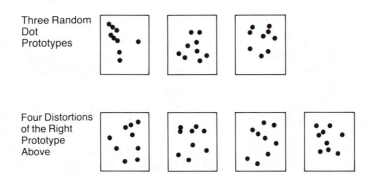

Figure 14–7. Sample stimuli from Posner and Keele's (1968)
   study of the acquisition of prototypes. (After Posner,
   1973. Reprinted by permission of the author.)

ure 14–8. Each of the stimuli to the right of the triangle prototype
shows a distortion of the prototype, with the degree of distortion increasing from left to right.

Thus, for each category, Posner and Keele had a prototype pattern and a set of distortions from it. The distorted patterns were such
that the average position of a given dot across all the distortions would
be the same as in the prototype. In order to see whether people would
abstract the prototypes from a set of distortions, Posner and Keele presented people with four distortions of each of the three prototypes
displayed in Figure 14–7. The person then learned to associate the
four distortions of each prototype with a single name. It is important
to note that during this training people did *not* know that the patterns
had been produced by distorting prototypes and the prototypes themselves were *never* presented. Nonetheless, later tests made it clear that
people had learned about the prototypes. In these tests people were
presented with a series of patterns to classify. Some were the same
distorted patterns they had seen during learning, some were other distortions they had not seen during learning, and some were the prototypes. The most remarkable finding was that people classified the pro-

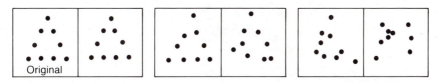

Figure 14–8. Distortions of the prototype of a triangle (left). The degree of
   distortion of this prototype increases from left to right. (After Posner,
   Goldsmith, & Welton, 1967. Copyright 1967 by the American Psychological Association. Reprinted by permission of the publisher and author.)

totypes just as accurately as the distortions they had learned on, whereas they were much poorer at classifying distortions presented for the first time. Moreover, when recognition memory for the patterns was tested (Posner, 1969), people tended to judge the prototypes as *old* even though they'd never seen them before.

The work of Posner and Keele demonstrates then, that people had learned about the prototype of a set of patterns, even though they had never seen the prototype itself, and even though they had not consciously tried to learn the concept. Furthermore, such implicit learning occurs even when there is no single element that is common to all concept members.

Concepts defined by sequential rules. People also learn implicitly concepts defined by simple left-to-right grammars of the sort we discussed in Chapter 8.

Think back now to the first problem you confronted in the Food for Thought section of this chapter. All the stimuli you memorized were produced by the finite state grammar shown in Figure 14–9. All the stimuli you memorized conform to this grammar in that they can be produced by beginning at START and following arrows from one node to another until END is reached. Thus, during training you were exposed to many exemplars corresponding to this grammatical concept. During testing you were asked to reveal how much you had learned about this underlying set of rules by differentiating items that conform to the rules from those that don't. If you were correct on more

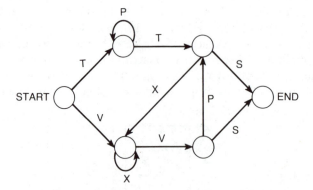

Figure 14–9. The left-to-right grammar from Reber (1976) which was used to generate the letter sequences in Table 14–1. (After Reber, 1976. Copyright 1976 by the American Psychological Association. Reprinted by permission of the publisher and author.)

than 50% of the new test items, you must have learned something about these constraints on what letters could follow each other.

In fact, this was a replication of the kinds of studies conducted by Reber and his colleagues (Reber, 1967; 1976; Reber & Lewis, 1977). Just as we did here, subjects were shown series of letter strings without knowing that all were drawn from a grammar. Reber obtained two major findings. First, people were consistently greater than the 50% correct they could have obtained by chance, usually averaging about 75% correct. Second, people were usually very poor at explaining the basis for their decisions. They were rarely able to verbalize the rules for deciding whether or not a test item conformed to the concept. I suggest that you try this experiment on some friends in order to see whether you replicate these findings.

Not only do people seem capable of learning about the grammar implicitly, but Reber (1976) has found that people actually do better when they are not trying to figure out rules (about 75% correct) than when they are (65% correct). This suggests that explicit hypothesis testing of the sort people use when they engage in explicit concept acquisition actually interferes with picking up the regularities in the stimulus sequences. This could be because the rules are rather complicated and the person's hypothesis pool does not contain appropriate hypotheses.

Notice, then, that Reber's findings indicate that we are remarkably sensitive to sequential regularities in the environment, even though we often find it difficult to state the nature of these regularities. It seems likely that this ability helps us to learn about the sequential regularities in our native language. Remember, though, that such abstraction of sequential regularities would not be sufficient for learning language, since as we saw in Chapter 8, many of the rule-governed aspects of human language cannot be described as a simple left-to-right grammar.

Abstraction of prototypes or drawing analogies from instances? We have seen, then, that even when people don't mean to do so, they are sensitive to regularities among the instances of a concept. They learn enough about these regularities to enable them to classify new stimuli as exemplars or nonexemplars of the concept, even though they are usually unable to state the bases for these decisions. What are people actually learning during such implicit acquisition? There are two general possibilities.

The first is that they are *implicitly abstracting regularities*. This has been the most favored explanation among those who studied implicit concept learning (e.g., Hull, 1920; Posner, 1969; Reber, 1967), although the exact terms used differ. According to this explanation, during exposure of the instances the person unconsciously abstracts regularities that are common to all members of a given category. Viewed in terms of network models, each time an exemplar of A is encountered, this automatically activates that memory node and the new information is added. Thus, at the memory node for the concept, the person is unconsciously tallying up the characteristics of the concept in the form of a composite. When a new item is presented for classification, the new item is compared with this stored composite (i.e., prototype) and the new item is classified as a member of the category to which it is most similar. According to this explanation, then, the abstraction is occurring during learning and the person stores away a composite or prototype of the instances, not a record of all the instances themselves.

The alternative possibility, however, is that people are *drawing analogies from instances*. According to this explanation, during learning, exemplars are stored away in separate memory nodes. During acquisition, then, there is simply the storage of instances with no abstraction of underlying regularities. Of course, given the inaccuracies induced by selective attention and forgetting, it is likely that the memory for these instances is often imperfect. During testing then, new stimuli are classified through analogy. The person asks, in effect, which earlier stimulus is this test item most similar to? The new stimulus is then assigned to the same class as the stored item to which it is most similar.

Even though the abstraction explanation has been more popular than the analogy from instances explanation in the past, recently Lee Brooks (1978) has argued that there is evidence that the latter is used, at least under some conditions of learning. Brooks has presented evidence based on the implicit learning of the artificial grammars that had been studied by Reber. In the first experiment we'll describe, Brooks chose two grammars, A and B, depicted in Figure 14–10. Brooks paired 15 letter strings from Grammar A with the response word *city* and 15 letter strings from Grammar B with the response word *animal*. His subjects, however, were not informed of the grammars. Rather they were given paired associate instructions which told them to learn to make the appropriate response to each of the 30 letter strings. After they had learned to make the appropriate responses, they were given a stack of 30 cards, each containing a letter string they had never seen before. These test items are shown at the bottom of Figure 14–10. Note that 10 were constructed from Grammar A (the *city* grammar), 10 from Grammar B (the *animal* grammar) and 10 from neither. Subjects were told that of the items in the deck, 10 should be assigned the response *city*, 10 the response *animal*, and 10 neither. Subjects then attempted to sort the cards, and all did so at much better than chance. Although people would be correct only 33% of the time by chance, most people were about 60% correct.

Notice that either of the theoretical explanations could account

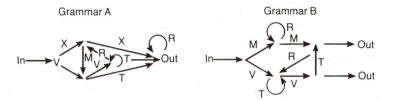

		Responses for Experiment 1	Responses for Experiment 2
	VVTRXRR	city	Paris
	VVTRX	city	zebra
	XMVTTRX	city	baboon
	VT	city	Cairo
	VTRR	city	tiger
Stimuli from Grammar A	VVRXRR	city	Oslo
	XMT	city	elephant
	XMTRRRR	city	Rome
	VVRMVRX	city	panda
	XMVRMT	city	Budapest
	XXRR	city	giraffe
	XMVRXRR	city	Moscow
	VVTTRMT	city	Tokyo
	XXRRRRR	city	lion
	VVRMTR	city	aardvark
	MRMRTTV	animal	Montreal
	VVT	animal	moose
	VVTRTTV	animal	Chicago
	MRRMRVT	animal	possum
	VRRM	animal	Halifax
Stimuli from Grammar B	MRRMRV	animal	Vancouver
	MRRRRRM	animal	bison
	VTTTTVT	animal	Detroit
	VV	animal	coyote
	MMRTVT	animal	rattlesnake
	MMRVTRV	animal	beaver
	MMRTV	animal	Boston
	VTTVTRV	animal	Toronto
	VTTV	animal	cougar
	VVTRVT	animal	New York

Stimuli for Testing Phase of Both Experiments

A	B	C
XXR	MRM	TRV
XMTR	MMRV	VVTVV
VVRX	MRMRV	MMMTV
VVRXR	MRMRTV	RMTTMR
VVTRXR	VIVT	VVVTVT
XMVRX	VVTRV	MTRVXT
XMVRXR	VVTRTV	RMRVTRR
VVRMT	VTVTRVT	TVTXTTR
VVRMTRR	MMRVT	VTRXMTM
XMVTRMT	MMRTTVT	XRXMVTV

Figure 14–10. The finite state grammars and stimulus strings used in Brooks' (1978) experiments on implicit concept acquisition. (After Brooks, 1978. Copyright 1978 by Lawrence Erlbaum Associates. Redrawn by permission of the author and publisher.)

for this performance. According to the abstraction explanation, during paired associate learning, the response *city* activated a concept node at which the person built up a composite record of the strings for *city*, and the response *animal* led to such a composite record of the strings associated with *animal*. During the sorting problem, then, the person compared the test item with each of these two abstractions and assigned it to the composite category to which it was most similar. If the test item was not similar to either category, it was assigned to the *neither* category. According to the analogy from instances explanation, on the other hand, during training the person stored away individual letter strings, each paired with one of the two responses. During sorting, each test item was compared with these individual letter strings and if the test item was similar to one of them, then it was assigned the same response as that instance.

Note that the experiment we have just described was one in which the two response categories were obvious during learning, so it is reasonable to argue (as the abstraction view does) that the person abstracted regularities for each of the two response classes during learning. In order to distinguish between these two alternatives experimentally, it is necessary to conduct an experiment in which the two categories are not obvious during training, since the two theories make different predictions in this case. Brooks conducted such an experiment, which is displayed in the right half of Figure 14–10. In this study, the same stimulus items drawn from Grammars A and B were used, but the responses were the city and country names shown in the right hand column of Figure 14–10. Note that about half of the Grammar A strings were paired with a city and about half with an animal name, so city-animal membership is not related to Grammar A versus B. Subjects completed paired associate learning as in the initial experiment, and then again were given the same stack of 30 test cards to sort. Now, however, it was pointed out to the subjects for the first time that half of the responses could be associated with the Old World (e.g., Paris, zebra, baboon, etc.), and half with the New World (e.g., Montreal, moose, Chicago, etc.). Their task was to sort the test items into New World, Old World, or neither. Of course, as you can see in the figure, during learning all the Old World items had occurred with stimuli from Grammar A and all the New World items with stimuli from Grammar B.

If performance during testing required that the subjects have abstracted some prototype for New World vs. Old World during training, then they should be very poor at this task. In fact, given the obvious animal names vs. city names distinction, it seems likely that had they been engaging in such abstraction, they would have attempted to build up two prototypes, one for animal and one for city, thus leading to very poor performance on the sorting task. On the other hand, if people are storing away instances and reasoning by analogy, then they should perform just as well in this experiment as they did in the previous one. That is, an individual test item such as *XXR* would call to mind a similar stored instance such as *XXRRR*. The person would then note that this is associated with giraffe and, since giraffe is Old World, would assign the test item to the Old World category. In fact, Brooks found that people performed just as well in this experiment (i.e., they were about 60% accurate) as they had in the previous study with obvious categories. This suggests that at least under some conditions, implicit concept learning relies not upon abstraction during learning, but upon drawing analogies from instances.

This distinction between abstraction and drawing analogies as the processes underlying implicit concept acquisition will undoubtedly receive more emphasis in the future. As Brooks notes, these possibilities are not necessarily contradictory. It seems likely that both can occur, with their relative importance being determined by the conditions under which learning occurs. We will return to this point at the end of our discussion of natural language concepts.

NATURAL LANGUAGE CONCEPTS

We have divided conceptual thinking into two general classes, explicit and implicit. Explicit acquisition occurs when people try to discover a concept. In such circumstances, people usually engage in hypothesis testing and the end result is a concept that the person can describe explicitly. In contrast, implicit acquisition occurs when the person is not attempting to learn a concept and the result is usually an intuitive concept, the basis of which the person cannot state.

So far we have considered only artificial concepts, designed for the laboratory, but what about natural language concepts? How do we learn to distinguish the stimuli to which the term *dog* should be applied from those to which the term *cat* should be applied? In this section we will consider the structure and conditions of learning of natural language concepts, and ask what earlier studies of explicit and implicit acquisition can tell us about natural concepts.

Structure of natural concepts. Before we can understand how natural language concepts are acquired, we need to know how they are structured. That is, we should study *what* is being acquired prior to, or at least simultaneously with, studying *how* it is acquired. This point was made most forcefully by Eleanor Rosch in a series of studies which we will be referring to again and again (e.g., Rosch, 1975a, 1975b, 1977, 1978; Rosch & Mervis, 1975; Rosch, Mervis, Gray, Johnson, & Boyes-Braem, 1976). Keep in mind throughout this discussion that we are focussing on the concepts themselves rather than on the processes by which they are acquired or the way in which they are represented in the mind. This is similar to studying the structure of language itself as part of our attempt to understand how people acquire and comprehend language. Recall that until psychologists looked seriously at the complex rule-governed nature of language, they were doomed to ignore some of the most fascinating puzzles that it poses. We will find that studying the structure of natural language concepts also reveals interesting new questions.

We will discuss four major characteristics of the structure of natural language concepts. First, *natural categories are ill defined or fuzzy.* Many of the experiments we discussed, particularly those concerned with explicit concept acquisition, used well-defined categories. That is there was some logical rule which defined class membership. Instances could be classified unambiguously once this rule was known. In contrast natural categories usually have fuzzy edges and are ill-defined, a point that has been argued most forcefully by the philosopher Wittgenstein (1958). His most famous quotation concerns the class of games. As he put it:

> Consider for example the proceedings we call "games." I mean board-games, card-games, ball-games, Olympic games, and so on. For if you look at them you will not see something that is common to *all*, but similarities, relationships, and a whole series of them at that. I can think of no better expression to characterize these similarities than "family resemblances."

It is easy to convince yourself that it is not only the category of games that lacks such defining features. What features are necessary and sufficient for something to be termed a *dog*? Not the ability to bark, surely for some dogs cannot, but they remain members of the category. Not four legs either, for even if a dog loses a leg in an accident it is still a dog.

A second characteristic of natural categories is that *in the real world, attributes do not occur independently, rather they tend to be correlated with each other.* In the Bruner, Goodnow, and Austin study discussed early in this chapter, the attributes were all independent of each other in that a given value, for example the color green, occurred equally often with each value of all other attributes (see Figure 14–2 again). Therefore, being told that the stimulus is green does not give you any basis for predicting the other attributes of the stimulus.

Anthropologists, philosophers, and psychologists have often assumed that the real world is like this as well, but a little thought will convince you that it isn't. Objects that have feathers are more likely to have the attribute of possessing wings than that of possessing wheels. Objects that have wheels are more likely to be made out of metal than out of cloth. Rosch has termed this tendency for real-world attributes to occur in clusters *real-world correlational structure.*

The existence of this real-world correlational structure is quite important for psychological issues, because it suggests that there are some natural bases of classification. Earlier, when they assumed that the world was made up of independently occurring attributes, psychologists and philosophers had assumed that people take a uniform world (much like the array of stimuli in Figure 14–2) and divide it up arbitrarily in order to form classes. This suggested the likelihood that such divisions were imposed arbitrarily by the members of a given culture, and that part of socialization was learning how the child's own culture divided up the world. The anthropologist Benjamin Whorf (1956) for example, argued that we divide up the world differently depending upon the linguistic community to which we are born. The existence of a real-world correlational structure suggests, however, that at least some classifications exist in the real world to be discovered, and that there might be similar divisions across widely ranging linguistic communities as long as they are exposed to the same correlational structure.

Rosch has argued, in fact, that real-world correlational structure is reflected in natural category systems. To understand this, consider Figure 14–11 which shows that there is both a horizontal and a vertical dimension to such taxonomies. The vertical dimension refers to the level of inclusion of a category. Thus, at the superordinate level we have categories like musical instrument. At the next level down we have categories like guitar, and at the lowest level we have particular type categories such as folk guitar and electric guitar. The horizontal dimension of classification refers to segmentation within each of these levels. Rosch has argued that the correlational structure of the real world, interacting with the characteristics of human cognition and the demands of communication have implications for both the vertical and the horizontal aspects of natural categories, as we will discuss in the remaining two characteristics of natural categories.

The third characteristic, then, is that *along the vertical dimension of taxonomies there is a basic level of classification.* Notice that the vertical dimension of Figure 14–11 indicates that a given object has more than one name. The object parked outside my study window might be called a vehicle, a car, a sports car, or a Corvette. Are all levels of categorization equally important or is one level more useful than the others?

Rosch has argued that there is a *basic level,* which she defines as the most inclusive level which reflects the perceived real-world correlational structure. That is, the basic level is the level at which items are most similar within a category and most different between categories. This basic level is indicated in Figure 14–11. In contrast

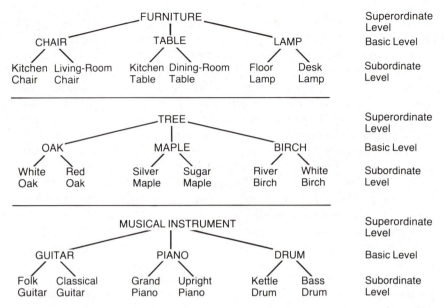

Figure 14–11. The horizontal and vertical dimensions in natural classification systems.

with the superordinate level, objects within a class at the basic level are quite similar to each other. In contrast with subordinate levels, objects within a class at the basic level are quite distinct from other classes. To verify that this is the case, Rosch and her colleagues (e.g., Rosch, Mervis, Gray, Johnson, & Boyes-Braem, 1976) have demonstrated three kinds of converging evidence for this definition of the basic level. First, Rosch gave people names at various levels of classification and asked them to list all attributes that are true of objects in that class. For example, try to list (or ask friends to do so) all the attributes held in common by all kinds of furniture. You probably won't come up with many common attributes for this superordinate level. On the other hand try to list all attributes held in common by all tables. You will probably come up with a number of attributes at this basic level. Now try to list all the attributes held in common by kitchen tables. You will probably name few more than you did for the basic level. Thus, the basic level is the most abstract level at which the members of a category have many attributes in common.

Similarly, Rosch found that when people were presented with all the category names in Figure 14–11 and asked to list for each the sequence of motor movements they use when dealing with members of this class, Rosch found that the basic level was the most abstract at which people could list motor movements in common. Thus, although you use a similar series of motor movements for all hammers, you use widely varying motor movements for different tools. Finally, Rosch superimposed drawings of a set of objects from each class and then drew averaged outlines of the class. For example, Rosch superimposed many pictures of chairs and combined them to form an average outline of a chair. She did the same for the category furniture and the subordinate category kitchen chair. These averaged drawings were presented to people for identification. Again, Rosch found that the basic level is the highest at which people can recognize averaged (i.e., composite) drawings. This suggests that the basic level is the most abstract level at which a spatial image can accurately depict the class as a whole.

Rosch's work, then, demonstrates that the basic level of categorization is that which most closely mirrors the perceived real-world correlational structure. Is there any sense in which this level is basic psychologically as well? The answer is "yes" on several counts.

First, *when we perceive and identify objects, we do so first at the basic level.* Evidence for this comes from both naming and picture verification tasks. When people are presented with a picture and asked to name it, Rosch and her colleagues (Rosch, Mervis, Gray, Johnson, & Boyes-Braem, 1976, Experiment 10) found that people virtually always use the basic level name (e.g., chair) rather than the superordinate (e.g., furniture) or the subordinate (kitchen chair). In addition, Rosch and her colleagues (Rosch, Mervis, Gray, Johnson, & Boyes-Braem, 1976, Experiment 7) gave people a picture verification task in which a name was presented followed after a brief duration by a picture. Subjects responded as quickly as possible, "yes" if the picture was a member of the category named and "no" otherwise. Basic level names led to faster decisions than either superordinate or subordinate names. These findings suggest, then, that objects are identified first at the basic level and that additional processing is required to go to super- or subordinate levels. In terms of network models, a picture activates first the concept node corresponding to the basic level category name, and activation then spreads (or is directed to) superordinate and subordinate concept nodes.

Second, *the basic level has primacy during child development.* Evidence for this comes from the fact that for most domains at least, this is the first level to which names are attached (Rosch, Mervis, Gray, Johnson, & Boyes-Braem, 1976, Experiment 11). We must interpret this finding with caution, however, since this could be due at least in part to the frequency with which words are heard by the child. When the child points at an object, the adult is more likely to say "car" than "vehicle." Stronger evidence comes from the fact that when children are given objects and asked to put them in piles that contain the "same type of thing," the basic level is the highest level at which the child is likely to arrange the objects. Thus, there is some evidence that the basic level is salient for young children.

Third, *basic level names emerge first during the evolution of language.* Here we have two particularly fascinating kinds of evidence, one from anthropological studies and one from linguistic studies of sign language. The anthropologist Berlin (1978) has studied the folk taxonomies of non-Western cultures for classifying the biological world. Berlin argues that all of the cultures he has studied reveal the kind of taxonomic structure depicted in Figure 14–11, and that there is a basic level of classification at which objects seem to "cry out to be named." At this basic level, virtually all classes are named in all cultures regardless of whether or not the distinction is culturally useful. For example, the class we term *pines* would be given a different name from that we term *oaks* even though neither tree performs an important function for the culture. On the other hand, subordinate levels are usually named only if the distinction is culturally important. For example, if two different kinds of pines are used for two different purposes, then they will be given distinctive names. Otherwise, they will simply both be termed *pines.* Similarly, superordinate levels often lack distinguishing names in many cultures, although there is often evidence that these classes are distinctive for the people. For example, the Tzeltal Maya of Southern Mexico lack words for *plant* and *animal.* However, it is clear that they are capable of distinguishing the two classes, since all plant forms are modified with the numerical classification *tehk* and all animal forms with *koht.* Thus, Berlin's anthropological data indicate that across cultures, categories at the basic level are the first to be named. In fact, they seem to be named for the same reason that mountains are climbed—because they are there. On the other hand superordinate and subordinate classes are named only if they are culturally important.

Other evidence on language evolution comes from the domain of American Sign Language. Recall that ASL is independent of spoken English and that it is a younger language which is still developing rapidly. It is of particular interest, then, to determine whether or not signs for classes at the basic level have developed more fully than those at superordinate and subordinate levels. Newport and Bellugi (1978) have presented fascinating evidence for the primacy of the basic level in ASL. They note that ASL usually has simple primary signs for the basic level. On the other hand, ASL rarely has primary signs at the superordinate level. Instead, when an individual wishes to convey a superordinate level category, he combines the signs for three or four basic level category names with the optional sign for *etc.* For example, to convey the idea VEHICLE the person might make signs for CAR, PLANE, TRAIN in rapid succession, possibly adding a sign for ETC. There is no fixed order in which the signs must occur, and in fact, the same basic level signs need not necessarily be used. In the same conversation, for example, the idea VEHICLE might be conveyed a second time by the string PLANE, CAR, BUS. When people use such strings, it is clear that their purpose is to construct a superordinate term rather than to just make a list. One thing that makes this clear is that the basic level signs are made in reduced form with only minor pauses and transitions, so that the length of time to produce the whole string (e.g., CAR, TRAIN, PLANE) is approximately the same as the time usually required to make a single sign. Thus, the signer attempts to make the string similar in duration to a single sign. In addition, it is clear that the speaker intends to make a superordinate rather than a list in many cases such as the one in which the person signs ME BUY NEW HAMMER-SCREWDRIVER-WRENCH-ETC, BUT NO SCREWDRIVER.

Again in the case of subordinate terms, ASL often has no single signs. Instead compounds are constructed of simple signs. For example, *kitchen chair* would be conveyed by the signs COOK-CHAIR. In many cases such subordinate compounds are conventionalized and standardized, so that they are used the same by all signers. This, of course, is analogous to the way in which spoken English often produces subordinate terms, such as *kitchen chair*, *sports car*, *sailboat*. Sometimes, however, signers find themselves without a standardized subordinate term, and they will often use mimetic depiction in such cases, acting out some salient property of the physical and/or functional attributes of the object to be named. An example of a signer creating a mimetic depiction of a grand piano is shown in Figure 14–12. In the construction of superordinate and subordinate terms, then, we again see sign language presenting a combination of the arbitrary,

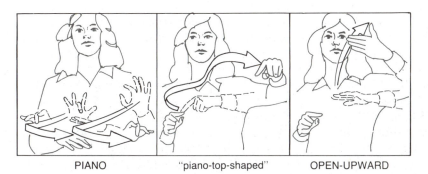

| PIANO | "piano-top-shaped" | OPEN-UPWARD |

Figure 14–12. An example of a signer creating a mimetic depiction of a grand piano (a subordinate level term). (From Newport & Bellugi, 1978. Copyright 1978 by Lawrence Erlbaum Associates. Redrawn by permission of the author and publisher.)

rule-governed nature of all language, combined with an exploitation of the special characteristics of the visual modality.

It is possible to express all levels of natural taxonomies in sign language, but the basic level is primary in that it is the only one for which there are always single sign equivalents. Presumably, this reflects the importance of the basic level in human thought and communication.

Having considered the vertical dimension of natural taxonomies, we turn finally to the horizontal. As we have indicated, *along the horizontal dimension, categories are structured in terms of family resemblance or as prototypes.* For contrast, recall again Bruner and his colleagues' stimuli depicted in Figure 14–2. Notice that for the categories Bruner studied, all exemplars of a class were equally "good" examples of that class. That is, all members of the class contained the defining attribute. Thus, the categories studied by Bruner and his colleagues lacked internal structure. On the other hand, natural categories are internally structured into a prototype (i.e., clearest case or best example of the category) and nonprototypes. We can tell that this is the case, because people usually agree on their judgments of category "goodness" or prototypicality, a point we discussed earlier in the chapter on semantic memory. For example, if asked to name the prototypical or best example of a dog, even the owners of a Chihuahua are unlikely to list that breed. Instead, people tend to pick a collie or perhaps a beagle. Furthermore, Rosch and her colleagues have demonstrated that those members judged to be prototypical of a category tend to be those that have the most attributes in common with other members of the same category and the fewest attributes in common with other categories. As Wittgenstein argued, natural categories are not defined by a set of criterial features, but by a general family resemblance. Prototypes are those members of a category which show the highest overall family resemblance.

Not only do natural categories appear to be internally structured around prototypical members, but the prototypicality of exemplars influences many aspects of performance. First, as we mentioned in the chapter on semantic memory, people make judgments of category membership faster for prototypes than for nonprototypes. For example, collie is judged to be a member of the class dog faster than is Chihuahua. Second, when children learn names, they attach the names first to the prototypical members of the category (e.g., Anglin, 1977). Prototypicality has an even greater effect on category membership judgments for young children than it does for adults (Rosch, 1973). Third, when people are asked to name the members of a category, the first and most frequently produced names are those of prototypical members (Rosch, 1975b). Fourth, in ASL when superordinates are produced by chaining category members, the members that are chained together are prototypical of the category (Newport & Bellugi, 1978). Thus, if a signer wished to convey the superordinate FURNITURE, he would probably chain together CHAIR-TABLE-BED, not RADIO-STOOL-CRIB.

We find, then, that natural concepts are structured in special ways that have not been characteristic of the concepts that have been studied in the laboratory. Notice that what we have said does not tell us the processes by which people acquire natural concepts, nor does it tell us how these structures are represented in the mind. The latter is a particularly important point. People often assume that when we say that natural categories are structured around prototypes we are thereby stating that these prototypes are represented in the mind as mental images. In fact, this is not necesssarily the case at all. The notion of prototypes is quite consistent with a model of knowledge that assumes a network model of the sort we discussed in the chapter on semantic memory. A prototype can be represented as a node containing a set of features, just as readily as by a mental image.

Acquisition of natural language concepts. Recall that when we talked about laboratory studies of concept acquisition we discussed three types of acquisition: hypothesis testing which occurred for explicit concepts, abstraction of prototypes, and drawing analogies from instances. Which of these, if any, is important in the acquisition of natural categories? We don't know yet, but it seems likely that all three are involved with their relative importance depending upon the conditions of acquisition and, perhaps, characteristics of the individual such as age. Let us consider each type in turn.

Given the differences between the structure of natural concepts and the structure of the concepts that have been studied in explicit concept acquisition, it seems unlikely that hypothesis testing alone can account for the acquisition of natural concepts. Nonetheless, we have already mentioned that adults, at least, tend to apply hypothesis testing any time they are presented with a concept learning problem in the laboratory. For example, Martin and Caramazza (1980) gave college students an explicit concept learning problem using schematic faces such as those shown in Figure 14–13. People were told that they should not expect to find a single defining feature or set of features for each category, but rather that members of each category would be defined by family resemblance. Nonetheless, Martin and Caramazza found that these young adults engaged in a form of hypothesis testing and that they developed decision trees based on the features of the faces, much like those Hunt (1962) found people using with well-defined concepts. Thus, among adults at least, it is possible that when they set out to acquire a new concept they search for a set of defining attributes using hypothesis testing.

Figure 14–13. The schematic faces used in Martin and Caramazza's (1980) study of explicit concept acquisition. (From Martin & Caramazza, 1980. Copyright 1980 by the American Psychological Association. Reprinted by permission of the publisher and author.)

Nonetheless, the conditions of real life acquisition are such that hypothesis testing cannot be used in any systematic fashion, at least by young children. It is possible that some form of abstraction is occurring, though as yet this has not been outlined clearly. Brooks (1978) has noted that the conditions of real world concept learning might often favor some form of analogy from instances. Typically the child is learning many concepts at once (not the single or perhaps pair of concepts usually presented in laboratory studies). This might make hypothesis testing difficult. Furthermore, for many of the important concepts, such as those corresponding to MOMMY, DADDY, DOG, SISTER, etc., for a long time the child sees only one exemplar. Thus, it is likely that he stores away this "best" example and then upon later experience analogizes from it. In fact, there is evidence that children do this, at least under some circumstances.

CHAPTER SUMMARY

In order to deal with the infinite variation in the world, we must segment it into conceptual classes within which nonidentical stimuli are treated as equivalent. In this chapter we examined how concepts are structured and learned, focusing first on explicit and then on implicit concepts. Explicit concepts differ from implicit in that they are learned intentionally and, after learning is complete, they can be described accurately by the learner.

Explicit concept learning has been studied using the concept identification task. Most adults solve such tasks by proposing and testing hypotheses, using either a partist or wholist strategy. The blank-trials procedure has made it possible to infer the hypotheses subjects are testing without requiring them to verbalize. This enables the study of hypothesis testing during concept learning among young children. Although children usually appear to test hypotheses somewhat less efficiently than young adults, there is evidence that their difficulties are due more to memory problems than to a lack of logical ability.

Studies of implicit concept acquisition have demonstrated that people are sensitive to regularities among class members even when they are not trying to learn a concept, and even when there is no defining attribute for the class. For example, people learn concepts that are defined by overall similarity to a prototype or by sequential rules. Whether implicit concepts are learned by abstracting prototypes or by drawing analogies from instances, or by some combination of the two, is a matter yet to be resolved.

In studying natural language concepts, it is first necessary to analyze their structure. Experimentation and observation have indicated four major characteristics of such structure. First, natural language categories are ill defined. Second, in the real world, attributes do not occur independently of each other. Third, within the vertical dimension of natural taxonomies there is a basic level of classification. Fourth, along the horizontal dimension of natural taxonomies, categories are structured in terms of family resemblance or prototypes. It is likely that explicit hypothesis testing, abstraction of prototypes, and drawing analogies from instances are all involved in the acquisition of natural language concepts, with their relative importance depending on the conditions of acquisition and on characteristics of the learner such as age.

SUGGESTED READING

The text by Cohen (1977) contains a clear, brief discussion of the major issues in concept learning and will send you to additional references. There are three books that were particularly influential in studies of explicit concept learning and all are good reading. These include Bruner, Goodnow, and Austin's *A Study of Thinking* (1956), Hunt's *Concept Learning: An Information Processing Problem* (1962), and Hunt, Marin, and Stone's *Experiments in Induction* (1966). An influential early paper on abstraction and implicit concept learning is the 1969 article by Posner. You will also find reprints of classic studies of concept identification in the edited books by Wason and Johnson-Laird (1968) and Johnson-Laird and Wason (1977). The best place to begin a more in-depth investigation of hypothesis testing theories of concept identification is Levine's (1975) volume, *A Cognitive*

Theory of Learning. An article by Millward and Spoehr (1973) reports another promising method for measuring hypothesis testing strategies. Finally, there is a single volume that provides the best place to gain a current picture of research and theory on conceptual thinking. This is the excellent book edited by Rosch and Lloyd (1978) entitled *Cognition and Categorization*. It contains a wide range of articles, including chapters on development, sign language, and cross-cultural work. The chapters by Garner and by Shepp are particularly noteworthy since they concern an important topic not discussed here, namely the psychological consequences and developmental implications of the distinction between integral and separable dimensions.

ABRAHAMSEN, A. A. *Child language: An interdisciplinary guide to theory and research.* Baltimore: University Park Press, 1977.

ABRAMS, K., and BEVER, T. G. Syntactic structure modifies attention during speech perception and recognition. *Quarterly Journal of Experimental Psychology,* 1969, *21,* 280–290.

ADAMSON, R. E. Functional fixedness as related to problem solving: A repetition of three experiments. *Journal of Experimental Psychology,* 1952, 44, 288–291.

AITCHISON, J. *The articulate mammal.* New York: McGraw-Hill, 1976.

AMMON, P. R., and AMMON, M. S. Effects of training black preschool children in vocabulary vs. sentence construction. *Journal of Educational Psychology,* 1971, 421–426.

ANDERS, T. R., FOZARD, J. L., and LILLYQUIST, T. D. The effects of age upon retrieval from short-term memory. *Developmental Psychology,* 1972, *6,* 214–217.

ANDERSON, C. M. B., and CRAIK, F. I. M. The effect of a concurrent task on recall from primary memory. *Journal of Verbal Learning and Verbal Behavior,* 1974, *13,* 107–113.

ANDERSON, J. R. *Language, memory, and thought.* Hillsdale, N.J.: Erlbaum, 1976.

ANDERSON, J. R. Arguments concerning representations for mental imagery. *Psychological Review,* 1978, *85,* 249–277.

ANDERSON, J. R. On the merits of ACT and information-processing psychology: A response to Wexler's review. *Cognition,* 1980, *8,* 73–88.

ANDERSON, J. R., and BOWER, G. H. *Human associative memory.* Washington, D.C.: Winston, 1973.

ANDERSON, J. R., KLINE, P. J., and LEWIS, C. H. A production system model of language processing. In M. A. Just and P. A. Carpenter (Eds.), *Cognitive processes in comprehension.* Hillsdale, N.J.: Erlbaum, 1977.

ANGLIN, J. *Word, object, and conceptual development.* New York: Norton & Company, 1977.

ANISFELD, M., and KNAPP, M. E. Association, synonymity, and directionality in false recognition. *Journal of Experimental Psychology,* 1968, *77,* 171–179.

ARCHER, E. J. A re-evaluation of the meaningfulness of all possible CVC trigrams. *Psychological Monographs,* 1960, *74.*

ATKINSON, R. C., HOLMGREN, J. E., and JUOLA, J. F. Processing time as influ-

References

enced by number of items in a visual display. *Perception & Psychophysics,* 1969, *6,* 321–326.

ATKINSON, R. C., and RAUGH, M. R. An application of the mnemonic keyword method to the acquisition of a Russian vocabulary. *Journal of Experimental Psychology: Human Learning and Memory,* 1975, *104,* 126–133.

ATKINSON, R. C., and SHIFFRIN, R. M. Human memory: A proposed system and its control processes. In K. W. Spence and J. T. Spence (Eds.), *The psychology of learning and motivation: Advances in research and theory* (Vol. 2). New York: Academic Press, 1968.

ATKINSON, R. C., and SHIFFRIN, R. M. The control of short-term memory. *Scientific American,* 1971, *225,* 82–90.

ATWOOD, M. E., and POLSON, P. G. A process model for water jug problems. *Cognitive Psychology,* 1976, *8,* 191–216.

AVERBACH, E. The span of apprehension as a function of exposure duration. *Journal of Verbal Learning and Verbal Behavior,* 1963, *2,* 60–64.

AVERBACH, E., and SPERLING, G. Short-term storage of information in vision. In C. Cherry (Ed.), *Information theory.* London: Butterworth, 1961.

BACH, M. J., and UNDERWOOD, B. J. Developmental changes in memory attributes. *Journal of Educational Psychology,* 1970, *61,* 292–296.

BADDELEY, A. D. A three-minute reasoning test based on grammatical transformation. *Psychonomic Science,* 1968, *10,* 341–342.

BADDELEY, A. D. *The psychology of memory.* New York: Basic Books, 1976.

BADDELEY, A. D. The trouble with levels: A reexamination of Craik and Lockhart's framework for memory research. *Psychological Review,* 1978, *85,* 139–152.

BADDELEY, A. D. Working memory and reading. In P. A. Kolers, M. E. Wrolstad, and H. Bouma (Eds.), *Processing of visible language* (Vol. 1). New York: Plenum Press, 1979.

BADDELEY, A. D. The concept of working memory: A view of its current state and probable future development. *Cognition,* 1981, *10,* 17–23.

BADDELEY, A. D., and HITCH, G. Working memory. In G. H. Bower (Ed.), *The psychology of learning and motivation* (Vol. 8). New York: Academic Press, 1974.

BADDELEY, A. D., and HITCH, G. Recency re-examined. In S. Dornic (Ed.), *Attention and performance VI.* New York: Academic Press, 1976.

BADDELEY, A. D., and LIEBERMAN, K. Spatial working memory. In R. Nickerson (Ed.), *Attention and performance VIII.* Hillsdale, N.J.: Erlbaum, 1980.

BADDELEY, A. D., and WARRINGTON, E. K. Amnesia and the distinction between long and short-term memory. *Journal of Verbal Learning and Verbal Behavior,* 1970, *9,* 176–189.

BALOTA, D. A., and ENGLE, R. W. Structural and strategic factors in the stimulus suffix effect. *Journal of Verbal Learning and Verbal Behavior,* 1981, *20,* 346–357.

BANKS, W. P. Encoding and processing of symbolic information in comparative judgments. In G. H. Bower (Ed.), *The psychology of learning and motivation* (Vol. 11). New York: Academic Press, 1977.

BANKS, W. P., and BARBER, G. Color information in iconic memory. *Psychological Review,* 1977, *84,* 536–546.

BANKS, W. P., and BARBER, G. Normal iconic memory for stimuli invisible to the rods. *Perception & Psychophysics,* 1980, *27,* 581–584.

BANKS, W. P., and FLORA, J. Semantic and perceptual processes in symbolic comparisons. *Journal of Experimental Psychology: Human Perception and Performance,* 1977, *3,* 278–290.

BARON, J. The word superiority effect: Perceptual learning from reading. In W. K. Estes (Ed.), *Handbook of learning and cognitive processes* (Vol. 6). Hillsdale, N.J.: Erlbaum, 1978.

BARTLETT, F. C. *Remembering: A study in experimental and social psychology.* London: Cambridge University Press, 1932.

BATTIG, W. F., and MONTAGUE, W. E. Category norms for verbal items in 56 categories: A replication and extension of the Connecticut category norms. *Journal of Experimental Psychology Monographs,* 1969, *80*(3, Pt. 2).

BEGG, I., and DENNY, J. P. Empirical reconciliation of atmosphere and conversion interpretations of syllogistic reasoning errors. *Journal of Experimental Psychology,* 1969, *81,* 351–354.

BEKERIAN, D. A., and BADDELEY, A. D. Saturation advertising and the repetition effect. *Journal of Verbal Learning and Verbal Behavior,* 1980, *19,* 17–25.

BELLUGI, U., and FISCHER, S. A comparison of sign language and spoken language. *Cognition,* 1972, *1,* 173–200.

BELLUGI, U., and KLIMA, E. S. The roots of language in the sign talk of the deaf. *Psychology Today,* 1972, *6,* 61–76.

BELLUGI, U., and KLIMA, E. S. Structural properties of American Sign Language. In L. S. Liben (Ed.), *Deaf children: Developmental perspectives.* New York: Academic Press, 1978.

BELLUGI, U., KLIMA, E. S., and SIPLE, P. Remembering in signs. *Cognition,* 1975, *3,* 93–125.

BELLUGI, U., and SIPLE, P. Remembering with and without words. In F. Bresson (Ed.), *Current problems in psycholinguistics.* Paris: Centre National de la Recherche Scientifique, 1974.

BERKO, J. The child's learning of English morphology. *Word,* 1958, *14,* 150–177.

BERLIN, B. Ethnobiological classification. In E. Rosch and B. B. Lloyd (Eds.), *Cognition and categorization.* Hillsdale, N.J.: Erlbaum, 1978.

BEVER, T. G. The cognitive basis for linguistic structures. In J. R. Hayes (Ed.), *Cognition and the development of language.* New York: Wiley, 1970.

BEVER, T. G., and CHIARELLO, R. J. Cerebral dominance in musicians and non-musicians. *Science,* 1974, *185,* 137–139.

BIRCH, H. G., and RABINOWITZ, H. S. The negative effect of previous experience on productive thinking. *Journal of Experimental Psychology,* 1951, *41,* 121–125.

BJORK, R. A. Short-term storage: The ordered output of a central processor. In F. Restle, R. M. Shiffrin, N. J. Castellan, H. Lindman, and D. B. Pisoni (Eds.), *Cognitive Theory* (Vol. 1). Hillsdale, N.J.: Erlbaum, 1975.

BLISS, J. C., Crane, H. D., Mansfield, P. K., and Townsend, J. T. Information available in brief tactile presentations. *Perception & Psychophysics,* 1966, *1,* 273–283.

BLOCK, N. (Ed.). *Imagery.* Cambridge, Mass.: MIT Press, 1981.

BOLINGER, D. L. *Aspects of language* (2nd ed.). New York: Harcourt Brace Jovanovich, 1975.

BOOLE, G. *An investigation of the laws of thought.* New York: Macmillan, 1854.

BOUSFIELD, W. A. The occurrence of clustering in the recall of randomly arranged associates. *Journal of General Psychology*, 1953, *49*, 229–240.

BOWER, G. H. Analysis of a mnemonic device. *American Scientist*, 1970, *58*, 496–510. (a)

BOWER, G. H. Organizational factors in memory. *Cognitive Psychology*, 1970, *1*, 18–46. (b)

BOWER, G. H. Mental imagery and associative learning. In L. Gregg (Ed.), *Cognition in learning and memory*. New York: Wiley, 1972.

BOWER, G. H. Cognitive psychology: An introduction. In W. K. Estes (Ed.), *Handbook of learning and cognitive processes* (Vol. 1). Hillsdale, N.J.: Erlbaum, 1975.

BOWER, G. H. Improving memory. *Human Nature*, 1978, *1*, 64–72.

BOWER, G. H. Mood and memory. *American Psychologist*, 1981, *36*, 129–148.

BOWER, G. H., GILLIGAN, S. G., and MONTEIRO, K. P. Selectivity of learning caused by affective states. *Journal of Experimental Psychology: General*, 1981, *110*, 129–148.

BOWER, G. H., and WINZENZ, D. Comparison of associative learning strategies. *Psychonomic Science*, 1970, *20*, 119–120.

BRADSHAW, J. L. Three interrelated problems in reading: A review. *Memory & Cognition*, 1975, *3*, 123–134.

BRAINE, M. D. S. On two types of models of the internalization of grammars. In D. I. Slobin (Ed.), *The ontogenesis of grammar*. New York: Academic Press, 1971.

BRAINE, M. D. S. On the relation between the natural logic of reasoning and standard logic. *Psychological Review*, 1978, *85*, 1–21.

BRANSFORD, J. D. *Human cognition*. Belmont, California: Wadsworth, 1979.

BRANSFORD, J. D., BARCLAY, J. R., and FRANKS, J. J. Sentence memory: A constructive versus interpretive approach. *Cognitive Psychology*, 1972, *3*, 193–209.

BRANSFORD, J. D., and FRANKS, J. J. The abstraction of linguistic ideas. *Cognitive Psychology*, 1971, *2*, 331–350.

BROADBENT, D. E. *Perception and communication*. London: Pergamon Press, 1958.

BROADBENT, D. E. *Decision and stress*. New York: Academic Press, 1971.

BROOKS, L. R. The suppression of visualization in reading. *Quarterly Journal of Experimental Psychology*, 1967, *19*, 289–299.

BROOKS, L. R. Spatial and verbal components of the act of recall. *Canadian Journal of Psychology*, 1968, *22*, 349–368.

BROOKS, L. R. Nonanalytic concept formation and memory for instances. In E. Rosch and B. B. Lloyd (Eds.), *Cognition and categorization*. Hillsdale, N.J.: Erlbaum, 1978.

BROWN, A., CAMPIONE, J., BRAY, N., and WILCOX, B. Keeping track of changing variables: Effect of rehearsal training and rehearsal prevention in normal and retarded adolescents. *Journal of Experimental Psychology*, 1973, *101*, 123–131.

BROWN, A., CAMPIONE, J. and MURPHY, M. Keeping track of changing variables: Long-term retention of a trained rehearsal strategy by retarded adolescents. *American Journal of Mental Deficiency*, 1974, *78*, 446–453.

BROWN, R., CAZDEN, C., and BELLUGI, U. The child's grammar from I to III. In

J. P. Hill (Ed.), *Minnesota symposium on child psychology* (Vol. 2). Minneapolis: University of Minnesota Press, 1969.

BROWN, R., and McNEILL, D. The "tip-of-the-tongue" phenomenon. *Journal of Verbal Learning and Verbal Behavior*, 1966, *5*, 325–337.

BRUNER, J. S. The course of cognitive growth. *American Psychologist*, 1964, *19*, 1–15.

BRUNER, J. S., GOODNOW, J. J., and AUSTIN, G. A. *A study of thinking*. New York: Wiley, 1956.

BRYANT, P. E., and TRABASSO, T. Transitive inferences and memory in young children. *Nature*, 1971, *232*, 456–458.

BUCCI, W. The interpretation of universal affirmative propositions. *Cognition*, 1978, *6*, 55–77.

BUCKHOUT, R. Eyewitness testimony. *Scientific American*, 1974, *231*, 23–31.

BUGELSKI, B. R. Words and things and images. *American Psychologist*, 1970, *25*, 1002–1012.

BYRNE, B., and SHEA, P. Semantic and phonetic memory codes in beginning readers. *Memory & Cognition*, 1979, *7*, 333–338.

CAMPIONE, J. C., and BROWN, A. L. Memory and metamemory development in educable retarded children. In R. V. Kail, Jr. and J. W. Hagen (Eds.), *Perspectives on the development of memory and cognition*. Hillsdale, N.J.: Erlbaum, 1977.

CAPLAN, D. Clause boundaries and recognition latencies for words in sentences. *Perception & Psychophysics*, 1972, *12*, 73–76.

CARNEY, A. E., WIDIN, G. P., and VIEMEISTER, N. F. Noncategorical perception of stop consonants differing in VOT. *Journal of the Acoustical Society of America*, 1977, *62*, 961–970.

CARPENTER, P. A., and JUST, M. A. Sentence comprehension: A psycholinguistic processing model of verification. *Psychological Review*, 1975, *82*, 45–73.

CARROLL, J. M., and BEVER, T. G. Sentence comprehension: A case study in the relation of knowledge and perception. In E. C. Carterette and M. P. Friedman (Eds.), *Handbook of perception* (Vol. 7). New York: Academic Press, 1976.

CERASO, J., and PROVITERA, A. Sources of error in syllogistic reasoning. *Cognitive Psychology*, 1971, *2*, 400–410.

CERMAK, L. S. *Improving your memory*. New York: McGraw-Hill, 1975.

CHAPMAN, L. J., and CHAPMAN, J. P. Atmosphere effect reexamined. *Journal of Experimental Psychology*, 1959, *58*, 220–226.

CHARNESS, N. Aging and skilled problem solving. *Journal of Experimental Psychology: General*, 1981, *110*, 21–38.

CHARNIAK, E. Toward a model of children's story comprehension. Unpublished doctoral dissertation, MIT, 1972.

CHASE, W., and CLARK, H. H. Mental operations in the comparison of sentences and pictures. In L. Gregg (Ed.), *Cognition in learning and memory*. New York: Wiley, 1972.

CHERRY, E. C. Some experiments on the recognition of speech, with one and with two ears. *Journal of the Acoustical Society of America*, 1953, *25*, 975–979.

CHERRY, E. C., and TAYLOR, W. K. Some further experiments upon the recognition of speech, with one and with two ears. *Journal of the Acoustical Society of America*, 1954, *26*, 554–559.

CHI, M. T. H. Short-term memory limitations in children: capacity or processing deficits? *Memory & Cognition*, 1976, *4*, 559–572.

CHOMSKY, N. *Syntactic structures*. The Hague: Mouton Publishers, 1957.

CHOMSKY, N. *Language and mind*. New York: Harcourt Brace Jovanovich, 1968.

CHOW, S. L., and MURDOCK, B. B. The effect of a subsidiary task on iconic memory. *Memory & Cognition*, 1975, *3*, 678–688.

CHOW, S. L., and MURDOCK, B. B. Concurrent memory load and the rate of readout from iconic memory. *Journal of Experimental Psychology: Human Perception and Performance*, 1976, *2*, 179–190.

CLARK, H. H. Linguistic processes in deductive reasoning. *Psychological Review*, 1969, *76*, 387–404.

CLARK, H. H., and CLARK, E. V. *Psychology and language*. New York: Harcourt Brace Jovanovich, 1977.

CLARK, H. H., and HAVILAND, S. E. Comprehension and the given-new contract. In R. O. Freedle (Ed.), *Discourse production and comprehension*. Norwood, N.J.: Ablex, 1977.

COHEN, G. *The psychology of cognition*. New York: Academic Press, 1977.

COHEN, M. R. *A preface to logic*. New York: Holt, 1944.

COLE, M., and SCRIBNER, S. *Culture and thought: A psychological introduction*. New York: Wiley, 1974.

COLE, M., and SCRIBNER, S. Cross-cultural studies of memory and cognition. In R. V. Kail, Jr. and J. W. Hagen (Eds.), *Perspectives on the development of memory and cognition*. Hillsdale, N.J.: Erlbaum, 1977.

COLE, R. A. (Ed.). *Perception and production of fluent speech*. Hillsdale, N.J.: Erlbaum, 1980.

COLE, R. A., and JAKIMIK, J. Understanding speech: How words are heard. In G. Underwood (Ed.), *Strategies of information processing*. London: Academic Press, 1978.

COLE, R. A., and JAKIMIK, J. A model of speech perception. In R. A. Cole (Ed.), *Perception and production of fluent speech*. Hillsdale, N.J.: Erlbaum, 1980.

COLLINS, A. M., and LOFTUS, E. F. A spreading activation theory of semantic processing. *Psychological Review*, 1975, *82*, 407–428.

COLLINS, A. M., and QUILLIAN, M. R. Retrieval time from semantic memory. *Journal of Verbal Learning and Verbal Behavior*, 1969, *8*, 240–247.

COLLINS, A. M., and QUILLIAN, M. R. How to make a language user. In E. Tulving and W. Donaldson (Eds.), *Organization of memory*. New York: Academic Press, 1972.

COLTHEART, M. Iconic memory: A reply to Professor Holding. *Memory & Cognition*, 1975, *3*, 42–48.

COLTHEART, M. Lexical access in simple reading tasks. In G. Underwood (Ed.), *Strategies of information processing*. New York: Academic Press, 1978.

COLTHEART, M. Iconic memory and visible persistence. *Perception & Psychophysics*, 1980, *27*, 183–228.

COLTHEART, M., LEA, C. D., and THOMPSON, K. In defense of iconic memory. *Quarterly Journal of Experimental Psychology*, 1974, *26*, 633–641.

CONRAD, R. Acoustic confusions in immediate memory. *British Journal of Psychology*, 1964, *55*, 75–84.

CONRAD, R. Short-term memory processes in the deaf. *British Journal of Psychology*, 1970, *61*, 179–195.

CONRAD, R. The chronology of the development of covert speech in children. *Developmental Psychology*, 1971, *5*, 398–405.

CONRAD, R. Speech and reading. In J. F. Kavanagh and I. G. Mattingly (Eds.), *Language by ear and by eye*. Cambridge, Mass.: MIT Press, 1972.

CONRAD, R. The reading ability of deaf school-leavers. *British Journal of Educational Psychology*, 1977, *47*, 138–148.

COOPER, W. E. Selective adaptation to speech. In F. Restle, R. M. Shiffrin, N. J. Castellan. H. Lindman, and D. B. Pisoni (Eds.), *Cognitive theory* (Vol. 1). Hillsdale, N.J.: Erlbaum, 1975.

COOPER, W. E. *Speech perception and production: Studies in selective adaptation*. Norwood, N.J.: Ablex, 1979.

CORCORAN, D. W. J. An acoustic factor in letter cancellation. *Nature*, 1966, *210*, 658.

CORCORAN, D. W. J. Acoustic factors in proof reading. *Nature*, 1967, *214*, 851.

CORCORAN, D. W. J., and WEENING, D. L. Acoustic factors in visual search. *Quarterly Journal of Experimental Psychology*, 1968, *20*, 83–85.

CORTEEN, R. S., and DUNN, D. Shock-associated words in a non-attended message: a test for momentary awareness. *Journal of Experimental Psychology*, 1974, *102*, 1143–1144.

CORTEEN, R. S., and WOOD, B. Autonomic responses to shock associated words in an unattended channel. *Journal of Experimental Psychology*, 1972, *97*, 308–313.

COSKY, M. J. Word length effects in word recognition. Unpublished Ph.D. dissertation, University of Texas at Austin, 1975.

CRAIK, F. I. M. The fate of primary memory items in free recall. *Journal of Verbal Learning and Verbal Behavior*, 1970, *9*, 143–148.

CRAIK, F. I. M., and JACOBY, L. L. A process view of short-term retention. In F. Restle, R. M. Shiffrin, N. J. Castellan, H. Lindman, and D. B. Pisoni (Eds.), *Cognitive theory* (Vol. 1). Hillsdale, N.J.: Erlbaum, 1975.

CRAIK, F. I. M., and LEVY, B. A. The concept of primary memory. In W. K. Estes (Ed.), *Handbook of learning and cognitive processes* (Vol. 4). Hillsdale, N.J.: Erlbaum, 1976.

CRAIK, F. I. M., and LOCKHART, R. S. Levels of processing: a framework for memory research. *Journal of Verbal Learning and Verbal Behavior*, 1972, *11*, 671–684.

CRAIK, F. I. M., and TULVING, E. Depth of processing and the retention of words in episodic memory. *Journal of Experimental Psychology: General*, 1975, *104*, 268–294.

CRAIK, F. I. M., and WATKINS, M. J. The role of rehearsal in short-term memory. *Journal of Verbal Learning and Verbal Behavior*, 1973, *12*, 599–607.

CRITCHLEY, M. *The dyslexic child*. London: Heinemann, 1970.

CROWDER, R. G. Visual and auditory memory. In J. F. Kavanagh and I. G. Mattingly (Eds.), *Language by ear and by eye*. Cambridge, Mass.: MIT Press, 1972.

CROWDER, R. G. Inferential problems in echoic memory. In P. Rabbitt and S. Dornic (Eds.), *Attention and performance V*. London: Academic Press, 1975.

CROWDER, R. G. *Principles of learning and memory*. Hillsdale, N.J.: Erlbaum, 1976.

CROWDER, R. G. Decay of auditory memory in vowel discrimination. *Journal of Experimental Psychology: Learning, Memory, and Cognition,* 1982, *8,* 153–162.

CROWDER, R. G., and MORTON, J. Precategorical acoustic storage (PAS). *Perception & Psychophysics,* 1969, *5,* 365–373.

CUNNINGHAM, J. P. Trees as memory representations for simple visual patterns. *Memory & Cognition,* 1980, *86,* 593–605.

CURTIS, H. S. Automatic movements of the larynx. *American Journal of Psychology,* 1900, *11,* 237–239.

CUTLER, A., and NORRIS, D. Monitoring sentence comprehension. In W. E. Cooper and E. C. T. Walker (Eds.), *Sentence processing: Psycholinguistic studies presented to Merrill Garrett.* Hillsdale, N.J.: Erlbaum, 1979.

CUTTING, J. E., and ROSNER, B. S. Categories and boundaries in speech and music. *Perception & Psychophysics,* 1974, *16,* 564–570.

DALE, P. S. *Language development: Structure and function* (2nd ed.), New York: Holt, 1976.

DANEMAN, M., and CARPENTER, P. A. Individual differences in working memory and reading. *Journal of Verbal Learning and Verbal Behavior,* 1980, *19,* 450–466.

DARLEY, C. F., TINKLENBERG, J. R., HOLLISTER, L. E., and ATKINSON, R. C. Marihuana and retrieval from short-term memory. *Psychopharmacologia,* 1973, *29,* 231–238.

DARWIN, C. J. The perception of speech. In E. C. Carterette and M. P. Friedman (Eds.), *Handbook of perception* (Vol. 7). New York: Academic Press, 1976.

DARWIN, C. J., and BADDELEY, A. D. Acoustic memory and the perception of speech. *Cognitive Psychology,* 1974, *6,* 41–60.

DARWIN, C. J., TURVEY, M. T., and CROWDER, R. G. An auditory analogue of the Sperling partial report procedure: Evidence for brief auditory storage. *Cognitive Psychology,* 1972, *3,* 255–267.

DAWSON, M. E., and SCHELL, A. M. Electrodermal responses to attended and nonattended significant stimuli during dichotic listening. *Journal of Experimental Psychology: Human Perception and Performance,* 1982, *8,* 315–324.

DAY, R. S., and BARTLETT, J. C. Separate speech and nonspeech processing in dichotic listening? *Journal of the Acoustical Society of America,* 1972, *51,* 79.

deGROOT, A. D. Perception and memory versus thinking. In B. Kleinmuntz (Ed.), *Problem solving.* New York: Wiley, 1966.

DELATTRE, P. C., LIBERMAN, A. M., and COOPER, F. S. Acoustic loci and transitional cues for consonants. *Journal of the Acoustical Society of America,* 1955, *27,* 769–773.

DELL, G. S., and NEWMAN, J. E. Detecting phonemes in fluent speech. *Journal of Verbal Learning and Verbal Behavior,* 1980, *19,* 608–623.

den HEYER, K., and BARRETT, B. Selective loss of visual and verbal information in STM by means of visual and verbal interpolated tasks. *Psychonomic Science,* 1971, *25,* 100–102.

DEUTSCH, D., and DEUTSCH, J. A. (Eds.). *Short-term memory.* New York: Academic Press, 1975.

DEUTSCH, J. A., and DEUTSCH, D. Attention: some theoretical considerations. *Psychological Review,* 1963, *70,* 80–90.

deVILLIERS, J. G., and deVILLIERS, P. A. *Language acquisition.* Cambridge, Mass.: Harvard University Press, 1978.

DICK, A. O. Iconic memory and its relation to perceptual processing and other memory mechanisms. *Perception & Psychophysics,* 1974, *16,* 575–596.

DICKSTEIN, L. S. Effects of instructions and premise order on errors in syllogistic reasoning. *Journal of Experimental Psychology: Human Learning and Memory,* 1975, *104,* 376–384.

DOLINSKY, R. Clustering in free recall with alternative organizational cues. *Journal of Experimental Psychology,* 1972, *95,* 159–163.

DOLLARD, J., and MILLER, N. E. *Personality and psychotherapy.* New York: McGraw-Hill, 1950.

DOMINOWSKI, R. L., and JENRICK, R. Effects of hints and interpolated activity on solution of an insight problem. *Psychonomic Science,* 1972, *26,* 335–338.

DONDERS, F. C. [On the speed of mental processes.] In W. G. Koster (Ed. and trans.), *Attention and performance II.* Amsterdam: North-Holland, 1969.

DOOST, R., and TURVEY, M. T. Iconic memory and central processing capacity. *Perception & Psychophysics,* 1971, *9,* 269–274.

DORNIC, S. (Ed.). *Attention and performance VI.* Hillsdale, N.J.: Erlbaum, 1977.

DOWNEY, J. E., and ANDERSON, J. E. Automatic writing. *American Journal of Psychology,* 1915, *26,* 161–195.

DRESHER, B. E., and HORNSTEIN, N. On some supposed contributions of artificial intelligence to the scientific study of language. *Cognition,* 1976, *4,* 321–398.

DRESHER, B. E., and HORNSTEIN, N. Reply to Schank and Wilensky. *Cognition,* 1977, *5,* 147–149. (a)

DRESHER, B. E., and HORNSTEIN, N. Reply to Winograd. *Cognition,* 1977, *5,* 379–392. (b)

DREYFUS, H. L. *What computers can't do.* New York: Harper & Row, 1972.

DUNCKER, K. On problem solving. *Psychological Monographs,* 1945, *58* (5, Whole No. 270).

EBBINGHAUS, H. [*Memory: A contribution to experimental psychology*] (H. A. Ruger and C. E. Bussenius trans.) New York: Dover Publications, Inc., 1964. (Originally published, 1885.)

EGETH, H. Attention and preattention. In G. H. Bower (Ed.), *The psychology of learning and motivation* (Vol. 11). New York: Academic Press, 1977.

EIMAS, P. D. A developmental study of hypothesis behavior and focusing. *Journal of Experimental Child Psychology,* 1969, *8,* 160–172.

EIMAS, P. D. Effects of memory aids on hypothesis behavior and focusing in young children and adults. *Journal of Experimental Child Psychology,* 1970, *10,* 319–336.

EIMAS, P. D. Speech perception in early infancy. In L. B. Cohen and P. Salapatek (Eds.), *Infant perception.* New York: Academic Press, 1975.

EIMAS, P. D. Developmental aspects of speech perception. In R. Held, H. Leibowitz, and H. L. Teuber (Eds.), *Handbook of sensory physiology: Perception.* New York: Springer-Verlag, 1978.

EIMAS, P. D., and CORBIT, J. D. Selective adaptation of linguistic feature detectors. *Cognitive Psychology,* 1973, *4,* 99–109.

EIMAS, P. D., and MILLER, J. L. Effects of selective adaptation on the perception of speech and visual patterns: Evidence for feature detectors. In H. Pick and R. Walk (Eds.), *Perception and experience.* New York: Plenum, 1978.

EIMAS, P. D., and MILLER, J. L. (Eds.). *Perspectives on the study of speech.* Hillsdale, N.J.: Erlbaum, 1981.

EIMAS, P. D., SIQUELAND, E. R., JUSCZYK, P., and VIGORITO, J. Speech perception in infants. *Science,* 1971, *171,* 303–306.

ERICKSON, J. R. A set analysis theory of behavior in formal syllogistic reasoning tasks. In R. L. Solso (Eds.), *Theories in cognitive psychology: The Loyola Symposium.* Potomac, Md.: Erlbaum, 1974.

ERICKSON, J. R. Research on syllogistic reasoning. In R. Revlin and R. E. Mayer (Eds.), *Human reasoning.* Washington, D.C.: V. H. Winston, 1978.

ERICKSON, T. D., and MATTSON, M. E. From words to meaning: A semantic illusion. *Journal of Verbal Learning and Behavior,* 1981, *20,* 540–551.

ERIKSEN, C. W., and COLLINS, J. F. Some temporal characteristics of visual pattern perception. *Journal of Experimental Psychology,* 1967, *74,* 476–484.

ERIKSEN, C. W., and COLLINS, J. F. Sensory traces versus the psychological moment in the temporal organization of form. *Journal of Experimental Psychology,* 1968, *77,* 376–382.

ERIKSEN, C. W., HAMLIN, R. M., and DAYE, C. Aging adults and rate of memory scan. *Bulletin of the Psychonomic Society,* 1973, *1,* 259–260.

ERIKSEN C. W., POLLACK, M. D., and MONTAGUE, W. E. Implicit speech: Mechanism in perceptual encoding? *Journal of Experimental Psychology,* 1970, *84,* 502–507.

ERVIN, S. Imitation and structural change in children's language. In E. H. Lenneberg (Ed.), *New directions in the study of language.* Cambridge, Mass.: MIT Press, 1964.

ESTES, W. K. Introduction to volume 4. In W. K. Estes (Ed.), *Handbook of learning and cognitive processes* (Vol. 4). Hillsdale, N.J.: Erlbaum, 1976.

EYSENCK, M. W. Levels of processing: A critique. *British Journal of Psychology,* 1978, *69,* 157–169. (a)

EYSENCK, M. W. Levels of processing: A reply to Lockhart and Craik. *British Journal of Psychology,* 1978, *69,* 177–178. (b)

FALMAGNE, R. J. (Ed.). *Reasoning: Representation and process.* Hillsdale, N.J.: Erlbaum, 1975.

FARB, P. *Word play: What happens when people talk.* New York: Alfred A. Knopf, 1974.

FEIGENBAUM, E. A., and FELDMAN, J. *Computers and thought.* New York: McGraw-Hill, 1963.

FELDMAN, J. Simulation of behavior in the binary choice experiment. In E. Feigenbaum and J. Feldman (Eds.), *Computers and thought.* New York: McGraw-Hill, 1963.

FILLMORE, C. J. The case for case. In E. Bach and R. T. Harms (Eds.), *Universals in linguistic theory.* New York: Holt, 1968.

FINKE, R. A., and KOSSLYN, S. M. Mental imagery acuity in the peripheral visual field. *Journal of Experimental Psychology: Human Perception and Performance,* 1980, *6,* 126–139.

FINKE, R. A., and KURTZMAN, H. S. Mapping the visual field in mental imagery. *Journal of Experimental Psychology: General,* 1981, *110,* 501–517.

FISCHLER, I. Associative facilitation without expectancy in a lexical decision task. *Journal of Experimental Psychology: Human Perception and Performance,* 1977, *3,* 18–26.

FLEXSER, A. J., and TULVING, E. Retrieval independence in recognition and recall. *Psychological Review*, 1978, *85*, 153–171.

FODOR, J. A., and BEVER, T. G. The psychological reality of linguistic segments. *Journal of Verbal Learning and Verbal Behavior*, 1965, *4*, 414–420.

FODOR, J. A., BEVER, T. G., and GARRETT, M. F. *The psychology of language.* New York: McGraw-Hill, 1974.

FODOR, J. A., and FRAZIER, L. Is the human sentence parsing mechanism an ATN? *Cognition*, 1980, *8*, 417–459.

FOREIT, K. G. Short-lived auditory memory for pitch. *Perception & Psychophysics*, 1976, *19*, 368–370.

FOSS D. J., and BLANK, M. A. Identifying the speech codes. *Cognitive Psychology*, 1980, *12*, 1–31.

FOSS, D. J., and HAKES, D. T. *Psycholinguistics: An introduction to the psychology of language.* Englewood Cliffs, N.J.: Prentice-Hall, 1978.

FOWLER, C. A., WOLFORD, G., SLADE, R., and TASSINARY, L. Lexical access with and without awareness. *Journal of Experimental Psychology: General*, 1981, *110*, 341–362.

FRANCOLINI, C. M., and EGETH, H. E. On the nonautomaticity of "automatic" activation: Evidence of selective seeing. *Perception & Psychophysics*, 1980, *27*, 331–342.

FRANK, H. S., and RABINOVITCH, M. S. Auditory short-term memory: Developmental changes in precategorical acoustic storage. *Child Development*, 1974, *45*, 522–526.

FRANKS, J. J., and BRANSFORD, J. D. Abstraction of visual patterns. *Journal of Experimental Psychology*, 1971, *90*, 65–74.

FRAZIER, L., and FODOR, J. D. The sausage machine: A new two-stage parsing model. *Cognition*, 1978, *6*, 291–325.

FREUD, S. [A note upon the "mystic writing-pad."] (J. Strachey, Trans.) *International Journal of Psycho-Analysis*, 1940, *21*, 469.

FRIEDMAN, L. (Ed.). *On the other hand.* New York: Academic Press, 1977.

FROMKIN, V. A. *Speech errors as linguistic evidence.* The Hague: Mouton, 1973.

FROMKIN, V. A., and RODMAN, R. *An introduction to language* (2nd ed.). New York: Holt, 1978.

FROST, N. Encoding and retrieval in visual memory tasks. *Journal of Experimental Psychology*, 1972, *95*, 317–326.

FULGOSI, A., and GUILFORD, J. P. Short-term incubation in divergent production. *American Journal of Psychology*, 1968, *81*, 241–246.

GALTON, F. *Inquiry into human faculty and its development.* New York: Macmillan, 1883.

GARNER, W. R. Aspects of a stimulus: Features, dimensions, and configurations. In E. Rosch and B. B. Lloyd (Eds.), *Cognition and categorization.* Hillsdale, N.J.: Erlbaum, 1978.

GARRETT, M. F., BEVER, T. G., and FODOR, J. A. The active use of grammar in speech perception. *Perception & Psychophysics*, 1966, *1*, 30–32.

GAZZANIGA, M. S. *The bisected brain.* New York: Appleton-Century-Crofts, 1970.

GAZZANIGA, M. S., and LeDOUX, J. E. *The integrated mind.* New York: Plenum, 1978.

GAZZANIGA, M. S., and SPERRY, R. W. Language after section of the cerebral commissures. *Brain,* 1967, *90,* 131–148.

GESCHWIND, N. Language and brain. *Scientific American,* 1972, *226,* 76–83.

GHOLSON, B., LEVINE, M. and PHILLIPS, S. Hypotheses, strategies and stereotypes in discrimination learning. *Journal of Experimental Child Psychology,* 1972, *13,* 423–446.

GIBSON, E. J., and LEVIN, H. *The psychology of reading.* Cambridge, Mass.: MIT Press, 1975.

GILHOOLY, K. J., and FALCONER, W. A. Concrete and abstract terms and relations in testing a rule. *Quarterly Journal of Experimental Psychology,* 1974, *26,* 355–359.

GLANVILLE, B. B., BEST, C. T., and LEVENSON, R. A cardiac measure of cerebral asymmetries in infant auditory perception. *Developmental Psychology,* 1977, *13,* 54–59.

GLENBERG, A. M. BRADLEY, M. M., STEVENSON, J. A., KRAUS, T. A., TKACHUK, M. J., GRETZ, A. L., FISH, J. H., and TURPIN, B. M. A two-process account of long-term serial position effects. *Journal of Experimental Psychology: Human Learning and Memory,* 1980, *6,* 355–369.

GOLDIN-MEADOW, S., and FELDMAN, H. The development of language-like communication without a language model. *Science,* 1977, *197,* 401–403.

GRAESSER, A. C., HOFFMAN, N. L., and CLARK, L. F. Structural components of reading time. *Journal of Verbal Learning and Verbal Behavior,* 1980, *19,* 135–151.

GREEN, D. W., and SHALLICE, T. Direct visual access in reading for meaning. *Memory & Cognition,* 1976, *4,* 753–758.

GREENO, J. G. Hobbits and orcs: Acquisition of a sequential concept. *Cognitive Psychology,* 1974, *6,* 270–292.

GREENO, J. G. Natures of problem-solving abilities. In W. K. Estes (Ed.), *Handbook of learning and cognitive processes* (Vol. 5). Hillsdale, N.J.: Erlbaum, 1978.

GRICE, H. P. *Logic and conversation.* The William James Lectures, Harvard University, 1967.

GROSJEAN, F. The perception of rate in spoken language and sign languages. *Journal of Psycholinguistic Research,* 1977, *22,* 408–413.

GUMMERMAN, K., and GRAY, C. R. Age, iconic storage, and visual information processing. *Journal of Experimental Child Psychology,* 1972, *13,* 165–170.

HABER, R. N. Information processing. In E. C. Carterette and M. P. Friedman (Eds.), *Handbook of perception* (Vol. 1). New York: Academic Press, 1974.

HABER, R. N., and STANDING, L. G. Direct measures of short-term visual storage. *Quarterly Journal of Experimental Psychology,* 1969, *21,* 43–54.

HABER, R. N., and STANDING, L. G. Direct estimates of apparent duration of a flash followed by visual noise. *Canadian Journal of Psychology,* 1970, *24,* 216–229.

HAGEN, J. W., and STANOVICH, K. G. Memory: Strategies of acquisition. In R. V. Kail, Jr. and J. W. Hagen (Eds.), *Perspectives on the development of memory and cognition.* Hillsdale, N.J.: Erlbaum, 1977.

HAKES, D. T. Effects of reducing complement constructions on sentence comprehension. *Journal of Verbal Learning and Verbal Behavior,* 1972, *11,* 278–286.

HALL, L. L., and BLUMSTEIN, S. E. The effect of vowel similarity and syllable length on acoustic memory. *Perception & Psychophysics*, 1977, *22*, 95–99.

HALLE, M., and STEVENS, K. N. Speech recognition: A model and a program for research. In J. A. Fodor and J. J. Katz (Eds.), *The structure of language: Readings in the philosophy of language*. Englewood Cliffs, N.J.: Prentice-Hall, 1964.

HANSON, V. L. Within category discriminations in speech perception. *Perception & Psychophysics*, 1977, *21*, 423–430.

HARDYCK, C. D., and PETRINOVITCH, L. R. Subvocal speech and comprehension level as a function of the difficulty level of reading material. *Journal of Verbal Learning and Verbal Behavior*, 1970, *9*, 647–652.

HARRIS, G. J., and FLEER, R. E. High speed memory scanning in mental retardates: Evidence for a central processing deficit. *Journal of Experimental Child Psychology*, 1974, *17*, 452–459.

HARRIS, R. J. Comprehension of pragmatic implications in advertising. *Journal of Applied Psychology*, 1977, *62*, 603–608.

HARRIS, R. J., and MONACO, G. E. Psychology of pragmatic implication: Information processing between the lines. *Journal of Experimental Psychology: General*, 1978, *107*, 1–22.

HART, J. T. Memory and the memory-monitoring process. *Journal of Verbal Learning and Verbal Behavior*, 1967, *6*, 685–691.

HASHER, L., and ZACKS, R. T. Automatic and effortful processes in memory. *Journal of Experimental Psychology: General*, 1979, *108*, 356–388.

HAVILAND, S. E., and CLARK, H. H. What's new? Acquiring new information as a process in comprehension. *Journal of Verbal Learning and Verbal Behavior*, 1974, *13*, 512–521.

HAYES, J. R., and SIMON, H. A. Understanding written problem instructions. In L. W. Gregg (Ed.), *Knowledge and cognition*. Potomac, Md.: Erlbaum, 1974.

HENLE, M. On the relation between logic and thinking. *Psychological Review*, 1962, *69*, 366–378.

HOLDING, D. H. Sensory storage reconsidered. *Memory & Cognition*, 1975, *3*, 31–41.

HOLLAN, J. D. Features and semantic memory: Set-theoretic or network model? *Psychological Review*, 1975, *82*, 154–155.

HORNBY, P. A. Surface structure and presupposition. *Journal of Verbal Learning and Verbal Behavior*, 1974, *13*, 530–538.

HUBEL, D. H., and WIESEL, T. N. Receptive fields, binocular interaction, and functional architecture in the cat's visual cortex. *Journal of Physiology*, 1962, *160*, 106–154.

HUEY, E. B. *The psychology and pedagogy of reading*. Cambridge, Mass.: MIT Press, 1968. (Original edition: Macmillan, 1908).

HULL, C. L. Quantitative aspects of the evolution of concepts: An experimental study. *Psychological Monographs*, 1920, *28*(1, Whole No. 123).

HULTSCH, D. F. Learning to learn in adulthood. *Journal of Gerontology*, 1974, *29*, 302–308.

HUNT, E. B. *Concept learning: An information processing problem*. New York: Wiley, 1962.

HUNT, E. B. What kind of computer is man? *Cognitive Psychology*, 1971, *2*, 57–98.

HUNT, E. B. Mechanics of verbal ability. *Psychological Review*, 1978, *85*, 109–130.

HUNT, E. B., and LANSMAN, M. Cognitive theory applied to individual differences. In W. K. Estes (Ed.), *Handbook of learning and cognitive processes* (Vol. 1). Hillsdale, N.J.: Erlbaum, 1975.

HUNT, E. B., and LOVE, T. How good can memory be? In A. W. Melton and E. Martin (Eds.), *Coding processes in human memory*. Washington, D.C.: V. H. Winston, 1972.

HUNT, E. B., LUNNEBORG, C., and LEWIS, J. What does it mean to be high verbal? *Cognitive Psychology*, 1975, *7*, 194–227.

HUNT, E. B., MARIN, J., and STONE, P. J. *Experiments in induction*. New York: Academic Press, 1966.

HUNT, E. B., and POLTROCK, S. E. The mechanics of thought. In B. H. Kantowitz (Ed.), *Human information processing: Tutorials in performance and cognition*. Hillsdale, N.J.: Erlbaum, 1974.

HUTTENLOCHER, J. Constructing spatial images: a strategy in reasoning. *Psychological Review*, 1968, *75*, 550–560.

HYDE, T. S., and JENKINS, J. J. Recall for words as a function of semantic, graphic, and syntactic orienting tasks. *Journal of Verbal Learning and Verbal Behavior*, 1973, *12*, 471–480.

JACKSON, M. D., and McCLELLAND, J. L. Processing determinants of reading speed. *Journal of Experimental Psychology: General*, 1979, *108*, 151–181.

JACOBS, J. Experiments on prehension. *Mind*, 1887, *12*, 75–79.

JAMES, W. *The principles of psychology*. New York: Henry Holt, 1890.

JENKINS, J. G., and DALLENBACH, K. M. Obliviscence during sleep and waking. *American Journal of Psychology*, 1924, *35*, 605–612.

JENKINS, J. J. Remember that old theory of memory? Well, forget it! *American Psychologist*, 1974, *29*, 785–795.

JOHNSON-LAIRD, P. N., LEGRENZI, P., and LEGRENZI, M. Reasoning and a sense of reality. *British Journal of Psychology*, 1972, *63*, 395–400.

JOHNSON-LAIRD, P. N., and STEEDMAN, M. The psychology of syllogisms. *Cognitive Psychology*, 1978, *10*, 64–99.

JOHNSON-LAIRD, P. N., and WASON, P. C. (Eds.). *Thinking: Readings in cognitive science*. Cambridge: Cambridge University Press, 1977.

JONES, G. V. Recognition failure and dual mechanisms in recall. *Psychological Review*, 1978, *85*, 464–469.

JONIDES, J., KAHN, R., and ROZIN, P. Imagery instruction improves memory in blind subjects. *Bulletin of the Psychonomic Society*, 1975, *5*, 424–426.

JORM, A. F. The cognitive and neurological basis of developmental dyslexia: A theoretical framework and review. *Cognition*, 1979, *7*, 19–33.

JUSCZYK, P. W. Infant speech perception: A critical appraisal. In P. D. Eimas and J. L. Miller (Eds.), *Perspectives on the study of speech*. Hillsdale, N.J.: Erlbaum, 1981.

JUST, M. A., and CARPENTER, P. A. (Eds.). *Cognitive processes in comprehension*. Hillsdale, N.J.: Erlbaum, 1977.

KAHNEMAN, D. *Attention and effort*. Englewood Cliffs, N.J.: Prentice-Hall, 1973.

KAIL, R. V., JR. *The development of memory in children.* San Francisco: W. H. Freeman, 1979.

KAIL, R. V., JR., and HAGEN, J. W. (Eds.), *Perspectives on the development of memory and cognition.* Hillsdale, N.J.: Erlbaum, 1977.

KAIL, R. V., JR., and SIEGEL, A. W. The development of mnemonic encoding in children: From perception to abstraction. In R. V. Kail, Jr. and J. W. Hagen (Eds.), *Perspectives on the development of memory and cognition.* Hillsdale, N.J.: Erlbaum, 1977.

KANT, I. [*Introduction to logic and essay on the mistaken subtilty of the four figures*] (T. K. Abbott, Trans.) New York: Longman's, 1885.

KAPLAN, R. M. Augmented transition networks as psychological models of sentence comprehension. *Artificial Intelligence,* 1972, *3,* 77–100.

KARMILOFF-SMITH, A., and INHELDER, B. If you want to get ahead, get a theory. In P. N. Johnson-Laird and P. C. Wason (Eds.), *Thinking: Readings in cognitive science.* Cambridge: Cambridge University Press, 1977.

KATZ, L., and WICKLUND, D. T. Letter scanning rate for good and poor readers in grades two and six. *Journal of Educational Psychology,* 1972, *63,* 363–367.

KAVANAGH, J. F., and CUTTING, J. E. (Eds.). *The role of speech in language.* Cambridge, Mass.: MIT Press, 1975.

KEARINS, J. M. Visual spatial memory in Australian Aboriginal children of desert regions. *Cognitive Psychology,* 1981, *13,* 434–460.

KEELE, S. W. *Attention and human performance.* Pacific Palisades, Cal.: Goodyear, 1973.

KEELE, S. W., and CHASE, W. G. Short-term visual storage. *Perception & Psychophysics,* 1967, *2,* 383–385.

KELLOGG, R. T. Is conscious attention necessary for long-term storage? *Journal of Experimental Psychology: Human Learning and Memory,* 1980, *6,* 379–390.

KEPPEL, G., and UNDERWOOD, B. J. Proactive inhibition in short-term retention of single items. *Journal of Verbal Learning and Verbal Behavior,* 1962, *1,* 153–161.

KERST, S. M., and HOWARD, J. H., JR. Mental comparisons for ordered information on abstract and concrete dimensions. *Memory & Cognition,* 1977, *5,* 227–234.

KIMURA, D. Cerebral dominance and the perception of verbal stimuli. *Canadian Journal of Psychology,* 1961, *15,* 166–171.

KIMURA, D. Functional asymmetry of the brain in dichotic listening. *Cortex,* 1967, *3,* 163–178.

KINGSLEY, P. R., and HAGEN, J. W. Induced versus spontaneous rehearsal in short-term memory in nursery school children. *Developmental Psychology,* 1969, *1,* 40–46.

KINTSCH, W. Notes on the structure of semantic memory. In E. Tulving and W. Donaldson (Eds.), *Organization of memory.* New York: Academic Press, 1972.

KINTSCH, W. *The representation of meaning in memory.* Hillsdale, N.J.: Erlbaum, 1974.

KINTSCH, W. More on recognition failure of recallable words: Implications for generation-recognition models. *Psychological Review,* 1978, *85,* 470–473.

KINTSCH, W., and GLASS, G. Effects of propositional structure upon sentence recall. In W. Kintsch (Ed.), *The representation of meaning in memory.* Hillsdale, N.J.: Erlbaum, 1974.

KINTSCH, W., and KENNAN, J. The psychological reality of text bases. In W. Kintsch (Ed.), *The representation of meaning in memory.* Hillsdale, N.J.: Erlbaum, 1974.

KINTSCH, W., and KOZMINSKY, E. Summarizing stories after reading and listening. *Journal of Educational Psychology,* 1977, *69,* 491–499.

KINTSCH, W., and VAN DIJK, T. A. Toward a model of text comprehension and production. *Psychological Review,* 1978, *85,* 363–394.

KLAHR, D., and ROBINSON, M. Formal assessment of problem-solving and planning processes in preschool children. *Cognitive Psychology,* 1981, *13,* 113–148.

KLAPP, S., ANDERSON, W. G., and BERRIAN, R. W. Implicit speech in reading reconsidered. *Journal of Experimental Psychology,* 1973, *100,* 368–374.

KLATZKY, R. L. *Human memory: Structures and processes* (2nd ed.). San Francisco: Freeman, 1980.

KLATZKY, R. L., and ATKINSON, R. C. Specialization of the cerebral hemispheres in scanning for information in short-term memory. *Perception & Psychophysics,* 1971, *10,* 335–338.

KLEIMAN, G. M. Speech recoding in reading. *Journal of Verbal Learning and Verbal Behavior,* 1975, *14,* 323–339.

KLIMA, E. S., and BELLUGI, U. *The signs of language.* Cambridge, Mass.: Harvard University Press, 1979.

KOBASIGAWA, A. Retrieval factors in the development of memory. In R. V. Kail, Jr., and J. W. Hagen (Eds.), *Perspectives on the development of memory and cognition.* Hillsdale, N.J.: Erlbaum, 1977.

KOESTLER, A. *The act of creation.* New York: Macmillan, 1964.

KOHLER, W. *The task of Gestalt psychology.* Princeton, N.J.: Princeton University Press, 1969.

KOLERS, P. A. Three stages of reading. In H. Levin and J. P. Williams (Eds.), *Basic studies on reading.* New York: Basic Books, 1970.

KORNBLUM, S. (Ed.). *Attention and performance IV.* New York: Academic Press, 1973.

KOSSLYN, S. M. Imagery and internal representation. In E. Rosch and B. B. Lloyd (Eds.), *Cognition and categorization.* Hillsdale, N.J.: Erlbaum, 1978.

KOSSLYN, S. M. *Image and mind.* Cambridge: Harvard University Press, 1980.

KOSSLYN, S. M. The medium and the message in mental imagery: A theory. *Psychological Review,* 1981, *88,* 46–66.

KOSSLYN, S. M., and POMERANTZ, J. R. Imagery, propositions, and the form of internal representations. *Cognitive Psychology,* 1977, *9,* 52–76.

KOSSLYN, S. M., and SCHWARTZ, S. P. A simulation of visual imagery. *Cognitive Science,* 1977, *1,* 265–295.

KRISTOFFERSON, M. W. Effects of practice on character-classification performance. *Canadian Journal of Psychology,* 1972, *26,* 540–560.

KUHL, P. K., and MILLER, J. D. Speech perception by chinchilla: Voiced-voiceless distinction in alveolar plosive consonants. *Science,* 1975, *190,* 69–72.

LABERGE, D., and SAMUELS, S. J. (Eds.), *Basic processes in reading: Perception and comprehension.* Hillsdale, N.J.: Erlbaum, 1977.

LACHMAN, R., LACHMAN, J. L., and BUTTERFIELD, E. C. *Cognitive psychology and information processing: An introduction.* Hillsdale, N.J.: Erlbaum, 1979.

LACKNER, J. R., and GARRETT, M. F. Resolving ambiguity: Effects of biasing context in the unattended ear. *Cognition,* 1973, *1,* 359–374.

LADEFOGED, P. *A course in phonetics.* New York: Harcourt Brace Jovanovich, 1975.

LADEFOGED, P., and BROADBENT, D. E. Information conveyed by vowels. *Journal of the Acoustical Society of Amerca,* 1957, *29,* 98–104.

LANDAUER, T. K. Rate of implicit speech. *Perceptual and Motor Skills,* 1962, *15,* 646.

LANDAUER, T. K., and FREEDMAN, J. L. Information retrieval from long-term memory: category size and recognition time. *Journal of Verbal Learning and Verbal Behavior,* 1968, *7,* 291–295.

LANDAUER, T. K., and MEYER, D. E. Category size and semantic memory retrieval. *Journal of Verbal Learning and Verbal Behavior,* 1972, *11,* 539–549.

LANE, H. *The wild boy of Aveyron.* Cambridge, Mass.: Harvard University Press, 1976.

LANSMAN, M., and HUNT, E. Individual differences in secondary task performance. *Memory & Cognition,* 1982, *10,* 10–24.

LASHLEY, K. S. The problem of serial order in behavior. In L. A. Jeffress (Ed.), *Cerebral mechanisms in behavior.* New York: Wiley, 1951.

LASKY, R. E., SYRDAL-LASKY, A., and KLEIN, R. E. VOT discrimination by four to six and a half month old infants from Spanish environments. *Journal of Experimental Child Psychology,* 1975, *20,* 215–225.

LEFFORD, A. The influence of emotional subject matter on logical reasoning. *Journal of General Psychology,* 1946, *30,* 127–151.

LETTVIN, J. Y., MATURANA, H. R., McCULLOCH, W. S., and PITTS, W. H. What the frog's eye tells the frog's brain. *Proceedings of the Institute of Radio Engineers,* 1959, *47,* 1940–1951.

LEVINE, M. Hypothesis behavior by humans during discrimination learning. *Journal of Experimental Psychology,* 1966, *71,* 331–338.

LEVINE, M. Hypothesis theory and nonlearning despite ideal S-R reinforcement contingencies. *Psychological Review,* 1971, *78,* 130–140.

LEVINE, M. *Hypothesis testing: A cognitive theory of learning.* Hillsdale, N.J.: Erlbaum, 1975.

LEVY, B. A. Reading: Speech and meaning processes. *Journal of Verbal Learning and Verbal Behavior,* 1977, *16,* 623–638.

LEWIS, J. Semantic processing of unattended messages using dichotic listening. *Journal of Experimental Psychology,* 1970, *85,* 225–228.

LIBEN, L. S. (Ed.). *Deaf children: Developmental perspectives.* New York: Academic Press, 1978.

LIBEN, L. S., NOWELL, R. C., and POSNANSKY, C. J. Semantic and formational clustering in deaf and hearing subjects' free recall of signs. *Memory & Cognition,* 1978, *6,* 599–606.

LIBERMAN, A. M. Some results of research on speech perception. *Journal of the Acoustical Society of America,* 1957, *29,* 117–123.

LIBERMAN, A. M., INGEMANN, F., LISKER, L., DELATTRE, P. C., AND COOPER, F. S. Minimal rules for synthesizing speech. *Journal of the Acoustical Society of America,* 1959, *31,* 1490–1499.

LIBERMAN, A. M., MATTINGLY, I. G., and TURVEY, M. T. Language codes and memory codes. In A. W. Melton and E. Martin (Eds.), *Coding processes in human memory.* New York: Wiley, 1972.

LIBERMAN, I. Y., SHANKWEILER, D., LIBERMAN, A. M., FOWLER, C., and FISCHER, F. W. Phonetic segmentation and recoding in the beginning reader. In A. S. Reber and D. Scarborough (Eds.), *Toward a psychology of reading: The proceedings of the CUNY Conference.* Hillsdale, N.J.: Erlbaum, 1977.

LIEBERMAN, P. On the evolution of language: A unified view. *Cognition,* 1973, *2,* 59–94.

LINDSAY, P. H., and NORMAN, D. A. *Human information processing* (2nd ed.). New York: Academic Press, 1977.

LISKER, L., and ABRAMSON, A. S. The voicing dimension: Some experiments in comparative phonetics. In *Proceedings of the Sixth International Congress of Phonetic Sciences,* Prague, 1967. Prague: Academia, 1970.

LOCKE, J. L. Phonemic effects in the silent reading of hearing and deaf children. *Cognition,* 1978, *6,* 175–187.

LOCKE, J. L., and LOCKE, V. Deaf children's phonetic, visual and dactylic coding in a grapheme recall task. *Journal of Experimental Psychology,* 1971, *89,* 142–146.

LOCKHART, R. S., and CRAIK, F. I. M. Levels of processing: A reply to Eysenck. *British Journal of Psychology,* 1978, *69,* 171–175.

LOFTUS, E. F. The malleability of human memory. *American Scientist,* 1979, *67,* 312–320.

LOFTUS, E. F., and MONAHAN, J. Trial by data: Psychological research as legal evidence. *American Psychologist,* 1980, *35,* 270–283.

LOFTUS, E. F., and PALMER, J. C. Reconstruction of automobile destruction: An example of the interaction between language and memory. *Journal of Verbal Learning and Verbal Behavior,* 1974, *13,* 585–589.

LOFTUS, E. F., and ZANNI, G. Eyewitness testimony: The influence of the wording of a question. *Bulletin of the Psychonomic Society,* 1975, *5,* 86–88.

LOFTUS, G. R., and LOFTUS, E. F. *Human memory: The processing of information.* Hillsdale, N.J.: Erlbaum, 1976.

LORAYNE, H., and LUCAS, J. *The memory book.* New York: Ballantine Books, 1974.

LOVELACE, E. A., POWELL, M., and BROOKS, R. J. Alphabetic position effects in covert and overt alphabetic recitation times. *Journal of Experimental Psychology,* 1973, *99,* 405–408.

LUCHINS, A. S. Mechanization in problem solving. *Psychological Monographs,* 1942, *54*(Whole No. 248).

LURIA, A. R. *The mind of a mnemonist.* New York: Basic Books, 1968.

McGEOCH, J. A. The influence of associative value upon the difficulty of nonsense-syllable lists. *Journal of Genetic Psychology,* 1930, *37,* 421–426.

McGEOCH, J. A. Forgetting and the law of disuse. *Psychological Review,* 1932, *39,* 352–370.

McGEOCH, J. A. *The psychology of human learning.* New York: Longman's, 1942.

McGHIE, A. *Pathology of attention.* Baltimore: Penguin Books, 1969.

McGUIGAN, F. J. Covert oral behavior during the silent performance of language tasks. *Psychological Bulletin,* 1970, *74,* 309–326.

McGuire, W. A syllogistic analysis of cognitive relationships. In M. Rosenberg and C. Hovland (Eds.), *Attitude organization and change*. New Haven: Yale University Press, 1960.

Mackay, D. G. Aspects of the theory of comprehension, memory and attention. *Quarterly Journal of Experimental Psychology*, 1973, *25*, 22–40.

McKeithen, K. B., Reitman, J. S., Rueter, H. H., and Hirtle, S. C. Knowledge organization and skill differences in computer programmers. *Cognitive Psychology*, 1981, *13*, 307–325.

MacLeod, C. M., Hunt, E. B., and Mathews, N. N. Individual differences in the verification of sentence-picture relationships. *Journal of Verbal Learning and Verbal Behavior*, 1978, *17*, 493–507.

McMahon, L. Grammatical analysis as part of understanding a sentence. Unpublished doctoral dissertation, Harvard University, 1963.

MacNeilage, P., and Ladefoged, P. The production of speech and language. In E. C. Carterette and M. P. Friedman (Eds.), *Handbook of perception* (Vol 7). New York: Academic Press, 1976.

McNeill, D. Developmental psycholinguistics. In F. Smith and G. A. Miller (Eds.), *The genesis of language*. Cambridge, Mass.: MIT Press, 1966.

Mahoney, M. J. *Scientist as subject: The psychological imperative*. Cambridge, Mass.: Ballinger, 1976.

Maier, N. R. F. Reasoning in humans: I. On direction. *Journal of Comparative Psychology*, 1930, *10*, 115–143.

Maier, N. R. F. Reasoning in humans: II. The solution of a problem and its appearance in consciousness. *Journal of Comparative and Physiological Psychology*, 1931, *12*, 181–194.

Makita, K. The rarity of reading disability in Japanese children. *American Journal of Orthopsychiatry*, 1968, *38*, 599–614.

Mandler, G. Organization and memory. In K. W. Spence and J. T. Spence (Eds.), *The psychology of learning and motivation: Advances in research and theory* (Vol. 1). New York: Academic Press, 1967.

Mann, V. A., Liberman, I. Y., and Shankweiler, D. Children's memory for sentences and word strings in relation to reading ability. *Memory & Cognition*, 1980, *8*, 329–335.

Marcel, A. J., and Patterson, K. E. Word recognition and production: Reciprocity in clinical and normal studies. In J. Requin (Ed.), *Attention and performance VII*. Hillsdale, N.J.: Erlbaum, 1978.

Mark, L. S., Shankweiler, D., Liberman, I. Y., and Fowler, C. A. Phonetic recoding and reading difficulty in beginning readers. *Memory & Cognition*, 1977, *5*, 623–629.

Marmor, G. S., and Zaback, L. A. Mental rotation by the blind: Does mental rotation depend on visual imagery? *Journal of Experimental Psychology: Human Perception and Performance*, 1976, *2*, 515–521.

Marslen-Wilson, W. D. Linguistic structure and speech shadowing at very short latencies. *Nature*, 1973, *244*, 522–523.

Marslen-Wilson, W. D., and Tyler, L. K. The temporal structure of spoken language understanding. *Cognition*, 1980, *8*, 1–71.

Marslen-Wilson, W. D., and Welsh, A. Processing interactions and lexical access during word recognition in continuous speech. *Cognitive Psychology*, 1978, *10*, 29–63.

Martin, R. C., and Caramazza, A. Classification in well-defined and ill-defined categories: Evidence for common processing strategies. *Journal of Experimental Psychology: General,* 1980, *109,* 320–353.

MASSARO, D. W. Preperceptual images, processing time, and perceptual units in auditory perception. *Psychological Review,* 1972, *79,* 124–145.

MASSARO, D. W. *Experimental psychology and information processing.* Chicago: Rand McNally, 1975.

MATHEWS, N. N., Hunt, E. B., and MACLEOD, C. M. Strategy choice and strategy training in sentence-picture verification. *Journal of Verbal Learning and Verbal Behavior,* 1980, *19,* 531–548.

MEDIN, D., and COLE, M. Comparative psychology and human cognition. In W. K. Estes (Ed.), *Handbook of learning and cognitive processes* (Vol. 1). Hillsdale, N.J.: Erlbaum, 1975.

MEHLER, J., SEGUI, J., and CAREY, P. Tails of words: monitoring ambiguity. *Journal of Verbal Learning and Verbal Behavior,* 1978, *17,* 29–37.

MELTON, A. W., and IRWIN, J. M. The influence of degree of interpolated learning on retroactive inhibition and the overt transfer of specific responses. *American Journal of Psychology,* 1940, *53,* 173–203.

METZLER, J., and SHEPARD, R. N. Transformational studies of the internal representation of three-dimensional objects. In R. L. Solso (Ed.), *Theories in cognitive psychology: The Loyola Symposium.* Potomac, Md.: Erlbaum, 1974.

MEYER, D. E. On the representation and retrieval of stored semantic information. *Cognitive Psychology,* 1970, *1,* 242–300.

MEYER, D. E., and ELLIS, G. B. Parallel processes in word-recognition. Paper presented at the meeting of the Psychonomic Society, San Antonio, Texas, November 5–7, 1970.

MEYER, D. E., and SCHVANEVELDT, R. W. Facilitation in recognizing pairs of words: evidence of a dependence between retrieval operations. *Journal of Experimental Psychology,* 1971, *90,* 227–234.

MEYER, D. E., SCHVANEVELDT, R. W., and RUDDY, M. G. Functions of graphemic and phonemic codes in visual word-recognition. *Memory & Cognition,* 1974, *2,* 309–321.

MILL, J. S. *A system of logic* (8th ed.). New York: Harper, 1874.

MILLER, G. A. The magical number seven, plus or minus two: Some limits on our capacity for processing information. *Psychological Review,* 1956, *63,* 81–97.

MILLER, G. A., GALANTER, E., and PRIBRAM, K. H. *Plans and the structure of behavior.* New York: Holt, 1960.

MILLER, G. A., and SELFRIDGE, J. A. Verbal context and the recall of meaningful material. *American Journal of Psychology,* 1950, *63,* 176–185.

MILLER, L. Has artificial intelligence contributed to an understanding of the human mind? A critique of arguments for and against. *Cognitive Science,* 1978, *2,* 111–128.

MILLWARD, R. B., and SPOEHR, K. T. The direct measurement of hypothesis sampling strategies. *Cognitive Psychology,* 1973, *4,* 1–38.

MILNER, B. Amnesia following operation on the temporal lobes. In C. W. M. Whitty and O. L. Zangwill (Eds.), *Amnesia.* London: Butterworths, 1966.

MILNER, B. Interhemispheric differences in the localization of psychological processes in man. *British Medical Bulletin,* 1971, *27,* 272–277.

MINSKY, M. A framework for representing knowledge. In P. H. Winston (Ed.), *The psychology of computer vision.* New York: McGraw-Hill, 1975.

MITROFF, I. I. *The subjective side of science.* Amsterdam: Elsevier, 1974.

MOELY, B. E. Organizational factors in the development of memory. In R. V. Kail and J. W. Hagen (Eds.), *Perspectives on the development of memory and cognition.* Hillsdale, N.J.: Erlbaum, 1977.

MORAY, N. Attention in dichotic listening: Affective cues and the influence of instructions. *Quarterly Journal of Experimental Psychology,* 1959, *11,* 56–60.

MORAY, N. *Attention: Selective processes in vision and hearing.* New York: Academic Press, 1970.

MORAY, N., BATES, A., and BARNETT, T. Experiments on the four-eared man. *Journal of the Acoustical Society of America,* 1965, *38,* 196–201.

MORGAN, C. S. A study in the psychology of testimony. *Journal of the American Institute of Criminal Law,* 1917, *8,* 222.

MORGAN, J. J., and MORTON, J. T. The distortion of syllogistic reasoning produced by personal convictions. *Journal of Social Psychology,* 1944, *20,* 39–59.

MORRISON, F. J., GIORDANI, B., and NAGY, I. Reading disability: An information-processing analysis. *Science,* 1977, *196,* 77–79.

MORRISON, F. J., HOLMES, D. L., and HAITH, M. M. A developmental study of the effect of familiarity on short-term memory. *Journal of Experimental Child Psychology,* 1974, *18,* 412–425.

MORSE, P. A. Infant speech perception: A preliminary model and review of the literature. In R. L. Schiefelbusch and L. Lloyd (Eds.), *Language perspectives—acquisition, retardation, and intervention.* Baltimore: University Park Press, 1974.

MORSE, P. A. Speech perception in the human infant and Rhesus monkey. In S. Harnad, H. D. Steklis, and J. Lancaster (Eds.), *Origins and evolution of language and speech.* New York: New York Academy of Sciences, 1977.

MORSE, P. A., and SNOWDEN, C. T. An investigation of categorical speech discrimination by rhesus monkeys. *Perception & Psychophysics,* 1975, *17,* 9–16.

MORTON, J. Categories of interference: Verbal mediation and conflict in card sorting. *British Journal of Psychology,* 1969, *60,* 329–346.

MORTON, J., and CHAMBERS, S. M. Some evidence for 'speech' as an acoustic feature. *British Journal of Psychology,* 1976, *67,* 31–45.

MORTON, J., MARCUS, S. M., and OTTLEY, P. The acoustic correlates of "speechlike": A use of the suffix effect. *Journal of Experimental Psychology: General,* 1981, *110,* 568–593.

MOYER, R. S., and BAYER, R. H. Mental comparison and the symbolic distance effect. *Cognitive Psychology,* 1976, *8,* 228–246.

MUENSTERBURG, H. *On the witness stand.* New York: McClure, 1908.

MURDOCK, B. B., JR. The serial position effect of free recall. *Journal of Experimental Psychology,* 1962, *64,* 482–488.

MURRAY, H. G., and DENNY, J. P. Interaction of ability level and interpolated activity (opportunity for incubation) in human problem solving. *Psychological Reports,* 1969, *24,* 271–276.

MUTER, P. Very rapid forgetting. *Memory & Cognition,* 1980, *8,* 174–179.

MYNATT, C. R., DOHERTY, M. E., and TWENEY, R. D. Confirmation bias in a simulated research environment: an experimental study of scientific inference. In P. N. Johnson-Laird and P. C. Wason (Eds.), *Thinking: Readings in cognitive science.* Cambridge: Cambridge University Press, 1977.

NAGEL, E. *Logic without metaphysics.* Free Press, 1956.

NEIMARK, E. D., and CHAPMAN, R. H. Development of the comprehension of logical quantifiers. In R. J. Falmagne (Ed.), *Reasoning: Representation and process.* Hillsdale, N.J.: Erlbaum, 1975.

NEISSER, U. *Cognitive psychology.* New York: Appleton-Century-Crofts, 1967.

NEISSER, U. Changing conceptions of imagery. In P. W. Sheehan (Ed.), *The function and nature of imagery.* New York: Academic Press, 1972.

NEISSER, U. *Cognition and reality.* San Francisco: Freeman, 1976.

NEISSER, U., and BECKLEN, R. Selective looking: attending to visually specified events. *Cognitive Psychology,* 1975, *7,* 480–494.

NELSON, T. O. Savings and forgetting from long-term memory. *Journal of Verbal Learning and Verbal Behavior,* 1971, *10,* 568–576.

NEWELL, A., SHAW, J. C., and SIMON, H. A. Elements of a theory of human problem solving. *Psychological Review,* 1958, *65,* 151–166.

NEWELL, A., and SIMON, H. A. *Human problem solving.* Englewood Cliffs, N.J.: Prentice-Hall, 1972.

NEWMAN, J., and DELL, G. The phonological nature of phoneme monitoring: a critique of some ambiguity studies. *Journal of Verbal Learning and Verbal Behavior,* 1978, *17,* 359–374.

NEWPORT, E. L., and BELLUGI, U. Linguistic expression of category levels in a visual-gestural language: A flower is a flower is a flower. In E. Rosch and B. B. Lloyd (Eds.), *Cognition and categorization.* Hillsdale, N.J.: Erlbaum, 1978.

NICKERSON, R. S. Binary classification reaction time: A review of some studies of human information-processing capabilities. *Psychonomics Monograph Supplement,* 1972, *4* (Whole No. 65), 275–318.

NICKERSON, R. S. (Ed.). *Attention and performance VIII.* Hillsdale, N.J.: Erlbaum, 1980.

NOBLE, C. E. Measurements of association value (a), rated associations (a'), and scaled meaningfulness (m') for the 2100 CVC combinations of the English alphabet. *Psychological Reports,* 1961, *8,* 487–521.

NORMAN, D. A. Toward a theory of memory and attention. *Psychological Review,* 1968, *75,* 522–536.

NORMAN, D. A. Memory while shadowing. *Quarterly Journal of Experimental Psychology,* 1969, *21,* 85–93.

NORMAN, D. A. *Memory and attention* (2nd ed.). New York: Wiley, 1976.

NORMAN, D. A., and BOBROW, D. G. On data-limited and resource-limited processes. *Cognitive Psychology,* 1975, *7,* 44–64.

NORMAN, D. A., and RUMELHART, D. E. A system for perception and memory. In D. A. Norman (Ed.), *Models of human memory.* New York: Academic Press, 1970.

NORMAN, D. A., RUMELHART, D. E., and the LNR Research Group. *Explorations in cognition.* San Francisco: Freeman, 1975.

O'BRIEN, E. J., and WOLFORD, C. R. Effect of delay in testing on retention of plausible versus bizarre mental images. *Journal of Experimental Psychology: Learning, Memory, and Cognition,* 1982, *8,* 148–152.

OFFENBACH, S. I. A developmental study of hypothesis testing and cue selection strategies. *Developmental Psychology,* 1974, *10,* 484–490.

OLSON, G. M., and CLARK, H. H. Research methods in psycholinguistics. In E. C. Carterette and M. P. Friedman (Eds.), *Handbook of perception* (Vol. 7). New York: Academic Press, 1976.

PAIVIO, A. Mental imagery in associative learning and memory. *Psychological Review*, 1969, *76*, 241–263.

PAIVIO, A. *Imagery and verbal processes*. New York: Holt, 1971.

PAIVIO, A. Language and knowledge of the world. *Educational Researcher*, 1974, *3*, 5–12.

PAIVIO, A., YUILLE, J. C., and MADIGAN, S. Concreteness, imagery, and meaningfulness values for 925 nouns. *Journal of Experimental Psychology Monograph Supplement*, 1968, *76* (1, Pt. 2).

PALMERO, D. S. Research on language acquisition: Do we know where we are going? In L. R. Goulet and P. B. Baltes (Eds.), *Theory and research in lifespan developmental psychology*. New York: Academic Press, 1970.

PALERMO, D. S. *Psychology of language*. Glenview, Illinois: Scott, Foresman, 1978.

PALMER, S. E. Fundamental aspects of cognitive representation. In E. Rosch and B. B. Lloyd (Eds.), *Cognition and categorization*. Hillsdale, N.J.: Erlbaum, 1978.

PARIS, S. G., and LINDAUER, B. K. Constructive aspects of children's comprehension and memory. In R. V. Kail and J. W. Hagen (Eds.), *Perspectives on the development of memory and cognition*. Hillsdale, N.J.: Erlbaum, 1977.

PENFIELD, W. The interpretive cortex. *Science*, 1959, *129*, 1719–1725.

PENG, F. C. C. *Sign language and language acquisition in man and ape*. Boulder, Colorado: Westview Press, 1978.

PERFETTI, C. A., and LESGOLD, A. M. Discourse comprehension and sources of individual differences. In M. A. Just and P. A. Carpenter (Eds.), *Cognitive processes in comprehension*. Hillsdale, N.J.: Erlbaum, 1977.

PETERSON, L. R., and PETERSON, M. J. Short-term retention of individual verbal items. *Journal of Experimental Psychology*, 1959, *58*, 193–198.

PETERSON, L. R., RAWLINGS, L., and COHEN, C. The internal construction of spatial patterns. In G. H. Bower (Ed.), *The psychology of learning and motivation* (Vol. 11). New York: Academic Press, 1977.

PETERSON, M. J. The retention of imagined and seen spatial matrices. *Cognitive Psychology*, 1975, *7*, 181–193.

PETITTO, L. A., and SEIDENBERG, M. S. On the evidence for linguistic abilities in signing apes. *Brain and Language*, 1979, *8*, 162–183.

PIAGET, J. *Judgment and reasoning in the child*. London: Routledge, 1928.

PIAGET, J. Intellectual evolution from adolescence to adulthood. *Human Development*, 1972, *15*, 1–12.

PIAGET, J., INHELDER, B., and SZEMINSKA, A. *The child's conception of geometry*. New York: Basic Books, 1960.

PISONI, D. B. Speech perception. In W. K. Estes (Ed.), *Handbook of learning and cognitive processes* (Vol. 6). Hillsdale, N.J.: Erlbaum, 1978.

PLATO. *The collected dialogues of Plato*. E. Hamilton and H. Cairns (Eds.). New York: Pantheon Books, Inc., 1963.

POINCAIRE, H. *The foundations of science*. New York: Science House, 1929.

POLLACK, R. H., PTASHNE, R. I., and CARTER, D. J. The effects of age and intelligence on the dark-interval threshold. *Perception & Psychophysics*, 1969, *6*, 50–52.

POLYA, G. *How to solve it*. Garden City, New York: Doubleday Anchor, 1957.

POON, L W., FOZARD, J. L., CERMAK, L. S., ARENBERG, D. and THOMPSON, L. W. *New directions in memory and aging*. Hillsdale, N.J.: Erlbaum, 1980.

540

References

POSNER, M. I. Abstraction and the process of recognition. In G. H. Bower and J. T. Spence (Eds.), *The psychology of learning and motivation* (Vol. 3). New York: Academic Press, 1969.

POSNER, M. I. *Cognition: An introduction.* Glenview, Illinois: Scott, Foresman and Company, 1973.

POSNER, M. I. Cumulative development of attentional theory. *American Psychologist,* 1982, *37,* 168–179.

POSNER, M. I., and BOIES, S. J. Components of attention *Psychological Review,* 1971, *78,* 391–408.

POSNER, M. I., BOIES, S. J., EICHELMAN, W. H., and TAYLOR, R. L. Retention of name and visual codes of single letters. *Journal of Experimental Psychology,* 1969, *79,* 1–16.

POSNER, M. I., GOLDSMITH, R., and WELTON, K. E. Perceived distance and the classification of distorted patterns. *Journal of Experimental Psychology,* 1967, *73,* 28–38.

POSNER, M. I., and KEELE, S. W. Decay of visual information from a single letter. *Science,* 1967, *158,* 137–139.

POSNER, M. I., and KEELE, S. W. On the genesis of abstract ideas. *Journal of Experimental Psychology,* 1968, *77,* 353–363.

POSNER, M. I., and KEELE, S. W. Retention of abstract ideas. *Journal of Experimental Psychology,* 1970, *83,* 304–308.

POSNER, M. I., and SNYDER, C. R. R. Attention and cognitive control. In R. Solso (Ed.), *Information processing and cognition: The Loyola Symposium.* Potomac, Md.: Erlbaum, 1975.

POSTMAN, L., and PHILLIPS, L. Short-term temporal changes in free recall. *Quarterly Journal of Experimental Psychology,* 1965, *17,* 132–138.

POSTMAN, L., and STARK, K. Role of response availability in transfer and interference. *Journal of Experimental Psychology,* 1969, *79,* 168–177.

POSTMAN, L., STARK, K., and FRASER, J. Temporal changes in interference. *Journal of Verbal Learning and Verbal Behavior,* 1968, *7,* 672–694.

POTTER, M. C., and FAULCONER, B. A. Time to understand pictures and words. *Nature,* 1975, *253,* 437–438.

POTTER, R. K., KOPP, G. A., and KOPP, H. G. *Visual speech.* New York: Dover, 1966.

PRESSLEY, M. Children's use of the keyword method to learn simple Spanish vocabulary words. *Journal of Educational Psychology,* 1977, *69,* 465–472.

PROUST, M. *Remembrance of things past.* New York: Random House, 1934.

PYLYSHYN, Z. W. What the mind's eye tells the mind's brain: A critique of mental imagery. *Psychological Bulletin,* 1973, *80,* 1–24.

QUILLIAN, M. R. Semantic memory. In M. Minsky (Ed.), *Semantic information processing.* Cambridge, Mass.: MIT Press, 1968.

RABBITT, P. M. A. Changes in problem solving ability in old age. In J. E. Birren and K. W. Schaie (Eds.), *Handbook of the psychology of aging.* New York: Van Nostrand Reinhold, 1977.

RABBITT, P. M. A., and DORNIC, S. (Eds.) *Attention and performance V.* London: Academic Press, 1975.

RAPHAEL, B. *The thinking computer: Mind inside matter.* San Francisco: Freeman, 1976.

RATCLIFF, R., and McKOON, G. Priming in item recognition: Evidence for the propositional structure of sentences. *Journal of Verbal Learning and Verbal Behavior,* 1978, *17,* 403–417.

RAUGH, M. R., and ATKINSON, R. C. A mnemonic method for learning of a second language vocabulary. *Journal of Educational Psychology,* 1975, *67,* 1–16.

REBER, A. S. Implicit learning of artificial grammars. *Journal of Verbal Learning and Verbal Behavior,* 1967, *6,* 855–863.

REBER, A. S. Implicit learning of synthetic languages: The role of instructional set. *Journal of Experimental Psychology: Human Learning and Memory,* 1976, *2,* 88–94.

REBER, A. S., and LEWIS, S. Implicit learning: An analysis of the form and structure of a body of tacit knowledge. *Cognition,* 1977, *5,* 333–361.

REBER, A. S., and SCARBOROUGH, D. (Eds.). *Toward a psychology of reading: The proceedings of the CUNY Conference.* Hillsdale, N.J.: Erlbaum, 1977.

REDDY, D. R. Speech recognition by machine: A review. *Proceedings of the IEEE,* 1976, *64,* 501–531.

REDDY, D. R. Machine models of speech perception. In R. A. Cole (Ed.), *Perception and production of fluent speech.* Hillsdale, N.J.: Erlbaum, 1980.

REED, G. *The psychology of anomalous experience: A cognitive approach.* London: Hutchinson University Library, 1972.

REITMAN, J. S. Mechanisms of forgetting in short-term memory. *Cognitive Psychology,* 1971, *2,* 185–195.

REITMAN, J. S. Without surreptitious rehearsal, information in short-term memory decays. *Journal of Verbal Learning and Verbal Behavior,* 1974, *13,* 365–377.

REITMAN, W. R. *Cognition and thought: An information processing approach.* New York: Wiley, 1965.

REMEZ, R. E. Adaptation of the category boundary between speech and nonspeech: A case against feature detectors. *Cognitive Psychology,* 1979, *11,* 38–57.

REMEZ, R. E. Susceptibility of a stop consonant to adaptation on a speech-nonspeech continuum: Further evidence against feature detectors in speech perception. *Perception & Psychophysics,* 1980, *27,* 17–23.

REQUIN, J. (Ed.). *Attention and performance VII.* Hillsdale, N.J.: Erlbaum, 1978.

RESTLE, F. The selection of strategies in cue learning. *Psychological Review,* 1962, *69,* 329–343.

REVLIN, R., and LEIRER, V. O. Understanding quantified categorical expressions. *Memory & Cognition,* 1980, *8,* 447–458.

REVLIN, R., LEIRER, V. O., YOPP, H., and YOPP, R. The belief-bias effect in formal reasoning: The influence of knowledge on logic. *Memory & Cognition,* 1980, *8,* 584–592.

REVLIN, R., and MAYER, R. E. (Eds.). *Human reasoning.* Washington, D.C.: V. H. Winston, 1978.

REVLIS, R. Syllogistic reasoning: Logical decisions from a complex data base. In R. Falmagne (Ed.), *Reasoning: Representation and process.* Hillsdale, N.J.: Erlbaum, 1975.(a)

REVLIS, R. Two models of syllogistic reasoning: Feature selection and conversion. *Journal of Verbal Learning and Verbal Behavior,* 1975, *14,* 180–195.(b)

542
References

REYNOLDS, A. G., and FLAGG, P. W. *Cognitive psychology.* Cambridge, Mass.: Winthrop, 1977.

RIPS, L. J., SHOBEN, E. J., and SMITH, E. E. Semantic distance and the verification of semantic relations. *Journal of Verbal Learning and Verbal Behavior,* 1973, *12,* 1–20.

RIPS, L. J., SMITH, E. E., and SHOBEN, E. J. Set-theoretic and network models reconsidered: A comment on Hollan's "Features and semantic memory." *Psychological Review,* 1975, *82,* 156–157.

ROBINSON, D. N. *The enlightened machine: An analytical introduction to neuropsychology.* Encino, Cal.: Dickenson, 1973.

ROSCH, E. H. On the internal structure of perceptual and semantic categories. In T. E. Moore (Ed.), *Cognitive development and the acquisition of language.* New York: Academic Press, 1973.

ROSCH, E. H. Cognitive reference points. *Cognitive Psychology,* 1975, *7,* 532–547.(a)

ROSCH, E. H. Cognitive representations of semantic categories. *Journal of Experimental Psychology: General,* 1975, *104,* 192–233.(b)

ROSCH, E. H. Classification of real-world objects: Origins and representations in cognition. In P. N. Johnson-Laird and P. C. Wason (Eds.), *Thinking: Readings in cognitive science.* Cambridge: Cambridge University Press, 1977.

ROSCH, E. H. Principles of categorization. In E. Rosch and B. B. Lloyd (Eds.), *Cognition and categorization.* Hillsdale, N.J.: Erlbaum, 1978.

ROSCH, E. H., and LLOYD, B. B. (Eds.). *Cognition and categorization.* Hillsdale, N.J.: Erlbaum, 1978.

ROSCH, E. H., and MERVIS, C. B. Family resemblances: Studies in the internal structure of categories. *Cognitive Psychology,* 1975, *7,* 573–605.

ROSCH, E. H., MERVIS, C. B., GRAY, W. D., JOHNSON, D. M., and BOYES-BRAEM, P. Basic objects in natural categories. *Cognitive Psychology,* 1976, *8,* 382–439.

ROWE, E. J., and ROWE, W. G. Stimulus suffix effects with speech and non-speech sounds. *Memory & Cognition,* 1976, *4,* 128–131.

ROZIN, P., PORITSKY, S., and SOTSKY, R. American children with reading problems can easily learn to read English represented by Chinese characters. *Science,* 1971, *171,* 1264–1267.

RUBENSTEIN, H., LEWIS, S. S., and RUBENSTEIN, M. A. Evidence for phonemic recoding in visual word recognition. *Journal of Verbal Learning and Verbal Behavior,* 1971, *10,* 645–657.

RUMELHART D. E. *Introduction to human information processing.* New York: Wiley, 1977.

RUMELHART, D. E., LINDSAY, P. H., and NORMAN, D. A. A process model for long-term memory. In E. Tulving and W. Donaldson (Eds.), *Organization of memory.* New York: Academic Press, 1972.

RUMELHART, D. E., and ORTONY, A. The representation of knowledge in memory. In R. C. Anderson, R. J. Spiro, and W. E. Montague (Eds.), *Schooling and the acquisition of knowledge.* Hillsdale, N.J.: Erlbaum, 1977.

RUNDUS, D. An analysis of rehearsal processes in free recall. *Journal of Experimental Psychology,* 1971, *89,* 63–77.

SABOL M. A., and DeROSA, D. V. Semantic encoding of isolated words. *Journal of Experimental Psychology: Human Learning and Memory,* 1976, *2,* 58–68.

SACHS, J. S. Recognition memory for syntactic and semantic aspects of connected discourse. *Perception & Psychophysics,* 1967, *2,* 437–442.

SAFFRAN, E. M., and MARIN, O. S. M. Immediate memory for word lists and sentences in a patient with deficient auditory short-term memory. *Brain and Language*, 1975, *2*, 420–433.

SAKITT, B. Locus of short-term visual storage. *Science*, 1975, *190*, 1318–1319.

SAKITT, B. Iconic memory. *Psychological Review*, 1976, *83*, 257–276.

SAKITT, B., and LONG, G. M. Spare the rod and spoil the icon. *Journal of Experimental Psychology: Human Perception and Performance*, 1979, *5*, 19–30.

SALAME, P., and BADDELEY, A. Disruption of short-term memory by unattended speech: Implications for the structure of working memory. *Journal of Verbal Learning and Verbal Behavior*, 1982, *21*, 150–164.

SALTHOUSE, T. A., and SOMBERG, B. L. Isolating the age deficit in speeded performance. *Journal of Gerontology*, 1982, *37*, 59–63.

SANDERS, A. F. (Ed.). *Attention and performance.* Amsterdam: North-Holland, 1967.

SANDERS, A. F. (Ed.). *Attention and performance III.* Amsterdam: North-Holland, 1970.

SAWUSCH, J. R. Peripheral and central processes in selective adaptation of place of articulation in stop consonants. *Journal of the Acoustical Society of America*, 1977, *62*, 738–750.

SCHANK, R., and the Yale AI Project. *SAM—A story understander.* Research Report No. 43. Yale University, Committee on Computer Science, 1975.

SCHANK, R., and ABELSON, R. *Scripts plans goals and understanding.* Hillsdale, N.J.: Erlbaum, 1977.

SCHANK, R., and WILENSKY, R. Response to Dresher and Hornstein. *Cognition*, 1977, *5*, 133–145.

SCHIANO, D. J., and WATKINS, M. J. Speech-like coding of pictures in short-term memory. *Memory & Cognition*, 1981, *9*, 110–114.

SCHLESINGER, H. S., and MEADOW, K. P. *Sound and sign: Childhood deafness and mental health.* Berkeley: University of California Press, 1972.

SCRIBNER, S. Recall of classical syllogisms: A cross-cultural investigation of error on logical problems. In R. J. Falmagne (Ed.), *Reasoning: Representation and process.* Hillsdale, N.J.: Erlbaum, 1975.

SCRIBNER, S. Modes of thinking and ways of speaking: Culture and logic reconsidered. In P. N. Johnson-Laird and P. C. Wason (Eds.), *Thinking: Readings in cognitive science.* Cambridge: Cambridge University Press, 1977.

SEAMON, J. G., and GAZZANIGA, M. S. Coding strategies and cerebral laterality effects. *Cognitive Psychology*, 1973, *5*, 249–256.

SEGAL, S. J., and FUSELLA, V. Influence of imaged pictures and sounds on detection of visual and auditory signals. *Journal of Experimental Psychology*, 1970, *83*, 458–464.

SEIDENBERG, M. S., and PETITTO, L. A. Signing behavior in apes: A critical review. *Cognition*, 1979, *7*, 177–215.

SELLS, S. B. The atmosphere effect: An experimental study of reasoning. *Archives of Psychology*, 136, *29*, 3–72.

SHALLICE, T. Neuropsychological research and the fractionation of memory systems. In L. Nilsson (Ed.), *Perspectives on memory research.* Hillsdale, N.J.: Erlbaum, 1979.

SHAND, M. A., and KLIMA, E. S. Nonauditory suffix effects in congenitally deaf signers of American Sign Language. *Journal of Experimental Psychology: Human Learning and Memory*, 1981, *7*, 464–474.

544
References

SHANKWEILER, D., and LIBERMAN, I. Y. Exploring the relations between reading and speech. In R. M. Knights and D. K. Bakker (Eds.), *Neuropsychology of learning disorders: Theoretical approaches.* Baltimore: University Park Press, 1976.

SHANNON, C. E., and WEAVER, W. *The mathematical theory of communication.* Urbana: University of Illinois Press, 1949.

SHAVER, P., PIERSON, L., and LANG, S. Converging evidence for the functional significance of imagery in problem solving. *Cognition,* 1974/5, *3,* 359–375.

SHEEHAN, P. W., and NEISSER, U. Some variables affecting the vividness of imagery in recall. *British Journal of Psychology,* 1969, *60,* 71–80.

SHEPARD, R. N. Form, formation, and transformation of internal representations. In R. L. Solso (Ed.), *Information processing and cognition: The Loyola Symposium.* Hillsdale, N.J.: Erlbaum, 1975.

SHEPARD, R. N., and FENG, C. A chronometric study of mental paper folding. *Cognitive Psychology,* 1972, *3,* 228–243.

SHEPARD, R. N., and METZLER, J. Mental rotation of three-dimensional objects. *Science,* 1971, *171,* 701–703.

SHEPARD, R. N., and PODGORNY, P. Cognitive processes that resemble perceptual processes. In W. K. Estes (Ed.), *Handbook of learning and cognitive processes* (Vol. 5). Hillsdale, N.J.: Erlbaum, 1978.

SHEPP, B. E. From perceived similarity to dimensional structure: A new hypothesis about perceptual development. In E. Rosch and B. B. Lloyd (Eds.), *Cognition and categorization.* Hillsdale, N.J.: Erlbaum, 1978.

SHIFFRIN, R. M. Information persistence in short-term memory. *Journal of Experimental Psychology,* 1973, *100,* 39–49.

SHIFFRIN, R. M. Short-term store: The basis for a memory system. In F. Restle, R. M. Shiffrin, N. J. Castellan, H. Lindman, and D. B. Pisoni (Eds.), *Cognitive theory* (Vol. 1). Hillsdale, N.J.: Erlbaum, 1975.

SHIFFRIN, R. M. Capacity limitations in information processing, attention, and memory. In W. K. Estes (Ed.), *Handbook of learning and cognitive processes* (Vol. 4). Hillsdale, N.J.: Erlbaum, 1976.

SHIFFRIN, R. M., and SCHNEIDER, W. Controlled and automatic human information processing: II. Perceptual learning, automatic attending, and a general theory. *Psychological Review,* 1977, *84,* 127–190.

SILVEIRA, J. Incubation: The effect of interruption timing and length on problem solution and quality of problem processing. Unpublished doctoral dissertation, University of Oregon, 1971.

SIMON, H. A. Rational choice and the structure of the environment. *Psychological Review,* 1956, *63,* 129–138.

SIMON, H. A. On the development of the processor. In S. Farnham-Diggory (Ed.), *Information processing in children.* New York: Academic Press, 1972.

SIMON, H. A. The structure of ill-structured problems. *Artificial Intelligence,* 1973, *4,* 181–202.

SIMON, H. A. How big is a chunk? *Science,* 1974, *183,* 482–488.

SIMON, H. A. *Models of thought.* New Haven: Yale University Press, 1979.

SIMON, H. A. Studying human intelligence by creating artificial intelligence. *American Scientist,* 1981, *69,* 300–309.

SIMON, H. A., and CHASE, W. G. Skill in chess. *American Scientist,* 1973, *61,* 394–403.

SIMPSON, M. E. and JOHNSON, D. M. Atmosphere and conversion errors in syllogistic reasoning. *Journal of Experimental Psychology*, 1966, *72*, 197–200.

SIPLE, P. (Ed.). *Understanding language through sign language research*. New York: Academic Press, 1978.

SKINNER, B. F. *The behavior of organisms*. New York: Appleton-Century-Crofts, 1938.

SLOBIN, D. I. Grammatical transformations and sentence comprehension in childhood and adulthood. *Journal of Verbal Learning and Verbal Behavior*, 1966, *5*, 219–227.

SLOBIN, D. I. Cognitive prerequisites for the acquisition of grammar. In C. A. Ferguson and D. I. Slobin (Eds.), *Studies of child language development*. New York: Holt, 1973.

SLOBIN, D. I. *Psycholinguistics* (2nd ed.). Glenview, Illinois: Scott, Foresman, 1979.

SMITH, A. D. Age differences in encoding, storage, and retrieval. In L. W. Poon, J. L. Fozard, L. S. Cermak, D. Arenberg, and L. W. Thompson (Eds.), *New directions in memory and aging*. Hillsdale, N.J.: Erlbaum, 1980.

SMITH, E. E. Theories of semantic memory. In W. K. Estes (Ed.), *Handbook of learning and cognitive processes* (Vol. 6). Hillsdale, N.J.: Erlbaum, 1978.

SMITH, E. E., SHOBEN, E. J., and RIPS, L. J. Structure and process in semantic memory: A featural model for semantic decisions. *Psychological Review*, 1974, *81*, 214–241.

SNYDER, C. R. C. Individual differences in imagery and thought. Unpublished doctoral dissertation, University of Oregon, 1972.

SOLOMONS, L., and STEIN, G. Normal motor automatism. *Psychological Review*, 1896, *3*, 492–512.

SPELKE, E., HIRST, W., and NEISSER, U. Skills of divided attention. *Cognition*, 1976, *4*, 215–230.

SPERLING, G. The information available in brief visual presentations. *Psychological Monographs*, 1960, *74* (Whole No. 498).

SPERLING, G. A model for visual memory tasks. *Human Factors*, 1963, *5*, 19–31.

SPRINGER, S. P., and DEUTSCH, G. *Left brain, right brain*. San Francisco: Freeman, 1981.

STANLEY, G. Visual memory processes in dyslexia. In D. Deutsch and J. A. Deutsch (Eds.), *Short-term memory*. New York: Academic Press, 1975.

STERNBERG, R. J. Component processes in analogical reasoning. *Psychological Review*, 1977, *84*, 353–378.

STERNBERG, R. J. Representation and process in linear syllogistic reasoning. *Journal of Experimental Psychology: General*, 1980, *109*, 119–159.

STERNBERG, R. J. Testing and cognitive psychology. *American Psychologist*, 1981, *36*, 1181–1189.

STERNBERG, S. High-speed scanning in human memory. *Science*, 1966, *153*, 652–654.

STERNBERG, S. Memory-scanning: Mental processes revealed by reaction-time experiments. *American Scientist*, 1969, *57*, 421–457.

STERNBERG, S. Memory scanning: New findings and current controversies. *Quarterly Journal of Experimental Psychology*, 1975, *27*, 1–32.

STOKOE, W. *Semiotics and human sign languages*. The Hague: Mouton, 1972.

STOKOE, W., CASTERLINE, D. and CRONEBERG, C. *A dictionary of American*

Sign Language on linguistic principles. Washington, D.C.: Gallaudet College Press, 1965.

STRANGE, W., and JENKINS, J. J. The role of linguistic experience in the perception of speech. In R. D. Walk and H. D. Pick (Eds.), *Perception and experience.* New York: Plenum, 1978.

STREETER, L. A. Language perception of 2-month-old infants shows effects of both innate mechanisms and experience. *Nature,* 1976, *259,* 39–41.

STROOP, J. R. Studies of interference in serial verbal reactions. *Journal of Experimental Psychology,* 1935, *18,* 643–662.

STUDDERT-KENNEDY, M. Speech perception. In N. J. Lass (Ed.), *Contemporary issues in experimental phonetics.* Springfield, Illinois: C. C. Thomas, 1976.

STUDDERT-KENNEDY, M., LIBERMAN, A. M., HARRIS, K. S., and COOPER, F. S. Motor theory of speech perception: A reply to Lane's critical review. *Psychological Review,* 1970, *77,* 234–249.

STUDDERT-KENNEDY, M., and SHANKWEILER, D. Hemispheric specialization for speech perception. *Journal of the Acoustical Society of America,* 1970, *48,* 579–594.

SWINNEY, D. A. Lexical access during sentence comprehension: (Re)consideration of context effects. *Journal of Verbal Learning and Verbal Behavior,* 1979, *18,* 645–660.

SWINNEY, D. A., and HAKES, D. T. Effects of prior context upon lexical access during sentence comprehension. *Journal of Verbal Learning and Verbal Behavior,* 1976, *15,* 681–689.

TERMAN, L. M., and MERRILL, M. A. *Measuring intelligence.* Boston: Houghton Mifflin, 1937.

TERVOORT, B. T. You me downtown movie fun? *Lingua,* 1968, *21,* 455–465.

THEIOS, J., SMITH, P. G., HAVILAND, S. E., TRAUPMANN, J., and MOY, M. C. Memory scanning as a serial, self-terminating process. *Journal of Experimental Psychology,* 1973, *97,* 323–336.

THOMAS, J. C. An analysis of behavior in the hobbits-orcs problem. *Cognitive Psychology,* 1974, *6,* 257–269.

THOMPSON, C. P., and BARNETT, C. Memory for product names: The generation effect. *Bulletin of the Psychonomic Society,* 1981, *18,* 241–243.

THOMSON, D. M., and TULVING, E. Associative encoding and retrieval: weak and strong cues. *Journal of Experimental Psychology,* 1970, *86,* 255–262.

THORNDIKE, E. L. *The psychology of learning.* New York: Teachers College, 1914.

TITCHENER, E. B. *Lectures on the elementary psychology of feeling and attention.* New York: Macmillan, 1908.

TOURANGEAU, R., and STERNBERG, R. J. Aptness in metaphor. *Cognitive Psychology,* 1981, *13,* 27–55.

TRABASSO, T., and BOWER, G. H. *Attention in learning: Theory and research.* New York: Wiley, 1968.

TRABASSO, T., RILEY, C. A., and WILSON, E. G. The representation of linear order and spatial strategies in reasoning: A developmental study. In R. J. Falmagne (Ed.), *Reasoning: Representation and process.* Hillsdale, N.J.: Erlbaum, 1975.

TREISMAN, A. M. Contextual cues in selective listening. *Quarterly Journal of Experimental Psychology,* 1960, *12,* 242–248.

TREISMAN, A., RUSSELL, R., and GREEN, J. Brief visual storage of shape and movement. In P. M. A. Rabbitt and S. Dornic (Eds.), *Attention and performance V*. London: Academic Press, 1975.

TSAL, Y. Symmetry and transitivity assumptions about a nonspecified logical relation. *Quarterly Journal of Experimental Psychology*, 1977, *29*, 677–684.

TULVING, E. Subjective organization in free recall of "unrelated" words. *Psychological Review*, 1962, *69*, 344–354.

TULVING, E. Subjective organization and effects of repetition in multi-trial free-recall learning. *Journal of Verbal Learning and Verbal Behavior*, 1966, *5*, 193–197.

TULVING, E. Episodic and semantic memory. In E. Tulving and W. Donaldson (Eds.), *Organization of memory*. New York: Academic Press, 1972.

TULVING, E., and DONALDSON, W. (Eds.). *Organization of memory*. New York: Academic Press, 1972.

TULVING, E., and PEARLSTONE, Z. Availability versus accessibility of information in memory for words. *Journal of Verbal Learning and Verbal Behavior*, 1966, *5*, 381–391.

TULVING, E., and THOMSON, D. M. Encoding specificity and retrieval processes in episodic memory. *Psychological Review*, 1973, *80*, 352–373.

TURING, A. M. Computing machinery and intelligence. *Mind*, 1950, *59*, 433–460.

TURVEY, M. T. Visual processing and short-term memory. In W. K. Estes (Ed.), *Handbook of learning and cognitive processes* (Vol. 5). Hillsdale, N.J.: Erlbaum, 1978.

TURVEY, M. T., and KRAVETZ, S. Retrieval from iconic memory with shape as the selection criterion. *Perception & Psychophysics*, 1970, *8*, 171–172.

TVERSKY, B. Pictorial and verbal encoding in a memory search task. *Perception & Psychophysics*, 1969, *4*, 225–233.

TWENEY, R. D., HEIMAN, G. W., and HOEMANN, H. W. Psychological processing of sign language: Effects of visual disruption on sign intelligibility. *Journal of Experimental Psychology: General*, 1977, *106*, 255–268.

TYLER, L. K., and MARSLEN-WILSON, W. D. The on-line effects of semantic context on syntactic processing. *Journal of Verbal Learning and Verbal Behavior*, 1977, *16*, 683–692.

TZENG, O. J. L., HUNG, D. L., and WANG, W. S-Y. Speech recoding in reading Chinese characters. *Journal of Experimental Psychology: Human Learning and Memory*, 1977, *3*, 621–630.

UNDERWOOD, B. J. "Spontaneous recovery" of verbal associations. *Journal of Experimental Psychology*, 1948, *38*, 429–439.

VAN DER VEUR, B. W. Imagery rating of 1,000 frequently used words. *Journal of Educational Psychology*, 1975, *67*, 44–56.

VIROSTEK, S., and CUTTING, J. E. Asymmetries for Ameslan handshapes and other forms in signers and nonsigners. *Perception & Psychophysics*, 1979, *26*, 505–508.

VON WRIGHT, J. M. Selection in visual immediate memory. *Quarterly Journal of Experimental Psychology*, 1968, *20*, 62–68.

VON WRIGHT, J. M. On the problem of selection in iconic memory. *Scandinavian Journal of Psychology*, 1972, *13*, 159–171.

VON WRIGHT, J. M., ANDERSON, K., and STENMAN, U. Generalization of conditioned GSRs in dichotic listening. In P. M. A. Rabbitt and S. Dornic (Eds.), *Attention and performance V*. New York: Academic Press, 1975.

548
References

WAGNER, D. A. The development of short-term and incidental memory: A cross-cultural study. *Child Development*, 1974, *45*, 389–396.

WAGNER, D. A. Memories of Morocco: The influence of age, schooling, and environment on memory. *Cognitive Psychology*, 1978, *10*, 1–28.

WALKER, E., GOUGH, P., and WALL, R. Grammatical relations and the search of sentences in immediate memory. *Proceedings of the Midwestern Psychological Association*, 1968.

WALSH, D. A., and BALDWIN, M. Age differences in integrated semantic memory. *Developmental Psychology*, 1977, *13*, 509–514.

WANNER, E. On remembering, forgetting, and understanding sentences. The Hague: Mouton, 1975.

WANNER, E. The ATN and the sausage machine: Which one is baloney? *Cognition*, 1980, *8*, 209–225.

WANNER, E., and MARATSOS, M. An ATN approach to comprehension. In M. Halle, J. Bresnan, and G. A. Miller (Eds.), *Linguistic theory and psychological reality*. Cambridge, Mass.: MIT Press, 1978.

WARREN, R. M. Perceptual restoration of missing speech sounds. *Science*, 1970, *167*, 393–395.

WASON, P. C. 'On the failure to eliminate hypotheses . . .'—a second look. In P. C. Wason and P. N. Johnson-Laird (Eds.), *Thinking and reasoning*. Harmondsworth: Penguin Books, 1968.

WASON, P. C. Self-contradictions. In P. N. JOHNSON-LAIRD and P. C. WASON (Eds.), *Thinking: Readings in cognitive science*. Cambridge: Cambridge University Press, 1977.

WASON, P. C., and JOHNSON-LAIRD, P. N. (Eds.). *Thinking and reasoning*. Baltimore: Penguin Books, 1968.

WASON, P. C. and JOHNSON-LAIRD, P. N. *Psychology of reasoning*. London: B. T. Batsford Ltd., 1972.

WASON, P. C., and SHAPIRO, D. Natural and contrived experience in a reasoning problem. *Quarterly Journal of Experimental Psychology*, 1971, *23*, 63–71.

WATKINS, M. J., and WATKINS, O. C. The postcategorical status of the modality effect in serial recall. *Journal of Experimental Psychology*, 1973, *99*, 226–230.

WATKINS, M. J., and WATKINS, O. C. A tactile suffix effect. *Memory & Cognition*, 1974, *2*, 176–180.

WATKINS, O. C., and WATKINS, M. J. The modality effect and echoic persistence. *Journal of Experimental Psychology: General*, 1980, *109*, 251–278.

WATSON, J. B. Psychology as the behaviorist views it. *Psychological Review*, 1913, *20*, 158–177.

WAUGH, N. C., and NORMAN, D. A. Primary memory. *Psychological Review*, 1965, *72*, 89–104.

WEXLER, K. A review of John R. Anderson's *Language, memory and thought*. *Cognition*, 1978, *6*, 327–351.

WHORF, B. L. *Language, thought, and reality: Selected writings of Benjamin Lee Whorf*, J. B. Carroll (Ed.). New York: Wiley, 1956.

WICKELGREN, W. A. Acoustic similarity and retroactive interference in short-term memory. *Journal of Verbal Learning and Verbal Behavior*, 1965, *4*, 53–61.

WICKELGREN, W. A. Distinctive features and errors in short-term memory for English consonants. *Journal of the Acoustical Society of America*, 1966, 39, 388–398.

WICKELGREN, W. A. The long and short of memory. *Psychological Bulletin*, 1973, 80, 425–438.

WICKELGREN, W. A. *How to solve problems: Elements of a theory of problems and problem solving*. San Francisco: Freeman, 1974.

WICKELGREN, W. A. More on the long and short of memory. In D. Deutsch and J. A. Deutsch (Eds.), *Short-term memory*. New York: Academic Press, 1975.

WICKENS, D. D. Characteristics of word encoding. In A. W. Melton and E. Martin (Eds.), *Coding processes in human memory*. New York: V. H. Winston, 1972.

WICKENS, D. D., BORN, D. G., and ALLEN, C. K. Proactive inhibition and item similarity in short-term memory. *Journal of Verbal Learning and Verbal Behavior*, 1963, 2, 440–445.

WILKINS, A. Conjoint frequency, category size, and categorization time. *Journal of Verbal Learning and Verbal Behavior*, 1971, 10, 382–385.

WILKINS, A., and STEWART, A. The time course of lateral asymmetries in visual perception of letters. *Journal of Experimental Psychology*, 1974, 102, 905–908.

WINDES, J. D. Reaction time for numerical coding and naming of numerals. *Journal of Experimental Psychology*, 1968, 78, 318–322.

WINOGRAD, T. A framework for understanding discourse. In M. A. Just and P. A. Carpenter (Eds.), *Cognitive processes in comprehension*. Hillsdale, N.J.: Erlbaum, 1977.

WINOGRAD, T. On some contested suppositions of generative linguistics about the scientific study of language. *Cognition*, 1977, 5, 151–179.

WINSTON, P. H. *Artificial intelligence*. Reading, Mass.: Addison-Wesley, 1977.

WITELSON, S., and PALLIE, W. Left hemisphere specialization for language in the newborn. *Brain*, 1973, 96, 641–646.

WITTGENSTEIN, L. [*Philosophical investigations* (2nd ed.)] (G. E. M. Anscombe, Trans.) Oxford: Blackwell, 1958.

WOOD, C. C., GOFF, W. R., and DAY, R. S. Auditory evoked potentials during speech perception. *Science*, 1971, 173, 1248–1251.

WOODWARD, A. E., BJORK, R. A., and JONGEWARD, R. H., JR. Recall and recognition as a function of primary rehearsal. *Journal of Verbal Learning and Verbal Behavior*, 1973, 12, 608–617.

WOODWORTH, R. S., and SELLS, S. B. An atmosphere effect in formal syllogistic reasoning. *Journal of Experimental Psychology*, 1935, 18, 451–460.

YATES, F. A. *The art of memory*. Chicago: University of Chicago Press, 1966.

YOUNG, R. M. Strategies and the structure of a cognitive skill. In G. Underwood (Ed.), *Strategies of information processing*. New York: Academic Press, 1978.

ZANGWILL, O. L. Some qualitative observations on verbal memory in cases of cerebral lesion. *British Journal of Psychology*, 1946, 37, 8–19.

Author Index

Subject Index